MODERN SOFTWARE DEVELOPMENT USING C# .NET

Richard Wiener

BROOKS/COLE

THOMSON LEARNING

Australia • Canada • Mexico • Singapore • Spain • United Kingdom • United States

BROOKS/COLE

™

THOMSON LEARNING

Modern Software Development Using C# .NET
Richard Wiener

Managing Editor	**Associate Product Manager**	**Cover Designer**
Mary Franz	Jennifer Smith	Steve Deschene
Senior Product Manager	**Senior Marketing Manager**	**Compositor**
Alyssa Pratt	Karen Seitz	GEX Publishing Services
Production Editor	**Senior Manufacturing Coordinator**	
Brooke Booth	Justin Palmeiro	
Developmental Editor	**Manufacturing Coordinator**	
Lisa Ruffolo	Suelaine Frongello	

For more information, contact Thomson Course Technology, 25 Thomson Place, Boston, MA 02210; or find us on the World Wide Web at *www.course.com*.

The Web addresses in this book are subject to change from time to time as necessary without notice.

For permission to use material from this text or product, contact us by
• Web: www.thomsonrights.com
• Phone: 1-800-730-2214
• Fax: 1-800-730-2215

ISBN 0-619-21759-6

This book is dedicated to my wife Hanne and children Erik, Marc, Daniel, and Anna. I love you all dearly.

Richard Wiener

CONTENTS

PART 1

THINKING AND USING OBJECT-ORIENTED PROGRAMMING   1

CHAPTER 1

Thinking and Using Object-Oriented Programming:
The Basics   3

CHAPTER 2

From Problem Definition to Classes: Object-Oriented Analysis and Design and the Software Life Cycle   47

PART 2

CLASS CONSTRUCTION   107

CHAPTER 4

The Basics of Class Construction   109

CHAPTER 6

Refactoring   205

CHAPTER 7

Programming with Threads   241

PART 3

EVENT HANDLING AND GUIS   271

CHAPTER 8

Delegates and Events in C#   273

CHAPTER 9

Form Classes and Event Handling   303

CHAPTER 12

Linear Data Structures and Their Applications 437

CHAPTER 13

Nonlinear Data Structures and Their Applications 493

CHAPTER 14

Standard Collections and Serialization 573

PART 5

PUTTING IT ALL TOGETHER   655

CHAPTER 16

Ecological Simulation   657

PREFACE

This textbook is intended for students taking a second course in computer science, CS 2, and is also suited for a modern software engineering course. The inspiration for this book comes from my own experience in industry, consulting, and teaching for many years at the University of Colorado, as well as from another Thomson Course Technology book, *Modern Software Development Using Java* by Paul Tymann and G. Michael Schneider, 2004.

The phrase "data structures" is purposely omitted from the title even though this book is aimed at CS 2 students, software engineering students, or intermediate-level professional software developers learning the .NET platform and C#. This book takes the view that students need to focus on modern software development issues first and data structures second. This is because the nature of programming and software development has changed dramatically over the past 15 years. Object-modeling and object-oriented programming (OOP) and problem solving have emerged into the mainstream in industry. It is now rare that programmers have to roll their own data structures as was the case when C, Pascal, Modula-2, and early versions of C++ were used.

Traditional data structure courses may present three or four distinct versions of a linked list (e.g., singly-linked, doubly-linked, circular, or array-based lists). Class time would be better spent briefly examining a sample implementation of a linked list, such as a doubly-linked list, and then discovering the many applications of linked lists by using the standard collection libraries. Through a detailed presentation of a doubly-linked list, students can acquire the linked-structure skills that are a fundamental part of computer problem solving.

With the advent of software development language frameworks, such as C# and .NET, which offer thousands of standard classes that support application program interfaces (APIs) in many application areas, the nature of CS 2 education should also be updated. C# and .NET include well-defined data structure classes (called standard collection classes) that allow programmers to solve problems using object-oriented data structures. CS 2 courses must therefore emphasize effectively using data structures rather than constructing them. This book provides this emphasis by presenting many applications that use data structure classes.

Because a well-educated computer scientist still needs to understand the basic skills associated with constructing linear linked structures as well as nonlinear structures such as unbalanced and balanced binary search trees and hash tables, this book includes several chapters on classic linear and nonlinear data structures. The rest of the book focuses on object-oriented software construction and modern software development using C# and .NET.

Because object-oriented programming and problem solving has emerged into the mainstream in industry, this book is intended to help readers build foundational skills in these areas and prepare for the real-world challenges that lie ahead. In particular, this book emphasizes the following topics:

- *The object-oriented framework*—Thinking and using object modeling and OOP effectively

- *Unified Model Language (UML)*—Understanding basic UML modeling and the concepts behind the notations

- *Events and graphic user interfaces (GUIs)*—Understanding event-handling and GUIs early allows students to work on interesting, GUI-based projects and to appreciate the richness of the Window Forms libraries and event-handling mechanisms that are provided in the .NET framework

- *The Observer pattern*—Understanding the Observer pattern and its use in constructing applications in which event notification and event handling play a central role

- *Effective class design*—Writing for reuse and learning the essential ingredients that need to be considered when constructing classes

- *Effective use of threads*—Using underlying hardware and operating system resources by learning to take advantage of pseudo parallel processing

- *C# and .NET*—Understanding how to effectively harness the C# language and .NET framework to build robust and efficient software systems

In addition, this book includes many carefully crafted examples, case studies, and exercises that illustrate the principles of modern software development and allow readers to see these principles and the C# language supported by .NET in action.

Instead of grouping exercises exclusively at the end of each chapter, many exercises are placed directly after an important principle is presented. Interspersing the exercises in this way allows readers to immediately use a principle and better understand it. Each exercise engages readers and requires them to more deeply explore the software development issue that is being presented. More traditional end-of-chapter exercises are also included.

Organization and Coverage

Part 1 of the book, "Thinking and Using Object-Oriented Programming," introduces students to the modeling notions and notations that have become fundamental in object-oriented problem solving in a variety of programming languages.

Chapter 1, "Thinking and Using Object-Oriented Programming: The Basics," presents the fundamentals of object-oriented problem solving. It reviews the concepts of object and class, encapsulation, inheritance, and polymorphism, and introduces UML notation to support these basic concepts.

Chapter 2, "From Problem Definition to Classes: Object-Oriented Analysis and Design and the Software Lifecycle," discusses the software development lifecycle and the processes of object-oriented analysis and design, illustrating these topics with many examples.

Chapter 3, "From Design to Implementation," uses a carefully constructed case study to demonstrate the transition from design concepts to implementation in C#. Some instructors may choose to defer a discussion of Chapter 3 until Part 2 of the book is completed.

Part 2 of the book, "Class Construction," presents the major features of C# .NET in a problem-solving and modern software development context.

Chapter 4, "The Basics of Class Construction," presents the features of a C# class and their significance in object-oriented software construction. It examines the unified type system so central in .NET and C# in particular, and discusses the use and importance of namespaces. It also introduces and explains conventions for naming the various features of a C# class, explores the concepts of commands and queries and the use of properties and indexers, and covers type-safe enumeration. The chapter also compares and contrasts important class concepts, including value types (through *struct*) and reference types (through *class*), static fields and methods, overriding and overloading, and rectangular and jagged arrays. During these comparisons, the chapter discusses important modifiers such as *ref*, *out*, *readonly*, and *sealed*, and illustrates overloaded operators. It concludes by examining the mechanism of exception handling. Although this chapter focuses on using these basic constructs in the context of problem solving, it can serve as an intensive review of the programming principles introduced in the CS1 course or as a concise introduction to the C# language.

Chapter 5, "More Advanced Class Construction," focuses on the effective construction of C# classes. The topics include avoiding protected fields, constructors and their pitfalls, overriding method *Equals*, cloning objects, using *StringBuilder* instead of *String*, constructing generic classes, constrained generic parameters and constructing generic methods. The student completing this chapter should not only understand the basic features of a C# class but also understand how to effectively build C# classes.

Chapter 6, "Refactoring," introduces the important concept of refactoring in which the methods and classes within an existing software system are reorganized to promote greater understandability and easier maintenance. This chapter uses a case study to demonstrate the steps of moving from a "POOP" solution (procedural object-oriented programming) to an OOP solution. Few books, if any, at this level present this increasingly important subject in modern software development.

Chapter 7, "Programming with Threads," introduces the subtle, challenging, and important approach of programming with threads to software development. It illustrates the features of C# .NET that support multithreaded programming with many examples.

Part 3 of this book, "Event Handling and GUIs," contains three chapters that present and illustrate the framework for event generation and handling that is a core part of the .NET framework and serves as the basis for graphical user interface development.

Chapter 8, "Delegates and Events in C#," introduces the delegate type as a first-class class, and presents examples that illustrate the use of delegates. It also examines the delegate modifier *event*, explores the differences between delegates and their close cousin, events, and then discusses events in GUI applications.

Chapter 9, "Form Classes and Event-Handling," introduces the use of the basic Windows Form classes that are available in the .NET framework. The chapter begins by discussing the Observer pattern and its use in GUI event-handling, and then revisits the refactoring case study presented in Chapter 6 to construct a GUI around the core classes that comprise the final refactoring. Upon completing this chapter, the student should be comfortable in writing GUI applications.

Chapter 10, "More Advanced GUI Construction," starts by showing how to design custom controls with event-handling hooks. It then presents a more advanced GUI application, Game of Dots and Boxes, which demonstrates the integration of graphics, mouse event handling, and other GUI-related topics that build upon the foundation established in Chapter 9.

Part 4 of the book is entitled "Data Structures," and covers recursion, classic linear data structures, nonlinear data structures (with particular emphasis on tree structures and hash tables), and the standard .NET collection classes and some applications.

Chapter 11, "Recursion," looks under the hood and examines how the runtime system manages recursive methods. This chapter introduces meta-notation, which allows readers to track and understand the details of the runtime stack during a recursion. Recursive algorithms play an important role in formulating algorithms that manipulate data structures.

Chapter 12, "Linear Data Structures and Their Applications," explores the classic data structures stack, queue, dequeue, priority queue, and various list types and their implementation in C#. It presents a maze application to provide a nontrivial application of stacks, and uses a long integer application to illustrate the use of lists. Each of the data structure classes presented features a generic implementation.

Chapter 13, "Nonlinear Data Structures and Their Applications," introduces the theory of binary trees and presents the implementation of generic binary search trees. It examines and implements two special and important balanced search trees, and presents complete implementation details for insertion and removal from AVL and Red/Black trees. Few texts, if any, present such details for AVL and Red/Black trees. This chapter also explores a GUI application that allows the display of binary search trees. This application shows the results of rotation on user-selected nodes as well as the results of insertion and removal from unbalanced, AVL, and Red/Black trees. The chapter concludes by discussing some theory associated with hash tables and implementing two algorithms for collision resolution.

Chapter 14, "Standard Collections and Serialization," presents the standard collection classes, both nongeneric and generic, in the .NET framework. It uses applications including a spelling checker, permutation groups of English words, palindrome tester, concordance, and infix to postfix conversion to show the standard collections in action. The chapter concludes with a discussion of object serialization.

Chapter 15, "Regular Expressions," introduces this important subject in modern software development. It uses many examples, both small and large, to illustrate the application of regular expressions. The main case study involves constructing a C# formatter, including designing and implementing a collection of regular expressions to parse and rebuild a C# source file so the output conforms to standard formatting conventions.

The final part of the book, Part 5, is entitled "Putting It All Together." A major GUI-based case study ties together many of the concepts and skills learned in the previous chapters. These include analysis and design with UML diagrams, principles of class construction, threads, event-notification and handling and the Observer Pattern, use of standard collections, and graphical user interface development.

Chapter 16, "Ecological Simulation," is the only chapter in Part 5. It features a major case study that explores the dynamic relationship between various species of predator and prey. The application is both fun and challenging.

Features

Modern Software Development Using Microsoft C# .NET includes the following features:

◆ **Chapter contents**. A brief list of topics appears at the beginning of each chapter so the student has an overview of the chapter contents.

◆ **Program listings**. Each chapter contains many illustrations of programming examples, including complete class and program listings, to demonstrate principles and concepts and to provide samples of working C# programs. Most listings are followed by discussions of the program statements that illustrate particular techniques or methods.

◆ **Figures**. Each chapter also provides graphics, such as drawings, UML diagrams, and screen shots of the programs' execution, to illustrate program features and to adhere to the principles of effective program design.

◆ **Summaries**. A summary that recaps the programming concepts covered follows each chapter.

◆ **Exercises**. Each chapter contains interesting exercises that allow students the opportunity to apply the concepts they have mastered. These exercises are provided within the chapter, usually following program listings, and at the end of the chapter, where students can synthesize what they have learned.

Supplemental Resources

The following ancillary materials are available when this book is used in a classroom setting. All of the teaching tools available with this book are available in the Instructor Downloads section of www.course.com.

◆ **Instructor's Manual:** Additional instructional material to assist in class preparation, including suggestions for lecture topics and a 14- and 16-week syllabus outline.

◆ **Solution Files:** Solutions to most exercises. (Due to the nature of programming, students' solutions may differ from these solutions and still be correct.)

◆ **Source Code:** Source code files, containing all of the C# source listings that students can study in preparation for completing the exercises in this book, are provided on the Thomson Course Technology Web site.

◆ **PowerPoint Presentations:** This book comes with Microsoft PowerPoint slides for each chapter. These are included as a teaching aid for classroom presentation, to make available to students on the network for chapter review, or to be printed for classroom distribution. Instructors can add their own slides for additional topics they introduce to the class.

◆ **Software:** The Express Edition of Visual C# .NET 2005 is available as an optional bundle with the text.

Suggested Teaching Sequence

This book was used by the author in a one-semester course entitled "Object-Oriented Programming Using C# .NET" using the following sequence of chapters: Chapters 1 and 2, Chapters 4, 5, 6, 7, 8, 9, 10, 14, 15, and Chapter 16. Chapters 11, 12, and 13, which concentrate on data structures, were omitted because the focus of the course was on software development using C#/ .NET.

For instructors who want to adhere more closely to the traditional data structure curriculum for CS 2, a logical sequence would be Chapters 4, 5, 7, 8, 9, 10, 11, 12, 13, and 14. This sequence provides a balance between enhancing programming and software development skills and an intensive presentation of basic and more advanced data structures.

Acknowledgments

The author is grateful to the following text reviewers: Barbara Doyle, Jacksonville University; Keyuan Jiang, Purdue University Calumet; and Rani Mikkilineni, Santa Clara University. Their reviews were always critical but constructive. Special thanks go to Lisa Ruffolo, the development editor, for her untiring efforts in making useful suggestions, and her continuous and vigorous encouragement at every stage of the writing effort. Special thanks also go to Alyssa Pratt, Senior Product Manager at Course Technology, for her encouragement and assistance at many important stages of this project.

Richard Wiener
Colorado Springs, Colorado

THINKING AND USING OBJECT-ORIENTED PROGRAMMING

This section of the book introduces an intellectual framework for a modern and powerful paradigm of software analysis, design, and implementation called object-oriented programming (OOP). The goal of this section is to present and illustrate the thought processes, notions, and notations that support the development of object-oriented software architecture with C#.

The first of three chapters in this section sets the stage for everything in this book by introducing "object think," a frame of reference for thinking about objects, and the basics of OOP. The second chapter in this section focuses on object-oriented problem analysis and design—going from problem specification to class discovery. The final chapter in this section introduces Unified Modeling Language (UML) notation. This notation will be used throughout the book and provides the basis for describing the architecture of an object-oriented software system.

CHAPTER 1

Thinking and Using Object-Oriented Programming: The Basics

1.1 ENCAPSULATION AND THE NOTIONS OF CLASS AND OBJECT

The world surrounding us is filled with objects of many types. Some of these objects are organic (people, animals, and plants), whereas others are manufactured by people (the computer, keyboard, and monitor being used to write this book).

For an object such as a person, it is reasonable to talk about the "state of being" for the person. "How are you feeling?" is a common greeting between friends and family members. Such a query is aimed at eliciting information about the internal state (physical or psychological) of the person being questioned. A response such as "I am feeling ill today" might lead to corrective action to change and improve the internal state of the person providing this response.

Although we cannot ask an inanimate object about its internal state, we might be able to measure it. For example, we might be interested in the current internal state of an oven. We need to know the current temperature inside of the oven before we can use it to roast beef. The same query might later be directed to the roast itself to determine whether it is cooked to satisfaction (rare, medium, or well-done) and is ready for eating. So probing an object, animate or inanimate, to obtain information about its internal state (or simply, state) is a common and reasonable thing to do. We call such a probe a **query** sent to the object.

It is also common to attempt to change the state of an object, particularly after we obtain information about its current state. If a person's temperature is found to be above normal, we can attempt to change the state (temperature) of the person by administering fever-control medication. If the temperature of the roast beef after several hours is still too low, we can increase the temperature within the oven. Such corrective action taken on an object (such as a person or oven) is called a **command**. The purpose of a command sent to an object is to change the object's state.

Software systems are often constructed by examining models of the problem being solved. Modeling has been the basis of many scientific disciplines. A model of a system represents an abstraction that captures the essence of the system's behavior. Models often provide a simplified but usable representation of a system to provide a tractable mechanism for problem solving.

We model the behavior of entities in the domain of software development using the concept of a **class**. These entities are the objects in the problem domain, and their behavior is the actions that may be taken on these objects. A class is a model of the behavior of a set of objects or instances of a class. One type of model is a data model that characterizes the state of the object as well as mechanisms for querying and changing this state.

The state information within a class is provided by an information model. The mechanism for querying this state is provided by one or more **query methods**. The mechanism for changing the internal state in a disciplined and controlled manner is provided by one or more **command methods**.

Consider the following examples that deal with everyday objects—fountain pens and cars—and the classes that describe the behavior of these objects.

Fountain pens are conceptually simple objects. A fountain pen can be modeled as being in one of two possible states: ink empty or ink not empty. The only action that may be taken on a pen to change its state is to fill the pen with ink. Table 1.1 describes a fountain pen class.

TABLE 1.1 Class *FountainPen*

Information Model	Values
inkState	empty, not empty
Command	
FillPen	
Query	
IsEmpty	false, true

Note: By convention a class name always starts with an uppercase character, just as a command or query name starts with an uppercase character. This naming convention comes from the Pascal programming language in which procedure and function names start with uppercase characters.

The class *FountainPen* described in Table 1.1 contains a single command and a single query and represents a simple model of these writing instruments. Such a model might be sufficient to represent the scenario of using the fountain pen as a writing instrument. In this context, all that is important to users is the presence of ink in the pen.

Absent from the class description is information about the pen's nib, color, thickness, and other physical features that might be of interest to a collector. If the software application that involves fountain pens requires such information, the *FountainPen* class would need to be modified to account for this additional behavior.

In addition to command and query methods, a class may define **constructor methods** whose purpose is to allow an initial state to be defined at the moment an object is created. In the absence of any explicit constructor methods, a default constructor method is always present. This default constructor method assigns default values for the initial state of the object being created.

Note: The behavior of a class is defined by the information model that characterizes the state of class instances (objects), the methods that access this information (query methods), the methods that modify this information (command methods), and the constructor methods that allow the user to set the initial state of an object as it is being created.

In contrast to fountain pens, cars are complex entities. The challenge in modeling a car is determining the features that are relevant and of interest in the domain of the application. The simplest context for modeling a car involves the need to drive the car without running out of fuel, engine oil, or air pressure in the tires. These are the "refillables" that need to be attended to from time to time. Table 1.2 provides a simple model for a car.

TABLE 1.2 Class *Car*

Information Model	Values
fuelState	Gallons remaining (fractional value such as 10.5 gallons)
Oil pressure	Value in pounds per square inch
Tire 1 pressure	Value in pounds per square inch (integer value such as 32 psi)
Tire 2 pressure	Value in pounds per square inch (integer value such as 32 psi)
Tire 3 pressure	Value in pounds per square inch (integer value such as 32 psi)
Tire 4 pressure	Value in pounds per square inch (integer value such as 32 psi)
Commands	
AddFuel	Specify the number of gallons (such as 10.5 gallons)
SetTirePressure	Specify the tire number and the new tire pressure (such as 3, 29 psi)
AddOil	Specify the number of quarts (such as 3 quarts)
Queries	
FuelRemaining	Number of gallons remaining
TirePressure	Must specify the tire number and returns value in psi
OilQuantity	Number of quarts

Each of the commands requires input parameters. Through these parameters, the desired changes to the internal state of the object receiving the command can be controlled. For example, the command *AddFuel* requires the user to specify the number of gallons that need to be added. The C# method signature might look as follows:

```
public void AddFuel(double gallonsToAdd) { … }
```

Such a command must be invoked through an object (instance) of class *Car*. Suppose we have created such an instance, *myCar,* and want to add 14.5 gallons to this vehicle. We can change the internal state of *myCar* by passing the value 14.5 to the *AddFuel* command as follows:

```
myCar.AddFuel(14.5);
```

To determine how much fuel is remaining, we can invoke the query *FuelRemaining* and output this value as follows:

```
double currentAmountOfFuel = myCar.FuelRemaining();
Console.WriteLine("Fuel remaining: " + currentAmountOfFuel);
```

An application accomplishes an action through an object (*myCar* in the previous examples).

In a car application, we would probably have many car objects coexisting in the application. Each of these car objects would have its own state. By changing the tire pressure in tire 4 of Marc's car, for example, we do not change the state of any of the other cars in the system.

```
marcsCar.SetTirePressure(4, 35); // Has no effect on other car
                                 // objects
```

Objects encapsulate their state. The only mechanism we have provided in class *Car* for changing the fuel within a car object is through the command *AddFuel*. The resulting quantity of fuel within a particular car object depends on the current fuel state of the car receiving the *AddFuel* command as well as the value of the parameter passed to this command.

Cars exist in many contexts, however. Suppose we are in the retail business of selling cars. Our concerns would not be related to tire pressure, oil pressure, or the fuel in a car. Instead, our concerns would involve engine choice, accessory packages, color, tire choice, lease versus loan versus cash purchase, and price.

Table 1.3 provides an alternative description of class *Car* that serves as a model for retail car sales.

TABLE 1.3 Alternative class *Car*

Information Model	Values
price	Amount in dollars and cents
engineType	An enumeration of choices (e.g., 160 hp 4 cylinder, 220 hp V6, 290 hp V8)
Accessory package	An enumeration of choices (e.g., cold weather package, sports package)
Color	An enumeration of choices (e.g., blue)
tireChoice	An enumeration of choices (17-inch sports tires, 16-inch all weather, 15-inch basic)
purchaseMethod	An enumeration of choices (e.g., loan, cash purchase, lease)
Commands	
SetEngineType	Specify the type of engine in the car
SetAccessoryPackage	Specify the particular accessory package to be installed in the car
SetColor	Specify the color of the car
SetTireChoice	Specify the tire type to be mounted on the car
SetPurchaseMethod	Specify the purchase method
SetPrice	Sets the price of the vehicle
Queries	
Price	Dollars and cents
Engine	The engine type
AccessoryPackage	A choice from an enumeration of packages
Color	The color of the car from the enumeration of possible colors
Tire	The tire type from the enumeration of possible tire types
PurchaseMethod	A choice from among the enumeration of purchase options

Suppose an object, *susansCar*, of type *Car* were created. A typical set of commands to invoke on *susansCar* as a prelude to ordering this car might be the following:

```
susansCar.SetEngineType(v6);
susansCar.SetAccessoryPackage(coldWeather);
susansCar.SetColor(red);
susansCar.SetTireChoice(mediumSized16Inch);
susansCar.SetPrice(22600.25);
```

The application domain dictates the model that is appropriate. For the driver, the first *Car* class represents a better model than the second car class. For the car retailer, the second *Car* class is a better model than the first.

Exercise 1.1

Write a description of a home thermostat system that is described by the following information model (state):

current temperature, desired temperature, heating system (on or off)

What objects are included in your description?

Exercise 1.2

Write a description of a clock class that is described by the following information model:

current time

The examples presented earlier deal with the modeling of real objects—pens and cars. In the world of software development, we often are required to model more abstract entities—things that are not physical objects. Consider the following example.

Suppose we want to design the model of a counter. A counter is an abstract entity that holds a count value, an integer. We use such an entity in an application where we need to keep track of how many times an event occurs.

Like other programming languages, the C# language provides the object type **int** (an alias for the reference value type **System.Int32**) to model integer values. It might seem that you need only this basic type to model a counter. Each time an event of interest is encountered, we increment our counter object as in the following example:

```
int counter;
// Some intervening code …
// Event of some interest occurs
counter++;
```

On the surface this seems just fine. At any instant, the value of the *int* object *counter* would represent the desired count value. The rules for objects of type *int* allow an assignment to an arbitrary integer value. The rules also allow the value of an *int* object to be modified by adding, subtracting, multiplying, or dividing the *int* value by another integer. So the following operations would be completely legal on the object *counter*:

```
counter += 70;
counter *= 20;
counter /= 4;
counter = 2006;
```

Although legal, none of these operations make sense when modeling the counter abstraction. The only allowable operation on a counter object should be *increment* (by 1).

The principle of encapsulation, realized through a class definition, provides and enforces a disciplined approach to changing the values that define the state of a class instance (an object). Consider the model of a counter class shown in Table 1.4, and then briefly examine a C# implementation of this class and a simple application.

TABLE 1.4 Class *Counter*

Information Model	Values
countValue	An integer that holds the current count
Command	
Increment	Add one to the internal countValue
Query	
CountValue	Return the current countValue

The class description in Table 1.4 presents a simple model of a counter. The only operation that can be applied to a *Counter* object to change its state (*countValue*) is through the command *Increment*. Then the *countValue* is increased by exactly one. The read-only property *CountValue* is used to access the state of a *Counter* object. Chapter 4 presents the details of class construction and the use of properties in detail.

Listing 1.1 presents the implementation of class *Counter* so that we can better understand the purpose and concept of encapsulation.

LISTING 1.1 Class *Counter* using encapsulation

```
namespace CounterEncapsulation {

    public class Counter {
        // Fields (describe the information model)
        private int countValue;

        // Command
        public void Increment() {
            countValue++;
        }
```

LISTING 1.1 Class *Counter* using encapsulation (continued)

```
        // Query Property
        public int CountValue { // Read-only property
            get {
                return countValue;
            }
        }
    }

    public class CounterApp {

        static void Main() {
            Counter myCounter = new Counter();
            for (int count = 0; count < 10000; count++) {
                myCounter.Increment();
            }
            Console.WriteLine("Value of myCounter: " +
                              myCounter.CountValue);
            Console.ReadLine();
        }
    }
}

/* Program output
Value of myCounter: 10000
*/
```

Discussion of Listing 1.1

◆ The information model of class *Counter* is represented by the fields of the class, in this case the field *countValue* of type *int*.

◆ The *Increment()* command changes the state of the object through which the command is invoked by adding one to the current *countValue*.

◆ The read-only property *CountValue* allows the current state (*countValue*) to be accessed.

◆ The *CounterApp* class exercises the *Counter* abstraction by creating an object *myCounter* of type *Counter*. This *Counter* object is incremented ten thousand times and then the count value is output.

◆ If an attempt were made to violate the encapsulation principle by doing the following, for example:

`myCounter.CountValue = 40;`

an error message would be displayed at compile time (only a portion of the error message is shown):

'CounterEncapsulation.Counter.CountValue' cannot be assigned to—it is read only.

◆ By encapsulating the *countValue* integer in class *Counter*, we provide only one mechanism for changing the *countValue*—through the command *Increment*.

◆ Through the model implemented in class *Counter*, we have been able to control changes to the ordinary *countValue* of type *int*.

Exercise 1.3

Explain why it would not be appropriate to include commands *Increment* and *Decrement* with the following signatures in class *Counter*:

```
public void Increment(int byAmount) {
    // Adds byAmount to the current value of countValue
}
public void Decrement(int byAmount) {
    // Subtracts byAmount from the current value of countValue
}
```

1.2 NAMING CONVENTIONS

Per the recommendation of Bertrand Meyer in his classic book *Object-Oriented Software Construction, Second Edition* (Prentice-Hall, 1997), query method names should be noun phrases and commands verb phrases. Constructor methods always have the name of the class in which they reside.

Some programmers use verb phrases for queries. These are often referred to as "accessors" or "getters." For example, in class *Counter* (see Listing 1.1), some programmers would create an access method *GetCount()*. This verb phrase puts emphasis on the process of getting a count value rather than on the type of entity that the query is returning (a count value). If all queries were to use the prefix "Get" followed by the type of quantity being sought, then the "Get" provides no additional information or value. It becomes a redundant appendage. By using a noun phrase that indicates the quantity that is being returned, the purpose of the query becomes much clearer.

For commands, verb phrases are appropriate because commands represent actions. These are often referred to as "mutators" or "setters." The command *Increment* in class *Counter* is an illustration of this. The command *AddFuel* from the first version of class *Car* is another example of a verb phrase that represents an action to be taken on the object through which the command is invoked.

These naming conventions are used throughout this book.

In the next section, we examine various types of relationships that may be defined between classes. These include **composition**, **aggregation**, **association** (strong and weak), and **inheritance**. The architecture of an object-oriented software system is defined by the classes that comprise the system and their relationships.

Basic UML notation is introduced in this chapter to support our discussion. Chapter 3 discusses UML notation in more detail.

1.3 AGGREGATION: WHOLE-PART RELATIONSHIPS

Objects are often built in terms of other objects. This leads us to consider the whole/part, or aggregation, relationship between classes. If the parts "belong to" the whole, the relationship is called composition or strong aggregation. If the parts are not owned by the whole but are simply there for the moment, the relationship is called the aggregation relationship. (Sometimes it's called weak aggregation.)

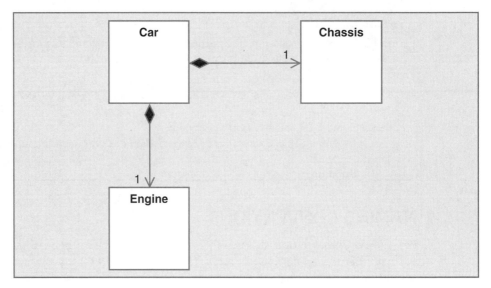

FIGURE 1.1 UML diagram for the *Car*, *Engine*, and *Chassis* classes

In a composition relationship, also called strong aggregation, if the whole is destroyed, so must all the parts be destroyed because they are owned by the whole. For example, if a classroom were destroyed, so would the chalkboard because it is an essential part of the classroom. In a business partnership, if one partner quits the company, the partnership is destroyed.

Consider class *Car* again. Its major and essential constituent parts include an engine and a chassis. Each of these parts is an object in its own right (instances of classes *Engine* and *Chassis*). We represent the relationship between these classes using UML notation as shown in Figure 1.1.

The two solid diamonds attached to class *Car* with association lines terminating at classes *Engine* and *Chassis* imply that *Car* is composed of these two classes and that these classes are an essential part of class *Car*.

The arrows indicate that the relationship is directed. That is, *Car* knows about *Engine* but *Engine* does not know about *Car*. The same is true for *Car* and *Chassis*.

Exercise 1.4

Discuss a class that has a composition relationship to at least two other classes. Explain why it is a composition relationship.

1.4 WEAK AGGREGATION

Another relationship between classes that represents a different kind of whole-part relationship is weak aggregation. If each constituent part of the whole is not essential for the integrity of the whole, the relationship is called a weak aggregation.

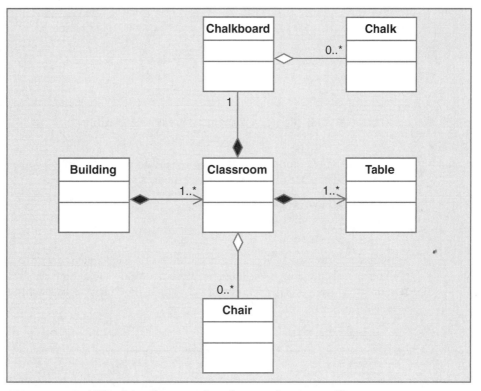

FIGURE 1.2 UML class diagram showing weak aggregation

Consider a classroom building that contains many classrooms, each containing tables that are bolted down, moveable chairs, a chalkboard, and chalk. How might we model the classes that describe these entities?

First we observe that the classrooms are an essential part of the building (they belong to the building). Within each classroom, the tables that are bolted down belong to each room. The chairs, although convenient, are not an essential part of each room. The chalkboard, being a fixture within the room, belongs to each room. The chalk is not considered to be an essential part of the chalkboard, although it is convenient to have a supply available. Based on this analysis, the UML class diagram shown in Figure 1.2 depicts the several classes and their relationships.

1.5 WEAK ASSOCIATION

If an object of another class is passed as a parameter into a method in a given class, this relationship between the two classes is called the "uses" relationship (the given class "uses" the class given by the parameter type).

FIGURE 1.3 UML diagram showing a weak association

As an example, consider a *Move* command in class *Player* in a game application. Suppose the signature of method *Move* is the following:

```
public void Move(Dice die) {
    // Details not shown
}
```

Classes *Player* and *Dice* are considered to be weakly associated because of the parameter passing shown earlier. The UML notation that depicts this relationship is shown in Figure 1.3. This relationship is called the "uses" relationship (e.g., *Player* uses *Dice*).

Exercise 1.5

Discuss two classes that have a weak association and explain why this is so.

1.6 INHERITANCE (GENERALIZATION/SPECIALIZATION RELATIONSHIPS)

One of the major pillars of object-oriented programming is inheritance. The inheritance relationship between two classes is a generalization/specialization relationship. A child class is designed to be a specialization of its parent. Most importantly, the child class must be able to logically stand in for its parent because it satisfies the "kind of" relationship. Consider class *Car* again and classes *SportsCar* and *Sedan*. It would be fair to state that a sports car is a "kind of car" and a sedan is a "kind of car." Each of these more specialized car classes could stand in and act as a substitute for a car object because they are more specialized types of car objects.

We show the inheritance relationship between classes *Car*, *SportsCar*, and *Sedan* in Figure 1.4. The broad-headed arrows point from child to parent.

Consider a more elaborate collection of vehicle classes to further illustrate the notion of inheritance, shown in the UML class diagram in Figure 1.5.

To conserve space, only a small sample of possible vehicle classes are shown in Figure 1.5. One must ask the question in every case where the inheritance relationship is shown whether the child class is a "kind of" its parent. This relationship is transitive. If B is a kind of A, and C is a kind of B, it follows that C is a kind of A. This certainly holds for the classes in Figure 1.5. For example, a young child's scooter is a kind

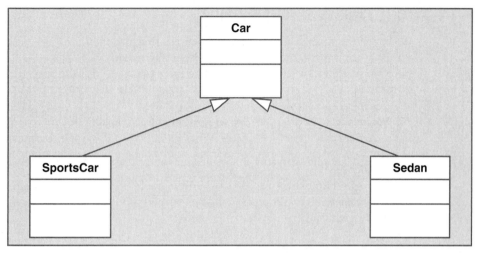

FIGURE 1.4 Inheritance relationship between classes *Car*, *SportsCar*, and *Sedan*

of unmotorized, land-based vehicle class. It should be able to stand in for *Vehicle*, *LandBased*, and *UnMotorized* if called upon to do so.

Exercise 1.6

Write an inheritance hierarchy based on everyday objects that surround you.

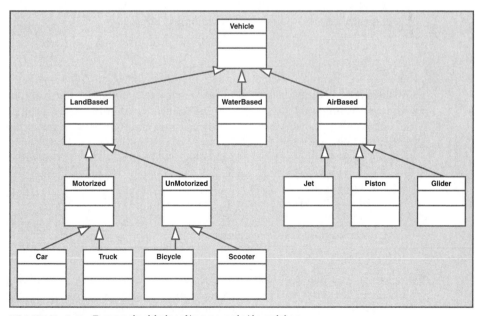

FIGURE 1.5 Expanded inheritance relationships

1.7 C# CLASS RELATIONSHIPS

We have been discussing classes and their relationship to other classes (strong aggregation, weak aggregation, weak association, and inheritance) as a basis for modeling software systems. This is an important activity that precedes the implementation of a software system. More details about such modeling in the context of object-oriented analysis and design will be presented in Chapter 2.

We must ground ourselves by seeing how the concepts presented in earlier sections affect the construction of C# classes. What does it mean if two C# classes have a strong or weak aggregation relationship, a weak association, or a generalization/specialization relationship?

If class relationships represent the blueprints of our software architecture, the construction of C# classes represents the finished product. Architecture sets the stage for building finished products.

1.7.1 C# Classes with Strong Aggregation

Consider the composition relationship between *Car*, *Engine*, and *Chassis* represented in Figure 1.1, and the following class *Car*:

```
public class Car {
    // Fields
    Engine theEngine = new Engine();
    Chassis theChassis = new Chassis();
    // Other details not shown
}
```

When an instance of class *Car* is created, *theEngine* and *theChassis* objects are automatically created. These objects belong to class *Car*.

1.7.2 C# Classes with Weak Aggregation

Consider the relationship between *Classroom* and *Chair* in Figure 1.2. Consider class *Classroom* as follows:

```
public class Classroom {
    // Fields
    Chair [] chairs;
    // Constructor
    public Classroom(Chair [] chairs) {
        this.chairs = chairs;
    // Other details not shown
}
```

When an instance of *Classroom* is created, an array, *chairs*, of *Chair* is passed as a parameter. This information is stored within the instance. The chairs are created and owned by another external class not shown, such as class *University*.

1.7.3 C# Classes with Weak Association

Consider again the weak association between class *Player* and *Dice* shown in Figure 1.3. Class *Player* "uses" class *Dice*.

A small portion of class *Player* is the following:

```
public class Player {
    // Command
    public void Move(Dice die) {
        die.Throw();
        // Other details not shown
    }
    // Other details not shown
}
```

1.7.4 C# Classes with Inheritance

Consider the classes *Car* and *Motorized* from Figure 1.5. Class *Car* is given as follows:

```
public class Car : Motorized {
    // Details not shown
}
```

The inheritance relationship in C# is given by the colon (:) operator that connects the child class to its parent. The child class is said to extend or be derived from the parent class.

Class *Car* acquires all the public and protected features (fields and methods) of class *Motorized*.

1.8 ABSTRACT CLASSES, POLYMORPHIC SUBSTITUTION, AND LATE-BINDING

We have seen that C# classes use fields (variables defined outside of a method within a class and global to the class) to represent the information structure or state of instances of the class. Class *Counter*, as you recall, used *countValue* (of type *int*) as its information structure to represent the state of a *Counter* object.

In many situations, we want to construct an inheritance hierarchy of classes in which the classes share the same fields but exhibit different behavior because of different implementations of one or more methods. In this situation, we might consider defining an abstract class and making it the root of the inheritance hierarchy.

An **abstract class** is a partially complete class in which one or more methods are left undefined and are declared abstract. No instances of an abstract class can be created. The fields and methods that are common to the concrete subclasses are factored out and placed in the abstract class. These fields and methods are acquired through inheritance in the concrete descendent classes. The methods declared as abstract must be completely implemented in each concrete subclass and serve to differentiate each of the subclasses.

We can construct a small software system that illustrates the use of abstract classes and leads to a discussion of polymorphic substitution and late-binding.

Suppose we collect an array of exam scores, each score of type double, and want to compute the average grade associated with these scores. We want to provide three distinct methods for computing the exam grade as follows:

1. Straight average of the scores (sum divided by the number of scores).

2. Straight average after dropping the lowest score.

3. Best weighted average in which a set of weights, each a fraction from 0.0 to 1.0, is specified and applied to each score so that the highest weight is applied to the highest score, the second highest weight to the second highest score, and so on.

Listing 1.2 shows the abstract class *Grading*.

LISTING 1.2 Abstract class *Grading*

```
using System;
namespace GradingApplication {
    public abstract class Grading {
        // Fields
        protected double[] grades;
        // Constructor
        public Grading(double[] theGrades) {
            grades = theGrades;
        }
        // Queries
        public abstract double AverageGrade();
        public abstract override String ToString();
    }
}
```

Discussion of Listing 1.2

◆ The abstract class *Grading* encapsulates an array of *double, grades*. The access specifier *protected* makes the field *grades* directly accessible in any subclass of *Grading*. Two abstract methods, *AverageGrade* and *ToString*, are specified. Each of the three concrete subclasses needs to implement these two methods.

We consider the first of these three concrete classes next. Class EqualWeights is presented in Listing 1.3.

LISTING 1.3 Class *EqualWeights*

```
using System;
namespace GradingApplication {
    public class EqualWeights : Grading {
        // Constructor
        public EqualWeights(double[] theGrades) : base(theGrades) {
        }
```

LISTING 1.3 Class *EqualWeights* (continued)

```
        // Queries
        public override double AverageGrade() {
            // Form average in ordinary way
            double sum = 0.0;
            int numberGrades = grades.Length;
            for (int i = 0; i < numberGrades; i++) {
                sum += grades[i];
            }
            return sum / numberGrades;
        }
        public override String ToString() {
            return "Using equal weights: ";
        }
    }
}
```

The class *EqualWeights* is shown as extending *Grading*. (It is a subclass of *Grading*.)

Discussion of Listing 1.3

◆ The constructor in the class takes an array of grades, *theGrades*, as input. It invokes the constructor inherited from the parent class *Grading* using the keyword *base*.

◆ The keyword **override** must be used in the signature for *AverageGrade*. This keyword indicates that the *AverageGrade* method is a redefinition of the parent class method, which in this case is an abstract method that contains no definition. This keyword override is a welcome requirement when redefining ancestor methods in a descendent class because it provides self-documentation about the intent of the subclass method. In other languages such as Java where redefinition is also possible, the absence of a keyword override requires the programmer to verify that a redefinition is taking place. The programmer does so by examining the method implementations in all ancestor classes and comparing them to the method implementation in the descendent class.

◆ The implementation details of *AverageGrade* in this class defines a local variable *sum*. A *for* loop iterates through all the scores in the *grades* array and increments *sum* by each score. This sum divided by the number of grades is returned.

Listing 1.4 presents the second concrete subclass of *Grading*, class *DropLowestGrade*.

LISTING 1.4 Class *DropLowestGrade*

```
using System;
namespace GradingApplication {
    public class DropLowestGrade : Grading {
        public DropLowestGrade(double [] grades) :
                                    base(grades) {
        }
```

LISTING 1.4 Class *DropLowestGrade* (continued)

```
        public override double AverageGrade() {
            /*
            Form average by taking straight average
            of all the grades minus the average grade
            */
            // Copy the grades array to gds, the sort gds
            double[] gds = new double[grades.Length];
            for (int i = 0; i < grades.Length; i++) {
                gds[i] = grades[i];
            }
            Array.Sort(gds);
            double sum = 0.0;
            for (int i = 1; i < grades.Length; i++) {
                sum += gds[i];
            }
            return sum / (grades.Length - 1);
        }
        public override String ToString() {
            return "Using drop lowest grade: ";
        }
    }
}
```

Discussion of Listing 1.4

◆ The method *AverageGrade* in class *DropLowestGrade* copies the scores in the field *grades* to a local array *gds*. It uses the static *Sort* method from class *Array* to sort the scores from smallest to largest. It then sums the scores excluding the first score (in index 0) and divides the sum by the length of the array minus one.

Exercise 1.7

Explain why it is desirable to copy the scores from the field *grades* to a local array *gds* before performing the sorting. What protection could be added to the code in method *AverageGrade* in class *DropLowestGrade* mentioned previously to protect the method from an error in the event that the number of scores in the grades array equals one? Add this additional protective code to method *AverageGrade*.

Listing 1.5 presents the third of the concrete classes that inherit from abstract class *Grading* and implements a best-weighted average approach to grading.

LISTING 1.5 Class *BestWeighted*

```
using System;
namespace GradingApplication {
    public class BestWeighted : Grading {

        // Fields
        private double [] weights;
```

LISTING 1.5 Class *BestWeighted* (continued)

```
        public BestWeighted(double [] grades,
                    double [] weights) : base(grades) {
        this.weights = weights;
    }
    public override double AverageGrade() {
        // Copy the grades and weights to gds and wts
        double [] wts = new double[weights.Length];
        double [] gds = new double[grades.Length];
        for (int i = 0; i < weights.Length; i++) {
            wts[i] = weights[i];
            gds[i] = grades[i];
        }
        Array.Sort(wts);
        Array.Sort(gds);
        double weightedAverage = 0.0;
        for (int i = 0; i < grades.Length; i++) {
            weightedAverage += gds[i] * wts[i];
        }
        return weightedAverage;
    }
    public override String ToString() {
        return "Using best weighted average: ";
    }
  }
}
```

Class *BestWeighted* defines a new field, *weights*, that is not present in the parent abstract class *Grading* or in the other two concrete classes. It is not uncommon when constructing hierarchies of classes to add fields in descendent classes. These represent new specialized behavior just as redefining ancestor class methods or adding new methods represent new specialized behavior.

Discussion of Listing 1.5

◆ The *AverageGrade* method in class *BestWeighted* creates two local array variables *wts* and *gds* and copies the values from the weights and grades fields to *wts* and *gds*, respectively.

◆ Each of these local arrays is then sorted using the static *Sort* method from class *Array*.

◆ Finally, the weighted average of the sorted grades and sorted weights is calculated by computing the sum of products of these two sorted arrays.

We have created a simple hierarchy of three subclasses that extend the abstract class Grading as shown in the UML class diagram in Figure 1.6.

The stereotype <> is used in class Grading to establish the abstract methods and the abstract class itself.

How might we use this hierarchy of classes in an application that requires different grading strategies? The answer to this question leads us to the two important concepts of polymorphic substitution and late-binding.

Suppose that we want to provide a menu that will allow the user to choose one of the three grading approaches. To make the application simpler, we will "hard wire" an array of four scores (exam grades) into the program.

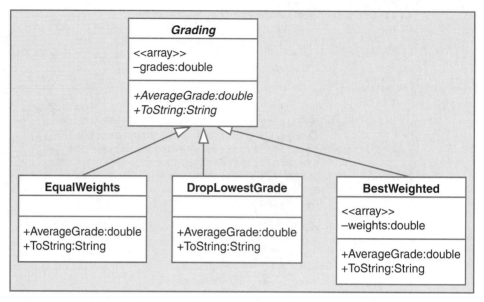

FIGURE 1.6 Three subclasses that extend the abstract class *Grading*

Our application will begin as follows:

```
using System;
namespace GradingApplication {
   public class GradingApp {
      static void Main() {
         double[] scores = { 90.0, 10.0, 80.0, 100.0 };
         double [] weights = { 0.4, 0.3, 0.2, 0.1 };
         Console.WriteLine("Scores: 90, 10, 80, 100");
         Console.WriteLine("Weights: 0.4, 0.3, 0.2, 0.1");
         bool done = false;
         while (!done) {
            Console.WriteLine("\n");
            Console.WriteLine("1 -> Use equal weights\n");
            Console.WriteLine("2 -> Use drop lowest grade\n");
            Console.WriteLine("3 -> Use weighted average\n");
            Console.WriteLine("Any other number to quit\n");
            Console.Write("Enter choice: ");
            String gradingMethodStr = Console.ReadLine();
            int gradingMethod =
              Convert.ToInt32(gradingMethodStr);
```

Using a non-object-oriented structured approach to programming, one might be tempted to continue with code as follows:

```
if (gradingMethod == 1) {
    EqualWeights grading = new EqualWeights(scores);
} else if (gradingMethod == 2) {
    DropLowestGrade grading = new DropLowestGrade(scores);
} else if ( ...
```

A better approach is used in Listing 1.6, which shows the entire grading application.

LISTING 1.6 Class *GradingApp*

```
using System;
namespace GradingApplication {
   public class GradingApp {
      static void Main() {
         double[] scores = { 90.0, 10.0, 80.0, 100.0 };
         double [] weights = { 0.4, 0.3, 0.2, 0.1 };
         Console.WriteLine("Scores: 90, 10, 80, 100");
         Console.WriteLine("Weights: 0.4, 0.3, 0.2, 0.1");
         bool done = false;
         while (!done) {
            Console.WriteLine("\n");
            Console.WriteLine("1 -> Use equal weights\n");
            Console.WriteLine("2 -> Use drop lowest grade\n");
            Console.WriteLine("3 -> Use weighted average\n");
            Console.WriteLine("Any other number to quit\n");
            Console.Write("Enter choice: ");
            String gradingMethodStr = Console.ReadLine();
            int gradingMethod =
               Convert.ToInt32(gradingMethodStr);
            Grading gradingObject = null;
            switch (gradingMethod) {
               case 1:
                  gradingObject =
new EqualWeights(scores); // Polymorphic substitution
                  break;
               case 2:
                  gradingObject =
new DropLowestGrade(scores); // Polymorphic substitution
                  break;
               case 3:
                  gradingObject =
new BestWeighted(scores, weights); // Polymorphic
                                                 // substitution
                  break;
               default:
                  done = true;
                  continue;
         }
         double average =
            gradingObject.AverageGrade(); // Late-binding
           String message =
            gradingObject.ToString(); // Late-binding
           Console.WriteLine(message + " the average grade = " +
                            average);
        }
      }
   }
}
```

Discussion of Listing 1.6

◆   A local variable *gradingObject* of type *Grading* is declared and initialized to null. The actual type of object that is created is either *EqualWeights*, *DropLowestGrade*, or *BestWeighted* depending on the user's input.

C# is a strongly typed language. Every identifier (field, local variable, and method parameter) must be declared to be of a well-defined type. The compiler enforces the type rules and does not, for example, allow an object of type *String* to be used where an object of type *int* is required.

Why is it legal to assign an object of type *EqualWeights*, *DropLowestGrade*, or *BestWeighted* to an object on the left side of the assignment of type *Grading* as done in the switch in Listing 1.6? The three assignment statements in which this is done are shown in boldface type in Listing 1.6.

Polymorphic substitution provides the basis for allowing this apparent violation of the type rules. This principle states that *an object from a descendent class may be used in place of an object from an ancestor class*. In this case, an object of type *EqualWeights*, type *DropLowestGrade*, or type *BestWeighted* can be used in place of an object of formal type *Grading*. The type *Grading* for *gradingObject* is used as a placeholder for one of the concrete descendent types.

Polymorphic substitution is a compile-time or static typing principle. It represents a relaxation of the strong typing rules to permit more flexibility in the software construction process.

Clearly the compiler (and for that matter, the programmer or the reader) cannot possibly know what choice the user will make for grading type while the program is running. Which of the three possible *AverageGrade* methods and which of the three possible *ToString* methods will the system dispatch when it encounters the two lines of code shown in boldface in Listing 1.6?

```
double average = gradingObject.AverageGrade();

String message = gradingObject.ToString();
```

Here the principle of late-binding applies. The runtime system binds the appropriate *AverageGrade* method based on the actual type of *gradingObject* rather than its formal type (*Grading*). The same is true for *ToString*. If the user chose "Use drop lowest grade" and the gradingObject is an instance of class *DropLowestGrade*, the version of *AverageGrade* and *ToString* implemented in class *DropLowestGrade* would be deployed.

Late-binding gets its name because the system attaches (binds) one of several possible methods to an object at runtime, in contrast to polymorphic substitution, which is a static or compile-time typing principle.

The combination of polymorphic substitution and late-binding promotes a flexible "pluggable" architecture. To dramatize this, we can perform some simple maintenance on the grading system.

Suppose we want to add a fourth concrete mechanism for computing a grade from the array of scores that is input. This fourth method for grading uses fixed weights, in which each score is multiplied by a weight without associating the best grade with the highest weight, and the second best grade with the second best weight as is done in class *BestWeighted*. We call the new concrete class that implements this grading strategy *FixedWeights*. Its details are presented in Listing 1.7.

LISTING 1.7 Class *FixedWeights*

```
using System;
namespace GradingApplication {
    public class FixedWeights : Grading {
        // Fields
        private double[] weights;
        // Constructor
        public FixedWeights(double [] grades,
            double [] weights) : base(grades) {
            this.weights = weights;
        }
        // Queries
        public override double AverageGrade() {
            double weightedAverage = 0.0;
            for (int i = 0; i < grades.Length; i++) {
                weightedAverage += grades[i] * weights[i];
            }
            return weightedAverage;
        }
        public override String ToString() {
            return "Using fixed weights: ";
        }
    }
}
```

It might be tempting to define class *FixedWeights* as a subclass of *BestWeighted* because *FixedWeights* also has two fields (*grades* and *weights*).

Exercise 1.8

Explain why it would not be appropriate to define class *FixedWeights* as a subclass of class *BestWeighted*.

Exercise 1.9

Modify Listing 1.6, class *GradingApp*, so that the user is presented with the fourth choice of "Use fixed weights" and the system can respond to this choice. Run this application and verify that when this fourth choice is made, the grade is computed accordingly (using the same hard-wired grades and weights as used in Listing 1.6).

The modified UML class diagram that accounts for the new concrete class *FixedWeights* is shown in Figure 1.7.

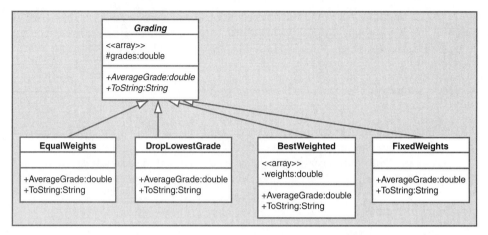

FIGURE 1.7 Modified UML class diagram with new concrete class *FixedWeights*

1.9 INTERFACES, POLYMORPHIC SUBSTITUTION, AND LATE-BINDING WITHOUT INHERITANCE

An interface is a special kind of C# class that supports polymorphic substitution and late-binding without inheritance. Like all classes, an interface is a type. All the methods declared in an interface must be abstract (no implementation details allowed) and no fields may be defined. Unlike an ordinary class, an interface cannot be extended (inherited from) by a concrete class. Only an interface can extend one or more interfaces. Concrete classes implement an interface. Because all the methods of an interface must be abstract, the abstract designator occurs by default and does not need to be explicitly stated.

By convention we always use an uppercase I in naming a C# interface.

The following code shows an example of an interface in the C# system:

```
public interface IComparable {
    /* Returns a positive value if the receiver is larger than
       obj, returns zero if the receiver object equals obj and
       returns a negative value if the receiver object is smaller
       than obj.
    */
    int CompareTo(Object obj);
}
```

This interface, like all interfaces, represents a contract that must be met by any class that implements this interface. For example, if *MyClass* implements this interface, its signature would be:

```
public MyClass : IComparable {
    // Must provide full implementation of CompareTo
}
```

The same colon (:) notation is used for implementing an interface as inheriting from a base class. This is unfortunate because it can easily lead to confusion. The *implements* keyword used in Java would be a much better choice in C#.

For the signature of *MyClass* shown in the preceding code, you read this as "MyClass implements the interface IComparable."

The compiler verifies that *MyClass* contains an implementation of *CompareTo*. In this sense, *MyClass* accepts the contract specified by the methods in the interface (only one method in this case). If *MyClass* fails to implement this method, it must be declared as an abstract class.

The contractual aspect of interfaces is used to great advantage in the C# libraries. For example, to sort a collection of objects, the objects must belong to a class that implements *IComparable*. The sort methods depend on the fact that each object in the collection responds to *CompareTo* with the semantics stated earlier.

In general, interfaces provide a framework for establishing a contractual context among concrete implementing classes. Each class among the implementing classes provides its own implementation of the required abstract methods declared in the interface. For example, the concrete classes that implement *IComparable* contain objects that may be compared to each other.

An interface may be used as a placeholder for any concrete class that implements the interface. The typing system allows any class that implements the interface to be used in place of the interface type. This is the principle of polymophic substitution once again.

The runtime system can dispatch the appropriate version of an abstract method declared in an interface if the method is invoked on an object that belongs to a class that implements the interface. In other words, late-binding applies to objects that belong to classes that implement an interface.

To bring these ideas to life, consider an interesting example that uses interfaces as its central architectural principle. We start by raising a philosphical question that applies to a dice game.

Suppose four six-sided dice are specially designed so that each die has a set of non-negative integers on each side of the die. Repeat values are legal, but the values on the four dice are distinct (no value on one die is equal to the same value on any other die). Suppose we play a game in which two dice from the set of four are thrown on a table with equal likelihood of landing on any of the six sides. The die with the higher number appearing on the top wins a point for the player who owns that die.

Two players choose one die each. On each throw of their die, the player with the higher number wins a point. Ties are not possible because the numbers on each die are distinct. The first player to score 100 points is the winner. Would you want to choose first so you can choose any of the four dice, allowing your challenger to choose from among the remaining three dice? Or would you rather choose second, giving your opponent the first choice among the four dice?

In some sense, we are asking the general question, "Is information useful and can we exploit it to our advantage?" It is assumed that the four dice would be available for each player's inspection before each chooses their die. The only question is whether to choose first or choose second.

The intuitive position would be to choose first. This is based on the assumption that if each die has distinct values (a tie is not possible), then it ought to be possible to determine which of the four dice is the best (has a higher probability of winning on each throw of the dice). The argument for choosing second would be based on the strange idea that for any die the first player chooses, there is always a better die in the set of four.

Before we resolve this question, let us construct a computer simulation where you, the user, choose first and the computer chooses second (from among the three remaining dice after you have made your choice). Listing 1.8 presents the interface for dice, *IDice*.

LISTING 1.8 Interface *IDice*

```
using System;
namespace DiceApplication {
    public interface IDice {
        // Commands
        void ThrowDie();
        // Read-only query property
        int LastThrow {
            get;
        }
    }
}
```

Discussion of Listing 1.8

◆   In order for a concrete class to fullfill the contract of interface *IDice* by implementing this interface, it must come up with an implementation of the *ThrowDie* command and the *LastThrow* property. (Properties are discussed in detail in Chapter 4. Don't be concerned with the programming details at this time.)

Before we answer the earlier question about whether it is better to choose first or second, let us construct a complete application that uses the four special dice even before we see these dice. The application shown in Listing 1.9 dramatizes the architectural simplicity and robustness of polymorphic substitution and late-binding using an interface and several classes that implement this interface.

LISTING 1.9 Class *DiceApp*

```
using System;
namespace DiceApplication {
    public class DiceApp {
        public static void Main() {
            try {
                // Prompt the user to choose one of the four
                // specialized die
                Console.Write(
            "Choose die 1, 2, 3 or 4 (any other number to exit): ");
                String choiceString = Console.ReadLine();
                int userDieChoice = Convert.ToInt32(choiceString);
```

LISTING 1.9 Class *DiceApp* (continued)

```
            while (userDieChoice >= 1 && userDieChoice <= 4) {
                int computerScore = 0;
                int playerScore = 0;
                IDice computerDie = null; // Placeholder
                IDice playerDie = null;   // Placeholder
                if (userDieChoice == 1) {
                    playerDie = new SpecialDie1(); // Poly sub
                    computerDie = new SpecialDie4(); // Poly sub
                } else if (userDieChoice == 2) {
                    playerDie = new SpecialDie2(); // Poly sub
                    computerDie = new SpecialDie1(); // Poly sub
                } else if (userDieChoice == 3) {
                    playerDie = new SpecialDie3(); // Poly sub
                    computerDie = new SpecialDie2(); // Poly sub
                } else if (userDieChoice == 4) {
                    playerDie = new SpecialDie4(); // Poly sub
                    computerDie = new SpecialDie3(); // Poly sub
                }
                // Play the game - user against the computer
                while (computerScore < 100 && playerScore < 100) {
                    computerDie.ThrowDie(); // Late-binding
                    playerDie.ThrowDie();   // Late-binding
                    if (computerDie.LastThrow >
                       playerDie.LastThrow) {
                       computerScore++;
                   } else {
                       playerScore++;
                   }
                }
                Console.WriteLine("The computer score: " +
                    computerScore +
                    " The player score: " +
                    playerScore);

        Console.Write(
        "\n\nChoose die 1, 2, 3 or 4 (any other number to exit): ");
                choiceString = Console.ReadLine();
                    userDieChoice = Convert.ToInt32(choiceString);
                }
            } catch (Exception ex) {
            }
        }
    }
}
```

Discussion of Listing 1.9

◆ The formal type of *computerDie* and *playerDie* is *IDice*. The interface is being used as a polymorphic placeholder for the actual type (either *SpecialDie1*, *SpecialDie2*, *SpecialDie3,* or *SpecialDie4*).

◆ After the user makes her choice, the computer makes its choice as shown in the *if, else if* construct.

◆ The *while* loop simulates the game. The command *ThrowDie* is invoked on *computerDie* and then on *playerDie*. The actual version of this command (there will be four distinct versions once the special die classes are constructed) is determined by the runtime system and is based on the actual type of *computerDie* and *playerDie*. This is an example of late-binding in action.

◆ When either *computerScore* or *playerScore* exceeds 100, the game ends.

All that remains is to define the four dice, answer the philosphical question discussed earlier (who goes first), and complete this application by implementing the four specialized die classes.

The four dice, called Efron dice (see "Tricky Dice Revisited" by Ivar Peterson, *www.sciencenews.org/articles/20020420/mathtrek.asp*):

Die 1: 0, 0, 4, 4, 4, 4

Die 2: 3, 3, 3, 3, 3, 3

Die 3: 2, 2, 2, 2, 6, 6

Die 4: 5, 5, 5, 1, 1, 1

Let us compare the strength of each die against another die from the set.

Die 1 is stronger than die 2. Of the 36 possible outcomes, die 1 wins whenever a 4 occurs. This occurs two-thirds of the time, so die 1 has two-to-one odds of beating die 2.

Die 2 is stronger than die 3. Die 2 wins whenever die 3 throws a 2. This occurs two-thirds of the time, so die 2 has two-to-one odds of beating die 3.

Die 3 is stronger than die 4. Die 3 wins whenever a 6 occurs on die 3 or whenever a 1 occurs on die 4. The number of possibilities for this to happen is $2 \times 6 + 4 \times 3 = 24 / 36$. So die 3 has two-to-one odds of beating die 4.

It would seem from this reasoning that die 1 should be stronger than die 4 since 1 is stronger than 2 and 2 is stronger than 3 and 3 is stronger than 4. But the opposite is true. Die 4 is twice as strong as die 1.

Exercise 1.10

Show that die 4 has 2 to 1 odds of beating die 1.

No matter which die the user chooses, the computer always chooses one that has twice the probability of winning a particular throw. (See the code in Listing 1.9 to confirm this.)

The dice are nontransitive. Although die1 > die2, die2 > die3, and die3 > die4, it does not follow that die1 > die4. The opposite is true.

A random number object is specified in class *RandomNumber* given in Listing 1.10. The random number object, *rnd*, is declared as a *public static* feature of this class and may be obtained through the class name *RandomNumber*. The static constructor serves to "warm up" the generator by accessing and throwing away 50,000 random values.

The four specialized die classes are presented in Listings 1.11–1.14.

LISTING 1.10 Class *RandomNumber*

```
using System;
namespace DiceApplication {

    public class RandomNumber {

        // Fields
        public static Random rnd = new Random();
        // Constructor
        static RandomNumber() {  // Executed once
            for (int i = 0; i < 50000; i++) {
                rnd.NextDouble();
            }
        }
    }
}
```

LISTING 1.11 Class *SpecialDie1*

```
using System;
namespace DiceApplication {
    // Models the special die 0, 0, 4, 4, 4, 4
    public class SpecialDie1 : IDice {
        // Fields
        private int lastThrow;
        // Commands
        public void ThrowDie() {
            if (RandomNumber.rnd.NextDouble() <= 1.0 / 3.0) {
                lastThrow = 0;
            } else {
                lastThrow = 4;
            }
        }
        // Read-only property query
        public int LastThrow {
            get {
                return lastThrow;
            }
        }
    }
}
```

LISTING 1.12 Class *SpecialDie2*

```
using System;
namespace DiceApplication {
    // Models the special die 3, 3, 3, 3, 3, 3
    public class SpecialDie2 : IDice {
        // Fields
        private int lastThrow;
```

LISTING 1.12 Class *SpecialDie2* (continued)

```csharp
        // Commands
        public void ThrowDie() {
            lastThrow = 3;
        }
        // Read-only property query
        public int LastThrow {
            get {
                return lastThrow;
            }
        }
    }
}
```

LISTING 1.13 Class *SpecialDie3*

```csharp
using System;
namespace DiceApplication {
    // Models the special die 2, 2, 2, 2, 6, 6
    public class SpecialDie3 : IDice {
        // Fields
        private int lastThrow;
        // Commands
        public void ThrowDie() {
            if (RandomNumber.rnd.NextDouble() <= 1.0 / 3.0) {
                lastThrow = 6;
            } else {
                lastThrow = 2;
            }
        }
        // Read-only property query
        public int LastThrow {
            get {
                return lastThrow;
            }
        }
    }
}
```

LISTING 1.14 Class *SpecialDie4*

```csharp
using System;
namespace DiceApplication {
    // Models the special die 5, 5, 5, 1, 1, 1
    public class SpecialDie4 : IDice {
        // Fields
        private int lastThrow;
```

LISTING 1.14 Class *SpecialDie4* (continued)

```
        // Commands
        public void ThrowDie() {
            if (RandomNumber.rnd.NextDouble() <= 1.0 / 2.0) {
                lastThrow = 5;
            } else {
                lastThrow = 1;
            }
        }
        // Read-only property query
        public int LastThrow {
            get {
                return lastThrow;
            }
        }
    }
}
```

The dice application may be modeled using a UML class diagram shown in Figure 1.8. The dotted lines with broad arrows indicate that a concrete class implements an interface.

Exercise 1.11

Explain and justify the implementation of method *ThrowDie* in class *SpecialDie1* in Listing 1.11.

Exercise 1.12

Explain and justify the implementation of method *ThrowDie* in class *SpecialDie2* in Listing 1.12.

Exercise 1.13

Explain and justify the implementation of method *ThrowDie* in class *SpecialDie3* in Listing 1.13.

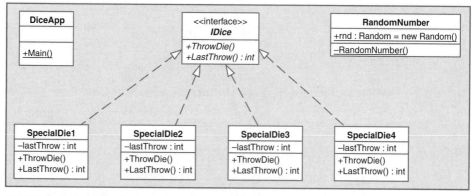

FIGURE 1.8 UML diagram for dice application

Exercise 1.14

Explain and justify the implementation of method *ThrowDie* in class *SpecialDie2* in Listing 1.14.

Exercise 1.15

Consider a four-person game in which each player is assigned one of the dice. The highest throw among the four dice wins a point. The first player to score 100 points wins the game.

What is the probability of each die winning a four-way toss?

Exercise 1.16

Simulate a game with the four dice competing against each other. The first die to score 100 points wins. Compare the outcome with the results of Exercise 1.15.

1.10 COMPARING OBJECTS

The C# framework provides two standard interfaces for comparing objects: *IComparable* (from namespace *System*) and *IComparer* (from namespace *System.Collections*). These interfaces are defined as follows:

```
public interface IComparable {
    /* Returns a positive value if the receiver is larger than
    obj, returns zero if the receiver object equals obj and
    returns a negative value if the receiver object is smaller
    than obj.
    */
    int CompareTo(Object obj);
}
public interface IComparer {
    /* Returns a positive value if x is greater than y,
    returns zero if object x equals object y,
    returns a negative value if object x is smaller
    than object y.
    */
    int Compare(Object x, Object y);
}
```

We consider an application that uses *IComparable* first.

1.10.1 C# Application that Illustrates the Use of IComparable

Consider the abstract class *GeometricFigure* presented in Listing 1.15.

LISTING 1.15 Abstract class *GeometricFigure*

```
using System;
namespace ComparingGeometricFigures {
    public abstract class GeometricFigure : IComparable {
        // Queries
        public abstract double area();
        public abstract double perimeter();
        public int CompareTo(Object obj) {
            if (obj is GeometricFigure) {
                GeometricFigure figure = (GeometricFigure)obj;
                if (this.area() == figure.area()) {
                    return 0;
                } else if (this.area() > figure.area()) {
                    return 1;
                } else {
                    return -1;
                }
            } else {
                throw new Exception("Cannot perform comparison");
            }
        }
        public abstract override String ToString();
    }
}
```

Abstract class *GeometricFigure* implements *IComparable* according to its declaration given in Listing 1.15. This implies that either it must implement the *CompareTo* method or it must obligate any of its concrete descendent classes to do this. In this case, the abstract class itself implements the *CompareTo* query.

Discussion of Listing 1.15

◆ According to the details in the *CompareTo* query, the *GeometricFigure* object receiving the *CompareTo* query is compared to the *GeometricFigure* object sent in as a parameter by comparing their areas. The *area* (as well as *perimeter*) method is abstract. Any concrete subclass of *GeometricFigure* will inherit this *CompareTo* method and will have completely implemented an *area* and *perimeter* method.

Listings 1.16 to 1.18 present the details of three concrete subclasses of *GeometricFigure* namely *Square*, *Rectangle*, and *RightTriangle*.

LISTING 1.16 Class *Square*

```
using System;
namespace ComparingGeometricFigures {
    public class Square : GeometricFigure {
        // Fields
        private double side;
```

LISTING 1.16 Class *Square* (continued)

```
        // Constructor
        public Square(double side) {
            this.side = side;
        }
        // Queries
        public override double area() {
            return side * side;
        }
        public override double perimeter() {
            return 4.0 * side;
        }
        public override String ToString() {
            return "Square of side " + side;
        }
    }
}
```

LISTING 1.17 Class *Rectangle*

```
using System;
namespace ComparingGeometricFigures {
    public class Rectangle : GeometricFigure {
        // Fields
        private double side1;
        private double side2;
        // Constructor
        public Rectangle(double side1, double side2) {
            this.side1 = side1;
            this.side2 = side2;
        }
        // Queries
        public override double area() {
            return side1 * side2;
        }
        public override double perimeter() {
            return 2.0 * (side1 + side2);
        }
        public override String ToString() {
            return
      "Rectangle with side1 = " + side1 + " side2 = " + side2;
        }
    }
}
```

LISTING 1.18 Class *RightTriangle*

```
using System;
namespace ComparingGeometricFigures {
    public class RightTriangle : GeometricFigure {
        // Fields
        private double leg1;
        private double leg2;
```

LISTING 1.18 Class *RightTriangle* (continued)

```
    // Constructor
    public RightTriangle(double leg1, double leg2) {
      this.leg1 = leg1;
      this.leg2 = leg2;
    }
    // Queries
    public override double area() {
      return 0.5 * leg1 * leg2;
    }
    public override double perimeter() {
      return leg1 + leg2 +
            Math.Sqrt(leg1 * leg1 + leg2 * leg2);
    }
    public override String ToString() {
        return
        "RightTriangle with leg1 = " + leg1 + " leg2 = " + leg2;
    }
  }
}
```

Listing 1.19 presents the details of a short application class. In this application class, an array of several geometric figure objects is declared. The largest and smallest geometric figures are determined and output to the console.

LISTING 1.19 Class *GeometricFigureApp*

```
using System;
namespace ComparingGeometricFigures {
    public class GeometricFigureApp {
      public static void Main() {
        GeometricFigure[] figures =
            {
              new Rectangle(3.0, 4.0), new Square(3.5),
              new RightTriangle(3.0, 4.0),
              new Rectangle(4.0, 2.0),
              new Square(2.0)
            }; // Polymorphic substitution used here
        // Find the largest value among the figures
        GeometricFigure largest = figures[0]; // Poly sub
         for (int index = 1; index < figures.Length; index++) {
            if (figures[index].CompareTo(largest) > 0) {
                largest = figures[index]; // Poly sub
            }
        }
        Console.WriteLine(
        // Late binding
        "The largest figure is " + largest.ToString());
```

LISTING 1.19 Class *GeometricFigureApp* (continued)

```
        // Find the smallest value among the figures
        GeometricFigure smallest = figures[0]; // Poly sub
        for (int index = 1; index < figures.Length; index++) {
            if (figures[index].CompareTo(smallest) < 0) {
                smallest = figures[index]; // Poly sub
            }
        }
        Console.WriteLine(
    // Late binding
    "The smallest figure is " + smallest.ToString());
        Console.ReadLine();
    }
  }
}
/* Program output
The largest figure is Square of side 3.5
The smallest figure is Square of side 2
*/
```

Discussion of Listing 1.19

◆ Polymorphic substitution and late-binding are used in Listing 1.19. In determining the largest value, we start by assuming this largest value is the *GeometricFigure* object in index 0. The actual type of object in index 0 is one of the three concrete class types (*Square*, *Rectangle*, or *RightTriangle*). The formal type is *GeometricFigure*, which is being used as a placeholder.

◆ As we iterate through the *figures* array, we use the inherited *CompareTo* method to determine whether the object *largest* must be replaced with one that is even larger. Once *largest* is found, late-binding allows us to deploy the *ToString* query for the actual object type associated with *largest*.

A UML class diagram that represents the relationship among the classes in the geometric figure application is shown in Figure 1.9.

Exercise 1.17

Change the implementation details of the *CompareTo* method in abstract class *GeometricFigure* (Listing 1.15). Rerun the application and compare the results with the version given in this book.

1.10.2 C# Application that Illustrates the Use of IComparer

Suppose we wish to determine the smallest and largest values in an array of objects. Consider the class *LargestSmallest* presented in Listing 1.20.

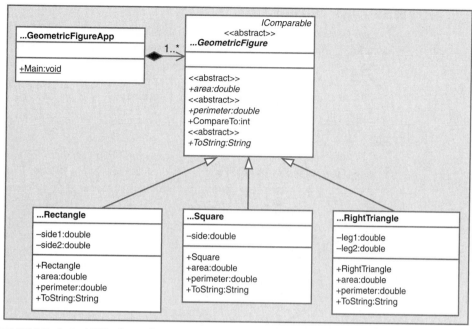

FIGURE 1.9 UML class diagram for the geometric figure application

LISTING 1.20 Class *LargestSmallest*

```
using System;
using System.Collections;
namespace LargestSmallestApplication {
   public class LargestSmallest {
      // Queries
      public Object Smallest(Object[] objects, IComparer
         comparer) {
         Object smallest = objects[0];
         for (int index = 1; index < objects.Length; index++) {
            if (comparer.Compare(objects[index], smallest) < 0) {
               smallest = objects[index];
            }
         }
         return smallest;
      }
      public Object Largest(Object[] objects, IComparer comparer) {
         Object largest = objects[0];
         for (int index = 1; index < objects.Length; index++) {
            if (comparer.Compare(objects[index], largest) > 0) {
               largest = objects[index];
            }
         }
         return largest;
      }
   }
}
```

Discussion of Listing 1.20

◆ Formal type *Object* is being used as a polymorphic placeholder for any type. The *comparer* parameter is an object whose formal type is *IComparer* but whose actual type is some concrete class that implements the *IComparer* interface. So the *comparer* object encapsulates behavior that describes how to compare two objects in the array passed in as the first parameter.

To illustrate the use of class *LargestSmallest*, we define a class *NameRecord* in Listing 1.21.

LISTING 1.21 Class *NameRecord*

```
using System;
namespace LargestSmallestApplication {

    public class NameRecord {
        // Fields
        private String firstName;
        private String lastName;
        private int idNumber;
        // Constructor
        public NameRecord(String firstName, String lastName,
                          int idNumber) {
            this.firstName = firstName;
            this.lastName = lastName;
            this.idNumber = idNumber;
        }
        // Read-only property queries
        public String FirstName {
            get {
                return firstName;
            }
        }
        public String LastName {
            get {
                return lastName;
            }
        }
        public int IDNumber {
            get {
                return idNumber;
            }
        }
        // Query
        public override String ToString() {
            return firstName + " " + lastName + " " + idNumber;
        }
    }
}
```

If our goal is to build an array of objects of type *NameRecord* and then find the smallest and largest objects of type *NameRecord* in the array, we first need to specify a mechanism (behavior) for comparing two objects of type *NameRecord*.

The *IComparer* interface provides the basis for doing this. Listing 1.22 presents the first of two concrete classes that implements the *IComparer* interface.

LISTING 1.22 Class *NameRecordComparer1*

```
using System;
using System.Collections;
namespace LargestSmallestApplication {
    public class NameRecordComparer1 : IComparer {
        /*
        Compare the concatenation of last name, first name, and
        ID number in the two NameRecord objects.
        */
        public int Compare(Object obj1, Object obj2) {
            NameRecord nameRecord1 = (NameRecord)obj1;
            NameRecord nameRecord2 = (NameRecord)obj2;
            String str1 = nameRecord1.LastName +
                          nameRecord1.FirstName +
                          nameRecord1.IDNumber;
            String str2 = nameRecord2.LastName +
                          nameRecord2.FirstName +
                          nameRecord2.IDNumber;
            return str1.CompareTo(str2);
        }
    }
}
```

The signature of the query method *Compare* matches the signature required by any concrete class that implements the *IComparer* interface. This *Compare* method takes two parameters of formal type *Object* as its parameters. But we are comparing *NameRecord* objects here, not entities of type *Object*. Therefore the first two lines of code in method *Compare* involve downcasts from *obj1* and *obj2* to *nameRecord1* and *nameRecord2*, respectively.

As a reminder, a downcast in C# does not convert or change the type of the object to which it applies. It is simply an assertion to the compiler and runtime system that the actual type of the object being downcast is equal to the type name used in the downcast (*NameRecord* in this case). The compiler then allows you to treat the object being downcast as if its formal type were equal to the type in the downcast. However, the runtime system verifies that the actual type of the object equals the type promised in the downcast. If not, a type cast exception is generated. So you cannot cheat. If one were to attempt to compare apples and oranges (a *NameRecord* object with, say, a *String* object), a type cast exception would be generated at runtime and of course the comparison would fail.

Discussion of Listing 1.22

◆   In Listing 1.22, two objects of type *NameRecord* are compared by forming a string given by the concatenation of the last name, first name, and ID number. The numeric value of the ID number is not used, but the lexical representation of the string. So the string "45" would be considered larger than the string "123".

A second alternative concrete class, *NameRecordComparer2*, is presented in Listing 1.23 for comparing two objects of type *NameRecord*.

LISTING 1.23 Class *NameRecordComparer2*

```
using System;
using System.Collections;
namespace LargestSmallestApplication {
    public class NameRecordComparer2 : IComparer {
        /*
            Compare the ID number of the two objects.
        */
        public int Compare(Object obj1, Object obj2) {
            NameRecord nameRecord1 = (NameRecord)obj1;
            NameRecord nameRecord2 = (NameRecord)obj2;
            return nameRecord1.IDNumber - nameRecord2.IDNumber;
        }
    }
}
```

Discussion of Listing 1.23

◆ Here the ID numbers of the two objects are compared in an ordinary numeric sense. Class *NameRecordComparer2* provides an entirely different mechanism for comparing objects than class *NameRecordComparer1*.

Listing 1.24 presents a short application class that demonstrates the use of the two comparer classes.

LISTING 1.24 Class *LargestSmallestApp*

```
using System;
using System.Collections;
namespace LargestSmallestApplication {
    public class LargestSmallestApp {
        public static void Main() {
            NameRecord[] records =
                {
                    new NameRecord("George", "Washington", 1234),
                    new NameRecord("John", "Adams", 4321),
                    new NameRecord("Harry", "Truman", 45678),
                    new NameRecord("Dwight", "Eisenhower", 123),
                    new NameRecord("George", "Bush", 1),
                    new NameRecord("George", "Bush", 2)
                };
            IComparer comparer1 = new NameRecordComparer1();
            IComparer comparer2 = new NameRecordComparer2();
            LargestSmallest largeSmall = new LargestSmallest();
            NameRecord largestNameRecord =
              (NameRecord) largeSmall.Largest(records, comparer1);
```

LISTING 1.24 Class *LargestSmallestApp* (continued)

```
                Console.WriteLine("Largest using comparer1: " +
                  largestNameRecord.ToString());
                NameRecord smallestNameRecord =
                  (NameRecord) largeSmall.Smallest(records, comparer1);
                Console.WriteLine(
                  "Smallest using comparer1: " +
                    smallestNameRecord.ToString());
                Console.WriteLine("\n");
                largestNameRecord =
                  (NameRecord) largeSmall.Largest(records, comparer2);
                Console.WriteLine(
                  "Largest using comparer2: " +
                    largestNameRecord.ToString());
                smallestNameRecord =
                  (NameRecord) largeSmall.Smallest(records, comparer2);
                Console.WriteLine(
                  "Smallest using comparer2: " +
                    smallestNameRecord.ToString());
                Console.ReadLine();
            }
        }
}
/* Program output
Largest using comparer1: George Washington 1234
Smallest using comparer1: John Adams 4321

Largest using comparer2: Harry Truman 45678
Smallest using comparer2: George Bush 1
*/
```

An array of six *NameRecord* objects is hard-wired into the application. Instances of classes *NameRecordComparer1* and *NameRecordComparer2* are generated in objects *comparer1* and *comparer2*, respectively.

Exercise 1.18

Explain the program output shown at the end of Listing 1.24.

Exercise 1.19

Create another class *NameRecordComparer3* that provides a third distinct mechanism for comparing two objects of type *NameRecord*. Add some additional code to class *LargestSmallestApp* that uses an object *comparer3* of type *NameRecordComparer3*, and repeat the computation and output of the largest and smallest *NameRecord* object based on *NameRecordComparer3*.

1.11 SUMMARY

This chapter has focused on the basics of object-oriented software technology:

◆   A class describes the behavior of objects (instances).

◆   The behavior of a class is defined by the information model that characterizes the state of class instances (objects), the methods that access this information (query methods), the methods that modify this information (command methods), and the constructor methods that allow the user to set the initial state of an object as it is being created.

◆   Commands are methods that modify the value of the information model but do not return information about the information model.

◆   Queries are methods that access portions of the information model but do not change the information.

◆   Constructors are methods that initialize the information model as an object is being created.

◆   Query methods should be named using nouns or noun phrases.

◆   Command methods should be named using verbs or verb phrases.

◆   Class names and method names start with an uppercase character.

◆   In a composition relationship, sometimes called strong aggregation, if the whole is destroyed so must all the parts be destroyed because they are owned by the whole.

◆   Another relationship between classes that represents a different kind of whole/part relationship is weak aggregation. If each constituent part of the whole is not essential for the integrity of the whole, the relationship is called a weak aggregation.

◆   If an object of one class is passed through a method parameter to another class, the two classes are said to be weakly associated. This relationship is also called the "uses" relationship.

◆   The inheritance relationship between two classes is a generalization/ specialization relationship. A child class is designed to be a specialization of its parent. Most importantly, the child class must be able to logically stand in for its parent because it satisfies the "kind of" relationship.

◆   An abstract class is a partially complete class in which one or more methods are left undefined and are declared abstract. The fields and methods that are common to the concrete subclasses are factored out and placed in the abstract class. These fields and methods are acquired through inheritance in the concrete descendent classes. The methods declared as abstract must be completely implemented in each concrete subclass.

◆   Polymorphic substitution states that an object from a descendent class may be used in place of an object from an ancestor class.

◆   Polymorphic substitution is a compile-time or static-typing principle. It represents a relaxation of the strong typing rules to permit more flexibility in the software construction process.

◆   Late-binding gets its name because the system attaches (binds) one of several possible methods in an inheritance hierarchy to an object at runtime, in contrast to polymorphic substitution, which is a static or compile-time typing principle.

◆   An interface is a special kind of C# class that supports polymorphic substitution and late-binding without inheritance.

◆   Like all classes, an interface is a type. All the methods declared in an interface must be abstract (no implementation details allowed), and no fields may be defined. Unlike an ordinary class, an interface cannot be extended (inherited from) by a concrete class. Only an interface can extend an interface. Concrete classes implement an interface.

◆   Because all the methods of an interface must be abstract, the abstract designator occurs by default and does not need to be explictly stated.

◆   By convention we always use an uppercase I in naming a C# interface.

1.12 ADDITIONAL EXERCISES

In this chapter, all of the exercises (Exercise 1.1–1.19) are directly related to the listings. They therefore follow the listings so that they appear in context, and are not repeated here.

CHAPTER 2

From Problem Definition to Classes: Object-Oriented Analysis and Design and the Software Life Cycle

This chapter examines the processes of object-oriented software engineering. Starting with problem specifications and followed by object-oriented analysis and design, artifacts are developed that document the analysis of the system and later its design. These steps set the stage for the implementation of the system.

It is difficult to describe these processes independent of some context—some actual problem. The challenge is finding a context that is simple enough to present in a single chapter. Another challenge is finding a problem that does not require specialized domain expertise. Simulations of relatively basic systems often provide a useful context from which to explore the processes that are used on a much larger scale when confronting real-world software development problems. In this chapter, a simulation of supermarket checkout lines provides the context for exploring object-oriented analysis (OOA) and object-oriented design (OOD). UML diagrams will be used throughout this chapter even though the goal of this chapter is not to focus on the mechanics of constructing such diagrams. The tutorial titled "Guide to UML Diagrams" at *www.dotnetcoders.com/web/learning/uml/* is intended for .NET coders who want to learn more about UML diagrams.

2.1 THE SOFTWARE LIFE CYCLE

In the development of large software systems, a considerable amount of preparatory work often precedes the actual development of code. This preparatory work involves creating many work products that are used to document the specifications, analysis, and design of the system. Some organizations such as the U.S. military have highly structured and formal processes requiring huge amounts of documentation, whereas other smaller organizations operate in a more ad-hoc manner.

The following steps generally performed during the life of a software system comprise the software life cycle:

1. Problem description
2. Specification based on the description
3. Analysis based on the specification
4. Design
5. Code development
6. Testing and verification
7. Maintenance

Each step is discussed in detail in the following sections. Maintenance is generally the most expensive part of the life cycle because it exists over the longest period of time, sometimes years after the initial software is released. The architecture of the system that is generated during the design phase often affects the cost of maintenance. A poorly designed system is often much more difficult and expensive to maintain.

2.2 SOFTWARE DEVELOPMENT FROM SPECIFICATION TO ANALYSIS

Formal specification languages have been developed to codify the process of stating the requirements of software systems. (For example, see V. Lopez, M. Malec, and J. Treur, *Comparing Formal Specification Languages for Complex Reasoning Systems*, pp. 258–282, Ellis Horwood.) This subject is beyond the scope of this book.

Most often, the specifications of a software system are expressed through declarations in English (or another natural language). These specifications are frequently the result of negotiation between the software provider and the customer who is commissioning the system. The specifications represent the problem definition. They are often incomplete, contradictory, and ambiguous. During analysis, defects in the specifications are usually revealed and corrected.

The final specification of a software system is sometimes encapsulated in a contract that binds the developer or development organization to the person or organization that is commissioning the software.

The goal of analysis is to clarify the working parts of the system under construction. To accomplish this goal, a team of software providers develops a model of the various parts and their relationship to each other. The work products built at the analysis stage are aimed at documenting the team's emerging understanding of the system.

During the analysis stage, the software development team identifies the use cases of the software to be built. These provide the basis for the analysis of the system. The team documents major scenarios associated with each use case. From an exploration of these scenarios emerges a clearer understanding of what parts constitute the system and what relationships the parts have among themselves. The team uses class diagrams, like the ones discussed in Chapter 1, to codify these relationships among parts.

Analysis is concerned with looking toward the problem domain to understand how the system works. Identifying the parts of the system helps to understand how the system works. In object-oriented analysis, identifying the parts means identifying the classes that model the problem domain.

Section 2.3 considers an example in detail to illustrate the process of object-oriented analysis, and Section 2.4 addresses object-oriented design.

2.2.1 Specifications of the Supermarket Checkout System

In this section, we design a simulation that models the checkout lines of a supermarket for a 12-hour period. At the end of this period, the doors to the supermarket close, but the customers in line are allowed to complete their service. An output file named SupermarketLog.txt must be generated in the same subdirectory as the application for each simulation run. This file must contain a sequential log of all critical events.

Assume specifically that the particular supermarket being simulated can have up to eight cashier stations numbered 1 to 8. There are two categories of cashiers: fast and slow. The time required for a cashier to process a customer is assumed to follow a uniform probability distribution, with the mean service time specified as user input and the maximum and minimum values 25 percent greater than or less than the mean. The typical average service time for a slow cashier is 200 seconds, and 60 seconds for a fast cashier. Even-numbered cashiers are assumed to be fast, and odd-numbered cashiers are assumed to be slow. The supermarket starts the day with only one cashier assigned to duty, cashier 1, who is a slow cashier.

At any time, if the shortest line equals or exceeds five customers, another cashier is immediately put on duty. If the idle time for any cashier exceeds four minutes (240 seconds), the cashier is taken off duty.

A cashier is assigned to duty by finding the first available off-duty cashier. To do so, the system scans the collection of cashiers sequentially from cashier 1 to cashier 8 or, with equal likelihood, it scans the collection of cashiers sequentially from 8 to 1 until it finds the first off-duty cashier. That cashier is put on duty.

When a customer arrives at the checkout area, he chooses the shortest available line. While waiting in line, if the longest line is longer by five or more people than the shortest line, the customer at the end of the longest line balks and joins the shortest line. This process is continued until the longest line has at most four people more than the shortest line.

The time between successive customer arrivals in the checkout area is also governed by a uniform probability density function, with maximum and minimum values plus or minus 20 percent of the mean time between customer arrivals. Each customer generated is sequentially assigned a number. Table 2.1 gives the mean time between successive customer arrivals as the day progresses (measured in hours after the supermarket opens for business).

TABLE 2.1 Mean time between successive customer arrivals

Hours	Average Time Between Customer Arrivals (Seconds)
0–1	50
1–3	15
4–6	30
7–9	10
10–12	35

The output of the program is a text file (SupermarketLog.txt) that contains a chronological log of all critical events. These critical events include:

1. The arrival time of a customer joining one of the cashier lines. The time of this event, the customer number, and the line number joined must be posted.

2. The departure time of a customer leaving one of the cashier lines. The cashier line number, the number of remaining customers in that line, and the total wait time of the departing customer and the customer number must be posted.

3. The event of a cashier put on duty. The cashier number and the time of this event must be posted.

4. The event of a cashier taken off duty. The cashier number and the time of this event must be posted.

5. The doors of the supermarket closing. No further customer arrivals can take place once this event has occurred.

6. The final statistics, including the average line length for all eight cashier lines, the average customer wait time for each of the cashier lines, and the number of customers served by each cashier line.

2.3 OBJECT-ORIENTED ANALYSIS

A **use-case diagram** depicts actors and actions that comprise the major usage patterns of the system being modeled. Stick figures are used to represent the major players in the system. Ovals are used to represent actions taken by the actors.

As an example, consider the use case of a customer choosing a line, waiting for a cashier, and then checking out and leaving the supermarket. Figure 2.1 presents a UML use-case diagram that depicts this activity.

The stick figures can be animate or inanimate objects. Figure 2.2 presents a more detailed UML use-case diagram.

Figure 2.2 shows the Simulation actor getting the customer arrival rate from the user input. The action, "Generate Customer," is triggered by the simulation. The "Generate Customer" action requires the support of the "Get current time" action. A Customer actor is the output of this action. The Simulation actor takes the action "Add/remove Cashier." The Customer actor takes the action "Choose Cashier line," and after it "waits in line," it reaches a Cashier actor. This Cashier actor takes the action "Checkout Customer," which uses the supporting actions "Update statistics" and "Get current time."

The focus in these use-case diagrams (Figures 2.1 and 2.2) is documenting how the system works in a most general way. As indicated earlier, this is the mission of analysis.

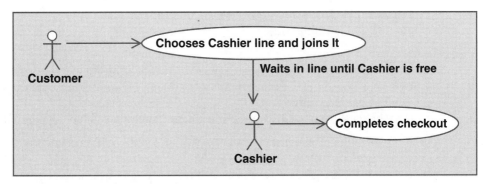

FIGURE 2.1 Use case of a customer choosing and joining a cashier line and being checked out

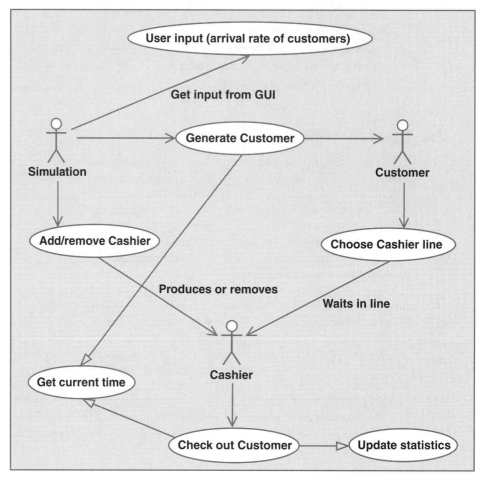

FIGURE 2.2 More detailed use-case diagram of a customer joining a
cashier line

From the detailed use case in Figure 2.2, we make our first attempt at discovering
the major domain classes that define the system. Figure 2.3 presents the UML class
diagram that does this.

The classes that are discovered and a short description of their responsibility follow:

◆ *Supermarket*—A supermarket controls the overall flow in the simulation. It is
associated with one or more cashiers.

◆ *Cashier*—A cashier is responsible for processing customers and posting statistics
involving wait time to a statistics object.

◆ *Clock*—A clock is responsible for keeping track of the current simulation time
and triggering critical events (e.g., generation of customers and service time of
customers).

◆ *Customer*—A customer is the main client object and is processed by cashiers.

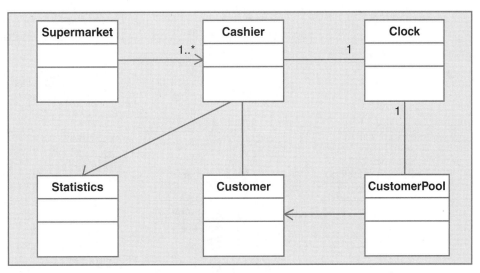

FIGURE 2.3 Initial analysis class diagram

◆ *customerPool*—The responsibility of the customerPool object is to generate customers at random instances in time. These instances are determined by the average customer arrival rate and found using a uniform probability distribution function. This function generates customers at times distributed uniformly across a specified range of values.

◆ *statistics*—The statistics object keeps track of average wait time for customers and line-length statistics for the cashier lines.

Our analysis of the supermarket simulation continues with a series of object-interaction UML diagrams based on the detailed use case in Figure 2.2. Each of these **object-interaction diagrams** represents an instance of the use case, and provides a path through the flow of events depicted in the use case. The goal of an object-interaction diagram, also called a **sequence diagram**, is to deepen our understanding of how the system works.

Following are a series of typical object-interaction diagrams for the supermarket simulation. The first, presented in Figure 2.4, focuses on the generation of a new customer. The diagram is composed of objects and the sequence of messages sent to these objects.

Figure 2.4 is a sequence diagram showing the interactions between objects that are needed to generate a new customer. The following four actions occur in sequence:

1. The *clock* object notifies the *customerPool* object that a new customer needs to be generated.
2. The *customerPool* object produces a new *customer*.
3. The *customerPool* object queries the uniform random number generator object for the next customer arrival time.
4. The *customerPool* object registers this next customer arrival time with the *clock*.

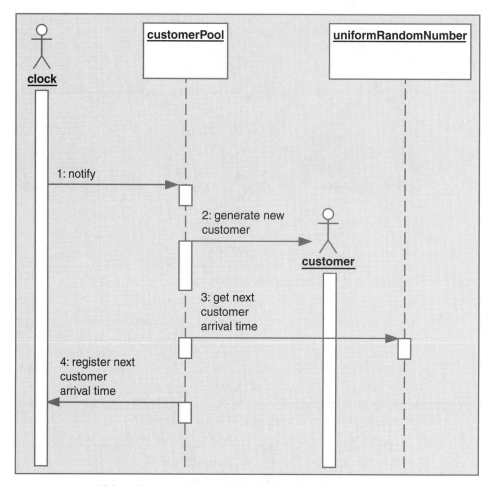

FIGURE 2.4 Object-interaction diagram depicting the generation of a new customer

This object-interaction diagram provides a more detailed picture and reflects a deeper understanding of how at least one aspect of the system works. This again is the goal of the analysis process.

From this sequence diagram, a new class is discovered, class *UniformRNG*. This second analysis class diagram is shown in Figure 2.5. Note that the class name *UniformRNG* in Figure 2.5 is not the same as the object name *uniformRandomNumber* in Figure 2.4. As the analysis evolves, it is acceptable to modify the names of classes.

The next object-interaction diagram shown in Figure 2.6 deals with the scenario of customer service and checkout.

The *clock* actor (object) is shown as notifying a *cashier* actor (object) that service time has elapsed. The *cashier* object obtains the first customer in the cashier queue (assuming that the cashier line is not empty and the cashier is not idle). The *cashier* object then processes the customer using the *statistics* object.

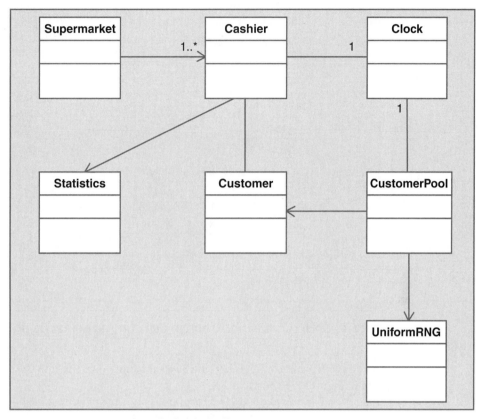

FIGURE 2.5 Second analysis class diagram

Many details about this transaction and the previous transactions are not dealt with at this stage of analysis. Our concern continues to be "how does the system work?" rather than "how will we build the system?".

Figure 2.7 depicts the object-interaction diagram that shows how a customer chooses a line to join. It too is an instance of the use case shown in Figure 2.2.

The object-interaction diagram (or sequence diagram) for adding and removing a cashier is shown in Figure 2.8.

The *supermarket* actor queries the *cashierCollection* object that it needs to check the line lengths in the current cashier lines. If the shortest line length equals or exceeds five, the *supermarket* object must create another cashier. The *supermarket* object also queries the *cashierCollection* object to see whether any idle time among the cashiers exceeds 240 seconds. If so, that cashier is removed from the system.

Details such as generating slow or fast cashiers are not dealt with at this early stage of analysis, and are better dealt with later at the design stage.

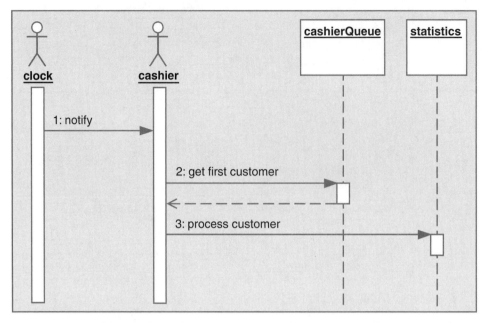

FIGURE 2.6 Object-interaction diagram depicting customer being processed

The class diagram can be updated based on a close examination of the sequence diagrams in Figures 2.6, 2.7, and 2.8.

This revised and expanded class diagram is shown in Figure 2.9.

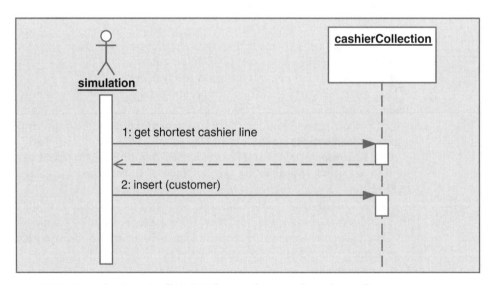

FIGURE 2.7 Sequence diagram for customer choosing a line

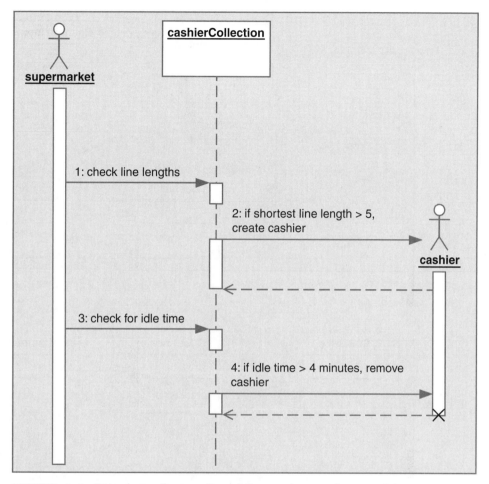

FIGURE 2.8 Sequence diagram for adding and removing a cashier

Class *CashierQueue* is added to the class diagram. Classes *Cashier* and *Customer* have an association with the new class *CashierQueue*. The need for these relationships comes from the sequence diagrams in Figures 2.6–2.8.

A customer is associated with one cashier line (queue). A cashier line is associated with a cashier and a cashier with a cashier line, forming a two-way association. A cashier is associated with a customer and a customer with a cashier, also forming a two-way association.

Whenever an object sends a message to another object in an object-interaction diagram (sequence diagram), the classes associated with the objects in the sequence diagram must have an appropriate relationship to enable the message passing.

Figure 2.10 shows an object-interaction diagram that depicts our analysis of balking logic, the logic that governs a customer's moving from a long line to a shorter line.

A revised class diagram is shown in Figure 2.11. Particular attention is given to the relationships between class *Clock* and other classes in the system.

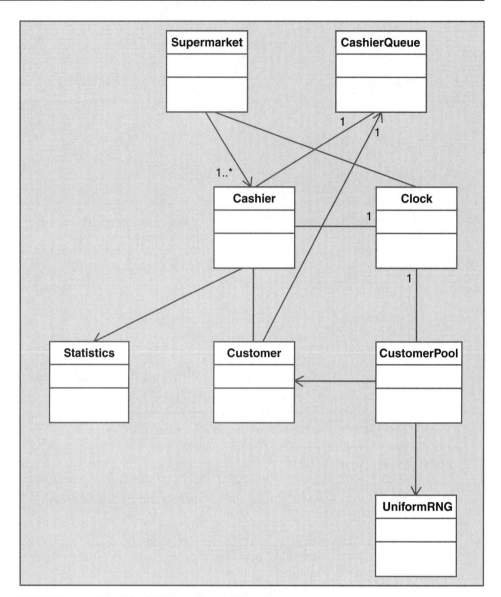

FIGURE 2.9 Updated UML analysis class diagram

The sequence diagram in Figure 2.10 is the most complicated so far. The *clock* object notifies a *balkingLogic* object to query the collection of cashier lines to find the longest and shortest lines. If the length of the longest line is at least five greater than the length of the shortest line, the last customer in the longest line is sent to the short-est line. This continues until the length condition no longer holds.

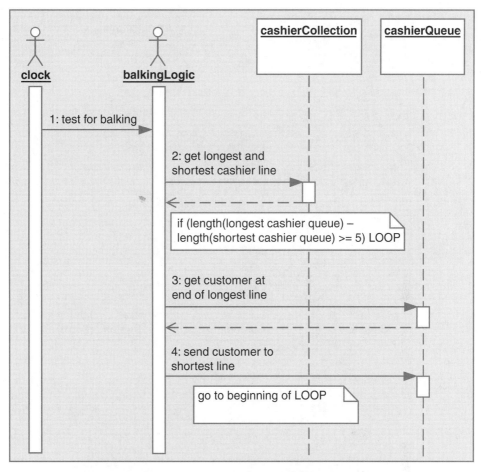

FIGURE 2.10 Sequence diagram of customer balking and going to shortest line

A new class *Collection* with an association with one or more *CashierQueue* classes is shown. Another new class *BalkingLogic* is shown with a reference to the collection of cashier lines, and *Clock* is also shown.

From the original analysis class diagram in Figure 2.3 containing six classes, examining object-interaction diagrams causes us to expand the number of classes discovered to ten.

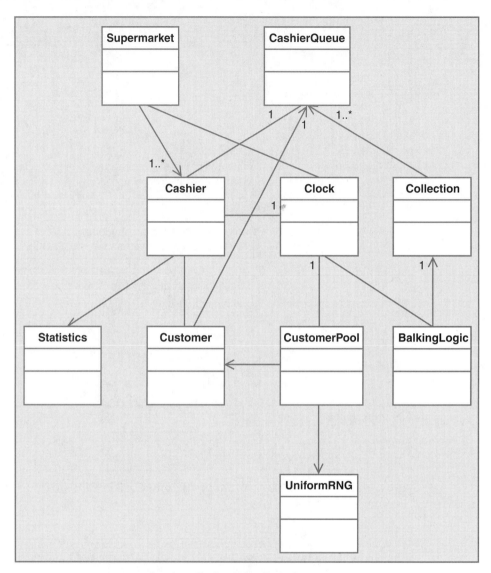

FIGURE 2.11 New revised analysis class diagram

2.4 OBJECT-ORIENTED DESIGN

If analysis has us looking toward the problem in an effort to deepen our understanding of the problem domain and how the system to be built works, design has us looking toward the solution. Our primary focus at the design stage is determining how to build the system so that it works as indicated in the analysis stage.

The work products created at the design stage are the same as those produced at the analysis stage but typically with more detail and refinement. What distinguishes analysis from design is state of mind—one's objective in producing the work product. As soon as the focus changes from how the system works to how to build it, the work changes from analysis to design. We are concerned at the design level with performance, thus efficiency. Our choices at the design level are influenced by the components available, such as a particular database system, GUI framework, or set of data structure components and collection classes. We must build the system with the materials provided to us. Part 4 of this book deals with data structure components.

This section continues the example started in Section 2.3 by proceeding with portions of the design of the supermarket simulation.

We examine next the scenario of updating the statistics object after a customer checks out. Because the preoccupation in this diagram is concerned with how to build the system and requires a greater level of detail, we have shifted from analysis to design. Often the boundary between analysis and design is murky. Surely as we focus on how the system is to be built, we also deepen our understanding of how the system works. The design sequence diagram for updating statistics is shown in Figure 2.12.

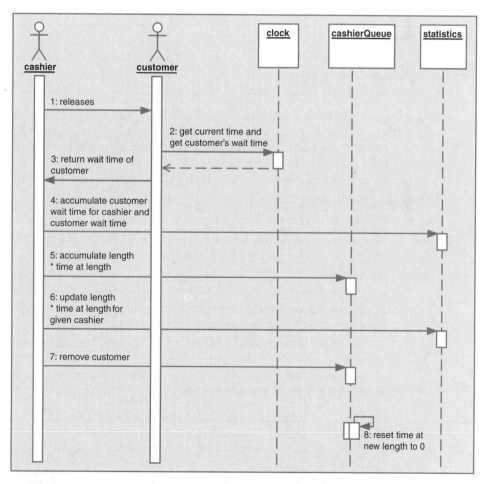

FIGURE 2.12 Design sequence diagram for updating statistics

The update of statistics begins when the cashier releases a customer. The customer queries the clock to obtain its release time from the system. The cashier commands the statistics object to accumulate the overall wait time based on this particular customer's wait time. The cashier commands the statistics object to accumulate the product of line length and the time at line length as a means to obtain the average line length across all cashiers, and then does the same to obtain the average line length for the particular cashier. The cashier removes the customer from the cashier queue. The time at the new length is reset to zero because the line length has just changed.

Similar sequence diagrams can be drawn that depict the statistics update when a customer joins a line and when a customer balks. In each of these cases, the accumulated length multiplied by time at the given length must be updated and the time at length reset to zero.

Exercise 2.1

Draw an "update statistics" sequence diagram dealing with the scenario where a customer joins the line.

Exercise 2.2

Draw an "update statistics" sequence diagram dealing with the scenario where a customer balks.

The analysis we have done in Section 2.3 suggests that we need to examine the behavior of class *Clock* in more detail. This class has many important responsibilities and provides the main event triggering mechanism throughout the simulation. Our focus will be on the design of this class.

We can start by reviewing the interactions between *Clock* and other classes.

1. The *clock* object periodically sends a *notify* message to the *balkingLogic* object in order to trigger the balking scenario. This happens after each clock tick.

2. The *clock* object sends a *notify* message to the *supermarket* object after each clock tick in order to trigger the add or remove cashier scenarios.

3. The *clock* object sends a *notify* message to the *customerPool* object only when a critical time event (time for a customer to arrive) has occurred. This event is asynchronous. As soon as this event occurs, the time for the next such customer arrival event is registered with the clock.

4. The *clock* object sends a *notify* message to a *cashier* object only when a critical time event (time for a customer to complete service) has occurred. This event is asynchronous. After this occurs, the next customer completion of service time is registered with the clock if the cashier's line is not empty.

From a careful analysis of these functions, we observe a design pattern and call it the Wakeup Call Pattern.

In a typical hotel, customers specify their desired wake up time and each request (customer-time pair) is logged in the hotel's computer system. Every morning, the computer rings customers at the time recorded for their wakeup call. The wakeup call actions are sorted in ascending time order. What the customer chooses to do after receiving this wakeup call is the customer's business. The only responsibility that the hotel has is in issuing the wakeup call.

We exploit this analogy in designing class *Clock* and using this wakeup call pattern.

We create an abstract class *Timeable* that interacts with interface *Clock*. Class *Timeable* represents any class that responds to the abstract command Wakeup(). In the supermarket simulation, these include concrete classes *Cashier*, *CustomerPool*, *Supermarket*, and *BalkingLogic*.

When a *Cashier* object receives the command *Wakeup()*, it releases a *Customer* object from the cashier queue and updates statistics (a critical event). When a *CustomerPool* object receives the command *Wakeup()*, it generates a new *Customer* object and sends it to one of the cashier lines. After each of these events, the *Timeable* object (*CustomerPool* or *Cashier*) registers itself and the time of the next critical event with the *Clock*.

The *Supermarket* and *BalkingLogic* objects also receive a *Wakeup()* command after each clock tick. The *Supermarket* object determines whether to add or remove a cashier in response to this wakeup call, and the *BalkingLogic* object determines whether any customers on the longest line transfer to the shortest line. After each clock tick, both the *Supermarket* and *BalkingLogic* objects register themselves and the time for the next wakeup call with the clock (the next clock tick).

The next four object-interaction diagrams shown in Figures 2.13–2.16 depict the wakeup calls for *cashier*, *customerPool*, *supermarket*, and *balkingLogic* objects.

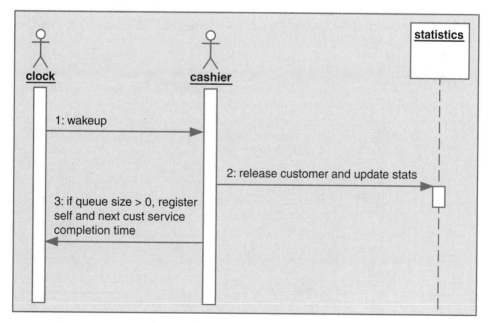

FIGURE 2.13 Wakeup call on *cashier* objects

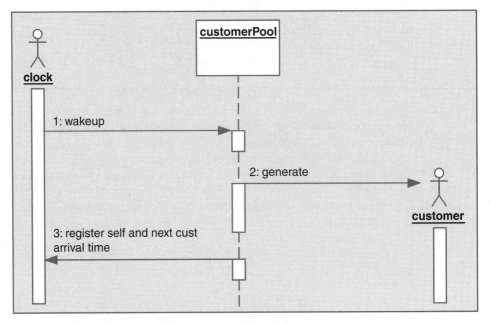

FIGURE 2.14 Wakeup call on *customerPool* objects

How do *Timeable* objects register with the *clock* object?

To answer this question, we need to discover another design class, class *TimeableAssociation*. This concrete class holds two fields: *criticalEventTime* (of type *double*) and *timeableObject* (of type *Timeable*). Each instance of *TimeableAssociation*

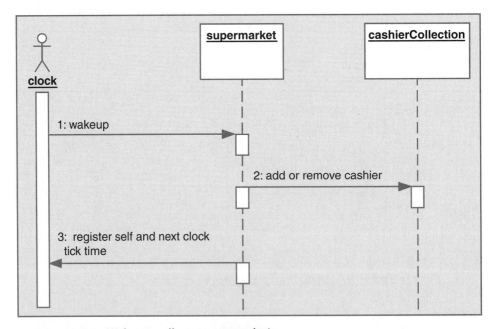

FIGURE 2.15 Wakeup call on *supermarket*

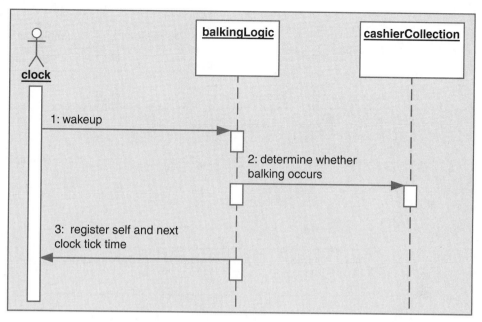

FIGURE 2.16 Wakeup call on *balkingLogic*

contains a floating-point number representing the time of the critical event time and the *Timeable* object that needs to obtain a wakeup call at the critical time. When a *CustomerPool* object, *Cashier* object, *Supermarket* object, or *BalkingLogic* object registers with the *Clock* object (requests the time of its next wakeup call), it creates a *TimeableAssociation* object and sends this *TimeableAssociation* object to the *Clock* object for registration.

Figure 2.17 shows the design classes that represent the wakeup call pattern and their relationship to each other.

The suffix "1" is added to many of the classes by the UML diagram tool because these classes appear earlier.

Four concrete classes are shown as extending the abstract class *Timeable*. This abstract class has a reference to class *Clock*. Class *Clock* is shown as having a composition relationship with a *Collection* class. This collection holds zero or more objects of type *TimeableAssociation*. Each *TimeableAssociation* object is shown as holding a *Timeable* object and containing a *criticalEventTime* object (type *double*).

Exercise 2.3

Based on the UML class diagram given in Figure 2.17, write the abstract class *Timeable* in C#.

The design work continues by refining some of the sequence diagrams produced earlier at the analysis stage. To illustrate the process, we consider one of these now.

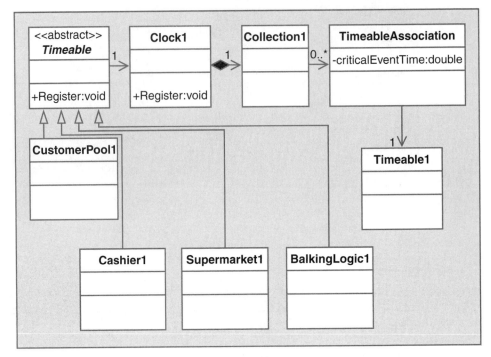

FIGURE 2.17 Classes for wake up call pattern

We revisit the object-interaction diagram that shows the adding and removing of a cashier. More details are provided at the design level, as shown in Figure 2.18.

As more details are provided in a succession of design-based object-interaction diagrams, the question naturally arises, When do we stop? At what point are we developing code in graphical format using UML sequence diagrams? That is an important and reasonable question. The goal of design is not to preempt implementation. The implementer (programmer) must be left with some freedom to interpret the design and implement accordingly. The goal of design is to produce the software architecture—an identification of the classes that comprise the system and their relationships to each other.

With many of the classes and their relationships already discovered (see Figures 2.11 and 2.17), the design process continues by focusing more closely on existing classes and providing more details. The behavior of these classes is formulated by identifying the fields (the information model) and actions (methods) of each.

We illustrate this process by considering several classes and focusing more closely on their behavior. We first consider the more detailed design of class *Customer*.

The information model of a customer contains its arrival time at one of the cashier lines and its start of service time. The difference between these times is the customer's wait time.

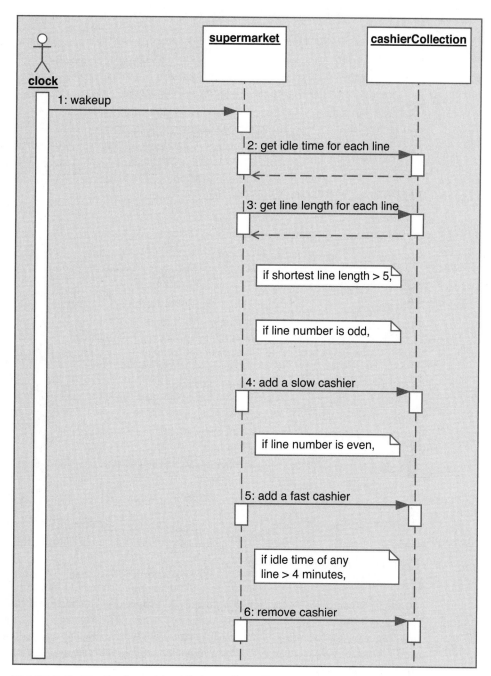

FIGURE 2.18 Design object-interaction diagram of adding/removing cashiers

The more detailed UML diagram for this class is shown in Figure 2.19.

Class *Customer*, although important and central to our supermarket system, is quite simple. Its design consists of two fields of type *double* and two properties that allow these fields to be get and set.

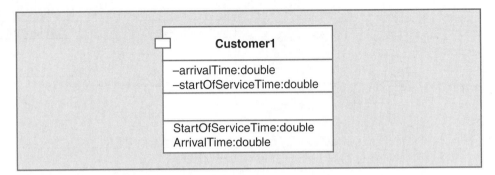

FIGURE 2.19 Design of class *Customer*

Figure 2.20 shows the design of class Cashier.

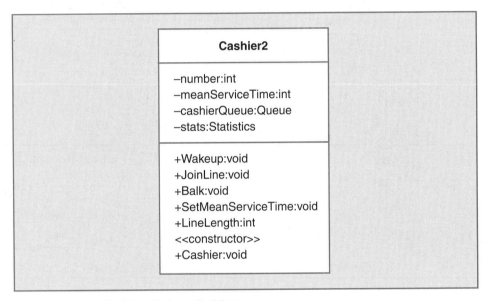

FIGURE 2.20 Design of class *Cashier*

The information model of class *Cashier* is designed so it contains a cashier number, the mean service time, a cashier queue, and a statistics object. Its methods include *Wakeup*, *JoinLine*, *Balk*, *SetMeanServiceTime*, and *LineLength*. These fields and methods are based on a close examination of the analysis and design sequence and class diagrams.

The last design class diagram is for class *CashierCollection*, as shown in Figure 2.21.

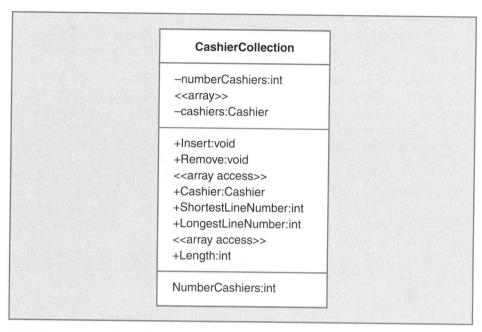

FIGURE 2.21 Design of class *CashierCollection*

2.5 REVISITING THE SOFTWARE LIFE CYCLE

We have examined aspects of the analysis and design stages of the software life cycle in earlier sections of this chapter. Recall that analysis is concerned with determining how a system works and design is concerned with determining how a system is built.

Design sets the stage for doing what most programmers enjoy doing the most—coding. After coding is testing, and then maintenance. We briefly examine coding, testing, and maintenance in the following sections.

2.5.1 Coding

Many software developers typically learn to code first, design second, and analyze third—exactly the opposite sequence of which industrial development takes place. As programming languages have evolved over the past half century, they have attempted to provide constructs that increase our ability to model myriad problem domains. Object-oriented languages provide one such approach to modeling a diversity of problem domains. The notions of encapsulation, inheritance, and polymorphism, discussed in some detail in Chapter 1, form the basis of this approach to software development and problem solving. To understand this, you need to understand the history of object-oriented programming languages.

Object technology has its roots in the SIMULA programming language. This language was designed by Ole-Johan Dahl and Kristen Nygaard at the Norwegian Computing Center in Oslo, Norway, between 1962 and 1967. In the mid 1970s, the Smalltalk language was developed in the United States at Xerox's Palo Alto Research Center. When the first commercial release of Smalltalk occurred in 1980, it provided a rekindling and rebirth of object technology. The programming languages Eiffel, C++, and Objective-C emerged in the 1980s as object technology gained its footing and increasing support in the IT industry. C++ became the dominant object-oriented language of the early to mid 1990s. In large measure because of the growing dissatisfaction with C++ felt by an increasing number of programmers and computer scientists, including James Gosling at Sun Microsystems, the Java programming language was born in the mid 1990s and became one of the dominant programming languages in the early 2000s. The C# programming language, part of the .NET Framework and designed by Anders Hejlsberg at Microsoft, represents an advance over Java and is only now coming into its own as a major object-oriented language.

Software is generally the most expensive part of a computer-based system, exactly the reverse of the way things were at the dawn of the computer age in the mid 1950s. At that time computers cost millions of dollars and software was provided at no extra cost. Now with reasonably powerful desktop computers costing as little as $500, software packages can cost more than the computer itself.

What continues to drive up the cost of software is the difficulty of producing it. Building from scratch is expensive. The advent of programming environments such as the standard Java classes with its thousands of classes and, more recently, the .NET Framework with its thousands of standard classes, has moved the development community away from the build-from-scratch approach that has prevailed for so long. Not only do the thousands of classes in the C# .NET libraries provide for reuse, but the framework provided in the hierarchy of standard library classes provides fertile opportunities for software development to benefit from an incremental development approach. These standard libraries provide frameworks for specialized application domains such as GUI development, for example. This previously difficult area of programming has become straightforward because of the powerful frameworks provided in both Java and C#. Integrated development environments (IDEs) such as Microsoft's Visual Studio or Borland's JBuilder have provided the programmer tremendous leverage in constructing GUI applications.

The mastery of these tools has become an important requirement in becoming an educated programmer. So has the mastery of the programming paradigm. One cannot use a modern and powerful programming language such as C# properly without understanding the underlying paradigm. This was illustrated in Chapter 1 when the concept of pluggable software was discussed and illustrated using abstract classes and interfaces along with polymorphic substitution and late-binding.

Modern programming languages such as C# provide constructs and frameworks that support a variety of important problem solving abstractions. Included among these are:

1. *Ability to spawn threads*—Processes that emulate parallel processing and make it possible to get more efficiency and better utilization from the underlying CPU.

2. *Exception handling*—The ability to control a program's response to error conditions that often arise because of faulty hardware or user errors.

3. *Streams*—The ability to write information to a variety of media including disks, remote computers on a distributed system or the Internet, printers, and other peripheral devices connected to the computer.

4. *Networks*—The ability to send and receive information to and from other computers.

The Java programming language was one of the first to provide strong support for these problem solving abstractions. The .NET Framework also does so. Whereas the Java framework was designed to provide this support across major programming platforms (i.e., Windows and Unix), the .NET Framework was created to provide support on the Windows platform but across many .NET programming languages. This book focuses on modern software development using the C# programming language and the .NET Framework.

Exercise 2.4

Write a brief account of the history of the major programming languages. Include FORTRAN, Algol, Lisp, C, Pascal, Basic, Modula-2, Ada, Eiffel, Smalltalk, Objective-C, C++, Perl, Java, Visual Basic, and C#. Include the dates of commercial release, and describe the language designer(s) and the application domains in which the language has been effectively used.

2.5.2 Testing

Although formal techniques have been devised for verifying the correctness of programs, these techniques are complex and typically usable on only small sections of a system. For this reason, software testing is often an empirical process that involves hand-crafted test cases whose goal is to ferret out any errors that are lurking in the system, particularly in its dark corners. From such testing, one has to make the leap (really a leap of faith) that the software system works for all possible test cases. This cannot ever be proven and is often wrong.

Software organizations often perform software testing in stages, beginning with white-box testing followed by black-box testing.

With white-box testing, the source code is available in configuring test cases. Individual modules are tested by themselves (classes in the case of object-oriented software) and later groups of modules (classes). This integration testing requires access to the source code of the software system being tested to configure tests of appropriate groups of classes.

Black-box testing does not provide access to the system's source code but only executable code. The testing is not based on the system's structure but on its specifications. This level of testing evaluates the performance of the system much more on the basis of how the user perceives the system. Criteria such as the software's mean time between failure, number of transactions per unit time, and other such performance measures can be evaluated.

It is common to release software along with known bugs or incomplete parts. Hopefully, these are documented in release notes. As bugs are corrected or incomplete parts are completed, new version numbers are attached to the software.

2.5.3 Maintenance

Maintenance is an ongoing process that involves the correction of errors detected during testing and reported by customers (corrective maintenance) and adding new features to the system (perfective maintenance).

Because of the long period during which maintenance occurs, it is generally the most expensive stage of the software development cycle. Often programmers who were not involved in the initial development are called upon to perform maintenance on the system. If the system is poorly documented (no analysis or design artifacts and poorly documented code), it is often very difficult to perform effective maintenance on the system and in extreme cases easier to rebuild the system from scratch than to try to decipher the existing code.

Refactoring is often done during software maintenance. The goal of refactoring is to simplify the existing code without changing its functionality. Code simplification offers the potential to reduce future maintenance costs. During refactoring, blocks of code that perform the same function and appear throughout the system are factored into methods that may be called from various parts of the system. Often methods are moved from one class to another in order to purify the mission of a class and produce less cohesion and more modularity among classes.

During the maintenance stage, new data structures and algorithms may be substituted based on changing hardware that supports the system. As shown later in the book, some data structures favor memory efficiency over speed, and others favor speed over memory efficiency. If the hardware environment surrounding the system changes, it may be appropriate to plug new data structures and algorithms into the system. The ability to do this without doing major damage to the existing architecture is dependent on whether the system has followed effective design practices.

The goal of this book is to inspire you to learn and use the skills that define modern software development. The C# language and .NET Framework provide a strong platform that supports this goal. The features of C# are best understood and best used when presented in the context of object-oriented software development. This is the approach that will be used throughout this book.

The next chapter demonstrates the path from architecture (analysis and design) to finished system by showing how the UML artifacts can be translated into a working C# software system.

The first task in Chapter 3 will be to translate the analysis and design artifacts developed for the supermarket checkout line simulation into a working software system. Then another complete but simpler example is presented that takes you from analysis to design to implementation.

2.6 SUMMARY

◆   Software development involves important preparatory steps that precede coding. A software system must be specified. Based on these specifications, analysis is performed.

◆   Analysis is concerned with determining how a system works, not how it is built. During analysis, major use cases are identified. From these, object-interaction diagrams that represent portions of a use case are constructed.

◆   The object-interaction diagrams provide the basis for the early analysis class diagrams. When the concern changes from how the system works to how the system is to be built, the focus changes from analysis to design.

- Design is concerned with efficiency. Classes that are not present in the problem domain are often discovered, or created, at the design stage. More detailed object-interaction diagrams lead to more detailed class diagrams. The fields and public methods of each class are developed in more detail during the design stage. This sets the stage for coding.

- Coding is most often supported by frameworks and tools. Frameworks supply myriad standard library classes that provide important functionality to support many important application domains. Development tools include integrated development environments that provide tremendous leverage for assembling standard components such as GUI widgets.

- Because of the complexity of many modern software systems, faults are often present in various parts of a software system. During the testing stage the goal is to isolate and repair these faults. White-box testing uses the source code of the application to formulate test cases that exercise individual classes and clusters of classes. Black-box testing exercises the system as the user will use it and measures the performance of the system and its adherence to the published specifications.

2.7 ADDITIONAL EXERCISES

Exercise 2.5

What are the preparatory stages of software development that precede actual coding?

Exercise 2.6

Explain in your own words how the wakeup pattern is used in the supermarket simulation.

Exercise 2.7

Find the version number of four commercial software packages.

Exercise 2.8

Answer true or false and explain:

1. Empirical testing can prove the presence of errors and prove that there are no errors.

2. Empirical testing typically allows one to cover every test case in a software system.

CHAPTER 3

From Design to Implementation

In Chapter 2, we examined the path from specifications to analysis to design. Using object-interaction diagrams and class diagrams, we modeled the architecture of a software system under construction.

In practice, even as early analysis progresses, it is common practice to build class prototypes using real code. Yes, coding often progresses in parallel with the analysis and design process. When a class is "discovered" at the analysis stage, the skeletal structure of the class can be formulated in C# code. As we deepen our understanding of classes and their relationship to other classes, we can use this understanding by adding more details to the prototypes. Eventually, the prototypes become fully implemented classes. We may therefore find ourselves well into the implementation stage before the design stage is completed. Grady Booch (see *Object-Oriented Analysis and Design with Applications*, Addison-Wesley, 1993) has called this approach "round-trip engineering." Some analysis is followed by some design, which is followed by some implementation, which is followed by some more analysis, and so on.

The first section of this chapter discusses the general relationships between UML design diagrams and the code that implements the design. The next section presents a relatively simple but complete case-study of a race game simulation. The process from analysis to design to implementation is presented. Finally, portions of the implementation of the supermarket simulation, introduced in the previous chapter, are examined to provide further insights into the process of going from design documentation to implementation.

It is not the intention of this chapter to teach the subtleties of class construction in C#. The next two chapters are dedicated to this task. Rather, this chapter shows the transition from a UML description of a system to an initial implementation. Therefore it is not necessary at this time that you concern yourself with a detailed understanding of the coding details presented.

3.1 FROM CLASS DIAGRAMS TO CODE

We have seen sequence diagrams and class diagrams used in Chapter 2 to describe the design architecture of a software system. Sequence diagrams present a dynamic model of the system being constructed; class diagrams present a static picture of the classes that comprise the system and their relationships to each other.

Let us review the evolution from design class diagrams to actual code. Does implementation (coding details) emerge unambiguously from a class diagram? The answer, unfortunately, is no. This despite the fact that development tools such as Together 6.1 provide support for "automatic" code generation from a UML class diagram. The code that is generated is often incorrect in capturing the subtleties of the architectural semantics. Typically, the automatically generated code is a rough approximation of the design semantics. It takes a good programmer/software architect to get the code right so that it faithfully represents the relationships implied by the class diagram and faithfully represents the relationships between the objects in the real system under construction. Without independent knowledge of the system under construction, it is difficult for a programmer to go from class design diagrams to code implementation.

We illustrate this point with several simple examples. Consider the UML class diagram given in Figure 3.1.

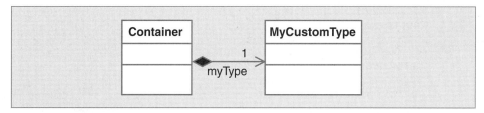

FIGURE 3.1 Simple example 1

Class *Container* is shown as having a strong aggregation relationship with respect to class *MyCustomType*. The cardinality is one and the association is directed from *Container* to *MyCustomType*. The skeletal structure of class *Container* is shown in Listing 3.1.

LISTING 3.1 Code for class Container

```
public class Container {

    // Fields
    private MyCustomType myType = new MyCustomType();

    // Other details not shown

}
```

In implementing class *Container*, the programmer has correctly identified *myType* as a field of *Container* and, most importantly, the responsibility of this class for creating an instance, *myType*, of *MyCustomType*. Suppose the relationship between *Container* and *MyCustomType* were as shown in Figure 3.2.

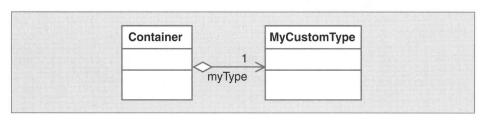

FIGURE 3.2 Simple example 2

Listing 3.2 presents a revised plausible implementation of class *Container* based on Figure 3.2.

LISTING 3.2 Revised class Container

```
public class Container {

    // Fields
    private MyCustomType myType;

    // Constructor
    public Container(MyCustomType input) {
        myType = input;
    }

    // Other details not shown

}
```

In the revised class *Container*, a reference, *myType*, to an object of *MyCustomType* is held as a field and passed to a *Container* object when it is being constructed. The responsibility for creating the instance *myType* that is held by the *Container* object lies outside of class *Container*.

Other objects in the system may also hold references to this *MyCustomType* object. *Container* does not own *myType* according to Figure 3.2. If several objects have internal references to the same *MyCustomType* object through their fields, any change induced in this object by one *Container* object will cause the values held by the other *Container* objects to change as well. This is generally not a desirable situation. This may be avoided by passing unique *MyCustomType* objects to each *Container* object as it is constructed.

A class diagram that shows yet another relationship between classes *Container* and *MyCustomType* is shown in Figure 3.3.

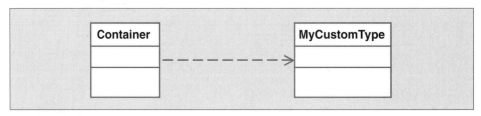

FIGURE 3.3 Simple example 3

Listing 3.3 shows a plausible implementation that follows from this design artifact.

LISTING 3.3 Another implementation of class Container

```
public class Container {

    // Command
    public void SomeMethod(MyCustomType customType) {
        // Details not shown
    }

    // Other details not shown

    }
}
```

In this third version of class *Container*, a parameter, *customType*, is passed to some method (shown as a command in this case but it could be any type of method). The information contained within the object *customType* is presumably used inside of this method. This is modeled in Figure 3.3 as a weak association between the two classes.

Finally, a class diagram that shows another possible relationship between class *Container* and *MyCustomType* is shown in Figure 3.4.

Class *Container* is shown as owning a collection of type *List*, which in turn holds references to zero or more *MyCustomType* objects. Listing 3.4 shows a plausible implementation of these classes.

Class *Container* is shown as holding an *elements* field, which it is responsible for creating. A command, *AddElement*, allows objects of type *MyCustomType* to be added to the *elements* list held by *Container*.

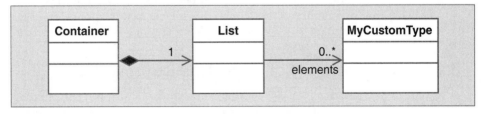

FIGURE 3.4 Simple example 4

LISTING 3.4 Example 4 of class Container

```
public class Container {

    // Fields
    private List elements = new List();

    // Command
    public void AddElement(MyCustomType customType) {
        elements.Add(customType);
    }

    // Other details not shown

}
```

Exercise 3.1

Show another plausible implementation of the design from Figure 3.2.

Exercise 3.2

Show another plausible implementation of the design from Figure 3.4.

3.2 SIMPLE CASE STUDY INVOLVING ANALYSIS, DESIGN, AND IMPLEMENTATION

To tie together the concepts presented in Part 1 of the book (Chapters 1, 2, and 3), a short but complete application is presented in this section. The analysis, design, and implementation of this application will be discussed. Many of the object-orientation (OO) concepts presented in Chapter 1 are used in this application. The UML tools illustrated in Chapters 2 and Section 3.1 are used here.

3.2.1 Specifications of Dice-Controlled Race Game

A game simulation is chosen for this case study because it is relatively simple to understand, yet it has sufficient complexity to provide the basis for illustrating the evolution from analysis to design to implementation. So here the means (showing the steps that take us from analysis and design models to a first implementation of the system) are more important than the end (producing a finished game simulation product).

We want to simulate a race among two or more players. The players move in sequence starting with player 1 and ending with player *n*. On each "move" a player goes forward or backward. As players move in sequence, the first player to move forward 100 or more units wins and the game is over.

The score a player receives on each move is determined by:

♦ The outcome of the throw of a fair die

♦ The relative position of the player who is moving with respect to the other players

♦ The response logic associated with the given player (the three distinct types of response logic are described in the following sections)

Some additional specifications are:

♦ Each player is associated with one of the three possible types of response logic.

♦ More than one player may have the same type of response logic.

♦ At random times, the same or one of the other two types of response logic replaces a player's response logic.

♦ It is the response logic associated with a player that determines how the die outcome and relative position of the other players affects the given player's change of position.

The following sections include details related to the three types of response logic.

Response Type 1

If a player's move is based on response type 1, its change in position is computed as:

The die throw + (position of leading player – player's position) / 2
If the die throw is 3, 4, 5, or 6, the change in position is positive; otherwise it is negative.

Response Type 2

If a player's move is based on response type 2, its change in position is computed as:

3 times the value of the die throw if the value is an even number; otherwise equal to the die throw if the value is an odd number
The change in position is always positive.

Response Type 3

If a player's move is based on response type 3, its change in position is computed as:

The die throw + (player's position – position of trailing player) / 2
If the die throw is 1 or 2, the change in position is positive; otherwise the change in position is negative.

A player holds a particular response type for a short duration. This duration is measured in number of moves. After the player has completed the requisite number of moves that are required in holding a particular response type, the player is reassigned either the same response type or one of the other two response types with an equal likelihood associated with being assigned each of the three possible response types. The requisite number of moves that a player must hold a particular response type is a randomly generated integer between two and five moves.

As the race progresses, and after each player's move, a line of textual output is sent to the console that specifies the player number and its current position. When the game is over, a final line of output must be written to the console that indicates the winner of the game.

3.2.2 Analysis of Race Game

The analysis begins by considering the major use cases of this system. Recall that a good use case represents a major piece of functionality from beginning to end. It usually involves several important classes in the system.

Because of the relative simplicity of this application, only the following use cases need to be considered:

◆   Game is initialized.

◆   Play game.

◆   Game assigns new response object to a player.

◆   Player makes a move.

◆   Determination of whether a player wins the game.

◆   Response object determines change in position for a given player.

Figure 3.5 depicts these use cases in a single diagram.

The *RaceGame* actor initializes the game. To support this, players are created and each player is assigned a response object. As the game is played, the winner is determined.

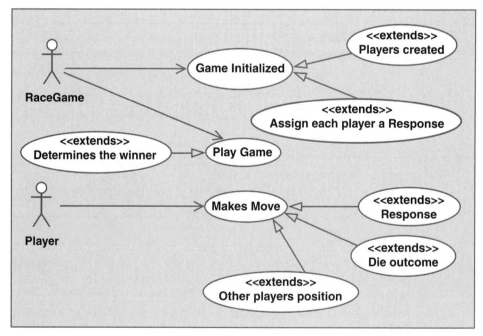

FIGURE 3.5 Use cases for race game

The *Player* actor makes a move. To support this, the response associated with the player, its die throw, and the position of the other players support the move outcome.

To clarify how the system works, we present several object-interaction diagrams. Figure 3.6 shows how the game is initialized.

The game object creates an array of player objects and creates and assigns four player objects to this array. It then creates a random number generator object.

Figure 3.7 depicts an object-interaction diagram that shows how a random response type is assigned to a player. A response type object (a concrete subclass of *Response*) is generated and assigned to a player object.

Figure 3.8 depicts an object-interaction diagram that shows how the game is played. Here a *game* actor initiates a **make move** command on a player even though the use case in Figure 3.5 shows a player actor doing this. This is because the use case in Figure 3.5 is very high-level and general, whereas the object-interaction diagram in Figure 3.8 is more detailed and specific.

The response life of the next player is obtained. If this response life is 0, a new randomly assigned response type is assigned to the player. The player is commanded to move. The new position of the player is output to the console.

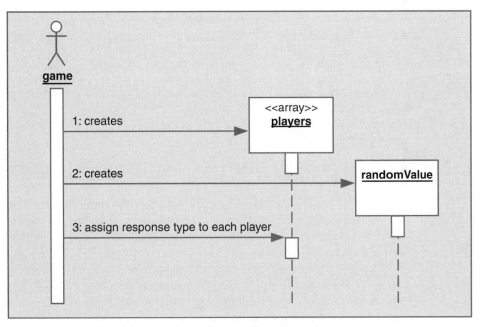

FIGURE 3.6 Object-interaction diagram for initializing game

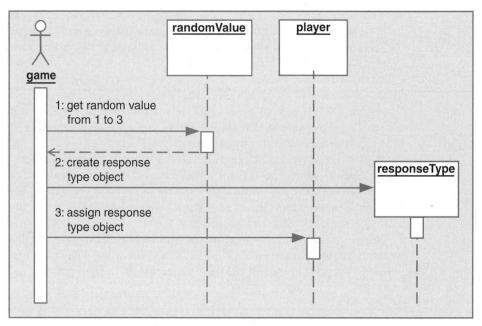

FIGURE 3.7 Object-interaction diagram for assigning random response type to player

From this analysis we identify the classes *Game*, *Player*, and *ResponseType*. A UML class diagram that depicts these classes is shown in Figure 3.9. A *Game* class is shown as owning a collection of *Player* objects each of which contains a *ResponseType* object.

3.2.3 Design of Race Game

The analysis diagram in Figure 3.9 does not show the three concrete response types. We refine this diagram by making the *ResponseType* class abstract and defining three concrete subclasses, *TypeOneResponse*, *TypeTwoResponse*, and *TypeThreeResponse*. This is shown in Figure 3.10.

The principle of polymorphic substitution is central to the design shown in Figure 3.10. Each *Player* object holds a placeholder of type *Response* as part of its information model. As the game progresses, concrete objects of *TypeOneResponse*, *TypeTwoResponse*, or *TypeThreeResponse* are held by each *Player* object.

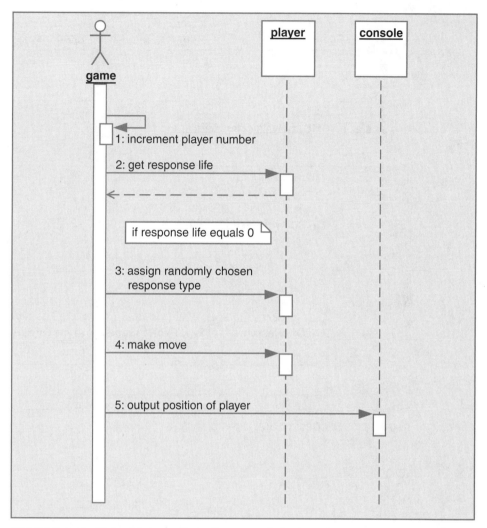

FIGURE 3.8 Object-interaction diagram of playing game

3.2.4 Implementation of Race Game

We are ready to implement this relatively simple system. We start by defining the abstract class *Response* in Listing 3.5.

The constructor in abstract class *Response* contains code that will be reused in the concrete subclass constructors. Each of the concrete subclasses needs to define *ChangeInPosition* according to the rules given in the problem specifications.

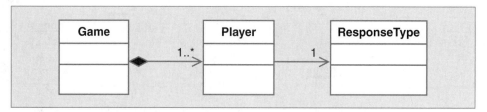

FIGURE 3.9 UML analysis class diagram

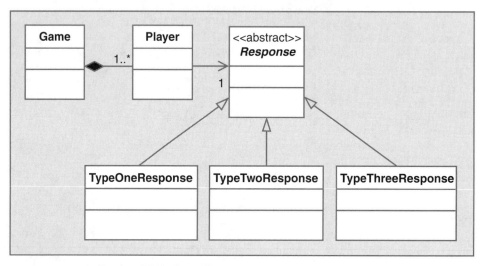

FIGURE 3.10 Design UML class diagram

LISTING 3.5 Abstract class Response

```
using System;
using System.Collections;

namespace RaceGame {

    public abstract class Response {

        // Fields
        protected Player[] players;
        protected int numberPlayers;
        protected int playerNumber;
        protected int responseLife;

        // Constructor
        public Response(Player[] players, int numberPlayers, int
                        playerNumber, Random randomValue) {
          this.players = players;
          this.numberPlayers = numberPlayers;
          this.playerNumber = playerNumber;
          responseLife = 2 + randomValue.Next(4);// Value from 2 to 5
        }

        // Commands
        public void DecrementResponseLife() {
          responseLife—;
        }

        // Queries
        /** Returns the player's change in position based on move */
        public abstract int ChangeInPosition(int dieThrow);

        public int ResponseLife {
            get {
                return responseLife;
            }
        }
    }
}
```

We consider the first concrete subclass of *Response*, *TypeOneResponse*, in Listing 3.6.

The *ChangeInPosition* query requires the keyword **override** in its signature because it is redefining the abstract method in the parent *Response* class. The constructor in the base class *Response* is used by invoking **base** and passing it the four parameters that are input to the *TypeOneResponse* constructor.

LISTING 3.6 Class TypeOneResponse

```
using System;

namespace RaceGame {

    public class TypeOneResponse : Response {

        // Constructor
        public TypeOneResponse(Player[] players, int numberPlayers,
            int playerNumber, Random randomValue) :
            base (players, numberPlayers, playerNumber, randomValue) {
        }

        // Queries
        public override int ChangeInPosition(int dieThrow) {
            // Compute highest position
            int highest = players[1].Position;

            for (int i = 2; i <= numberPlayers; i++) {
                if (players[i].Position > highest) {
                    highest = players[i].Position;
                }
            }
            int change = dieThrow
                        + (highest -
                            players[playerNumber].Position) / 2;
            return (dieThrow > 2) ? change : -change;
        }
    }
}
```

Exercise 3.3

Discuss how the *ChangeInPosition* method in class *TypeOneResponse* satisfies the rules for change in position given in the problem specifications.

Listings 3.7 and 3.8 show the remaining concrete subclasses *TypeTwoResponse* and *TypeThreeResponse*.

LISTING 3.7 Class TypeTwoResponse

```csharp
using System;

namespace RaceGame {

    public class TypeTwoResponse : Response {

        // Constructor
        public TypeTwoResponse(Player[] players, int numberPlayers,
            int playerNumber, Random randomValue) :
            base (players, numberPlayers, playerNumber, randomValue) {
        }

        // Queries
        public override int ChangeInPosition(int dieThrow) {
            return (dieThrow % 2 == 0) ? 3 * dieThrow : dieThrow;
        }
    }
}
```

LISTING 3.8 Class TypeThreeResponse

```csharp
using System;

namespace RaceGame {

    public class TypeThreeResponse : Response {

        // Constructor
        public TypeThreeResponse(Player[] players, int numberPlayers,
            int playerNumber, Random randomValue) :
            base(players, numberPlayers, playerNumber, randomValue) {
        }

        // Queries
        public override int ChangeInPosition(int dieThrow) {

            // Compute lowest position
            int lowest = players[1].Position;

            for (int i = 2; i <= numberPlayers; i++) {
                if (players[i].Position < lowest) {
                    lowest = players[i].Position;
                }
            }
            int change = dieThrow +
                    (players[playerNumber].Position - lowest) / 2;
            return (dieThrow > 2) ? -change : change;
        }
    }
}
```

Exercise 3.4

Discuss how the *ChangeInPosition* method in class *TypeTwoResponse* satisfies the rules for change in position given in the problem specifications.

Exercise 3.5

Discuss how the *ChangeInPosition* method in class *TypeThreeResponse* satisfies the rules for change in position given in the problem specifications.

We consider class Player in Listing 3.9.

LISTING 3.9 Class Player

```
using System;
using System.Collections;

namespace RaceGame {

    public class Player {

        // Fields
        private int position;
        private int playerNumber;
        private Response response; // Placeholder
        private Random randomValue;

        // Constructor
        public Player(int number, Random randomValue) {
            this.randomValue = randomValue;
            playerNumber = number;
        }

        // Commands
        public void AssignResponse(Response response) {
            this.response = response;
        }

        public void MakeMove() {
            response.DecrementResponseLife();
            position +=
                response.ChangeInPosition(1 + randomValue.Next(6));
        }

        // Queries
        public int ResponseLife {
            get {
                return response.ResponseLife;
            }
        }
```

LISTING 3.9 Class Player (continued)

```
        public int Position {
            get {
                return position;
            }
        }

        public bool Wins() {
            return position >= 100;
        }

        public int PlayerNumber {
            get {
                return playerNumber;
            }
        }
    }
}
```

Exercise 3.6

Discuss the details of the *MakeMove* command in class *Player*. Is this an example of late-binding?

It should be clear from Listings 3.5–3.9 that only a single instance of class *Random* exists. This instance is passed to a concrete response type at the time it is created. The same is true of class *Player*. It is the *Game* class, presented in Listing 3.10, that creates and owns the random number object. Some sample output is shown after class *Game*.

LISTING 3.10 Class Game

```
using System;
using System.Collections;

namespace RaceGame {

    public class Game {

        // Fields
        private Player[] players;
        private Random randomValue = new Random();
        private int numberPlayers;
        // Constructor
        public Game(int numberPlayers) {
            this.numberPlayers = numberPlayers;
            players = new Player[numberPlayers + 1];// Natural indexing
```

LISTING 3.10 Class Game (continued)

```
            // Warm up random number generator
            for (int i = 0; i < 50000; i++) {
                randomValue.NextDouble();
            }



            // Create Player objects
            for (int i = 1; i <= numberPlayers; i++) {
                players[i] = new Player(i, randomValue);
            }

            // Assign random Response type to each player
            for (int playerNumber = 1; playerNumber <= numberPlayers;
                    playerNumber++) {
                AssignRandomResponse(players[playerNumber]);
            }
        }

        // Commands
        public void AssignRandomResponse(Player player) {

            // Assign a random Response object to specified player
            switch (1 + randomValue.Next(3)) {
                case 1:    // Player gets TypeOneResponse
                    player.AssignResponse(new TypeOneResponse(
                            players, numberPlayers,
                            player.PlayerNumber, randomValue));
                    break;
                case 2:    // Player gets TypeTwoResponse
                    player.AssignResponse(new TypeTwoResponse(
                        players, numberPlayers,
                        player.PlayerNumber, randomValue));
                    break;
                case 3:    // Player gets TypeThreeResponse
                    player.AssignResponse(new TypeThreeResponse(
                        players, numberPlayers,
                        player.PlayerNumber, randomValue));
                    break;
            }
        }
        public void Play() {
            int playerNumber = 0;
            do {
                playerNumber++;
                if (playerNumber > numberPlayers) {
                    playerNumber = 1;
                }
```

LISTING 3.10 Class Game (continued)

```
                    // Assign new response object to player if response
                    // life is zero
                    if (players[playerNumber].ResponseLife == 0) {
                        AssignRandomResponse(players[playerNumber]);
                    }

                    // Make move and output result to Console
                    players[playerNumber].MakeMove();
                    Console.WriteLine("Player " + playerNumber +
                                " position: " +
                                players[playerNumber].Position);
                } while (!players[playerNumber].Wins());

                Console.WriteLine("\n\nPlayer " + playerNumber +
                            " wins the game.");
                Console.ReadLine();
            }

            public static void Main() {
                Game game = new Game(4); // Create a four player game
                game.Play();
            }
        }
    }
}

/* Sample Output
Player 1 position: 18
Player 2 position: -3
Player 3 position: 12
Player 4 position: -11
Player 1 position: 36
Player 2 position: -13
Player 3 position: -1
Player 4 position: 15
Player 1 position: 42
Player 2 position: -41
Player 3 position: 21
Player 4 position: 0
Player 1 position: 60
Player 2 position: -92
Player 3 position: 78
Player 4 position: 45
Player 1 position: 73
Player 2 position: -2
Player 3 position: 34
Player 4 position: 50
Player 1 position: 77
Player 2 position: -6
```

LISTING 3.10 Class Game (continued)

```
Player 3 position: 11
Player 4 position: 55
Player 1 position: 119


Player 1 wins the game.
*/
```

Exercise 3.7

Compare the implementation details of the constructor in class *Game* with the object-interaction diagram shown in Figure 3.7.

Exercise 3.8

Compare the implementation details of the *AssignRandomResponse* command in class *Game* with the object-interaction diagram shown in Figure 3.8.

Exercise 3.9

Compare the implementation details of the *Play* command in class *Game* with the object-interaction diagram shown in Figure 3.9.

Exercise 3.10

To demonstrate that polymorphic substitution and late-binding, both featured in the design of the Race Game, provide the basis for relatively easy maintenance, make the following changes to the source code of the Race Game application:

1. Change the number of players from four to ten.

2. Add three more response types with the same rules for assigning response types to players and lifetime of response types to players (equal likelihood of any response type and lifetimes from 2 to 5 units of time). The three new response types have the following rules:

    Response Type4—The change in position is negative and is given by three times the die throw if the die throw is 1, 2, 3, or 4; otherwise there is no change in position.

    Response Type5—The change in position is positive and is given by three times the die throw if the die throw is 1, 2, 3, 4 or 5; otherwise there is no change in position.

    Response Type6—The change in position is always positive and equal to twice the die throw.

3. End the game when a player reaches 1000 instead of 100.

3.3 REVISITING THE SUPERMARKET SIMULATION

To further illustrate the process of going from design artifacts to implementation, we focus on a few of the classes related to the wakeup call pattern described in Chapter 2 in connection with the supermarket simulation.

The design class for the wakeup call pattern is shown in Figure 3.11. *PriorityQueue* replaces *Collection* since we need to order objects on the basis of their critical event time. *Supermarket* and *BalkingLogic* are removed for simplicity.

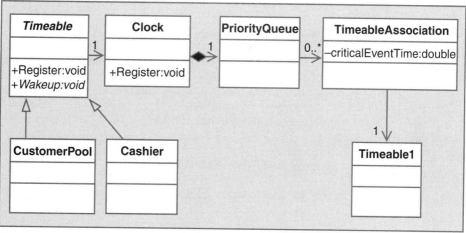

FIGURE 3.11 Design class diagram for wakeup call pattern

Recall that *Timeable* objects of type *CustomerPool* are sent a "wakeup call" by the *Clock* object whenever it is time to generate a new *Customer* object. Likewise, *Cashier* objects are sent a "wakeup call" by the *Clock* object whenever it is time to complete a customer service. When either the *CustomerPool* object or one of the *Cashier* objects registers with the *Clock* object, it is encapsulated in an object of type *TimeableAssociation*, which holds the *Timeable* object along with its critical event time. This *TimeableAssociation* object is inserted into a *PriorityQueue* queue. The object with the smallest *criticalEventTime* value is at the front of this queue.

We consider abstract class *Timeable*. Its details are shown in Listing 3.11. The *Wakeup* command is shown as abstract.

A protected field, *Clock*, is specified. This *Clock* field is inherited and is accessible in all the concrete subclasses of *Timeable*. The clock is not owned by a *Timeable* object, and a reference to the clock must be passed in as a parameter to the constructor in each *Timeable* subclass.

The concrete method *Register* takes a critical event time as input. It then invokes the *Register* command on the clock, passing itself (the *Timeable* object) as the first parameter. When the clock sends a wakeup call to the objects it holds, it is the *Timeable* object that receives the wakeup call. Therefore, it is essential that this object is passed to the *Register* method using the self-reference keyword, **this**.

The abstract *Wakeup* command must be defined in each of the concrete subclasses of *Timeable*.

Listing 3.12 presents the details of class *Clock*. This class is one of the most important in the entire implementation because it is the centerpiece of the event notification through its wakeup call dispatching mechanism.

In class *Clock*, the field *currentTime* is modified each time the *Tick* command is invoked. This causes the value of *currentTime* to be incremented by one unit. This time is accessible using the read-only property *CurrentTime*.

LISTING 3.11 Class Timeable

```
using System;

namespace SupermarketCheckout {

    // The base class for classes Cashier and CustomerPool
    public abstract class Timeable {

        // Fields
        protected Clock clock;

        // Commands
        public abstract void Wakeup();

        public void Register(double criticalEventTime) {
            clock.Register(this, criticalEventTime);
        }
    }
}
```

LISTING 3.12 Class Clock

```
using System;
using System.Collections;

namespace SupermarketCheckout {

    // Holds Timeable objects, each with a critical event time
    public class Clock {

        // Fields
        private PriorityQueue sleepers = new PriorityQueue();
        private double currentTime = 0.0;
        // Commands
        public void Register(Timeable timeableObject,
                             double criticalEventTime) {
            TimeableAssociation timeableAssociation =
                    new TimeableAssociation(timeableObject,
                                            criticalEventTime);
            sleepers.Insert(timeableAssociation);
        }
```

LISTING 3.12 Class Clock (continued)

```
        // Send Wakeup command to sleepers whose time has come
        public void SendWakeUpCalls() {
            while (sleepers.NumberElements > 0 &&
                currentTime >= sleepers.FirstItem.CriticalEventTime)
{

                sleepers.FirstItem.TimeableObject.Wakeup();
                sleepers.Remove();
            }
        }

        public void Tick() {
            currentTime++;
        }

        // Properties
        public double CurrentTime { // Read-only
            get {
                return currentTime;
            }
        }
    }
}
```

Another important field of class *Clock* is *sleepers* of type *PriorityQueue* (whose details we will not show). The *sleepers* field holds the collection of <*Timeable*, critical event time> pairs (of type *TimeableAssociation*) ordered by the critical event times in ascending order. When the command *SendWakeUpCalls* is invoked on the *Clock* object, all sleeper objects whose critical event time is equal to or less than the current clock time are sent the *Wakeup* command. The *FirstItem* property of the *PriorityQueue* class is used to obtain the *TimeableAssociation* object with the smallest critical event time. The *TimeableObject* property extracts the *Timeable* object from the *TimeableAssociation*. After sending the *Wakeup* command to the *Timeable* object, the *TimeableAssociation* object is deleted from the priority queue.

The *Register* command in *Clock* creates a new *TimeableAssociation* object (2-tuple) and inserts it into the *sleepers* priority queue. Listing 3.13 presents the details of class *TimeableAssociation*.

LISTING 3.13 Class TimeableAssociation

```
using System;
using System.Collections;

namespace SupermarketCheckout {
```

LISTING 3.13 Class TimeableAssociation (continued)

```csharp
/**
 * An association between a timeable object and a critical event
 * time. Must implement Comparable so that instances can be
 * compared.
 */
public class TimeableAssociation : IComparable {

    // Fields
    private Timeable timeableObject;
    private double criticalEventTime;

    // Constructor
    public TimeableAssociation(Timeable timeableObject,
                               double criticalEventTime) {
        this.timeableObject = timeableObject;
        this.criticalEventTime = criticalEventTime;
    }

    // Properties
    public Timeable TimeableObject {
        get {
            return timeableObject;
        }
    }

    public double CriticalEventTime {
        get {
            return criticalEventTime;
        }
    }

    // Queries
    public int CompareTo(Object other) {
        TimeableAssociation timeableAssoc =
                            (TimeableAssociation) other;
        if (this.criticalEventTime <
                timeableAssoc.CriticalEventTime) {
            return -1;
        } else if (this.criticalEventTime ==
                timeableAssoc.CriticalEventTime) {
            return 0;
        } else {
            return 1;
        }
    }
}
}
```

TimeableAssociation implements the *IComparable* interface because we must be able to compare instances of this type. Without this ability, the priority queue could not determine the "smallest" object and order its objects properly.

As you recall from the examples of *CompareTo* in Chapter 1, a downcast to the object type being compared is mandatory. The critical event times are used as the basis for comparing two *TimeableAssociation* objects.

We conclude this section by examining the transition from design to a first implementation of class *CustomerPool*. The early analysis object-interaction diagram is shown in Figure 3.12.

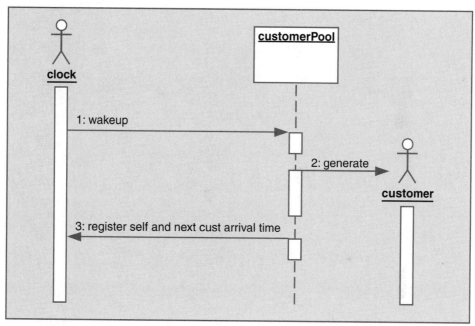

FIGURE 3.12 Early analysis object-interaction diagram for *CustomerPool* class

Figure 3.12, although useful in understanding the basic mission of the *CustomerPool* class, lacks design details. We correct this by presenting a more detailed design stage object-interaction diagram in Figure 3.13.

The *CustomerPool* object receives a *Wakeup* command from the clock. The *CustomerPool* object queries the clock for the current time. The next customer number is obtained, and this number plus the current clock time are used to generate the next *Customer* object. The time of arrival of the next customer is obtained. The *CustomerPool* object registers itself and this next arrival time with the clock.

Now a change in design occurs. Instead of notifying the supermarket object with a wakeup call each second to determine whether to add or remove a cashier, the *cashierCollection* object is queried to determine whether the shortest line is equal to or greater than five in size or whether a cashier has been idle for more than four minutes. This simplification will not affect the simulation statistics because it is only when a customer arrives that it matters how many cashiers are on duty. The newly generated customer is commanded to join the shortest line only after a cashier is added or removed, as needed.

From the sequence diagram in Figure 3.13 emerge the details of method *Wakeup* in class *CustomerPool*. These details as well as the rest of class CustomerPool are presented in Listing 3.14. Class *CustomerPool* is shown as extending abstract class *Timeable* as indicated in the class diagram of Figure 3.11.

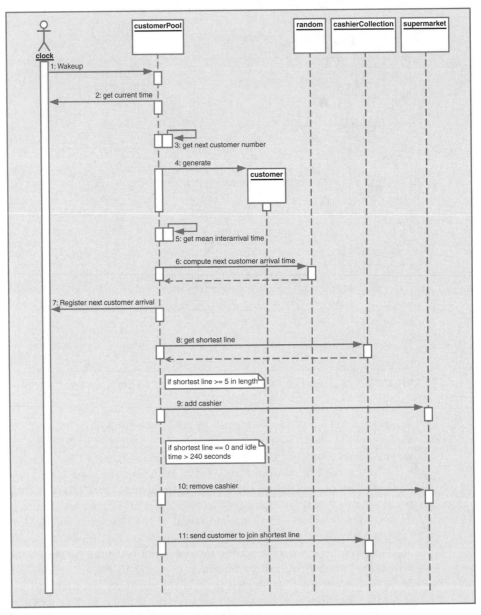

FIGURE 3.13 More detailed object-interaction diagram of CustomerPool wakeup

Five fields define the information model of *CustomerPool*:

◆ *customer*—Step 4 in the object-interaction diagram requires the *CustomerPool* object to generate a customer.

◆ *supermarket*—Step 9 in the object-interaction diagram requires the *CustomerPool* object to generate a cashier in the supermarket.

◆ *cashierCollection*—Step 8 in the object-interaction diagram requires the *CustomerPool* object to obtain the shortest line from the cashier collection.

◆ *customerNumber*—Step 3 in the object-interaction diagram requires the *CustomerPool* object to generate a customer number.

◆ *openForBusiness*—Although not shown in the object-interaction diagram, the purpose of this field is to shut down the further generation of customers when the elapsed time for the simulation has ended.

LISTING 3.14 Class CustomerPool

```
using System;

namespace SupermarketCheckout {

    public class CustomerPool : Timeable {

        // Fields
        private Customer customer;
        private Supermarket supermarket;
        private CashierCollection cashierCollection;
        private int customerNumber;
        private bool openForBusiness = true;

        // Constructor
        public CustomerPool(Clock clock, Supermarket supermarket,
                            CashierCollection cashierCollection) {
            this.clock = clock;
            this.supermarket = supermarket;
            this.cashierCollection = cashierCollection;
            Register(0.0);
        }

        // Commands
        public override void Wakeup() {
            if (openForBusiness) {
                double meanArrivalTime;
                double currentTime = clock.CurrentTime;
                customerNumber++;
                customer = new Customer(customerNumber, currentTime);
                if (currentTime <= 1 * 3600.0) {
                    meanArrivalTime = 50.0;
                } else if (currentTime <= 3 * 3600.0) {
                    meanArrivalTime = 15.0;
```

LISTING 3.14 Class CustomerPool (continued)

```
    } else if (currentTime <= 6 * 3600.0) {
        meanArrivalTime = 30.0;
    } else if (currentTime <= 9 * 3600.0) {
        meanArrivalTime = 10.0;
    } else {
        meanArrivalTime = 35.0;
    }
    double smallestArrivalTime =
        (1.0 - Application.ArrivalTimeFraction) *
            meanArrivalTime;
    double largestArrivalTime =
        (1.00 + Application.ArrivalTimeFraction) *
            meanArrivalTime;
    double nextCriticalTime = currentTime +
        smallestArrivalTime +
            Application.RandomValue.NextDouble() *
            (largestArrivalTime - smallestArrivalTime);
    Register(nextCriticalTime);
    int shortestLine = cashierCollection.ShortestLine();
    int shortestLineLength =
        cashierCollection.ShortestLineLength();
    if (shortestLineLength == 0 &&
        currentTime -
            cashierCollection.Cashier(shortestLine).
                                    StartIdleTime >
        Application.IdleTimeThreshold &&
            cashierCollection.NumberOnDutyCashiers > 1) {
        supermarket.RemoveCashier(shortestLine);
        shortestLine = cashierCollection.ShortestLine();
    } else if (cashierCollection.NumberOnDutyCashiers <
            Application.MaxNumberCashiers &&
            shortestLineLength >= 5) {
        supermarket.AddCashier();
        shortestLine = cashierCollection.ShortestLine();
    }
    cashierCollection.Cashier(shortestLine).
                                JoinLine(customer);
    Application.OutputFile.WriteLine("Customer " +
        customerNumber +
        " generated at " + currentTime +
        " seconds. Joined line " + shortestLine +
        " Line length = " +
        cashierCollection.Cashier(shortestLine).
                        LineLength + ".");
    }
```

LISTING 3.14 Class CustomerPool (continued)

```
        }

        public void CloseForBusiness() {
            openForBusiness = false;
        }
    }
}
```

Exercise 3.11

Correlate the details of Listing 3.14 with Figure 3.13. Are there any actions specified in the object-interaction diagram that are not accounted for in the source listing? Are there any actions specified in the source listing that are not accounted for in the object-interaction diagram?

3.4 SUMMARY

♦ In this chapter, we examined two applications that show the steps from analysis to design to implementation.

♦ From use cases, object-interaction diagrams that typically represent instances of a use case are developed. Each object shown in an object-interaction diagram is associated with a class that defines the behavior of the object (the information model, commands, and queries that the object encapsulates).

♦ Analysis class diagrams are formulated from the object-interaction diagrams. The connections between classes must provide support for the messages that are passed between objects in the interaction diagrams.

♦ Analysis evolves to design as our concern changes from what the system does to how we build it. More detailed object-interaction diagrams and class diagrams are constructed.

♦ Implementation follows design closely but still allows for further refinements and discoveries that may change the design. Each stage of our work deepens our understanding of previous stages and of the overall system.

♦ It is not uncommon to implement prototypes of classes with minimal functionality as these classes are discovered during early analysis. As the analysis and design processes evolve, so do the prototypes. By the time design is completed, the implementation is well under way. The advantage of this quasi-parallel approach to development is that each stage of work provides insights into all other stages, so doing some early implementation helps to clarify analysis and design work.

3.5 ADDITIONAL EXERCISES

Exercise 3.12

Write a portion of a plausible class *Car* based on the class diagram originally shown in Figure 1.1 and repeated in Figure 3.14.

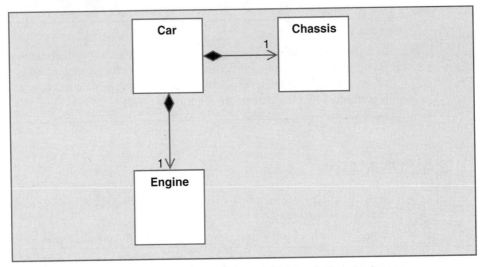

FIGURE 3.14 UML diagram for the *Car, Engine*, and *Chassis* classes

Exercise 3.13

Write a portion of a plausible class *Classroom* based on the class diagram originally shown in Figure 1.2 and repeated in Figure 3.15.

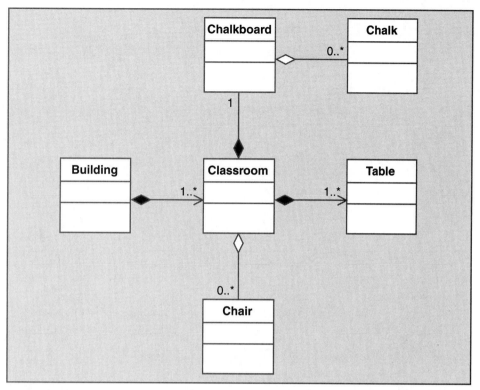

FIGURE 3.15 UML class diagram showing weak aggregation

Exercise 3.14

Write a portion of a plausible class *Player* based on the class diagram originally shown in Figure 1.3 and repeated in Figure 3.16.

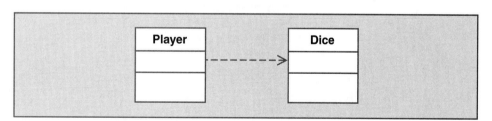

FIGURE 3.16 UML diagram showing a weak association

PART 2

CLASS CONSTRUCTION

Class construction forms the basis of software implementation in C# and .NET and the basis for object-oriented programming. This section of the book focuses on principles of class construction.

The basics of class construction are presented in Chapter 4. This includes namespaces, assemblies, access qualifiers, properties, indexers, type-safe enumeration, static members, value (*struct*) and reference (*class*) types, overriding and overloading, new points of specialization, overloading operators, the parameter modes *ref* and *out*, the *sealed* specifier, rectangular arrays and jagged arrays, destructors, and exceptions.

Chapter 5 deals with more advanced principles of class construction with a focus on creating robust and reusable classes. Such classes must often include features for determining the equality and comparison of instances, a *ToString* query that allows for a textual representation of an instance, a hash code that associates a unique integer with each instance, shallow and deep copying of objects from the class, and enabling iteration through the *foreach* construct. Finally, the exciting and new capability of generic classes that contain one or more generic parameters is introduced.

Chapter 6 deals with refactoring. This important and often ignored activity involves rebuilding classes after an initial design and implementation is complete. This is accomplished by factoring code that appears in several locations into support methods, moving existing methods from one class to another often with the requirement that their signatures are modified, and renaming entities to provide for easier understandability and maintenance. Minor and major refactoring is illustrated using the refactoring tools provided in .NET 2005.

Chapter 7 focuses on the construction of thread classes. Creating and deploying thread classes provides opportunities to achieve performance improvements as well as simplification of design. Modern operating systems such as Unix, Windows 2000, and Windows XP support threaded programming. The event-handling mechanisms provided in .NET utilize threads.

Several thread-centric case studies are presented that showcase the benefits achievable with thread classes.

CHAPTER 4

The Basics of Class Construction

In implementing the two case studies in the earlier chapters, we used some principles that will be discussed in detail in this chapter and in Chapter 5. The main focus in Part 1 was on showing how object modeling provides the basis for implementation. We focus here on software implementation using objects. The basis for accomplishing this is through class construction.

Classes form the brick and mortar of software construction in C# and in any object-oriented language. To implement a C# software system is to construct classes. There are some basic principles of class construction that are examined and illustrated in this chapter. While focusing on class construction, we also examine and review important features of the C# language that relate to the effective construction of classes and object-oriented programming.

4.1 UNIFIED TYPE SYSTEM IN C#

One of the C# language's most significant advances compared to Java and C++ is its unified type system. Every entity (for example, a field, local variable, or method parameter) is an object type. In contrast, there are two universes of types in Java: primitive types and object types. This duality of types in Java has led to unnecessary clutter and distracting overhead in building Java software systems and in learning the Java programming language. The designers of the C# language were bold and innovative in creating the unified type system in which every type of entity is an object. This has led to a uniform object model and cleaner coding.

Although every entity type in C# is an object, some objects enjoy value semantics whereas others enjoy reference semantics. Variables with value semantics are allocated on the system stack or inline, whereas reference variables are allocated on the system heap. Automatic garbage collection ensures that all reference variables are deallocated and their memory recycled when they are no longer needed. For efficiency reasons, variables such as basic integer or double types, characters, and Boolean (*bool* in C#) have value semantics. The mere declaration of such variables causes storage to be allocated and brings such objects to life. The **struct** is a class with value semantics. We examine and further define the *struct* type later in this chapter. Storage for a *struct* object is deallocated when it goes out of scope.

All C# types derive from a single base type, *Object*. This means that all types (structs, concrete classes, abstract classes, interfaces, delegates—to be introduced in Chapter 8—enums—to be introduced later in this chapter—and arrays) share the same basic functionality. This includes being converted to a string, being serialized, or being stored in a collection.

This unified approach to types makes C# a pure object-oriented language. The only other two pure object-oriented languages among major languages are Eiffel and Smalltalk. Other object-oriented programming languages including C++, Java, and Objective-C are hybrid languages that contain non-object types as well as object types.

In a typed language such as C#, every field, local variable, and method parameter must have a specified type. Knowledge of the type determines the values that the variable can hold and the operations that can be performed on the variable. Because all C# variables are objects, an object's class description completely characterizes the values and operations relevant to the variable. In other words, the class description of every variable completely characterizes the behavior of the variable.

When a variable of a simple type such as *int* (alias for class *System.Int32*) is added to a collection, such as an *ArrayList*, the object is boxed (held as an object of type *System.Int32*). When the object is removed from the collection, it must be unboxed (converted back to the simple representation). This is accomplished using a downcast.

Boxing and **unboxing** are a basic part of C#'s type system. Boxing automatically converts any value-type to a reference-type. Unboxing is an explicit operation that extracts a value type from a reference type.

To illustrate and dramatize the fact that all variables in C# are objects, and that simple types can be added and removed from containers through boxing and unboxing, consider the code in Listing 4.1.

LISTING 4.1 Numeric types are object types—boxing and unboxing

```
using System;
using System.Collections;
namespace BoxingUnBoxing {
    public class BoxingUnBoxingExample {
        static void Main() {
            Object obj1 = 17; // 17 is of type System.Int32
            Object obj2 = 18; // 18 is of type System.Int32
            String str = obj1.GetType().ToString();
            Console.WriteLine(str);
```

LISTING 4.1 Numeric types are object types—boxing and unboxing (continued)

```
            // GetType query sent directly to the object 17
            Console.WriteLine(17.GetType().ToString());
            // ToString query sent directly to object 17
            Console.WriteLine(17.ToString());
            int sumValues = (int) obj1 + (int) obj2;
            Console.WriteLine("sumValues = " + sumValues);
            // Add objects of type double to ArrayList
            ArrayList myList = new ArrayList();
            // Load myList with double value objects
            for (int i = 0; i < 100; i++) {
                myList.Add(Math.Sin(i));
            }
                // Output the sum of myList[0] and myList[1]
            double value1 = (double)myList[0];
            double value2 = (double)myList[1];
            Console.WriteLine("myList[0] + myList[1] = " +
                                (value1 + value2));
            // Obtain the sum of the objects in myList
            double sum = 0.0;
            foreach (double value in myList) {
                sum += value;
            }
            Console.WriteLine("sum = " + sum);
            Console.ReadLine();
        }
    }
}
/* Output
System.Int32
System.Int32
17
sumValues = 35
myList[0] + myList[1] = 0.841470984807897
sum = 0.379194627449339*/
```

The following assignment:

```
Object obj1 = 17;
```

is legal because *17* is an instance of class *System.Int32*. The principle of **polymorphic substitution**, discussed in Chapter 1, allows the formal type *Object* to be replaced by the actual type *System.Int32*, which is a descendent of class *Object*.

The query *GetType().ToString()* invoked on *obj1* returns the name of the class to which *obj1* belongs. As shown in the output, the name of this class is *System.Int32*. The same query can be invoked on the object *17*, itself producing the same output.

The object *17* responds to the *ToString()* method as is evident by the following statement:

```
Console.WriteLine(17.ToString());
```

In summing the values of *obj1* and *obj2*, each must be unboxed (converted back to *int*) because entities of formal type *Object* cannot be added. The downcast, (*int*), is used to achieve this. This is a type-safe operation because the runtime system ensures that the actual types of *obj1* and *obj2* are *int* (*System.Int32*).

After creating an object, *myList*, of type *ArrayList*, this container is filled with objects of type *double* (*System.Double*) using the following code:

```
for (int i = 0; i < 100; i++) {
    myList.Add(Math.Sin(i));
}
```

To add the values in index 0 and index 1 of the *ArrayList*, we access *myList[0]* and *myList[1]*. But the formal type stored in any *ArrayList* is *Object*. Therefore, a downcast must be performed in order to add the two values to produce the sum that is output. This is accomplished using the following code:

```
double value1 = (double)myList[0];
double value2 = (double)myList[1];
Console.WriteLine("myList[0] + myList[1] = " + (value1 + value2));
```

Lastly, the sum of values in the *ArrayList* is sought. The *foreach* iteration, enabled in class *ArrayList*, is used as follows:

```
double sum = 0.0;
foreach (double value in myList) {
    sum += value;
}
```

In this iteration, a downcast is implied by declaring *value* to be of type *double*. If the actual type that was stored in *myList* were not of type *double*, a runtime exception would be generated as follows:

```
Unhandled Exception: System.InvalidCastException: Specified cast is
not valid.
```

4.2 NAMESPACES

C# software systems typically contain many classes, each defining a set of specialized behaviors specified by their fields and public methods. When two or more developers are working on the same application, as is often required in building modern software systems, it is important to be able to manage the global namespace to ensure that there are no clashes of class names.

C# uses the **namespace** keyword to control global clashes of class names. A namespace may contain one or more public as well as non-public classes. These classes may be stored in a single file or in separate files. Each of the files declares the namespace before the classes within the namespace.

It is recommended that a C# namespace be used to contain logically coherent C# classes, the same as a package in Java. Such coherent classes are designed to support a common purpose (e.g., GUI classes, Math classes, and File I/O classes).

The source listing given in Listing 4.2 illustrates some of the options using namespaces. Because the example is not associated with a meaningful application, the entire application is contained within a single source file, *NamespaceApplication.cs.*

LISTING 4.2 Tutorial application involving namespaces

```
using System;
namespace Namespace1 {
    public class MyClass {

        public void Talk() {
            System.Console.WriteLine("In MyClass in Namespace1");
            System.Console.ReadLine();
        }
        static void Main() {
            MyClass appObject = new MyClass();
            appObject.Talk();
            Namespace2.MyClass object1 = new Namespace2.MyClass();
            object1.Talk();

            AnotherClass object2 = new AnotherClass();
            object2.Talk();
            Namespace3.MyClass object3 =
                new Namespace3.MyClass();
            object3.Talk();
            Namespace3.Namespace4.MyClass object4 =
                    new Namespace3.Namespace4.MyClass();
            object4.Talk();
        }
    }
}
namespace Namespace2 {
    public class MyClass {
        public void Talk() {
            System.Console.WriteLine("In MyClass in Namespace2");
            System.Console.ReadLine();
        }
    }
}
namespace Namespace1 {
    public class AnotherClass {
        public void Talk() {
            System.Console.WriteLine("In AnotherClass in
                Namespace1");
            System.Console.ReadLine();
        }
    }
}
```

LISTING 4.2 Tutorial application involving namespaces (continued)

```
namespace Namespace3 {
   public class MyClass {
      public void Talk() {
         System.Console.WriteLine("In MyClass in Namespace3");
         System.Console.ReadLine();
      }
   }
   namespace Namespace4 {
      public class MyClass {
         public void Talk() {
            System.Console.
               WriteLine("In MyClass in Namespace3.Namespace4");
            System.Console.ReadLine();
         }
      }
   }
}
/* Output
In MyClass in Namespace1
In MyClass in Namespace2
In AnotherClass in Namespace1
In MyClass in Namespace3
In MyClass in Namespace3.Namespace4
*/
```

Discussion of Listing 4.2

- There are four classes named *MyClass* in Listing 4.2. Each of these has a command *Talk()* that outputs namespace information to the console.

- Method *Main()* declares and initializes an *appObject* of type *MyClass*. It sends *appObject* the *Talk()* command. Because method *Main()* is inside of namespace *Namespace1*, the output "In MyClass in Namespace1" reflects the fact that the *Talk* method within *Namespace1.MyClass* is invoked.

- Next in *Main()*, object1 is declared and initialized as an instance of *Namespace2.MyClass*.

- This shows how the namespace qualifier can be used to avoid name clashes among the four *MyClass* names.

- Next, object2 is declared and initialized as an instance of *AnotherClass* in *Namespace1*. Following this, object3 is declared and initialized as an instance of *MyClass* in *Namespace3*.

- Finally, object4 is declared and initialized as an instance of *MyClass* in the nested namespace within *Namespace3*. This is accomplished using the following code:

```
Namespace3.Namespace4.MyClass object4 =
         new Namespace3.Namespace4.MyClass();
```

- The dot operator is used to indicate nested namespaces in this case.

A fully qualified class name always consists of the namespace (connected by dots in the case of nested namespaces) followed by a dot followed by the class name.

The keyword **using** at the beginning of a C# file allows one to use an unqualified name for a class. For example, the class *Brush* in namespace *System.Drawing* has a qualified name, *System.Drawing.Brush*. If the user includes the following statement:

```
using System.Drawing;
```

at the beginning of the file containing a reference to *Brush*, then the reference to *Brush* can be made without requiring *System.Drawing.Brush* but only *Brush*.

4.3 ASSEMBLIES

Before proceeding to the main subject of class construction, we review the mechanism of assemblies in the .NET framework because classes are a component of assemblies and assemblies play a fundamental role in the .NET framework.

Assemblies are the unit of deployment in a .NET software system. They are also the basis for tracking versions and ensuring security. The .NET common language runtime (CLR) uses the metadata contained within an assembly to load the assembly and supporting libraries, handle version support, perform type validation, and enforce security.

There are several file formats for an assembly:

◆ *.exe*—An executable that contains one entry point through method *Main()*

◆ *.dll*—A type library that can be used by other assemblies

◆ *.netmodule*—A module containing a nonexecutable collection of compiled code for use in other assemblies

An assembly contains a manifest with metadata, one or more modules, and resource files (bitmaps, etc).

The manifest defines:

◆ The name of the assembly

◆ The version of the assembly (major and minor version numbers)

◆ The culture that the assembly supports (the native language, format for time, decimals, etc.)

◆ The files that comprise the assembly

◆ The types that are exported by the assembly

◆ The references to other assemblies required to support the given assembly

◆ General information including the owner of the copyright, and so forth.

Modules are units written in some .NET language and useful for constructing a .NET application from different .NET-compliant languages. Modules can be combined to form an assembly. Modules by themselves cannot be used by the CLR. A module can contain types from more than one namespace.

To construct a module using the C# compiler from the command line use:

csc /target:module /out:MyModule.netmodule SourceFile1.cs SourceFile2.cs

Listing 4.3 presents the details of a simple *Counter* class. Using the command line compiler, we generate a file *Counter.dll* as follows:

csc /target:library Counter.cs

We then compile the *CounterApp* class, presented in Listing 4.4 as follows:

csc /reference:Counter.dll CounterApp.cs

The resulting file is *CounterApp.exe*.

Library assemblies provide the basis for shipping custom libraries that contain user-defined classes to a remote user. The author of the *CounterApp* class needs the *Counter.dll* file in order to assemble the *CounterApp.exe* file (assembly).

LISTING 4.3 Class Counter for producing the assembly Counter.dll

```
using System;
namespace Assemblies {

   public class Counter {
      // Fields
      private int count;
      // Constructors
      public Counter() {
         count = 0;
      }
      public Counter(int initialValue) {
         count = initialValue;
      }
      // Properties
      public int Count { // Read-only property
         get {
            return count;
         }
      }
      // Commands
      public void Reset() {
         count = 0;
      }
      public void Increment() {
         count++;
      }
   }
}
```

LISTING 4.4 Class CounterApp in a separate assembly

```
using System;
using Assemblies;
namespace CounterApp {

   public class CountApp {
```

LISTING 4.4 Class CounterApp in a separate assembly (continued)

```
        public static void Main() {
            Counter myCounter = new Counter(20);
            for (int i = 1; i <= 20; i++) {
                myCounter.Increment();
            }
            Console.WriteLine("myCounter.Count = " +
                myCounter.Count);
        }
    }
}
/* Program output
myCounter.Count = 40
*/
```

4.3.1 Creating and Using a Multifile Assembly

The assembly linker (al.exe) is used to combine modules into an assembly. The modules may be generated from different .NET languages. Here we use the two C# classes presented in the previous section, Listings 4.3 and 4.4, to produce two modules. These are combined into an assembly file (.exe file) that may be run.

The steps that are used to produce two modules and then combine them into a single assembly are the following:

Produce the module *Counter.netmodule* as follows:

csc /target:module Counter.cs -> Counter.netmodule

Produce the module *CounterApp.netmodule* as follows:

csc /addmodule:Counter.netmodule /target:module CounterApp.cs -> CounterApp.netmodule

The /addmodule:Counter.netmodule is needed because *CounterApp* contains references to class *Counter* that the linker must resolve.

Link the two modules using the al.exe (assembly linker) as follows:

al /out:CounterApp.exe /target:exe /main:CounterApp.CountApp.Main CounterApp.netmodule Counter.netmodule -> CounterApp.exe

4.4 CLASS NAMES AND OTHER NAMING CONVENTIONS

Perhaps one of the most important features of a class is its name. Because classes represent models of problem domain entities, their names should reflect this.

Class names are used when creating objects using the object creation operator **new** followed by the constructor that always has the name of the class. Class names are used when declaring the type for a field, local variable, or method parameter because a class is a user-defined type. A well-chosen class name therefore promotes program readability and maintainability.

By convention, all class names must begin with an uppercase character. There are no exceptions to this important rule. If multiple-word identifiers are used in constructing a class name, uppercase characters should be used at the beginning of each word. Some examples of possible class names are: *MyClass*, *CounterApplication*, *TaxComputation*, and *GeometricFigure*. The class name should communicate useful information about the purpose or application of the class. Obscure names such as *classB* should be avoided.

The C# language provides aliases to some classes: **object** for *Object* and **string** for *String*. We will avoid the use of these aliases because they represent a violation of the class naming rule stated earlier.

In addition to class names, a consistent mechanism for choosing other identifier names (method name, local variable name, and parameter name) is most important. The source code that you write represents the final documentation of the product being constructed. Useful information may be gleaned from the formation of a name. A well-formatted program that uses a consistent set of rules for naming the various entities that comprise your application lets others easily understand and maintain your code.

By convention, a lowercase character must be used as the first character in naming a field, local variable, or parameter. If the name involves multiple words, uppercase characters are used to identify the multiple words (e.g., *torqueOnWheel*).

Some object-oriented languages including Smalltalk and Java use a lowercase character as the first character of a method. C# uses uppercase characters as the first character of a method name. Examples include *IsEmpty*, *SetTime*, *Reset*, and *ElapsedTime*.

Finally, constants are named using all uppercase characters and the underscore to separate multiple words in a constant identifier. Some examples include: POUNDS_PER_TON and COEFFICIENT_OF_FRICTION.

4.5 ACCESS SPECIFIERS: PUBLIC, PROTECTED, PRIVATE, INTERNAL

The visibility of the fields and methods of a class are specified using an access modifier such as **public**, **protected**, **private**, or **internal**.

Fields or methods declared **private** are accessible only within the class in which they are defined. Fields or methods declared **protected** are accessible within the class in which they are defined as well as within any descendent class. Fields or methods defined as **public** (and it is most unusual to declare a field to be public) are accessible within the class in which they are defined as well as within any other class in the system. Fields or methods declared as **internal** are accessible within the same assembly.

The *internal* and *protected* modifiers may be combined (e.g., *protected internal int value;*) to provide accessibility to all descendent classes and all classes within the same assembly.

If no access specifier is declared for a field or method, it assumes a default of *private*.

Recall from Chapter 1 that the principle of encapsulation suggests the importance of controlling the accessibility of fields through the commands in a class that are designed to modify the internal state (field values) of the objects on which they are invoked. Therefore, it is normal to specify fields as either *private* or *protected*.

The commands that define and provide the mechanism for modifying the values of fields are normally declared as *public*. This enables them to be invoked from any class in the system. Private methods are typically used to support the implementation of a public method. They are for internal class use only.

4.6 THE PARTS OF A CLASS

A class description contains many features and represents a model of some aspect of the problem domain. As we have seen, the fields of a class model the information structure of each object that is an instance of the class. The methods control and limit how we can change the values within the information structure or access the current state of an instance. C# classes contain other artifacts in addition to fields, constructors, commands, and queries. These include indexers, enum constants, and static fields and methods. Table 4.1 summarizes the possible features of a class with a brief description of each feature. We examine some of these features in more detail later in this chapter.

TABLE 4.1 Parts of a class

Class Feature	Description
Field	An object that defines all or part of the internal state of an instance.
Constructor	A method with the name of the class that is used to initialize a class instance as it is created. All classes without an explicit constructor have a default constructor with no parameters. In that case fields assume their default values (0 for numeric types, false for Boolean types, and null for reference types).
Command method	A method that is capable of modifying the value of one or more fields and thereby changing the internal state of an instance. The return type of a command method is always void.
Query method	A method that is capable of returning the value of one or more fields and thereby returning state information about an instance. The return type of a query method is never void.
Property	An alternative mechanism for setting or getting the values of one or more fields.
Indexer	Provides the ability for an object to be associated with an index, emulating the behavior of an array object.
Enum	Provides type-safe enumeration constants.
Other methods	May change the internal state of an instance as well as return information about its state.
Static field or method	Accessible only through the class name. No state information about an instance can be used.

4.7 PROPERTIES

Properties are a wonderful feature of C#, first introduced in Delphi Pascal by the language designer Anders Hejlsberg, who also designed C#. Properties let you control the access of a field that needs to set or get field information. Through a property, a field may be specified as read-only, write-only, or read-write. Direct access to a field is possible using a property, but does not compromise the integrity of the underlying field data. On the surface, using a read-only property appears similar to using a public field. The difference is that access is possible everywhere without the ability to modify the value of the field. Modifying the value of a field can be done only with a command method or a read-write or write-only property.

Listing 4.5 presents a simple application that introduces properties.

Properties are defined for each of the three private fields, *importantValue1*, *importantValue2*, and *importantValue3*.

LISTING 4.5 Simple application that uses properties

```
using System;
namespace IntroducingProperties {
    public class SimplePropertiesApplication {
        // Fields
        private int importantValue1;
        private double importantValue2;
        private String importantValue3;
        // Constructor
        public SimplePropertiesApplication(int importantValue1) {
            this.importantValue1 = importantValue1;
        }
        // Properties
        public int ImportantValue1 { // Read-only property
            get {
                return importantValue1;
            }
        }
        public double ImportantValue2 { // Write-only property
            set {
                importantValue2 = value; // value is a reserved word
            }
        }
        public String ImportantValue3 { // Read-write property
            get {
                return importantValue3;
            }
            set {
                importantValue3 = value; // value is a reserved word
            }
        }
    }
```

LISTING 4.5 Simple application that uses properties (continued)

```
        public override String ToString() {
            return "importantValue1: " + importantValue1 +
                " importantValue2: " + importantValue2 +
                " importantValue3: " + importantValue3;
        }
        public static void Main() {
            SimplePropertiesApplication app =
                new SimplePropertiesApplication(17);
            app.ImportantValue2 = 14;   // Write-only property
            app.ImportantValue3 = "ABCDEFG"; // Read-write
              property
            Console.WriteLine("importantValue1 = " +
              app.ImportantValue1); // Read-only
            Console.WriteLine(app.ToString());
            Console.ReadLine();
        }
    }
}
```

Discussion of Listing 4.5

♦   The first property, *ImportantValue1*, is a read-only property. Once the value of the field is set through the constructor, it cannot be changed but only read. Suppose an attempt were made to assign a value to this field through the property using the following statement:

```
app.ImportantValue1 = 12;
```

The compiler would display the following error message:

```
Error: Property or indexer
'IntroducingProperties.SimplePropertiesApplication.ImportantValue1'
cannot be assigned to -- it is read only
```

♦   The second property, *ImportantValue2*, is a write-only property. Suppose an attempt were made to access the value of the field using the property using the following statement:

```
double result = app.ImportantValue2;
```

The compiler would display the following error message:

```
Error: The property or indexer
 'IntroducingProperties.SimplePropertiesApplication.ImportantValue2'
cannot be used in this context because it lacks the get accessor
```

♦   The third property, *ImportantValue3*, is a read-write property. The value of the *importantValue3* field can be accessed and set.
    The "set" portion of the *ImportantValue3* property is:

```
set {
 importantValue3 = value;
}
```

The keyword **value** represents the right side of an assignment statement that involves the property such as in:

```
ImportantValue3 = "Hello";
```

Here *value* would be "Hello".

Properties are sometimes referred to as "smart-fields."

Abstract properties can be defined in an abstract class or interface, as the following example that uses an interface demonstrates. Consider the interface *GeometricFigure* in Listing 4.6 and the concrete class *Square* that implements this interface.

LISTING 4.6 Abstract Property

```
using System;
namespace AbstractProperties {
    public interface GeometricFigure {
        // Query
        double Area { // abstract read-only property
            get;
        }
    }
    // Concrete class that implements the interface
    public class Square : GeometricFigure {
        // Fields
        private double side;
        // Constructor
        public Square(double side) {
            this.side = side;
        }
        // Properties
        public double Area {
            get {
                return side * side;
            }
        }
    }
}
```

Exercise 4.1

If class *GeometricFigure* were an abstract class instead of an interface, what keyword would you need to insert in front of the type *double* in the *Area* property?

Properties can encapsulate more complex behavior than simply setting or getting the value of a field, as shown in the application in Listing 4.7.

The write-only *Filename* property not only sets the value of the *filename* field but creates a file for writing and writes the text "Testing, testing, 123" in that file.

LISTING 4.7   More complex use of property

```
using System;
using System.IO;
namespace MoreComplexProperty {
    public class FileApplication {
        // Fields
        private String filename;
        private StreamWriter outputFile;
        // Property
        public String Filename { // Write-only property
            set {
                filename = value;
                outputFile = new StreamWriter(
                            new FileStream(filename,
                                        FileMode.Create,
                                        FileAccess.Write));
                outputFile.WriteLine("Testing, testing, 123");
                outputFile.Close();
            }
        }
        public static void Main() {
            FileApplication app = new FileApplication();
            app.Filename = "Testing.Txt";
        }
    }
}
```

Listing 4.8 shows another example of a class that contains a property that does more than simply access or assign a value to a field.

The read-write property *RandomValue* provides access to the *randomValue* field as well as allowing an assignment to this field. In addition to assigning a random number object to the *randomValue* field, the *set* property warms up the random number generator by generating 100,000 values and throwing them away.

LISTING 4.8   Another example of properties

```
using System;
namespace ComplexProperty2 {
    public class ContainsRandom {
        // Field
        private Random randomValue;
        // Property
        public Random RandomValue { // Read-write property
            get {
                return randomValue;
            }
```

LISTING 4.8 Another example of properties (continued)

```
        set {
            randomValue = value;
            // Warms up random number generator
            for (int i = 0; i < 100000; i++) {
                randomValue.NextDouble();
            }
        }
    }
  }
}
```

Exercise 4.2

Write a method *Main* in class *ContainsRandom* that exercises the *set* property of the RandomValue field shown in Listing 4.8.

4.8 INDEXERS: PROPERTIES WITH AN INDEX

An indexer provides a natural way to index elements in a class that encapsulates a collection using the bracket syntax of the array type. An indexer is a class property with an index.

Through the use of an indexer, *myCars[1] = "Ford"*, *myCars[2] = "Toyota"*, *myCars[3] = "Saab"* could be legal assignments on a class that encapsulates car names.

Listing 4.9 presents a class that defines an indexer that supports the type of assignment to *myCars* given above.

The information model for this class contains an array, *cars*, of type *String* initialized to seven *String* values.

The property *Size* is an example of a read-only property that does not simply return the value of a field. It returns the length of the field *cars* in this case.

Indexers must always use the keyword **this** and return a type, which is *String* in this case. Following the keyword *this* must be a left square bracket, one or more indices, and a right square bracket. The indexer in this case uses natural indexing by requiring the user to input an integer index between 1 and 7.

LISTING 4.9 A class containing an indexer

```
using System;
namespace IndexerApplication {
    public class CarCollection {
        private String[] cars = {"Ford", "Toyota", "Saab", "Volvo",
                                 "Chevy", "Dodge", "Mercedes"};
```

LISTING 4.9 A class containing an indexer (continued)

```
        // Properties
        public int Size { // Read-only property
            get {
                return cars.Length;
            }
        }
        public String this[int index] { // Read-write property
            get {
                if (index >= 1 && index <= 7) {
                    return cars[index - 1];
                } else {
                    return "Illegal index";
                }
            }
            set {
                if (index >= 1 && index <= 7) {
                    cars[index - 1] = value;
                }
            }
        }
    }
}
```

A simple application class that exercises the features of class *CarCollection* is shown in Listing 4.10.

The read-only property *Size* is used in controlling the upper-bound of the for-loop in method *Main()*.

The read-write indexer property is used to assign the String "Audi" to the second index in *myCars*.

Without looking closely, it appears that *myCars* is an array type, though it is not. It is an instance of class *CarCollection* that contains an indexer.

LISTING 4.10 Class CarCollectionApp

```
using System;
namespace IndexerApplication {
    public class CarCollectionApp {
        public static void Main() {
            CarCollection myCars = new CarCollection();
            for (int index = 1; index <= myCars.Size; index++) {
                Console.WriteLine(myCars[index]);
            }
            Console.WriteLine();
            myCars[2] = "Audi";
            for (int index = 1; index <= myCars.Size; index++) {
                Console.WriteLine(myCars[index]);
```

LISTING 4.10 Class CarCollectionApp (continued)

```
            }
            Console.ReadLine();
        }
    }
}
/* Output
Ford
Toyota
Saab
Volvo
Chevy
Dodge
Mercedes
Ford
Audi
Saab
Volvo
Chevy
Dodge
Mercedes
*/
```

Exercise 4.3

Write a class *MyFriends* that contains an indexer that provides access to the names of your friends.

4.9 TYPE-SAFE ENUMERATION

Many software applications require enumeration constants. Examples include days of the week, months of the year, playing cards, or the parts of a machine.

In older programming languages such as C or Pascal, enumeration constants can be defined that are surrogates for integers. They are not type-safe because they obey the ordinary rules of integers (for example, they can be added or multiplied). C# provides a type-safe mechanism for defining enumeration constants. Although each enumeration constant can be associated with a numeric value, this value cannot be directly used as we shall see as follows.

Consider the following *enum*:

```
public enum Month : byte { // byte is a short int
    January = 1, February = 2, March = 3, April = 4, May = 5,
    June = 6, July = 7, August = 8, September = 9,
    October = 10, November = 11, December = 12
}
```

The *enum Month* has all the characteristics of a class.

An expression that declares a local variable of type *Month* and assigns it the value *February* would be:

```
Month value = Month.February;
```

The name of an *enum* class must always be used when accessing any of its constants. That is what makes it type-safe. The following segment of code is illegal and would not compile:

```
Month value = Month.March;
if (value == 3) {
    // Details not shown
}
```

This code would produce the following error:

```
Error: Operator '==' cannot be applied to operands of type 'Month' and
'int'
```

The correct expression would be:

```
if (value == Month.March) {
    // Details not shown
}
```

The requirement that the name of an *enum* class always precede one of its constants not only makes the use of *enum* type-safe as indicated earlier, but makes the code more readable.

The next application presented in Listings 4.11 and 4.12 uses one- and two-dimensional indexers as well as an *enum* class to support some date computations.

Suppose you want to build a class that enables you to obtain the day of the year for any input date that is specified. Consider how this is done in the application that follows.

LISTING 4.11 Class DateComputation

```
using System;
namespace TypeSafeEnumeration {
  public enum Month : int {
    January = 1, February = 2, March = 3, April = 4, May = 5,
    June = 6, July = 7, August = 8, September = 9,
    October = 10, November = 11, December = 12
  }
   public class DateComputation {
    // Fields
    private String [] daysOfWeek = {"Sunday", "Monday",
     "Tuesday", "Wednesday", "Thursday", "Friday",
     "Saturday"};
    // Natural indexing
    private int [] startingDayOfMonth =
        {0, 0, 31, 59, 90, 120, 151,
           181, 212, 243, 273, 304, 334}; // Natural indexing
```

LISTING 4.11 Class DateComputation (continued)

```
        // Indexers (properties)
        // Returns the day corresponding to day of week
        public String this[int index] {
           get { // Read-only indexer
              return daysOfWeek[index - 1];
           }
        }
        // Returns the day within the year
        public int this[Month month, int day, int year] {
           get { // Read-only indexer
              int dayOfYear = startingDayOfMonth[(int) month] +
                 day;
              if (!IsLeapYear(year) || (int) month <= 2) {
              return dayOfYear;
              } else {
              return dayOfYear + 1;
              }
           }
        }
      private bool IsLeapYear(int year) {
         return (year % 4 == 0 && year % 100 != 0) ||
                year % 400 == 0;
      }
    }
}
```

LISTING 4.12 Class DateComputationApp

```
using System;
namespace TypeSafeEnumeration {
   public class DateComputationApp {
      public static void Main() {
        DateComputation date =
           new DateComputation(); // Application object
        System.Console.WriteLine("The third day of the week = " +
                              date[3]);
        System.Console.
           WriteLine("The day of the year for 3/1/2000 is: " +
                    date[Month.March, 1, 2000]);
        System.Console.
           WriteLine("The day of the year for 3/1/2003 is: " +
                    date[Month.March, 1, 2003]);
        System.Console.
           WriteLine("The day of the year for 12/31/2000 is: " +
                    date[Month.December, 31, 2000]);
        System.Console.
           WriteLine("The day of the year for 12/31/2004 is: " +
                    date[Month.December, 31, 2004]);
```

LISTING 4.12 Class DateComputationApp (continued)

```
            System.Console.
                WriteLine("The day of the year for 12/31/2005 is: " +
                        date[Month.December, 31, 2005]);
            System.Console.ReadLine();
            /* Compiler errors omitted since enum constants are type
               safe.
                if (Month.March == 3) {
                    Console.WriteLine("Found third month of year.");
                }
                int result = Month.March + Month.April;
                */
            }
        }
    }
    /* Application output
    The third day of the week = Tuesday
    The day of the year for 3/1/2000 is: 61
    The day of the year for 3/1/2003 is: 60
    The day of the year for 12/31/2000 is: 366
    The day of the year for 12/31/2004 is: 366
    The day of the year for 12/31/2005 is: 365
    */
```

The *enum Month* (shown earlier) is declared as a standalone class that is nested inside of the namespace *TypeSafeEnumeration* and is therefore accessible anywhere within this namespace.

The array field *daysOfWeek* that initializes an array of eight *String* values using natural indexing is supported by a read-only indexer that takes a single index and returns the name of the day of the week associated with the integer index.

Another array field, *startingDayOfMonth*, initializes an array of 13 integer values that represent the day of the year associated with the first day of each of the 12 months. Natural indexing is used (the value in index 0 is not used).

Another read-only indexer is defined on three indices—month, day, and year—and returns the day of the year as an integer. Let us examine closely how this indexer works.

The day of the year is computed as follows:

```
int dayOfYear = startingDayOfMonth[(int) month] + day;
```

The *month* parameter is downcast to an *int* and used as an index in the *startingDayOfMonth* array field. This value plus the value of the day parameter determines the day of the year in years that are not leap years.

If the month is less than or equal to 2 (January or February) or the year is not a leap year, the indexer returns the value computed above. Otherwise it returns the value computed above plus 1 to reflect the fact that the year is a leap year.

Exercise 4.4

Carefully explain how the *IsLeapYear* query works.

Exercise 4.5

Explain why compiler errors would be generated if the commented code at the end of Listing 4.12 were uncommented.

Exercise 4.6

Write a class, *MyCourses*, that contains an enumeration of all the courses that you are currently taking. This *enum* should be nested inside of your class *MyCourses*. Your class should also have an array field that provides a short description (as a *String*) of each of your courses. Write an indexer that takes one of your enumerated courses as an index and returns the *String* description of the course.

4.10 VALUE TYPES AND STRUCT

All value types in C# are either of type *struct* or *enum*.

Recall that a struct is a class in which the keyword *struct* is used in place of the keyword *class*. An example is shown in Listing 4.13.

LISTING 4.13 Struct Point

```
using System;
namespace StructApp1 {
    // This class has value semantics
    public struct Point {
        // Fields
        private int x;
        private int y;
        // Constructor
        public Point(int x, int y) {
            this.x = x;
            this.y = y;
        }
        // Properties
        public int X { // Read-write property
            get {
                return x;
            }
            set {
                x = value;
            }
        }
```

LISTING 4.13 Struct Point (continued)

```
        public int Y { // Read-write property
            get {
                return y;
            }
            set {
                y = value;
            }
        }
         // Queries
        public override bool Equals(Object obj) {
            Point other = (Point)obj;
            return other.x == x && other.y == y;
        }
        public override int GetHashCode() {
            return x ^ y;
        }
        public override String ToString() {
            return "<" + x + ", " + y + ">";
        }
    }
}
```

When an instance of a *struct* is created, its memory is allocated on the stack or inline if it's a field of a class. The memory allocated to a *struct* contains the member data instead of a reference to the data as in the case of a class. Finally, instances of a struct are disposed of as soon as they go out of scope. They are not garbage collected like instances of a class. The struct type does not support inheritance even though it inherits from *System.ValueType*.

4.10.1 Special Rules for struct Types

1. It is illegal to define a constructor containing no parameters for a *struct*. The compiler implicitly defines such a constructor for a *struct* that sets its fields to their default values.

2. An instance of a *struct* is allocated memory at its point of declaration. The object creation operator *new* is not needed. But if the object creation operator *new* followed by a constructor is not used, all the fields of the *struct* take their default values.

3. The fields of a *struct* cannot be explicitly initialized.

4. A variable of type *struct* can never be assigned the value *null*.

5. A *struct* can contain the same member types as a class. These include constants, fields, methods, properties, and so on. A *struct* cannot contain a destructor because no garbage collection pertains to *struct* types.

6. A copy of a complete *struct* is created when performing an assignment from one *struct* variable to another, passing a *struct* variable to a method parameter that is a *struct* type, or returning a *struct* type from a method.

4.10.2 Considerations in Choosing a struct

1. A *struct* should generally be relatively small in its feature set (number of fields and methods).

2. In a memory-sensitive environment in which the deallocation of storage for a *struct* occurs by simply going out of scope (in contrast to having to wait for garbage collection), a *struct* type is attractive.

3. If an application frequently needs to assign a *struct* variable (e.g., by passing the variable to a method parameter), the overhead might become significant because a complete copy of the *struct* is made, in contrast to passing only a simple reference in the case of an ordinary class instance.

4. Methods that are frequently invoked are probably better served by classes because the overhead of implicit boxing may offset the benefit gained by having a *struct* stack-based.

5. If a *struct* type is to be held by a collection, the *Equals* method or *GetHashCode* method will cause the *struct* to be repeatedly boxed, causing a performance penalty.

Compare the performance of *struct Point* defined in Listing 4.13 with a similar *PointClass* defined in Listing 4.14. The *PointApplication* class that compares the performance of the class-based point with the struct-based point is presented in Listing 4.15.

LISTING 4.14 Class PointClass

```
using System;
namespace StructApp1 {
    public class PointClass {
        // Fields
        private int x;
        private int y;
        // Constructor
        public PointClass(int x, int y) {
            this.x = x;
            this.y = y;
        }
        // Properties
        public int X { // Read-write property
            get {
                return x;
            }
            set {
                x = value;
            }
        }
```

LISTING 4.14 Class PointClass (continued)

```csharp
        public int Y { // Read-write property
            get {
                return y;
            }
            set {
                y = value;
            }
        }
        // Queries
        public override bool Equals(Object obj) {
            PointClass other = (PointClass)obj;
            return other.x == x && other.y == y;
        }
        public override String ToString() {
            return "<" + x + ", " + y + ">";
        }
        public override int GetHashCode() {
            return x ^ y;
        }
    }
}
```

LISTING 4.15 Class PointApplication

```csharp
using System;
using ElapsedTime;
namespace StructApp1 {
    public class PointApplication {
        // Commands
        public Point Twice(Point pt) {
            return new Point(2 * pt.X, 2 * pt.Y);
        }
        public PointClass Twice(PointClass pt) {
            return new PointClass(2 * pt.X, 2 * pt.Y);
        }
        public static void Main() {
            PointApplication app = new PointApplication();
            Point pt1 = new Point(4, 5);
            PointClass pt2 = new PointClass(4, 5);
            Timing timer = new Timing();
            timer.StartTiming();
            for (int i = 0; i < 100000000; i++) {
                Point result = app.Twice(pt1);
            }
```

LISTING 4.15 Class PointApplication (continued)

```
                timer.EndTiming();
                Console.WriteLine(
                "Time for value type point: " + timer.ElapsedTime());
                timer = new Timing();
                timer.StartTiming();
                for (int i = 0; i < 100000000; i++) {
                    PointClass result = app.Twice(pt2);
                }
                timer.EndTiming();
                Console.WriteLine(
                "Time for reference type point: " + timer.ElapsedTime());
                Console.ReadLine();
            }
        }
    }
/* Program output
Time for value type point: 4.953125
Time for reference type point: 3.484375
*/
```

The method *Twice* is overloaded in class *PointApplication*. The compiler can distinguish which version to bind to based on whether the argument passed is of type *Point* or of type *PointClass*.

Each of the overloaded methods *Twice* is invoked 100 million times in a loop while being timed using a *Timing* class that is shown in Listing 4.16.

LISTING 4.16 Class Timing

```
using System;
namespace ElapsedTime {
    // Used for bench marking code segments
    public class Timing {
        // Fields
        private long startTicks, endTicks;
        public void StartTiming () {
            DateTime t = DateTime.Now;
            startTicks = t.Ticks;
        }
        public void EndTiming () {
            DateTime t = DateTime.Now;
            endTicks = t.Ticks;
        }
        public double ElapsedTime () {
            return (endTicks - startTicks) / 10000000.0;
        }
    }
}
```

Exercise 4.7

Research and explain how method *StartTiming* works in class *Timing*.

Exercise 4.8

Research and explain how method *EndTiming* works in class *Timing*.

Exercise 4.9

Research and explain how method *ElapsedTime* works in class *Timing*.

The class-based point runs in 70 percent of the time that the struct-based point runs. This confirms the earlier observation that applications that need to assign or return struct types frequently (as Listing 4.15 requires) may be less efficient.

Suppose we add the following code segment to method *Main* in Listing 4.15:

```
Point pt1Copy = pt1;
PointClass pt2Copy = pt2;
Console.WriteLine("pt1Copy: " + pt1Copy.ToString());
Console.WriteLine("pt12opy: " + pt2Copy.ToString());
// Change pt1
pt1.X = 50;
pt1.Y = 60;
// Change pt2
pt2.X = 50;
pt2.Y = 60;
// Output the two point copies again
Console.WriteLine("pt1Copy: " + pt1Copy.ToString());
Console.WriteLine("pt12opy: " + pt2Copy.ToString());
```

The output produced follows:

```
Before copying - pt1Copy: <4, 5>
Before copying - pt2Copy: <4, 5>
After copying - pt1Copy: <4, 5>
After copying - pt2Copy: <50, 60>
```

It is evident that when the struct-based *pt1* is changed, this has no effect on *pt1Copy*. But when the class-based *pt2* is changed, this causes *pt2Copy* to be changed since *pt2Copy* is just another reference to the same storage as *pt2* and not an independent copy of *pt2*.

Figure 4.1 shows the effect of a value object assignment versus a reference object assignment. Consider the following code:

```
valueObj2 = valueObj1; // struct types
refObj2 = refObj1; // class types
```

where *valueObj1* and *valueObj2* are *struct* types (value semantics) and *refObj1* and *refObj2* are ordinary class types (reference semantics).

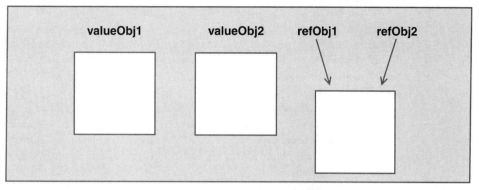

FIGURE 4.1 Value assignment versus reference assignment

All the simple types in C# are aliases to *struct* types. Table 4.2 presents the simple types and their associated *struct* types.

TABLE 4.2 Simple types and their associated struct types

Simple Type	Associated struct Type	Range of Values
bool	System.Boolean	false, true
sbyte	System.SByte	–128 to 127
byte	System.Byte	0 to 255
short	System.Int16	–32768 to 32767
ushort	System.UInt16	0 to 655535
int	System.Int32	–2147483648 to 2147483647
uint	System.UInt32	0 to 4294967295
long	System.Int64	–9223372036854775808 to 9223372036854775807
ulong	System.UInt64	0 to 18446744073709551615
float	System.Single	32–bit double precision
double	System.Double	64–bit double precision
decimal	System.Decimal	128–bit high precision decimal with 28 significant digits
char	System.Char	2–byte Unicode

4.11 STATIC FIELDS AND METHODS

Static members play a specialized role in class construction and should be used only when justified. Static methods do not have access to the local state (nonstatic fields) of the class. For this reason, they must be invoked through the class name and not through a class instance (an object).

To use a style of software development called POOP (procedural object-oriented programming) instead of OOP, one can define all methods as static, and then pass needed information in through parameters. Only beginners in an object language or the uninformed would resort to this approach. One of the major benefits of OOP is the localization of information (data) within an object. This benefit is lost when static methods are used.

When is it justified or appropriate to define a static method? The answer is simple: whenever you believe that an operation or computation defined within the static method is of universal importance and does not depend on local information stored within a particular object. Mathematical functions fit this description. For example, in computing the sine of an angle, you do not need the local state information of an object but only the value of the angle for which you wish to compute the sine. This angle should be passed to the function through a parameter. Another example would be a sorting routine. Only the array of information to be sorted needs to be passed through a parameter to the sort method. Most importantly, mathematical functions and sorting routines are of universal importance because they are used across many applications.

The litmus test to justify the use of a static method is as follows:

◆ Is the method of universal importance (outside the domain of the given class)?

◆ Can the method comfortably work independently of data local to any object?

If the answer is yes to both questions, then the method should probably be declared static.

In C#, static methods *cannot* be accessed through an object, as in Java. Access is done through the name of the class containing the static method followed by the dot operator followed by the name of the static method.

What about static fields?

Public fields that are declared static become part of the global namespace of your application. Often this is useful if constants need to be available among many classes within your application. In such cases the use of static fields, often placed in a separate class that defines all such global application constants, is justified and useful. Recall class *Application* in the supermarket checkout simulation in Chapter 3. It contained static public constants that were needed throughout the simulation.

Static constructors are used to initialize static fields in a class. Only one static constructor may be defined per C# class. Access modifiers are not allowed on static constructors.

The next application illustrates a legitimate use of static methods and a static constructor. Using static methods and two interesting algorithms, we approximate the value of the square root of a positive number and approximate the value of pi. The field *randomValue* is **private static**—it needs to be *static* to be accessible within the static method *ApproximatePI* and needs to be *private* to make it inaccessible to the user.

Listing 4.17 presents both static methods.

LISTING 4.17 Static methods for approximating the square root and pi

```
using System;
namespace StaticMethods {
    public class MathUtilities {
        static MathUtilities() {
            randomValue = new Random();
            // Warm-up random number generator
            for (int i = 0; i < 100000; i++) {
                randomValue.NextDouble();
            }
        }
        // Fields
        private static Random randomValue;
        public static decimal SquareRoot(decimal x,
                                    decimal precision) {
            decimal y = x;
            while (Math.Abs(y * y - x) > precision) {
                y = (y + x / y) / 2;
            }
            return y;
        }
        public static double ApproximatePI(int NumberPoints) {
            int hits = 0;
            double x, y;
            for (int i = 0; i < NumberPoints; i++) {
                x = randomValue.NextDouble();
                y = randomValue.NextDouble();
                if (x * x + y * y <= 1.0)
                    hits++;
            }
            return 4.0 * hits / NumberPoints;
        }
    }
}
```

Discussion of Listing 4.17

- Class *MathUtilities* contains a static field *randomValue* of type *Random*. The static constructor initializes this static field and invokes *NextDouble* 100,000 times to warm up the random number generator.

- The static method *SquareRoot* takes two inputs. The first is the positive number whose square root is sought. The second is the precision desired. The smaller the precision is, the better the approximation but the longer the computation. Both input parameters are of type decimal. This provides the most accurate basis for the approximation. The suffix "m" is used to denote a decimal literal.

Exercise 4.10

By researching this classic square-root algorithm, carefully explain how static method *SquareRoot* works. In particular, why does the sequence of values y = (y + x / y) / 2 get closer and closer to the square root of x?

The basis for the approximation to pi, given by the static method *ApproximatePI*, may be gleaned from Figure 4.2.

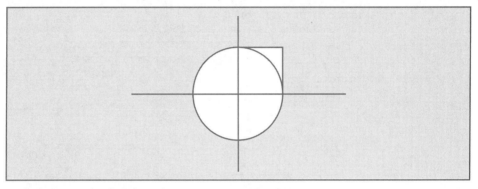

FIGURE 4.2 Calculating pi

If the circle has a radius of 1, then the area of the circle is equal to π. Therefore the quadrant of the circle inside the rectangle has an area of π / 4. The ratio of this area to the rectangle that it is embedded in equals $(\pi / 4) / 1 = \pi / 4$.

This leads to the following simulation:

1. Generate a random point by generating an x coordinate between 0 and 1 and a y coordinate between 0 and 1.

2. Determine whether the generated random point lies inside the quadrant of the circle by seeing whether $x^2 + y^2 <= 1$. Each time this inequality is satisfied, increment a hit counter by 1.

3. After generating many random points, the ratio of hits to points generated should roughly approximate the number π / 4. Therefore the number π is approximately equal to 4 times the ratio of hits to points generated.

Exercise 4.11

Explain how the code in static method *ApproximatePI* carries out the simulation outlined above.

4.12 OVERRIDING, OVERLOADING, AND INHERITANCE

As you have seen in Chapters 1–3, inheritance is one of the major architectural relationships between classes and provides a model of generalization-specialization among classes.

A base class, a class at the root of an inheritance hierarchy of classes, can declare a method as **virtual**. A *virtual* method is intended to be redefined in a descendent class. In a descendent class that redefines the method, the keyword **override** must be used and the signature of the redefined method must be identical to the signature of the virtual method in the base class. The requirement that *override* be used when redefining descendent methods provides self-documentation in the code and is therefore desirable.

If a descendent class contains a method with a signature that is identical to a nonvirtual method that is defined in the base class, the descendent class method is considered to overload the base-class method. The C# compiler warns of this situation because it is not considered a good design—the overloaded descendent class method effectively blocks access to the base-class method. The C# compiler warning suggests that you use the keyword *new* to clarify your intention to overload the base-class method. It is recommended that you avoid this practice of overloading nonvirtual base-class methods in subclasses.

If you attempt to redefine a virtual base-class method in a subclass without using the *override* keyword, a compiler warning is generated suggesting that if you want to overload the virtual method, you use the keyword *new*. Again this practice is not recommended.

It is strongly recommended that you only define a descendent class method with a signature that matches a base-class signature when the base-class method is *virtual*, and that you use the *override* keyword in the descendent class. Then you are redefining the base-class method. This is a common activity in subclasses.

Listing 4.18 presents a tutorial application that illustrates these ideas.

LISTING 4.18 Application that involves overriding

```
using System;
namespace Overriding {
    public class BaseClass {
        // Fields
        protected int baseClassValue;
        // Constructor
        public BaseClass(int value) {
            baseClassValue = value;
        }
        public BaseClass() {
            baseClassValue = 0;
        }
        // Commands
        public virtual void SomeImportantOperation() {
            baseClassValue += 500;
        }
```

LISTING 4.18 Application that involves overriding (continued)

```
        // Queries
        public override string ToString() {
            return "baseClassValue: " + baseClassValue;
        }
    }
}
using System;
namespace Overriding {
    public class ChildClass : BaseClass {
        // Constructor
        public ChildClass(int value) : base(value) {
        }
        public ChildClass() : base() {
        }
        // Commands
        public override void SomeImportantOperation() {
            baseClassValue *= 2;
        }
    }
}


using System;
namespace Overriding {
    public class OverrideApplication {
        public static void Main() {
            BaseClass obj = new ChildClass(20);
            obj.SomeImportantOperation();
            Console.WriteLine(obj.ToString());
            Console.ReadLine();
        }
    }
}
/* Output
baseClassValue: 520
baseClassValue: 25
*/
```

Discussion of Listing 4.18

Three classes are defined in Listing 4.18.

◆   Class *BaseClass* defines a protected field *baseClassValue*, accessible in all
    descendent classes. A virtual method *SomeImportantOperation()* is also defined.

◆   Class *ChildClass* redefines *SomeImportantOperation()*. It provides two
    constructors that use the inherited code from the *BaseClass* constructor by
    explicitly invoking *base*.

◆ The application class *OverrideApplication* declares *obj* with formal type *BaseClass* but actual type *ChildClass*. Polymorphic substitution, discussed in Chapter 1, allows this. The method *SomeImportantOperation()* is invoked on *obj* and late-binding uses the *ChildClass* version of this method.

Exercise 4.12

What happens to the output in Listing 4.18 if the keyword *override* is removed from method *SomeImportantOperation* in class *ChildClass*? Explain.

4.13 NEW POINTS OF SPECIALIZATION

The **new** modifier may be used in front of the *virtual* modifier to cause a new point of specialization within the class hierarchy. Polymorphism will prevail in overridden versions of the method in classes that are descendents of the class containing the *new virtual* method. In all classes above this class, the method will be treated as nonvirtual.

To illustrate how a new point of specialization can be created, we revisit the application presented in Listing 4.18. The modified application appears in Listing 4.19.

LISTING 4.19 Revised application that includes a new point of specialization

```
using System;
namespace Overriding {
    public class ChildClass : BaseClass {
        // Constructor
        public ChildClass(int value) : base(value) {
        }
        public ChildClass() : base() {
        }
        // Commands
        public new virtual void SomeImportantOperation() {
            baseClassValue *= 2;
        }
    }
}
using System;
namespace Overriding {
    public class GrandChildClass : ChildClass {
        // Constructor
        public GrandChildClass(int value) : base(value) {
        }
        public GrandChildClass() : base() {
        }
        // Commands
        public override void SomeImportantOperation() {
            baseClassValue /= 2;
        }
    }
}
```

LISTING 4.19 Revised application that includes a new point of specialization (continued)

```
using System;
namespace Overriding {
    public class OverrideApplication {
        public static void Main() {
            BaseClass obj = new ChildClass(20);
            obj.SomeImportantOperation();
            Console.WriteLine(obj.ToString());
            ChildClass obj2 = new GrandChildClass(50);
            obj2.SomeImportantOperation();
            Console.WriteLine(obj2.ToString());
            Console.ReadLine();
        }
    }
}
/* Output
baseClassValue: 520
baseClassValue: 25
*/
```

Discussion of Listing 4.19

◆   Class *BaseClass* is the same as in Listing 4.18. The revised *ChildClass* uses the following signature for its method *SomeImportantOperation*:

```
public new virtual void SomeImportantOperation() { ... }
```

The keyword *new* establishes a new point of specialization. Late-binding prevails only from class *ChildClass* downward in the inheritance hierarchy. This is illustrated in the revised class *OverrideApplication*.

◆   In this case when method *SomeImportantOperation* is invoked on *obj*, the *BaseClass* version is used because late-binding no longer prevails on any class above the new point of specialization. When this same method is invoked on *obj2*, late-binding is evident by the output.

4.13.1 Fragile Base Class Problem

The ability to create a new point of specialization in a class hierarchy was introduced in C# to provide a mechanism for coping with the fragile base-class problem. This problem occurs when the implementation details of a virtual method in a base-class are modified without changing the signature of the method. When this happens, all overridden methods in descendent classes become suspect and in many cases simply unusable.

The problem may go unnoticed because when the system is recompiled against the new base class, no compilation errors are produced. (This would not be the case if the signature of one or more virtual methods were changed.)

If one becomes aware of such a change to a base class, perhaps the best workaround is to redefine the point of specialization from the base class to the highest accessible class that you have control over. By doing this, you will break the dependency of your methods on the base-class methods. You might also need to modify the details of your methods. But at least the control has been provided to let you attempt this. In other languages such as Java or C++, which do not offer this level of control, the effects of changing the base class might be potentially more devastating.

The best way to solve the problem of a fragile base class is to avoid it. The owner of a base class should not tamper with implementation details of virtual methods. To do otherwise is to commit a major design infraction with potentially high costs.

4.14 ACCESS MODIFIERS REF, OUT, READONLY, AND SEALED

Several other important access modifiers may be used in the construction of classes. These include *ref*, *out*, *readonly*, and *sealed*.

4.14.1 The sealed Modifier

The modifier **sealed** may be used as part of a class declaration, as shown in the following code:

```
public sealed class MyClass {
    // Details not shown
}
```

No subclass can inherit from a sealed class such as *MyClass*.

The *sealed* modifier may also be used as part of a method declaration in front of the *override* modifier, as in the following code:

```
public sealed override MyMethod() {
    // Details not shown
}
```

No further redefinition of a sealed override method such as *MyMethod* above is allowed.

4.14.2 The readonly Modifier

A field can be tagged with the **readonly** modifier. Such a field can be initialized at its point of declaration or within an instance constructor. If the field is static, then a static constructor must be used to initialize the field. Once initialized, the value of the field cannot be modified by a method command.

4.14.3 The ref and out Modifiers

The **ref** or **out** modifier may be used in the formal signature of a method and in invoking the method.

The **ref** modifier used in front of a method parameter type causes any change that is made within the method to the parameter value to be returned through the parameter value. The ref parameter must be initialized.

The **out** modifier used in front of a method parameter type causes the value assigned to the parameter within the method to be returned through the parameter value.

A simple tutorial example that demonstrates the use of the *ref* and *out* modifiers is presented in Listing 4.20.

LISTING 4.20 The *ref* and *out* modifiers

```
using System;
namespace OtherModifiers {
    public sealed class Modifiers {
        // Command
        public void ProduceSomeValue(out int someValue) {
            someValue = 17;
        }
        public void ChangeSomeValue(ref int someValue) {
            someValue *= 5;
        }
        public static void Main() {
            Modifiers app = new Modifiers();
            int value = 0;
            app.ProduceSomeValue(out value);
            Console.WriteLine("value: " + value);
            app.ChangeSomeValue(ref value);
            Console.WriteLine("value: " + value);
            Console.ReadLine();
        }
    }
}
/* Output
value: 17
value: 85
*/
```

Discussion of Listing 4.20

◆ When the method *ProduceSomeValue()* is invoked in method *Main()*, the *out* modifier is required. This provides additional self-documentation within the code.

◆ Similarly, when the *ChangeSomeValue()* method is invoked within *Main()*, the *ref* modifier is required. This too provides additional self-documentation within the code.

◆ A method that uses a *ref* modifier in front of one of its parameters is said to be of type in/out.

We shall see in Part 4 of the book that *ref* parameters are particularly useful in implementing recursive algorithms on data structures.

4.15 OVERLOADING OPERATORS

Operator overloading allows the convenience of operators to be defined in lieu of methods in a class. Although this capability may seem wonderful at first glance, if it is not used with great self-discipline and care, it can cause major problems.

Probably the most logical domain for overloading operators is the mathematical domain where custom classes that have a natural interpretation for operations such as "+" or "−"or "++" exist.

A conservative approach to overloading operators is to avoid their use unless their use is compelling.

The following binary operators may be overloaded in pairs in C#:

== and !=

> and <

>= and <=

When a binary operator such as "*" is overloaded, the corresponding compound assignment operator is implicitly overloaded (e.g., the *= operator).

Overloaded operators must be *static* and use the keyword **operator**. A typical overloaded operator signature is given as follows:

```
public static bool operator == (Fraction f1, Fraction f2) {
    // Details not shown
}
```

Here the equals operator "==" is overloaded in a class that takes two objects of type *Fraction* and compares them.

Typical usage would be:

```
if (f1 == f2) {
    // Details not shown
}
```

where *f1* and *f2* are objects of type *Fraction*.

As an example that illustrates the overloading of operators, we define a class *Fraction* that encapsulates the behavior of a rational number.

Consider the class *Fraction* in Listing 4.21. You the reader shall be asked to be a partner in implementing this class because it uses some of the principles presented thus far in this chapter.

LISTING 4.21 Portions of Class Fraction

```
using System;
namespace Fractions {
    /*
     * Models the behavior of a rational number
     */
    public class Fraction {
        // Fields
        private int numerator;
        private int denominator = 1;
        // Constructors
        public Fraction() {
            numerator = 0;
            denominator = 1;
```

LISTING 4.21 Portions of Class Fraction (continued)

```
    }
    public Fraction(int numerator, int denominator) {
        if (denominator == 0) {
            throw new Exception("Cannot have zero denominator.");
        }
        this.numerator = numerator;
        this.denominator = denominator;
        Reduce();
    }
    public Fraction(int numerator) {
        this.numerator = numerator;
        denominator = 1;
    }
    // Properties
    public int Numerator {
        get {
            return numerator;
        }
        set {
            numerator = value;
            Reduce();
        }
    }
    public int Denominator {
        get {
            return denominator;
        }
        set {
            if (value == 0) {
                throw new Exception("Cannot have zero denominator");
            }
            denominator = value;
            Reduce();
        }
    }
    // Static overloaded operators
    public static bool operator ==(Fraction f1, Fraction f2) {
        return (f1.numerator == f2.numerator &&
                f1.denominator == f2.denominator);
    }
    public static bool operator !=(Fraction f1, Fraction f2) {
        return !(f1 == f2);
    }
    public static bool operator >(Fraction f1, Fraction f2) {
        // Exercise
    }
    public static bool operator <(Fraction f1, Fraction f2) {
        // Exercise
    }
```

LISTING 4.21 Portions of Class Fraction (continued)

```
public static Fraction operator +(Fraction f1, Fraction f2) {
    return (new Fraction(f1.numerator * f2.denominator +
                f2.numerator * f1.denominator,
                f1.denominator * f2.denominator));

}
public static Fraction operator -(Fraction f1, Fraction f2) {
    // Exercise
}
public static Fraction operator *(Fraction f1, Fraction f2) {
    // Exercise
}
public static Fraction operator /(Fraction f1, Fraction f2) {
    // Exercise
}
// Queries related to comparison
public override bool Equals(Object obj) {
    // Exercise
}
public override int GetHashCode() {
    double value = (double)numerator / denominator;
    return value.GetHashCode();
}


// Queries related to conversion
public double ToDouble() {
    return (double)numerator / denominator;
}
// Queries related to display
public override String ToString() {
    String sign = "";
    if (numerator == 0) {
        return "0";
    }
    if (numerator * denominator < 0) {
        sign = "-";
    }
    if (denominator == 1) {
        return sign + Math.Abs(numerator);
    }
    return sign + Math.Abs(numerator) + "/" +
                                Math.Abs(denominator);
}
// Internal use
private Fraction Reduce() {
    int gcd = Math.Abs(numerator) > Math.Abs(denominator) ?
            Math.Abs(denominator) : Math.Abs(numerator);
```

LISTING 4.21 Portions of Class Fraction (continued)

```
              if (gcd == 0) {
                  return this;
              }
              while (gcd != 1 &&
                     (numerator % gcd != 0 || denominator % gcd != 0)) {
                  gcd--;
              }
              numerator /= gcd;
              denominator /= gcd;
              return this;
          }
      }
  }
```

Discussion of Listing 4.21

◆ Class *Fraction* contains two fields, *numerator* and *denominator*, each of type *int*. Three constructors allow a *Fraction* object to be initialized as it is created. The first takes no parameters and sets the numerator to 0 and denominator to 1 (fraction with value 0). The second allows the user to specify the numerator and denominator, and the third allows the user to specify only the numerator. If the user specifies a value of 0 for the denominator, a runtime exception is thrown with the message "Cannot have zero denominator."

◆ The private method *Reduce* uses one of the oldest mathematical algorithms, the Euclid algorithm, for obtaining a least common denominator.

Exercise 4.13

Research the Euclid algorithm for finding the least common denominator of a fraction. Show that the code in private method *Reduce* forces the numerator and denominator to be in simplest form (e.g., 6 / 18 reduces to 1 / 3).

The overloaded "==" operator compares the numerators and denominators of the two fractions and returns true if they are the same. Because both fractions must be in simplest form, this strategy works.

The overloaded "+" operator creates and returns a new *Fraction* object, as shown, making sure to send the new object the *Reduce* query as part of the *return* statement.

Exercise 4.14

Write the details of the overloaded operator ">".

Exercise 4.15

Write the details of the overloaded operator "<".

Exercise 4.16

Write the details of the overloaded operator "–".

Exercise 4.17

Write the details of the overloaded operator "*".

Exercise 4.18

Write the details of the overloaded operator "/".

Exercise 4.19

Write the details of the method *Equals*.

Exercise 4.20

Write a main application class *FractionApplication*. In this class create three *Fraction* objects with values f1 = <–1, 2>, f2 = <1, 2> and f3 = <5, 10>.

Test to see whether fraction f1 equals f2 and if so, output this fact to the console. Output the value of f1 * f2. Output the value of f2 – f1. Finally, output the value of f1 / f2.

4.16 ARRAYS

Arrays provide efficient support for managing indexable collections of objects and are often an important part of a C# class. There are two distinct types of multidimensional arrays in C#, rectangular and jagged.

All arrays inherit from the abstract base class *System.Array* that inherits from *System.Object*.

Because of the special importance and widespread use of arrays, the notation for creating instances of class *Array* is special.

Suppose you want to create an instance of an array, *data*, which holds 1000 values of type *int*. You may accomplish this as follows:

```
int [] data = new int[1000];
```

The index range of an array goes from 0 to one less than its size. So for the array *data*, given above, the index range is from 0 to 999. An attempt to access or assign to an index outside of this range will produce an *IndexOutOfBounds* exception.

The values in *data* are automatically assigned 0, by default. If, for example, you want to assign the value 23 at index 129, you would achieve this as follows:

```
data[129] = 23;
```

To access the value at index 814 and assign it to result, you would achieve this as follows:

```
int result = data[814];
```

4.16.1 Rectangular Arrays

Suppose you want to store rows and columns that model a matrix of double values. In particular, you want to hold 20 rows and 40 columns of such data. You could achieve this by declaring *matrix* as follows:

```
double [,] matrix = new double[20, 40];
```

The row index of this two-dimensional array goes from 0 to 19, and the column index from 0 to 39.

To assign a value of 1.25 to the element in the fourth row and sixth column, you would do this as follows:

```
matrix[3, 5] = 1.25;
```

A first index of 3 is used because rows start at index 0 so the fourth row would be at index 3. Likewise, the sixth column would be at index 5. If one wishes to use natural indexing, it would be necessary to over-dimension the array by one in each of its dimensions and then ignore row 0 and column 0.

There are several static methods that are useful on one-dimensional arrays. These are summarized in Table 4.3.

TABLE 4.3 Static methods for one-dimensional arrays

Type	Description
Array.Clear	Sets each element to its default value
Array.Length	Returns the number of elements in the array
Array.Rank	Returns the number of dimensions in the array
Array.BinarySearch	Searches an array for a key value (one-dimensional only)
Array.Copy	Copies a portion of an array into another array
Array.CopyTo	Copies an entire array to another array
Array.Sort	Sorts the elements of a one-dimensional

Listing 4.22 shows the use of some of these static methods.

LISTING 4.22 Static methods from class Array in action

```
using System;
namespace ArrayMethods {
    public class ArrayMethodsInAction {
    // Fields
```

LISTING 4.22 Static methods from class Array in action (continued)

```csharp
        private double[] data =
              { 2.6, 2.1, 2.8, -3.4, -3.2, 1.9, 5.1, 0.65 };
    // Commands
    public void Display(double[] data) {
        foreach (double value in data) {
            System.Console.Write(value + " ");
        }
        System.Console.WriteLine();
    }
    static void Main(string[] args) {
        ArrayMethodsInAction app =
                new ArrayMethodsInAction();
        // One dimensional array manipulations
        double[] dataCopy = new double[app.data.Length];
        // Copy data to dataCopy starting at index 0
        app.data.CopyTo(dataCopy, 0);
        Console.Write("dataCopy: ");
        app.Display(dataCopy);
        // Using quick-sort, sort data
        Array.Sort(app.data);
        Console.Write("Sorted data: ");
        app.Display(app.data);
        // Using Copy, copy 4 elements of data to newData
        double[] newData = new double[app.data.Length];
        Array.Copy(app.data, newData, 4);
        Console.Write("4 elements of data copied to newData: ");
        app.Display(newData);
        // Do a binary search for the value 2.1
        int index = Array.BinarySearch(app.data, 2.1);
        System.Console.WriteLine("index after binary search: " +
                                    index);
        System.Console.ReadLine();
    }
  }
}
/* Output
dataCopy: 2.6 2.1 2.8 -3.4 -3.2 1.9 5.1 0.65
Sorted data: -3.4 -3.2 0.65 1.9 2.1 2.6 2.8 5.1
4 elements of data copied to newData: -3.4 -3.2 0.65 1.9 0 0 0 0
index after binary search: 4
*/
```

Exercise 4.21

Go to the MSDN documentation for each of the static methods given above Listing 4.22. Write the signature of each of these methods along with a brief explanation of how the method works.

4.16.2 Jagged Arrays

In addition to supporting rectangular arrays, C# also supports jagged arrays. Consider the following array:

```
int [][] data = new int[2][];
```

Here *data* is a one-dimensional array containing two arrays, each of undefined size. Suppose you want to set the size of row 0 to 50 and row 1 to 100. Consider the following code:

```
data[0] = new int[50];
data[1] = new int[100];
```

This array is **jagged** because its rows have different lengths.
A simple example of jagged arrays is presented in Listing 4.23.

LISTING 4.23 Simple example of jagged arrays

```
using System;
namespace JaggedArrays {
    public class JaggedArraysInAction {
        static void Main() {
            int[][] data = new int[2][];
            Console.Write("What is the size of row 0: ");
            String str1 = Console.ReadLine();
            Console.Write("What is the size of row 1: ");
            String str2 = Console.ReadLine();
            int sizeRowZero = Convert.ToInt32(str1);
            int sizeRowOne = Convert.ToInt32(str2);
            data[0] = new int[sizeRowZero];
            data[1] = new int[sizeRowOne];
            // Load up jagged array
            for (int col = 0; col < sizeRowZero; col++) {
                data[0][col] = col;
            }
            for (int col = 0; col < sizeRowOne; col++) {
                data[1][col] = col;
            }
            // Compute the sum of values in the jagged array
            int sum = 0;
            for (int row = 0; row < 2; row++) {
                for (int col = 0; col < data[row].Length; col++) {
                    sum += data[row][col];
                }
            }
            Console.WriteLine("sum = " + sum);
            Console.ReadLine();
        }
    }
}
```

Discussion of Listing 4.23

◆ The user is prompted to enter the size of rows 0 and 1. After initializing each row to its proper size, the sum of values in the jagged array is computed as follows:

```
int sum = 0;
for (int row = 0; row < 2; row++) {
    for (int col = 0; col < data[row].Length; col++) {
        sum += data[row][col]; // Note the use of jagged index
notation
    }
}
```

◆ The *Length* attribute of each row is used to control the upper bound on the inner for-loop.

◆ Note the use of jagged index notation, which uses rectangular brackets for each array index, in contrast to rectangular index notation, which uses a comma-separated list.

4.16.3 An Application Using Rectangular and Jagged Arrays

We next consider a more serious application that demonstrates the use of rectangular and jagged arrays as well as the use of the static *Sort* method from class *Array*.

Suppose that you have a matrix that represents student grades. Column 0 is a one-dimensional array of *String* values representing student names. Each additional column represents the grades on a separate exam. Consider the two-dimensional rectangular array *grades* given as follows:

```
String[,] grades = {
    {"Smith Robert", "60", "70", "80", "90"},
    {"Abbot John", "70", "80", "90", "100"},
    {"Markus Susan", "99", "98", "97", "96"},
    {"Cull Megan", "20", "40", "60", "80"},
    {"Simmons Frank", "0", "20", "40", "60"},
    {"Edwards Ryan", "30", "20", "10", "0"}
};
```

Here there are six rows of data with the grades represented as string values. To sort any column of grades, the string values must be converted to entities of type *double*.

We want to write a class that sorts the entire matrix based on either the name column (from lexically smallest to largest name, i.e., alphabetically) or from largest to smallest based on any of the numeric columns. When sorting any of the columns, the rows in the other columns should move with the rows in the column of keys being sorted. Can this be accomplished using the *Array.Sort* method in class *System.Array*? The answer is yes. The mechanism for accomplishing this is not trivial, but instructive.

Implementing a solution to this problem provides a practical opportunity to explore jagged and rectangular type arrays.

The documentation for one of the overloaded methods of the *Sort* method in class *Arrays* indicates the following:

```
public static void Sort(
   Array keys,
   Array items,
   IComparer comparer
);
```

where *keys* is the one-dimensional array that contains the keys to sort; *items* is the one-dimensional array (jagged array) that contains the items that correspond to each of the keys in the *keys* array; and *comparer* is an instance of a class that implements *IComparer*, which has a required *Compare* method that determines how objects that are being sorted are compared. The signature of the required *Compare* method is:

```
public int Compare(Object obj1, object obj2);
```

The return value is positive if *obj1* is greater than *obj2*, zero if they are equal, otherwise negative.

As shown earlier, we define the underlying type in our *grades* matrix as *String* even though most of the cells in the matrix are of type double. Because it is easy to convert a *String* representation of a double to a numeric type *double*, this appears to be the best choice for the underlying type.

The *CompareObjects* class defined below allows us to sort a column (one-dimensional array) of objects in either ascending or descending order based on the value of the Boolean parameter *ascending* that is passed to the constructor:

```
public class CompareObjects : IComparer { // Implements IComparer
   // Fields
   private bool ascending = true;
   // Constructor
   public CompareObjects(bool ascending) {
      this.ascending = ascending;
   }
   public int Compare(Object obj1, Object obj2) {
      // obj1 and obj2 will be either of type double or String
      IComparable c1 = obj1 as IComparable;
      IComparable c2 = obj2 as IComparable;
      if (c1 == null || c2 == null) {
         throw new
         Exception("Comparing objects that are not comparable");
      }
      if (c1.CompareTo(c2) > 0) {
         return ascending ? 1 : -1;
      } else if (c1.CompareTo(c2) == 0) {
         return 0;
      } else {
         return ascending ? -1 : 1;
      }
```

```
        }
    }
```

The declarations:

```
IComparable c1 = obj1 as IComparable; // Downcast obj1 to IComparable
IComparable c2 = obj2 as IComparable; // Downcast obj2 to IComparable
```

return *null* for *c1* or *c2* if either *obj1* or *obj2* are not of type *IComparable*, otherwise serve as a downcast to type *IComparable*. Because the actual types of *obj1* and *obj2* will be either *String* or *double* (*System.Double*), the values of *c1* and *c2* will never be *null*. A well-defined *CompareTo* method is part of the protocol of standard classes *String* and *System.Double*.

If the Boolean field *ascending* is true, the *Compare* query returns 1 if *c1* is greater than *c2;* otherwise it returns −1. This is what allows this Boolean field to control whether the *Array.Sort* method produces ascending or descending ordering.

Listing 4.24 presents the complete class *StudentGrades*. A detailed analysis follows.

LISTING 4.24 Class StudentGrades

```
using System;
using System.Collections;
namespace SortingGrades {
    public class CompareObjects : Icomparer {
        // Fields
        private bool ascending = true;
        // Constructor
        public CompareObjects(bool ascending) {
            this.ascending = ascending;
        }
        public int Compare(Object obj1, Object obj2) {
            // obj1 and obj2 will be either of type double or String
            IComparable c1 = obj1 as IComparable;
            IComparable c2 = obj2 as IComparable;
            if (c1 == null || c2 == null) {
                throw new
                Exception("Comparing objects that are not comparable");
            }
            if (c1.CompareTo(c2) > 0) {
                return ascending ? 1 : -1;
            } else if (c1.CompareTo(c2) == 0) {
                return 0;
            } else {
                return ascending ? -1 : 1;
            }
        }
    }
    public class StudentGrades {
        // Fields
        private int rows, cols;
        private String[,] scores;
```

LISTING 4.24 Class StudentGrades (continued)

```
// Constructor
public StudentGrades(String[,] scores, int rows, int cols) {
    this.scores = scores;
    this.rows = rows;
    this.cols = cols;
}


/*
 * This method rearranges all the rows using the elements
 * in the given column as the key values for sorting
 */
public void SortGrades(int keyCol, bool ascending,
                       bool stringType) {
  // If stringType is false, it is assumed that sorting is on
  // type double
  // Define the keyColumn
  String[] keyColumn = new String[rows];
  for (int row = 0; row < rows; row++) {
      keyColumn[row] = scores[row, keyCol];
  }
  // Define the elements as an array of arrays
  String[][] elements = new String[rows][]; // Jagged array
  for (int row = 0; row < rows; row++) {
      elements[row] = new String[cols]; // Initialize a row
      for (int col = 0; col < cols; col++) {
          elements[row][col] = scores[row, col];
      }
  }
  double[] keyValues = null;
  if (!stringType) {
      keyValues = new double[rows];
      for (int index = 0; index < rows; index++) {
          keyValues[index] =
              Convert.ToDouble(keyColumn[index]);
      }
  }
  // Use the static Sort method in class Array
  if (stringType) {
      Array.Sort(keyColumn, elements,
              new CompareObjects(ascending));
  } else {
      Array.Sort(keyValues, elements,
              new CompareObjects(ascending));
  }
  for (int row = 0; row < rows; row++) {
      for (int col = 0; col < cols; col++) {
          scores[row, col] = elements[row][col];
```

LISTING 4.24 Class StudentGrades (continued)

```
            }
        }
    }
    public void DisplayGrades() {
        for (int row = 0; row < rows; row++) {
            System.Console.WriteLine();
            for (int col = 0; col < cols; col++) {
                System.Console.Write(scores[row, col] + "\t\t");
            }
        }
        System.Console.WriteLine(
            "\n--------------------\n");
    }
    static void Main() {
        String[,] grades = {
          {"Smith Robert", "60", "70", "80", "90"},
          {"Abbot John",   "70", "80", "90", "100"},
          {"Markus Susan", "99", "98", "97", "96"},
          {"Cull Megan", "20", "40", "60", "80"},
          {"Simmons Frank", "0", "20", "40", "60"},
          {"Edwards Ryan", "30", "20", "10", "0"}
      };
        StudentGrades app = new StudentGrades(grades, 6, 5);
        app.DisplayGrades();
        app.SortGrades(0, true, true);
        app.DisplayGrades();
        app.SortGrades(1, false, false);
        app.DisplayGrades();
        app.SortGrades(3, true, false);
        app.DisplayGrades();
        System.Console.ReadLine();
    }
  }
}
/* Output
Smith Robert        60          70          80          90
Abbot John          70          80          90          100
Markus Susan        99          98          97          96
Cull Megan          20          40          60          80
Simmons Frank       0           20          40          60
Edwards Ryan        30          20          10          0
-----------------------------------------------------------------

Abbot John          70          80          90          100
Cull Megan          20          40          60          80
Edwards Ryan        30          20          10          0
Markus Susan        99          98          97          96
```

LISTING 4.24 Class StudentGrades (continued)

```
 Simmons Frank      0            20           40           60
 Smith Robert       60           70           80           90
 ------------------------------------------------------------

 Markus Susan       99           98           97           96
 Abbot John         70           80           90           100
 Smith Robert       60           70           80           90
 Edwards Ryan       30           20           10           0
 Cull Megan         20           40           60           80
 Simmons Frank      0            20           40           60
 ------------------------------------------------------------

 Edwards Ryan       30           20           10           0
 Simmons Frank      0            20           40           60
 Cull Megan         20           40           60           80
 Smith Robert       60           70           80           90
 Abbot John         70           80           90           100
 Markus Susan       99           98           97           96
 ------------------------------------------------------------
*/
```

Discussion of Listing 4.24

◆ The constructor in class *StudentGrades* takes the rectangular array of *String* values as input as well as the number of rows and number of columns. Our focus is on the *SortGrades* method.

◆ The one-dimensional local array variable *keyColumn* is loaded with *String* values from the column that is to act as the key values for sorting the matrix.

◆ A jagged array, *elements*, is constructed from the rectangular array held in the field *scores*. Note that the assignment to elements uses the jagged index format on the left and the rectangular index format on the right:

```
elements[row][col] = scores[row, col];
```

If the field *stringType* is *false* (the row that is being used as a key is not the row of names), a one-dimensional array, *keyValues*, of type *double* is loaded with the key values converted from *String* to *double*.

◆ The static *Sort* method from class *Array* is invoked using either the *keyColumn* or *keyValues* array as the first parameter, the jagged array *elements* as the second parameter, and a new instance of the *CompareObjects* (implements *IComparer*) class as the third parameter. The result of sorting is stored in the jagged *elements* array.

◆ Finally, the sorted results in the jagged elements array are copied to the field *scores*. Note once again the use of rectangular indexing in the *scores* array and jagged indexing in the *elements* array.

Exercise 4.22

Explain the output from Listing 4.24 that is shown by doing a careful analysis of method *Main*.

4.17 DESTRUCTORS AND GARBAGE COLLECTION

Destructor methods are used by the common language runtime system to reclaim memory resources. A destructor must take the name of its class and be preceded by a tilde (~). The following code shows an example of a destructor:

```
public class SomeClass {
    ~SomeClass() {
        // Details not shown
    }
}
```

Only one destructor may be defined in a C# class. It cannot take any parameters. A *struct* cannot define a destructor because its memory is managed on the stack. A destructor is not inherited by a descendent class.

Destructors cannot be explicitly invoked. They are under the control of the automatic garbage collector. The garbage collector does not guarantee when or whether a destructor will be invoked. Furthermore, the garbage collector does not guarantee the order in which objects are destroyed.

A destructor would typically be defined when it is desirable to clean up resources before deallocating storage for an instance of the class containing the destructor.

As a general rule, C# destructors should be used with great care and frugality because of the lack of control the programmer has regarding when and whether the destructor is called. Because, according to the .NET documentation, objects with destructors are deallocated more slowly than objects without destructors, this could impose an unintended penalty on performance.

4.18 EXCEPTION HANDLING

There are two major categories of errors in an application that can cause exceptions to be generated:

1. Logical errors in the program itself. Typical errors in this category include an attempt to access an array using an index that is out of the range of the array, an attempt to invoke a method on an object with a *null* value, or a division by zero.

2. Errors that are out of the control of the programmer. Typical errors in this category include a user input error (e.g., the user is expected to input a numeric value but instead inputs a string of non-numeric characters), a disk drive failure when attempting to read or write a file, or an out of memory error if too much storage is requested by the program.

Through a process of rigorous testing, one always hopes to eliminate all errors in the first category before the software is released to customers. But the second category of error is always lurking and must be dealt with.

The mechanism for handling an exception generated by the system is through **try-catch** blocks. In general, try-catch blocks are set up as follows:

```
try {
    // Code that may generate an exception
} catch (SomeExceptionClass1 exception1) {
    // Code to handle the exceptions of type SomeExceptionClass1
} catch (SomeExceptionClass2 exception2) {
    // Code to handle the exceptions of type SomeExceptionClass2
} catch {
    // Code that handles any exception not caught by the other
    // exception blocks
} finally {
    // Code that executes unconditionally
}
```

An exception can be generated programmatically using the keyword **throw**. The following statement shows an example:

```
throw new SomeExceptionClass();
```

Here, an exception object of type *SomeExceptionClass* is generated.

The root class of the C# exception hierarchy is *System.Exception*. You can construct specialized exception classes that are descendents of this root class.

We consider a simple and typical application that uses exception handling. Suppose you want to take input from a user in the form of five numeric values and return the sum of these values. Consider first Listing 4.25, which attempts this without exception handling.

LISTING 4.25 Taking user input without exception handling

```
using System;
namespace ExceptionHandling {
    public class UserInput {
        // Fields
        private int[] values = new int[5];
        // Commands
        public void GetUserInput() {
            Console.Write("Enter value 1: ");
            String value1Str = Console.ReadLine();
            values[0] = Convert.ToInt32(value1Str);
            Console.Write("Enter value 2: ");
            String value2Str = Console.ReadLine();
            values[1] = Convert.ToInt32(value2Str);
            Console.Write("Enter value 3: ");
            String value3Str = Console.ReadLine();
            values[2] = Convert.ToInt32(value3Str);
```

LISTING 4.25 Taking user input without exception handling (continued)

```
                Console.Write("Enter value 4: ");
                String value4Str = Console.ReadLine();
                values[3] = Convert.ToInt32(value4Str);
                Console.Write("Enter value 5: ");
                String value5Str = Console.ReadLine();
                values[4] = Convert.ToInt32(value5Str);
            }
            // Queries
            public int Sum() {
                int sum = 0;
                for (int i = 0; i < values.Length; i++) {
                    sum += values[i];
                }
                return sum;
            }
            public static void Main() {
                UserInput app = new UserInput();
                app.GetUserInput();
                Console.WriteLine(
                        "Sum of values input by user: " + app.Sum());
                Console.ReadLine();
            }
        }
    }
```

Suppose the user provides the following input:

```
Enter value 1: 1
Enter value 2: Hello
```

The application would terminate and display the following exception message:

```
Unhandled Exception: System.FormatException: Input string was not in a
correct format.
```

The application can be protected from this type of abnormal termination using relatively simple exception handling, as shown in Listing 4.26.

LISTING 4.26 Exception handling to protect user input

```
using System;
namespace ExceptionHandling {
    public class UserInput {
        // Fields
        private int[] values = new int[5];
        // Commands
        public void GetUserInput() {
            for (int index = 0; index < 5; index++) {
                bool error = true;
```

LISTING 4.26 Exception handling to protect user input (continued)

```
                    while (error) {
                        try {
                            Console.Write(
                                "Enter value " + (index + 1) + ": ");
                            String valueStr = Console.ReadLine();
                            values[index] = Convert.ToInt32(valueStr);
                            error = false;
                        } catch {
                            error = true;
                        }
                    }
                }
            }
            // Queries
            public int Sum() {
                int sum = 0;
                for (int i = 0; i < values.Length; i++) {
                    sum += values[i];
                }
                return sum;
            }
            static void Main() {
                UserInput app = new UserInput();
                app.GetUserInput();
                Console.WriteLine(
                        "Sum of values input by user: " + app.Sum());
                Console.ReadLine();
            }
        }
    }


            Carefully examine the for-loop in method GetUserInput:

    for (int index = 0; index < 5; index++) {
        bool error = true;
        while (error) {
            try {
            Console.Write("Enter value " + (index + 1) + ": ");
            String valueStr = Console.ReadLine();
            values[index] = Convert.ToInt32(valueStr);
            error = false;
        } catch {
            error = true;
            }
        }
    }
```

If an exception is generated during the conversion from *valueStr* to *values[index]*, the value of *error* is set to true; otherwise it is set to false. An error value of true causes the while loop to continue. The user is prompted to enter a value for (*index + 1*). This prompting continues until the user enters a string that corresponds to a valid integer. So the exception handling in the *catch* block forces the system to obtain a fresh input from the user until the user gets it right.

Exercise 4.23

Why are the parentheses necessary around index + 1 in the *Console.Write* statement in method *GetUserInput* in Listing 4.26?

4.19 SUMMARY

- Every entity, field, local variable, or method parameter in C# is an object type.

- Object types have either value semantics or reference semantics.

- All value types in C# are either of type struct or enum. Simple types such as int, double, decimal, and bool are all struct types.

- Memory for a struct variable is allocated at its point of declaration for a local variable or field. The fields of a *struct* object may be initialized using the operator *new* followed by a constructor with one or more parameters.

- It is illegal to define a constructor containing no parameters for a *struct*. The compiler implicitly defines such a constructor for a *struct* that sets its fields to their default values.

- An instance of a *struct* is allocated memory at its point of declaration. The object creation operator *new* is not needed. But if the object creation operator *new* followed by a constructor is not used, all the fields of the *struct* take their default values.

- The fields of a *struct* cannot be explicitly initialized.

- A variable of type *struct* can never be assigned the value *null*.

- A *struct* class can contain the same member types as a non-*struct* class. These include constants, fields, methods, and properties. A *struct* cannot contain a destructor because no garbage collection pertains to *struct* types.

- A copy of a complete *struct* is created when performing an assignment from one *struct* variable to another, passing a *struct* variable to a method parameter that is a *struct* type, or returning a *struct* type from a method.

- Value types are automatically boxed when added to a collection or when compared. They need to be unboxed when removed from a collection.

- Namespaces are used to control global clashes of class names. A namespace may contain one or more public as well as nonpublic classes.

- Assemblies are the unit of deployment in a .NET software system. They are also the basis for versioning and security. The .NET common language runtime (CLR) uses the metadata contained within an assembly to load the assembly and supporting libraries, handle version support, perform type validation, and enforce security.

- By convention, all class names must begin with an uppercase character. There are no exceptions to this important rule. If multiple-word identifiers are used in constructing a class name, uppercase characters should be used at the beginning of each word.

- Fields or methods declared **private** are accessible only within the class in which they are defined. Fields or methods declared **protected** are accessible within the class in which they are defined as well as within any descendent class. Fields or methods defined as **public** (and it is most unusual to declare a field to be public) are accessible within the class in which they are defined as well as within any other class in the system. Fields or methods declared as **internal** are accessible within the same assembly.

- Properties enable one to control the access of a field that needs to set or get field information. Through a property, a field may be made to be read-only, write-only, or read-write.

- An indexer provides a natural way to index elements in a class that encapsulates a collection using the bracket syntax of the array type. An indexer is a class property with an index.

- The *enum* construct provides a type-safe mechanism for defining enumeration constants.

- Static methods do not have access to the local state (nonstatic fields) of a class. For this reason they must be invoked through the class name and not through a class instance (an object).

- To justify the use of a static method, one should verify that the method is of universal importance (outside the domain of the given class) and that the method comfortably stands independent of data local to any object.

- A *virtual* method is intended to be redefined in a descendent class. In a descendent class that redefines the method, the keyword **override** must be used and the signature of the redefined method must be identical to the signature of the virtual method in the base class.

- The **new** modifier may be used in front of the *virtual* modifier to cause a new point of specialization within the class hierarchy. Polymorphism will prevail in overridden versions of the method in classes that are descendents of the class containing the *new virtual* method. In all classes above this class, the method will be treated as nonvirtual.

- There are two distinct types of multidimensional arrays in C#, rectangular and jagged. All arrays inherit from the abstract base class *System.Array*, which that inherits from *System.Object*. Rectangular arrays use a comma to separate index values while jagged arrays use rectangular brackets to separate index values.

- Only one destructor may be defined in a C# class. It cannot take any parameters. A *struct* cannot define a destructor because its memory is managed on the stack. A destructor is not inherited by a descendent class.

- Destructors cannot be explicitly invoked. They are under the control of the automatic garbage collector. The garbage collector does not guarantee when or whether a destructor will be invoked. Furthermore, the garbage collector does not guarantee the order in which objects are destroyed.

- There are two major categories of errors in an application that can cause exceptions to be generated: logical errors in the program itself and errors that are out of the control of the programmer.

- Exceptions are handled using try-catch blocks.

4.20 ADDITIONAL EXERCISES

In this chapter, all of the exercises (Exercises 4.1–4.23) are directly related to the listings. They therefore follow the listings so that they appear in context, and are not repeated here.

CHAPTER 5

More Advanced Class Construction

The effective construction of C# classes is the main theme of this chapter. It examines some common pitfalls associated with class construction and proposes solutions to the problems. The chapter looks at constructor pitfalls, redefining the *Equals* method from class *Object*, cloning objects, and using *StringBuilder* instead of *String* objects, the important and new feature of generic classes and the new and important feature of enumerators that enable the use of the *foreach* iteration for the instances of a class.

5.1 AVOIDING PROTECTED FIELDS

Fields earmarked as *protected* in a base class are directly accessible in all descendent classes. As a consequence, an assignment to a base-class field made in a remote descendent class, many levels down in a class hierarchy, may not be easy to decipher and understand unless the programmer making this field assignment has intimate knowledge of the base class that contains the field whose value is being modified. Another consequence of making direct assignments to base-class fields in a descendent class is that if the information structure of the base class is changed and the base-class field is removed, the descendent classes that have made direct assignments to this base-class field is broken.

We begin by exploring an alternative to using protected fields to provide accessibility to base-class fields in descendent classes. Consider Listing 5.1 in which a protected field in a base class is given an assignment in a grandchild class. Then consider an alternative approach to the class construction.

LISTING 5.1 Direct assignment to a protected field in a base class

```csharp
using System;
namespace UsingProtectedFields {
    public class BaseClass {
      // Fields
        protected int someCrypticValue;
        public override string ToString() {
            return "" + someCrypticValue;
        }
      // Other details not shown
    }
    public class ChildClass : BaseClass {
      // Details not shown
    }
    public class GrandChildClass : ChildClass {
      // Commands
      public void SomeCommand() {
          someCrypticValue = 10; // Assignment to base -class field
      }
      public static void Main() {
          GrandChildClass app = new GrandChildClass();
          app.SomeCommand();
          Console.WriteLine(app.ToString());
```

LISTING 5.1 Direct assignment to a protected field in a base class (continued)

```
            Console.ReadLine();
        }
    }
}
```

Unless the programmer who is implementing *SomeCommand* in *GrandChildClass* has knowledge of the details of the *BaseClass*, the following assignment may not be easy to understand:

```
someCrypticValue = 10;
```

Suppose the base class is modified later as shown in Listing 5.2.

LISTING 5.2 Modified BaseClass

```
public class BaseClass {
      // Fields
      private int crypticValue;
      private Information importantInfo;
      // Properties
      public int BaseClassValue {
          get {
              return crypticValue;
          }
          set {
              crypticValue = value;
              importantInfo.ImportantValue = crypticValue;
              importantInfo.AnotherCrypticValue =
                        10 * crypticValue;
          }
      }
      // Queries
      public override String ToString() {
          return "crypticValue: " + crypticValue +
              " importantInfo: " + importantInfo.ToString();
      }
      // Other features of class not shown
      private struct Information {
          private int importantValue;
          private int anotherCrypticValue;
          // Properties
          public int ImportantValue { // Read-write property
              get {
                  return importantValue;
              }
```

LISTING 5.2 Modified BaseClass (continued)

```
            set {
                importantValue = value;
            }
        }
        public int AnotherCrypticValue { // Read-write property
            get {
                return anotherCrypticValue;
            }
            set {
                anotherCrypticValue = value;
            }
        }
        // Query
        public override String ToString() {
          return " importantValue: " + importantValue +
                " anotherCrypticValue: " + anotherCrypticValue;
        }
    }
}
```

Discussion of Listing 5.2

◆ In the modified version of *BaseClass*, the previously protected field *crypticValue* is now declared as a *private* field. A *private struct*, Information, is defined as part of the information structure of *BaseClass*. The fields *importantValue* and *anotherCrypticValue* define the information content of the *Information struct*. Two read-write properties allow set and get access to these fields.

◆ The *public* property *BaseClassValue* in *BaseClass* is used to access *crypticValue* and assign a value to *crypticValue* and *importantInfo* as follows:

```
public int BaseClassValue {
    get {
      return crypticValue;
    }
    set {
      crypticValue = value;
        importantInfo.ImportantValue = crypticValue;
        importantInfo.AnotherCrypticValue = 10 * crypticValue;
    }
}
```

◆ The method *SomeCommand*, in *GrandChildClass* is revised as follows:

```
public void SomeCommand() {
    Value = 10;
}
```

By using the *BaseClassValue* property of *BaseClass* instead of a direct assignment to a protected field as in Listing 5.1, the system has been made more robust (i.e., resistant to change).

So the question remains, should you always avoid defining protected fields in a base class? The answer may depend on the complexity of the application, the number of subclasses, and whether two or more programmers will be touching the code. If the code is relatively complex and contains many subclasses, and two or more programmers will be maintaining the code, avoiding protected fields is probably a sensible choice.

The example presented earlier makes a case for not using protected fields and instead using public properties to control access to base-class private fields.

5.2 CONSTRUCTORS AND THEIR PITFALLS

A subtle but common pitfall related to constructors is examined and exposed in this section. Consider the class *BaseClass* in Listing 5.3, which contains a method *CanBeRedefined*.

LISTING 5.3 Base class with method CanBeRedefined

```
public class BaseClass {
    // Constructor
    public BaseClass() {
        Console.WriteLine("In Ancestor constructor");
        this.CanBeRedefined();
    }
    public virtual void CanBeRedefined() {
        Console.WriteLine("In CanBeRedefined in class Ancestor");
    }
}
```

Clearly the intention of the *virtual* method *CanBeRedefined* is to encourage a redefinition of this method in one or more descendent classes. So what could be wrong with this seemingly innocent scenario? Consider a complete application that uses *BaseClass* in Listing 5.4.

LISTING 5.4 Pitfall related to constructors exposed

```
using System;
namespace ConstructorPitfall {
    public class BaseClass {
        // Constructor
        public BaseClass() {
            Console.WriteLine("In BaseClass constructor");
            this.CanBeRedefined();
        }
        public virtual void CanBeRedefined() {
            Console.WriteLine("In CanBeRedefined in class
                BaseClass");
        }
    }
```

LISTING 5.4 Pitfall related to constructors exposed (continued)

```
public class Descendent : BaseClass {
  private Random randomValue;
  public Descendent() {
     Console.WriteLine("In Descendent constructor");
     randomValue = new Random();
  }
  public override void CanBeRedefined() { // Redefinition
     Console.WriteLine("In CanBeRedefined in class
       Descendent");
     Console.WriteLine(randomValue.NextDouble().ToString());
  }
  static void Main() {
     Descendent obj = new Descendent();
     obj.CanBeRedefined();
     Console.ReadLine();
  }
}
}
```

Discussion of Listing 5.4

◆ Class *Descendent* is derived from *BaseClass*. It contains a field *randomValue* of type Random. Its constructor initializes the field *randomValue*. The method *CanBeRedefined* generates a random value from 0.0 to 1.0 and outputs its value to the console. Method *Main* declares and initializes a local variable object of type *Descendent* and invokes the command *CanBeRedefined*. All of this looks innocent enough, and the output from method *Main* is as follows.

```
In BaseClass constructor
In CanBeRedefined in class Descendent
Unhandled Exception: System.NullReferenceException: Object reference
  not set to an instance of an object.
    at ConstructorPitfall.Descendent.CanBeRedefined() …
```

◆ A "NullReferenceException" exception is generated in method *CanBeRedefined* in class *Descendent* one line below the console output statement "In CanBeRedefined in class Descendent".

◆ You can trace the execution of this application up to the runtime crash. Following is the first line of code in *Main*:

```
Descendent obj = new Descendent();
```

This line causes the inherited *BaseClass* constructor to be executed. This accounts for the first line of output to the console, "In BaseClass constructor".

Following is the second line of code in the BaseClass constructor:

```
this.CanBeRedefined();
```

This line causes the method *CanBeRedefined* in class *Descendent* to be invoked because *this* is of type *Descendent*. This explains the second line of console output, "In CanBeRedefined in class Descendent".

The attempt to invoke *NextDouble* in the second line of code in class Descendent's *CanBeRedefined* method causes the runtime error because *randomValue* has not yet been initialized and has a default value *null*.

The cause of this problem is that the *BaseClass* constructor invokes a method that can be redefined in some descendent class (*CanBeReDefined* in this case). This is the pitfall to avoid leading to the following general principle:

Never invoke a method within a base-class constructor that can be redefined in some descendent class.

5.3 OVERRIDING METHOD EQUALS FROM CLASS OBJECT

When designing classes for potential reuse in many applications, be sure to consider whether it is appropriate to redefine the *Equals* method inherited by default from class *Object*. The default *Equals* method from *Object* considers two objects to be equal in value only if they have the same memory reference. Often this default meaning of *Equals* is incorrect. Often it is essential to override the *Equals* method based on field values.

The following simple class *SimplePoint* presented in Listing 5.5 illustrates this principle. The *GetHashCode* query is needed whenever method *Equals* is redefined. The *GetHashCode* query associates every object with an integer value. Two objects that are equal to each other should produce the same hash code value. This hash code value is needed when objects are stored in certain types of collections. This subject is discussed in Chapter 14.

LISTING 5.5 Class SimplePoint

```
using System;
namespace MakingAPoint {
    public class SimplePoint {
        // Fields
        private int xCoordinate, yCoordinate;
        // Constructor
        public SimplePoint(int x, int y) {
            xCoordinate = x;
            yCoordinate = y;
        }
        // Properties
        public int XCoordinate {
            get { // Read-only property
                return xCoordinate;
            }
        }
```

LISTING 5.5 Class SimplePoint (continued)

```csharp
        public int YCoordinate {
            get { // Read-only property
                return yCoordinate;
            }
        }
        /*
        public override bool Equals(Object obj) {
            if (!(obj is SimplePoint)) {
                return false;
            }
            SimplePoint other = (SimplePoint)obj;
            return other.xCoordinate == xCoordinate &&
                    other.yCoordinate == yCoordinate;
        }
        public override int GetHashCode() {
            return xCoordinate ^ yCoordinate;
        }
        */
        public override String ToString() {
            return "<" + xCoordinate + ", " + yCoordinate + ">";
        }
    }
    public class SimplePointApplication {
        public static void Main() {
            SimplePoint point1 = new SimplePoint(3, 5);
            SimplePoint point2 = new SimplePoint(3, 5);
            if (point1.Equals(point2)) {
                Console.WriteLine("Two points are equal.");
            } else {
                Console.WriteLine("Two points are not equal.");
            }
            point2 = point1;
            // Points now share same memory reference
            if (point1.Equals(point2)) {
                Console.WriteLine("Two points are equal.");
            } else {
                Console.WriteLine("Two points are not equal.");
            }
            Console.ReadLine();
        }
    }
}
/* Output
   Two points are not equal.
   Two points are equal.
*/
}
```

With the redefined method *Equals* commented out, as shown in Listing 5.5, the output indicates that the point objects *point1* and *point2* are initially not equal. This is because without a redefinition of the *Equals* method, the default *Equals* method from *Object*, which compares the memory references only, is operational. Using this *Equals*, any two points that do not share the same memory reference would be considered unequal. After assigning *point2* to *point1*, the two memory references are now the same and the default *Equals* method indicates that the points are equal. In reality there is only one point object with the two names *point1* and *point2*.

If we uncomment the *Equals* method as in the following code, the program works as expected.

```
public override bool Equals(Object obj) {
    if (!(obj is SimplePoint)) {
    return false;
    }
    SimplePoint other = (SimplePoint)obj;
    return other.xCoordinate == xCoordinate &&
        other.yCoordinate == yCoordinate;
}
```

This specialized version of *Equals*, customized for our *SimplePoint* class, compares two points by seeing whether they each have the same values for their *xCoordinate* and *yCoordinate* fields. The *if* block checks to see whether the parameter *obj* is of type *SimplePoint* and if not, a value *false* is returned (we cannot compare apples and oranges).

So far this approach is fairly straightforward. Let's see what happens if we create a subclass, *PointWithThickness*, in the same namespace *MakingAPoint* as shown in Listing 5.6. A revised method *Main* is shown in class *SimplePointApplication*.

LISTING 5.6 Subclass PointWithThickness

```
public class PointWithThickness : SimplePoint {
    // Fields
    private int thickness;
    // Constructor
    public PointWithThickness(int x, int y, int thickness) :
      base(x, y) {
        this.thickness = thickness;
    }
    public override bool Equals(Object obj) {
        if (!(obj is SimplePoint)) {
            return false;
        }
```

LISTING 5.6 Subclass PointWithThickness (continued)

```
            if (!(obj is PointWithThickness)) {
                return obj.Equals(this);
            }
            PointWithThickness other = (PointWithThickness)obj;
            return base.Equals(obj) && other.thickness ==
              thickness;
        }
        public override int GetHashCode() {
            return XCoordinate ^ XCoordinate +
                thickness.GetHashCode();
        }
    }
    public class SimplePointApplication {
        public static void Main() {
            PointWithThickness p1 = new PointWithThickness(1, 2, 5);
            SimplePoint p2 = new SimplePoint(1, 2);
            PointWithThickness p3 = new PointWithThickness(1, 2, 3);
            Console.WriteLine("p1.Equals(p2)= " + p1.Equals(p2));
            Console.WriteLine("p2.Equals(p3)= " + p2.Equals(p3));
            Console.WriteLine("p1.Equals(p3)= " + p1.Equals(p3));
            Console.ReadLine();
        }
    }
```

Discussion of Listing 5.6

◆ A specialized field *thickness* of type *int* is introduced in subclass *PointWithThickness*. We focus on its redefined method *Equals*. The goal is to define two points of type *PointWithThickness* as equal only if their coordinate values are the same and their thickness is the same. This seems simple enough. Let's dissect the method *Equals* shown in Listing 5.6.

◆ The *if* block verifies that the parameter *obj* is of type *SimplePoint* or *PointWithThickness*. This is because the "is" operator returns true if *obj* is of type *SimplePoint* or any of its descendents.

◆ The second *if* block is deployed if the parameter *obj* is of type *SimplePoint*. Because of late binding, the *Equals* method from class *SimplePoint* that simply compares the coordinate values of the two points is used in this case.

◆ Finally, if the parameter *obj* is of type *PointWithThickness*, the points are defined as equal if their coordinates are the same (from *base.Equals(obj)*) and their thickness values are identical (*other.thickness == thickness*).

Exercise 5.1

What do you expect as the output of method *Main* in Listing 5.6 and why?

Exercise 5.2

What is wrong with method *Equals* in class *PointWithThickness*?

Because of the importance of Exercises 5.1 and 5.2, the solution to both exercises is presented on the next page. Attempt to answer both questions before continuing this section on the next page.

The output in Listing 5.6 is:

```
p1.Equals(p2)= True

p2.Equals(p3)= True

p1.Equals(p3)= False
```

This presents a problem because it violates the sacred principle of transitivity. We have the application indicating that *p1* equals *p2* and *p2* equals *p3*, but *p1* does not equal *p3*.

The first comparison does not use thickness information. It compares only the coordinates of the points. The same is true of the second comparison. The third comparison is not thickness blind, and returns false because the thickness of the two points that are being compared are unequal even though their coordinates are the same.

The *Equals* method in class *PointWithThickness* is defective because it fails the transitivity test.

Exercise 5.3

Repair the *Equals* method in *PointWithThickness*.

Because of the importance of Exercise 5.3, a solution to this exercise is presented on the next page. Attempt your solution without reading further in this section.

Class *RevisedPointWithThickness* in namespace *MakingAPoint*, presented in Listing 5.7, solves the problem of the defective *Equals* method of Listing 5.6. Composition is required instead of inheritance. It can be shown that when a subclass adds one or more fields, the *Equals* method will always fail unless a composition relationship is used.

LISTING 5.7 Class RevisedPointWithThickness

```
public class RevisedPointWithThickness {
  // Fields
  private SimplePoint point;
  private int thickness;
  // Constructor
  public RevisedPointWithThickness(int x, int y, int thickness) {
      point = new SimplePoint(x, y);
      this.thickness = thickness;
  }
  public SimplePoint AsPoint() {
      return point;
  }
```

LISTING 5.7 Class RevisedPointWithThickness (continued)

```
public override bool Equals(Object obj) {
    if (!(obj is RevisedPointWithThickness)) {
        return false;
    }
    RevisedPointWithThickness other =
        (RevisedPointWithThickness) obj;
    return other.point.Equals(point) &&
            other.thickness == thickness;
}
public override int GetHashCode() {
    return point.XCoordinate ^ point.XCoordinate +
        thickness.GetHashCode();
}
}
```

Discussion of Listing 5.7

◆ Composition is used instead of inheritance. Class *RevisedPointWithThickness* is composed of a point object of type *SimplePoint* and a field *thickness* of type *int*.

◆ The first *if* block returns false unless the parameter *obj* is of type *RevisedPointWithThickness*. This prevents simple points and points with thickness from ever being considered equal to each other.

◆ The problem of transitivity being violated is repaired using this revised class.

Exercise 5.4

Write a revised method *Main* in class *SimplePointApplication* using objects of class *RevisedPointWithThickness* and indicate the output.

Exercise 5.5

Indicate what if anything is wrong with method *Equals* in class *CaseInsensitiveString* given below. Repair this *Equals* method if it is defective.

```
using System;
namespace EqualsMethod {

    public sealed class CaseInsensitiveString {
        // Fields
        private String str;
        // Constructor
        public CaseInsensitiveString (String str) {
            this.str = str;
        }

        public override bool Equals (Object obj) {
            if (obj is CaseInsensitiveString) {
```

```
            return str.Equals(((CaseInsensitiveString) obj).str,
               StringComparison.CurrentCultureIgnoreCase);
         }
         if (obj is String) {
            return str.Equals((String) obj,
               StringComparison.CurrentCultureIgnoreCase);
         }
         return false;
      }
      public override int GetHashCode() {
         return str.ToLower().GetHashCode();
      }
      static void Main() {
         CaseInsensitiveString s1 = new CaseInsensitiveString("AbCD");
         CaseInsensitiveString s2 = new CaseInsensitiveString("aBcd");
         if (s1.Equals(s2)) {
            Console.WriteLine("s1 equals s2");
         } else {
            Console.WriteLine("s1 does not equal s2");
         }
      }
   }
}
```

5.4 CLONING OBJECTS

Cloning has been in the news in recent years with Dolly the sheep and discussions about human cloning. To clone is to produce an autonomous entity containing features that duplicate those in another entity that is the source of the cloning.

In programming, cloning an object involves producing a new instance of a class, the target, and copying the features of the source instance to the target instance. An important question is whether the target instance continues to depend on the source object. In principle, it should not. In practice, it often does, as we shall see shortly.

There are two types of copying: shallow and deep copying. The former copies references but not the content of the references. As a result, the target reference becomes another name for the source reference. Any change made to the source or target after the copy affects the other. With deep copying, an independent autonomous target is created with the content of the source copied to the target and with no residual dependency between the source and the target.

When one reference-type object such as *object1* is assigned to another reference-type object such as *object2*, a shallow copy is created, as in the following code.

```
object2 = object1;
```

Any subsequent change to *object1* appears to affect *object2* because they are both names for the same storage. Copying an object using either the semantics of shallow or deep copy is called cloning. A standard C# interface *IClonable* provides the contract for cloning. Any C# class that defines a *Clone* method must implement the interface *IClonable*. This interface is given as follows:

```
public interface IClonable {
    Object Clone();
}
```

We examine the subtleties of cloning by considering an example involving a class named *Sheep*. Consider class *Sheep* in Listing 5.8 along with several other support classes. The standard collection class *Hashtable* is used in this example. This important collection class as well as other important standard collections are the subject of Chapter 14. An indexer in *Hashtable* allows a unique key to be assigned a value. The indexer also allows the value to be obtained using the key.

LISTING 5.8 Class Sheep

```
using System;
using System.Collections;
namespace Cloning {
    public class Sheep : ICloneable {
        // Fields
        private String name;
        private Person owner = new Person();
                // A standard C# collection explained in Chapter 14
        private Hashtable attributes = new Hashtable();
        // Constructor
        public Sheep(String name, String owner, String color,
                    double weight) {
            this.name = name;
            SetOwnerName(owner);
            SetColor(color);
            SetWeight(weight);
        }
        // Properties
        public String Name {
            get {
                return name;
            }
            set {
                name = value;
            }
        }
        public void SetOwnerName(String ownerName) {
            owner.Name = ownerName;
        }
```

LISTING 5.8 Class Sheep (continued)

```csharp
        public void SetColor(String color) {
            attributes["Color"] = color;
        }
        public void SetWeight(double weight) {
            attributes["Weight"] = weight;
        }
        // Queries
        public String OwnerName() {
            return owner.Name;
        }
        public String Color() {
            return (String) attributes["Color"];
        }
        public double Weight() {
            return (double) attributes["Weight"];
        }
        public override String ToString() {
            return "Name: " + this.name + "\nOwner: " +
            OwnerName() +
                "\nColor: " + Color() + "\nWeight: " +
            Weight();
        }
        public Object Clone() {
            return this.MemberwiseClone();
        }
    }
    public class Person {
        // Fields
        private String name;
        public Person() { }
        public Person(String name) {
            this.name = name;
        }
        // Properties
        public String Name {
            get {
                return name;
            }
            set {
                name = value;
            }
        }
    }
    public class CloningApp {
      static void Main() {
        // Farmer Joe's perfect sheep
        Sheep sheep1 = new Sheep("Wooly", "Farmer Joe",
```

LISTING 5.8 Class Sheep (continued)

```
                    "White and Black", 123.7);
            Console.WriteLine("Sheep 1 before cloning: \n" +
                sheep1.ToString() + "\n");
            // Make clone and sell it to Farmer Frank
            Sheep sheep2 = (Sheep) sheep1.Clone();
            sheep2.SetOwnerName("Farmer Frank");
            sheep2.Name = "Patches";   // New owner changes its name
            sheep2.SetWeight(150.6);   // New owner overfeeds sheep
            sheep2.SetColor("Green"); // New owner dyes its coat
            // Output results
            Console.WriteLine("Sheep1 after cloning: \n" +
              sheep1.ToString() + "\n");
            Console.ReadLine();
        }
    }
}
```

The information structure of class *Sheep* is given by its three fields, *name*, *owner*, and *attributes*. The *owner* field is an instance of class *Person* (defined after class *Sheep*). The field *attributes* is an instance of *Hashtable*, an important standard collection class (which, as indicated earlier, takes key-value pairs with unique key objects).

Class *Person* is a simple class containing a single field *name* and a read-write property *Name* that allows access to this field.

The *Clone* method in *Sheep*, shown in the following code, invokes the *MemberwiseClone* method inherited from class *Object*.

```
public Object Clone() {
    return this.MemberwiseClone();
}
```

This method performs a shallow copy in producing the new *Sheep* object. Recall that a shallow copy means that all reference-type fields have their references copied rather than their content copied. Class *Sheep* has one reference type *String* object, *name*, and two additional reference-type fields, *owner* and *attributes*. Because *String* objects are immutable (i.e., one cannot change the content of a *String* object after it is created), the assignment of one *String* object to another such as in *str2 = str1* makes it appear that the contents of object *str1* are copied to *str2*. Only one *String* object is actually stored in memory with two distinct references to it (*str1* and *str2*). Figure 5.1 depicts the shallow copy of the sheep objects.

Following is the output of the sheep cloning application in Listing 5.8:

```
Sheep 1 before cloning:
Name: Wooly
Owner: Farmer Joe
```

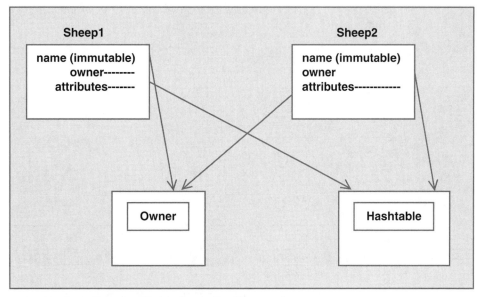

FIGURE 5.1 Copying fields from the Sheep class

```
Color: White and Black
Weight: 123.7
Sheep1 after cloning:
Name: Wooly
Owner: Farmer Frank
Color: Green
Weight: 150.6
```

As is evident in the output, when the owner of cloned *sheep2* is changed, the owner of *sheep1* is also changed. Likewise, when the color and weight of cloned *sheep2* is changed, these values are changed in *sheep1*. Cloning has failed because of the shallow copying of the sheep objects. We need to explore a mechanism for achieving a deep copy in producing *sheep2*. Consider the revised method *Clone*.

```
public Object Clone() {
    Sheep newSheep = (Sheep)this.MemberwiseClone();
    // Set the fields of the new Sheep object
    newSheep.owner = (Person)this.owner.Clone();
    newSheep.attributes = (Hashtable)this.attributes.Clone();
    return newSheep;
}
```

In this revised method, a local and autonomous sheep object, *newSheep*, is created. Its fields are then set to equal those of the owner and containing the attributes.

After installing the revised *Clone* method, the output of Listing 5.8 becomes the following:

```
Sheep 1 before cloning:
Name: Wooly
Owner: Farmer Joe
Color: White and Black
Weight: 123.7
Sheep1 after cloning:
Name: Wooly
Owner: Farmer Joe
Color: White and Black
Weight: 123.7
```

Exercise 5.6

Write the *Clone* method in class *Person* that the revised method *Clone* in class *Sheep* now requires.

To explore another potential pitfall associated with class construction, we consider next the cloning of mammals.

Listing 5.9 presents the details of interface *DeepCopy* and class *Mammal* that implements this interface.

LISTING 5.9 Class Mammal

```csharp
using System;
using System.Collections;
namespace DeepCloning {
   public interface IDeepCopyable {
      Object DeepCopy();
   }
   public class Mammal : IDeepCopyable {
     // Fields
     private Hashtable attributes = new Hashtable();
     // Constructor
     public Mammal(String name) {
        attributes["Name"] = name;
     }
     // Properties
     public Hashtable Attributes {
        get {
            return attributes;
        }
     }
   }
```

LISTING 5.9 Class Mammal (continued)

```
    // Queries
    public virtual Object DeepCopy() {
      // Using a constructor to implement clone
      Mammal newMammal = new Mammal((String)attributes["Name"]);
      newMammal.attributes = (Hashtable)attributes.Clone();
      return newMammal;
    }
    public override String ToString() {
      return "Name: " + attributes["Name"];
    }
  }
}
```

Discussion of Listing 5.9

◆ Class *Mammal* contains a field, *attributes*, which like class *Sheep* in Listing 5.8 uses the standard *Hashtable* collection for the *attributes* type.

◆ The *DeepCopy* method appears at first glance to be clever at doing its job because it declares a new autonomous *newMammal* object and returns it. Its cloning is based on a call to its constructor *Mammal*. We reserve final judgment until later.

We consider next class *Dog* defined in the same namespace as *Mammal*. This class inherits from *Mammal* and implements *IDeepCopyable*. Its details are given in Listing 5.10.

LISTING 5.10 Class Dog

```
    public class Dog : Mammal, IDeepCopyable {
      // Fields
      private ArrayList tricks;
      // Constructor
      public Dog(String name, String breed, ArrayList tricks) :
            base(name) {
        Attributes["Breed"] = breed;
        this.tricks = tricks;
      }
      // Queries
      public override Object DeepCopy() {
        // Create a new dog object
        Dog newDog = (Dog)base.DeepCopy();
        // Set the newDog attributes to the source attributes
        newDog.tricks = (ArrayList)tricks.Clone();
        return newDog;
      }
      public override String ToString() {
        String s = base.ToString() + "\nBreed: " +
              Attributes["Breed"] +
              "\nTricks:";
        for (int i = 0; i < tricks.Count; i++) {
          s = s + "\n" + tricks[i];
        }
        return s;
      }
    }
```

The *DeepCopy* method in *Dog* creates a new autonomous dog object, *newDog*, and sets its *tricks* field (of standard collection class *ArrayList*) by cloning the *tricks* field. Again, at least on the surface, this appears to be a clever and successful way to construct this class.

Finally an application class, *CloneDogApp*, is created. Its details are shown in the following code.

```
public class CloneDogApp {
    static void Main() {
        ArrayList tricks = new ArrayList();
        tricks.Add("Roll over");
        tricks.Add("Fetch");
        tricks.Add("Stay");
        Dog tara = new Dog("Tara", "Border Collie", tricks);
        Dog taraClone = (Dog)tara.DeepCopy();
        Console.WriteLine(tara);
        Console.WriteLine();
        Console.WriteLine(taraClone);
        Console.WriteLine();
        Console.ReadLine();
    }
}
```

When the *CloneDogApp* application is run, the output is as follows:

```
Unhandled Exception: System.InvalidCastException: Specified cast is not
valid on line 54.
```

The failure occurs when the code on line 54 is executed, as shown in the following code.

```
Dog newDog = (Dog)base.DeepCopy();
```

Exercise 5.7

Explain why the *InvalidCastException* is generated when line 54 is executed.

Hint: What type of object does the *Mammal* constructor always produce?

This leads to another important class construction principle:

Never implement a *Clone* method by invoking the constructor of the containing class.

Exercise 5.8

Repair the *DeepCopy* method in Listing 5.9. Run the *CloneDogApp* and verify that your solution works.

5.5 USING STRINGBUILDER INSTEAD OF STRING

A common and potentially expensive pitfall is using objects of type *String* instead of *StringBuilder* when repeatedly concatenating string objects. As indicated earlier, objects of type *String* are immutable. Standard class *StringBuilder* presents a mutable reference type that may be used as an alternative to *String* when appropriate.

Listing 5.11 illustrates the pitfall of using class *String* when *StringBuilder* would be more appropriate.

LISTING 5.11 Comparing the use of String and StringBuilder

```
using System;
using System.Collections;
using System.Text;
using ElapsedTime;
namespace StringandStringBuilder {
    public class StringApp {
        // Fields
        private String str;
        private StringBuilder strB;

        static void Main() {
            Timing t = new Timing();
            StringApp app = new StringApp();
            t.StartTiming();
            for (int i = 0; i < 100000; i++) {
                app.str += "A";
            }
            t.EndTiming();
            Console.WriteLine(
            "Time for 100,000 String concatenates: " +
                t.ElapsedTime());

            app.strB = new StringBuilder();
            t.StartTiming();
            for (int i = 0; i < 1000000; i++) {
                app.strB.Append("A");
            }
            t.EndTiming();
            Console.WriteLine(
            "Time for 100,000 StringBuilder appends: " +
                t.ElapsedTime());
            Console.ReadLine();
        }
    }
}
/* Output
Time for 100,000 String concatenates: 11.484375
Time for 100,000 StringBuilder appends: 0.03125
*/
```

The execution times shown in the output dramatically illustrate the benefit of using the *Append* method of *StringBuilder* as an alternative to the concatenate operation of *String*. When you need to perform a number of modifications to a *String* object, the overhead associated with creating a new *String* object each time can be costly. Using a *StringBuilder* object does not necessitate a new object being created with each change of the string. There are other useful methods in class *StringBuilder* including *Insert*, *Remove*, and *Replace*.

5.6 GENERICS

There has long been a need in programming to be able to create a generic container class (a class that contains objects of some generic type) whose operations are not based on the type of objects being held in the container. Prior to Version 2.0 of C#, there was no way to achieve this in C#.

With the advent of object-oriented languages and an omnipresent class *Object* from which all classes descend, the temptation or requirement (as in the case of earlier versions of C#) to achieve generic behavior through polymorphism has been present.

In a landmark paper "Genericity versus Inheritance" published in the ACM SIGPLAN Notices, Vol 21, No 11 in 1986, Bertrand Meyer presents a clear case that using polymorphism through inheritance is the wrong way to achieve generic behavior.

Exercise 5.9

Read this landmark paper and summarize its content (*www.inf.ethz.ch/personal/meyer/publications/acm/geninh.pdf*).

A class is generic if it contains one or more generic parameters. When an instance of such a class is created, the specific type for each generic parameter must be specified.

Consider the signature of the following generic class:

```
public class MyGenericClass<T> {

    // Details not shown

}
```

An instance of this class may be created as follows:

```
MyGenericClass<String> myObject = new MyGenericClass<String>();
```

Here the generic parameter *T* is replaced by *String*.

We demonstrate some of the benefits of generic classes in the next example. Consider class *MyClass*, which is not generic. Its details are shown in Listing 5.12.

LISTING 5.12 Class MyClass

```
using System;
namespace FirstGenericClass {
    public class MyClass {
        // Fields
        private Object someObject;
        // Properties
        public Object SomeObject { // Read-write
            get {
                return someObject;
            }
            set {
                someObject = value;
            }
        }
    }
}
```

MyClass holds *someObject* as a private field and provides get and set access to this field through the public property *SomeObject*.

We construct an application that uses *MyClass* and requires class *Counter*, given in Listing 5.13.

LISTING 5.13 Class Counter

```
using System;
namespace FirstGenericClass {
    public class Counter {
        // Fields
        private int count;
        // Properties
        public int Count { // Read-only
            get {
                return count;
            }
        }
        // Commands
        public void Increment() {
            count++;
        }
    }
}
```

Class *Application* is given in Listing 5.14.

LISTING 5.14 Class Application

```
using System;
namespace FirstGenericClass {
    public class Application {
        public static void Main() {
            Counter counter1 = new Counter();
            for (int i = 0; i < 50; i++) {
                counter1.Increment();
            }
            Counter counter2 = new Counter();
            for (int i = 0; i < 150; i++) {
                counter2.Increment();
            }
            Counter counter3 = new Counter();
            for (int i = 0; i < 200; i++) {
                counter3.Increment();
            }
            Object [] objects = {
              new MyClass(),
              new MyClass(),
              new MyClass() };
            ((MyClass) objects[0]).SomeObject = counter1;
            ((MyClass) objects[1]).SomeObject = counter2;
            ((MyClass) objects[2]).SomeObject = counter3;
            for (int i = 0; i < 3; i++) {
                int countValue =
                    ((Counter)((MyClass)
                                objects[i]).SomeObject).Count;
                Console.WriteLine("objects[" + i + "].Count = " +
                                countValue);

            }
            Console.ReadLine();
        }
    }
}
/* Output
objects[0].Count = 50
objects[1].Count = 150
objects[2].Count = 200
*/
```

Discussion of Listing 5.14

◆ In class *Application*, three *Counter* objects, *counter1*, *counter2*, and *counter3*, are initialized and incremented 50 times, 150 times, and 200 times, respectively.

◆ An array, *objects*, of type *Object* is created and initialized with three instances of *MyClass*. Using the set property, *SomeObject*, the three *Counter* objects are inserted into array locations 0, 1, and 2. The downcast (*MyClass*) is required since the formal type at each index location in objects is *Object*, whereas the actual type is *MyClass*.

◆ A for loop accesses each of the entities stored in the *objects* array.

Let's examine the assignment statement that accesses each entity and uses a pair of downcasts to convert it to an integer value *countValue*.

```
int countValue = ((Counter)((MyClass) objects[i]).SomeObject).Count;
```

The entity, objects[i], is of type *Object*. The first downcast, (*MyClass*), allows the get property, *SomeObject*, to be used to obtain the object at index i. The formal type returned by *SomeObject* is *Object*, whereas the actual type is *Counter*. The second downcast, (*Counter*), allows the *Count* get property to be used to return the integer *countValue* to the left side of the assignment.

To make this application more readable, we introduce our first generic class, *MyGenericClass*, in Listing 5.15.

LISTING 5.15 Class MyGenericClass

```
using System;
using System.Collections.Generic;
namespace FirstGenericClass {
    public class MyGenericClass<T> {
        // Fields
        private T someObject;
        // Properties
        public T SomeObject {
            get {
                return someObject;
            }
            set {
                someObject = value;
            }
        }
    }
}
```

The property *SomeObject* returns an entity of generic type *T*.

A revised class *Application2* presented in Listing 5.16 demonstrates the use of *MyGenericClass*.

LISTING 5.16 Class Application2

```
using System;
using System.Collections.Generic;
namespace FirstGenericClass {
    public class Application2 {
        public static void Main() {
            Counter counter1 = new Counter();
            for (int i = 0; i < 50; i++) {
                counter1.Increment();
            }
```

LISTING 5.16 Class Application2 (continued)

```
                Counter counter2 = new Counter();
                for (int i = 0; i < 150; i++) {
                    counter2.Increment();
                }
                Counter counter3 = new Counter();
                for (int i = 0; i < 200; i++) {
                    counter3.Increment();
                }
                MyGenericClass<Counter> [] objects =
                        { new MyGenericClass<Counter>(),
                          new MyGenericClass<Counter>(),
                          new MyGenericClass<Counter>() };
                objects[0].SomeObject = counter1;
                objects[1].SomeObject = counter2;
                objects[2].SomeObject = counter3;
                for (int i = 0; i < 3; i++) {
                    int countValue = objects[i].SomeObject.Count;
                    Console.WriteLine("objects[" + i + "].Count = " +
                                      countValue);
                }
                Console.ReadLine();
            }
        }
    }
```

Discussion of Listing 5.16

◆ The array, *objects*, in *Application2* is declared to be of type *MyGenericClass<Counter>* and initialized with three objects of this type.

◆ The assignments of *counter1*, *counter2*, and *counter3* to the *objects* array requires no downcasts because the object types on the right side of the assignment match the type specified by the generic instance, *MyGenericClass<Counter>*.

◆ In accessing the integer *countValue* in the for loop, no downcasts are required in the following assignment.

```
int countValue = objects[i].SomeObject.Count;
```

This follows because *objects[i].SomeObject* is of type *Counter* (the generic instance) so that *Count* can be directly applied to this type.

   The code in *Application2* is easier to read than the corresponding code in class *Application* because no downcasts are required.

Exercise 5.10

What would be the consequence of the following assignment in method *Main* of *Application2*:

```
objects[2].SomeObject = "My name is Tom";
```

In general, the use of generic container classes provides for more readable code. When a generic instance is created, the programmer's intentions are documented in the code itself. If you try to insert an object whose type differs from the type specified when the instance of the generic container is created, C# displays a compile-time error. This is better than a runtime error, which would occur when using the older approach to constructing generic containers. Discovering errors at compile-time is always superior to discovering errors at runtime.

5.6.1 Constrained Generic Parameters

The parameters specified in a generic class may be constrained. A generic parameter may be constrained by specifying that it must implement a particular interface or extend a particular class.

Consider the following class declaration:

```
public class MyGenericClass<T> : IComparable where T :
    IComparable {
// Details not shown
}
```

This declaration implies that *MyGenericClass* contains a generic parameter *T* that must implement the *IComparable* interface. In addition, the class itself must implement this interface (define a method *CompareTo*).

Listing 5.17 presents the details of such a class.

LISTING 5.17 Class MyGenericClass with a generic parameter

```
using System;
using System.Collections.Generic;
namespace ConstrainedGenericApplication {
    public class MyGenericClass<T> : IComparable
        where T : IComparable {
        // Fields
        private T someObject;
        public T SomeObject {
            get {
                return someObject;
            }
            set {
                someObject = value;
            }
        }
        public int CompareTo(Object obj) {
            MyGenericClass<T> other = (MyGenericClass<T>)obj;
            return someObject.CompareTo(other.SomeObject);
        }
    }
}
```

LISTING 5.17 Class MyGenericClass with a generic parameter (continued)

```
public class Application {
  public static void Main() {
      MyGenericClass<int> object1 = new MyGenericClass<int>();
      MyGenericClass<int> object2 = new MyGenericClass<int>();
      object1.SomeObject = 20;
      object2.SomeObject = 16;
      if (object2.CompareTo(object1) < 0) {
        Console.WriteLine("object2 is smaller than object1.");
      } else {
          Console.WriteLine(
            "object 2 is not smaller than object1.");
      }
      Console.ReadLine();
    }
  }
}
```

The method *CompareTo* in *MyGenericClass* uses the downcast (*MyGenericClass<T>*) in assigning *obj* to *other*. Because we are assured that *other.SomeObject* is of some type that implements *IComparable*, we compare *someObject* to *other.SomeObject*.

Exercise 5.11

What would be the consequence of not constraining the generic parameter T in Listing 5.17?

5.6.2 Generic Methods

Methods may be defined that contain one or more generic parameters even though the class in which they are defined contains no generic parameters.

Consider the static method *SelectionSort* that contains the constrained generic parameter *T*. Its signature is the following:

```
public static void SelectionSort<T>(T [] data, int size)
    where T : IComparable {
  // Details not shown
}
```

The constraint on the generic parameter *T* is that it must be an instance of a class that implements the *IComparable* interface. This makes sense because to sort an array of values, the values must be comparable otherwise there would be no way to determine the smallest, the next smallest, and so on.

Consider the details of generic sorting. We shall use one of the simplest sorting algorithms available—one that you probably learned in your Computer Science 1 (CS 1) course—the selection sort. With selection sort, the largest value is tentatively assumed to exist in the first array position (index 0). Then all values in index locations from 1 to the largest index (*size* − 1) are consecutively compared against the tentative largest. If a value is found that is larger than this tentative largest, the tentative largest is updated and its index stored. When this first major iteration of the algorithm is completed, the largest value is swapped with the value in the right-most index location. Now the largest value in the array has been put where it needs to be—in the largest index location of the array.

During the second major iteration, the largest index location is excluded from the process so the array is effectively shortened in size by one value. The largest value is again obtained, excluding the value in the largest index location. It is swapped with the value in the next to the largest index location.

The major iterations continue in this way, each time reducing the effective size of the array by one in order to preserve the ordering from largest to next to largest, ..., which are found after each major iteration.

Listing 5.18 presents the details of the generic sorting along with a brief application class that exercises the algorithm.

LISTING 5.18 Class Sorting

```
using System;
using System.Collections.Generic;
namespace GenericSorting {
    public class Sorting {
        public static void SelectionSort<T>(T [] data, int size)
            where T : IComparable {
            for (int outerIndex = size - 1; outerIndex >= 1;
                outerIndex--) {
                // Find the largest value in data
                T largest = data[0];
                int indexLargest = 0;
                for (int innerIndex = 1; innerIndex <= outerIndex;
                    innerIndex++) {
                    if (data[innerIndex].CompareTo(largest) > 0) {
                        // found value larger than largest
                        largest = data[innerIndex];
                        indexLargest = innerIndex;
                    }
                }
                /* Interchange data[indexLargest] with
                    data[outerIndex];
                */
                    T temp = data[indexLargest];
                    data[indexLargest] = data[outerIndex];
                data[outerIndex] = temp;
            }
        }
    }
}
```

LISTING 5.18 Class Sorting (continued)

```
public class Application {
    public static void Main() {
        double[] myData =
            { 2.5, -1.3, -0.75, 1.5, 2.4, -0.5, 0.75, 1.0 };
        Sorting.SelectionSort(myData, myData.Length);
        for (int i = 0; i < myData.Length; i++) {
            Console.Write(myData[i] + "  ");
        }
        Console.WriteLine();
        Console.ReadLine();
    }
}
}
```

Exercise 5.12

Step through the code in method *SelectionSort* and explain in detail how it works. Focus in particular on each statement that involves the generic parameter *T*. Explain how the *CompareTo* method is used and what justifies its use.

Exercise 5.13

Recall or research the bubble sort algorithm from CS 1. Add a static method *BubbleSort* to class *Sorting* that contains a constrained generic parameter, *T*, and that implements the bubble sort algorithm.

Add additional code to the *Application* class to test your *BubbleSort* method.

5.6.3 Summary of the Benefits of Generic Classes

Generic container classes move type checking from the runtime system to the compiler, thus making code safer. They also provide a mechanism for self-documentation because when a generic container instance is created, the type of objects to be placed in the container is specified in the code itself. Finally, generic classes remove the need for cluttering your code with downcasts. This makes the code easier to read and maintain.

5.7 ENUMERATORS

Container classes (i.e., classes that hold and organize collections of objects) are the focus of Part 4 of this book. We introduce the subject of enumerators here because it is an important subject related to more advanced class construction even though its major application is in connection with container classes.

Iteration through a container class allows each object in the container to be visited exactly once. Any class that is to support an enumerator must implement the *IEnumerable* interface. Such a class must meet the contract of implementing the *GetEnumerator* method that returns an instance of *IEnumerator*.

A class that implements *IEnumerator* must meet the contract of implementing:

1. The read-only property *Current*, which returns the element in the collection that the cursor is currently pointing to).

2. The method *MoveNext*, which returns a value true if the enumerator has successfully advanced to the next element in the collection and false if there is no next element in the collection.

3. The method *Reset*, which restores the cursor so that it points to the first element in the collection.

All of the standard collection classes that will be studied in Part 4 of the book implement *IEnumerable*.

The **foreach** construct provides a simple mechanism for iterating through a collection object that is an instance of a class that implements *IEnumerable*.

We illustrate the use of the *foreach* construct on the standard *ArrayList* collection class in Listing 5.19.

An *ArrayList* containing four objects of type *String* is created. Using the *foreach* iteration construct, the names are output.

LISTING 5.19 Use of foreach construct

```
using System;
using System.Collections;
namespace Iteration {
    public class IterationApplication {
        static void Main() {
            ArrayList myList = new ArrayList();
            myList.Add("Erik");
            myList.Add("Anna");
            myList.Add("Marc");
            myList.Add("Daniel");
            foreach (String name in myList) {
                Console.WriteLine(name);
            }
            Console.ReadLine();
        }
    }
}
```

An alternative way to iterate through the *ArrayList* would be:

```
IEnumerator iterator = myList.GetEnumerator();
bool result = iterator.MoveNext();
while (result && iterator.Current != null) {
    String name = (String)iterator.Current;
      Console.WriteLine(name);
    result = iterator.MoveNext();
}
```

The *foreach* construct clearly provides a simpler mechanism for accomplishing the iteration through the *ArrayList* container.

Version 2.0 of C# allows you to enable a *foreach* iteration in any container class that you construct. Your class must define an iteration block that contains one or more **yield return** statements. The sequence of reserved words "yield return" is used to define the collection objects that are returned in the foreach iteration. We illustrate this process next.

Consider class *MyContainer* in Listing 5.20. Because *IEnumerable<T>* inherits from *IEnumerable* (a change made to C# Version 2.0 shortly before its final release), it is necessary to define a nongeneric form of *GetEnumerator*.

LISTING 5.20 Class MyContainer

```
using System;
using System.Collections.Generic;
using System.Collections;
namespace EnablingIteration {
   public class MyContainer : IEnumerable<String> {
     // Fields
     private List<String> myPossessions = new List<String>();
     // Commands
     public void Add(String item) {
           myPossessions.Add(item);
     }
     // Iterator
     public IEnumerator<String> GetEnumerator() {
         for (int index = 0; index < myPossessions.Count; index++) {
             yield return myPossessions[index];
         }
     }
   }
   /* Code to satisfy new requirement that IEnumerable<T> inherits

          from IEnumerable */
          IEnumerator IEnumerable.GetEnumerator() {
       return null;
   }
 }
   public class IterationApplication {
     public static void Main() {
         MyContainer container = new MyContainer();
         container.Add("Violin");
         container.Add("Guitar");
         container.Add("Canon Digital Camera");
         container.Add("Saab Sedan");
         foreach (String things in container) {
             Console.WriteLine(things);
         }
         Console.ReadLine();
     }
   }
}
```

LISTING 5.20 Class MyPossessions (continued)

```
/* Output
Violin
Guitar
Canon Digital Camera
Saab Sedan
*/
```

Discussion of Listing 5.20

◆   The class is shown as implementing a generic version of *IEnumerable* holding the *String* type. It is therefore under contract to implement the generic *IEnumerator* interface that holds a *String* type.

◆   The private field *myPossessions* is declared as an instance of a generic *List* holding type *String*.

◆   The method *GetEnumerator* returns a generic *IEnumerator* that holds a *String*. In this iteration method, a yield return statement is used to construct the values that comprise the iteration. These values consist of the *String* objects in the *myPossessions* list.

◆   Class *IterationApplication*, also presented in Listing 5.20, demonstrates the use of the *foreach* iteration on an object of type *MyContainer*.

Exercise 5.14

Replace the foreach iterator in method *Main* of the *IterationApplication* class and use the method *MoveNext* and the read-only property *Current* to achieve the same end result.

5.8 PARTIAL CLASSES

Version 2.0 of C# allows a class definition to be distributed over several source files. Integrated development environments such as Visual Studio take advantage of this capability by embedding initialization code in a separate file from the code the user develops even though both are part of the same class.

The keyword **partial** is used to achieve this. In GUI applications, as seen in Chapter 9, the method *InitializeComponent*, is embedded in a partial class that is segregated from the partial class that the user creates in defining the behavior of the GUI component.

To further illustrate, *MyClass* might be written is several parts by using the following code:

```
public partial class MyClass {
    // Details not shown
}
public partial class MyClass {
    // Other details not shown
}
```

5.9 SUMMARY

◆ Fields earmarked as *protected* in a base class are directly accessible in all descendent classes. As a consequence, an assignment to a base-class field made in a remote descendent class may not be easy to decipher and understand unless the programmer making this field assignment has intimate knowledge of the base class that contains the field whose value is being modified.

◆ Never invoke a method within a base-class constructor that can be redefined in some descendent class.

◆ When designing classes for potential reuse in many applications, consider whether it is appropriate to redefine the *Equals* method inherited by default from class *Object*. The default *Equals* method from *Object* considers two objects to be equal in value if and only if they have the same memory reference. Often this default meaning of *Equals* is incorrect.

◆ There are two types of copying: shallow and deep copying. The former copies references but not the content of the references. As a result, the target reference becomes another name for the source reference. Any change made to the source or target after the copy affects the other. With deep copying, an independent autonomous target is created with the content of the source copied to the target and with no residual dependency between the source and the target.

◆ Never implement a *Clone* method by invoking the constructor of the containing class.

◆ A common and potentially expensive pitfall is using objects of type *String* instead of *StringBuilder* when repeatedly concatenating string objects. Objects of type *String* are immutable. That means that once a *String* object is constructed, its contents cannot be changed. Standard class *StringBuilder* presents a mutable reference type that may be used as an alternative to *String* when appropriate.

◆ In a landmark paper "Genericity versus Inheritance" published in the ACM SIGPLAN Notices, Vol 21, No 11 in 1986, Bertrand Meyer presents a clear case that using polymorphism through inheritance to achieve generic behavior is the wrong way to achieve generic behavior.

◆ In general, the use of generic container classes provides for more readable code. When a generic instance is created, the programmer's intentions are documented in the code itself. Any attempt on the part of the programmer to insert an object whose type differs from the type specified when the instance of the generic container is created produces a compile-time error. This is better than a runtime error that would occur when using the older approach to constructing generic containers. Discovering errors at compile time is always superior to discovering errors at runtime.

◆ The parameters specified in a generic class may be constrained. A generic parameter may be constrained by specifying that it must implement a particular interface or extend a particular class.

◆ Methods may be defined that contain one or more generic parameters even though the class that they are defined within contains no generic parameters.

◆ Generic container classes move type-checking from the runtime system to the compiler thus making code safer.

◆ Generic classes provide for a mechanism for self-documentation because when a generic container instance is created, the type of objects that are intended to be placed inside the container is specified in the code itself.

◆ Generic classes remove the need for cluttering your code with downcasts. This makes the code easier to read and maintain.

◆ Iteration through a container class allows each object in the container to be visited exactly once. Any class that is to support an enumerator must implement the *IEnumerable* interface. Such a class must meet the contract of implementing the *GetEnumerator* method that returns an instance of *IEnumerator*.

◆ A class that implements *IEnumerator* must meet the contract of implementing: 1) the read-only property *Current*, which returns the element in the collection to which the cursor is currently pointing; 2) the method *MoveNext*, which returns a value true if the enumerator has successfully advanced to the next element in the collection and false if there is no next element in the collection; and 3) the method *Reset*, which restores the cursor so that it points to the first element in the collection.

◆ The foreach construct provides a simple mechanism for iterating through a collection object that is an instance of a class that implements *IEnumerable*.

◆ Using the keyword partial, Version 2.0 of C# allows a class definition to be distributed over several source files.

5.10 ADDITIONAL EXERCISES

Exercise 5.15

Write class *Counter*, presented in Listing 5.13, as two partial classes. The first partial class should contain the queries and the second the commands.

Exercise 5.16

Illustrate the problem of a constructor invoking a method that can be redefined by creating another example that demonstrates this pitfall.

Exercise 5.17

Define an *Equals* method for class *MyContainer* presented in Listing 5.20.

Exercise 5.18

Write a method *DeepClone* for class *MyContainer* presented in Listing 5.20.

Exercise 5.19

Demonstrate your knowledge of enumerators by writing a class of your own that contains an enumerator. Verify that the foreach construct works on objects of your class by writing a short application class that contains method *Main*. In this method *Main*, construct an object of your class and demonstrate the use of the *foreach* iteration on this object.

CHAPTER 6

Refactoring

Refactoring is redesign aimed at improving existing software without adding new functionality. Like any design activity, it is a process that is guided by basic principles, experience, and creativity.

The goal of refactoring is to make the resulting software system easier to understand and maintain as future changes are made in response to new requirements. Through a disciplined process of rebuilding classes, the architecture of a software system is refined and enhanced during refactoring without changing the observable behavior of the system. Only the internal structure of the system is improved.

Many organizations are reluctant to encourage or support refactoring activity because of the fear that defects, or bugs, may be introduced as classes are modified and rebuilt. They believe that the expenditures are not commensurate with the benefits, because in the end, no new functionality is added to a refactored system. In some cases, such a view is short-sighted—the long-term benefits of having a system that is easier to understand because its parts fit together more logically may lower the amortized cost of development.

Refactoring is typically performed incrementally. A series of modifications from minor to major is undertaken. These modifications include renaming an entity such as a class, method, or parameter; moving a field from one class to another; changing the number of parameters in a method; pulling code out of a method to extract a new method; moving a method up or down an inheritance hierarchy; extracting a super class in order to be able to factor common behavior (fields or methods); and replacing a branching construct with polymorphism.

At each stage of refactoring, careful testing must be done to ensure that the external behavior of the system is unchanged. Unit testing (see *http://junit.org/index.htm* or *www.nunit.org*) has become an activity widely used with refactoring.

It is difficult to know when refactoring is needed and when it is completed. As a complex software system evolves, refactoring is often performed at various times during the development cycle.

During the earlier stages of development, many of the same activities that are done later during more formal refactoring form the basis for development itself. This includes adding parameters to a method; renaming a field, method, or class; breaking a large method into smaller parts; and performing the other activities cited earlier that constitute refactoring.

6.1 PRINCIPLES USED IN REFACTORING

Some of the refactoring principles and techniques that are becoming more widely used and accepted are presented in an important book that is becoming a classic: *Refactoring: Improving the Design of Existing Code* by Martin Fowler, Kent Beck, John Brant, William Opdyke, and Don Roberts, Addison-Wesley (1999). Fowler talks about code that needs refactoring as having some characteristic "smells."

Table 6.1 includes some "smells" that can serve as an indicator that refactoring is needed. The first column includes the name of the smell, the second provides a short description of the problem, and the third offers possible solutions.

TABLE 6.1 "Smells" that suggest the need for refactoring

Smell (Symptom)	Brief Description	Possible Remedy
Long method	Mission is overly ambitious	Extract one or more methods. Replace method with method object.
Large class	Too many fields and methods	Extract class. Extract subclass.
Long parameter list	Method unnecessarily complicated because of the myriad of items passed into it	Remove parameters and ensure that through the reduced input information, the method can access anything that it needs to complete its business.
Poor identifier name	Identifier name that does not provide self-documentation within an application	Rename identifier.
Comments	A comment should provide clarification regarding why the specified code is being used, which often happens when the method is poorly named	Rename method. Extract method. Use an assertion.
Dead code	Local variables or parameters that are not being used for anything	Remove the code.
Data groups	A class that contains clumps of data	Extract class.
Classes with data only	Class contains only fields and set/get properties	Use move method to encapsulate operations with the data.
Subclasses that block ancestor class behavior	A subclass that cannot use or must block behavior inherited by an ancestor class	Push down method. Push down field.
Codependency	Two classes that are too interdependent	Change bidirectional association to directed association. Move method. Move field. Extract class.
Ill-conceived class	Class that does not perform a well-defined mission	Remove class.
Long message chains	One object is used to get another, which is used to get still another, and so on	Extract method. Move method.

TABLE 6.1 "Smells" that suggest the need for refactoring (continued)

Smell (Symptom)	Brief Description	Possible Remedy
Too much delegation	When a class delegates too much of its behavior to another class	Remove this class. Replace delegation with inheritance.
Too much generality	Code that is too general in an attempt to anticipate future changes	Collapse hierarchy.

Let us consider two of the "smells" listed in Table 6.1 and discuss their solution in more detail.

6.1.1 Long Method

Comments and white-space delimiters often provide a clue about where to extract a private method with the goal of shortening and simplifying the method in which the code is embedded. The extracted method should provide a simple and well-defined mission. The mission of the extracted code is what is important, not its length. One should never arbitrarily extract methods from a given method only to shorten the original method.

In the process of creating extracted private methods that support a given method, duplication or near duplication of functionality may be discovered. Using parameter modification, two or more such extracted methods might be combined into a single supporting method.

The goal of method extraction is to manage complexity through functional decomposition. The overhead of additional method calls should generally not be a consideration. Intellectual overhead, which is a measure of the programmer's intellectual cycles (thinking time) that must be expended in understanding and maintaining the software, is typically much more expensive than the often immeasurable extra machine cycles that extracted methods may entail.

6.1.2 Long Parameter List

Replace one or more parameters with a parameter object. This involves creating a class that contains a group of logically related parameters that appear in the long parameter list. The parameter list may be shortened by sending an object of the new class to replace the individual parameters in the original parameter list.

A collected reference that includes important articles on refactoring may be found at *www.refactoring.com/reflist.html*.

It is difficult and tedious to discuss refactoring out of the context of an example. The list of refactoring techniques has become overwhelming, especially when the techniques are presented without the context of some application. (For example, see Martin Fowler's list of refactoring techniques in *www.refactoring.com/catalog/index.html*.)

It is not the intent of this chapter to duplicate the lists of techniques and explanations of refactoring cited earlier. That would require another book of considerable size and add little in the way of new information.

The next section presents a case study in refactoring that demonstrates many of the techniques cited earlier.

6.2 CASE STUDY IN REFACTORING

It is believed that refactoring is best learned and inspired by example. Such an example is presented in this section. The case study illustrates some of the basic refactoring techniques typically used. Refactoring is shown in action by examining the evolution from an initial implementation whose architecture is poorly conceived to revised solutions that gradually improve in the quality of their internal architecture.

This case study journeys through five separate solutions to the problem. The complete source code for each solution is available at the Course Technology Web site (*www.course.com*) under the link for this book. Only key portions of this code will be presented and discussed.

To benefit fully from this journey from one solution to the next, put on your code-slogging hiking boots; the only way to understand refactoring is to observe it at close range.

6.2.1 Specifications of the "OOPLY" Game

The game of "OOPLY," inspired by the classic game of Monopoly, is specified. Unlike Monopoly, there is no human intervention in this game. The software system, through its various behaviors, is responsible for playing a complete game, presenting the user with output in the form of a log file to be described later, and presenting the final scores at the end.

The game contains 10 board positions and four players initialized to start at position 1. The players move in sequence starting with player 1. When a player moves, it rolls a die with an equal probability of outcomes from 1 to 6, and then moves that number of board positions forward. Board position 10 connects to board position 1 as a closed system.

The game ends in one of two ways: 1) Each player has moved 5000 times (each sequence of four moves is defined as a **move cycle**); 2) One of the players is out of money. When the game ends, the player with the most cash is declared the winner. Only a player's available cash is counted, not property.

Each of the players is randomly assigned one of three investment strategies (Random Strategy, Aggressive Strategy, or Conservative Strategy) at the beginning of the game. Each player starts with an account balance of $5000. As the game progresses, the original investment strategy is replaced with another. Such swaps occur from time to time for each player as the game progresses. Players have no control over these investment strategy swaps.

There are two kinds of board positions, chance and property positions. If a player lands on a chance position, the following actions may occur:

◆ The player may immediately acquire additional money.

◆ The player may immediately lose some money.

◆ The player may get a replacement investment strategy or retain the same investment strategy.

If a player lands on a property position, the following actions may occur:

◆ If the property is not owned, the player is offered the opportunity to purchase the property at a preset price associated with the board position. The player's decision to purchase or not purchase is based on the investment strategy that it currently has.

◆ If the property is owned by another player, the player must pay a fixed rental fee directly to the player who owns the property. The rent is based on the number of investment units (the Monopoly equivalent of houses) built on the property by the owner and the cost of the property.

◆ If the property is owned by the player who has landed on the property, the player is offered the opportunity to purchase from zero to five additional investment units. These investment units on an owned property offer the advantage of increasing the rental fee obtained if another player lands on the property. There is no limit on the total number of investment units that can be "built" on an owned property. The decision regarding the number of investment units to purchase (from zero to five) on the current turn is based on the player's current investment strategy (more details following).

The output log file must be updated at the conclusion of every player's move. Several sample output chunks are shown, each occurring after a player's move.

```
Move cycle: 723
Player 2 moved from position 4 to 9.
Current investment strategy: 3
Position 9: Property position with cost of $1200
Current owner: None
Current number of investment units: 0
Action: Purchase the property.
New investment strategy: 3
New number of investment units: 0
Change in total cash for player: -$1200
Summary of cash for each player: A: $2045, B: $7210, C: $615, D: $1290
Move cycle: 980
Player 2 moved from position 6 to 9.
Current investment strategy: 1
Position 9: Property position with cost of $1200
Current owner: Player 2
Current number of investment units: 2
Action: Add 3 investment units
New investment strategy: 1
```

```
New number of investment units: 5
Change in total cash for player: -$1800
Summary of cash for each player: A: $6500, B: $200, C: $6150, D: $150
Move cycle: 1420
Player 1 moved from position 7 to 9.
Current investment strategy: 2
Position 9: Property position with cost of $1200
Current owner: Player 2
Current number of investment units: 5
Action: Pay rent to Player 2
New investment strategy: 2
New number of investment units: 5
Change in total cash for player: -$420
Summary of cash for each player: A: $1500, B: $2000, C: $7850, D: $1150
```

Following are the specifications for board positions:

The position is a property position. The purchaser of a property cannot purchase investment units during the move in which it acquires the property but only on subsequent moves to the property. If another player lands on your property, rent is one-tenth the cost of the property. Rent is increased by one-tenth the cost of each additional investment unit. Investment units cost half as much as the property. Up to five investment units can be purchased on any given turn when landing on your own property. The number of investment units purchased depends on the investment strategy held by the owner of the property.

A property position is therefore uniquely characterized by its cost.

◆ **Position 1**—If a player *lands on* or *passes* this board position, the player "earns" $200 (like passing "Go" in Monopoly). That is the only function of position 1.

◆ **Position 2**—This is a property position. Its cost is $2000. Based on the rules for property given above, its rent is $200. Investment units cost $1000 each. For each investment unit on the property, the rent goes up by $100.

◆ **For position 3**—This is a chance position. If a player lands on this position, it receives a new investment strategy randomly chosen from the remaining two with equal likelihood.

◆ **For position 4**—This is a chance position. A player landing on this position has its cash amount changed by a random integer uniformly distributed from –$300 to $200.

◆ **For position 5**—This is a property position. Its cost is $500.

◆ **For position 6**—This is a property position. Its cost is $800.

◆ **For position 7**—This is a chance position. A player landing on this position has its cash amount changed by a random integer uniformly distributed from –$500 to $300.

◆ **For position 8**—This is a chance position. A player landing on this position must "throw" the die and move again.

- **For position 9**—This is a property position. Its cost is $1200.

- **For position 10**—This is a chance position. If a player lands on this position, it receives a new investment strategy randomly chosen from 1 to 3 with equal likelihood. It is possible that it will receive the same investment strategy that it already has (one-third probability).

It was stated earlier that when a player is offered the option of purchasing a property (when landing on a property that is not owned) or offered the option of purchasing from zero to five investment units when landing on its own property, its decision is based on its current investment strategy. The algorithms for each of the three investment strategies follow:

A player has the Random Strategy. When offered the opportunity to purchase a property, a player flips a fair coin to decide whether to purchase the property provided it has more cash than the cost of the property. Its decision to purchase between zero and five investment units when landing on its own property is made by choosing a uniformly distributed random integer from 0 to 5. It will purchase the investment units providing it has more cash than the cost of the units. For example, if the random integer chosen is 3 and the player lacks the cash to buy three units, it buys no units.

A player has the Aggressive Strategy. When offered a property that is not owned, a player always purchases the property if it has more cash than the cost of the property. When given an opportunity to buy between zero and five additional investment units, a player always purchases the largest number that it can afford. That is, a player tries to purchase five units if it has the cash. If not, it will try to purchase four units, and so on. After such a purchase, a player must have at least one dollar left.

A player has the Conservative Strategy. When offered the opportunity to purchase a property that is not owned, a player purchases the property provided that the player has more than five times the cost of the property in current cash. When offered the opportunity to purchase between zero and five investment units, the player will purchase as many investment units as it can subject to the following constraints: 1) It has more than five times as much cash as the total outlay for the additional investment units; 2) The rent already earned from the property exceeds one-fourth the cost of the additional investment units.

When a player runs out of money because it lands on another player's property and must pay rent, or a chance board position imposes a monetary penalty, it cannot take a loan or sell its property or investment units to acquire additional cash. Property and investment units are not deemed to have any monetary value for avoiding bankruptcy. Their only value is in acquiring wealth during the game. When a player runs out of cash, the game ends. The player who currently has the most cash is the winner.

6.2.2 Initial Solution

The initial solution might be typical of one developed by someone relatively inexperienced with object technology. It relies on many global constants and takes little advantage of the OOP paradigm.

The initial software system contains the following 17 classes:

Player—Models each of the four players

Position—Factors behavior common to all board positions

Position1 (inherits from Position)—Models the first board position

Position2 (inherits from Position)—Models the second board position

Position3 (inherits from Position)—Models the third board position

Position4 (inherits from Position)—Models the fourth board position

Position5 (inherits from Position)—Models the fifth board position

Position6 (inherits from Position)—Models the sixth board position

Position7 (inherits from Position)—Models the seventh board position

Position8 (inherits from Position)—Models the eighth board position

Position9 (inherits from Position)—Models the ninth board position

Position10 (inherits from Position)—Models the tenth board position

RandomStrategy—Models the random investment strategy

AggressiveStrategy—Models the aggressive investment strategy

ConservativeStrategy—Models the conservative investment strategy

OOPLYApp—Point of entry that initializes and starts the game

GlobalConstants—Contains constants needed throughout the system

The class diagram in Figure 6.1 shows a bird's eye view of the classes. The class *GlobalConstants* is shown in Listing 6.1. Its fields include:

RandomValue—A globally accessible random number generator

PlayerPosition—An array of *int* that contains each player's position

RentCollected—An array of *int* that contains the rent collected by each player

InvestmentStrategyName—An array of String that contains the name of the investment strategy for each player

Position—An array that contains the 10 position objects

DieThrow—The outcome from 1 to 6 of a die throw

LogFile—A file opened for writing the simulation events as they occur

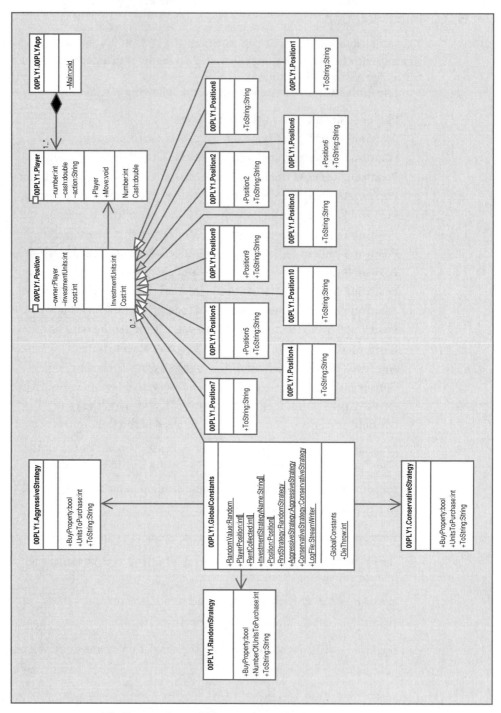

FIGURE 6.1 Bird's eye view of classes for Solution 1

LISTING 6.1 Class GlobalConstants

```
using System;
using System.IO;
namespace OOPLY1 {
   public class GlobalConstants {
      // Fields
      public static Random RandomValue = new Random();
      // Index 0 not used to achieve more natural indexing
      public static int[] PlayerPosition = new int[5];
      public static int[] RentCollected = new int[5];
      public static String[] InvestmentStrategyName = new
         String[5];
      public static Position[] Position =
         {null, new Position1(), new Position2(), new Position3(),
         new Position4(), new Position5(), new Position6(),
         new Position7(), new Position8(), new Position9(),
         new Position10() };
      public static RandomStrategy RndStrategy = new
         RandomStrategy();
      public static AggressiveStrategy AggressiveStrat =
         new AggressiveStrategy();
      public static ConservativeStrategy ConserveStrategy =
         new ConservativeStrategy();

      // Warmup the random number generator
      static GlobalConstants() {
         for (int i = 0; i < 100000; i++) {
             RandomValue.NextDouble();
         }
         PlayerPosition[1] = 1;
         PlayerPosition[2] = 1;
         PlayerPosition[3] = 1;
         PlayerPosition[4] = 1;
      }
      // Queries
      public static int DieThrow() {
         return RandomValue.Next(1, 7);
      }
      public static StreamWriter LogFile = new StreamWriter(
             new FileStream("Log.txt", FileMode.Create,
                FileAccess.Write));
   }
}
```

We look next at the three investment strategy classes. These are presented in Listing 6.2.

LISTING 6.2 Investment strategy classes

```csharp
using System;
namespace OOPLY1 {
   public class RandomStrategy {
      public bool BuyProperty(double price, Player player) {
         if (player.Cash > price)
            return GlobalConstants.DieThrow() <= 3; // Flip coin
         else
            return false;
      }
      public int NumberOfUnitsToPurchase(double price, Player
                                                     player) {
         int numberUnits = GlobalConstants.RandomValue.Next(0, 6);
         if (player.Cash > numberUnits * price / 2.0)
            return numberUnits;
         else
            return 0;
      }
      public override String ToString() {
         return "Random Strategy";
      }
   }
}

using System;
namespace OOPLY1 {
   public class AggressiveStrategy {

      public bool BuyProperty(double price, Player player) {
         return player.Cash > price;
      }
      public int UnitsToPurchase(double price, Player player) {
         if (player.Cash > 5 * price / 2.0)
            return 5;
         else if (player.Cash > 4 * price / 2.0)
            return 4;
         else if (player.Cash > 3 * price / 2.0)
            return 3;
         else if (player.Cash > 2 * price / 2.0)
            return 2;
         else if (player.Cash > price / 2.0)
            return 1;
         else
            return 0;
      }
      public override String ToString() {
         return "Aggressive Strategy";
      }
   }
}
```

LISTING 6.2 Investment strategy classes (continued)

```csharp
using System;
namespace OOPLY1 {
    public class ConservativeStrategy {
        public bool BuyProperty(double price, Player player) {
            return player.Cash > 5.0 * price;
        }
        public int UnitsToPurchase(double price, Player player) {
            if (GlobalConstants.RentCollected[player.Number] <
                price / 8.0) {
                return 0;
            }
            if (player.Cash > 25 * price / 2.0)
                return 5;
            else if (player.Cash > 20.0 * price / 2.0)
                return 4;
            else if (player.Cash > 15.0 * price / 2.0)
                return 3;
            else if (player.Cash > 10.0 * price / 2.0)
                return 2;
            else if (player.Cash > 5.0 * price / 2.0)
                return 1;
            else
                return 0;
        }
        public override String ToString() {
            return "Conservative Strategy";
        }
    }
}
```

Exercise 6.1

Explain the first *if* block in class *ConservativeStrategy*:

```csharp
if (GlobalConstants.RentCollected[player.Number] <
            price / 8.0) {
    return 0;
}
```

Listing 6.3 presents the details of class *OOPLYApp*, the main entry point for the application.

LISTING 6.3 Class OOPLYApp

```csharp
using System;
namespace OOPLY1 {
    public class OOPLYApp {
        static void Main(string[] args) {
            int turn = 1;
            int moveCycle = 1;
            // Initialize players
            Player player1 = new Player(1, 5000);
            Player player2 = new Player(2, 5000);
            Player player3 = new Player(3, 5000);
            Player player4 = new Player(4, 5000);
            for (int playerNumber = 1; playerNumber <= 4;
                    playerNumber++) {
                switch (GlobalConstants.RandomValue.Next(1, 4)) {
                    case 1:
                    GlobalConstants.
                      InvestmentStrategyName[playerNumber] =
                            "Random Strategy";
                        break;
                    case 2:
                    GlobalConstants.
                      InvestmentStrategyName[playerNumber] =
                            "Aggressive Strategy";
                        break;
                    case 3:
                    GlobalConstants.
                      InvestmentStrategyName[playerNumber] =
                            "Conservative Strategy";
                        break;
                }
            }
            while (moveCycle <= 5000 && player1.Cash > 0 &&
                    player2.Cash > 0 &&
                    player3.Cash > 0 &&
                    player4.Cash > 0) {
                switch (turn) {
                    case 1:
                        player1.Move(moveCycle);
                        break;
                    case 2:
                        player2.Move(moveCycle);
                        break;
                    case 3:
                        player3.Move(moveCycle);
                        break;
                    case 4:
                        player4.Move(moveCycle);
                        break;
                }
```

LISTING 6.3 Class OOPLYApp (continued)

```
                    GlobalConstants.LogFile.WriteLine(
                        "Summary of cash for each player: 1: $" +
                        player1.Cash + " 2: $" + player2.Cash +
                        " 3: $" + player3.Cash + " 4: $" +
                        player4.Cash);
                    turn++;
                    if (turn == 5) {
                        turn = 1;
                        moveCycle++;
                    }
                }
                // Display the winner
                GlobalConstants.LogFile.WriteLine();
                GlobalConstants.LogFile.WriteLine("GAME IS OVER.");
                GlobalConstants.LogFile.Close();
            }
        }
    }
```

The *Move* command is invoked on each *Player* object in turn in the while loop in method *Main*. Listing 6.4 presents portions of this initial version of this important class *Player*.

Note: Please examine the full source listing for class *Player* in the Chapter 6 folder provided with the files for this book.

LISTING 6.4 Initial version of class Player

```
using System;
namespace OOPLY1 {
    public class Player {
        // Fields
        private int number;
        private double cash;
        private String action;
        // Constructor
        public Player(int number, double cash) {
            this.number = number;
            this.cash = cash;
        }
        // Properties
        public double Cash { // Read-write
            get {
                return cash;
            }
            set {
                cash = value;
            }
```

LISTING 6.4 Initial version of class Player (continued)

```
        }
        public int Number { // Read-only
            get {
                return number;
            }
        }
        // Commands
        public void Move(int moveCycle) {
          action = "";
          GlobalConstants.LogFile.WriteLine();
          GlobalConstants.LogFile.WriteLine(
            "Move cycle: " + moveCycle); int currentPosition =
                GlobalConstants.PlayerPosition[number];
          int dieThrow = GlobalConstants.DieThrow();
          int newPosition = currentPosition + dieThrow;
          if (newPosition > 10) {
              newPosition -= 10;
              Cash += 200; // For passing "G0"
              action += "Passed go and collected $200. ";
          }
          GlobalConstants.PlayerPosition[number] = newPosition;
          GlobalConstants.LogFile.WriteLine("Player " + number +
            " moved from position " + currentPosition +
            " to " + newPosition);
          GlobalConstants.LogFile.WriteLine(
            "Current investment strategy: " +
                GlobalConstants.InvestmentStrategyName[number]);
          int playerPosition =
                GlobalConstants.PlayerPosition[number];
          if (playerPosition == 2 || playerPosition == 5 ||
              playerPosition == 6 || playerPosition == 9) {
              Position pos =
                GlobalConstants.Position[playerPosition];
            Player owner = pos.Owner;
            int cost = pos.Cost;
            if (owner == null) { // No one owns the property
              // Determine whether to purchase property
              if (GlobalConstants.InvestmentStrategyName[number]
                    == "Random Strategy") {
                  if (GlobalConstants.RndStrategy.BuyProperty
                        (cost, this)) {
                      pos.Owner = this;
                      Cash -= cost;
                      action += "Purchased property for " + cost;
                      // Output to the console—see data files
                } else {
                      action = "Could not purchase property";
                      // Output to the console—see data files
                  }
```

LISTING 6.4   Initial version of class Player (continued)

```
                    } else if (GlobalConstants.
                       InvestmentStrategyName
                       [number] == "Aggressive Strategy") {
                      if (GlobalConstants.AggressiveStrat.
                          BuyProperty(cost, this)) {
                        pos.Owner = this;
                        Cash -= cost;
                        action += "Purchased property for " + cost;
                        // Output to the console—see data files
                      }
                  } else if
                     (GlobalConstants.
                      InvestmentStrategyName[number] ==
                        "Conservative Strategy") {
                      if (GlobalConstants.ConserveStrategy.
                          BuyProperty(cost, this)) {
                        pos.Owner = this;
                        Cash -= cost;
                        action += "Purchased property for " + cost;
                        // Output to the console—see data files
                      } else {
                          action = "Could not purchase property";
                          // Output to the console—see data files
                      }
                  }
              } else if (this == owner) { // player owns the property
                  if (GlobalConstants.InvestmentStrategyName
                      [number] == "Random Strategy") {
                      int unitsToPurchase =
                        GlobalConstants.RndStrategy.
                            NumberOfUnitsToPurchase(cost, this);
                      Cash -= unitsToPurchase * cost / 2;
                      action += "Purchased " + unitsToPurchase +
                          " investment units for " +
                          (unitsToPurchase * cost / 2);
                      // Output to the console—see data files
                  } else if
                     (GlobalConstants.InvestmentStrategyName
                         [number] == "Aggressive Strategy") {
                      int unitsToPurchase =
                        GlobalConstants.AggressiveStrat
                              .UnitsToPurchase(cost, this);
                      Cash -= unitsToPurchase * cost / 2;
                      action += "Purchased " + unitsToPurchase +
                          " investment units for " +
                          (unitsToPurchase * cost / 2);
                      // Output to the console—see data files
                  } else if (GlobalConstants.InvestmentStrategyName
                     [number] == "Conservative Strategy") {
```

LISTING 6.4   Initial version of class Player (continued)

```
                        int unitsToPurchase =
                            GlobalConstants.ConserveStrategy.
                                UnitsToPurchase(cost, this);
                        Cash -= unitsToPurchase * cost / 2;
                        action += "Purchased " + unitsToPurchase +
                            " investment units for " +
                            (unitsToPurchase * cost / 2);
                        // Output to the console—see data files
                    }
                } else { // Must pay rent
                    int investmentUnits = pos.InvestmentUnits;
                    Cash -= (cost / 10 + investmentUnits * cost / 20);
                    action += "Paying rent to " +
                            pos.Owner.Number + ".";
                    pos.Owner.Cash +=
                        (cost / 10 + investmentUnits * cost / 20);
                    GlobalConstants.RentCollected[pos.Owner.Number] +=
                        (cost / 10 + investmentUnits * cost / 20);
                    GlobalConstants.LogFile.WriteLine("Owner: Player" +
                        pos.Owner.Number);
                    // Output to the console—see data files
                }
            } else if (playerPosition == 4 || playerPosition == 7) {
                if (playerPosition == 4) {
                    int chance = GlobalConstants.
                        RandomValue.Next(-300, 201);
                    Cash += chance;
                    // See data files for details
                } else {
                    int chance = GlobalConstants.
                        RandomValue.Next(-500, 301);
                    Cash += chance;
                    // See data files for details
                }
            } else if (playerPosition == 3 || playerPosition == 10) {
                action += "Change in investment strategy from " +
                    GlobalConstants.InvestmentStrategyName[number];
                // See data files for details
            }
        }
    }
}
```

The size and complexity of class *Player* is an abomination (long method "smell"). It is a classic example of procedural programming with objects. All actions for a player are determined by accessing and then updating information that is stored in the *GlobalConstants* class. Significant refactoring is in order.

Before starting this refactoring, the relatively simple class *Position* is presented in Listing 6.5. Class *Position* contains only three fields and associated set and get methods. If you recall from Section 6.1, this is one of the bad "smells" that suggests the need for refactoring.

LISTING 6.5 Class Position

```
public class Position {
      // Fields
      private Player owner;
      private int investmentUnits;
      private int cost;
      // Queries
      public int Cost {
          get {
              return cost;
          }
          set {
              cost = value;
          }
      }
      public int InvestmentUnits {
          get {
              return investmentUnits;
          }
          set {
              investmentUnits = value;
          }
      }
      public Player Owner {
          get {
              return owner;
          }
          set {
              owner = value;
          }
      }
  }
```

Five solutions are produced for the OOPLY game. The first two solutions use many global arrays and represent more of a structured approach than an object-oriented approach to programming. The final refactoring changes this relationship so that board positions are in the dominant positions when interacting with the players that move across them. This leads to dramatic simplification of the system.

The refactored system is significantly shorter than the original and much easier to understand and maintain. This is accomplished without making any changes to the functionality of the system.

The second solution in namespace OOPLY2, available for inspection in the Chapter 6 folder provided with the files for this book, does little except extract private methods from the many blocks of code that write output to the console. From an architectural viewpoint, this second refactoring is minor and provides little improvement.

We focus instead on the third solution, which represents a major refactoring and major improvement to the architecture of the system.

6.2.3 First Major Refactoring

There are currently 10 *Position* subclasses, one for each board position. Although you could argue that this represents a realistic mapping from the problem domain, it in no way takes advantage of our ability to factor common behavior into super classes. So an important task in this major refactoring is to clarify board behavior by generating appropriate super class abstractions. We do this by recognizing that there are three distinct types of board positions: property positions, chance positions, and new strategy positions. This leads to the "discovery" of classes *PropertyPosition*, *ChancePosition*, and *NewStrategyPosition*.

Another important goal of this round of refactoring is to strip out all the global arrays that hold player position information, player strategy information, rent collected information, and the array of position objects. All that will remain in the *GlobalConstants* class will be the random number object, *RandomValue*, and the output file, *LogFile*.

To accomplish this, it is necessary that each *Player* object hold a position object and investment strategy object in its information structure as fields. From the three concrete investment strategy classes we must extract an interface, *InvestmentStrategy*, that can be used as a polymorphic placeholder for any one of the three concrete investment strategy types.

This interface is given in Listing 6.6.

LISTING 6.6 Interface InvestmentStrategy

```
public interface InvestmentStrategy {
  bool BuyProperty(double price, Player player);
  int NumberOfUnitsToPurchase(double price, Player player);
  String ToString();
}
```

The three concrete investment strategy classes each meet the contract mandated by this interface because they implement the queries *BuyProperty* and *NumberOfUnitsToPurchase*. The details are the same as in Listing 6.2.

```
public class RandomStrategy : InvestmentStrategy {
  // See Listing 6.2 for details
}
```

The revised class *Player* contains the fields *number*, *cash*, *pos*, and *strategy* as follows:

```
public class Player {
// Fields
```

```
private int number;
private double cash;
private Position pos;
private InvestmentStrategy strategy;
```

It can be seen in this field structure that the interface *InvestmentStrategy* is being used as a placeholder for any one of its concrete implementing class instances.

Each *Position* object is linked to the next *Position* object by adding a field *next* of type *Position* to this class.

The all-important and revised *Move* command in class *Player* is shown in Listing 6.7.

LISTING 6.7 Revised method Move in class Player

```
public void Move(int moveCycle) {
   action = "";
   GlobalConstants.LogFile.WriteLine();
   GlobalConstants.LogFile.WriteLine(
      "Move cycle: " + moveCycle);
   int currentPosition = pos.PositionNumber;
   int dieThrow = GlobalConstants.DieThrow();
   int newPosition = currentPosition + dieThrow;
   if (newPosition > 10) {
     newPosition -= 10;
     Cash += 200; // For passing "GO"
     action += "Passed go and collected $200. ";
   }
   // Advance pos
   for (int count = 1; count <= dieThrow; count++) {
     pos = pos.Next;
   }
   GlobalConstants.LogFile.WriteLine("Player " + number +
      " moved from position " + currentPosition +
      " to " + newPosition);
   GlobalConstants.LogFile.WriteLine(
      "Current investment strategy: " + strategy.ToString());
   int playerPosition = pos.PositionNumber;
   if (pos is PropertyPosition) {
     PropertyPosition propertyPosition = (PropertyPosition) pos;
     Player owner = ((PropertyPosition)pos).Owner;
     int cost = propertyPosition.Cost;
     if (owner == null) { // No one owns the property
        // Determine whether to purchase property
        if (strategy.BuyProperty(cost, this)) {
           propertyPosition.Owner = this;
           Cash -= cost / 2;
           action += "Purchased property for " + (cost / 2);
              OutputToLogFile1(cost);
        } else {
```

LISTING 6.7 Revised method Move in class Player (continued)

```
            action = "Could not purchase property";
            OutputToLogFile2(); // See data files for details
        }
    } else if (this == owner) { // player owns the property
        int unitsToPurchase =
            strategy.NumberOfUnitsToPurchase(cost, this);
        Cash -= unitsToPurchase * cost / 20;
        action += "Purchased " + unitsToPurchase +
                    " investment units for " +
                    (unitsToPurchase * cost / 20);
        propertyPosition.InvestmentUnits += unitsToPurchase;
        OutputToLogFile(propertyPosition, cost,
            unitsToPurchase); // see data files
    } else { // Must pay rent
        int investmentUnits = propertyPosition.InvestmentUnits;
        Cash -= (cost / 10 + investmentUnits * cost / 20);
        action += "Paying rent to " +
                    propertyPosition.Owner.Number + ".";
        propertyPosition.Owner.Cash +=
            (cost / 10 + investmentUnits * cost / 20);
        propertyPosition.RentCollected +=
                    (cost / 10 + investmentUnits * cost / 20);
        // See data files for OutputToLogFile3
        OutputToLogFile3(propertyPosition, cost, investmentUnits);
    }
} else if (pos is ChancePosition) {
    if (playerPosition == 4) {
        int chance = GlobalConstants.RandomValue.Next(-400, 201);
        Cash += chance;
        action +=
        "Chance position 4 causes change in cash to be " +
            chance;
        OutputToLogFile4(chance); // See data files
    } else {
        int chance = GlobalConstants.RandomValue.Next(-500, 301);
        Cash += chance;
        action +=
            "Chance position 7 causes change in cash to be " +
                chance;
            OutputToLogFile4(chance); // See data files
    }
} else if (pos is NewStrategyPosition) {
    action += "Change in investment strategy from " +
            strategy.ToString();
    ((NewStrategyPosition)pos).ChangeStrategy(this);
    action += " to " + strategy.ToString();
    OutputToLogFile5(); // See data files
```

LISTING 6.7 Revised method Move in class Player (continued)

```
    } else if (playerPosition == 8) {
       GlobalConstants.LogFile.WriteLine(
              "Landed on position 8. Must move again.");
       Move(moveCycle); // Recursive method invocation
    } else if (playerPosition == 1) {
       GlobalConstants.LogFile.WriteLine(
              "Landed on position 1 and collected $200.");
    }
  }
}
```

We observe first that the method, although still quite long, is significantly shorter than Listing 6.4. More importantly, all dependencies on the global arrays that were the centerpiece of the earlier implementations are gone.

Exercise 6.2

Explain in words, and in some detail, the revised class *Player* in Listing 6.7.

The new class *PropertyPosition* is presented in Listing 6.8.

LISTING 6.8 Class PropertyPosition

```
public class PropertyPosition : Position {
   // Fields
   private Player owner;
   private int investmentUnits;
   private int cost;
   private int rentCollected;
   // Constructor
   public PropertyPosition(int cost) {
      this.cost = cost;
   }
   // Queries
/* Get set properties Cost, InvestmentUnits, RentCollected and
 * owner—See Web site for code
 */

}
```

The same concern that was indicated earlier concerning class *Position*—that it contained only fields and get/set accessors—is raised again with class *PropertyPosition*. More refactoring will be needed.

Class *ChancePosition* is shown in Listing 6.9.

LISTING 6.9 Class ChancePosition

```
public class ChancePosition : Position {
   // Fields
   private int lowerBound, upperBound;
   // Constructor
   public ChancePosition(int lowerBound, int upperBound) {
     this.lowerBound = lowerBound;
     this.upperBound = upperBound;
   }
   // Read-only properties
   public int LowerBound {
     get {
        return lowerBound;
     }
   }
   public int UpperBound {
     get {
        return upperBound;
     }
   }
}
```

Finally, the simplified class *GlobalConstants* is shown in Listing 6.10.

LISTING 6.10 Revised class GlobalConstants

```
public class GlobalConstants {
   // Fields
   public static Random RandomValue = new Random();
   public static StreamWriter LogFile = new StreamWriter(
     new FileStream("Log.txt",
       FileMode.Create, FileAccess.Write));
   // Warmup the random number generator
   static GlobalConstants() {
     for (int i = 0; i < 100000; i++) {
       RandomValue.NextDouble();
     }
   }
   // Queries
   public static int DieThrow() {
     return RandomValue.Next(1, 7);
   }
}
```

The application class, *OOPLYApp*, is revised as well and is shown in Listing 6.11.

LISTING 6.11 Revised class OOPLYApp

```
/*
 *  Major changes made to system.  Removed classes
 *  Postion1 ... Postion10.
 *  Added interface InvestmentStrategy.
 *  Added class Position.
 *  Added class PropertyPosition.
 *  Added class ChancePosition.
 *  Added class NewStrategyPosition.
 *  Removed all of the global static arrays.
 *  The only global variables are RandomValue and LogFile
 */

using System;

namespace OOPLY3 {

    public class OOPLYApp {
        // Fields
        private Player[] player = new Player[5];
        private Position pos1, pos2, pos3, pos4, pos5, pos6, pos7,
                   pos8, pos9, pos10;

    static void Main() {
        OOPLYApp app = new OOPLYApp();
        int turn = 1;
        int moveCycle = 1;
        app.InitializeBoardPositions();
        app.InitializePlayers();
        app.AssignRandomStrategies();
        while (moveCycle <= 5000 && app.player[1].Cash > 0 &&
          app.player[2].Cash > 0 && app.player[3].Cash > 0 &&
          app.player[4].Cash > 0) {
          app.player[turn].Move(moveCycle);
          GlobalConstants.LogFile.WriteLine(
            "Summary of cash for each player: 1: $" +
              app.player[1].Cash + " 2: $" + app.player[2].Cash +
            " 3: $" + app.player[3].Cash +
            " 4: $" + app.player[4].Cash);
          turn++;
          if (turn == 5) {
            turn = 1;
            moveCycle++;
          }
        }

        GlobalConstants.LogFile.WriteLine();
        GlobalConstants.LogFile.WriteLine("GAME IS OVER.");
        GlobalConstants.LogFile.Close();
    }
}
```

LISTING 6.11 Revised class OOPLYApp (continued)

```
    private void InitializeBoardPositions() {
      pos1 = new Position();
      pos1.PositionNumber = 1;
      pos2 = new PropertyPosition(2000);
      pos2.PositionNumber = 2;
      pos1.Next = pos2;
      pos3 = new NewStrategyPosition(true);
      pos3.PositionNumber = 3;
      pos2.Next = pos3;
      pos4 = new ChancePosition(-300, 200);
      pos4.PositionNumber = 4;
      pos3.Next = pos4;
      pos5 = new PropertyPosition(500);
      pos5.PositionNumber = 5;
      pos4.Next = pos5;
      pos6 = new PropertyPosition(800);
      pos6.PositionNumber = 6;
      pos5.Next = pos6;
      pos7 = new ChancePosition(-500, 300);
      pos7.PositionNumber = 7;
      pos6.Next = pos7;
      pos8 = new Position();
      pos8.PositionNumber = 8;
      pos7.Next = pos8;
      pos9 = new PropertyPosition(1200);
      pos9.PositionNumber = 9;
      pos8.Next = pos9;
      pos10 = new NewStrategyPosition(false);
      pos10.PositionNumber = 10;
      pos9.Next = pos10;
      pos10.Next = pos1;
    }
    private void InitializePlayers() {
      for (int playerNumber = 1;
             playerNumber <= 4; playerNumber++) {
        player[playerNumber] = new Player(playerNumber, 5000);
        player[playerNumber].Pos = pos1;
      }
    }
    private void AssignRandomStrategies() {
      for (int playerNumber = 1; playerNumber <= 4;
             playerNumber++) {
        int outcome = GlobalConstants.RandomValue.Next(1, 4);
        if (outcome == 1) {
          player[playerNumber].Strategy = new RandomStrategy();
        } else if (outcome == 2) {
          player[playerNumber].Strategy =
            new AggressiveStrategy();
        } else {
```

LISTING 6.11 Revised class OOPLYApp (continued)

```
            player[playerNumber].Strategy =
              new ConservativeStrategy();
        }
      }
    }
  }
```

Exercise 6.3

Explain in words, and in some detail, the actions represented in class *OOPLYApp* in Listing 6.11.

Progress has been made with the major refactoring shown in the source listings presented in this section. Is more refactoring needed? If so, why?

We first examine the architecture of the system following the refactoring that has just been completed. This is shown in Figure 6.2.

A close examination of class *Player* in Listing 6.7 reveals that many of the important actions that a player takes in response to landing on a particular board position are done through the *Position* field held by the player. Some examples of such action through the *Position* object include:

```
if (pos is PropertyPosition) {
   PropertyPosition propertyPosition = (PropertyPosition) pos;
   Player owner = ((PropertyPosition)pos).Owner;
   int cost = propertyPosition.Cost;
   if (owner == null) { // No one owns the property
   // Determine whether to purchase property
     if (strategy.BuyProperty(cost, this)) {
       propertyPosition.Owner = this;
       propertyPosition.Owner.Cash +=
       cost / 10 + investmentUnits * cost / 20);
       propertyPosition.RentCollected +=
       cost / 10 + investmentUnits * cost / 20);
       ((NewStrategyPosition)pos).ChangeStrategy(this);
```

In the current evolution of the system, it is clear that player objects are in the driver's seat and position objects are subordinate to player objects. This is also evident in the class diagram in Figure 6.2. Yet as demonstrated earlier, many of the important player actions are achieved through the position object held by each player.

Before tackling these issues and doing another round of major refactoring, some minor refactoring is in order.

6.2.4 Minor Refactoring

The interface *InvestmentStrategy* is shown in the following code. It is held by each *Player* as a placeholder for a concrete investment strategy from one of the three concrete classes that implement this interface.

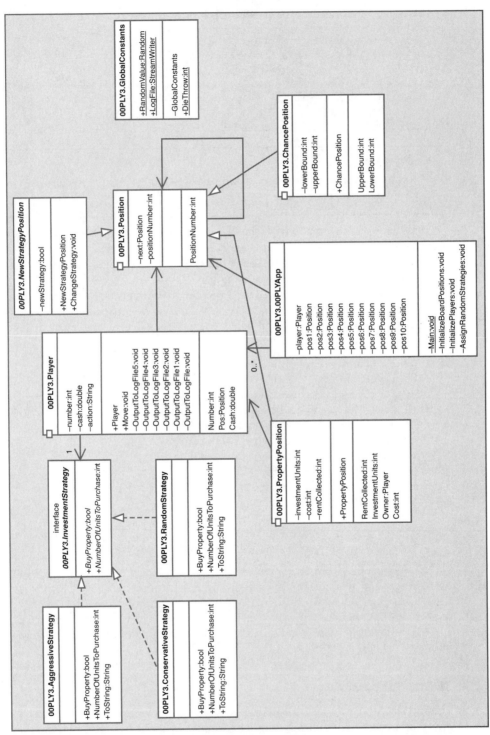

FIGURE 6.2 System after first major refactoring

```
public interface InvestmentStrategy {
   bool BuyProperty(double price, Player player);
   int NumberOfUnitsToPurchase(double price, Player player);
   String ToString();
}
```

We can reduce the number of parameters in each of the public methods from two to zero parameters if we convert this interface to an abstract class and include a field *holder*, of type *Player*. That is, each *InvestmentStrategy* object holds the *Player* that is attached to it.

The revised abstract class *InvestmentStrategy* is shown in Listing 6.12.

LISTING 6.12 New abstract class InvestmentStrategy

```
abstract public class InvestmentStrategy {
   // Fields
   private Player holder;
   // Constructor
   public InvestmentStrategy(Player holder) {
     this.holder = holder;
   }
   // Queries
   public Player Holder {
     get {
       return holder;
     }
     set {
       holder = value;
     }
   }
   public abstract bool BuyProperty();
   public abstract int NumberOfUnitsToPurchase();
}
```

One of the three concrete subclasses, *AggressiveStrategy*, is shown in Listing 6.13.

LISTING 6.13 Class AggressiveStrategy

```
public class AggressiveStrategy : InvestmentStrategy {
   // Constructor
   public AggressiveStrategy(Player holder) : base(holder) {
   }

   public override bool BuyProperty() {
     return Holder.Cash > ((PropertyPosition) Holder.Pos).Cost;
   }
   public override int NumberOfUnitsToPurchase() {
     int price = ((PropertyPosition)Holder.Pos).Cost;
     if (Holder.Cash > 5 * price / 2.0)
       return 5;
```

LISTING 6.13 Class AggressiveStrategy (continued)

```
      else if (Holder.Cash > 4 * price / 2.0)
        return 4;
      else if (Holder.Cash > 3 * price / 2.0)
        return 3;
      else if (Holder.Cash > 2 * price / 2.0)
        return 2;
      else if (Holder.Cash > price / 2.0)
        return 1;
      else
        return 0;
    }
    public override String ToString() {
      return "Aggressive Strategy";
    }
}
```

Exercise 6.4

By carefully inspecting Listing 6.13, explain how the two parameters that were previously present in the methods *BuyProperty* and *NumberOfUnitsToPurchase* are now absent.

6.2.5 Another Round of Major Refactoring

To overcome the problem about *Player* objects being dominant and *Position* objects subordinate, we add an abstract method *ProcessPlayer* to class *Position*, which now becomes an abstract class. This enables board positions to process the players that march across them rather than player objects having to process the position objects that they contain as they move across the board. This represents a major redesign of the system.

Listing 6.14 presents the revised abstract class *Position*.

LISTING 6.14 New abstract class Position

```
// Placeholder for hierarchy of position classes
abstract public class Position {
  // Fields
  private Position next; // Link to next position
  private int positionNumber;
  // Properties
  public Position Next {
    get {
      return next;
    }
    set {
      next = value;
```

LISTING 6.14 New abstract class Position (continued)

```
      }
    }
    public int PositionNumber {
      get {
        return positionNumber;
      }
      set {
        positionNumber = value;
      }
    }
    // Commands
    public abstract void ProcessPlayer(Player player);
    public void OutputToLogFile(Player player) {
      GlobalConstants.LogFile.WriteLine(
        "Owner: " + player.ToString());
    }
}
```

The benefits of this major change are immediately and dramatically evident in the revised class *Player* presented in Listing 6.15.

LISTING 6.15 Revised class Player

```
public class Player {
    // Fields
    private int number;
    private double cash;
    private Position pos;
    private InvestmentStrategy strategy;
    // Constructor
    public Player(int number, double cash) {
      this.number = number;
      this.cash = cash;
    }
    // Public get/set properties for cash, number, strategy and
    // pos not shown

    public override String ToString() {
      return "Player " + number;
    }
    // Commands
    public void Move(int moveCycle) {
      GlobalConstants.LogFile.WriteLine();
      GlobalConstants.LogFile.WriteLine("Move cycle: " +
        moveCycle);
        int currentPosition = pos.PositionNumber;
        int dieThrow = GlobalConstants.DieThrow();
```

LISTING 6.15 Revised class Player (continued)

```
      int newPosition = currentPosition + dieThrow;
      if (newPosition > 10) {
        newPosition -= 10;
        Cash += 200; // For passing "GO"
        GlobalConstants.LogFile.WriteLine(
          "Passed go and collected $200. ");
      }
      // Advance pos
      for (int count = 1; count <= dieThrow; count++) {
        pos = pos.Next;
      }
      GlobalConstants.LogFile.WriteLine(
        "Player " + number +
        " moved from position " + currentPosition +
        " to " + newPosition);
      GlobalConstants.LogFile.WriteLine(
        "Current investment strategy: " + strategy.ToString());
      pos.ProcessPlayer(this);
      int playerPosition = pos.PositionNumber;
      if (playerPosition == 8) {
          GlobalConstants.LogFile.WriteLine(
            "Landed on position 8. Must move again.");
          Move(moveCycle);
      } else if (playerPosition == 1) {
          GlobalConstants.LogFile.WriteLine(
            "Landed on position 1 and collected $200.");
      }
    }
  }
}
```

The following command yields control to the *Position* object that the player has just moved to and allows it to dominate the business between the two objects. This represents a major improvement and simplification in the design.

```
pos.ProcessPlayer(this);
```

Exercise 6.5

After examining the revised class *Player* in Listing 6.15, carefully explain the interaction between player objects and their current position.

The *ProcessPlayer* command in revised class *PropertyPosition* is shown in Listing 6.16.

LISTING 6.16 ProcessPlayer command in class PropertyPosition

```
public override void ProcessPlayer(Player player) {
  if (owner == null) {
    // Determine whether property can be purchased
    if (player.Strategy.BuyProperty()) {
      player.Cash -= cost;
      owner = player;
      GlobalConstants.LogFile.WriteLine("Purchased property");
      GlobalConstants.LogFile.WriteLine("Change in cash: -$" +
        cost);
    }
  } else if (owner == player) {
    // Determine whether investment units can be purchased
    int numberUnits = player.Strategy.NumberOfUnitsToPurchase();
    investmentUnits += numberUnits;
    player.Cash -= numberUnits * cost / 2.0;
    GlobalConstants.LogFile.WriteLine(
      "Purchased " + numberUnits +
      " investment units resulting in ownership of " +
      investmentUnits + " investment units.");
    GlobalConstants.LogFile.WriteLine(
      "Change in cash: -$" + numberUnits * cost / 2.0);
  } else if (owner != player) {
    // Determine the rent that must be paid to the owner
    int rent = cost / 10 + cost * investmentUnits / 20;
    owner.Cash += rent;
    player.Cash -= rent;
    RentCollected += rent;
    GlobalConstants.LogFile.WriteLine(
      "Property owned by " + owner.ToString());
    GlobalConstants.LogFile.WriteLine("Investment units: " +
      investmentUnits);
    GlobalConstants.LogFile.WriteLine(
      "Paid rent to player: " + owner.ToString());
    GlobalConstants.LogFile.WriteLine("Change in cash: -$" +
      rent);
  }
}
```

Most of the action in this method can now be accomplished using the data stored in the *Position* object. Only a few actions are done through the *Player* object that is passed as a parameter to this method.

Exercise 6.6

After examining the code in Listing 6.16, carefully explain how a property position object processes the player that has just landed on it.

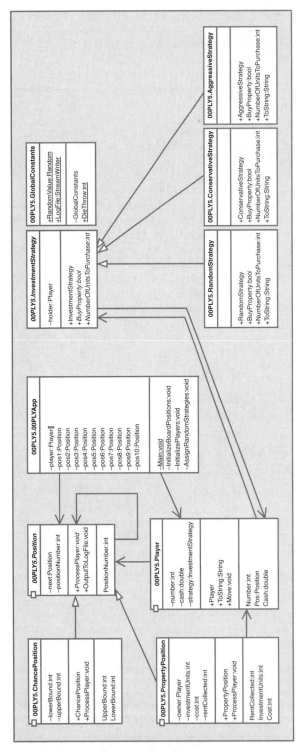

FIGURE 6.3 Bird's eye view of architecture

The *ProcessPlayer* method in class *ChancePosition* is given in Listing 6.17.

LISTING 6.17 Method ProcessPlayer in class ChancePosition

```
public override void ProcessPlayer(Player player) {
   int amountWon = GlobalConstants.RandomValue.Next(lowerBound,
                                               upperBound + 1);
   player.Cash += amountWon;
   GlobalConstants.LogFile.WriteLine(
     "Chance position (" + lowerBound + ", " + upperBound +
     ")");
   GlobalConstants.LogFile.WriteLine("Change in cash: $" +
     amountWon);
}
```

A revised UML diagram that shows the architecture of the system following this latest round of major refactoring is given in Figure 6.3.

6.3 SUMMARY

We have presented five solutions to the OOPLY game. The first two solutions use many global arrays and represent more of a structured approach than an object-oriented approach to programming.

The first major refactoring removes the system's reliance on the global arrays. The interaction between players and board positions is dominated by players. The final refactoring changes this relationship so that board positions are in the dominant positions when interacting with the players that move across them. This leads to dramatic simplification of the system.

The refactored system is significantly shorter than the original (please examine the full source listings for OOPLY5 and compare them to the full source listings for OOPLY1) and much easier to understand and maintain. This was accomplished without making any changes to the functionality of the system.

6.4 ADDITIONAL EXERCISES

To demonstrate the importance of refactoring in producing a simpler architecture, the following projects involve making small changes to the game specification and seeing how they can be handled using the original OOPLY1 implementation versus the final OOPLY5 implementation.

For each exercise, implement the revised specifications first using the source code in OOPLY1 and next using the source code in OOPLY5. Upon the completion of each mini-project, specified following, write a short summary of your impressions about which of the two architectures better supports the needed maintenance and why. As a prelude to doing these exercises, make sure you have the full source code for OOPLY1 and OOPLY5 in the Chapter 6 folder of the files provided with this book.

Exercise 6.7

Suppose an eleventh board position is introduced with the following specifications: The amount of cash that a player landing on this eleventh position is given equals 10 times the total of all rent receipts obtained to date from all properties held by the player landing on this position. The new board position connects back to position 1.

Exercise 6.8

Suppose a different eleventh board position from that of Exercise 6.7 is introduced with the following specifications: A player landing on this board position is entitled to take one-tenth the cash from each of the other three players. The new board position connects back to position 1.

Exercise 6.9

Another eleventh board position is introduced (in place of those suggested in Exercises 6.7 and 6.8) with specifications as follows: A player landing on this eleventh board position is allowed to immediately move to any of its current properties, if any, without collecting $200 for "passing go." Upon going to one of its current properties, it may purchase additional investment units according to the normal rules. You are free to formulate any reasonable algorithm for determining which particular property to go to if more than one is owned by the player. If no properties are owned by the player, it does not move from this new position.

Exercise 6.10

Two more additional players are introduced into the game. Implement the revised game with the original 10 board positions.

CHAPTER 7

Programming with Threads

C# and .NET support programming with threads. **Threads** provide a logical partitioning of processing into pseudo-parallel processes. On a single-processor computer, each thread is executed in a time slice (a predetermined and small interval of CPU time). On such a machine, threads compete for processor time. One thread may end up dominating all or most of the processor time. On multiple-processor computers, the operating system assigns threads to each processor and attempts to distribute the workload equally, leading to computational efficiency.

Modern operating systems use threads extensively. It is typical to have dozens of threads running at the same time performing background tasks. Supercomputers have been constructed that assign entire processes to separate processors. These machines allow complex computations to be performed in parallel. Parallel hardware architecture can be used to great advantage only if clever algorithms provide the basis for partitioning a problem into parallel pieces. The same is true of threads that provide pseudo-parallelism.

There are two dominant types of time slicing: cooperative and preemptive multitasking. In the latter, threads may be interrupted without their consent. In the former, a thread must yield control before it may be interrupted. Many UNIX systems use cooperative multitasking, whereas Windows uses preemptive multitasking. In a language like Java, which runs on both UNIX and Windows platforms, a threaded application may behave differently on each platform because of differences in the mode of time slicing. Because .NET and C# run mainly on Windows platforms, this may be less of a problem. There exists an implementation of .NET, Mono, that runs under Linux (*www.monoproject.com/about/index.html*). You need to be aware of the differences in time slicing and the effects that this can have on threaded programs if running .NET on another operating system.

Programming with threads is challenging and potentially rewarding. This chapter introduces and illustrates programming with threads. Because of the advanced nature of this subject, this chapter does not present the subject in its entirety, but focuses on the most important and basic aspects of programming with threads using C# and .NET.

7.1 CONSTRUCTING SIMPLE THREADS

Class *Thread* exists in the *System.Threading* namespace and cannot be extended. Therefore any class that uses threads must create thread objects within the class. Listing 7.1 demonstrates how to spawn two simple threads within a C# application.

LISTING 7.1 Spawning two simple threads

```
using System;
using System.Threading;
namespace SimpleThreads {

    public class SpawningThreadsApp {
```

LISTING 7.1 Spawning two simple threads (continued)

```
    //Fields
    private Thread thread1;
    private Thread thread2;

    private void Method1() {
      for (int i = 0; i < 10; i++) {
        Console.WriteLine("i = " + i);
        Thread.Sleep(200); // 200 milliseconds pause
      }
    }

    private void Method2() {
      for (int i = 0; i < 10; i++) {
        Console.WriteLine("i = " + 100 * i);
        Thread.Sleep(100); // 100 milliseconds pause
      }
    }

    static void Main(string[] args) {
      SpawningThreadsApp app = new SpawningThreadsApp();
      app.thread1 = new Thread(new ThreadStart(app.Method1));
      app.thread2 = new Thread(new ThreadStart(app.Method2));
      app.thread1.Start();
      app.thread2.Start();
      Console.ReadLine();
    }
  }
}
/* Program output
i = 0
i = 0
i = 100
i = 1
i = 200
i = 300
i = 2
i = 400
i = 500
i = 3
i = 600
i = 700
i = 4
i = 800
i = 900
i = 5
i = 6
i = 7
i = 8
i = 9
*/
```

The two methods, *Method1* and *Method2*, each serve as threads in Listing 7.1. Fields *thread1* and *thread2* are initialized as thread objects in method *Main*.

Consider field *thread1*. It is brought to life as a thread object using the following statement:

```
app.thread1 = new Thread(new ThreadStart(app.Method1));
```

The *Thread* constructor expects an instance of the *ThreadStart* delegate, a method that has no parameters and returns void. This delegate object is constructed using the *ThreadStart* delegate constructor and the name of the method that is to serve as a thread. Because delegates are the subject of Chapter 8, no further explanation of delegates will be made here. For now, note that the name of a method whose signature contains no parameters and that returns void (*Method* in this case) must be passed as a parameter using the idiom of programming shown in Listing 7.1. If an attempt were made to pass a method that contains one or more parameters or returns anything other than void, the compiler would flag this as an error.

When a thread variable is brought to life as a thread object, as shown in the preceding line of code, the thread must still be started. This is accomplished by invoking the *Start* command on the thread object as shown in method *Main* of Listing 7.1.

In general, the following code serves as programming mechanism for creating a thread object and then starting it:

```
Thread threadObject = new Thread(new
                    ThreadStart(NameOfThreadMethod));
threadObject.Start();
```

Each of the threads in Listing 7.1 (*Method1* and *Method2*) runs for loops that output the values from 0 to 9 in increments of 1 and from 0 to 900 in increments of 100. Punctuating each for loop is a static method, *Thread.Sleep*, that pauses the execution of the loop and provides the practical benefit that during this pause, the thread controller can pass control to the other competing thread.

Exercise 7.1

What would the output of Listing 7.1 be if both *Thread.Sleep* commands were removed from the for loops?

The program output shows the predisposition of the *Method2* thread to dominate because the *Method1* thread pauses for twice the duration as the *Method2* thread.

Consider another example that involves the relatively simple use of threads. Suppose you want to have a clock thread notify the console every second by posting the time and the progress of a meaningful computation that is taking place. This allows the progress of the computation to be displayed on the console every second.

We demonstrate this by implementing a computational process that involves filling a list with prime numbers that are equal to or greater than 10,000,000,000,001. We choose such a large starting value to ensure that the computational effort is significant and takes place "in parallel" with the clock that outputs the progress of the computation.

The size of the emerging list of very large prime numbers is output along with the time every second.

First consider the following method that models the computational process (which will become a thread once the pieces are put together):

```
public void ComputeLargePrimes() {
    decimal potentialPrime = 10000000000001;
    bool isPrime = true;
    while (time < thresholdTime) {
    // time controlled by clock thread
      decimal trialDivisor = 3;
      isPrime = true;
      while (isPrime &&
         (double) trialDivisor <=
          Math.Sqrt((double) potentialPrime)) {
        if (potentialPrime % trialDivisor == 0) {
          isPrime = false;
        }
        trialDivisor += 2;
      }
      if (isPrime) {
        largePrimes.Add(potentialPrime);
      }
      potentialPrime += 2;
    }
    this.OutputPrimes();
}
```

We start with the tentative assumption that the potential prime number is prime. As odd-valued trial divisors are generated, starting with 3 and ending with the square root of the potential prime number, if a trial divisor is found that divides evenly into the potential prime, the value of *isPrime* is changed to false and a new potential prime number is generated. If no trial divisor is found that divides with zero remainder into the potential prime number, the potential prime number is added to the list, *largePrimes*, of decimal values.

Exercise 7.2

Explain why the trial divisors in method *ComputeLargePrimes* have an upper bound equal to the square root of the potential prime number.

Listing 7.2 presents the complete application that creates the computation and clock threads.

LISTING 7.2 Progress of computation using a clock thread

```csharp
using System;
using System.Threading;
using System.Collections.Generic;

namespace ComputationClockThread {

    public class BigPrimes {

        // Field
        private List<decimal> largePrimes = new List<decimal>();
        private int thresholdTime;
        private int time = 0;
        private Thread thread1, thread2;

        // Constructor
        public BigPrimes(int thresholdTime) {
            this.thresholdTime = thresholdTime;
            thread1 = new Thread(new ThreadStart(Clock));
            thread2 = new Thread(new ThreadStart(ComputeLargePrimes));
            thread1.Start();
            thread2.Start();
        }

        // Method threads
        public void ComputeLargePrimes() {
            decimal potentialPrime = 10000000000001;
            bool isPrime = true;
            while (time < thresholdTime) {
                decimal trialDivisor = 3;
                isPrime = true;
                while (isPrime &&
                        (double) trialDivisor <=
                        Math.Sqrt((double) potentialPrime)) {
                    if (potentialPrime % trialDivisor == 0) {
                        isPrime = false;
                    }
                    trialDivisor += 2;
                }
                if (isPrime) {
                    largePrimes.Add(potentialPrime);
                }
                potentialPrime += 2;
            }
            this.OutputPrimes();
        }
```

LISTING 7.2 Progress of computation using a clock thread (continued)

```
      public void Clock() {
        while (time < thresholdTime) {
          Thread.Sleep(1000); // Pause for one second
          time++;
          Console.Write("Time: " + time);
          Console.WriteLine(
          " Size of list of big primes: " + largePrimes.Count);
        }
      }

      public void OutputPrimes() {
        Console.Write("Time: " + time);
        Console.WriteLine(
        " Size of list of big primes: " + largePrimes.Count);
        foreach (decimal value in largePrimes) {
          Console.WriteLine(value);
        }
        Console.ReadLine();
      }
    }

    public class PrimeApplication {
      public static void Main() {
        BigPrimes bigPrimes = new BigPrimes(20);
      }
    }
}
/* Output
Time: 1   Size of list of big primes: 0
Time: 2   Size of list of big primes: 1
Time: 3   Size of list of big primes: 2
Time: 4   Size of list of big primes: 2
Time: 5   Size of list of big primes: 2
Time: 6   Size of list of big primes: 3
Time: 7   Size of list of big primes: 4
Time: 8   Size of list of big primes: 4
Time: 9   Size of list of big primes: 5
Time: 10  Size of list of big primes: 5
Time: 11  Size of list of big primes: 6
Time: 12  Size of list of big primes: 7
Time: 13  Size of list of big primes: 8
Time: 14  Size of list of big primes: 8
Time: 15  Size of list of big primes: 9
Time: 16  Size of list of big primes: 10
Time: 17  Size of list of big primes: 10
Time: 18  Size of list of big primes: 11
Time: 19  Size of list of big primes: 11
Time: 20  Size of list of big primes: 12
Time: 20  Size of list of big primes: 13
```

LISTING 7.2 Progress of computation using a clock thread (continued)

```
10000000000037
10000000000051
10000000000099
10000000000129
10000000000183
10000000000259
10000000000267
10000000000273
10000000000279
10000000000283
10000000000313
10000000000343
10000000000391
*/
```

The fields of class *BigPrimes* include a generic *List* with base-type *decimal* specified. Two thread fields are also defined and have default values of null, like all reference type fields. Finally, fields *thresholdTime* and *time* are defined.

The constructor in class *BigPrimes* takes as input the threshold time and assigns it to the field of the same name. The two methods *Clock* and *ComputeLargePrimes* are defined as program code to be executed by the thread objects *thread1* and *thread2*. Following this initialization, both threads are started.

The *Clock* method (thread1) executes a while loop that terminates when the *time* field is no longer less than the value of *thresholdTime*. Within this loop, a pause of 1000 milliseconds (1 second) occurs. Then the *time* value is incremented by one. Then the current time and the size of the *largePrimes* list is displayed on the console.

Method *Main* in class *PrimeApplication* creates an instance of *BigPrimes* passing the value 20 as parameter.

Exercise 7.3

Estimate how many prime numbers would be output in 20 seconds if the first potential prime number were ten times as large. Modify the source code in Listing 7.2 and see how good your estimate was.

Exercise 7.4

Write a C# application that has five threads running at the same time. Each thread displays on the console the following five strings ten times each: "AAA", "BBB", "CCC", "DDD", "EEE". Write the application so that the output gives roughly equal priority to each of the five threads and the outputs from each are interleaved.

7.2 THE LOCK CONSTRUCT

When two or more threads are accessing data that is available to each thread, you often need to control access to the data to prevent one thread from writing to the common data while another is reading the common data.

C# and .NET provide constructs for controlling such thread access and making the use of such threads safe. You can use a **lock** block within a thread. The structure of this block is the following:

```
lock (anObject) {
    // Code in the block
}
```

The locked object, *anObject*, cannot have its value changed by another thread while the code in the block is executed. It is called a mutually exclusive lock or mutex lock. The lock is released when the block is exited. Then another thread can lock the same object.

All the fields within a class containing a thread can be locked using code similar to the following:

```
lock(this) {
    // Code in the block
}
```

To illustrate the use of the locks, we construct an application that spawns three threads. Each thread has access to a list of integers. The first thread adds the value 1 to the list every half second. The second thread removes an integer in the list every second. The third thread sums the numbers in the list every five seconds. Listing 7.3 presents this application.

The field *commonData* is a *List* with *int* as the base-type. The field *sumOfCommonData* is set by the thread *SumCommonData*. The constructor initializes and starts the three threads. The *InsertIntegers* thread adds the value one 30 times at intervals of one-half second. The *RemoveIntegers* thread removes the 30 integers at intervals of one second. The *SumCommonData* thread forms the sum of the values in *List* every five seconds.

Within each thread, the *commonData* object that is shared by the three threads is locked while the appropriate operation is performed. This prevents the *foreach* iterator in the *SumCommonData* thread from failing because the number of elements within *List* has changed while the summation is taking place. If you were to remove the locks from the threads such a failure is guaranteed.

LISTING 7.3 Use of locks

```
using System;
using System.Collections.Generic;
using System.Threading;

namespace SynchronizingAccess {

    public class InformationAccess {

        // Fields
        private List<int> commonData = new List<int>();
        private int sumOfCommonData; // Computed in SumCommonData
```

LISTING 7.3 Use of locks (continued)

```
    private Thread thread1, thread2, thread3;

    // Constructor
    public InformationAccess() {
      thread1 = new Thread(new ThreadStart(InsertIntegers));
      thread2 = new Thread(new ThreadStart(SumCommonData));
      thread3 = new Thread(new ThreadStart(RemoveIntegers));
      thread1.Start();
      thread2.Start();
      thread3.Start();
    }

    // Thread commands
    public void InsertIntegers() {
      for (int index = 1; index <= 30; index++) {
        lock (commonData) {
          commonData.Add(1);
        }
        Thread.Sleep(500); // Add number 1 every 1/2 second
      }
    }

    public void RemoveIntegers() {
      for (int index = 1; index <= 30; index++) {
        lock (commonData) {
          commonData.RemoveAt(0);
        }
        Thread.Sleep(1000);
        // Remove number from commonData every second
      }
    }

    public void SumCommonData() {
      for (;;) {
        lock (commonData) {
          sumOfCommonData = 0;
          foreach (int value in commonData) {
            sumOfCommonData += value;
          }
        }
        Console.WriteLine("Sum: " + sumOfCommonData);
        Thread.Sleep(5000); // Perform sum every 5 seconds
      }
    }
    static void Main() {
      InformationAccess app = new InformationAccess();
    }
  }
}
```

LISTING 7.3 Use of locks (continued)

```
/* Output
Sum:  1
Sum:  4
Sum:  10
Sum:  15
Sum:  9
Sum:  4
Sum:  0
Sum:  0
Sum:  0
*/
```

Exercise 7.5

After carefully examining the code in Listing 7.3, explain the output shown.

Locks are used in general to protect a thread that is accessing a critical section of code from the intrusion of another thread. When the critical section of code is completed and the lock is released, the runtime system selects one of the waiting threads, allows it to enter the critical section, and relocks the critical section until the critical section is completed.

7.3 CLASS MONITOR

Class *Monitor* in namespace *System.Threading* contains useful static methods for controlling threaded access to critical sections of code. An instance of the *Monitor* class cannot be created.

Static commands that can be invoked through class *Monitor* include the following:

- *Enter(Object obj)*—Acquires an exclusive lock on the object, obj
- *Exit(Object obj)*—Releases the lock on the object, obj
- *Pulse(Object obj)*—Notifies a thread that is waiting to acquire a lock on the object about the state of the object
- *PulseAll(Object obj)*—Notifies all threads waiting to acquire a lock on the object about the state of the object
- *bool TryEnter(Object obj)*—Attempts to set a lock on the object; the return value determines whether the lock has been obtained
- *bool TryEnter(Object obj, int millisecondsTimeout)*—Attempts, for the specified time, to acquire a lock on the object
- *bool Wait(Object obj)*—Releases a lock on the object and blocks the current thread until a new lock is acquired later
- *bool Wait(Object obj, int millisecondsTimeout)*—Releases the lock on the object and blocks the current thread until it reacquires the lock or the specified time elapses

The combination of *Enter* and *Exit* simulates the *lock* construct. The use of some of these constructs are illustrated in the next section.

7.4 DEADLOCKS

As indicated at the beginning of this chapter, programming with threads can be challenging. One of the basic challenges of developing a multithreaded application is coping with the presence of deadlocks. As the name implies, a deadlock occurs when two threads are in a blocked state, each waiting for the other to complete a task, with neither thread able to complete the task. The consequence is that program execution comes to a stop and the application stops running.

Next is a classic demonstration of deadlock. The example has been presented in many forms with many names (including mailbox and producer/consumer).

As in the book *Modern Software Development Using Java* by Tymann and Scheider (Brooks/Cole, 2004), the following example uses the producer/consumer model. Figure 7.1 is inspired by the one that appears in Chapter 11 of this book.

The Buffer allows the producer to add an object and the Consumer can remove an object from the Buffer.

Consider the generic interface *Buffer*, given in Listing 7.4. An object of "generic" type T is specified as a parameter.

LISTING 7.4 Interface Buffer

```
// Provides a connection between a producer and consumer
interface Buffer<T> {
  // Adds an item if the buffer is empty
    void Add(T obj);
  // Removes an item if the buffer is not empty
    void Remove();
}
```

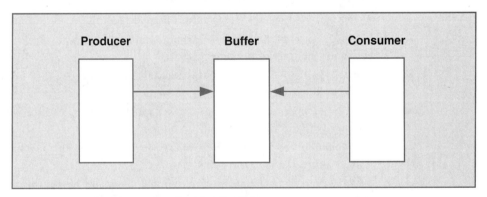

FIGURE 7.1 Producer/consumer model

Listing 7.5 presents a concrete implementation, *BufferWithDeadlock*, of this generic class.

LISTING 7.5 Class BufferWithDeadlock

```
public class BufferWithDeadlock<T> : Buffer<T> {
  // Fields
  private T item;         // Item currently held in the buffer
  private bool isEmpty = true;
     // Returns true if the buffer is empty
     // Commands
  public void Add(T item) {
    lock (this) {
      // Do nothing while the buffer is not empty
      while (!isEmpty) {
          ;
      }

      this.item = item;
      isEmpty = false;
      Console.WriteLine("Just added item to buffer.");
    }
  }

  public void Remove() {
    lock (this) {
      // Do nothing while the buffer is empty
      while (isEmpty) {
          ;
      }

      isEmpty = true;
      item = default(T); // null if T is a reference type
      Console.WriteLine("Just removed item from buffer.");
    }
  }

  // Property query
  public T Item {
    get {
        return item;
    }
  }
}
```

Finally a short application class, *BufferApplication*, is shown in Listing 7.6. Although this simple application does not spawn any threads, it does illustrate the deadlock fault that is designed into class Buffer.

LISTING 7.6 Class BufferApplication

```
public class BufferApplication {
   public static void Main() {
      BufferWithDeadlock<int> buffer =
         new BufferWithDeadlock<int>();
      buffer.Add(20);
      buffer.Remove();
      buffer.Remove();   // Causes deadlock
      buffer.Add(15);
      Console.ReadLine();
   }
}
```

The second *Remove* invocation puts the system into deadlock. The lock is acquired by the *Remove* method. The while loop continues to run as long as the buffer is empty. This lock makes it impossible for an item to be added to the buffer. The application stalls because of this deadlock.

Exercise 7.6

Explain how method *Add* in class *BufferWithDeadlock* works.

Exercise 7.7

Explain how method *Remove* in class *BufferWithDeadlock* works.

Exercise 7.8

What changes would you make to class *BufferWithDeadlock* to ensure that no deadlock occurs?

7.5 SYNCHRONIZATION

A lock may be placed on an object to secure a critical section (the block that is locked) from other threads that also want to access the critical section. Such locks should be used only when needed because they impose a performance penalty. This section introduces and illustrates the use of additional constructs that support the synchronization of multiple threads.

Consider first the *Join* command. This method, invoked on a thread object, may be used to detect when the thread terminates. The method *Join* is overloaded. All versions return a Boolean (*bool*). The value returned is true if the thread receiving the *Join* command terminated and false if it timed out.

A one-parameter version of *Join* has the following signature:

bool Join (int millisecondTimeout)

A typical usage is shown in the following code:

```
if (someThread.Join(1000)) {
    // Some action
} else {
    // Some other action
}
```

The *if* block is executed if *someThread* terminates within one second; otherwise the *else* block is executed indicating that *someThread* timed out after one second.

When the version of *Join* without parameters is invoked on a thread, the calling thread is blocked until the receiving thread (thread receiving the *Join* command) is terminated. When a time-out parameter is used, the calling thread is blocked until the receiving thread is terminated or the time-out has been completed.

The next few source listings explore the effect of *Join*. Listing 7.7 defines two threads, *thread1* and *thread2*, associated with methods *ThreadMethod1* and *ThreadMethod2*, that output consecutive integers from 0 to 24 using a for loop.

The output shows that each thread takes control and produces a partial output of the consecutive integers from 0 to 24. Specifically, *thread1* outputs the values from 0 to 6 before *thread2* takes over and outputs its values from 0 to 4. *Thread1* takes over again and continues its output from 7 to 23, then *thread2* continues its output from 5 to 24, completing its work, and finally *thread1* outputs its last value, 24.

LISTING 7.7 Two threads without join

```
using System;
using System.Threading;

namespace ExploringJoin {

    public class JoinApplication {

        // Fields
        private Thread thread1, thread2;

        // Constructor
        public JoinApplication() {
            thread1 = new Thread(new ThreadStart(ThreadMethod1));
            thread2 = new Thread(new ThreadStart(ThreadMethod2));
            thread1.Start();
            thread2.Start();
        }

        public void ThreadMethod1() {
            for (int i = 0; i < 25; i++) {
                Console.WriteLine("In ThreadMethod1: i = " + i);
            }
        }
```

LISTING 7.7 Two threads without join (continued)

```
      public void ThreadMethod2() {
        for (int i = 0; i < 25; i++) {
            Console.WriteLine("In ThreadMethod2: i = " + i);
        }
      }

      static void Main() {
        JoinApplication app = new JoinApplication();
        Console.ReadLine();
      }
    }
}
/* Output
In ThreadMethod1: i = 0
In ThreadMethod1: i = 1
In ThreadMethod1: i = 2
In ThreadMethod1: i = 3
In ThreadMethod1: i = 4
In ThreadMethod1: i = 5
In ThreadMethod1: i = 6
In ThreadMethod2: i = 0
In ThreadMethod2: i = 1
In ThreadMethod2: i = 2
In ThreadMethod2: i = 3
In ThreadMethod2: i = 4
In ThreadMethod1: i = 7
In ThreadMethod1: i = 8
In ThreadMethod1: i = 9
In ThreadMethod1: i = 10
In ThreadMethod1: i = 11
In ThreadMethod1: i = 12
In ThreadMethod1: i = 13
In ThreadMethod1: i = 14
In ThreadMethod1: i = 15
In ThreadMethod1: i = 16
In ThreadMethod1: i = 17
In ThreadMethod1: i = 18
In ThreadMethod1: i = 19
In ThreadMethod1: i = 20
In ThreadMethod1: i = 21
In ThreadMethod1: i = 22
In ThreadMethod1: i = 23
In ThreadMethod2: i = 5
In ThreadMethod2: i = 6
In ThreadMethod2: i = 7
In ThreadMethod2: i = 8
In ThreadMethod2: i = 9
In ThreadMethod2: i = 10
In ThreadMethod2: i = 11
```

LISTING 7.7 Two threads without join (continued)

```
In ThreadMethod2:  i = 12
In ThreadMethod2:  i = 13
In ThreadMethod2:  i = 14
In ThreadMethod2:  i = 15
In ThreadMethod2:  i = 16
In ThreadMethod2:  i = 17
In ThreadMethod2:  i = 18
In ThreadMethod2:  i = 19
In ThreadMethod2:  i = 20
In ThreadMethod2:  i = 21
In ThreadMethod2:  i = 22
In ThreadMethod2:  i = 23
In ThreadMethod2:  i = 24
In ThreadMethod1:  i = 24
*/
```

Suppose the following line of code is added to the constructor in Listing 7.7:

```
thread1.Join();
```

That causes *thread1* first to output all its values from 0 to 24 followed by *thread2* doing the same. No interleaving of output from the two threads occurs.

The effect of the *Join* command invoked on *thread1* is to cause *thread2* to wait until *thread1* has terminated.

Table 7.1 presents the various states of a C# thread.

TABLE 7.1 States of a C# thread

Thread State (Enumeration)	Meaning
Aborted	The thread is stopped.
AbortRequested	Abort() has been invoked but the thread is still running.
Background	The thread terminates when the thread that spawned it terminates.
Running	The thread is running.
Stopped	The thread has been terminated.
Suspended	The thread has been suspended by the Suspend() command.
SuspendRequested	The thread has received the Suspend() command but is still running.
Unstarted	The thread has been initialized but has not received the Start() command.
WaitSleepJoin	The thread has been blocked because it has received either Wait or Sleep or has invoked Join on another thread.

The methods *Abort* and *Suspend* have the potential to create deadlocks or put a locked object into an inconsistent state. Instead of suspending or halting a thread using these methods, use global switches (fields of type *bool*) that may be set by other threads to accomplish these goals. These methods have been deprecated in .NET 2005.

Listing 7.8 continues exploring synchronization by examining a more complex application.

LISTING 7.8 Application that uses Monitor commands

```
using System;
using System.Threading;
using System.Collections;

namespace MonitorDemonstration {

    public class MonitorApplication {

        const int loopUpperBound = 10;

        // Fields
        private ArrayList list;

        // Constructor
        public MonitorApplication() {
            list = new ArrayList();
        }

        // Threads
        public void FirstThread() {
            int index = 0;

            lock (list) {
                while (index < loopUpperBound) {
                    /* Join the queue of threads wishing to lock the
                    list if the list is busy. */
                    Monitor.Wait(list);   // Released by PulseAll

                    // Add three elements
                    list.Add(index);
                    Console.WriteLine("FirstThread(): list.Add(" +
                            index + ")");
                    index++;
                    list.Add(index);
                    Console.WriteLine("FirstThread(): list.Add(" +
                            index + ")");
                    index++;
                    list.Add(index);
                    Console.WriteLine("FirstThread(): list.Add(" +
                            index + ")");
```

LISTING 7.8 Application that uses Monitor commands (continued)

```
              // Allow all waiting threads to compete
              Monitor.PulseAll(list);
              index++;
        }
    }
}

public void SecondThread() {
  lock (list) {
    // Allow all waiting threads to compete
    Monitor.PulseAll(list);

    // Wait in the loop, while the list is busy.
    // Exit on the time-out if no Pulse is received
    while (Monitor.Wait(list, 1000)) {
      // Remove the first element
      int value = (int) list[0];
      list.RemoveAt(0);
      Console.WriteLine(
  "SecondThread(): list.RemoveAt(0). Value removed = " +
          value.ToString());
      // Remove the first element
      value = (int)list[0];
      list.RemoveAt(0);
      Console.WriteLine(
  "SecondThread(): list.RemoveAt(0). Value removed = " +
          value.ToString());
      // Remove the first element
      value = (int)list[0];

      list.RemoveAt(0);
      Console.WriteLine(
  "SecondThread(): list.RemoveAt(0). Value removed = " +
          value.ToString());

      // Release the waiting thread.
      Monitor.PulseAll(list);
    }
  }
}

public void ThirdThread() {
  int index = 0;

  lock (list) {
    while (index < loopUpperBound) {
      /* Join the queue of threads wishing to lock the
         list */
      // if the list is busy.
```

LISTING 7.8 Application that uses Monitor commands (continued)

```
        Monitor.Wait(list, 100);

        //Push two elements
        list.Add(index);
        Console.WriteLine("ThirdThread(): list.Add(" +
                index + ")");
        index++;
        list.Add(index);
        Console.WriteLine("ThirdThread(): list.Add(" +
                index + ")");
        index++;
        list.Add(index);
        Console.WriteLine("ThirdThread(): list.Add(" +
                index + ")");

        // Release the waiting thread.
        Monitor.PulseAll(list);
        index++;
      }
    }
  }

// Queries
public int ArrayCount() {
  return list.Count;
}

static void Main() {
  // Create the MonitorSample object
  MonitorApplication app = new MonitorApplication();

  // Create the first thread
  Thread firstThread =
  new Thread(new ThreadStart(app.FirstThread));

  // Create the second thread
  Thread secondThread =
    new Thread(new ThreadStart(app.SecondThread));

  // Create the third thread
  Thread thirdThread =
    new Thread(new ThreadStart(app.ThirdThread));

  // Start threads
  firstThread.Start();
  secondThread.Start();
  thirdThread.Start();
```

LISTING 7.8 Application that uses Monitor commands (continued)

```
        // Wait to the end of the three threads
        firstThread.Join();
        secondThread.Join();
        thirdThread.Join();

        // Print the number of queue elements.
        Console.WriteLine("Array Count = " +
            app.ArrayCount().ToString());
      }
    }
}
/* Output
FirstThread(): list.Add(0)
FirstThread(): list.Add(1)
FirstThread(): list.Add(2)
SecondThread(): list.RemoveAt(0). Value removed = 0
SecondThread(): list.RemoveAt(0). Value removed = 1
SecondThread(): list.RemoveAt(0). Value removed = 2
FirstThread(): list.Add(3)
FirstThread(): list.Add(4)
FirstThread(): list.Add(5)
SecondThread(): list.RemoveAt(0). Value removed = 3
SecondThread(): list.RemoveAt(0). Value removed = 4
SecondThread(): list.RemoveAt(0). Value removed = 5
FirstThread(): list.Add(6)
FirstThread(): list.Add(7)
FirstThread(): list.Add(8)
SecondThread(): list.RemoveAt(0). Value removed = 6
SecondThread(): list.RemoveAt(0). Value removed = 7
SecondThread(): list.RemoveAt(0). Value removed = 8
FirstThread(): list.Add(9)
FirstThread(): list.Add(10)
FirstThread(): list.Add(11)
SecondThread(): list.RemoveAt(0). Value removed = 9
SecondThread(): list.RemoveAt(0). Value removed = 10
SecondThread(): list.RemoveAt(0). Value removed = 11
ThirdThread(): list.Add(0)
ThirdThread(): list.Add(1)
ThirdThread(): list.Add(2)
SecondThread(): list.RemoveAt(0). Value removed = 0
SecondThread(): list.RemoveAt(0). Value removed = 1
SecondThread(): list.RemoveAt(0). Value removed = 2
ThirdThread(): list.Add(3)
ThirdThread(): list.Add(4)
ThirdThread(): list.Add(5)
SecondThread(): list.RemoveAt(0). Value removed = 3
SecondThread(): list.RemoveAt(0). Value removed = 4
SecondThread(): list.RemoveAt(0). Value removed = 5
ThirdThread(): list.Add(6)
```

LISTING 7.8 Application that uses Monitor commands (continued)

```
ThirdThread(): list.Add(7)
ThirdThread(): list.Add(8)
SecondThread(): list.RemoveAt(0). Value removed = 6
SecondThread(): list.RemoveAt(0). Value removed = 7
SecondThread(): list.RemoveAt(0). Value removed = 8
ThirdThread(): list.Add(9)
ThirdThread(): list.Add(10)
ThirdThread(): list.Add(11)
SecondThread(): list.RemoveAt(0). Value removed = 9
SecondThread(): list.RemoveAt(0). Value removed = 10
SecondThread(): list.RemoveAt(0). Value removed = 11
Array Count = 0
*/
```

Exercise 7.9

Carefully explain the operation of the application in Listing 7.8.

Exercise 7.10

What would the consequence of removing the three *Join* operations in method *Main* be and why?

Exercise 7.11

What would the consequence of removing all the static *Monitor* methods in addition to removing the three *Join* operations in method *Main* be and why?

7.6 EVENT LISTENER AND NOTIFICATION APPLICATION USING THREADS

Threads are often used in applications that notify listener objects that some event has occurred. In Part 3 of this book, you examine such applications in considerable detail. A listener object, as its name implies, listens for an event notification and then executes an action in response to this event notification. This section informally introduces the context of event notification using threads without presenting all of the formal machinery that will be introduced in Part 3 of the book.

We start by defining an interface, *INotification*, in a namespace *Notification*. All additional classes presented in this section are also assumed to be defined in this same namespace.

Listing 7.9 presents the *INotification* interface.

LISTING 7.9 Interface INotification

```
namespace Notification {
  public interface INotification {
    void NotificationReceived(NotificationEvent e);
  }
}
```

The method *NotificationReceived*, in interface *INotification*, has a parameter, *e*, of type *NotificationEvent*. Listing 7.10 presents the details of this class.

LISTING 7.10 Class NotificationEvent

```
public class NotificationEvent {
  // Fields
  private int eventValue; // The event value
  private Object source;

  // Constructor
  public NotificationEvent(Object source, int eventValue) {
    this.eventValue = eventValue;
    this.source = source;
  }

  // Property
  public int EventValue {
    get {
      return eventValue;
    }
  }
}
```

An object of type *NotificationEvent* contains an integer eventValue and a source of type generic placeholder type *Object*.

The general nature of class *NotificationEvent* allows it to be used to transmit general information from an event source to an event listener.

Class *Notify* is presented in Listing 7.11. It contains a *listener* field of type *INotification*. The *listener* is assigned using the command *AddNotificationListener*.

When an instance of *Notify* is created, its constructor initializes a thread that executes the *NotifyMethod* block of code. When a listener is defined through the *AddNotificationListener* command, the thread is started. This thread generates a *NotificationEvent* every 600 milliseconds and passes this event as a parameter to a *NotificationReceived* method that is invoked on the listener object. The *Notify* object, *this*, and the current count, updated every 200 milliseconds, are used to construct the *NotificationEvent* passed to the listener object.

Class *Listener*, shown in Listing 7.12, responds to this event.

LISTING 7.11 Class Notify

```
public class Notify {
  // Fields
  private int count = 0;
  private INotification listener = null;
  private Thread thread;

  // Constructor
  public Notify() {
    thread = new Thread(new ThreadStart(NotifyThread));
  }

  // Commands
  public void NotifyThread() {
    for (; ; ) { // Infinite loop
      Thread.Sleep(200);
      count++;

      // Fire an event every third time
      if (count % 3 == 0) {
        Console.WriteLine("value = " + count);

        // Fire the event
        if (listener != null) {
          listener.NotificationReceived(
            new NotificationEvent(this, count));
        } else {
          Console.WriteLine("listener = null");
        }
      }
    }
  }

  public void AddNotificationListener(INotification listener) {
    if (this.listener == null) { // Allow only one listener
      this.listener = listener;
      thread.Start();
    }
  }

  public void RemoveNotificationListener(INotification listener) {
    if (this.listener != null) {
      listener = null;
    }
  }
}
```

Class *Listener* contains and creates an instance, *notify*, of class *Notify*. It registers itself (using *this*) as the listener to the notify object. As soon as the registration is performed through *notify.AddNotificationListener(this)*, *NotifyThread* starts.

The *Listener* event handler, *NotificationReceived*, displays the event number extracted from the *NotificationEvent* object on the console and simulates computational work that takes two seconds using the *Thread.Sleep(2000)* command.

This is a common scenario involving an event notifier that invokes an event handler in a method that performs a heavy computational load.

LISTING 7.12 Class Listener

```
public class Listener : INotification {
  // Fields
  private Notify notify;

  // Constructor
  public Listener() {
    notify = new Notify();
    notify.AddNotificationListener(this); // Registers listener
  }

  // Commands
  public void NotificationReceived(NotificationEvent evt) {
    Console.WriteLine("Received event number: " +
                      evt.EventValue);
    Thread.Sleep(2000); // Simulates time-intensive computation
  }
}
```

A short application class, *NotificationApplication*, is shown in Listing 7.13.

LISTING 7.13 Class NotificationApplication

```
public class NotificationApplication {
  static void Main() {
    Listener listener = new Listener();
  }
}
```

The UML diagram shown in Figure 7.2 shows the architecture of the application.

Exercise 7.12

Explain the UML diagram in Figure 7.2. In particular, why are there dependency relationships shown between classes *Notify* and *INotification* and between *Listener* and *NotificationEvent*?

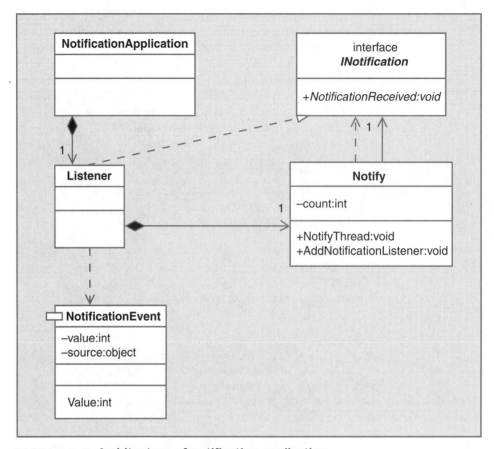

FIGURE 7.2 Architecture of notification application

The output of the Notification application is interesting and important. Only the initial portion of this output is shown because it will run forever or until the user presses the Ctrl+Alt+Del keys.

Application Output

```
value = 3
Received event number: 3
value = 6
Received event number: 6
value = 9
Received event number: 9
value = 12
Received event number: 12
value = 15
Received event number: 15
```

Something is wrong. Given the disparity between the one-fifth-second pause within the *NotifyThread* and the two second hold imposed by the listener to this event source thread, you would expect many more output values posted to the console from the infinite loop in the *NotifyThread* than the outputs to the console generated in class *Listener*.

This is not what happens. The actual output reveals a one-to-one correspondence between the output posted within the infinite loop and the output posted from the *listener* object.

This can be explained by the fact that the listener holds up the event source from firing every 600 milliseconds as the code indicates it should. Because the *Notify* class is created independent of any listener, we need to find a mechanism for ensuring that it works as designed—notifying a listener every 600 milliseconds and not being affected by the workload of the listener.

We need to modify the design of the system to decouple the notify mechanism in the infinite loop of the *NotifyThread* method from the listener's *NotificationReceived* method. It is the latter method that causes the difficulty in the present design.

The solution to this problem is to design an adapter class that is a listener to the *Notify* class. When it receives an event notification from the *Notify* class (in its *NotificationReceived* handler), it queues the event and releases it to its listener, the *Listener* class. This adapter pattern is useful in creating a bridge between the needs of the event source (class *Notify*) and class *Listener*.

Only the details of the new *NotifyAdapter* class and the redesigned *Listener* class are shown in Listing 7.14. The other classes remain the same as in the previous implementation.

The standard C# collection class *Queue* is used in this application. Its details are presented and discussed in Chapter 14.

Exercise 7.13

Based on the new class *NotifyAdapter* and the redesigned class *Listener* shown in Listing 7.14, draw a revised UML class diagram.

LISTING 7.14 Redesigned notification system

```
public class NotifyAdapter : INotification {

   // Fields
   private Queue queue = new Queue(); // Standard .NET class
   private INotification listener;
   private Thread thread;

   public NotifyAdapter(INotification listener, Notify notify) {
      this.listener = listener;
      notify.AddNotificationListener(this); // Registers itself
      thread = new Thread(new ThreadStart(AdapterThread));
      thread.Start();
   }
```

LISTING 7.14 Redesigned notification system (continued)

```
  public void NotificationReceived(NotificationEvent evt) {
    lock (queue) {
      queue.Enqueue(evt);
    }
  }

  public void AdapterThread() {
    for (; ; ) {

      // Clone the queue so it does not tie anyone else up
      Queue tempQueue;

      lock (queue) {
        tempQueue = (Queue)queue.Clone();
        queue.Clear();
      }

      // Empty the queue in FIFO order and notify listener
      while (tempQueue.Count > 0) {
        NotificationEvent evt =
            (NotificationEvent)tempQueue.Dequeue();
        listener.NotificationReceived(evt);
      }
    }
  }
}

public class Listener : INotification {

  // Fields
  private NotifyAdapter adapter;

  // Constructor
  public Listener() {
    adapter = new NotifyAdapter(this, new Notify());
  }

  // Commands
  public void NotificationReceived(NotificationEvent evt) {
    Console.WriteLine("Received event number: " +
                                      evt.EventValue);
    Thread.Sleep(2000); // Simulates computational work
  }
}
```

The *NotifyAdapter* class provides a bridge between the revised *Listener* class and the old *Notify* class. Because it implements *INotification*, it is a listener class itself. *NotifyAdapter* registers itself with the instance of *Notify* that is passed into its constructor. Each time it receives the *NotificationReceived* message, it adds a *NotificationEvent* object to its queue.

AdapterThread, initialized and started in the *NotifyAdapter* constructor, defines a *tempQueue* object and initializes it by cloning the *queue* while placing a lock on the *queue*. It then clears the *queue* and then uses the contents of *tempQueue* when sending *NotificationReceived* messages to the *listener* object registered with it. In the meantime, fresh *NotificationEvent* objects can be stored in the *queue*. This is especially important if the *Notify* object generates events faster than the listener object can absorb the notifications being sent by *tempQueue*.

The revised *Listener* class holds an instance of *NotifyAdapter*. When creating this instance, it passes itself and a new instance of *Notify*. The adapter object sends notifications to this listener using the mechanism in its *AdapterThread* as described earlier.

Exercise 7.14

Explain why it is not necessary for any class in the redesigned system to hold a *Notify* object in one of its fields.

Exercise 7.15

Monitor the size of the *queue* in the *NotifyAdapter* class and describe how the size of the queue changes over time.

7.7 SUMMARY

◆ Threads provide a logical partitioning of processing into pseudo-parallel processes. On a single-processor computer, each thread is executed in a time slice (a predetermined and small interval of CPU time).

◆ To derive tangible benefits from the use of threads that provide pseudo-parallelism, it is necessary to devise algorithms that allow pieces of a problem to be performed in parallel.

◆ The following code shows the programming mechanism for creating a thread object and then starting it:

```
Thread threadObject = new Thread(new ThreadStart(NameOfThreadMethod));
threadObject.Start();
```

◆ When two or more threads are accessing data that is available to each thread, it is often important to control access to the data to prevent one thread from writing to the common data while another is reading the common data.

◆ Locks are used to protect a thread that is accessing a critical section of code from the intrusion of another thread. When the critical section of code is completed and the lock is released, the runtime system selects one of the waiting threads, allows it to enter the critical section, and relocks the critical section until the critical section is completed.

◆ One of the basic challenges of developing a multithreaded application is coping with the presence of deadlocks. As the name implies, a deadlock occurs when two threads are in a blocked state, each waiting for the other to complete a task, with neither thread able to complete the task. The consequence is that program execution comes to a stop and the application stops running.

◆ When the version of *Join* without parameters is invoked on a thread, the calling thread is blocked until the receiving thread (thread receiving the *Join* command) is terminated. When a time-out parameter is used, the calling thread is blocked until the receiving thread is terminated or the time-out has been completed.

7.8 ADDITIONAL EXERCISES

Exercise 7.16

Research the use of class *ReaderWriterLock*. Explain why it is used and write a simple application that demonstrates its use.

Exercise 7.17

Describe the various ways that a thread can go from the run state to the wait state.

EVENT HANDLING
AND GUIS

GUIs have become an important and standard mechanism for presenting output to a user and obtaining input from the user in a variety of application domains. Chapters 8, 9, and 10 focus on graphical user interface (GUI) development and event handling in the .NET framework using C#.

Event handling provides the infrastructure that allows software to respond to button clicks, menu selections, or other user actions. In addition to supplying the backbone for GUI applications, event handling provides a general pattern of programming that enables information generated in one portion of an application to communicate with other portions of the application, notifying them when critical events have occurred. The Observer Pattern, explored in this part of the book, provides the basis for this type of communication.

Chapter 8 presents the programming mechanisms available in C# and .NET for firing events from event sources and notifying listener methods that may be distributed throughout the software system. This is accomplished using delegate and event types.

Chapters 9 and 10 introduce standard and commonly used GUI components including *Form*, *Button*, *Panel*, *Checkbox*, *Textbox*, and other useful components that form the basis of GUI development. The integration of event handling and GUI development is introduced in these chapters.

Although GUI development is typically assisted by an integrated development environment (IDE) such as Visual Studio, this book does not discuss the use of any particular IDE even though much of the code relating to the layout of GUI components is generated automatically by such an IDE tool. This code would be tedious to construct by hand.

CHAPTER 8

Delegates and Events in C#

8.1 USING DELEGATES AS FIRST-CLASS CLASSES

Recall that classes provide the basis for encapsulating behavior (through methods) and state (through the fields defined in the class). Furthermore, the classic notion of abstract data type, a unification of data and the operations that may be performed on the data, is realized by the class construct. Classes provide the basis for spawning objects, each object being an instance of a class. It is through objects that the work of an application is accomplished. Each object holds internal information (its current state) and can take actions (defined by the methods the object may respond to) on other objects or on itself.

This chapter explores a different type of C# class, a delegate. **Delegate** classes are designed to encapsulate a method signature. Instances of a delegate class are specific and fully defined methods that satisfy the signature specified in the delegate class.

The following *TemperatureConversion* class provides an example of a delegate class, two instances, and the invocation of the instances:

```
// This class is defined within some namespace
public delegate double TemperatureConversion(double
                          inputTemperature);


// This method is defined inside of the same namespace as the
// delegate
public double FahrenheitToCentigrade(double
                          fahrenheitTemperature) {
    return (fahrenheitTemperature - 32.0) * 5.0 / 9.0;
}


// This method is defined inside of the same namespace as the
// delegate
public double CentigradeToFahrenheit(double
                          centigradeTemperature) {
    return centigradeTemperature * 9.0 / 5.0 + 32.0;
}


// Inside of some method within the same namespace as the
// delegate


// convertFahrenheitToCentigrade is an instance of the delegate
TemperatureConversion convertFahrenheitToCentigrade =
    new TemperatureConversion(FahrenheitToCentigrade);


// convertCentigradeToFahrenheit is an instance of the delegate
TemperatureConversion convertCentigradeToFahrenheit =
    new TemperatureConversion(CentigradeToFahrenheit);


// Each instance of the delegate is invoked
double centigradeTemperature =
      convertFahrenheitToCentigrade(75.0);
```

```
double fahrenheitTemperature =
     convertCentigradeToFahrenheit(25.0);
```

In the simplest sense, a delegate type provides the basis for an object-oriented, type-safe mechanism for treating methods as objects and passing method references as parameters without having to use pointers as in C or C++. Delegate types (classes) form the basis of event handling throughout the .NET framework. As shown in the preceding code, they can also be used in a context removed from event handling. Another example of a delegate class declaration is the following:

```
public delegate void TakeAction();
```

Some possible methods that can be defined as instances of the *TakeAction* delegate include:

```
public void MyAction() {
   Console.WriteLine("In MyAction");
}

public void AnotherMethod() {
   Console.WriteLine("In AnotherMethod");
}
```

Instances of the *TakeAction* delegate can be created as follows:

```
TakeAction action1 = new TakeAction(MyAction);
TakeAction action2 = new TakeAction(AnotherMethod);
TakeAction action3 = action1 + action2; // Invocation list
```

The delegate instance, *action3*, may be invoked as follows:

```
action3();
```

Because the delegate instance *action3* was formed by "adding" the delegate instances *action1* and *action2*, when *action3* is invoked, it causes the invocation list containing *action1* and *action2* to be activated in the order the invocation list is constructed (that is, *action1* followed by *action2*).

When an invocation list of delegate instances is built, it is common for the delegate type to return void. If a nonvoid type is specified (as in the case of *TemperatureConversion* earlier), only the value returned by the last method in the invocation list would be returned.

The following code shows an attempt to create a delegate instance of *TakeAction*:

```
public void ThirdMethod(double first) {
   /* Details not shown*/
}
TakeAction action4 = new TakeAction(ThirdMethod); // Compiler error
```

These statements fail at compile time because the signature of *ThirdMethod* does not match the required signature specified in the *TakeAction* delegate class.

A delegate class may be defined anywhere that an ordinary class may be defined within a namespace and have the same access modifiers (public, protected, and private) as a regular class. So a delegate class is a first-class class. Like all classes, it characterizes the behavior of its instances, in this case methods that satisfy the delegate method signature.

Suppose you want to compare the efficiency of several sorting algorithms. You could define a generic delegate *Sorting* class as follows:

```
public delegate void Sorting<T>(ref T [] data, int size)
    where T: IComparable;
```

This generic method specification requires instances to take as the first parameter an array of some generic type that implements the *IComparable* interface (has a *CompareTo* method defined that allows values of type T to be compared with each other). If you think about it, the only requirement that is needed for a set of elements to be sorted is that the elements can be compared to each other. This is represented by the *where T : IComparable* constraint on the generic parameter.

The second parameter, *size*, specifies the number of elements in the array that are to be sorted. It is not always the case that the array to be sorted is completely filled with elements that are to be sorted. (If this were always the case we could eliminate the *size* parameter and use *data.Length* in place of *size*.) This *size* parameter allows only a portion of the array to be sorted.

We look at the use of this delegate in the context of comparing the sort times of two simple sorting methods, **selection-sort** and **bubble-sort**. We shall create generic instances using two different type parameters—type *int* (an alias for class *System.Int32*) and a user-defined class *NameRecord*. Our *NameRecord* class needs to implement the *IComparable* interface in order for the Sorting instance to work. Listing 8.1 presents the details of our user-defined *NameRecord* class.

LISTING 8.1 Class NameRecord

```
public class NameRecord : IComparable { // Implements IComparable

    // Fields
    private String lastName;
    private String firstName;
    private int idNumber;

    // Constructor
    public NameRecord(String lastName, String firstName,
                      int idNumber) {
        this.lastName = lastName;
        this.firstName = firstName;
        this.idNumber = idNumber;
    }

    // Properties
    public String LastName { // Read-only
        get {
            return lastName;
        }
    }
}
```

LISTING 8.1 Class NameRecord (continued)

```
    public String FirstName { // Read-only
        get {
            return firstName;
        }
    }

    public int IDNumber { // Read-only
        get {
            return idNumber;
        }
    }

    /**
     * Compare the concatenation of lastname and firstname
     */
    public int CompareTo(Object obj) {
        NameRecord nameRecord = (NameRecord)obj;
        return (lastName +
            firstName).CompareTo(nameRecord.lastName +
                nameRecord.firstName);
    }
}
```

The required *CompareTo* query method, with the signature specified in the *IComparable* interface, performs a downcast from formal type *Object* to actual type *NameRecord*. This is necessary so that the concatenation of the *lastName* and *firstName* values of the receiver object can be compared to the concatenation of the name record's *lastName* and *firstName* values. This comparison is done using the *CompareTo* query of class *String*.

Listing 8.2 uses this *NameRecord* class and the generic *Sorting* delegate in a complete sorting application.

LISTING 8.2 Generic sorting delegate in action

```
using System;
using System.Collections.Generic;
using System.Text;
namespace SortingWithDelegate {

    public delegate void Sorting<T>(ref T[] data, int size)
            where T : IComparable;

    public class NameRecord : IComparable {
    // See Listing 8.1 for details
    }

    public class Timing {
        // Fields
        private long startTicks, endTicks;
```

LISTING 8.2 Generic sorting delegate in action (continued)

```
        public void StartTiming() {
            DateTime t = DateTime.Now;
            startTicks = t.Ticks;
        }

        public void EndTiming() {
            DateTime t = DateTime.Now;
            endTicks = t.Ticks;
        }

        public double ElapsedTime() {
            return (endTicks - startTicks) / 10000000.0;
        }
    }

    public class SortingMethods {

        // Fields
        private Timing time = new Timing();
        private const int ARRAYSIZE = 10000;

        // Constructor
        public SortingMethods() {
            Sorting<double> sortSelectDouble = new
                Sorting<double>(SelectionSort);
            Sorting<double> sortBubbleDouble = new
                Sorting<double>(BubbleSort);
            Sorting<NameRecord> sortSelectNames = new
                Sorting<NameRecord>(SelectionSort);
            Sorting<NameRecord> sortBubbleNames = new
                Sorting<NameRecord>(BubbleSort);

            // Benchmark selection sort on 10,000 doubles
            double[] doubleData = new double[ARRAYSIZE];
            for (int i = 0; i < ARRAYSIZE; i++) {
                doubleData[i] = Math.Cos(10 * i);
            }
            time.StartTiming();
            sortSelectDouble(ref doubleData, ARRAYSIZE);
            time.EndTiming();
            Console.WriteLine(
            "Elapsed time for selection-sort of size 10,000 = " +
                        time.ElapsedTime() + " seconds.");
            Console.WriteLine("Numbers are sorted: " +
            IsSorted(doubleData, ARRAYSIZE));

            // Benchmark bubble sort on 10,000 doubles
            doubleData = new double[ARRAYSIZE];
            for (int i = 0; i < ARRAYSIZE; i++) {
                doubleData[i] = Math.Cos(10 * i);
            }
```

LISTING 8.2 Generic sorting delegate in action (continued)

```
            time.StartTiming();
            sortBubbleDouble(ref doubleData, ARRAYSIZE);
            time.EndTiming();
            Console.WriteLine(
            "Elapsed time for bubble-sort of size 10,000 = " +
                            time.ElapsedTime() + " seconds.");
            Console.WriteLine("Numbers are sorted: " +
            IsSorted(doubleData, ARRAYSIZE));

            // Benchmark selection-sort on 10,000 NameRecords
            NameRecord [] namesData = new NameRecord[ARRAYSIZE];
            for (int i = 0; i < ARRAYSIZE; i++) {
                namesData[i] = new NameRecord("ABCDEFG" + i,
                "HIJKLMNOP" + i, i);
            }
            time.StartTiming();
            sortSelectNames(ref namesData, ARRAYSIZE);
            time.EndTiming();
            Console.WriteLine(
            "Elapsed time for selection-sort of size 10,000 names
                = " + time.ElapsedTime() + " seconds.");
            Console.WriteLine("Numbers are sorted: " +
            IsSorted(namesData, ARRAYSIZE));

            // Benchmark bubble-sort on 10,000 NameRecords
            namesData = new NameRecord[ARRAYSIZE];
            for (int i = 0; i < ARRAYSIZE; i++) {
                namesData[i] = new NameRecord("ABCDEFG" + i,
                    HIJKLMNOP" + i, i);
            }
            time.StartTiming();
            sortBubbleNames(ref namesData, ARRAYSIZE);
            time.EndTiming();
            Console.WriteLine(
            "Elapsed time for bubble-sort of size 10,000 names =
                " + time.ElapsedTime() + " seconds.");
            Console.WriteLine("Numbers are sorted: " +
            IsSorted(namesData, ARRAYSIZE));
            Console.ReadLine();
    }

// Returns true if data in ascending order otherwise false
public bool IsSorted<T>(T[] data, int size)
    where T : IComparable {
    // Exercise 8.5
}

    // A potential instance of delegate Sorting
    public void SelectionSort<T>(ref T[] data, int size)
        where T : IComparable {
        for (int i = size; i >= 1; i--) {
            // Get the largest value
            T largest = data[0];
            int index = 0;
```

LISTING 8.2 Generic sorting delegate in action (continued)

```
                  for (int j = 1; j < i; j++) {
                      if (data[j].CompareTo(largest) > 0) {
                          index = j;
                          largest = data[j];
                      }
                  }

                  // Interchange data[index] and data[i - 1]
                  T temp = data[i - 1];
                  data[i - 1] = data[index];
                  data[index] = temp;
              }
          }

          // Another potential instance of delegate Sorting
          public void BubbleSort<T>(ref T[] data, int size)
              where T : IComparable {
              int index1, index2;
              T temp;
              bool exchanged;

            for (index1 = size - 1; index1 >= 2; index1--) {
              exchanged = false;
              for (index2 = 0; index2 <= index1 - 1; index2++) {
                  if (data[index2].CompareTo(data[index2 + 1]) > 0) {
                      // Interchange elements
                      temp = data[index2];
                      data[index2] = data[index2 + 1];
                      data[index2 + 1] = temp;
                      exchanged = true;
                  }
              }
              if (!exchanged) { // Early termination of outer loop
                  break;
                  }
              }
          }

          static void Main() {
              // Create instances of delegate Sorting
              new SortingMethods();
          }
      }
}

/* Output
Elapsed time for selection-sort of size 10,000 = 1.234375 seconds.
Numbers are sorted: True
Elapsed time for bubble-sort of size 10,000 = 1.59375 seconds.
Numbers are sorted: True
Elapsed time for selection-sort of size 10,000 names = 26.453125
seconds.
Numbers are sorted: True
```

LISTING 8.2 Generic sorting delegate in action (continued)

```
Elapsed time for bubble-sort of size 10,000 names = 5.078125
seconds.
Numbers are sorted: True
*/
```

Analysis of Listing 8.2

A namespace *SortingWithDelegate* is created. Four public classes are defined within this namespace. The public generic *Sorting* delegate class is defined first. Next, *NameRecord*, presented in Listing 8.1, is defined. Then a *Timing* class is defined. It uses the *Now* property of the *DateTime* class to obtain the current date and the *Ticks* property to obtain the current internal clock time. Finally, the *SortingMethods* class that contains the main driver method *Main* is defined.

In class *SortingMethods*, the constructor defines four instances of the *Sorting* delegate, *sortSelectDouble*, *sortBubbleDouble*, *sortSelectNames*, and *sortBubbleNames*, as follows:

```
Sorting<double> sortSelectDouble = new
      Sorting<double>(SelectionSort);
Sorting<double> sortBubbleDouble = new
      Sorting<double>(BubbleSort);
Sorting<NameRecord> sortSelectNames = new
      Sorting<NameRecord>(SelectionSort);
Sorting<NameRecord> sortBubbleNames = new
      Sorting<NameRecord>(BubbleSort);
```

The first two of these *Sorting* delegate instances use *double* as the generic type parameter, and the last two use *NameRecord* as the generic parameter.

The classic methods *SelectionSort* and *BubbleSort* are defined in class *SortingMethods*. It is assumed that the reader is familiar with these elementary sorting routines. As a reminder, *SelectionSort* finds the largest element in the *data* array passed to it by reference. It swaps this largest element with the element in the largest index location (the rightmost element). It then repeats the process, only this time finding the largest element among the data elements that do not include the rightmost element. It swaps this second largest element with the element one index to the left of the rightmost element. It iteratively continues this process until the entire array is placed in ascending order. Because the element type in the *data* array is generic (type T) and T must implement *IComparable*, the required *CompareTo* method is used to compare two values of this generic type. This is done as follows (see the generic *SelectionSort* earlier):

```
if (data[j].CompareTo(largest) > 0) {
```

Method *BubbleSort* compares adjacent elements two at a time, interchanging their position if the first is larger than the second. When the first iteration is completed, the largest of the data elements is forced to the rightmost position. This process is repeated, only this time excluding the rightmost element from consideration (because it has already been placed where it belongs). Further iterations shrink the size of the array by one each time until all *data* elements are in ascending order. A Boolean *exchanged* variable allows for possible early termination of the outer loop if no further interchanges are needed.

Exercise 8.1

Show in detail and step by step the process of using *SelectionSort* to sort the following double values: {2.6, 1.7, -6.8, -4.1, 12.1, 4.5, 9.1, 8.7}.

Exercise 8.2

Show in detail and step by step the process of using *BubbleSort* to sort the following double values: {2.6, 1.7, -6.8, -4.1, 12.1, 4.5, 9.1, 8.7}.

Exercise 8.3

Which of the two sorting methods appears to be faster and why?

Exercise 8.4

If you double the size of a given array, approximately what effect would this have on the sorting time for each of the two sorting methods?

Benchmarking a typical sorting method that uses a specific base-type is accomplished as follows:

```
time.StartTiming();
sortSelectDouble(ref doubleData, ARRAYSIZE);
time.EndTiming();
```

Here the array *doubleData* is filled with a set of values from the *Cos* function in class *Math*. The *sortSelectDouble* is an instance of delegate *Sorting*.

To confirm that each of the sorting methods actually performs its task correctly (i.e., produces an ascending sequence of values in the array), an *IsSorted* query is defined. The details are not shown because Exercise 8.5 asks you to write these details.

Exercise 8.5

Write the implementation of generic method *IsSorted* with the following signature:

```
public bool IsSorted<T>(T[] data, int size)
        where T : IComparable
```

Exercise 8.6

Explain why *SelectionSort* is faster when sorting the array of type double compared with *BubbleSort* but slower when sorting the array of base-type *NameRecord*.

Exercise 8.7

Find another sorting method and add it to class *SortingMethods*. Modify the constructor in this class so that you can benchmark its performance as in the two existing sorting methods.

Exercise 8.8

Define a class *NameRecord2* that is similar to class *NameRecord* except that it compares two objects using each object's *idNumber* value. Add this class to namespace *SortingWithDelegate* and add appropriate code to class *SortingMethods* that enables you to benchmark your sorting algorithms when *NameRecord2* is used.

8.2 ANOTHER APPLICATION OF DELEGATES

Suppose you want to write a method that takes as input a user-defined mathematical function with one independent variable. A sample function might be f(x) = 3x^2 + 2x + 6.

The method to be implemented must construct a table with two columns, x and f(x). The method must contain a parameter that indicates the starting value of independent variable x, the ending value, and the increment. The method must then fill the table with values of the input function based on the starting and ending values specified and the increment that is given. The output that is generated by this method should be directed to the console. Consider Listing 8.3.

LISTING 8.3 Table of user-supplied mathematical functions

```
using System;
namespace FunctionTable {

    public delegate double Function(double x);

    public class ConstructingFunctionTable {

        public void BuildTable(Function f, double startValue,
                               double endValue, double increment)
{
            Console.WriteLine("x\t\t\tf(x)");
            for (double x = startValue; x <= endValue;
                x += increment) {
                Console.WriteLine(String.Format(
                "{0:f}\t\t\t\t{1:f}", x,  f(x)));
            }
            Console.ReadLine();
        }
```

LISTING 8.3   Table of user-supplied mathematical functions (continued)

```
        private double function1(double x) {
            return 3.0 * x * x + 2.0 * x + 6.0;
        }

        private double function2(double x) {
            return 1.0 / (1.0 - x);
        }

        static void Main() {
            ConstructingFunctionTable app =
              new ConstructingFunctionTable();
            Function f1 = new Function(app.function1);
            app.BuildTable(f1, -2.0, 2.0, 0.5);
            Console.WriteLine("\n\n");
            Function f2 = new Function(app.function2);
            app.BuildTable(f2, 0.95, 0.99, 0.01);
            Console.WriteLine("\n\n");
            app.BuildTable(Math.Sin, 0.0, 2.0, 0.5);
        }
    }
}

/*
Output
x                              f(x)
-2.00                          14.00
-1.50                          9.75
-1.00                          7.00
-0.50                          5.75
0.00                           6.00
0.50                           7.75
1.00                           11.00
1.50                           15.75
2.00                           22.00

x                              f(x)
0.95                           20.00
0.96                           25.00
0.97                           33.33
0.98                           50.00
0.99                           100.00

x                              f(x)
0.00                           0.00
0.50                           0.48
1.00                           0.84
1.50                           1.00
2.00                           0.91
*/
```

Discussion of Listing 8.3

◆ Delegate class *Function* is defined in the namespace *FunctionTable* as the following statement:

```
public delegate double Function(double x);
```

◆ The first parameter of method *BuildTable* is of type *Function*. This provides a type-safe mechanism for passing a function as a parameter to a method. An instance, *f1*, of the delegate class *Function* is created as follows:

```
Function f1 = new Function(app.function1);
```

◆ The *BuildTable* command is invoked through an *app* object of type *ConstructingFunctionTable* (the class that contains *BuildTable*). The delegate object, *f1*, is passed to *BuildTable* using the following statement:

```
app.BuildTable(f1, -2.0, 2.0, 0.5);
```

It is generally not a good practice to use type double as the type for an index variable in constructing a for loop, as is done in method *BuildTable*. Because of the computer's inability to represent floating-point types exactly, the table being constructed probably does not contain an entry for the ending value specified. Because the goal of this simple application is to provide an example of the use of delegates, no further corrective action is taken to overcome this problem.

8.3 EVENTS AS DELEGATE MODIFIERS

The keyword **event** is used as a delegate modifier. So an event type is a modified delegate type and, like a delegate type, encapsulates a method signature. Event types are typically used in the context of the Observer Pattern in which an event occurs in one class (the model class) and notifies one or more listeners often in separate observer classes to take some action in response to the critical event in the model class. Chapter 9 discusses the Observer Pattern in some detail.

Although one can use the keyword *event* to modify any delegate declaration, the typical use of event types in the .NET framework is the following:

```
public delegate void EventHandler(Object sender, EventArgs e);

public event EventHandler someEvent;
```

Delegate class *EventHandler* and class *EventArgs* are defined in namespace *System*. You will see many examples of events of type *EventHandler* in the next chapter that deal with *WinForm* classes and event handling in a GUI context. For now, this chapter examines event types in the more general context of the Observer Pattern.

In contrast to a delegate instance, an event instance can be invoked only within the class that declares it. When an event object is invoked, all delegate instances registered with the event are fired. If the event has no registered listeners, it has the value *null*. Event instances must be added (registered) with the event type using the "+=" operator.

To illustrate event types, consider a class *Counter* that counts the number of tries and the number of critical events in a general programming context. The *Increment* method takes a Boolean parameter. If true, the number of critical events is incremented by one. The number of tries is always incremented by one when the *Increment* method is invoked. When the number of critical events equals a specified critical event threshold (specified in the constructor to *Counter*), an event is fired that contains two parameters of type *int* (*System.Int32*).

Listing 8.4 presents all the details of this application.

LISTING 8.4 Counting critical events: an introduction to event handling

```
#region Using directives

using System;
using System.Collections.Generic;
using System.Text;

#endregion

namespace EventTutorial {

    public delegate void SpecialEventHandler(int first,
        int second);

    public class EventContainer {

      public event SpecialEventHandler someEvent;

      public void OnSomeEvent(int first, int second) {
          if (someEvent != null) {
              someEvent(first, second);
          }
      }
    }

    /**
    * A model class that fires events when the number of tries
    * equals the critical event count.
    */
    public class Counter {

      // Fields
      private int numberTries;
      private int criticalEventCount;
      private int criticalEventThreshold;
      private EventContainer eventContainer = new EventContainer();

      // Constructor
      public Counter(int triggerEventThreshold) {
          criticalEventThreshold = triggerEventThreshold;
      }
```

LISTING 8.4 Counting critical events: an introduction to event handling
(continued)

```
// Properties
public int NumberTries {
    get {
        return numberTries;
    }
}

public int CriticalEventCount {
    get {
        return criticalEventCount;
    }
}

// Commands
public void Register(SpecialEventHandler eventHandler) {
    eventContainer.someEvent += eventHandler;
}

/**
 * If criticalEvent parameter is true, increment
 * criticalEventCount.
 * Always increment numberTries.
 * If criticalEventCount equals criticalEventThreshold,
 * fire someEvent in the EventContainer object.
 */
public void Increment(bool criticalEvent) {
    numberTries++;
    if (criticalEvent) {
        criticalEventCount++;
    }
    if (criticalEventCount == criticalEventThreshold) {
        // Fire OnSomeEvent
        eventContainer.OnSomeEvent(numberTries,
          criticalEventThreshold);
    }
}
}

public class Observer {

  // Constructor
  public  Observer(Counter c) {
      // Register method Handler as listener
      c.Register(Handler);
  }

  public void Handler(int first, int second) {
      Console.WriteLine("It took " + first +
        " uniformly distributed random numbers from 0 to 1" +
        " to get " +
        second + " numbers equal or greater than 0.5");
      Console.ReadLine();
  }
```

LISTING 8.4 Counting critical events: an introduction to event handling (continued)

```
    }

    public class EventApplication {

        static void Main() {
            Random rnd = new Random();
            // Define a Counter with a critical event value of 10
            Counter myCounter = new Counter(10);
            Observer myCounterObserver = new Observer(myCounter);
            for (int i = 0; i < 10000; i++) {
                myCounter.Increment(rnd.NextDouble() >= 0.5);
            }
        }
    }
}
/* Sample Output
It took 22 uniformly distributed random numbers from 0 to 1 to get
10 numbers equal or greater than 0.5

It took 23 uniformly distributed random numbers from 0 to 1 to get
10 numbers equal or greater than 0.5

It took 24 uniformly distributed random numbers from 0 to 1 to get
10 numbers equal or greater than 0.5

It took 25 uniformly distributed random numbers from 0 to 1 to get
10 numbers equal or greater than 0.5

It took 26 uniformly distributed random numbers from 0 to 1 to get
10 numbers equal or greater than 0.5
*/
```

An analysis of Listing 8.4 is shown in Figure 8.1.

Five classes define the architecture of this application: Delegate *SpecialEventHandler*, *EventContainer*, *Counter*, *Observers*, and *EventApplication*.

The UML diagram in Figure 8.1 shows each of the five classes and their relationship to each other. Class *Counter* owns an *EventContainer* object that is used to register listener methods. *EventApplication* owns *Counter* and *Observer* objects. *Observer* has a weak association with *Counter* and is responsible for registering its *Handler* method with the *Counter* object passed to its constructor. This allows the *Observer* object to write to the console whenever the *Counter* that it has registered with reports that the specified number of critical events has occurred. This report is initiated by the *Counter* object firing the *OnSomeEvent* method.

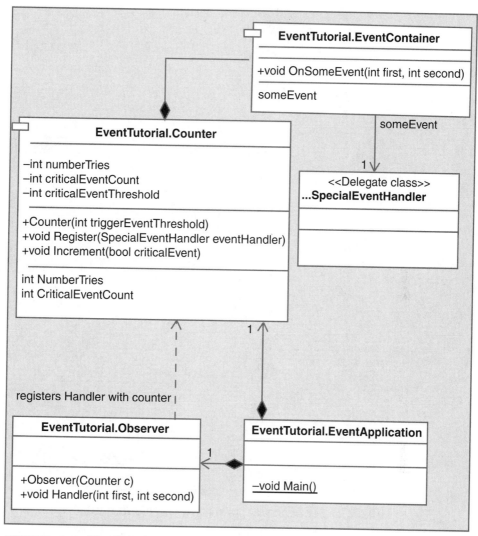

FIGURE 8.1 The five classes in the application

The sequence diagram in Figure 8.2 shows the eight steps that enable the *myCounter* object to fire a notification, which is received by *myCounterObserver* and then outputs information to the console.

The main application object creates *myCounter* with a threshold of 10. The *myCounter* object creates and owns an *EventContainer* object. A new *Observer* object, *myCounterObserver*, is created. It registers its *Handler* method as a listener for *myCounter*. The main application sends the *Increment* commands to *myCounter*. When the critical number of events has occurred, *myCounter* fires the *OnSomeEvent* command to its *eventContainer*. It notifies *myCounterObserver*, which posts output to the Console.

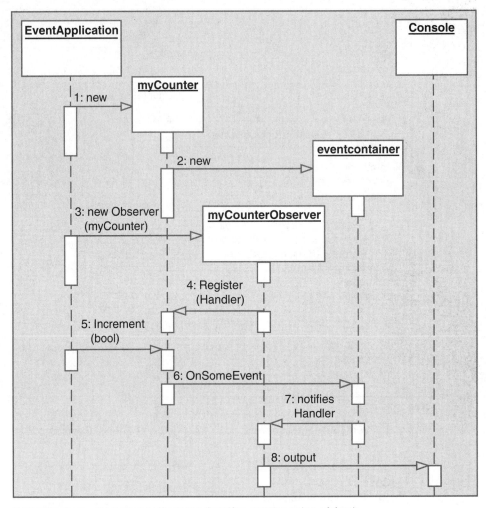

FIGURE 8.2 Sequence diagram for the *myCounter* object

Now in more detail, in namespace *EventTutorial*, a delegate class *SpecialEventHandler* is defined as shown in the following statement:

```
public delegate void SpecialEventHandler(int first, int second);
```

Next, class *EventContainer* is defined so that it encapsulates *someEvent*, which is an event type that modifies the *SpecialEventHandler* delegate.

Class *Counter* is the most important and interesting. Its state consists of the number of tries, the number of critical events, the critical event threshold, and an object of type *EventContainer*. A register method allows an observer class to add a listener method to the invocation list of *someEvent* contained within the *EventContainer* object. The "+=" operator is used to accomplish this as follows:

```
public void Register(SpecialEventHandler eventHandler) {
    eventContainer.someEvent += eventHandler;
}
```

The *Increment* method uses the *OnSomeEvent* command on its *EventContainer* object to fire *someEvent*, which conveys the number of tries and the critical event threshold to all listener methods. Recall that *someEvent* cannot be directly invoked outside of the *EventContainer* class.

The *Observer* class takes a *Counter* object in its constructor and registers its *Handler* method with the *Counter* object that is sent in.

The *EventApplication* class that contains method *Main* creates a *Counter* object, *myCounter*, with a critical event threshold of 10. An *Observer* object, *myCounterObserver*, is also created with *myCounter* passed as a parameter to its constructor. The following for loop defines a critical event as a uniformly distributed random number from 0 to 1 having a value equal to or greater than 0.5:

```
for (int i = 0; i < 10000; i++) {
    myCounter.Increment(rnd.NextDouble() >= 0.5);
}
```

Any Boolean condition could be substituted for this simple one. It is assumed that 10,000 values are sufficient to achieve the threshold of 10 outcomes (the average number of tries would be 20).

The advantage of using this Observer Pattern with event types is that the model class, in this case class *Counter*, does not need to know anything about its listener method or methods. The counter merely does its work of enumerating tries and critical events and fires *someEvent* (indirectly through the *OnSomeEvent* method) to whoever is listening when the number of critical events equals the specified threshold. This distribution of responsibility promotes greater modularity and maintainability in software.

Exercise 8.9

Consider the following two C# classes:

```
using System;
using System.Threading;

namespace Exercise {

    public class EventSource {

        // Fields
        private Random rnd = new Random();
        private int distance;
```

```
    // Commands
    public void RandomWalk() {
        for (int count = 1; count <= 50; count++) {
        distance += -2 + rnd.Next(5); // from -2 to 2
            Thread.Sleep(250);  // Time delay of 1/4 second
        }
    }
}


public class EventResponse {

    // Fields
    private EventSource source = new EventSource();

    static void Main() {
        EventResponse app = new EventResponse();
        app.source.RandomWalk();
    }
}
}
```

Each time the field *distance* in class *EventSource* has a magnitude greater than 2 (less than −2 or greater than 2), an event must be fired and propagated to an event listener in class *EventResponse*. The *distance* value must be transmitted to the event listener (event handler method) in class *EventResponse*, which then outputs the distance value to the console.

Add appropriate code within namespace *Exercise* that provides the machinery to fire events from method *RandomWalk* (in class *EventSource*) and handle (listen to) these events in class *EventResponse* by using an event handler method *Response* that you must write.

Your solution must include a delegate definition, an event declaration, an event handler method (called *Response*—you define its signature) in class *EventResponse*, and a mechanism for registering the *Response* method with the event source.

8.4 DIFFERENCES BETWEEN EVENTS AND DELEGATES

Because the keyword **event**, whenever present, is used as a modifier on a delegate type, it might be tempting to conclude that it is really the same as a delegate type.

The first reason for defining a delegate type as an event type (using the **event** modifier) is purely communicative. It suggests a context in which the Observer Pattern will be used.

In terms of differences of substance, an event type may be declared within an interface whereas a delegate type cannot. This is quite important and alone provides a significant distinction between ordinary delegate types and delegate types that are modified to be event types.

As mentioned earlier, another distinction is that event types can be invoked only from within the class in which they are defined, whereas this constraint does not apply to delegate types.

Finally, events may be treated like properties with the **add** and **remove** constructs. This capability of event types is illustrated in the following code:

```
// Invocation list held as an array of type MyEventHandler
private MyEventHandler [] events = new MyEventHandler[5];


public event MyEventHandler someEvent {
    // Add an event to the invocation list
    add {
      int i;
      for (i = 0; i < 5; i++) {
        if (events[i] == null) {
          events[i] = value;
        }
      }
      if (i == 5) {
        Console.WriteLine("Event list is full.");
      }
    }
    // Remove an event from the invocation list
    remove {
      // Details not shown
    }
}
```

8.5 EVENTS IN GUI APPLICATIONS

Chapter 9 deals with *Form* classes and event handling. This chapter introduces and illustrates some simple uses of event types in the context of GUI programming.

As indicated in Section 8.3, the cornerstone of GUI event handling is the delegate class *EventHandler* and its associated event type.

```
public delegate void EventHandler(Object sender, EventArgs e);


public event EventHandler someEvent;
```

Consider a simple form that contains a single button. How do we handle button clicks?

It is common for the method that handles (or responds to) a button click to be in the same class as the button itself. There is no requirement for this. The source of an event may be in one class and its listener in another class.

Consider the simple class *ButtonResponse* shown in the following code in which the button handler is in a separate class from the button itself. There could be several button handlers, each in a separate method (possibly in separate classes) and all registered with the *Click* event type. They would be invoked in the order they were registered.

```
namespace GUIEvents {

    public class ButtonResponse {

      // Constructor
      public ButtonResponse(Button btn) {
          btn.Click +=
              new EventHandler(this.ButtonClickHandler);
      }


      private void ButtonClickHandler(Object sender, EventArgs e) {
          MessageBox.Show("Button is clicked.");
      }
    }
}
```

Click is an event type defined in class *Button*. It modifies the *EventHandler* delegate class.

```
// In Class Button
public event EventHandler Click;
```

In the constructor, *ButtonResponse*, the private *ButtonClickHandler* method, with the required signature, is defined as an instance of the *EventHandler* delegate class and part of the invocation list of the *Click* event type.

Consider another example, this one from a real application, a text editor. The text editor requires a dynamic menu list of recently opened files. This list is stored on disk. There are two issues here. One is to load the list of filenames and add them to the file menu. The other is to associate a menu-click handler with each of the filenames. This is essential so that when the user clicks a filename on the File menu, appropriate action is taken (in this case opening the file and displaying its content).

Examine only a small portion of this task, the part that involves event handling. You do not need to understand the details and nuances of the following code, but you should recognize and understand how the *OnMenuItemClick* method is added to the invocation list of a new *MenuItem* object. Once again, event types and their associated delegate (*EventHandler* in this case) play a central role.

```
// lastFileNames is a collection of String objects
int count = 0;
foreach (String filename in lastFileNames) {
    if (count < 10) {
      fileMenu.MenuItems.Add(new MenuItem(filename,
        new EventHandler(OnMenuItemClick)));
      count++;
    }
}
```

```
private void OnMenuItemClick(object sender, System.EventArgs e) {
    MenuItem menuItem = (MenuItem) sender;
    filename = menuItem.Text;
    // Remaining details not shown
}
```

As each new *MenuItem* object is added to the collection of *MenuItems*, the name of the menu item (*filename*) is the first parameter, and a new instance of *EventHandler* (an event *OnMenuItemClick*) is registered with the new menu item.

In the *OnMenuItem* event handler, the filename is retrieved from the sender parameter by downcasting it to *MenuItem* and then obtaining its *Text* property.

8.6 FINAL APPLICATION THAT FEATURES EVENT HANDLING

In this section, you examine an application that models the ups and downs of a particular stock using a simplistic one-dimensional random walk model. In such a model, the value of a stock is assumed to change by plus or minus a specified number of units after every time unit (such as one hour). A notification is generated each time a stock changes more than a specified number of units above or below its initial value. A collection of brokers who control the stock must receive this notification. The range within which a stock can change every time unit and the threshold above or below which the collection of brokers who control the stock must be notified are specified when the stock is created (using its constructor).

We shall design and implement a C# application that satisfies the specification given above. This application involves delegates, events, and threads. We begin by defining a namespace *Stocks* and a delegate class *StockNotification*. This is shown in Listing 8.5.

LISTING 8.5 Delegate StockNotification

```
using System;
using System.Collections.Generic;
using System.Text;

namespace Stocks {
    public delegate void StockNotification(String stockName,
        int currentValue,
        int numberChanges);
}
```

This delegate is designed so that when an event of this type is fired, the stock's name, value, and the number of changes in value can be sent to the listener.

Class *Stock* is presented in Listing 8.6.

LISTING 8.6 Class Stock

```csharp
using System;
using System.Collections.Generic;
using System.Text;
using System.Threading; // For Sleep command

namespace Stocks {
   public class Stock {
      // Fields
      private String name;
      private int initialValue;
      private int maxChange;
      private int notificationThreshold;
      private int currentValue;
      private Random rnd = new Random();
      private int numberChanges;
      private Thread thread;

      // Events
      public event StockNotification stockEvent;

      // Constructor
      public Stock(String name, int startingValue, int maxChange,
            int threshold) {
         this.name = name;
         initialValue = startingValue;
         currentValue = initialValue;
         this.maxChange = maxChange;
         notificationThreshold = threshold;
         thread = new Thread(new ThreadStart(Activate));
         thread.Start();
      }

      public void Activate() {
         for (;;) {
            Thread.Sleep(500);  // 1/2 second
            ChangeStockValue();
         }
      }

      private void ChangeStockValue() {
         currentValue += rnd.Next(1, maxChange);
         numberChanges++;
         if (Math.Abs(currentValue - initialValue) >
            notificationThreshold) {
               FireEvent();
         }
      }

      private void FireEvent() {
         stockEvent(name, currentValue, numberChanges);
      }
   }
}
```

When a stock object is created, its *Activate* thread is started. This causes its value to be modified every 500 milliseconds. If its value changes from its initial value by more than the specified *notificationThreshold*, the *FireEvent* method is invoked. This invokes the *stockEvent* (of event-type *StockNotification*) and multicasts a notification to all listeners who have registered with *stockEvent*.

It is essential that the *Activate* method be spawned as a thread, otherwise the infinite loop that periodically changes its value would dominate the CPU and not allow any other stocks to come into play.

Listing 8.7 presents class *StockBroker*.

LISTING 8.7 Class StockBroker

```
#region Using directives
using System;
using System.Collections.Generic;
using System.Text;
#endregion
namespace Stocks {

    public class StockBroker {
        // Fields
        private String brokerName;
        private List<Stock> stocks = new List<Stock>();

        // Constructor
        public StockBroker(String brokerName) {
            this.brokerName = brokerName;
        }

        // Properties
        public List<Stock> Stocks {
            get {
                return stocks;
            }
        }

        public String BrokerName {
            get {
                return brokerName;
            }
        }

        // Commands
        public void AddStock(Stock stock) {
            stocks.Add(stock);
            stock.stockEvent += new StockNotification(Notify);
        }
```

LISTING 8.7 Class StockBroker (continued)

```
      public void Notify(String name, int value, int
         numberChanges) {
         Console.WriteLine("Broker name: " + brokerName +
                         " Stock name: " + name +
                         " Stock value: " + value +
                         " Number changes: " + numberChanges);
      }
   }
}
```

Class *Stockbroker* has fields *brokerName* and *stocks*, a *List* of *Stock*. This latter field is not used in this application but could be used to obtain the stocks currently controlled by a given broker. The *AddStock* method registers the *Notify* listener with the stock (in addition to adding it to the list of stocks held by the broker). This *Notify* method outputs to the console the name, value, and number of changes of the stock whose value is out of the range given by the stock's notification threshold.

Finally, Listing 8.8 presents a main driver class, *StockApplication*.

LISTING 8.8 Class StockApplication

```
#region Using directives
using System;
using System.Collections.Generic;
using System.Text;
#endregion

namespace Stocks {

   public class StockApplication {

      static void Main() {
         Stock stock1 = new Stock("Valuable", 160, 5, 15);
         Stock stock2 = new Stock("Cheap", 30, 2, 6);
         Stock stock3 = new Stock("Medium", 90, 4, 10);
         Stock stock4 = new Stock("Precious", 500, 20, 50);

         StockBroker b1 = new StockBroker("Broker 1");
         b1.AddStock(stock1);
         b1.AddStock(stock2);

         StockBroker b2 = new StockBroker("Broker 2");
         b2.AddStock(stock1);
         b2.AddStock(stock3);
         b2.AddStock(stock4);

         StockBroker b3 = new StockBroker("Broker 3");
         b3.AddStock(stock1);
         b3.AddStock(stock3);
```

LISTING 8.8 Class StockApplication (continued)

```
            StockBroker b4 = new StockBroker("Broker 4");
            b4.AddStock(stock1);
            b4.AddStock(stock2);
            b4.AddStock(stock3);
            b4.AddStock(stock4);


        }
    }
}


/* Portion of program output
Broker name: Broker 2 Stock name: Precious Stock value: 558 Number
changes: 4
Broker name: Broker 4 Stock name: Precious Stock value: 558 Number
changes: 4
Broker name: Broker 2 Stock name: Precious Stock value: 562 Number
changes: 5
Broker name: Broker 4 Stock name: Precious Stock value: 562 Number
changes: 5
Broker name: Broker 2 Stock name: Medium Stock value: 101 Number
changes: 5
Broker name: Broker 3 Stock name: Medium Stock value: 101 Number
changes: 5
Broker name: Broker 4 Stock name: Medium Stock value: 101 Number
changes: 5
Broker name: Broker 2 Stock name: Precious Stock value: 565 Number
changes: 6
Broker name: Broker 4 Stock name: Precious Stock value: 565 Number
changes: 6
Broker name: Broker 2 Stock name: Medium Stock value: 102 Number
changes: 6
Broker name: Broker 3 Stock name: Medium Stock value: 102 Number
changes: 6
Broker name: Broker 4 Stock name: Medium Stock value: 102 Number
changes: 6
Broker name: Broker 2 Stock name: Medium Stock value: 105 Number
changes: 7
Broker name: Broker 2 Stock name: Precious Stock value: 580 Number
changes: 7
Broker name: Broker 3 Stock name: Medium Stock value: 105 Number
changes: 7
Broker name: Broker 4 Stock name: Medium Stock value: 105 Number
changes: 7
Broker name: Broker 4 Stock name: Precious Stock value: 580 Number
changes: 7
Broker name: Broker 1 Stock name: Cheap Stock value: 37 Number
changes: 7
Broker name: Broker 4 Stock name: Cheap Stock value: 37 Number
changes: 7
*/
```

The architecture of this application is shown in the UML diagram in Figure 8.3.
StockApplication owns several *StockBroker* objects and several *Stock* objects. A public event. *stockEvent* (of type *StockNotification*), is defined in class *Stock*.

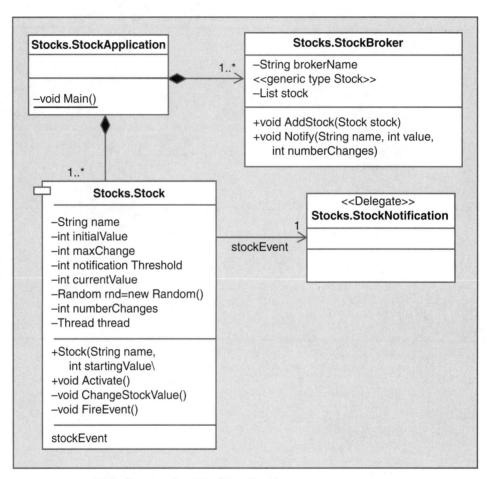

FIGURE 8.3 UML diagram for StockApplication

The sequence diagram in Figure 8.4 shows the steps that are involved in creating a listener and fire events that are received by the listener.

The main application class creates *stock1* and *broker1*. It then uses *AddStock* to add *stock1* to *broker1*'s stocks list. The *broker1* object registers its *Notify* listener method to *stock1*'s *someEvent* object (an instance of the *StockNotification* delegate). When *stock1* invokes its *FireEvent* method, the *Notify* method (listener) in *broker1* is invoked. This method then provides output to the console.

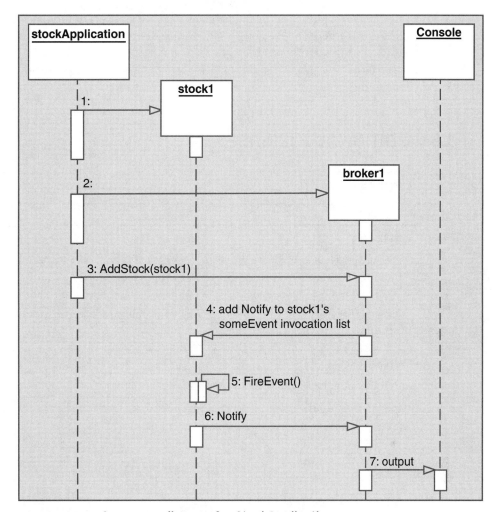

FIGURE 8.4 Sequence diagram for StockApplication

8.7 SUMMARY

- ◆ Delegates are full-fledged classes that encapsulate a method signature.
- ◆ Delegates may be defined anywhere a class definition is permitted.
- ◆ Delegate types may be used anywhere any type can be used (e.g., parameter to method, local variable, and field).
- ◆ An event is a delegate modifier.
- ◆ An event may be used in an interface declaration whereas a delegate cannot.
- ◆ An event may have *add* and *remove* accessors defined.

◆ Events are typically defined when a model class needs to notify one or more listener methods in the same or separate classes of some event. The Observer Pattern is frequently used.

◆ The event type is used throughout the .NET framework as the basis for event handling.

8.8 ADDITIONAL EXERCISES

Exercise 8.10

Research the Observer Pattern and explain in your own words how it works.

Exercise 8.11

Using the *Sorting* delegate, define your own instance of this delegate:

```
public delegate void Sorting<T>(ref T [] data, int size)
    where T: IComparable;
```

Create a short application that exercises your delegate instance (performs sorting).

Exercise 8.12

Suppose a delegate, *Function*, is defined as follows:

```
public delegate double Function(double x);
```

Write a method *Area* with the following signature:

```
public double Area(Function f, double lowerLimit,
                   double upperLimit,
                   double rectangleWidth)  {
   // You write the details
}
```

This signature approximates the area under the function, *f*, from *lowerLimit* to *upperLimit* using a series of rectangles of specified width (parameter *rectangleWidth*). The area is to be approximated by adding the areas of the approximating rectangles between the lower limit and the upper limit.

Write an entire application that tests your *Area* query by creating instances of the delegate *Function* that have well-known areas.

CHAPTER 9

Form Classes and Event Handling

Graphical user interface (GUI)-based programming is strongly supported by the .NET framework and tools such as Visual Studio. Many programmers (the author included) find GUI-based applications enjoyable to write because they involve the design and construction of a human-computer interface. Such an interface is much more interesting and user friendly than a simple text-based screen. Along with the enjoyment comes a challenge. In order to master the craft of developing GUI-based applications, one needs to learn how to manage the asynchronous events that are typically triggered by user input such as clicking or dragging the mouse, entering information in a text box, clicking a menu item, or clicking a choice in a combo box.

Support for GUI programming in .NET is provided by the classes in the *System.Windows.Forms* namespace. The many classes that support GUI programming are referred to as the *WinForm* classes. If you learn the basics of form programming in any .NET language such as Visual Basic or Visual C++ .NET, it is easy to carry those skills over to C#.

GUI programming has its roots in the Smalltalk development environment developed by Alan Kay at Xerox Palo Alto Research Center (Parc) in the late 1970s and made it officially available in 1980. The desktop programming metaphor pioneered in Smalltalk found its way first onto the Apple Lisa and shortly afterward the early Apple Macintosh computers. The huge growth in popularity of the Macintosh computer attests to the popularity among users of the friendly and intuitive graphical user interface that set the Macintosh apart from other computers during this era.

Visual Basic was created by Allan Cooper as a prototype called Ruby in 1988 and released as VB 1 (Version 1 of Visual Basic) at Window's World in March 1991. This early version of Visual Basic was a marriage of QuickBasic and Ruby. By June 1993, Visual Basic evolved to Version 3, which included the Jet Access Engine and reporting tools. The appeal of Visual Basic during this period was its simplicity compared to other programming languages and its growing support for GUI programming. A cottage industry involving many companies building Visual Basic "widgets" (visual components that could be plugged into a Visual Basic framework) was created. For many programmers, particularly ones with little formal training or programming experience, Visual Basic remained the first and only programming language that was used. Visual Basic, probably more than any language before it, established the culture of GUI programming.

Borland capitalized on this culture when it released Version 1 of Delphi Pascal in May 1995. This GUI-based language/framework was more complex and more powerful than Visual Basic. As a compiled language, it was much more efficient than Visual Basic. The inventor of Delphi Pascal, Anders Hejlsberg (also the inventor of Borland's famous Turbo Pascal), went on to become the chief architect of Microsoft's C# language. Delphi, like Visual Basic, was not an object-oriented language, and therefore its framework was not easily extensible.

It was not until the late 1990s that a truly powerful object-oriented language was harnessed to a rich GUI framework when Java 1.1 was released by Sun MicroSystems. Java's chief architect, James Gosling, was interested in promoting a standard GUI framework along with the language—something that was notably missing in C++.

The tremendous popularity and rapid acceptance of Java demonstrated how the programming community welcomed such a GUI framework. C++ included several major and competing nonstandard frameworks. This made it difficult and frustrating to port applications from one vendor's C++ development system to another.

The birth of .NET in the early 2000s provides another rich GUI framework that sits behind all the .NET languages. As shown in the previous chapter, its event-handling system is based on delegation. This is in sharp contrast to Java, which does not support delegates.

The goals of this chapter are to introduce the .NET Form classes, examine some of the most widely used GUI visual components from this framework, and show these components in action through GUI-based case studies.

It is not the objective of this chapter to present a comprehensive reference on Form classes. The MSDN documentation provides such a reference. Erik Brown's 715-page book, *Windows Forms Programming With C#* (Manning 2002), is another comprehensive reference.

This chapter does not present and illustrate the use of every visual component. Once you have mastered the use of the most basic components and have become familiar with the metaphor of GUI programming, particularly event handling, it is relatively easy to learn how to use other GUI components when they are needed.

From this chapter onward most of the applications that will be presented will be GUI based. It is useful to use an integrated development environment (IDE) when constructing GUI applications. Although this book was developed using Visual Studio .NET 2005 as the IDE, it is not the purpose of this chapter to teach or promote any particular IDE. Learning to use a particular IDE is the responsibility of the reader.

9.1 SIMPLE GUI PROGRAMMING

We begin with the simplest GUI application—one that writes the message, "Welcome to the world of GUI Programming" on the screen. But as we will see, even this simple task requires some infrastructure. Fortunately, all of the major IDEs provide this infrastructure for the programmer. As the user places visual components such as buttons or text boxes or other standard components on the design form, the IDE automatically generates C# code. This code is responsible for creating and initializing the visual component object and placing it on the form at the location indicated by the user (programmer). It would be a tedious process to produce this code by hand.

The static method *Application.Run* initiates the application. Its signature is:

```
public void Run(Form form)
```

This method makes the form sent as a parameter visible and starts an event thread that polls the system for user-actuated events such as clicking a button or typing in a text box.

Listing 9.1 shows the details of class *WelcomeMessageApplication*. The Run method creates an anonymous object of type *WelcomeMessage* as its argument and displays the *WelcomeMessage* form.

LISTING 9.1 Class WelcomeMessageApplication

```
using System;
using System.Collections.Generic;
using System.Windows.Forms;

namespace Welcome {

    public class WelcomeMessageApplication {

        public static void Main() {
            Application.Run(new WelcomeMessage());
        }
    }
}
```

Form class *WelcomeMessage* is presented in Listing 9.2.

LISTING 9.2 Class WelcomeMessage

```
using System;
using System.Collections.Generic;
using System.ComponentModel;
using System.Data;
using System.Drawing;
using System.Windows.Forms;

namespace Welcome {

    public partial class WelcomeMessage : Form {

        public WelcomeMessage() {
            InitializeComponent();
        }
    }
}
```

Please note the use of the keyword *partial*. This was inserted by the IDE in producing the boilerplate code. The constructor invokes the command *InitializeComponent*. This command is implemented in the other portion of this partial class and is shown in Listing 9.3.

All of the details presented in Listing 9.3 were produced by the IDE. The only visual design done by the author was to set the *Text* property of the form to "Welcome Message", drop a *Label* component onto the main form (named *welcomeLabel*), set its *Text* property to the string "Welcome to the world of GUI Programming", set the font to 12 point, and set its foreground color to red. These settings were all performed using the visual design tool in the IDE. In turn, it produced the code shown in Listing 9.3.

LISTING 9.3 Other portion of partial class WelcomeMessage

```
namespace Welcome {

    public partial class WelcomeMessage {

        private System.ComponentModel.IContainer components = null;

        // Clean up any resources being used.
        protected override void Dispose(bool disposing) {
            if (disposing && (components != null)) {
                components.Dispose();
            }
            base.Dispose(disposing);
        }

        #region Windows Form Designer generated code

        /// <summary>
        /// Required method for Designer support - do not modify
        /// the contents of this method with the code editor.
        /// </summary>
        private void InitializeComponent() {
            this.welcomeLabel = new System.Windows.Forms.Label();
            this.SuspendLayout();
            //
            // welcomeLabel
            //
            this.welcomeLabel.AutoSize = true;
            this.welcomeLabel.Font = new System.Drawing.Font(
                "Microsoft Sans
                Serif", 12F, System.Drawing.FontStyle.Regular,
                System.Drawing.GraphicsUnit.Point, ((byte)(0)));
            this.welcomeLabel.ForeColor =
                System.Drawing.Color.Red;
            this.welcomeLabel.Location =
                new System.Drawing.Point(25, 147);
            this.welcomeLabel.Name = "welcomeLabel";
            this.welcomeLabel.Size =
                new System.Drawing.Size(319, 21);
            this.welcomeLabel.TabIndex = 0;
            this.welcomeLabel.Text =
                "Welcome to the world of GUI Programming";
            //
```

LISTING 9.3 Other portion of partial class WelcomeMessage (continued)

```
            // WelcomeMessage
            //
            this.AutoScaleBaseSize =
                new System.Drawing.Size(5, 13);
            this.BackgroundImageLayout =
                System.Windows.Forms.ImageLayout.None;
            this.ClientSize = new System.Drawing.Size(381, 320);
            this.Controls.Add(this.welcomeLabel);
            this.Name = "WelcomeMessage";
            this.Text = "Welcome Message";
            this.ResumeLayout(false);
            this.PerformLayout();


        }

        #endregion

        private System.Windows.Forms.Label welcomeLabel;
    }
}
```

A screenshot of the completed application is shown in Figure 9.1.

When the application is launched, the form (window) containing the message appears in the upper-left corner of the screen. It is often desirable for a GUI application to launch with a form that is centered on the screen.

FIGURE 9.1 Screenshot of GUI application

This may be accomplished by adding one line of code directly underneath the *InitializeComponent* command in the *WelcomeMessage* constructor. This line of code is:

```
// Center form on the user's screen
this.SetBounds((Screen.GetBounds(this).Width / 2) -
                    (this.Width / 2),
               (Screen.GetBounds(this).Height / 2) -
                    (this.Height / 2),
              this.Width, this.Height, BoundsSpecified.Location);
```

The property *Width* is used in connection with the static method *Screen.GetBounds(this)* to obtain the width (in pixels) of the screen. The *Height* property is used in a similar way to obtain the height of the screen (in pixels). The expressions *this.Width* and *this.Height* are used to obtain the width and height of the form. As an alternative, .NET provides a property called *StartPosition*. It can be assigned as follows: *this.StartPosition = FormStartPosition.CenterScreen*.

Exercise 9.1

Explain how the *this.SetBounds* command shown above centers the form on the user's screen. Your reasoning should be based on how the screen width and form width are used to set the screen rectangle.

As additional visual components are positioned onto the main form, the length of the *InitializeComponent* method grows. Happily the IDE produces the code in response to the user moving visual components around the form. If the code is edited, the effect is immediately evident in the visual designer.

Although it is clearly possible to produce a GUI application from scratch, without the assistance of an IDE, this is not recommended because so many of the details are tedious and best done by the IDE.

Some very simple event handling is next introduced in this application. Suppose that in response to the user clicking the mouse when it is over the *welcomeLabel* component a modal dialog box with the message "You have clicked the welcome message" is displayed, as shown in Figure 9.2.

FIGURE 9.2 Welcome message

To accomplish this, an instance of the *Click* event handler is created within the *InitialComponent* method as follows:

```
this.welcomeLabel.Click += new
                System.EventHandler(this.welcomeLabel_Click);
```

Recall from Section 8.5 that the *Click* event is declared in class *Button* as follows:

```
public event EventHandler Click;
```

The delegate instance, *welcomeLabel_Click*, is given as follows:

```
private void welcomeLabel_Click(object sender, EventArgs e) {
    MessageBox.Show("You have clicked the welcome message.");
}
```

The static *Show* method from class *MessageBox* is used to produce the modal dialog box. The *Label* component, like many other standard *Form* components, is wired to trigger the *Click* event when the mouse button is depressed (clicked) inside of the component.

Visual Studio and Borland's C# Builder automate the production of the *Click* event handler instance when the user double-clicks the component in the visual designer. In addition to constructing the event handler, it also creates the skeletal structure of the event handler method (*welcomeLabel_Click* in this case).

Although *Button* components are normally associated with mouse clicks, any component may have a *Click* event handler associated with it. Within most IDEs, users can select from a list of events that can be associated with an event handler that the user can write.

9.2 CLASS CONTROL

Class *Control* in the *System.Windows.Forms* namespace encapsulates the functionality used by all *Form* controls. Class *Control* is found in the following hierarchy:

> Object
>   MarshalByRefObject
>   ComponentModel.Component
>   Control

Table 9.1 lists some public properties, methods, and events contained within class *Control*.

TABLE 9.1 Features of class Control

Public Properties	Description
AllowDrop	If true, allows drag and drop operations within the control
Anchor	Determines the edges for the control
BackColor	Determines the background color of the control
ContextMenu	Gets or sets the context menu of the control

TABLE 9.1 Features of class Control (continued)

Public Properties	Description
Controls	Gets or sets the collection of controls contained by this control
ClientRectangle	Gets the client area of the control
Cursor	Gets or sets the cursor to display when the mouse is over the control
Enabled	Gets or sets whether the control is enabled
Location	Gets or sets the Top and Left properties of the control
Parent	Gets or sets the parent control
TabIndex	Gets or sets the tab index of the control
TabStop	Determines whether the user can use the Tab key to give focus to the control
Text	Gets or sets the text associated with the control
Visible	Gets or sets the visibility of the control and any controls that are contained within the control
Public Methods	
BringToFront	Brings the control to the front of the z-order
GetNextControl	Returns the next or previous control in the tab order
Invalidate	Forces a paint message to be sent to the control
PointToClient	Converts a screen location to client coordinates
Public Events	
Click	Triggered when the mouse is depressed within the control
KeyPress	Triggered when a key is pressed while the control has the focus
MouseUp	Triggered when a mouse button is released within the control
Paint	Occurs when part or all of the control needs to be repainted

Because all controls are components, they therefore implement the *IComponent* and *IDisposable* interfaces. When a control is no longer needed, the *Dispose* command should be invoked on the control in order to free any resources used by the control.

9.3 BASIC CONTROLS

Basic controls that are frequently used in building GUI applications include *Panel*, *GroupBox*, *TextBox*, *Button*, *Label*, *ComboBox*, *ListBox*, *CheckBox*, and *RadioButton*.

We construct a simple application whose principal purpose is to bring on stage the controls listed above. Once these controls have made their presence known, we examine several of them in more detail.

Figure 9.3 displays the user interface of our simple application.

The ComboBox with title "Relationship" contains the choices shown in Figure 9.4.

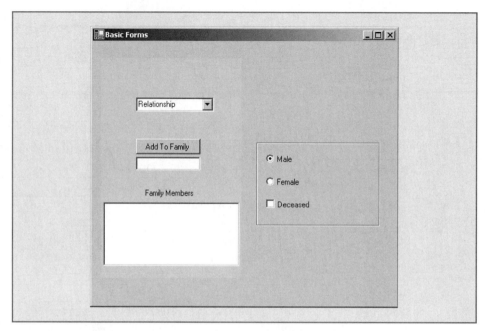

FIGURE 9.3 User interface for simple GUI application

Exercise 9.2

Name the visual components used in Figure 9.3.

Most of the code for this application is automatically generated by the IDE. After some of the visual components are dropped onto the design form, they are immediately renamed in order to promote program readability.

Listing 9.4 presents the source-code details of this application. The code that is not automatically generated is shown in boldface type.

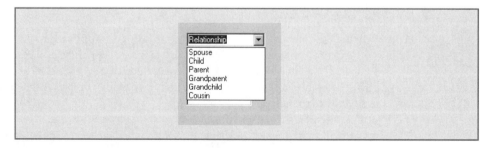

FIGURE 9.4 Relationship ComboBox

LISTING 9.4 Source code for GUI application

```
using System;
using System.Collections.Generic;
using System.Windows.Forms;

namespace BasicControls {

   public class BasicFormsApp {

      static void Main() {
         Application.Run(new BasicFormsUI());
      }
   }
}

using System.ComponentModel;
using System.Data;
using System.Drawing;
using System.Windows.Forms;

namespace BasicControls {

   partial class BasicFormsUI : Form {

   private System.Windows.Forms.Panel panel1;
      private System.Windows.Forms.ListBox familyMembersListBox;
      private System.Windows.Forms.Label label2;
      private System.Windows.Forms.TextBox addToFamilyBox;
      private System.Windows.Forms.Button addToFamilyBtn;
      private System.Windows.Forms.ComboBox comboBox;
      private System.Windows.Forms.GroupBox groupBox2;
      private System.Windows.Forms.CheckBox checkBox;
      private System.Windows.Forms.RadioButton femaleBtn;
      private System.Windows.Forms.RadioButton maleBtn;

      public BasicFormsUI() {
         InitializeComponent();
         // Center form on the user's screen
         this.SetBounds((Screen.GetBounds(this).Width / 2)
            - (this.Width / 2),
            (Screen.GetBounds(this).Height / 2) -
            (this.Height / 2), this.Width,
             this.Height, BoundsSpecified.Location);
      }

      private void addToFamilyBtn_Click(object sender,
         EventArgs e) {
         if (addToFamilyBox.Text.Trim().Length == 0) {
            MessageBox.Show("Must enter a family name.");
         } else {
```

LISTING 9.4 Source code for GUI application (continued)

```
            String gender = maleBtn.Checked ?
                        " (Male)" : " (Female)";
            String relationship = (String) comboBox.SelectedItem;
            familyMembersListBox.Items.Add(addToFamilyBox.Text +
                        gender + " <" + relationship + ">");
            addToFamilyBox.Text = "";
        }
      }
    }
  }

namespace BasicControls {

  partial class BasicFormsUI {

    private System.ComponentModel.IContainer components = null;


    protected override void Dispose(bool disposing) {
      if (disposing && (components != null)) {
          components.Dispose();
      }
      base.Dispose(disposing);
    }

    private void InitializeComponent() {
    /* Details automatically generated by IDE and not shown here.
    /*

    }
  }
}
```

As shown in Listing 9.4, only a small quantity of code is written by the programmer. The rest is generated by the IDE in response to dropping and aligning visual components onto the design form. The IDE provides tremendous leverage in quickly constructing the simple GUI application.

Suppose we want to disable all the visual components attached to form *BasicFormsUI*. We can use the *Controls* property of the main form to accomplish this as follows:

```
foreach (Control control in this.Controls) {
    control.Enabled = false;
}
```

Using your favorite (or available) IDE, implement the application shown in Figure 9.3.

9.4 EVENT HANDLING

GUI components generate events in response to user actions such as clicking a button, entering text in a *TextBox*, making a selection in a *ComboBox*, checking a *CheckBox*, or simply moving or clicking the mouse over a control. Because the main purpose of a graphical user interface is to elicit input from a user, it should be clear that event handling plays a central role in the construction of GUI applications because it is through event handling that the application is programmed to respond to the user's inputs.

As shown earlier, event types provide the basis for event handling. There are more than 60 events defined for a *TextBox*. This is typical of GUI controls. For example, *TextBox* includes *Click*, *Enter*, *KeyDown*, *KeyPress,* and *TextChanged*.

Within method *InitializeComponent* we might bring these events to life using the following code:

```
this.textBox.Click += new System.EventHandler(this.textBox_Click);
this.textBox.KeyDown +=
  new System.Windows.Forms.KeyEventHandler(this.textBox_KeyDown);
this.textBox.KeyPress +=
  new System.Windows.Forms.KeyPressEventHandler
    (this.textBox_KeyPress);
this.textBox.Enter +=
  new System.EventHandler(this.textBox_Enter);
this.textBox.TextChanged +=
  new System.EventHandler(this.textBox_TextChanged);
```

Each of the five constructor calls shown in the preceding code adds an event handler to the list of handlers triggered when the user performs the operation associated with the event.

Exercise 9.4

Build a simple GUI application that contains a single *TextBox* control embedded in a *Form*. Implement event handlers for the five events shown above that work as follows:

```
MessageBox.Show("In event handler xxx");
```

where "xxx" is the name of the event handler.

Suppose we want to replace or duplicate the functionality of the "Add To Family" button in Figure 9.3 by having the "Enter" key trigger the same response as the "Add To Family" button currently does. So when the user has entered the name of a family member and wishes it to be recorded in the list box control, the user types the "Enter" key following the last character that is entered in the text box. This is a natural kind of user input.

The code that accomplishes this using the *KeyUp* event is:

```
// In method InitializeComponent
this.addToFamilyBox.KeyUp +=
    new System.Windows.Forms.KeyEventHandler
        (this.addToFamilyBox_KeyUp);


private void addToFamilyBox_KeyUp(object sender, KeyEventArgs e) {
    if (e.KeyCode == Keys.Enter) {
      if (addToFamilyBox.Text.Trim().Length == 0) {
        MessageBox.Show("Must enter a family name.");
      } else {
        String gender = maleBtn.Checked ? " (Male)" : " (Female)";
        String relationship = (String)comboBox.SelectedItem;
        familyMembersListBox.Items.Add(addToFamilyBox.Text +
            gender + " <" + relationship + ">");
        addToFamilyBox.Text = "";
      }
    }
}
```

A *ListBox* control is used not only to display a set of items but also to select one or more items from the display. Items can be added to or deleted from a *ListBox* control as an application is running.

To illustrate this, suppose we wish to be able to select one or more family members in the list box control and display their names using *MessageBox.Show*. A new button, "Output Selection," is added to the GUI as shown in Figure 9.5.

The "Click" handler for this new button contains the code for obtaining the selected lines in the list box control and outputting them using *MessageBox.Show*.

```
// In method InitializeComponent
this.familyMembersListBox.SelectionMode =
    System.Windows.Forms.SelectionMode.MultiSimple;


private void selectionBtn_Click(object sender, EventArgs e) {
    ListBox.SelectedObjectCollection family =
      familyMembersListBox.SelectedItems;
    String familyMembers = "";
    foreach (String member in family) {
      familyMembers += member + "\n";
    }
    MessageBox.Show(familyMembers);
}
```

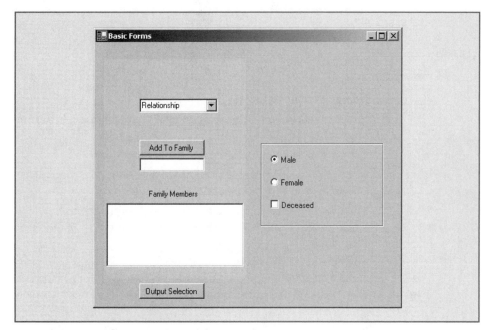

FIGURE 9.5 Revised simple GUI

The *SelectionMode* property is set with the value *MultiSimple*. This allows multiple lines in the list box control to be selected.

The "get" property *SelectedItems* is used to obtain a *ListBox.SelectedObjectCollection* family. The *foreach* iteration is used to capture each *String* object in this collection. The collection of newline separated string values is output.

The two radio buttons in Figure 9.5 are embedded in a *GroupBox* control. This allows them to enjoy the mutually exclusive behavior that we wish to achieve (when one button is selected, the other is deselected).

Learning the myriad details associated with each GUI control is a massive undertaking and is not recommended. With each control having dozens of properties and dozens of event types, the best way to discover the rich functionality associated with a particular control is to use the control in some application. The Property View in your IDE (both Visual Studio and C# Builder have Property Views) presents a list of all the properties whose values you may set and all the event types that you may associate with a custom handler that you design. The needs of your application will direct you to use the IDE so that the control meets these needs.

Exercise 9.5

Add appropriate code to the "Add To Family" button handler so that <Deceased> is displayed if the *CheckBox* component is checked.

Exercise 9.6

Construct a complete temperature conversion GUI application with the following specifications:

1. The user must enter the starting temperature that defines the beginning of a range of temperatures.

2. The user must enter the ending temperature that defines the end of the range of temperatures.

3. The user must enter the increment in temperature.

4. If the user fails to provide these three data entries, a modal dialog message is emitted that directs the user to comply with the input requirements.

5. The user must indicate whether the conversion within the range of temperatures given is from Fahrenheit to centigrade or from centigrade to Fahrenheit.

6. The output must be displayed in two aligned columns using a *RichTextBox* control. The left column contains the values in the range of temperatures specified, and the right column contains the equivalent temperatures after conversion.

7. You are free to design the user interface so that it meets the general requirements given.

9.5 COMPUTATIONS IN A GUI

It is a fairly common practice to perform a computation within a GUI event handler. Often the computation involves one or more loop constructs. Because the computation is performed in the event dispatch thread (the same thread that responds to GUI events such as closing down a window or clicking a button), these GUI functions are temporarily disabled while the CPU is preoccupied with completing the computation. This manifests itself to the user with the symptom that all GUI controls seem to be locked. In fact, they are locked while the CPU performs the time-intensive computation. The application cannot even be exited using a normal control such as clicking the "x". In time-consuming applications this can be most frustrating. Another possible problem stemming from the same cause would be output to a control that is delayed until the computation is completed even though the programmer designed the code to provide output while the computation is in progress or even before the computation started. Once started, the computation seizes total control of the machine.

The pattern of programming that should be used to overcome this disabling of the GUI while allowing the computation to proceed in "parallel" is shown in the following code:

```
private void ComputationThread() {
    Thread.Sleep(100);
    // Time-intensive computation not shown
}
```

```
private void PerformComputation_EventHandler(Object sender,
                                            System.EventArgs e) {
   Thread computation =
     new Thread(new ThreadStart(this.ComputationThread));
     computation.Start();
}
```

Here it is assumed that the event handler *PerformComputation_EventHandler* is triggered by some GUI-based user input. Instead of running the computation directly in this event handler, a thread, *computation*, is spawned and started in the event handler. The details of the computation are put in the thread method.

Exercise 9.7

Construct a simple GUI application that contains a single button with the label "Start Computation". The Click event should initiate a process given by three nested loops, each going from 1 to 100,000,000. In the innermost loop, the values of integer variables a and b are multiplied (where a is assigned the value 4 and b the value 5). Construct the application so that while this massive computation is taking place, the user may exit the application, resize the window, minimize the window, or in general retain control of the GUI. Use the pattern of programming shown earlier to achieve your objective.

9.6 SIMPLE GRAPHICS

C# provides namespaces, classes, methods, and events for supporting applications with graphical capabilities. The *System.Drawing* namespace and class *Graphics* provide functionality for drawing shapes such as lines, rectangles, circles, ellipses, and polygons. The namespace *System.Drawing.Drawing2D* is used for drawing and filling more complex shapes. We introduce only simple shapes in this chapter.

Drawing shapes is accomplished by sending commands to a *Graphics* object. Table 9.2 lists several commands in class *Graphics* and sample usage. Brush is an abstract class so it is necessary to use one of its concrete subclasses such as *SolidBrush* or *TextureBrush*.

TABLE 9.2 A few useful commands in class Graphics

Command	Sample Code Assuming a Graphics Object, graphics

DrawRectangle(System.Drawing.Pen, float x, float y, float width, float height)	graphics.DrawRectangle(
	    new Pen(Color.Black, 2), 10,10,
	      100, 150);

FillRectangle(System.Drawing.Brush, float x, float y, float width, float height)	graphics.FillRectangle (new SolidBrush(Color.Red), 10, 10, 100, 50);

DrawLine(System.Drawing.Pen, float x, float y, float width, float height)	graphics.DrawLine(new
	   Pen(Color.Black,2), 10 ,10 ,100,
	    50);

Pen objects are used in drawing shapes and *Brush* objects are used in filling shapes.

Following is an illustrative application that demonstrates the use of several commands from the *Graphics* class:

```
using System;
using System.Collections.Generic;
using System.ComponentModel;
using System.Data;
using System.Drawing;
using System.Windows.Forms;

namespace SimpleGraphics {

    partial class SimpleGraphics : Form {

        public SimpleGraphics() {
            InitializeComponent();
        }

        private void drawBtn_Click(object sender, EventArgs e) {
            // Obtain graphics context of Panel
            Graphics graphics = panel.CreateGraphics();
            graphics.DrawArc(new Pen(Color.Red, 5),
                    new Rectangle(20, 20, 100, 100), 0, 90);
            graphics.DrawLine(new Pen(Color.Green, 10), 50, 50, 200,
                        200);
            graphics.DrawRectangle(new Pen(Color.Black, 1), 0, 0, 50,
                        50);
            graphics.FillRectangle(new SolidBrush(Color.Black), 0, 0,
                        50, 50);
            graphics.DrawCurve(new Pen(Color.OrangeRed, 5),
              new Point [] {new Point(50, 50),
              new Point(60, 60), new Point(70, 70),
              new Point(80, 80), Point(90, 90),
              new Point(100, 100)});
            graphics.DrawLines(new Pen(Color.Black, 20),
              new Point[] {new Point(200, 200),
              new Point(220, 220),
              new Point(230, 230),
              new Point(240, 240)});
        }
    }
}
```

Only the nongenerated code is shown in this partial class. The shapes that are produced by the code shown are shown in Figure 9.6.

In the next section, we construct a real application using graphical shapes.

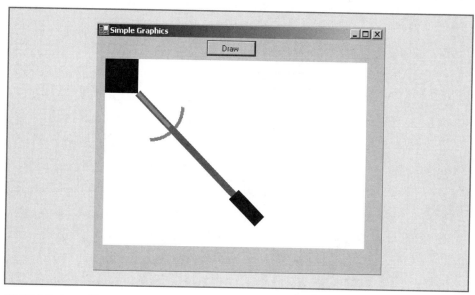

FIGURE 9.6 Shapes produced by the preceding code

9.7 MODEL-VIEW DESIGN (OBSERVER PATTERN)

Recall the Smalltalk language/environment, developed at Xerox Parc, set the stage for much of the GUI frameworks that have evolved over the past 25 years. It was also through Smalltalk that a powerful principle of GUI programming emerged—the Model-View-Controller pattern (MVC) that has more recently evolved into the **Observer Pattern**.

Trygve Reenskaug (in Oslo, Norway) is credited with formulating the MVC concept while visiting Xerox Parc in the 1970s. The first significant paper published on MVC was "A Cookbook for Using the Model-View-Controller User Interface Paradigm in Smalltalk-80," by Glenn Krasner and Stephen Pope, published in the August/September 1988 issue of the *Journal of Object-Oriented Programming* (Richard Wiener, Editor, SIGS Publications).

The Observer Pattern separates the computational aspects of the software architecture, the **model**, from the display or GUI aspects, the **view**. Whenever something of interest occurs within a model object, notification is sent to one or more view objects that display information to the user. More generally, the Observer Pattern defines a one-to-many relationship between objects so that when one object changes its state, its dependents are notified.

A UML diagram that depicts the design pattern is given in Figure 9.7.

9.7.1 Application that Illustrates the Observer Pattern

An application is to be constructed that tests the reaction time and mouse agility of a user. Using a track bar, the user chooses the width (which is the same as the height) of the squares that will be displayed on the screen, each at a randomly chosen location.

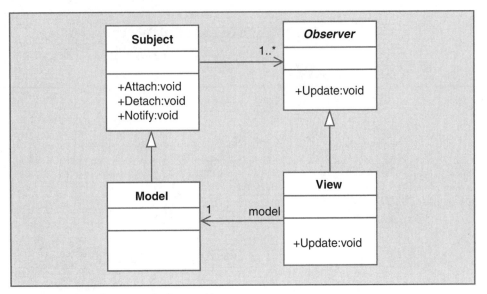

FIGURE 9.7 Observer design pattern

The reaction-time test begins with squares generated at random locations every five seconds. The user must click the left mouse button anywhere inside the square that is generated. If five consecutive squares are generated by the computer that are not "hit" by the user (user successfully clicking the mouse within the square before the next square is generated), the reaction test ends. The user's score is output and is measured in terms of the total number of hits achieved during the test.

But there is more ...

◆ If the user's hit occurs before 90 percent of the delay time has elapsed, the delay time is reduced by a factor of 0.8.

◆ Squares that are hit by the user are to be filled with red until the next unfilled square is generated. All squares except the current square are to be colored blue.

A screen shot of the application running is given in Figure 9.8. An Observer Pattern approach will be taken in designing the software. A namespace *ReactionTime* is defined. Within this namespace, a delegate class *Notification* containing no parameters is declared. Next, a *ReactionTimeModel* class is constructed. This class has five fields:

◆ *delayTime (in milliseconds)*—controls how often notifications to display a square are sent to the view

◆ *thread*—the method that periodically fires a notification to the view informing it to display a randomly located square

♦ *timer*—an instance of class TimeInterval that measures elapsed time

♦ *stopThread*—a Boolean value that when set to true stops the thread

♦ *consecutiveMisses*—counts the number of consecutive times a square has been generated that is not hit by the user

♦ *totalHits*—counts the number of times that the user has hit the randomly located square

A public event, *notify*, of type *Notification* is declared. The constructor initializes the field values for *delayTime*, *totalHits*, and *consecutiveMisses*. It then spawns the thread by launching the thread method *TriggerView*.

A *Register* method allows the view to register itself with the model so that it can be notified.

The *TriggerView* thread method runs in a for-loop controlled by the Boolean *stopThread* field. *Thread.Sleep*(delayTime) is used to control the frequency of notifications to the view that it should generate the next randomly located square. Each time a notification is sent to the view the value of *consecutiveMisses* is incremented by one.

The method *StopTiming* allows the view to signal to the model that the user has hit a square. The *totalHits* value is incremented by one, and the value of *consecutiveMisses* is reset to zero. If the elapsed time from the moment the square is displayed to the time the user hits the square is less than 90 percent of the current delay time, the delay time is reduced by 0.8. This makes the game more and more challenging to play over time.

Listing 9.5 presents the source code details.

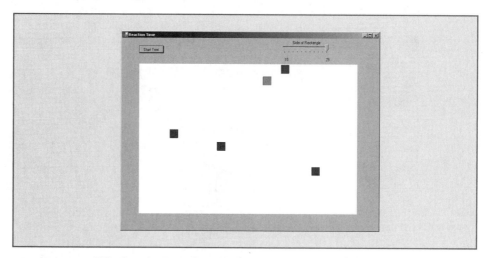

FIGURE 9.8 Window in Reaction Time application

LISTING 9.5 Class ReactionTimeModel

```
using System;
using System.Collections.Generic;
using System.Text;
using System.Threading;
using System.Windows.Forms;

namespace ReactionTime {

    public delegate void Notification();

    public class ReactionTimeModel {

        private int delayTime; // In milliseconds
        private Thread thread;
        private TimeInterval timer = new TimeInterval();
        private bool stopThread = false;
        private int consecutiveMisses;
        private int totalHits;

        public event Notification notify;

        // Constructor
        public ReactionTimeModel() {
            delayTime = 5000;
            totalHits = 0;
            consecutiveMisses = 0;
            thread = new Thread(new ThreadStart(TriggerView));
            thread.Start();
        }

        // Commands
        public void Register(Notification update) {
            notify += new Notification(update);
        }

        public void StopThread() {
            stopThread = true;
        }

        public void TriggerView() {
            for (; !stopThread; ) {
               Thread.Sleep(delayTime);
               if (notify != null) {
                    notify(); // Using the registered update method
                    consecutiveMisses++;
                    if (consecutiveMisses == 6) {
                        this.StopThread();
                        MessageBox.Show(
    "Game is over since you have missed 5 consecutive boxes.");
```

LISTING 9.5   Class ReactionTimeModel (continued)

```
                      MessageBox.Show(
   "You have achieved " + totalHits + " hits during the game.");
                  }
                      timer.StartTiming();
              }
          }
      }


      public void StopTiming() {
          timer.EndTiming();
          totalHits++;
          consecutiveMisses = 0;
          if (timer.ElapsedTime() < 0.9 * delayTime) {
              delayTime = 4 * delayTime / 5;
          }
      }
  }

  public class TimeInterval {
      // Fields
      private long startTicks, endTicks;

      public void StartTiming() {
          DateTime t = DateTime.Now;
          startTicks = t.Ticks;
      }

      public void EndTiming() {
          DateTime t = DateTime.Now;
          endTicks = t.Ticks;
      }

      public double ElapsedTime() { // In milliseconds
          return (endTicks - startTicks) / 10000.0;
      }
  }
}
```

The *Register* method adds the *update* method sent in by the view.
Listing 9.6 presents the details of the view, class *ReactionTimeUI*.

LISTING 9.6 Class ReactionTimeUI

```
using System;
using System.Collections.Generic;
using System.ComponentModel;
using System.Data;
using System.Drawing;
using System.Windows.Forms;
using System.Threading;

namespace ReactionTime {

    partial class ReactionTimeUI : Form {

        // Fields
        private ReactionTimeModel model;
        private Graphics g;
        private Random randomValue = new Random();
        private float x, y; // Produced by GenerateSquare
        private float side = 15;

        public ReactionTimeUI() {
            InitializeComponent();
            // Center form on the user's screen
            this.SetBounds((Screen.GetBounds(this).Width / 2) -
                (this.Width / 2),
                (Screen.GetBounds(this).Height / 2) -
                (this.Height / 2), this.Width, this.Height,
                BoundsSpecified.Location);
            g = panel.CreateGraphics();
        }

        public void GenerateSquare() {
            g.FillRectangle(new SolidBrush(Color.Blue), x, y,
                        side, side);
            // Get random x and y coordinates
            x = (float) (randomValue.NextDouble() * panel.Width * 0.8);
            y = (float)(randomValue.NextDouble() * panel.Height * 0.8);
            g.DrawRectangle(new Pen(
                new SolidBrush(Color.Black)), x, y, side, side);
        }

        private void ReactionTimeUI_FormClosing(object sender,
                                FormClosingEventArgs e) {
            model.StopThread();
            Thread.Sleep(500);
        }
```

LISTING 9.6 Class ReactionTimeUI (continued)

```
    private void panel_MouseDown(object sender,
            MouseEventArgs e) {
      int mouseX = e.X;
      int mouseY = e.Y;
      if (mouseX >= x && mouseX <= x + side &&
            mouseY >= y && mouseY <= y + side) {
          model.StopTiming();
          g.FillRectangle(new SolidBrush(Color.Red), x, y, side,
                    side);
      }
    }

    private void sideTrackBar_ValueChanged(object sender,
                                    EventArgs e) {
        side = sideTrackBar.Value;
    }

    private void startTestBtn_Click(object sender, EventArgs e) {
        if (model != null) {
            model.StopThread();
        }
        model = new ReactionTimeModel();
        model.Register(GenerateSquare);
        g.Clear(Color.White);
    }
  }
}
```

The view class contains five fields:

◆ *model*—an instance of ReactionTimeModel presented in Listing 9.5

◆ *g*—the graphics context for the panel component

◆ *randomValue*—a random number object used to produce squares at random locations

◆ *x, y*—the coordinates of the upper-left corner of each square that is randomly generated

◆ *side*—the dimension, in pixels, of each square

Each time the user clicks the "Start Test" button, a new model is constructed and the method *GenerateSquare* is registered with the model. The method *GenerateSquare* fills the existing square with blue, generates random coordinates *x* and *y*, and generates a new square using these random coordinates. It is typical to use a *Panel* component for rendering graphics. That is done in this application. The location and background color of a *Panel* component can be controlled by the user.

The *GenerateSquare* listener is triggered in time intervals given by the model's current *delayTime*, as described earlier. These time intervals get shorter as the test progresses. Each time the user clicks the mouse, the *panel_MouseDown* event handler is triggered. If the mouse coordinates are within the current square, the command *StopTiming* is sent to the model. The square is colored red until the next square is generated.

The automatically generated code, mainly in method *InitializeComponent*, is not shown but may be obtained along with the completed application on the Course Technology Web site.

Exercise 9.8

You will notice when you run the application that two squares are initially displayed, with one of them colored blue. Although this does not affect the correctness of the hit count, it is annoying. Revise the application so that only one square is presented initially.

Exercise 9.9

Modify the application so that the user's score (number of hits) is displayed in a noneditable text box above the panel containing the squares. Each time the user starts a new test, this value must be reset to zero.

A UML diagram that displays the architecture of the completed application is shown in Figure 9.9.

Exercise 9.10

Explain in words the relationships between the classes shown in the UML diagram of Figure 9.9.

9.7.2 ANOTHER APPLICATION OF THE OBSERVER PATTERN: ADDING A GUI TO THE OOPLY GAME

The OOPLY game presented in Chapter 6 sets the stage for another, more extensive example of using GUI controls and the Observer Pattern.

The presentation follows the chronology of the actual development. All the thinking and steps that convert the console-based application that contains the 11 model classes *AggressiveStrategy*, *ChancePosition*, *ConservativeStrategy*, *OOPLYApp*, *GlobalConstants*, *InvestmentStrategy*, *NewStrategyPosition*, *Player*, *Position*, *PropertyPosition*, and *RandomStrategy* to a GUI application that depicts the game as it progresses using a graphical user interface are explained.

The first challenge is to construct the graphical user interface using the standard *Windows.Form* components that we have been discussing. Here, the support of an IDE is indispensable. Using an IDE, there is no actual coding required during the construction of this GUI. Only the names of the controls need to be thoughtfully chosen because the IDE creates objects using these names.

After several hours of tinkering, a screenshot of the design view of the GUI is shown in Figure 9.10. The ten positions are shown, each using a separate *Panel* component. The most complex of these, the property positions, contain two read-only

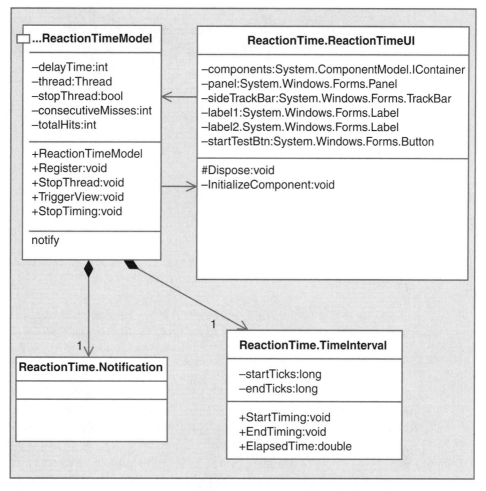

FIGURE 9.9 UML class diagram for Reaction Time application

TextBox controls that contain the owner of the property and the number of units purchased for the property.

A *Button* control is used to allow the user to throw a die for the player whose name appears on the button. The outcome of the die throw is shown in a read-only *Textbox* control.

Five read-only *TextBox* controls appear in a separate *Panel* at the bottom and are used to output the move number and the cash of each of the four players.

The numerals 1, 2, 3, and 4, shown in red in position 1, represent the starting position of each of the four players. As players move around the board, their current positions are shown by placing their number onto the position that they occupy.

Exercise 9.11

Using your favorite C#/.NET IDE, construct the GUI shown in Figure 9.10.

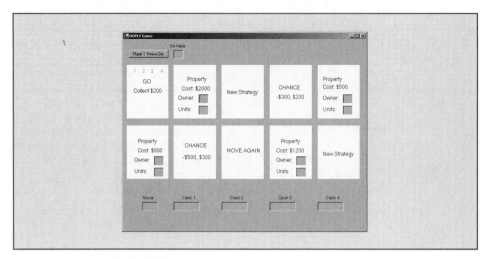

FIGURE 9.10 GUI for OOPLY game

As these words are being written, there are two disparate pieces that must be welded together. There is the IDE-generated code for the class OOPLYUI that sits behind the GUI shown in Figure 9.10 and the 11 classes produced earlier (and described in Chapter 6) that represent the problem domain and architectural model of the system.

We want to vest as much responsibility with the model classes as possible because these classes were designed to handle the interactions between the entities that comprise the game. When events in the model classes occur that require the GUI to be updated, these model classes need to notify the GUI. This forms the basis for the Observer Pattern.

Following is a catalog of the events of interest in the model that require notification of the GUI:

1. Die throw for player must be displayed.

2. Player moves to a new board position and its number must be displayed at the new position and removed at the old position.

3. A new move cycle occurs (a move cycle includes one move for each player or a total of four moves) and must be displayed.

4. Player landing on a property position purchases the property so the owner must be displayed.

5. Player landing on its own property purchases investment units. The total number of investment units sitting on this property must be displayed.

6. One or more players have their cash changed because of the purchase of a property or investment units, having to pay rent to another player (in which case two players have their cash changed), passing Go and collecting $200 or landing on a chance position and either gaining or losing cash.

7. Player becomes bankrupt and game ends. GUI must be notified.

Class *OOPLYApp* in the console version is changed to class *Game*. Its method *Main* is removed. A new class *OOPLYApp*, which is produced by the IDE, contains method *Main* and constructs an instance of OOPLYUI.

A careful analysis of the list of GUI updates that are required suggests the need for events to be triggered in classes *Game* (in response to a die throw, a player changing its position, new move cycle, or the game ending), *PropertyPosition* (in response to the property being purchased, rent being paid to the owner by a player other than the owner landing on it, or investment units being purchased by the owner of the property), *ChancePosition* (in response to a player having its cash value changed). Following is a summary of the needed events:

- *Game* needs to update GUI when the user clicks the "Throw Die" button. The value of the die throw and the player who has thrown the die must be displayed.

- *Game* needs to update GUI when a player changes its position. Its number must be displayed in the new position and removed from the old position.

- *Game* needs to update GUI when the move cycle has been incremented.

- *Game* needs to update GUI when a player becomes bankrupt and game ends.

- *Game* needs to update GUI when a player passes Go and has its cash increased.

- *PropertyPosition* needs to update GUI when a player purchases property (both its cash changes and the owner of the property must be displayed).

- *PropertyPosition* needs to update GUI when a non-owning player pays rent to the owner of the property (the cash values of these two players must be updated).

- *PropertyPosition* needs to update the GUI when an owning player purchases one or more investment units (its cash value changes and the total number of units changes).

- *ChancePosition* needs to update the GUI when a player's cash changes.

We have identified the need for nine event types and event handlers.

The event firing and handling between class *Game* acting as an event source and class *OOPLYUI* acting as an event handler (observer) is straightforward. Five public delegate types are declared at namespace scope in the file containing class *Game*. These are given as follows:

```
// Delegate classes
public delegate void PlayerNewPositionNotification
        (int playerNumber, int oldPosition, int newPosition);

public delegate void MoveCycleNotification(int moveCycle);

public delegate void GameOverNotification();

public delegate void DieValueNotification(int dieValue);

public delegate void PassedGoNotification(int playerNumber, int cash);
```

The parameters in each delegate type are designed to allow the *OOPLYUI* class to update its GUI appropriately.

The *PlayerNewPositionNotification* delegate has its parameters designed so that it informs the *OOPLYUI* class about the player that has moved, its old position, and its new position. This provides sufficient information to move the number representing the player from the old position to the new position by making the *Label* control representing the old position invisible and the *Label* representing the new position visible. To accomplish this a matrix of *Label* components is stored as a field in the *OOPLYUI* class.

The *PassedGoNotification* delegate provides the player number and cash to *OOPLYUI* in order to permit it to update the player's cash display.

Exercise 9.12

Explain the parameters in the remaining three delegate types given earlier.

Class *Game* provides public event types for each of the delegate types, as shown in the following code:

```
public event PlayerNewPositionNotification playerMoveEvent;

public event MoveCycleNotification newMoveCycleEvent;

public event GameOverNotification gameOverEvent;

public event DieValueNotification dieValueEvent;

public event PassedGoNotification passedGoEvent;
```

Commands that allow the observer class *OOPLYUI* to register its handlers with the *game* object are provided. The command for registering the *playerMoveEvent* is given as follows:

```
public void RegisterForNewPositionNotification
          (PlayerNewPositionNotification update) {
   playerMoveEvent += new PlayerNewPositionNotification(update);
}
```

In the constructor in class *OOPLYUI*, the following line of code accomplishes the registration:

```
game.RegisterForNewPositionNotification(NewPlayerPositionHandler);
```

The event-handling link is completed with method *NewPlayerPositionHandler* in class *OOPLYUI*, which is implemented as follows:

```
public void NewPlayerPositionHandler(int playerNumber,
          int oldPosition, int newPosition) {
   dieValueLbl.Text = "Die Value For Player " + playerNumber;
   label[oldPosition, playerNumber].Visible = false;
   label[newPosition, playerNumber].Visible = true;
}
```

Here the matrix of *Label* controls that hold the numerals 1 through 4 in each *Panel* control representing a position is used to simulate the move of a player.

Figure 9.11 shows the steps involved in displaying the move of a player from one position to another.

Recall from our earlier discussion that:

◆ *PropertyPosition* needs to update the GUI when a player purchases property (both its cash changes and the owner of the property must be displayed).

◆ *PropertyPosition* needs to update the GUI when a non-owning player pays rent to the owner of the property (the cash values of these two players must be updated).

◆ *PropertyPosition* needs to update the GUI when an owning player purchases one or more investment units (its cash value changes and the total number of units changes).

ChancePosition needs to fire one event type:

◆ *ChancePosition* needs to update the GUI when a player's cash changes.

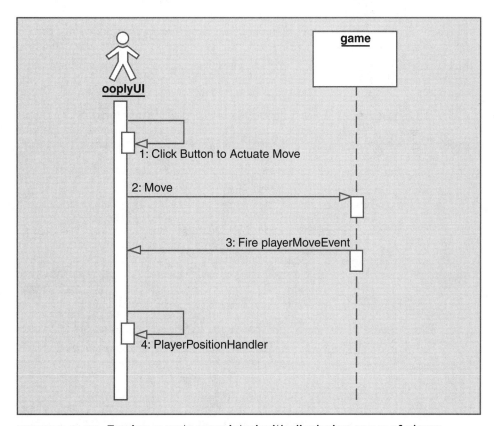

FIGURE 9.11 Tracing events associated with displaying move of player

The *OOPLYUI* class creates an instance of *Game* and therefore can register its event handlers with the *game* object as we illustrated previously. But the *OOPLYUI* class has no direct contact with either class *PropertyPosition* or class *ChancePosition*. The *Position* objects are private and internal to the *Game* class. So how can we register the four *OOPLYUI* handlers of interest with the three *PropertyPosition* objects or the two *ChancePosition* objects?

The answer is we cannot.

But because class *Game* creates the position objects it can register listeners with the three property position objects and the two chance position objects. Class *Game* must then have handlers that can fire events to the *OOPLYUI* class when it receives notification from the position objects. In other words, class *Game* both responds to events and fires events—it acts as an observer and event source. This requires that *Game* declare event types and allow class *OOPLYUI* to register handlers with these event types so that it can respond to the events that originate with the position objects.

In summary, when an event of interest occurs in one of the property position objects (e.g., a property is acquired by a player), the property position object fires an appropriate event that is listened to (handled) by the *game* object. The game object's handler merely transmits this event to the *OOPLYUI* object by firing its own event to the handler in the *OOPLYUI* class that has registered with the *Game* class.

We show the relevant segments of code for one such scenario starting in class *PropertyPosition* and ending in class *OOPLYUI*.

The *ProcessPlayer* command in class *PropertyPosition* shows three events fired and is presented in Listing 9.7. The three lines of code that fire events are shown in boldface.

LISTING 9.7 Move method in class PropertyPosition

```
public override void ProcessPlayer(Player player) {
   if (owner == null) {
    // Determine whether property can be purchased
    if (player.Strategy.BuyProperty()) {
      player.Cash -= cost;
      owner = player;
      purchasedPropertyEvent(player.Number); // Fire event
      // Code to output to log file not shown
    } else if (owner == player) {
      // Determine whether invest units can be purchased
      int numberUnits =
          player.Strategy.NumberOfUnitsToPurchase();
          investmentUnits += numberUnits;
          player.Cash -= numberUnits * cost / 2;
          purchasedInvestmentUnitsEvent(player.Number,
              investmentUnits); // Fire event
          // Code to output to log file not shown
    } else {
      // Determine the rent that must be paid to the owner
      int rent = cost / 10 + cost * investmentUnits / 20;
```

LISTING 9.7 Move method in class PropertyPosition (continued)

```
      owner.Cash += rent;
      player.Cash -= rent;
      RentCollected += rent;

      rentPaidEvent(player.Number, owner.Number);  // Fire event
      // Code to output to log file not shown
    }
  }
}
```

The first several lines of code in class *Game* that register three event handlers with property position two are shown below:

```
private void InitializeBoardPositions() {
    pos1 = new ChancePosition(0, 0);
    pos1.PositionNumber = 1;
    pos2 = new PropertyPosition(2000);
    pos2.PositionNumber = 2;

((PropertyPosition)pos2).RegisterPurchasedPropertyNotification
    (PurchasePropertyHandler);
((PropertyPosition)pos2).RegisterInvestmentUnitsNotification
    (PurchaseInvestmentUnitsHandler);
((PropertyPosition)pos2).RegisterRentPaidNotification
    (RentPaidHandler);
pos1.Next = pos2;
```

Exercise 9.13

Explain why the downcast *(PropertyPosition)* must be used in the code segment shown above.

The three delegate types in class *Game* that provide the basis for the three event types that are used to transmit information from the property position objects to the GUI class are shown in the following code:

```
public delegate void PurchasePropertyNotification
    (int playerNumber,
        int cash, int propertyPosition);

public delegate void PurchaseInvestmentUnitsNotification(
    int player,
        int cash, int propertyPosition, int totalUnits);
```

```
public delegate void PaidRentNotification(int fromPlayer,
    int fromCash,
        int toPlayer, int toCash);
```

The number of parameters in these delegate types is different than the number of parameters in the corresponding delegate types given in class *PropertyPosition*. This is so because the *Game* object needs to inform the *OOPLYUI* object about more details relevant to the updating of display information—information that is directly available to the *game* object but not the *OOPLYUI* object.

As an example, the following *PurchaseInvestmentUnitsHandler* method in class *Game* takes the two parameters, *playerNumber* and *totalUnits*, as input and fires the *purchaseInvestmentUnitsEvent*:

```
public void PurchaseInvestmentUnitsHandler(int playerNumber,
    int totalUnits) {
  purchaseInvestmentUnitsEvent(playerNumber,
            player[playerNumber].Cash,
            player[playerNumber].Pos.PositionNumber,
            totalUnits); // Transmit event
}
```

The *Game* object can use the two pieces of input data and generate the four values that the *OOPLYUI* object needs in order to perform its update of the display.

The details of class *Game* and its associated delegate types are presented in Listing 9.8.

LISTING 9.8 Class Game

```
using System;
using System.Windows.Forms;

namespace OOPLY {

    // Delegate classes
    public delegate void PlayerNewPositionNotification(int
        playerNumber, int oldPosition, int newPosition);
    public delegate void MoveCycleNotification(int moveCycle);
    public delegate void GameOverNotification();
    public delegate void DieValueNotification(int dieValue);
    public delegate void PassedGoNotification(int playerNumber,
                                        int cash);

    public delegate void PurchasePropertyNotification
        (int playerNumber,
         int cash, int propertyPosition);
    public delegate void PurchaseInvestmentUnitsNotification(
         int player, int cash, int propertyPosition,
         int totalUnits);
    public delegate void PaidRentNotification(int fromPlayer,
         int fromCash, int toPlayer, int toCash);
```

LISTING 9.8 Class Game (continued)

```
public delegate void ChanceNotification(int playerNumber,
    int cash);

public class Game {

  // Events generated within class Game
  public event PlayerNewPositionNotification playerMoveEvent;
  public event MoveCycleNotification newMoveCycleEvent;
  public event GameOverNotification gameOverEvent;
  public event DieValueNotification dieValueEvent;
  public event PassedGoNotification passedGoEvent;


  // Events generated within class PropertyPosition
  public event PurchasePropertyNotification
            purchasePropertyEvent;
  public event PurchaseInvestmentUnitsNotification
            purchaseInvestmentUnitsEvent;
  public event PaidRentNotification paidRentEvent;

  // Events generated within class ChancePosition
  public event ChanceNotification chanceEvent;

  // Fields
  private Player[] player = new Player[5];
  private Position pos1, pos2, pos3, pos4, pos5, pos6, pos7,
                pos8, pos9, pos10;
  private int turn = 1;
  private int moveCycle = 1;

  // Constructor
  public Game() {
     InitializeBoardPositions();
     InitializePlayers();
     AssignRandomStrategies();
  }

  // Commands
  public void RegisterForNewPositionNotification(
            PlayerNewPositionNotification update) {
        playerMoveEvent +=
            new PlayerNewPositionNotification(update);
  }
```

LISTING 9.8 Class Game (continued)

```
    public void RegisterForMoveCycleNotification
             (MoveCycleNotification update) {
      newMoveCycleEvent +=
        new MoveCycleNotification(update);
    }

    public void RegisterForGameOverNotification
             (GameOverNotification update) {
      gameOverEvent += new GameOverNotification(update);
    }

    public void RegisterDieValueNotification(
             DieValueNotification update) {
      dieValueEvent += new DieValueNotification(update);
    }

    public void RegisterForPassedGoNotification
             (PassedGoNotification update) {
      passedGoEvent += new PassedGoNotification(update);
    }

    public void RegisterForChanceNotification(ChanceNotification
             update) {
      chanceEvent += new ChanceNotification(update);
    }

    public void Move(int dieThrow) {
      dieValueEvent(dieThrow);  // Fire event
      int oldPos = player[turn].Pos.PositionNumber;
      if (moveCycle <= 5000 && player[1].Cash > 0 &&
                    player[2].Cash > 0 &&
                    player[3].Cash > 0 &&
                    player[4].Cash > 0) {
        player[turn].Move(moveCycle, dieThrow);
        int newPos = player[turn].Pos.PositionNumber;
        if (newPos < oldPos) {
           passedGoEvent(turn, player[turn].Cash); // Fire evt
        }
        playerMoveEvent(turn, oldPos, newPos); // Fire event
        // Output to log file not shown
        if (newPos == 8) {
           // Output to log file not shown
          MessageBox.Show(
"Player " + turn + " landed on position 8 - Must Move Again");
            Move(GlobalConstants.DieThrow());
        } else {
          turn++;
        if (turn == 5) {
            turn = 1;
```

LISTING 9.8 Class Game (continued)

```
            moveCycle++;
            newMoveCycleEvent(moveCycle); // Fire event
      }
  }
  } else {
    // Output to log file not shown
    gameOverEvent(); // Fire event
  }
}

  public void PurchasePropertyHandler(int playerNumber) {
    // Transmit event from PropertyPosition
    purchasePropertyEvent(playerNumber,
        player[playerNumber].Cash,
        player[playerNumber].Pos.PositionNumber);
  }

  public void PurchaseInvestmentUnitsHandler(int playerNumber,
                                         int totalUnits) {
    // Transmit event
    purchaseInvestmentUnitsEvent(playerNumber,
        player[playerNumber].Cash,
        player[playerNumber].Pos.PositionNumber, totalUnits);
  }

  public void RentPaidHandler(int fromPlayer, int toPlayer) {
    // Transmit event
    paidRentEvent(fromPlayer, player[fromPlayer].Cash,
                  toPlayer, player[toPlayer].Cash);
  }

  public void RegisterForPurchasePropertyNotification(
        PurchasePropertyNotification update) {
    purchasePropertyEvent +=
        new PurchasePropertyNotification(update);
  }

  public void RegisterForPurchaseInvestmentUnitsNotification(
          PurchaseInvestmentUnitsNotification update) {
    purchaseInvestmentUnitsEvent +=
        new PurchaseInvestmentUnitsNotification(update);
  }

  public void RegisterForPaidRentNotification(
          PaidRentNotification update) {
    paidRentEvent += new PaidRentNotification(update);
  }
```

LISTING 9.8   Class Game (continued)

```
public void ChancePositionHandler(int playerNumber) {
  // Transmit event
  chanceEvent(playerNumber, player[playerNumber].Cash);
}

private void InitializeBoardPositions() {
  pos1 = new ChancePosition(0, 0);
  pos1.PositionNumber = 1;
  pos2 = new PropertyPosition(2000);
  pos2.PositionNumber = 2;

  ((PropertyPosition)pos2).
      RegisterPurchasedPropertyNotification(
      PurchasePropertyHandler);
   ((PropertyPosition)pos2).
      RegisterInvestmentUnitsNotification(
              PurchaseInvestmentUnitsHandler);
   ((PropertyPosition)pos2).
      RegisterRentPaidNotification(RentPaidHandler);
   pos1.Next = pos2;
   pos3 = new NewStrategyPosition(true);
   pos3.PositionNumber = 3;
   pos2.Next = pos3;
   pos4 = new ChancePosition(-300, 200);
   pos4.PositionNumber = 4;
   ((ChancePosition)pos4).
      RegisterChancePositionNotification(
              ChancePositionHandler);
   pos3.Next = pos4;
   pos5 = new PropertyPosition(500);
   pos5.PositionNumber = 5;
   ((PropertyPosition)pos5).
      RegisterPurchasedPropertyNotification(
              PurchasePropertyHandler);
   ((PropertyPosition)pos5).
      RegisterInvestmentUnitsNotification(
              PurchaseInvestmentUnitsHandler);
   ((PropertyPosition)pos5).
      RegisterRentPaidNotification(RentPaidHandler);
   pos4.Next = pos5;
   pos6 = new PropertyPosition(800);
   pos6.PositionNumber = 6;
   ((PropertyPosition)pos6).
      RegisterPurchasedPropertyNotification(
              PurchasePropertyHandler);
   ((PropertyPosition)pos6).
      RegisterInvestmentUnitsNotification(
              PurchaseInvestmentUnitsHandler);
```

LISTING 9.8 Class Game (continued)

```
        ((PropertyPosition)pos6).
            RegisterRentPaidNotification(RentPaidHandler);
        pos5.Next = pos6;
        pos7 = new ChancePosition(-500, 300);
        pos7.PositionNumber = 7;
        ((ChancePosition)pos7).
            RegisterChancePositionNotification(
                    ChancePositionHandler);
        pos6.Next = pos7;
        pos8 = new ChancePosition(0, 0);
        pos8.PositionNumber = 8;
        pos7.Next = pos8;
        pos9 = new PropertyPosition(1200);
        pos9.PositionNumber = 9;
        ((PropertyPosition)pos9).
            RegisterPurchasedPropertyNotification(
                    PurchasePropertyHandler);
        ((PropertyPosition)pos9).
            RegisterInvestmentUnitsNotification(
                    PurchaseInvestmentUnitsHandler);
        ((PropertyPosition)pos9).
            RegisterRentPaidNotification(RentPaidHandler);
        pos8.Next = pos9;
        pos10 = new NewStrategyPosition(false);
        pos10.PositionNumber = 10;
        pos9.Next = pos10;
        pos10.Next = pos1;
    }

    private void InitializePlayers() {
        for (int playerNumber = 1; playerNumber <= 4;
          playerNumber++) {
          player[playerNumber] = new Player(playerNumber, 5000);
          player[playerNumber].Pos = pos1;
        }
    }

    private void AssignRandomStrategies() {
        for (int playerNumber = 1; playerNumber <= 4;
            playerNumber++) {
            int outcome = GlobalConstants.RandomValue.Next(1, 4);
            if (outcome == 1) {
                player[playerNumber].Strategy =
                  new RandomStrategy(player[playerNumber]);
            } else if (outcome == 2) {
                player[playerNumber].Strategy =
                  new AggressiveStrategy(player[playerNumber]);
            } else {
```

LISTING 9.8 Class Game (continued)

```
                player[playerNumber].Strategy =
                    new ConservativeStrategy(player[playerNumber]);
            }
        }
    }
}
```

Exercise 9.14

Explain in detail the code for *InitializeBoardPositions* given in Listing 9.8.

Exercise 9.15

Explain in detail the code for the handler methods given in Listing 9.8 (methods that include the word "Handler" in their name).

Exercise 9.16

Explain in detail how method *Move* works.

The portion of class *OOPLYUI* that is not generated by the IDE and that involves event handlers and other important GUI-related code is presented in Listing 9.9.

LISTING 9.9 Class OOPLYUI

```
using System;
using System.Collections.Generic;
using System.ComponentModel;
using System.Data;
using System.Drawing;
using System.Windows.Forms;
using System.Threading;

namespace OOPLY {

    partial class OOPLYUI : Form {

        // Fields
        private Label [,] label = new Label[11, 5];
        private Game game = new Game();
        private int playerTurn = 1; // Used only for button text

        public OOPLYUI() {
            InitializeComponent();
            // Center form on the user's screen code not shown

            // Register event handlers
            game.RegisterForMoveCycleNotification(NewMoveCycleHandler);
            game.RegisterForNewPositionNotification(
                NewPlayerPositionHandler);
```

LISTING 9.9 Class OOPLYUI (continued)

```
game.RegisterForGameOverNotification(GameOverHandler);
game.RegisterDieValueNotification(DieValueHandler);
game.RegisterForPassedGoNotification(PassedGoHandler);
game.RegisterForPurchasePropertyNotification(
    PurchasePropertyHandler);
game.RegisterForPurchaseInvestmentUnitsNotification(
    PurchaseInvestmentUnitsHandler);
game.RegisterForPaidRentNotification(RentPaidHandler);
game.RegisterForChanceNotification(ChanceHandler);

// Assign matrix of labels to control player display
label[1, 1] = label1111;
label[1, 2] = label1122;
label[1, 3] = label1133;
label[1, 4] = label1144;
label[2, 1] = label2211;
label[2, 2] = label2222;
label[2, 3] = label2233;
label[2, 4] = label2244;
label[3, 1] = label3311;
label[3, 2] = label3322;
label[3, 3] = label3333;
label[3, 4] = label3344;
label[4, 1] = label4411;
label[4, 2] = label4422;
label[4, 3] = label4433;
label[4, 4] = label4444;
label[5, 1] = label5511;
label[5, 2] = label5522;
label[5, 3] = label5533;
label[5, 4] = label5544;
label[6, 1] = label6611;
label[6, 2] = label6622;
label[6, 3] = label6633;
label[6, 4] = label6644;
label[7, 1] = label7711;
label[7, 2] = label7722;
label[7, 3] = label7733;
label[7, 4] = label7744;
label[8, 1] = label8811;
label[8, 2] = label8822;
label[8, 3] = label8833;
label[8, 4] = label8844;
label[9, 1] = label9911;
label[9, 2] = label9922;
label[9, 3] = label9933;
label[9, 4] = label9944;
label[10, 1] = label1011;
label[10, 2] = label1022;
```

LISTING 9.9 Class OOPLYUI (continued)

```
        label[10, 3] = label1033;
        label[10, 4] = label1044;
        for (int row = 1; row <= 10; row++) {
            for (int col = 1; col <= 4; col++) {
                if (row > 1) {
                    label[row, col].Visible = false;
                }
                    label[row, col].ForeColor = Color.Red;
            }
        }
    }

    private void throwDieBtn_Click(object sender, EventArgs e) {
        int dieValue = GlobalConstants.DieThrow();
        playerTurn++;
        if (playerTurn == 5) {
            playerTurn = 1;
        }
      throwDieBtn.Text = "Player " + playerTurn + " throws die";
      game.Move(dieValue); // Notifies model
    }

    public void NewMoveCycleHandler(int moveCycle) {
        moveBox.Text = "  " + moveCycle;
    }

    public void NewPlayerPositionHandler(int playerNumber,
      int oldPosition, int newPosition) {
      dieValueLbl.Text = "Die Value For Player " + playerNumber;
      label[oldPosition, playerNumber].Visible = false;
      label[newPosition, playerNumber].Visible = true;
    }

    public void DieValueHandler(int dieValue) {
      dieValueBox.Text = " " + dieValue;
    }

    public void PassedGoHandler(int playerNumber, int cash) {
        switch (playerNumber) {
          case 1: cash1Box.Text = "$" + cash; break;
          case 2: cash2Box.Text = "$" + cash; break;
          case 3: cash3Box.Text = "$" + cash; break;
          case 4: cash4Box.Text = "$" + cash; break;
        }
    }

    public void PurchasePropertyHandler
      (int playerNumber, int cash, int propertyPosition) {
        switch (propertyPosition) {
```

LISTING 9.9　Class OOPLYUI (continued)

```
          case 2:
            ownerP2.Text = "" + playerNumber;
            switch (playerNumber) {
              case 1: cash1Box.Text = "$" + cash; break;
              case 2: cash2Box.Text = "$" + cash; break;
              case 3: cash3Box.Text = "$" + cash; break;
              case 4: cash4Box.Text = "$" + cash; break;
          }
            break;
          case 5:
            ownerP5.Text = "" + playerNumber;
            switch (playerNumber) {
              case 1: cash1Box.Text = "$" + cash; break;
              case 2: cash2Box.Text = "$" + cash; break;
              case 3: cash3Box.Text = "$" + cash; break;
              case 4: cash4Box.Text = "$" + cash; break;
            }
            break;
          case 6:
              ownerP6.Text = "" + playerNumber;
              switch (playerNumber) {
                case 1: cash1Box.Text = "$" + cash; break;
                case 2: cash2Box.Text = "$" + cash; break;
                case 3: cash3Box.Text = "$" + cash; break;
                case 4: cash4Box.Text = "$" + cash; break;
              }
              break;
          case 9:
              ownerP9.Text = "" + playerNumber;
              switch (playerNumber) {
                case 1: cash1Box.Text = "$" + cash; break;
                case 2: cash2Box.Text = "$" + cash; break;
                case 3: cash3Box.Text = "$" + cash; break;
                case 4: cash4Box.Text = "$" + cash; break;
              }
              break;
      }
  }

  public void PurchaseInvestmentUnitsHandler(int playerNumber,
            int cash, int propertyPosition,
                int totalUnits) {
    switch (propertyPosition) {
      case 2:
        unitsP2.Text = "" + totalUnits;
        switch (playerNumber) {
          case 1: cash1Box.Text = "$" + cash; break;
          case 2: cash2Box.Text = "$" + cash; break;
          case 3: cash3Box.Text = "$" + cash; break;
```

LISTING 9.9 Class OOPLYUI (continued)

```
                      case 4: cash4Box.Text = "$" + cash; break;
                  }
                  break;
            case 5:
              unitsP5.Text = "" + totalUnits;
              switch (playerNumber) {
                case 1: cash1Box.Text = "$" + cash; break;
                case 2: cash2Box.Text = "$" + cash; break;
                case 3: cash3Box.Text = "$" + cash; break;
                case 4: cash4Box.Text = "$" + cash; break;
              }
              break;
            case 6:
              unitsP6.Text = "" + totalUnits;
              switch (playerNumber) {
                case 1: cash1Box.Text = "$" + cash; break;
                case 2: cash2Box.Text = "$" + cash; break;
                case 3: cash3Box.Text = "$" + cash; break;
                case 4: cash4Box.Text = "$" + cash; break;
              }
              break;
            case 9:
              unitsP9.Text = "" + totalUnits;
              switch (playerNumber) {
                case 1: cash1Box.Text = "$" + cash; break;
                case 2: cash2Box.Text = "$" + cash; break;
                case 3: cash3Box.Text = "$" + cash; break;
                case 4: cash4Box.Text = "$" + cash; break;
              }
              break;
          }
        }

  public void RentPaidHandler
    (int fromPlayer, int fromPlayerCash, int toPlayer,
                  int toPlayerCash) {
    MessageBox.Show(
      "Rent paid by player " + fromPlayer + " to " + toPlayer);
    switch (fromPlayer) {
      case 1: cash1Box.Text = "$" + fromPlayerCash; break;
      case 2: cash2Box.Text = "$" + fromPlayerCash; break;
      case 3: cash3Box.Text = "$" + fromPlayerCash; break;
      case 4: cash4Box.Text = "$" + fromPlayerCash; break;
    }
    switch (toPlayer) {
      case 1: cash1Box.Text = "$" + toPlayerCash; break;
      case 2: cash2Box.Text = "$" + toPlayerCash; break;
      case 3: cash3Box.Text = "$" + toPlayerCash; break;
      case 4: cash4Box.Text = "$" + toPlayerCash; break;
```

LISTING 9.9 Class OOPLYUI (continued)

```
        }
    }

    public void ChanceHandler(int playerNumber, int cash) {
        switch (playerNumber) {
            case 1:
                cash1Box.Text = "$" + cash;
                break;
            case 2:
                cash2Box.Text = "$" + cash;
                break;
            case 3:
                cash3Box.Text = "$" + cash;
                break;
            case 4:
                cash4Box.Text = "$" + cash;
                break;
        }
    }

    public void GameOverHandler() {
        throwDieBtn.Enabled = false;
        MessageBox.Show("GAME IS OVER");
        Application.Exit();
    }
  }
}
```

A screenshot of the game in action during the sixth move cycle is presented in Figure 9.12. All of the property positions are owned, and three of the four property

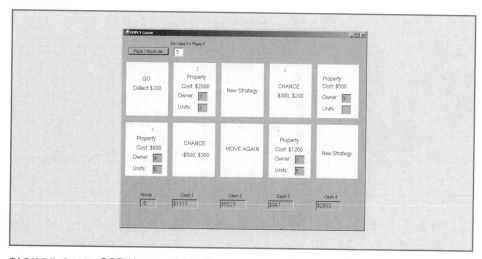

FIGURE 9.12 OOPLY game in action

positions already have investment units on them. At this moment in the game, Player 2 is ahead, probably because she did not purchase any property.

Exercise 9.17

Do you see any obvious opportunities for refactoring in the code of Listing 9.9?

Exercise 9.18

Draw a UML sequence diagram that depicts the actions associated with an owner of a property position purchasing investment units. You must trace the events that start in class *PropertyPosition* and end in class *OOPLYUI*.

Exercise 9.19

Draw a UML sequence diagram that depicts the actions associated with a player landing on a chance position. You must trace the events that start in class *ChancePosition* and end in class *OOPLYUI*.

9.8 SOME MAINTENANCE ON THE OOPLY GUI

Suppose we want to allow the user to automate the game play instead of having to click the button to throw the die each time you wish a player to move. Another button, "Automate Play," is created for this purpose. When the user clicks this button, the original throw die button is disabled. Move commands are generated every one-half second. The moves of players must continue to be shown in the GUI. If the user wishes to abort the program execution before the game completes itself, this should be possible by clicking the "x" in the upper-right corner of the window.

The design form for this modified OOPLY game is shown in Figure 9.13.

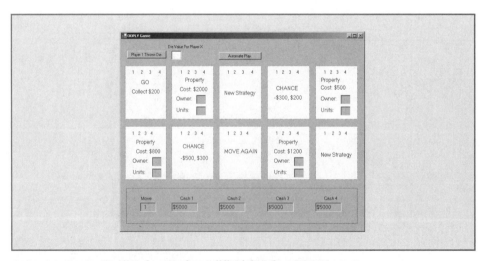

FIGURE 9.13 Design form of modified GUI for OOPLY game

The challenge in getting this to work is getting the GUI to redisplay itself every one-half second after a move has occurred. We want also to disable any modal dialog messages to the screen if the game is on automatic pilot.

We need to make several modifications and additions to class *Game* and class *OOPLYUI*. Two fields are added to class *OOPLYUI*, as shown in the following code:

```
// Two new fields
private bool playToEnd = false;  // Controls modal dialog box displays
private Thread thread;  // Used for automatic play
```

In the *RentPaidHandler* method, the command *MessageBox.Show* modal dialog is now made conditional as follows:

```
if (!playToEnd) {
   MessageBox.Show("Rent paid by player " + fromPlayer + " to " +
                   toPlayer);
}
```

The same is true of all other invocations of *MessageBox.Show*. This protects the automatic play mode from being interrupted by such messages.

The handler for the "Automatic Play" button is implemented as follows:

```
private void playToEndBtn_Click(object sender, EventArgs e) {
   throwDieBtn.Enabled = false;
   playToEndBtn.Enabled = false;
   playToEnd = true;
   game.PlayContinuously = true;
   if (thread == null) {
     thread = new Thread(new ThreadStart(game.PlayToEnd));
     thread.Start();
   }
}
```

The changes to class *Game* include the following new field:

```
private bool playContinuously = false;
```

Changes also include a write-only property, *PlayContinuously*, and a thread command, *PlayToEnd*. The details of this new command are as follows:

```
public void PlayToEnd() {
   for (; playContinuously; ) {
   Move(GlobalConstants.DieThrow());
     Thread.Sleep(500);
   }
}
```

As long as the Boolean field *playContinuously* is true, a *Move* command is issued every 500 milliseconds (1/2 second).

Why is *PlayToEnd* started as a separate thread rather than simply being invoked as an ordinary method? The answer is that we want to retain control of the GUI while the for-loop executes and issues *Move* commands. Without retaining this control, the user would not be able to exit the application while the automatic moves were still in progress.

There is still a subtle but important problem that must be overcome. As it stands now, the GUI does not refresh itself in response to the automatically generated *Move* commands. It is necessary to command each control in the GUI to refresh itself in each GUI event handler. A new private method, *RefreshComponents*, is added to class *OOPLYUI* and is given as follows:

```
private void RefreshComponents() {
   foreach (Control control in this.Controls) {
     control.Refresh();
   }
}
```

This method is invoked as the last line of code within each of the event handlers in class *OOPLYUI*. As is evident from the preceding code, each control is told to refresh itself.

The final obstacle that must be overcome is shutting the system down. As it stands, if the user clicks the "x" in the upper-right corner of the window to exit the application, the thread in the GUI continues to run even after the rest of the application has quit.

A *FormClosed* handler is used to trap the action of the user clicking the "x" button. This handler is implemented as follows:

```
private void OOPLYUI_FormClosed(object sender, FormClosedEventArgs e)
{
   playToEnd = false;
   game.PlayContinuously = false;
   if (thread != null && thread.IsAlive) {
     thread.Abort(); // Stops the thread in class Game
   }
   RefreshComponents();
}
```

Likewise the thread in class *Game* must be stopped when the game naturally ends. The *GameOver* handler is rewritten as follows:

```
public void GameOverHandler() {
   throwDieBtn.Enabled = false;
   MessageBox.Show("GAME IS OVER");
   if (thread != null && thread.IsAlive) {
     thread.Abort();
   }
   RefreshComponents();
   Application.Exit();
}
```

9.9 SUMMARY

- Support for GUI programming in .NET is provided by the classes in the *System.Windows.Forms* namespace. The classes that support GUI programming are referred to as the *Form* classes.

- In order to master the craft of developing GUI-based applications, you need to learn how to manage the asynchronous events that are typically triggered by a user input such as clicking or dragging the mouse, entering information in a text box, clicking a menu item, or clicking a choice in a combo box.

- Class *Control* in the *System.Windows.Forms* namespace encapsulates the functionality used by all *Form* controls.

- The basic controls that are frequently used in building GUI applications include *Panel*, *GroupBox*, *TextBox*, *Button*, *Label*, *ComboBox*, *ListBox*, *CheckBox*, and *RadioButton*.

- GUI components generate events in response to user actions such as clicking a button, entering text in a *TextBox*, making a selection in a *ComboBox*, checking a *CheckBox*, or simply moving or clicking the mouse over a control.

- The Smalltalk language/environment, developed at Xerox Parc, set the stage for much of the GUI frameworks that have evolved over the past 25 years. It was also through Smalltalk that a powerful principle of GUI programming emerged—the Model-View-Controller pattern (MVC) that has more recently evolved into the Observer Pattern.

- The Observer Pattern separates the computational aspects of the software architecture, the model, from the display or GUI aspects, the view. Whenever something of interest occurs within a model object, notification is sent to one or more view objects that display information to the user. More generally, the Observer Pattern defines a one-to-many relationship between objects so that when one object changes its state, its dependents are notified.

9.10 ADDITIONAL EXERCISE: A GUI PROJECT

Exercise 9.20

Download the source code for the console-based version of the Race Game presented in Chapter 3, Section 3. Using the Observer Pattern, develop a GUI that displays the progress of the game as each of the players moves toward and away from the finish line (500 units from the starting line). You are free to design the graphical user interface anyway you like.

CHAPTER 10

More Advanced GUI Construction

10.1 EVENT-HANDLING HOOKS WITHIN YOUR CUSTOM CONTROLS

In the previous chapter, we examined event handling using standard .NET controls. In this section we take the next step—creating your own custom control with hooks for user-defined event handling. Such custom controls are often needed in applications in which the functionality of a standard control is insufficient.

A custom control is typically a GUI class that is derived from *System.Windows. Forms.UserControl*, or some other *WinForm* class. It is created with the expectation that you and others will use this component in your own application work. In addition to providing properties that affect the appearance of the control (size, color, etc.), it is customary that you provide event-handling services that allow the user's application to register listeners and consume events generated within your component.

Before showing a practical example of this, we outline the steps generally required to accomplish this task for a custom component called *MyControl*. The steps are outlined in the next section.

10.1.1 General Steps Involved in Creating a Custom Control

Declare a top-level stand-alone delegate class that provides the template for event handling outside of your component. Suppose we call this delegate *MyControlEventHandling*. The code that we have so far is the following:

```
namespace CustomEventServices {

    public delegate void MyControlEventHandling(Object sender,
                                        MyControlEventArgs e);

    public class MyControl : UserControl {
        // Details not shown
    }

        // Other details not shown
}
```

The signature in the delegate conforms to the usual event-handling signature used throughout the .NET libraries.

The second parameter of the delegate implies that we will be creating our own subclass of the standard *EventArgs* class. After doing this, the structure of our system is as follows:

```
namespace CustomEventServices {

    public delegate void MyControlEventHandling(Object sender,
                                        MyControlEventArgs e);
```

```
    public class MyControlEventArgs : EventArgs {
        // Details not shown
    }


    public class MyControl : UserControl {
        // Details not shown
    }


        // Details not shown
}
```

Next, we must create an event field within the custom component *MyControlEventArgs*, say *MyControlHandler*. In addition, we need to create a private virtual method with one parameter of type *MyControlEventArgs* that fires the *MyControlHandler* event. Let us call this method *OnMyControlEvent*.

Finally, a *Register* method is included that allows a user of your custom control to register a listener—an instance of the *MyControlEventHandling* delegate.

```
namespace CustomEventServices {

    public delegate void MyControlEventHandling(Object sender,
                                        MyControlEventArgs e);


    public class MyControlEventArgs : EventArgs {
        // Details not shown
    }


    public class MyControl : UserControl {
    // Fields
    private event MyControlEventHandler MyControlHandler;

        // Commands
        public void Register(MyControlEventHandling instance) {
            MyControlHandler += new MyControlEventHandling(instance);
        }

        private void OnMyControlEvent(MyControlEventArgs e) {
            if (MyControlHandler ! = null) {
                MyControlHandler(this, e);
            }

            // Other details not shown
        }
    }
}
```

The *OnMyControlEvent* method will be invoked within your *MyControl* class whenever something happens that should trigger event notification among all registered listeners.

10.1.2 Case Study: Multiple Choice Custom Controls

Suppose we wish to implement a custom control that automates the process of constructing multiple choice questions in a simple GUI form. In constructing an instance of our custom control class *MultipleChoice*, the user must specify:

◆ A multiple choice question (as a String)

◆ Four possible answers (each as a String)

◆ The correct answer (number from 1 to 4)

Following is a code segment containing a sample instance of *MultipleChoice*. The results are shown in Figure 10.1.

```
MultipleChoice question1 = new MultipleChoice(
        "Which fraction is closest to 1/2", 2,
          "My answer is 2/3.",
          "My answer is 6/14.",
          "My answer is 3/5.",
          "My answer is 5/7.");
```

When the user clicks one of the four colored boxes, the box is filled and the correct answer is displayed at the bottom as shown in Figure 10.2.

The custom *MultipleChoice* control is derived from class *System.Windows.Form*. It must present the user with two event-handler hooks—one for displaying the correct solution and one for handling any input that the user provides.

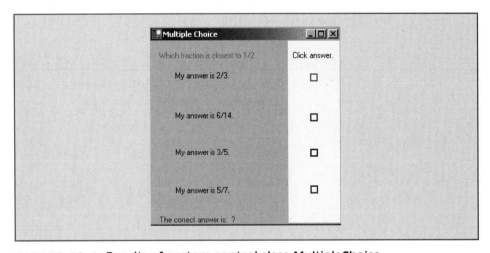

FIGURE 10.1 Results of custom control class *MultipleChoice*

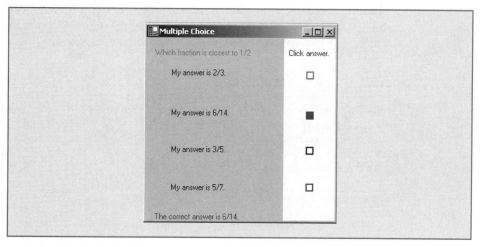

FIGURE 10.2 Selecting an answer in the Multiple Choice control

The application that deploys the custom *MultipleChoice* control must be able to register its event handlers with the instance of *MultipleChoice*.

Listing 10.1 presents delegate class *MulipleChoiceEventHandling* and class *MultipleChoiceEventArgs*. Both of these classes play a support role in building our custom control.

LISTING 10.1 Support classes for custom control

```
namespace CustomEventServices {
    public delegate void MultipleChoiceEventHandling(Object sender,
                        MultipleChoiceEventArgs e);
    public class MultipleChoiceEventArgs : EventArgs {
        // Fields
        private int winner;

        // Constructor
        public MultipleChoiceEventArgs(int winner) {
            this.winner = winner;
        }

        // Properties
        public int Winner { // Read-only property
            get {
                return winner;
            }
        }
    }
}
```

Class *MultipleChoiceEventArgs*, a specialization of class *EventArgs*, contains a private integer field, *winner*, and a read-only property that allows access to this value. The custom control class *MultipleChoice* is presented in Listing 10.2.

LISTING 10.2 Class MultipleChoice

```
using System;
using System.Drawing;
using System.Collections;
using System.ComponentModel;
using System.Windows.Forms;

namespace CustomEventServices {

    public class MultipleChoice: Form {
        // Fields
        private int correctAnswer;
        private Graphics panelGraphics;

        // Events
        private event MultipleChoiceEventHandling
                        MultipleChoiceHandler;

        // GUI components
        private Panel panel;
        private Container components = null;
        private Label answer1Lbl;
        private Label answer2Lbl;
        private Label answer3Lbl;
        private Label answer4Lbl;
        private Label questionLbl;
        private String[] answers = new String[5]; // Holds the answers
        private Label correctAnswerLbl;

        // Constructor
        public MultipleChoice(String question,
                            int correctAnswer, String answer1,
                            String answer2, String answer3,
                            String answer4) {
            InitializeComponent();
            this.correctAnswer = correctAnswer;
            panelGraphics = panel.CreateGraphics();
            Answers[1] = Answer1 = answer1;
            Answers[2] = Answer2 = answer2;
            Answers[3] = Answer3 = answer3;
            Answers[4] = Answer4 = answer4;
            Question = question;
            this.panel.Paint +=
                new PaintEventHandler(paintPanel);
```

LISTING 10.2 Class MultipleChoice (continued)

```
        }

        // Properties
        public String [] Answers {
            get {
                return answers;
            }
            set {
                answers = value;
            }
        }

        public int CorrectAnswer {
            get {
                return correctAnswer;
            }
            set {
                correctAnswer = value;
            }
        }

        public String Question {
            get {
                return questionLbl.Text;
            }
            set {
                questionLbl.Text = value;
            }
        }

        public String Answer1 {
            get {
                return answer1Lbl.Text;
            }
            set {
                answer1Lbl.Text = value;
            }
        }

        public String Answer2 {
            get {
                return answer2Lbl.Text;
            }
            set {
                answer2Lbl.Text = value;
            }
        }
```

LISTING 10.2 Class MultipleChoice (continued)

```
        public String Answer3 {
           get {
              return answer3Lbl.Text;
           }
           set {
              answer3Lbl.Text = value;
           }
        }

        public String Answer4 {
           get {
              return answer4Lbl.Text;
           }
           set {
              answer4Lbl.Text = value;
           }
        }

        // Commands
        public void Register(MultipleChoiceEventHandling instance) {
           MultipleChoiceHandler += new
                       MultipleChoiceEventHandling(instance);
        }

        public void SetCorrectAnswer(String answer) {
            correctAnswerLbl.Text = answer;
        }

        public virtual void
              OnMultipleChoiceEvent(MultipleChoiceEventArgs e) {
           if (MultipleChoiceHandler != null) {
             MultipleChoiceHandler(this, e);
           }
        }

        // Method dispose not shown

        private void panelMouseDown(Object sender, MouseEventArgs e) {
           int x = e.X;
           int y = e.Y;
            if (x >= 35 && x <= 45) {
              if (y >= 50 && y <= 60) {
                    panelGraphics.FillRectangle(
                  new SolidBrush(Color.Red), 35, 50, 10, 10);
                    OnMultipleChoiceEvent(
                  new MultipleChoiceEventArgs(1));
                } else if (y >= 110 && y <= 120) {
                    panelGraphics.FillRectangle(
                  new SolidBrush(Color.Blue), 35,
```

LISTING 10.2 Class MultipleChoice (continued)

```
                                          110, 10, 10);
            OnMultipleChoiceEvent(
            new MultipleChoiceEventArgs(2));
      } else if (y >= 163 && y <= 173) {
            panelGraphics.FillRectangle(
            new SolidBrush(Color.Black), 35,
                                    163, 10, 10);
            OnMultipleChoiceEvent(
            new MultipleChoiceEventArgs(3));
      } else if (y >= 218 && y <= 228) {
            panelGraphics.FillRectangle(
            new SolidBrush(Color.DarkGreen), 35, 218,
                                    10, 10);
            OnMultipleChoiceEvent(
            new MultipleChoiceEventArgs(4));
      }
   }
}

private void paintPanel(Object sender, PaintEventArgs e) {
   panelGraphics.DrawString("Click answer.", Font,
        new SolidBrush(Color.Black), 5, 15);
   panelGraphics.DrawRectangle(
        new Pen(Color.Red, 2),35, 50, 10, 10);
   panelGraphics.DrawRectangle(
        new Pen(Color.Blue, 2), 35, 110, 10, 10);
   panelGraphics.DrawRectangle(
        new Pen(Color.Black, 2), 35, 163, 10, 10);
   panelGraphics.DrawRectangle(
        new Pen(Color.DarkGreen, 2), 35, 218, 10, 10);
}

// Automatically generated code from IDE not shown
   }
}
```

Exercise 10.1

Explain in detail how method *panelMouseDown* works.

We show the *MultipleChoice* custom control in action by constructing a simple application class *MultipleChoiceApp*. Its user interface is shown in Figure 10.3 and coding details are shown in Listing 10.3.

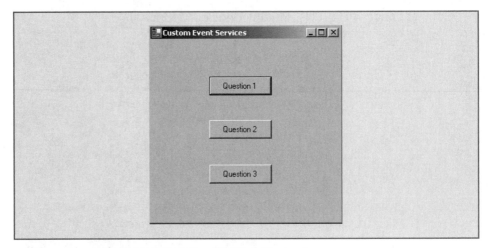

FIGURE 10.3 User interface for *MultipleChoiceApp*

LISTING 10.3 Class MultipleChoiceApp

```
using System;
using System.Drawing;
using System.Collections;
using System.ComponentModel;
using System.Windows.Forms;
using System.Data;

namespace CustomEventServices {

    public class MultipleChoiceApp : Form {

        // Fields
        private MultipleChoice question1;
        private MultipleChoice question2;
        private MultipleChoice question3;

        // Visual components
        private System.ComponentModel.Container components = null;
        private Button question1Btn;
        private Button question2Btn;
        private Button question3Btn;

        public MultipleChoiceApp() {
          InitializeComponent();
          // Center form on the user's screen
          this.SetBounds((Screen.GetBounds(this).Width / 2) -
                    (this.Width / 2),
                    (Screen.GetBounds(this).Height / 2) -
                    (this.Height / 2),
```

LISTING 10.3 Class MultipleChoiceApp (continued)

```
                            this.Width, this.Height,
                    BoundsSpecified.Location);
    }

    public void AnswerHandler1(Object sender,
                    MultipleChoiceEventArgs e) {
      MessageBox.Show(question1.Answers[e.Winner]);
    }

    public void CorrectAnswerHandler1(Object sender,
                    MultipleChoiceEventArgs e) {
        String correctAnswer =
        question1.Answers[question1.CorrectAnswer].
                    Replace("My", "The correct");
        question1.SetCorrectAnswer(correctAnswer);
    }

    public void CorrectAnswerHandler2(Object sender,
                    MultipleChoiceEventArgs e) {
        String correctAnswer =
            question2.Answers[question2.CorrectAnswer].
                    Replace("My", "The correct");
        question2.SetCorrectAnswer(correctAnswer);
    }

    public void CorrectAnswerHandler3(Object sender,
                    MultipleChoiceEventArgs e) {
        question3.SetCorrectAnswer(
            "L'hospital's rule says the limit is 1.");
    }

    public void AnswerHandler3(Object sender,
                    MultipleChoiceEventArgs e) {
        MessageBox.Show(
        // The following String is broken for display
        // purposes but not broken in the code editor
        "L'hospital's rule from calculus states that one must
        take the derivative of the numerator and the
        denominator separately and then take limit as x ->
        0");
    }

    protected override void Dispose( bool disposing ) {
        if( disposing ) {
            if (components != null) {
                components.Dispose();
            }
        }
    }
```

LISTING 10.3 Class MultipleChoiceApp (continued)

```
        base.Dispose( disposing );
    }

    // Additional code automatically generated from IDE not shown

    static void Main() {
        Application.EnableVisualStyles();
        Application.Run(new MultipleChoiceApp());
    }

    private void question1Btn_Click(object sender, EventArgs e) {
        question1 = new MultipleChoice(
        "Which fraction is closest to 1/2", 2,
            "My answer is 2/3.",
            "My answer is 6/14.",
            "My answer is 3/5.",
            "My answer is 5/7.");
        question1.Register(AnswerHandler1);
        question1.Register(CorrectAnswerHandler1);
        question1.Show();
    }

    private void question2Btn_Click(object sender, EventArgs e) {
        question2 = new MultipleChoice(
        "Who was the youngest US president", 3,
            "My answer is Bill Clinton",
            "My answer is Jimmy Carter",
            "My answer is John F. Kennedy",
            "My answer is George W. Bush");
        question2.Register(CorrectAnswerHandler2);
        question2.Show();
    }

    private void question3Btn_Click(object sender, EventArgs e) {
        question3 = new MultipleChoice(
        "What is the limit of sin(x) / x as x -> 0?", 1,
            "My answer is 1",
            "My answer is 0",
            "My answer is 1/2",
            "My answer is 10");
        question3.Register(AnswerHandler3);
        question3.Register(CorrectAnswerHandler3);
        question3.Show();
    }
    }
}
```

The ease with which the main application is able to produce customized multiple choice questions and associated event handlers should be evident from Listing 10.3. Examples from grade-school arithmetic, politics, and mathematics are used to demonstrate the custom control in action. For a commercial application, the questions and answers would be stored in a database or a flat file and not hard-coded into the application. Hard-coding was done to simplify the presentation and allow the focus to be on the development of the custom component.

Exercise 10.2

Explain in detail how the application class shown in Listing 10.3 works.

Exercise 10.3

Construct one more *MultipleChoice* question object in Listing 10.3 and appropriate event handlers that support the question object.

10.2 MORE ADVANCED GUI APPLICATION: GAME OF DOTS AND BOXES

The game of dots and boxes is often first played as a child. A grid of dots is created, say a 4 x 4 grid with 16 dots, as shown in Figure 10.4.

FIGURE 10.4 Grid of 4 x 4 boxes for the game of Dots and Boxes

Players move alternately. When a player moves, she may draw a line between two adjacent dots. The objective is to produce as many boxes as possible. A box is captured by four lines connecting four adjacent dots. Each time a box is captured, a colored square, say red for one player, blue for the other player, is placed inside the box just captured. When a player captures a box, she must move again. When no further lines can be drawn, the player who has captured the most boxes wins the game. When playing on paper, the player's initials can be used in place of the colored rectangles.

Figure 10.5 shows a game in progress in which the red player has captured two boxes and the blue player one box.

What makes this game ideally suited for children is that it can be played quickly and provides opportunities for the player to improve with experience.

The game has been studied extensively and found to be much deeper than it may first appear. In fact, no winning strategy is known. The classic reference dealing with the mathematics of dots and boxes is presented in *The Dots-and-Boxes Game* by Elwyn Berlekamp, A.K. Peters, 2000. This University of California at Berkeley mathematician has spent many years researching this fascinating game. In his book, he presents different strategies of play from simple to quite complex.

We shall not be preoccupied with the mathematics of the game. Our concern will be in constructing an application in which the user plays against the computer. We will initially allow the computer three levels of play: Novice, Beginner, and Intermediate. None of these levels would pose a serious challenge to an advanced player. At the Intermediate level, some testing indicates that users who have not carefully studied the game would tend to lose to the computer more often than win.

In playing against the computer, the user moves first, then the computer generates a counter-move. Later we can upgrade the game and allow the user to determine

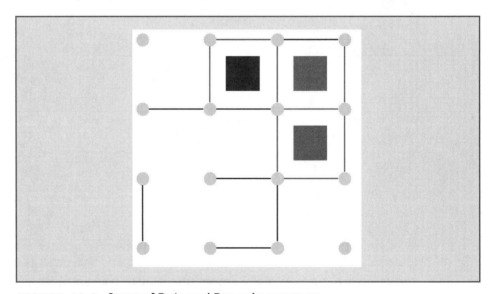

FIGURE 10.5 Game of Dots and Boxes in progress

whether he or the computer moves first. Of course if a box is captured by either the user or computer, another move following this capture is mandated.

The playing area should allow a 4 x 4 or 5 x 5 or 6 x 6 grid of dots. When a user moves his mouse over the grid, a gray line must be drawn between dots when the mouse is near the line that would connect two adjacent dots. When the player's mouse is moved away, the gray line must disappear. Only when the player clicks his mouse when the temporary gray line appears does the gray line become a red line indicating that the user has completed a move. If the move results in the capture of a box, a filled red rectangle must be displayed inside of this box (as in Figure 10.5) and the user must move again. Otherwise, the computer must make the next move. Its line must be colored blue. If its move results in the capture of a box, a blue-filled rectangle must be drawn inside of the box that it just captured, and it must move again. It is possible for the computer to capture a long chain of boxes during a move, because after the capture of one box it must move again. The same is true of the player.

Let us carefully define the three strategies of play.

At the Novice level, the computer makes a random choice among the remaining possible lines that may be drawn. This implies that it will often not capture a box even if one is available for capture.

At the Beginner level, the computer first attempts to capture a box if one is available. If this is not possible, the computer makes a random choice among the remaining possible lines that may be drawn.

At the Intermediate level, the computer first attempts to capture a box if one is available. If this is not possible, it attempts to find a line, from among the remaining lines, that will not allow the human user to capture a box. If no such choice is possible, it chooses one of the remaining lines at random allowing the user to capture a box.

After a careful consideration of the problem domain, the following classes are identified:

◆ **Line**—Models the line-segments that connect adjacent dots

◆ **Model**—Holds information about the entire grid, including lines already drawn as well as remaining lines that may be drawn

◆ **BoxesUI**—Contains the graphical user interface for the application

We first examine the non-user-interface classes, *Line* and *Model*.
The state information needed by a *Line* object is:

◆ **row, col**—The row and column that defines the upper-left dot coordinate of the line

◆ **horizontal**—Determines whether the line is horizontal or vertical

◆ **lineColor**—The color of the line

◆ **sequenceNumber**—The sequence number of the line relative to the other lines that are drawn

Listing 10.4 presents the details of class *Line*.

LISTING 10.4 Class Line

```
using System;
using System.Drawing;

namespace DotsBoxes {

    public class Line {
        // Fields
        private int row, col;
        private bool horizontal;
        private Color lineColor;
        private int sequenceNumber;

        public Line(int row, int col, bool horizontal) {
            this.row = row;
            this.col = col;
            this.horizontal = horizontal;
            sequenceNumber = 0;
        }

        public Line(int row, int col, Color lineColor,
                    bool horizontal) {
            this.row = row;
            this.col = col;
            this.lineColor = lineColor;
            this.horizontal = horizontal;
             sequenceNumber = 0;
        }

        // Properties
        public int Row {
            get {
                return row;
            }
        }

        public int Col {
            get {
                return col;
            }
        }

        public bool Horizontal {
            get {
                return horizontal;
            }
        }
```

LISTING 10.4 Class Line (continued)

```
        public Color LineColor {
            get {
                return lineColor;
            }
            set {
                lineColor = value;
            }
        }

        public int SequenceNumber {
            get {
                return sequenceNumber;
            }
            set {
                sequenceNumber = value;
            }
        }

        public override bool Equals(Object obj) {
            // Color blind comparison
            if (!(obj is Line)) {
                return false;
            }
            Line other = (Line) obj;
            return row == other.row && col == other.col &&
                horizontal == other.horizontal;
        }

    // Needed because the Equals method is overridden
        public override int GetHashCode() {
            if (horizontal) {
                return row ^ col;
            } else {
                return - (row ^ col); // Exclusive or operator
            }
        }

        // Query
        public override String ToString() {
            return "<" + row + "," + col + "> " +
                    (horizontal ? "horizontal" : "vertical");
        }
    }
}
```

Next, the *Model* class is presented. This class is more complex and holds the logic for the three types of moves outlined previously.

We present the details of class *Model* in stages so that each stage may be explained carefully. Listing 10.5 shows the fields and constructors of class *Model*.

The *enum* keyword is used to create a distinct type with the named constants (*Novice, Beginner, Intermediate*) representing integral values of 0, 1, and 2.

LISTING 10.5 Fields and constructor of class Model

```
namespace DotsBoxes {

    public enum LevelOfPlay {Novice, Beginner, Intermediate};

    public class Model {
        // Fields
        private ArrayList grayLines = new ArrayList();
        private ArrayList lines = new ArrayList();
        private int gridSize;
        private ArrayList remainingLines = new ArrayList();
        private Random randomValue = new Random();
        private LevelOfPlay level = LevelOfPlay.Intermediate;
        private int row, col;      // Set by ComputerMove
        private bool horizontal; // Set by ComputerMove

        // Constructor
        public Model(int size) {
            gridSize = size;
            // Build list of remaining lines
            for (int row = 1; row <= gridSize; row++) {
                for (int col = 1; col <= gridSize; col++) {
                    if (col != gridSize) {
                        remainingLines.Add(
                            new Line(row, col, true));
                    }
                    if (row != gridSize) {
                        remainingLines.Add(
                            new Line(row, col, false));
                    }
                }
            }
        }
```

There are nine fields defined in the *Model* class. Fields *lines*, *grayLines*, and *remainingLines* are defined as standard type *ArrayList*. You will recall that this standard type is essentially a dynamic array.

The field *gridSize* specifies the number of dots in each row and column. This value is set by the user in the UI class and passed to the model as a parameter in the model's constructor.

The other fields of class *Model* include a random number object, *randomValue*, a *level* object (that specifies the level of play for the computer), the row and column of the line, and whether this line is horizontal or vertical.

The constructor fills the array list *remainingLines*.

Exercise 10.4

Explain the nested for loops in the constructor in class *Model*:

```
for (int row = 1; row <= gridSize; row++) {
    for (int col = 1; col <= gridSize; col++) {
        if (col != gridSize) {
            remainingLines.Add(
                new Line(row, col, true));
        }
        if (row != gridSize) {
            remainingLines.Add(
                new Line(row, col, false));
        }
    }
}
```

In particular, why is it necessary to exclude *gridSize* from the value of the *col* and *row* index using the *if* clause?

Next, we present the remaining details of class *Model* in Listing 10.6 and then examine and discuss each of the computer move strategies.

LISTING 10.6 Class Model

```
using System;
using System.Collections;

namespace DotsBoxes {

    public enum LevelOfPlay {Novice, Beginner, Intermediate};

    public class Model {
        // See Listing 10.5 for fields and constructor

        // Properties
        public bool Horizontal {
            get {
                return horizontal;
            }
        }
```

LISTING 10.6 Class Model (continued)

```
public int Row {
   get {
      return row;
   }
}

public int Col {
   get {
      return col;
   }
}

public LevelOfPlay Level {
   get {
      return level;
   }
   set {
      level = value;
   }
}

public ArrayList Lines {
   get {
      return lines;
   }
}

public ArrayList RemainingLines {
   get {
      return remainingLines;
   }
}

// Commands
public void ComputerMove() {
    if (level == LevelOfPlay.Novice) {
       NoviceMove();
    } else if (level == LevelOfPlay.Beginner) {
       BeginnerMove();
    } else if (level == LevelOfPlay.Intermediate) {
       IntermediateMove();
    }
}

public void RemoveLine(Line line) {
    remainingLines.Remove(line);
}

public void AddLine(Line line) {
    lines.Add(line);
```

LISTING 10.6 Class Model (continued)

```
    }

    public void AddGrayLine(Line line) {
        grayLines.Add(line);
    }

    public void ClearGrayLines() {
        grayLines.Clear();
    }

    // Queries
    public int NumberRemainingLines() {
        return remainingLines.Count;
    }

    public bool ContainsGrayLine(Line line) {
        return grayLines.Contains(line);
    }

    public bool ContainsLine(Line line) {
        return lines.Contains(line);
    }

    public Line RandomLineFromRemainingLines() {
        return (Line)remainingLines[randomValue.
                Next(remainingLines.Count)];
    }

    public bool CanMoveUp(int row, int col) {
        if (row == 1) {
            return false;
        } else {
            return lines.Contains(new Line(row - 1, col, false));
        }
    }

    public bool CanMoveRight(int row, int col) {
        if (col == gridSize) {
            return false;
        } else {
            return lines.Contains(new Line(row, col, true));
        }

    }

    public bool CanMoveDown(int row, int col) {
        if (row == gridSize) {
            return false;
```

LISTING 10.6 Class Model (continued)

```
        } else {
            return lines.Contains(new Line(row, col, false));
        }
    }

    public bool CanMoveLeft(int row, int col) {
        if (col == 1) {
            return false;
        } else {
            return lines.Contains(new Line(row, col - 1, true));
        }
    }

    /* Returns true if the presence of a horizontal line
     * starting at row, col produces a box when moving
     * down, left, and up.
     */
    public bool HaveBoxHorizontalDown(int row, int col) {
        return CanMoveDown(row, col + 1) &&
            CanMoveLeft(row + 1, col + 1) &&
            CanMoveUp(row + 1, col);
    }

    /* Returns true if the presence of a horizontal line
     * starting at row, col produces a box when moving
     * up, left, and down.
     */
    public bool HaveBoxHorizontalUp(int row, int col) {
        return CanMoveUp(row, col + 1) &&
            CanMoveLeft(row - 1, col + 1) &&
            CanMoveDown(row - 1, col);
    }

    /* Returns true if the presence of a vertical line
     * starting at row, col produces a box when moving
     * right, up, and left.
     */
    public bool HaveBoxVerticalRight(int row, int col) {
        return CanMoveRight(row + 1, col) &&
            CanMoveUp(row + 1, col + 1) &&
            CanMoveLeft(row, col + 1);
    }

    /* Returns true if the presence of a vertical line
     * starting at row, col produces a box when moving
     * left, up, and right.
     */
    public bool HaveBoxVerticalLeft(int row, int col) {
        return CanMoveLeft(row + 1, col) &&
```

LISTING 10.6 Class Model (continued)

```
                    CanMoveUp(row + 1, col - 1) &&
                    CanMoveRight(row, col - 1);
        }

        private void ScrambleRemainingLines() {
            ArrayList scrambledLines = new ArrayList();
            while (remainingLines.Count > 0) {
                Line randomLine = RandomLineFromRemainingLines();
                scrambledLines.Add(randomLine);
                remainingLines.Remove(randomLine);
            }
            remainingLines = (ArrayList) scrambledLines.Clone();
        }

        private void PickRandomLine() {
            if (NumberRemainingLines() > 0) {
                // Pick a line from remaining lines at random
                Line randomLine = RandomLineFromRemainingLines();
                row = randomLine.Row;
                col = randomLine.Col;
                horizontal = randomLine.Horizontal;
            }
        }

        private bool PickLineToCaptureBox() {
        // Capture a box if possible
            ScrambleRemainingLines(); // Randomize remaining lines
            foreach (Line line in RemainingLines) {
                row = line.Row;
                col = line.Col;
                horizontal = line.Horizontal;
                if (horizontal) {
                    if (HaveBoxHorizontalDown(row, col) ||
                        HaveBoxHorizontalUp(row, col)) {
                        return true;
                    }
                } else {
                    if (HaveBoxVerticalRight(row, col) ||
                        HaveBoxVerticalLeft(row, col)) {
                        return true;
                    }
                }
            }
            return false;
        }

        private void NoviceMove() {
            PickRandomLine();
```

LISTING 10.6 Class Model (continued)

```
    }

    private void BeginnerMove() {

        if (PickLineToCaptureBox()) {
            return;
        } else {
          PickRandomLine();
        }
    }

    private void IntermediateMove() {
        /* Close a box if possible otherwise choose a line that
            prevents opponent from next closing a box otherwise
            pick a line at random.
        */
        if (PickLineToCaptureBox()) {
            return;
        }

        ScrambleRemainingLines();
        foreach (Line line in RemainingLines) {
        row = line.Row;
        col = line.Col;
        horizontal = line.Horizontal;
        this.AddLine(new Line(row, col, horizontal));
        if (horizontal) {
            if (!HaveBoxVerticalLeft(row, col + 1) &&
                !HaveBoxVerticalLeft(row - 1, col + 1) &&
                !HaveBoxVerticalRight(row, col) &&
                !HaveBoxVerticalRight(row - 1, col) &&
                !HaveBoxHorizontalDown(row - 1, col) &&
                    !HaveBoxHorizontalUp(row + 1, col)

                                                    ) {
                // Opponent cannot get box with addition of
                // line
                lines.Remove(
                        new Line(row, col, horizontal));
                return;
            }
        } else {
            if (!HaveBoxHorizontalUp(row + 1, col  - 1) &&
                !HaveBoxHorizontalDown(row, col - 1) &&
                !HaveBoxHorizontalDown(row, col) &&
                !HaveBoxHorizontalUp(row + 1, col) &&
                !HaveBoxVerticalLeft(row, col + 1) &&
                    !HaveBoxVerticalRight(row, col - 1)
                ) {
```

LISTING 10.6 Class Model (continued)

```
                      // Opponent cannot get box with addition of
                      // line
                      lines.Remove(
                                  new Line(row, col, horizontal));
                      return;
                }
            }
            lines.Remove(new Line(row, col, horizontal));
        }

        if (NumberRemainingLines() > 0) {
            PickRandomLine();
        }
    }
  }
}
```

Class *Model* has the usual set of read and read-write properties. We note that the properties *Horizontal*, *Row*, *Col*, *Lines*, and *RemainingLines* are read-only because the values they return are modified through public commands in the class.

Several important public queries support the logic of computer moves. These include *CanMoveUp*, *CanMoveRight*, *CanMoveDown*, and *CanMoveLeft*. Each of these queries takes a row and column as input.

Let us consider one of these queries in detail, say, *CanMoveLeft*. If the column is the furthest to the left ($col == 1$), the query returns false because there cannot be a line to the left of column 1. Otherwise, the query returns the outcome of determining whether the *ArrayList lines* contains a horizontal line that starts at the given row and at $col - 1$.

Exercise 10.5

Explain the queries *CanMoveRight*, *CanMoveDown*, and *CanMoveUp* in class *Model*.

Several additional public queries support the logic of computer moves. These include *HaveBoxHorizontalDown*, *HaveBoxHorizontalUp*, *HaveBoxVerticalRight*, and *HaveBoxVerticalLeft*. Each of these queries takes a row and column as input.

Let us consider one of these, *HaveBoxVerticalLeft*. This query returns true if the presence of a vertical line starting at *row, col* produces a box when moving left, up, and right from *row, col*.

The outcome of this query, assuming a vertical line from *<row, col>* to *<row + 1, col>*, is:

```
return CanMoveLeft(row + 1, col) && CanMoveUp(row + 1, col - 1) &&
       CanMoveRight(row, col - 1);
```

The first query assures that there is a connection between the points <row + 1, col> and <row + 1, col − 1>. The second query assures that there is a connection between the points <*row + 1, col − 1*> and <*row, col − 1*>, and the third query assures a connection between the points <*row, col − 1*> and <*row, col*>.

Exercise 10.6

Explain the query *HaveBoxHorizontalDown*.

Exercise 10.7

Explain the query *HaveBoxHorizontalUp*.

Exercise 10.8

Explain the query *HaveBoxVerticalRight*.

We examine next several important private support methods.

Method *ScrambleRemainingLines* randomly rearranges the order of the existing *ArrayList, remainingLines*.

Exercise 10.9

Explain how method *ScrambleRemainingLines* works.

Method *RandomLineFromRemainingLines* accesses a random index from the *ArrayList remainingLines* as follows:

```
return (Line) remainingLines[randomValue.Next(remainingLines.Count)];
```

The downcast is essential because the formal type returned by any *ArrayList* is *Object* whereas the known actual type is *Line*. This method is used to implement the support method *PickRandomLine*.

The method *PickLineToCaptureBox* first randomizes the *ArrayList remainingLines*. This method violates the command/query protocol used throughout this book. It changes the internal state of the model object by changing its *row* and *col* fields, and it also returns a Boolean value that indicates whether a box was able to be captured (true if a box was captured and false if a box could not be captured). An iteration through each line in the *ArrayList remainingLines* allows each line to be tested. The reason for invoking *ScrambleRemainingLines* before entering the iteration is to allow a box to be randomly chosen in the event that several boxes can be captured.

Exercise 10.10

Explain how each line in the iteration, *foreach (Line line in RemainingLines)*, is tested to determine whether it can capture a box.

The method *NoviceMove* invokes *PickRandomLine*. As indicated earlier, this implies that the computer will not capture a box that could be captured unless by luck it randomly chooses the correct line for accomplishing this.

The method *BeginnerMove* attempts first to capture a box by invoking *PickLineToCaptureBox*. If this method returns true, the method is exited. The field values of *row*, *col*, and *horizontal* define the line that has captured the box. If the method returns false (a box could not be captured), a randomly chosen line is chosen for the computer move.

The method *IntermediateMove* first attempts to capture a box using *PickLineToCaptureBox*. An immediate exit occurs if a box is captured.

Next, iterating over each of the remaining lines, the randomly chosen line is temporarily added to the *ArrayList lines*. If the temporarily added line is horizontal, then if the Boolean condition:

```
!HaveBoxVerticalLeft(row, col + 1) &&
!HaveBoxVerticalLeft(row - 1, col + 1) &&
!HaveBoxVerticalRight(row, col) &&
!HaveBoxVerticalRight(row - 1, col) &&
!HaveBoxHorizontalDown(row - 1, col) &&
!HaveBoxHorizontalUp(row + 1, col)
```

is true, the temporary line is removed from the *ArrayList lines* and the method is exited because the line defined by *row*, *col*, and *horizontal* will not allow the opponent (the user) to capture a box.

Exercise 10.11

Assume the line being tested is horizontal. Explain why the Boolean condition given above, if true, guarantees that the user will not be able to capture a box when the computer chooses the line defined by *row*, *col*, and *horizontal*.

If the randomly chosen line in the iteration is vertical, then if the Boolean condition:

```
!HaveBoxHorizontalUp(row + 1, col - 1) &&
!HaveBoxHorizontalDown(row, col - 1) &&
!HaveBoxHorizontalDown(row, col) &&
!HaveBoxHorizontalUp(row + 1, col) &&
!HaveBoxVerticalLeft(row, col + 1) &&
!HaveBoxVerticalRight(row, col - 1)
```

is true, the temporary line is removed from the *ArrayList lines* and the method is exited. The user will not be able to capture a box because of the computer's move.

Exercise 10.12

Assume the line being tested is vertical. Explain why the Boolean condition given previously, if true, guarantees that the user will not be able to capture a box when the computer chooses the line defined by *row*, *col*, and *horizontal*.

If no line among the remaining lines can be found that prevents the user from capturing a box, then a randomly chosen line is chosen from among the remaining lines. This randomly chosen line will allow the user to capture a box.

The *Model* class provides the infrastructure and core logic that supports the playing of the game. What remains is to design and implement the graphical user interface that allows the user to choose the grid size, the level of play, and most importantly the red line connecting two dots that defines the user's move. The GUI must then convert the computer's move to another line, colored blue. If either the computer or the user captures a box, a filled rectangle colored either blue or red signifies this captured box. The current score must be displayed, and the cumulative score over a series of games must also be displayed. Other user interface controls are needed to start a new game, quit an existing game prematurely, choose the size of the grid, and choose the level of play.

A screenshot of the completed application is shown in Figure 10.6.

A group box control is used to hold the three radio buttons that offer a choice of grid sizes. A combo box offers the user the choice of the level of play. A New Game button, not shown, appears initially and after the end of a game. A game can be ended prematurely by clicking the Quit This Game button. The game is credited to the computer and the New Game button, above the Grid Size group box, becomes visible. Another group box containing two noneditable text boxes is used to hold the total number of wins for the user (you) and the computer. Finally, two labels are used to hold the user's score and the computer score for a given game. A check box (with default of checked) allows the user to toggle sequence numbers on and off. The presence of sequence numbers is very useful in performing a post-mortem analysis of a game—typically to determine why the computer beat you.

The dots and lines are drawn within a *Panel* component using the graphics context of the *Panel*.

We focus next on the details of this user interface encapsulated in class *BoxesUI*. We will not present the code that is automatically generated by the IDE but focus instead on the programmer-generated code. Because the source listing for class *BoxesUI* is lengthy, as is typical for UI classes, only select portions of the class will be presented and discussed. The reader is encouraged to examine the full source code for this class after downloading the code from the book's Web site.

The fields in class *BoxesUI* are given in Listing 10.7.

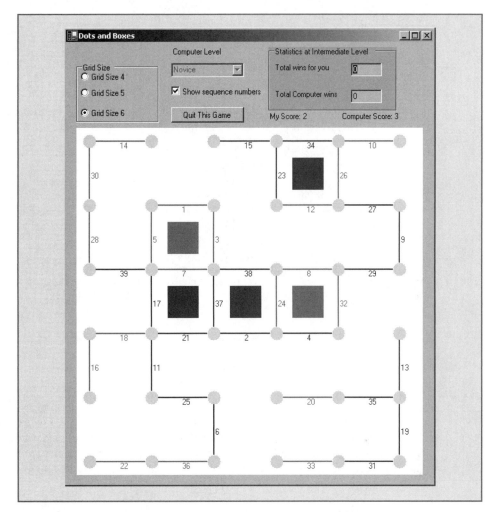

FIGURE 10.6 Screenshot of Dots and Boxes game in action

LISTING 10.7 Fields in class BoxesUI

```
public class BoxesUI : Form {

    // Fields
    private int gridSize;
    private Graphics panelGraphics;
    private Model model;
    private int space;
    private int computerScore, personScore;
    private int totalPlayerWins, totalComputerWins;
    private bool capturedBox; // Set after each line is drawn
    private bool canDrawLine;
```

LISTING 10.7 Fields in class BoxesUI (continued)

```
private int sequenceNumber = 1;
private bool gameOver = false;
```

The dots that are graphically rendered in the *Panel* are generated by method *DrawDots*. This method is shown in Listing 10.8.

LISTING 10.8 Method DrawDots

```
private void DrawDots() {
    panelGraphics = panel.CreateGraphics();
    panelGraphics.Clear(Color.White);
    for (int row = 0; row < gridSize; row++) {
        for (int col = 0; col < gridSize; col++) {
            panelGraphics.DrawArc(
                new Pen(new SolidBrush(Color.Line), 10),
                new Rectangle(15 + row * (120 - 4 * gridSize),
                15 +  col * (120 - 4 * gridSize), 10, 10), 0, 360);
        }
    }
}
```

It is tedious to read as well as write the kind of code that is in method *DrawDots*. First, the panel is cleared of any existing graphics by using the *Clear* method and the background color (white) of the *Panel*. Next, the matrix of dots is drawn.

The *DrawArc* method in class *Graphics* is used. The angle of the arc is shown as 360 (in degrees). The color of each dot is Lime. The spacing between dots is a function of the grid size.

Exercise 10.13

After studying Listing 10.8, explain the basis for the spacing between dots and how it relates to the grid size.

As the user moves his mouse across the panel, an event handler must determine whether to draw a gray line indicating a potential connection between two dots. The event handling that accomplishes the drawing and erasing of such gray lines is presented in Listing 10.9.

LISTING 10.9 Methods for managing gray lines

```
private void panel_MouseMove(object sender,
            System.Windows.Forms.MouseEventArgs e) {
    ClearGrayLines();
```

LISTING 10.9 Methods for managing gray lines (continued)

```
        int x = e.X;
        int y = e.Y;
        DrawGrayLine(x, y);
}

private void ClearGrayLines() {
    // Clear any gray vertical line that may be present
    for (int row = 1; row <= gridSize; row++) {
        for (int col = 1; col <= gridSize; col++) {
            if (model.ContainsGrayLine(new Line(row, col, false))) {
                model.ClearGrayLines();
                panelGraphics.DrawLine(
                    new Pen(new SolidBrush(Color.White), 2),
                        20 + (col - 1) * space,
                        30 + space * ( row - 1),
                        20 + (col - 1) * space, 10 + space * row);
            }
        }
    }

    // Clear any gray horizontal line that may be present
    for (int row = 1; row <= gridSize; row++) {
        for (int col = 1; col <= gridSize; col++) {
            if (model.ContainsGrayLine(
                new Line(row, col, true))) {
            model.ClearGrayLines();
            panelGraphics.DrawLine(
                new Pen(new SolidBrush(Color.White), 2),
                30 + (col - 1) * space,
                20 + space * ( row - 1),
                10 + col * space, 20 + space * (row - 1));
            }
        }
    }
}



private void DrawGrayLine(int x, int y) {
    // Determine whether to draw gray vertical line
    space = 120 - 4 * gridSize;
    for (int row = 1; row < gridSize; row++) {
        for (int col = 1; col <= gridSize; col++) {
            if (!model.ContainsLine(new Line(row, col, false)) &&
                x >= 15 + (col - 1) * space &&
                x <= 50 + (col - 1) * space &&
                y >= 35 + space * (row - 1) && y <= space * row) {
                model.AddGrayLine(new Line(row, col, false));
                panelGraphics.DrawLine(
```

LISTING 10.9 Methods for managing gray lines (continued)

```
                new Pen(new SolidBrush(Color.Gray), 2),
                20 + (col - 1) * space,
                30 + space * ( row - 1),
                20 + (col - 1) * space, 10 + space * row);
      }
    }
  }


  // Determine whether to draw gray horizontal line
  for (int col = 1; col < gridSize; col++) {
    for (int row = 1; row <= gridSize; row++) {
      if (!model.ContainsLine(new Line(row, col, true)) &&
        y >= 15 + (row - 1) * space &&
        y <= 35 + (row - 1) * space &&
        x >= 35 + space * (col - 1) && x <= space * col) {
      model.AddGrayLine(new Line(row, col, true));
        panelGraphics.DrawLine(
          new Pen(new SolidBrush(Color.Gray), 2),
          30 + (col - 1) * space,
          20 + space * ( row - 1),
          10 + col * space, 20 + space * (row - 1));
      }
    }
  }
}
```

The details of method *DrawGrayLine* in Listing 10.9 were arrived at somewhat experimentally. The hot zone surrounding each line that connects adjacent dots was determined. These zones are dependent on a *space* variable, which is dependent on the grid size.

Exercise 10.14

Explain how the model object is used in method *DrawGrayLine*.

The mouse up event handler is used to determine if the user wishes to draw a line that connects two adjacent dots. The details of this event handler are shown in Listing 10.10.

LISTING 10.10 Method panel_MouseUp

```
private void panel_MouseUp(object sender,
        System.Windows.Forms.MouseEventArgs e) {
```

LISTING 10.10 Method panel_MouseUp (continued)

```
    if (gameOver) {
          MessageBox.Show("Game is over. Must start a new game."
);
          return;
    }
    if (model != null) {
        int x = e.X;
        int y = e.Y;
        ClearGrayLines();
        UserDrawLine(x, y);
        if (!capturedBox && model.NumberRemainingLines() > 0) {
            if (canDrawLine) {
                ComputerMove();
            }
            while (model.NumberRemainingLines() > 0 && capturedBox)
{
                if (canDrawLine) {
                    ComputerMove();
                }
            }
        }
        levelComboBox.Enabled = false;
        if (model.NumberRemainingLines() == 0 && !gameOver) {
            if (personScore > computerScore) {
                totalPlayerWins++;
            } else if (computerScore > personScore) {
                totalComputerWins++;
            }
            UpdateStats();
            newGameBtn.Visible = true;
            gameOver = true;
        }
    }
}
```

First, if the user clicks the mouse after the game is over a modal dialog message is displayed on the screen that advises the user that "Game is over. Must start a new game."

All gray lines are cleared from the graphics panel. The method *UserDrawLine* (to be described next) is invoked with the current coordinate values of the mouse. The Boolean field, *canDrawLine*, is set by the *UserDrawLine* method. If the user's mouse is within a hot zone of a line that is still among the lines remaining, this field is set to true, otherwise to false.

Only if the value of *canDrawLine* is true will the *ComputerMove* command be invoked. The computer continues to move if there are still remaining lines and field *capturedBox* is true.

The *UserDrawLine* method alluded to above is presented in Listing 10.11.

LISTING 10.11 Method UserDrawLine

```
private void UserDrawLine(int x, int y) {
    Color color = Color.Red;
    canDrawLine = false;
    // Determine whether to draw vertical line
    if (model != null) {
        capturedBox = false;
        space = 120 - 4 * gridSize;
        for (int row = 1; row < gridSize; row++) {
            for (int col = 1; col <= gridSize; col++) {
                if (x >= 15 + (col - 1) * space &&
                    x <= 50 + (col - 1) * space &&
                    y >= 35 + space * (row - 1) &&
                    y <= space * row) {
                    if (!model.ContainsLine(
                        new Line(row, col, false))) {
                    canDrawLine = true;
                    Line newLine =
                        new Line(row, col, Color.Red, false);
                    newLine.SequenceNumber = sequenceNumber;
                    model.AddLine(newLine);
                    if (model.HaveBoxVerticalLeft(row, col)) {
                        panelGraphics.FillRectangle(
                            new SolidBrush(color),
                            45 + (col - 2) * space,
                            45 + space * (row - 1),
                            space / 2, space / 2);
                        capturedBox = true;
                        personScore++;
                        personScoreLbl.Text =
                            "My Score: " + personScore;
                    }
                    if (model.HaveBoxVerticalRight(row, col)) {
                        panelGraphics.FillRectangle(
                            new SolidBrush(color),
                            45 + (col - 1) * space,
                            45 + space * (row - 1),
                            space / 2, space / 2);
                        capturedBox = true;
                        personScore++;
                        personScoreLbl.Text =
                            "My Score: " + personScore;
                    }
                    panelGraphics.DrawLine(
                        new Pen(new SolidBrush(Color.Red), 2),
                        20 + (col - 1) * space,
                        30 + space * ( row - 1),
                        20 + (col - 1) * space,
                        10 + space * row);
                    if (sequenceNumbersBox.Checked) {
```

LISTING 10.11 Method UserDrawLine (continued)

```
                        float xPos =
                    (float)(20 + (col - 1) * space);
                          float yPos =
                    (float)30 + space * (row - 1) + 35;
                       panelGraphics.DrawString("" +
                    sequenceNumber, Font,
                    new SolidBrush(Color.Red),
                    xPos, yPos);
                            }
                          sequenceNumber++;
                 model.RemoveLine( // From remaining lines
                    new Line(row, col, false));
                 } else {
                    capturedBox = true; // Forces player to move
                                        // again
             }
           }
         }
       }
   }
   // Determine whether to draw horizontal line
   if (model != null) {
       for (int col = 1; col < gridSize; col++) {
           for (int row = 1; row <= gridSize; row++) {
               if (y >= 15 + (row - 1) * space &&
                   y <= 35 + (row - 1) * space &&
                   x >= 35 + space * (col - 1) &&
                     x <= space * col) {
                   if (!model.ContainsLine(
                       new Line(row, col, true))) {
                   Line newLine =
                   new Line(row, col, Color.Red, true);
                   newLine.SequenceNumber = sequenceNumber;
                     model.AddLine(newLine);
                   canDrawLine = true;
                   if (model.HaveBoxHorizontalDown(row,
                             col)) {
                       panelGraphics.FillRectangle(
                           new SolidBrush(color),
                           45 + (col - 1) * space,
                           45 + space * (row - 1),
                           space / 2, space / 2);
                       capturedBox = true;
                       personScore++;
                       personScoreLbl.Text =
                           "My Score: " + personScore;
                   }
                   if (model.HaveBoxHorizontalUp(row,
                             col)) {
```

LISTING 10.11 Method UserDrawLine (continued)

```
                          panelGraphics.FillRectangle(
                             new SolidBrush(color),
                             45 + (col - 1) * space,
                             45 + space * (row - 2),
                             space / 2, space / 2);
                          capturedBox = true;
                          personScore++;
                          personScoreLbl.Text =
                             "My Score: " + personScore;
                       }
                       panelGraphics.DrawLine(
                          new Pen(new SolidBrush(Color.Red),
                          2), 30 + (col - 1) * space,
                          20 + space * ( row - 1),
                          10 + col * space,
                          20 + space * (row - 1));
                             if (sequenceNumbersBox.Checked) {
                                float xPos =
                             (float)30 + (col - 1) * space + 35;
                                   float yPos =
                             (float)20 + space * (row - 1);
                                   panelGraphics.DrawString(
                             "" + sequenceNumber,
                             Font,
                             new SolidBrush(Color.Red),
                             xPos, yPos);
                                }
                                sequenceNumber++;
                       model.RemoveLine( // From remainingLines
                          new Line(row, col, true));
                    } else {
                    capturedBox = true; // Forces
                                        // player to move again
                 }
              }
           }
         }
       }
     }
   }
```

Exercise 10.15

Explain the details of method *UserDrawLine* given in Listing 10.11.

Listing 10.12 contains the details of methods *ComputerMove* and *ComputerDrawLine*.

LISTING 10.12 Methods ComputerMove and ComputerDrawLine

```
private void ComputerMove() {
    Thread.Sleep(250);        // To artificially slow down game
      model.ComputerMove(); // Model generates the computer's line
    ComputerDrawLine(model.Row, model.Col, model.Horizontal);
}

private void ComputerDrawLine(int row, int col, bool horizontal) {
    capturedBox = false;
    if (!horizontal) {
        // Draw vertical line
        space = 120 - 4 * gridSize;
        Line newLine = new Line(row, col, Color.Blue, false);
        newLine.SequenceNumber = sequenceNumber;
        model.AddLine(newLine);
        if (model.HaveBoxVerticalLeft(row, col)) {
            panelGraphics.FillRectangle(
                new SolidBrush(Color.Blue), 45 + (col - 2) * space,
                45 + space * (row - 1), space / 2, space / 2);
            capturedBox = true;
            computerScore++;
            computerScoreLbl.Text =
                "Computer Score: " + computerScore;
        }
        if (model.HaveBoxVerticalRight(row, col)) {
            panelGraphics.FillRectangle(
                new SolidBrush(Color.Blue), 45 + (col - 1) * space,
                45 + space * (row - 1), space / 2, space / 2);
            capturedBox = true;
            computerScore++;
            computerScoreLbl.Text =
                "Computer Score: " + computerScore;
        }
        panelGraphics.DrawLine(
            new Pen(new SolidBrush(Color.Blue), 2),
            20 + (col - 1) * space,
            30 + space * ( row - 1),
            20 + (col - 1) * space, 10 + space * row);
            if (sequenceNumbersBox.Checked) {
                float xPos = (float)(20 + (col - 1) * space);
                float yPos = (float)30 + space * (row - 1) + 35;
                panelGraphics.DrawString(
                "" + sequenceNumber, Font,
                new SolidBrush(Color.Blue), xPos, yPos);
            }
            model.RemoveLine(new Line(row, col, false));
    } else {
        // Draw horizontal line
        Line newLine = new Line(row, col, Color.Blue, true);
        newLine.SequenceNumber = sequenceNumber;
```

LISTING 10.12 Methods ComputerMove and ComputerDrawLine (continued)

```
        model.AddLine(newLine);
        if (model.HaveBoxHorizontalDown(row, col)) {
            panelGraphics.FillRectangle(
                new SolidBrush(Color.Blue), 45 + (col - 1) * space,
                45 + space * (row - 1), space / 2, space / 2);
            capturedBox = true;
            computerScore++;
            computerScoreLbl.Text =
                "Computer Score: " + computerScore;
        }
        if (model.HaveBoxHorizontalUp(row, col)) {
            panelGraphics.FillRectangle(
                new SolidBrush(Color.Blue), 45 + (col - 1) * space,
                45 + space * (row - 2), space / 2, space / 2);
            capturedBox = true;
            computerScore++;
            computerScoreLbl.Text =
                "Computer Score: " + computerScore;
        }
        panelGraphics.DrawLine(
            new Pen(new SolidBrush(Color.Blue), 2),
            30 + (col - 1) * space,
            20 + space * ( row - 1),
            10 + col * space, 20 + space * (row - 1));
        if (sequenceNumbersBox.Checked) {
            float xPos = (float)30 + (col - 1) * space + 35;
            float yPos = (float)20 + space * (row - 1);
            panelGraphics.DrawString(
                "" + sequenceNumber,
                Font, new SolidBrush(Color.Blue), xPos, yPos);
        }
        model.RemoveLine(new Line(row, col, true));
    }
    sequenceNumber++;
}
```

The *ComputerMove* method introduces an artificial time delay of 250 milliseconds in order to create a slower rhythm for the computer's move. The model object is sent the *ComputerMove* command. Depending on the level of play recorded with the model, the model will generate a line defined by *row*, *col*, and *horizontal*. These values are obtained from the model using the properties with the same name (*Row*, *Col*, and *Horizontal*).

Exercise 10.16

Explain the details of method *ComputerDrawLine* in Listing 10.12.

In reviewing the code in classes *Model* and *BoxesUI*, one can see the distribution of responsibility between the model and view classes. Each of these classes is already complex enough. If the two classes were mixed into one big class, the complexity would become overwhelming and maintenance would be thwarted.

10.3 RESIZING AND REPAINTING

An important issue when displaying graphics, as in this Dots and Boxes game, is repainting the panel whenever the panel becomes "invalidated." This can happen if another control, such as a modal dialog box, is superimposed in front of the panel or if the form containing the panel is minimized and then restored in size. Without some explicit intervention to restore the graphics, these events and others like them would remove part or all of the graphics being displayed. Clearly we must make the application resilient to such disturbances.

We accomplish this by defining two event handlers for the *Panel* component: Resize and Repaint. The handler that responds to these events uses the model object to re-create each line. Listing 10.13 presents the details of these two event handlers and their support methods.

LISTING 10.13 Handling resizing and repainting of the Panel

```
private void BoxesUI_Resize(object sender, System.EventArgs e) {
    RestoreLines();
}

private void panel_Paint(object sender, PaintEventArgs e) {
    RestoreLines();
}

private void RestoreLines() {
    if (model != null && model.Lines != null) {
        DrawDots();
        // Get lines from model
        ArrayList lines = model.Lines;
        foreach (Line line in lines) {
        Color lineColor = line.LineColor;
                int sequenceNumber = line.SequenceNumber;
                RecreateLine(lineColor, sequenceNumber,
                        line.Row, line.Col, line.Horizontal);
            }
        }
    }

private void RecreateLine(Color lineColor, int sequenceNumber,
                    int row, int col, bool horizontal) {
    capturedBox = false;
```

LISTING 10.13 Handling resizing and repainting of the Panel (continued)

```
    if (!horizontal) {
        // Draw vertical line
        space = 120 - 4 * gridSize;
        if (model.HaveBoxVerticalLeft(row, col)) {
            panelGraphics.FillRectangle(
                new SolidBrush(lineColor), 45 + (col - 2) * space,
                45 + space * (row - 1), space / 2, space / 2);
            capturedBox = true;
        }
        if (model.HaveBoxVerticalRight(row, col)) {
            panelGraphics.FillRectangle(
                new SolidBrush(lineColor), 45 + (col - 1) * space,
                45 + space * (row - 1), space / 2, space / 2);
            capturedBox = true;
        }
        panelGraphics.DrawLine(
                new Pen(new SolidBrush(lineColor), 2),
                20 + (col - 1) * space,
                30 + space * ( row - 1), 20 + (col - 1) * space,
                10 + space * row);
        if (sequenceNumbersBox.Checked) {
                float xPos = (float)(20 + (col - 1) * space);
            float yPos = (float)30 + space * (row - 1) + 35;
                panelGraphics.DrawString("" + sequenceNumber,
                    Font, new SolidBrush(lineColor), xPos, yPos);
        }
    } else {
        // Draw horizontal line
        if (model.HaveBoxHorizontalDown(row, col)) {
            panelGraphics.FillRectangle(
                new SolidBrush(lineColor), 45 + (col - 1) * space,
                45 + space * (row - 1), space / 2, space / 2);
            capturedBox = true;
        }
        if (model.HaveBoxHorizontalUp(row, col)) {
            panelGraphics.FillRectangle(
                new SolidBrush(lineColor), 45 + (col - 1) * space,
                45 + space * (row - 2), space / 2, space / 2);
            capturedBox = true;
        }
        panelGraphics.DrawLine(
            new Pen(new SolidBrush(lineColor), 2),
            30 + (col - 1) * space,
            20 + space * ( row - 1), 10 + col * space,
            20 + space * (row - 1));
        if (sequenceNumbersBox.Checked) {
            float xPos = (float)30 + (col - 1) * space + 35;
            float yPos = (float)20 + space * (row - 1);
```

LISTING 10.13 Handling resizing and repainting of the Panel (continued)

```
                        panelGraphics.DrawString("" + sequenceNumber,
                        Font, new SolidBrush(lineColor), xPos, yPos);
            }
        }
    }
```

Exercise 10.17

Explain the code in Listing 10.13.

To demonstrate the benefit of the current architecture, we shall undertake some maintenance in the next section.

10.4 MORE ADVANCED AND ADVANCED LEVELS OF PLAY IN DOTS AND BOXES

Note: You might want to skip this section upon the first reading of this book. The implementation of the More Advanced and Advanced levels of play use recursion. Understanding and using recursion is an extremely important subject in modern software development and algorithm design. It is presented in Chapter 11 because it is closely related to the subject of data structures, the subject of Part 4 of the book. You may wish to continue a first reading of this section without becoming concerned about the use of recursion. This will provide you with an introduction and flavor for the use and power of recursion. You may then return to this section for a more intensive reading after completing the presentation of recursion in Chapter 11.

Suppose we are charged with the task of adding a more advanced level of play to the existing game of Dots and Boxes described and presented in Section 10.2.

Because of the clear delineation and separation of responsibility between classes *Model* and *BoxesUI* described in Section 10.2, this maintenance will be straightforward and deal mainly with class *Model*.

At the Intermediate level of play, if the computer cannot choose a line that will deny the user the ability to capture a box, it chooses a random line from among its remaining lines. This has the effect of randomly selecting the box that the user can capture if there are in fact two or more boxes that the user can capture. This random choice might lead the user to not only capture the given box but subsequently capture a long chain of boxes that includes the captured box.

The new level of play, "More Advanced," replaces the random choice described previously as follows: For each possible line among the remaining lines that allows the user to capture a box, the length of the chain of boxes that the user will be able to capture is determined. The line that is associated with the smallest chain of boxes that the user will be able to capture is chosen by the computer instead of leaving the choice to chance. In the event that there are two or more lines that would lead to the same smallest chain of boxes that the user could capture, one of these lines is chosen at random.

We illustrate the situation in Figure 10.7.

Following the capture of the box in the lower right using line 14, the computer chose line 15 on the left boundary of the grid. Any line that the computer would have chosen would allow the user to capture a box. The computer randomly chose the line shown as line 15. It made a bad choice. The user would be able to capture all the remaining boxes because a chain of size seven includes the first box that the user can capture. The user would capture these seven boxes and then give the final box in the upper-left corner to the computer. The score would be seven for the user, two for the computer.

If the computer had chosen a horizontal line starting with the upper-left dot, the user would capture the upper-left box, but then be forced to place a line within the chain of seven boxes allowing the computer to capture these boxes. The score would be eight for the computer and one for the user.

In order to implement this more advanced strategy, we need to augment the *Model* class so that it can compute the size of a chain that includes the box captured by the user. Then the computer can be guided in giving up the box to the user that is associated with the smallest size chain (size 1 in the case given previously).

The first simple task in performing our software maintenance is to change the *enum*, *LevelOfPlay*, as follows:

```
public enum LevelOfPlay {Novice, Beginner, Intermediate,
                    MoreAdvanced, Advanced};
```

In class *Model*, we add a field, *chains*, of type *ArrayList*. Each object to be inserted into this *ArrayList* will be an *ArrayList* of type *Line*. These lines (in the second

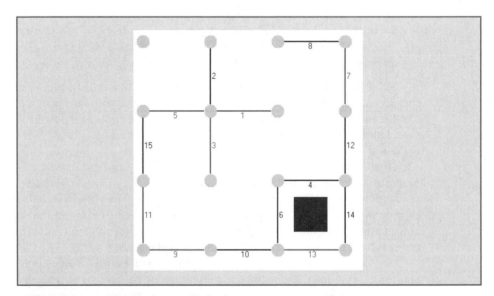

FIGURE 10.7 More advanced strategy

ArrayList contained with the *ArrayList chains*) define each chain and would be the lines in the boxes that are captured by the user if the original line is selected.

We also add an integer field *chainCount* that represents the number of distinct chains in the grid.

Listing 10.14 presents the details of method *ComputeChains*. This important new support method loads the *chains* field with a collection of *ArrayList* objects, each of which defines the collection of lines that define a chain.

LISTING 10.14 Method ComputeChains

```
private void ComputeChains() {
    chains = new ArrayList();
    chainCount = -1;
    foreach (Line line in RemainingLines) {
        int row = line.Row;
        int col = line.Col;
    bool horizontal = line.Horizontal;
        // Test to see whether line is in an existing chain
        bool inExistingChain = false;
        for (int index = 0; index <= chainCount; index++) {
        if (((ArrayList)chains[index]).Count > 1 &&
                ((ArrayList)chains[index]).Contains(line)) {
                inExistingChain = true;
            }
        }

        if (!inExistingChain) {
        chainCount++;
            chains.Add(new ArrayList());
            if (horizontal) {
                ExtendChain(new Line(row - 1, col, true));
                ExtendChain(new Line(row - 1, col, false));
                ExtendChain(new Line(row - 1, col + 1, false));
                ExtendChain(new Line(row + 1, col, true));
                ExtendChain(new Line(row, col + 1, false));
                ExtendChain(new Line(row, col, false));
            } else {
                ExtendChain(new Line(row, col, true));
                ExtendChain(new Line(row, col + 1, false));
                ExtendChain(new Line(row + 1, col, true));
                ExtendChain(new Line(row, col - 1, true));
                ExtendChain(new Line(row, col - 1, false));
                ExtendChain(new Line(row + 1, col - 1, true));
            }
        }
    }
}
```

The iteration produces each available line among the remaining lines. It first tests to see whether that line is already contained in one of the existing chains. If it is not, *chainCount* is incremented by one. A new *ArrayList* object is added to the *chains ArrayList*.

The recursive method *ExtendChain*, to be described following, is invoked six times. The exact sequence of *ExtendChain* commands is based on whether the line under consideration is horizontal or vertical.

Each of the six *ExtendChain* commands is based on the lines that can expand the evolving chain in the possible directions that it can grow.

Let us consider in detail the first three of the six *ExtendChain* method arguments if the line is horizontal. The horizontal line under consideration is shown at row 2 and column 1 (the second line down) in Figure 10.8.

The first *ExtendChain* argument is:

```
new Line(row - 1, col, true)
```

This represents a horizontal line in the box just north at the north (top) end of the box. It is identified as red in Figure 10.8. This line is one of the six that allows for the expansion of the chain in a northerly direction.

The second *ExtendChain* argument is:

```
new Line(row - 1, col, false)
```

It represents the line identified as blue in Figure 10.8, and allows for the expansion of the chain in a northwesterly direction.

The third *ExtendChain* argument is:

```
new Line(row - 1, col + 1, false)
```

This green colored line (identified in Figure 10.8) allows for the expansion of the chain in a northeasterly direction.

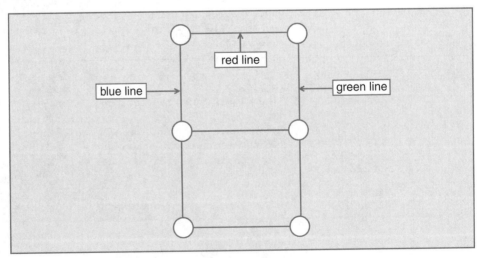

FIGURE 10.8 First *ExtendChain* method argument

Exercise 10.18

Explain the remaining nine invocations of *ExtendChain* in method *ComputeChains*.

The recursive method *ExtendChain* is presented in Listing 10.15.

LISTING 10.15 Method ExtendChain

```
/*
 * This recursive method attempts to expand the boundaries
 * of a chain in the six possible directions depending on whether
 * the line is horizontal or vertical.
 */

private void ExtendChain(Line line) {
    if (remainingLines.Contains(line)) {
        if (!((ArrayList) chains[chainCount]).Contains(line)) {
        ((ArrayList) chains[chainCount]).Add(line);
            int row = line.Row;
            int col = line.Col;
            bool horizontal = line.Horizontal;
            if (horizontal) {
                ExtendChain(new Line(row - 1, col, true)); // N
                ExtendChain(new Line(row - 1, col, false)); // NW
                ExtendChain(new Line(row - 1, col + 1, false)); // NE
                ExtendChain(new Line(row + 1, col, true)); // S
                ExtendChain(new Line(row, col + 1, false)); // E
                ExtendChain(new Line(row, col, false)); // W
            } else {
                ExtendChain(new Line(row, col, true)); // N
                ExtendChain(new Line(row, col + 1, false)); // E
                ExtendChain(new Line(row + 1, col, true)); // S
                ExtendChain(new Line(row, col - 1, true)); // NW
                ExtendChain(new Line(row, col - 1, false)); // W
                ExtendChain(new Line(row + 1, col - 1, true)); // SW
            }
        }
    }
}
```

Only if the input line that represents the potential boundary of the chain expansion is among the remaining lines and is not currently in the chain being formed do we recursively attempt to expand it further in each of the six possible directions based on whether the line is horizontal or vertical (see Exercise 10.18). The recursion ends when no further lines within the collection, *remainingLines*, can be found or the line is already included in the expanding chain.

Listing 10.16 presents a portion of the details of method *MoreAdvancedMove*.

LISTING 10.16 A portion of method MoreAdvancedMove

```
private void MoreAdvancedMove() {
    // Capture a box if possible, otherwise choose a line
    // that prevents opponent from next closing a box
    // otherwise pick a line that provides the shortest
    // chain of boxes that opponent can capture.

    /* Beginning details identical to method IntermediateMove
       and not shown.
    */
    if (NumberRemainingLines() > 0) {
        ComputeChains();
        int shortestChain = ((ArrayList)chains[0]).Count;
        int indexShortestChain = 0;
        for (int i = 1; i < chains.Count; i++) {
          int count = ((ArrayList) chains[i]).Count;
            if (count < shortestChain && count > 0) {
                shortestChain = count;
                indexShortestChain = i;
            }
        }
        Line line = (Line)
            ((ArrayList) chains[indexShortestChain])[0];
        row = line.Row;
        col = line.Col;
        horizontal = line.Horizontal;

    }
}
```

The downcast *(ArrayList)* is used in several places in the code given above. This is needed whenever accessing the *ArrayList* object contained within the *ArrayList* chains because the formal type in all *ArrayList* collections is *Object*. The actual type is *ArrayList*.

Experience in testing the More Advanced Move strategy among the several players who have tried it suggests that it adds a considerable measure of improvement to the computer's playing ability.

The final addition in level of play is Advanced Move. It is based on a principle cited in the book *"Dots and Boxes Game: Sophisticated Child's Play"* by Elwyn Berlekamp. He defines a chain as containing three or more boxes. His long chain rule is the following:

If you are the first player, try to make the number of initial dots plus the eventual long chains an even number. If you are the second player, make this sum an odd number. That would imply that if you are the second player (the computer) and the grid size is 4 x 4 or 6 x 6 (an even number of initial dots), you would like to make the number of long chains an odd number.

We have already built most of the infrastructure needed to implement this long chain rule of Berlekamp. Only a short support method *NumberChains* that counts the number of chains of size three or greater is needed. The method *AdvancedMove* that is added to class *Model* is presented in Listing 10.17.

LISTING 10.17 Portions of method AdvancedMove

```
private int NumberChains() {
    ComputeChains();
        int returnValue = 0;
    for (int i = 0; i < chains.Count; i++) {
        if (((ArrayList)chains[i]).Count >= 4) {
            returnValue++;
        }
    }
    return returnValue;
}

private void AdvancedMove() {
    /*
     * Same as MoreAdvanced except when choosing box that
     * will not allow opponent to capture box:
     * If number of grid lines is even (4 x 4 or 6 x 6):
     *    If computer moves second, try to make move that creates an
     *    odd number of chains (a chain is defined as having 3 or
     *    more boxes).
     *    If computer moves first try to make move that creates
     *    an even number of chains.
     * If number of grid lines is odd (5 x 5):
     *    If computer moves second, try to make move that creates
     *    an even number of chains.
     *    If computer moves first, try to make move that creates
     *    an odd number of chains.
     */
    if (PickLineToCaptureBox()) {
        return;
    }
    bool foundLine = false;
    ScrambleRemainingLines();
    foreach (Line line in RemainingLines) {
        row = line.Row;
        col = line.Col;
        horizontal = line.Horizontal;
        this.AddLine(new Line(row, col, horizontal));
        if (horizontal) {
            if (!HaveBoxVerticalLeft(row, col + 1) &&
                    !HaveBoxVerticalLeft(row - 1, col + 1) &&
                    !HaveBoxVerticalRight(row, col) &&
                    !HaveBoxVerticalRight(row - 1, col) &&
                    !HaveBoxHorizontalDown(row - 1, col) &&
```

LISTING 10.17 Portions of method AdvancedMove (continued)

```
                            !HaveBoxHorizontalUp(row + 1, col)) {
                            // Opponent cannot get box with addition of line
                            int numberOfChains = NumberChains();
                            // Long chain rule:  Berlekamp
                            if ( (((gridSize == 4 || gridSize == 6) &&
                                    !computerMovesFirst ) ||
                                    (gridSize == 5 && computerMovesFirst)) &&
                                        numberOfChains % 2 == 1) {
                                lines.Remove(new Line(row, col, horizontal));
                                    return;
                        } else if ((((gridSize == 4 || gridSize == 6)
                                    && computerMovesFirst) ||
                                    (gridSize == 5 && !computerMovesFirst)) &&
                                        numberOfChains % 2 == 0) {
                            lines.Remove(new Line(row, col, horizontal));
                                return;
                        } else {
                            foundLine = true;
                                lines.Remove(new Line(row, col, horizontal));
                        }
                    }
            } else {
                // Details similar to above and not shown
            }

            /*  Remaining details the same as MoreAdvancedMove
    }
```

Although lengthy, the basic idea in Listing 10.17 is to find a line that prevents the user from capturing a box and makes either an even or odd number of chains based on the grid size and whether the computer moves first or second. This consideration is now needed because the final addition to the application is the presence of a new check box that determines whether the computer or the user moves first when starting a new game. A Boolean field, *computerMovesFirst*, and an associated write-only (set) property are added to class *Model*.

The final GUI is shown in Figure 10.9. Here the computer is shown as having moved first in a 6 x 6 game being played at the Advanced level.

You are encouraged to download the completed game and see how well you can play against the computer at each of its five levels of play.

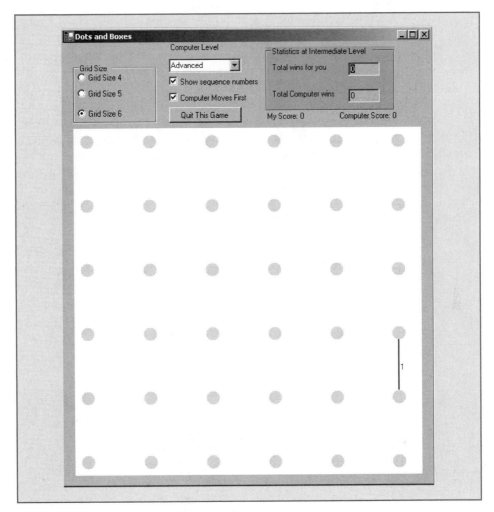

FIGURE 10.9 Final GUI for Dots and Boxes game

10.5 SUMMARY

◆ A custom control is typically a GUI class that is derived from
System.Windows.Forms.UserControl.

◆ In addition to providing properties that affect the appearance of your custom
control (size, color, etc.), it is customary that you provide event-handling
services that allow the user's application to register listeners and consume
events generated within your component.

◆ An important issue when displaying graphics is repainting the panel whenever
the panel becomes "invalidated." This can happen if another control, such as a
modal dialog box, is superimposed in front of the panel or if the form containing
the panel is minimized and then restored in size. Without some explicit

intervention to restore the graphics, these events and others like them would remove part or all of the graphics being displayed.

◆ A relatively short case study that demonstrates the steps that are typically involved in constructing a custom control is presented.

◆ Another case study that provides another demonstration of the importance and power of separating the computational aspects of the model from the view is presented. Five different algorithms (Novice, Beginner, Intermediate, More Advanced, and Advanced) for playing dots and boxes are presented. A GUI application that allows the user to add a line between adjacent dots with the objective of capturing as many boxes as possible is constructed.

10.6 ADDITIONAL EXERCISES

In this chapter, all of the exercises (Exercises 10.1-10.18) are directly related to the listings. They therefore follow the listings so that they appear in context, and are not repeated here.

DATA STRUCTURES

An important technique of programming, **recursion**, briefly introduced and used in Chapter 10, is presented in Chapter 11 in some detail. Recursion is not only a technique of programming but also a mechanism for thinking and software design. Many of the algorithms that are used in Chapter 13 to implement tree structures use recursion. Important algorithms that lie outside of the domain of data structures also use recursion. These include two classic sorting algorithms that are presented in Chapter 11.

Container types in software development are used to hold and efficiently access information. Data structures represent the implementation of a container type. The study of data structures, including the algorithms for inserting information into a container, deleting information from a container, and accessing information within a container, has served as the foundation and basis for CS 2 courses for several decades.

Data structures such as stack, queue, priority queue, deque, linked list, binary search tree, balanced search tree, and hash table are considered classic because they have been and continue to be used in countless applications and have been studied for decades. In fact, they form the building blocks of many important applications.

In addition to recursion, this part of the book examines these classic data structures and provides you with the skills needed to manipulate linked structures and understand the subtleties of nonlinear structures.

Chapter 11 focuses on recursion and some applications. Chapter 12 examines classic linear data structures. Chapter 13 studies nonlinear data structures with particular emphasis on tree structures and hash tables. Chapter 14 presents the standard .NET collection classes and some applications.

CHAPTER 11

Recursion

An important technique of programming, **recursion**, briefly introduced and used in the previous chapter, is presented here in some detail. Recursion is not only a technique of programming but more importantly a mechanism for thinking and software design. Many of the algorithms that are used in Chapter 13 to implement binary search trees use recursion. Many important algorithms that lie outside of the domain of data structures also use recursion.

A careful examination of what happens "under the hood" when a recursive method is invoked is conducted. Two important and classic sorting algorithms, Quick Sort and Merge Sort, are presented as applications of recursion.

11.1 INTRODUCTION TO RECURSION

A method is recursive if within its body it calls itself. In mathematics, a recursive function is defined in terms of itself. In general, a structure is recursive if it is defined in terms of itself. For example, a tree data structure is defined as having a root node. This root node has child nodes, each of which may serve as the root node of a sub-tree (another tree structure rooted within the original tree structure). So here the definition of a tree involves the use of a tree.

The factorial function, n!, from mathematics, may be defined as follows:

$n! = n * (n - 1)!$

This definition is recursive because the computation of n factorial is replaced with the computation of (n–1) factorial.

Recursive methods generally satisfy the following conditions:

◆ The method invokes itself one or more times.

◆ The method contains a sentinel parameter that is used to stop further recursive calls from occurring and thus eventually stopping the recursion from continuing forever. There is a base terminating case that is the simplest or smallest size problem that can be solved.

◆ The body of the recursive method must drive the value of the sentinel parameter in a manner that will eventually stop the recursion from continuing.

Listing 11.1 shows the implementation of the factorial function as a recursive method. All three conditions are satisfied by this recursive method.

LISTING 11.1 Recursive method Factorial

```
public decimal Factorial(decimal value) {
    if (value > 0) {
        return value * Factorial(value - 1);
    } else {
        return 1;
    }
}
```

Exercise 11.1

Embed the *Factorial* method in a class *FactorialApp* and show the computation of 13!.

When the sentinel parameter, *value*, is driven down to 0, no further recursive calls occur and the value of 1 is returned (corresponding to 0!).

Before digging deeper into the mechanics of recursion, we consider another relatively simple example—computing the average value of numbers within an array.

To see how such a recursive method is designed, consider the average value of the following:

```
x[i]; i = 1..n.
```

$$\text{Average}[n] = \sum_{i=1}^{n} x[i] / n = x[n] / n + \sum_{i=1}^{n-1} x[i] / n = x[n] / n + (n-1) / n * \text{Average}[n-1]$$

Listing 11.2 presents the details of recursive method *Average*.

LISTING 11.2 Recursive method Average

```
public double Average(double[] values, int n) {
    if (n == 1) {
        return values[0];
    } else {
        return values[n - 1] / n +
                (n - 1.0) / n * Average(values, n - 1);
    }
}
```

11.2 LOOKING AT RECURSION FROM UNDER THE HOOD

Insight into the inner workings of the recursive method *Average* of Listing 11.2 may be obtained by inserting output commands into the recursive method to capture the flow of control, as shown in Listing 11.3. An alternative would be to set a watch window using a debugger such as the one integrated with Visual Studio.

LISTING 11.3 Closely observing the mechanics of method Average

```
using System;

namespace Recursion {

    public class RecursionApp {

        private double Average(double[] values, int n) {
            if (n == 1) {
```

LISTING 11.3 Closely observing the mechanics of method Average (continued)

```
                    Console.WriteLine("n  = 1:  return " + values[0]);
                    return values[0];
                } else {
                    Console.WriteLine("n = " + n + ": return " +
                            values[n - 1] / n + " + " + (n - 1.0) +
                            " / " + n + " * Average(values," +
                            (n - 1) + ")");
                    return values[n - 1] / n +
                            (n - 1.0) / n * Average(values, n - 1);
                }
            }


        static void Main(string[] args) {
            RecursionApp app = new RecursionApp();
            double[] data = { 2.0, 4.0, 6.0, 7.0, 9.0 };
            Console.WriteLine("Average[5] = " + app.Average(data, 5));
            Console.ReadLine();
        }
    }
}

/* Program output
n = 5: return 1.8 + 4 / 5 * Average(values,4)
n = 4: return 1.75 + 3 / 4 * Average(values,3)
n = 3: return 2 + 2 / 3 * Average(values,2)
n = 2: return 2 + 1 / 2 * Average(values,1)
n  = 1:  return 2
Average[5] = 5.6
*/
```

From the output it is clear that when the method is invoked with n = 5, the value returned is expressed in terms of the Average(values, 4), which in turn causes a value to be returned in terms of Average(values, 3), which in turn causes a value to be returned in terms of Average(values, 2), which in turn causes a value to be returned in terms of Average(values, 1). It is only when n = 1 that the first numeric value is generated, a value of 2. Through the backtracking process, the values when n = 2, then n = 3, then n = 4, and finally n = 5 are produced, returning 5.6 as the result.

Exercise 11.2

Using the output of Listing 11.3, verify that the correct average value of 5.6 is produced. To accomplish this, "walk" up the chain of recursive calls starting with n = 1, then n = 2, and so on, until the value at n = 5 is produced.

To understand the mechanics of recursion, we need to understand two basic principles that govern the internal operation of recursion:

1. Just before a recursive call, all local variables and parameters are copied onto an internal stack and held until the recursive call is completed. This internal stack is managed by the runtime system and is not directly accessible to the programmer.

2. When a recursive call is completed (the end brace of the recursive method has been reached), the local variables and parameters that were saved on the internal stack are removed from this stack and restored. The flow of control is returned to one line below the recursive call.

The stack data structure is examined in detail in Chapter 12. For now, you need to know only that a stack defines a last-in, first-out structure so that the oldest item inserted is the last item removed, the next to the oldest item inserted is the next to the last item to be removed, and so on, and the youngest item inserted is the first item to be removed. If one envisions the data piled on top of each other, then the top of the pile would correspond to the most recent item inserted and the first item that can be removed. The bottom of the pile would hold the first (oldest) item to have been inserted and the last item that can be removed.

The mechanism described above in which a snapshot of local variables and parameters taken just before a recursive call is held in an internal stack and released from the stack just after the recursive call forms the basis for understanding the mechanics of recursion.

We illustrate these mechanics by considering a more challenging example of recursion. Consider the following recursive method:

```
public void DoItRecursively(int value) {
    if (value != 0) {
        DoItRecursively(value / 2);
        Console.WriteLine(value);
        DoItRecursively(value / 2);
    }
}
```

Suppose this method were invoked with the argument *value* initially equal to 10.

A diagramming technique is introduced that permits a detailed examination of the inner workings of this and any other recursive method.

Table 11.1 contains three columns. The first column indicates the action taken. The second column shows the internal system stack from left to right. The most recent item added to the system stack is shown to the left, with older items progressing to the right in a comma-separated list. The output is shown in the third column.

Because there are two recursive calls within the body of *DoItRecursively*, it is important to distinguish whether the parameter *value* that is inserted onto the stack is caused by the first or second recursive call. This is important to know so that when the recursive call is completed, control can be directed to either the line just below the first or just below the second recursive call.

Whenever the parameter *value* is inserted onto the internal stack just before the second recursive call is made, an asterisk is placed in front of the number that represents the parameter *value*. Later, when the information is removed from the internal stack, if the number has an asterisk in front, program control is directed to one line below the second recursive call. Without such an asterisk, control is directed to the line directly below the first recursive call (the output to the console).

Using the asterisk in this way as a meta-symbol makes the analysis of the inner workings of the recursion straightforward, although as we shall see it is still tedious.

So tighten your seat belt and get ready for a ride in performing a part of the analysis of *DoItRecursively* when the input value is set to 10.

We use the term "push" to indicate inserting an item onto the internal stack. We use the term "pop" to indicate removing an item from the internal stack.

TABLE 11.1 Details of DoItRecursively

Action	Internal System Stack (left is top)	Output
Top: DoItRecursively (10)		
push value = 10 onto stack	10	
Top: DoItRecursively (5)		
push value = 5 onto stack	5 , 10	
Top: DoItRecursively (2)		
push value = 2 onto stack	2 , 5 , 10	
Top: DoItRecursively (1)		
push value = 1 onto stack	1 , 2 , 5 , 10	
Top: DoItRecursively (0)		
pop stack; restore value = 1	2 , 5 , 10	1
push value = *1 onto stack	*1 , 2 , 5 , 10	
Bottom: DoItRecursively (0)		
pop stack; restore value = *1	2 , 5 , 10	
pop stack; restore value = 2	5 , 10	2
push value = *2 onto stack	*2 , 5 , 10	
Bottom: DoItRecursively (1)		
push value = 1 onto stack	1 , *2 , 5 , 10	
Top: DoItRecursively (0)		
pop stack; restore value = 1	*2 , 5 , 10	1
push value = *1 onto stack	*1 , *2 , 5 , 10	
Bottom: DoItRecursively (0)		
pop stack; restore value = *1	*2 , 5 , 10	
pop stack; restore value = *2	5 , 10	
pop stack; restore value = 5	10	5
push value *5 onto stack	*5 , 10	
Bottom: DoItRecursively (2)		

TABLE 11.1 Details of DoItRecursively (continued)

Action	Internal System Stack (left is top)	Output
push value = 2 onto stack	2 , *5, 10	
Top: DoItRecursively (1)		
push value = 1 onto stack	1 , 2 , *5 , 10	
Top: DoItRecursively (0)		
pop stack; restore value = 1	2, *5, 10	1
push value = *1 onto stack	*1, 2, *5, 10	
Bottom: DoItRecursively (0)		
pop stack; restore value = *1	2, *5, 10	
pop stack, restore value 2	*5, 10	2
push value = *2	*2, *5, 10	
Bottom: DoItRecursively (1)		
push value = 1 onto stack	1, *2, *5, 10	
Top: DoItRecursively (0)		
pop stack; restore value = 1	*2, *5, 10	1
push value = *1 onto stack	*1, *2, *5, 10	
Bottom: DoItRecursively (0)		
pop stack; restore value = *1	*2, *5, 10	
pop stack; restore value = *2	*5, 10	
pop stack; restore value = *5	10	
pop stack; restore value = 10	empty	10
push value = *10 onto stack	*10	
Top: DoItRecursively (5)		
push value = 5 onto stack	5 , *10	History repeats

The first recursive calls to *DoItRecursively* cause the internal stack to hold the values 1, 2, 5, 10 (the value of 1—the most recent value—pushed onto the stack and the value 10—the oldest value—pushed onto the stack). This is shown in the first eight lines in Table 11.1.

When the call to *DoItRecursively(0)* occurs, the *if* block is bypassed and the ending brace is finally reached. Then as shown in line 10 of Table 11.1, the value of 1 is popped from the stack, control is returned to the output statement, and the value of 1 is output to the console. Line 11 shows the value of 1 being pushed onto the stack in preparation for the second recursive call. The meta-symbol "*" is inserted in front of the 1 to establish that it is caused by the second recursive call.

Whenever a value tagged with the asterisk is popped from the stack, the next value on the stack is immediately popped because control is returned below the second recursive call, which causes the end brace of the recursive method to be reached. This is illustrated in lines 20 to 24 in Table 11.1.

Table 11.1 represents only half of the "action" involved in the analysis of the recursion. The "history repeats" indication in the lower-right cell of the table suggests the same sequence of output follows from the internal stack containing 5, *10.

The total output when *DoItRecursively(10)* is invoked is:

```
1
2
1
5
1
2
1
10
1
2
1
5
1
2
1
```

Who might think that so much output would result from a three-line recursive method? It is typical for recursive methods to be capable of performing a lot of computation.

Exercise 11.3

Continue the table and show that the remaining output is:

```
1
2
1
5
1
2
1
```

Exercise 11.4

Perform an analysis similar to that presented in Table 11.1 for the method *DoItRecursively2* given as follows (assume that the value 10 is sent in).

```
public void DoItRecursively2(int value) {
    if (value != 0) {
        DoItRecursively2(value / 2);
        Console.WriteLine(value);
        DoItRecursively2(value / 3);
        Console.WriteLine(value);
        DoItRecursively2(value / 4);
```

```
        }
}
```

Show that the output is:

1

1

2

2

5

1

1

5

1

1

10

1

1

3

1

1

3

10

1

1

2

2

To further demonstrate the mechanisms of recursion, we consider the application presented in Listing 11.4.

LISTING 11.4 Further exploring the mechanics of recursion

```
using System;

namespace Snapshots {

    public class SnapshotsApp {

        public void RecursiveMethod(int sentinelValue) {
            Console.WriteLine("sentinelValue = " + sentinelValue);
            int localValue1 = 2 * sentinelValue;
            int localValue2 = sentinelValue / 2;
```

LISTING 11.4 Further exploring the mechanics of recursion (continued)

```
            if (localValue1 + localValue2 > 5) {
                RecursiveMethod(sentinelValue / 3);
                Console.WriteLine("localValue1: " + localValue1);
                Console.WriteLine("localValue2: " + localValue2);
            }
        }

        static void Main(string[] args) {
            SnapshotsApp app = new SnapshotsApp();
            app.RecursiveMethod(25);
            Console.ReadLine();
        }
    }
}
```

Table 11.2 shows the details of the inner workings of this recursive method.

TABLE 11.2 Analysis of RecursiveMethod in Listing 11.4

Action	Stack (top on left) <localValue1, localValue2>	Output
RecursiveMethod(25)		Sentinel value = 25
	<50, 12>	
RecursiveMethod(8)		Sentinel value = 8
	<16, 4>, <50, 12>	
RecursiveMethod(2)		Sentinel value = 2
	<50, 12>	localValue1: 16 localValue2: 4
		localValue1: 50 localValue2: 12

The internal stack contains a two-tuple set *<localValue1, localValue2>*. When *RecursiveMethod* is invoked with the argument set to 25, the two-tuple <50, 12> is pushed onto the internal system stack because *localValue1* is 50 and *localValue2* is 12.

When *RecursiveMethod* is invoked with the argument set to 8 (25 / 3), the two-tuple <16, 4> is pushed on top of the existing <50, 12> because *localValue1* is 16 and *localValue2* is 4.

Finally, when *RecursiveMethod* is invoked with the sentinel parameter set to 2 (8 / 3), no further recursive calls are executed because *localValue1* is 4 and *localValue2* is 1 and their sum does not exceed 5. This causes the end brace of the recursive method to be reached. The internal stack is popped, removing the two-tuple <16, 4> from the stack. This causes the output shown in column 3. The end brace of the recursive method is again reached. This causes the final popping of the internal stack, with the values <50, 12> popped from the stack and output as shown in column 3.

11.3 SOME PRACTICAL EXAMPLES OF RECURSION

The examples presented in Section 11.2 were tutorial in nature. In this section we present two practical examples of recursion. Further practical applications of recursion will be presented in Section 11.4 and Chapter 13 in connection with the implementation of nonlinear data structures.

11.3.1 Binary Search Using Recursion

A relatively simple, but important, application of recursion is performing a binary search of an array. This can also be accomplished using iteration. However, because of the nature of binary search, where we examine the middle element and reduce the scope of the search, recursion provides for an elegant and compact solution.

Suppose we have a sorted array containing values of type *double*. We wish to determine whether a particular value is present in the sorted array.

Consider method *BinarySearch* presented in Listing 11.5.

LISTING 11.5 Method BinarySearch

```
public int BinarySearch(double[] data,
                        double searchFor, int low, int high) {
    int mid;
    if (low > high) {
        return -1; // searchFor not in array
    } else {
        mid = (low + high) / 2;
        if (searchFor == data[mid]) {
            return mid;
        } else {
            if (searchFor < data[mid]) {
                return BinarySearch(data, searchFor, low, mid - 1);
            } else {
                return BinarySearch(data, searchFor, mid + 1, high);
            }
        }
    }
}
```

Exercise 11.5

Explain how method *BinarySearch* in Listing 11.5 works.

Exercise 11.6

Write an application that "hard-wires" the array values as follows:

`double[] values = { -0.5, -0.25, 0.0, 0.15, 0.34, 1.2, 6.7, 9.1 };`

Using the method *BinarySearch* it determines first whether the value 0.17 is present and next whether the value 0.15 is present. If present, it outputs to the console the index containing the values being searched for.

11.3.2 Permutations Using Recursion

The next application of recursion is more complex. Suppose we have an array of objects. We want to output every permutation of the objects. There are n! such permutations for an array of size n. For example, if the objects stored in the array were String objects with values A, B, and C, the output of the recursive *Permute* method would be:

A B C
A C B
B A C
B C A
C B A
C A B

Listing 11.6 presents the static method *Permute*. The method is defined in terms of a generic parameter T of any object type. The method is declared static because it is of universal importance.

A simple application that exercises method *Permute* is defined in Listing 11.7 along with a support class *Person*.

LISTING 11.6 Recursive method Permute

```
using System;

namespace Permutations {

    public class Permutation {

        public static void Permute<T>(T[] input, int size) {
            int index = size - 1;
            T temp;

            if (size > 1) {
                Permute(input, index);
                for (int value = index - 1; value >= 0; value—) {
                    // Interchange the objects at index and value
                    temp = input[index];
                    input[index] = input[value];
                    input[value] = temp;
                    Permute(input, index);
                    // Interchange the objects at index and value
                    temp = input[index];
                    input[index] = input[value];
                    input[value] = temp;
                }
            } else {
                for (int i = 0; i < input.Length; i++) {
                    Console.Write(input[i] + " ");
                }
                Console.WriteLine();
            }
        }
    }
```

LISTING 11.6 Recursive method Permute (continued)

```
        }
}
```

LISTING 11.7 Application of method Permute

```
using System;

namespace Permutations {

    public class Person {
        // Fields
        private String name;
        private int id;

        public Person(String name, int id) {
            this.name = name;
            this.id = id;
        }

        public override String ToString() {
            return "<" + name + ", " + id + ">";
        }
    }
}

using System;

namespace Permutations {

    public class PermutationApp {

        public static void Main() {
            Person person1 = new Person("Jake", 2);
            Person person2 = new Person("Blake", 1);
            Person person3 = new Person("Snake", 3);

            Permutation.Permute<Person>(
                new Person[] { person1, person2, person3 }, 3);

            Console.ReadLine();
        }
    }
}
/* Program output
<Jake, 2> <Blake, 1> <Snake, 3>
<Blake, 1> <Jake, 2> <Snake, 3>
<Jake, 2> <Snake, 3> <Blake, 1>
<Snake, 3> <Jake, 2> <Blake, 1>
<Snake, 3> <Blake, 1> <Jake, 2>
<Blake, 1> <Snake, 3> <Jake, 2>
*/
```

For those not faint of heart, the most challenging exercise regarding recursion is given in Exercise 11.7.

Exercise 11.7

Show how static recursive method *Permute*, given in Listing 11.6, works by performing a detailed analysis on the three *Person* objects used in the *PermutationApp* class of Listing 11.7.

11.4 TWO CLASSIC AND EFFICIENT RECURSIVE SORTING ALGORITHMS

In this section two classic and important sorting algorithms, Quick Sort and Merge Sort, are presented. These sorting algorithms are important because they are extremely efficient. They are classic because they have been deployed in countless applications for decades.

11.4.1 Quick Sort

Quick Sort was developed by Tony Hoare (Oxford University) and is considered the fastest sorting algorithm ever devised. The Quick Sort algorithm is an example of a divide-and-conquer algorithm, in which a large problem is partitioned into a series of smaller and smaller problems. The solutions to the smaller problems are woven together to form the solution to the larger problem. This is accomplished using recursion.

The outer structure of method *QuickSort* is presented in Listing 11.8.

LISTING 11.8 Outer structure of QuickSort

```
public static void QuickSort(double[] data, int low, int high) {
    int partitionIndex;

    if (high - low > 0) {
        partitionIndex = Partition(data, low, high);
        QuickSort(data, low, partitionIndex - 1);
        QuickSort(data, partitionIndex + 1, high);
    }
}
```

The method *Partition*, presented in Listing 11.9, shuffles the numbers in *data* between *low* and *high* so that all the numbers between *low* and *partitionIndex* are less than or equal to all the numbers between *partitionIndex* and *high*. The genius of this algorithm lies in the implementation of the method *Partition*.

Before we concern ourselves with the details of method *Partition*, let us explain the reasoning behind the relatively simple recursive *QuickSort* method shown in Listing 11.8.

Let us suppose that the *Partition* method were to partition the data between indices *low* and *high* so that the partition index was roughly halfway between *low* and *high*. Then the problem of sorting all the data between *low* = 0 and *high* = *size* − 1 would be replaced by the two problems of sorting the *data* array between *low* and *partitionIndex* − 1 and between *partitionIndex* + 1 and *high*. When this is accomplished, the entire array would be sorted because the *Partition* method forces all the numbers to the left of *partitionIndex* to be equal or less in value than all the numbers to the right of *partitionIndex*. If the left side of the array (portion of the array with index values less than *partitionIndex*) is sorted separately from the right side of the array (portion of the array with index values greater than *partitionIndex*), then because all the sorted numbers in the left side of the array are equal to or smaller than all the numbers in the right side of the array, it follows that the entire array is sorted.

But each of the two recursive calls to *QuickSort* causes the left as well as the right side of the array to be further divided into two more regions. Each of these four regions is then divided to produce eight regions. This recursive process continues until the sentinel condition, *high* − *low* > 0, fails.

It is easier to comprehend the high-level strategy that forms the basis of the relatively simple recursive method shown in Listing 11.8 than actually to follow the low-level details of the recursion. Once the mechanics of recursion are understood (see Section 11.2), it is not necessary to go through the sometimes painful details of diagramming each and every recursive method that you design. It is better to reason about the recursion at a higher level, as we have done in the case of the recursive *QuickSort* method in Listing 11.8.

We examine the important *Partition* method shown in Listing 11.9.

LISTING 11.9 Method Partition

```
private static int Partition(double[] data, int low, int high) {
    int index1, index2;
    double temp, partitionValue;

    partitionValue = data[low];
    index1 = low;
    index2 = high + 1;

    // Move index1 to the right until a value
    // greater than partitionValue is found
    do {
        index1++;
    } while (data[index1] <= partitionValue && index1 < high);

    // Move index2 to the left until a value smaller
    // than partitionValue is found
    do {
        index2--;
    } while (data[index2] > partitionValue);

    while (index1 < index2) {
        // Interchange the values at index1 and index2
        temp = data[index1];
        data[index1] = data[index2];
        data[index2] = temp;

        // Continue to move index1 to the right until a value
        // greater than partitionValue is found
```

LISTING 11.9 Method Partition (continued)

```
        do {
            index1++;
        } while (data[index1] <= partitionValue);

        // Continue to move index2 to the left until a value
        // smaller than partitionValue is found
        do {
            index2--;
        } while (data[index2] > partitionValue);
    }
    // Exchange the values at low and index2
    if (low != index2) {
        temp = data[low];
        data[low] = data[index2];
        data[index2] = temp;
    }
    return index2; // Partition index
}
```

Let us "walk" through the important *Partition* method of Listing 11.9 for an array given as follows:

10	20	14	4	2	18	12	16	8	6

The partition value is 10 (the value to the left).

After iteration 1 (in which *index1* is moved to the right and *index2* moved to the left), *index1* equals 1 and *index2* equals 9. The two values corresponding to index1 and index2 are shown in large boldface type.

10	**20**	14	4	2	18	12	16	8	**6**

After interchanging these values, the modified array data is as follows:

10	6	14	4	2	18	12	16	8	20

After iteration 2 (in which *index1* is moved further to the right and *index2* moved further to the left), the values corresponding to *index1* and *index2* are again shown in large boldface:

10	6	**14**	4	2	18	12	16	**8**	20

After interchanging these values, the modified array data is as follows:

10	6	8	4	2	18	12	16	14	20

After iteration 3 (in which *index1* is moved further to the right and *index2* moved further to the left), the values corresponding to *index1* and *index2* are again shown in large boldface:

10	6	8	4	**2**	**18**	12	16	14	20

But *index1* equals 5 and *index2* equals 4. Because *index1* is no longer less than *index2*, the final step is to interchange the partition value on the left with the value at *index2*. The array resulting from this final step is shown below with the partition value shown in large boldface.

2   6   8   4   **10**   18   12   16   14   20

As expected, all the values to the left of the partition value are equal to or smaller than all the values to the right of the partition value. It should be clear from this example how the *Partition* method guarantees the result that it promises.

How efficient is Quick Sort? If the range between *low* and *high* were roughly bisected, on the average, it would take $log_2(n)$ recursive calls before *low* were no longer less than *high*. This is the number of times that one can divide a number by 2 before the answer is equal or less than 1.

Each recursive call requires the invocation of *Partition*. Because this method uses simple loops to accomplish its work, the amount of computational work is directly proportional to the size of the array (*high − low*) being processed. Because this can never be greater than *n* (the size of the entire array), the complexity of quick sort is $n * log_2 n$.

In contrast, all the simple sorting algorithms (Selection Sort and Bubble Sort) are of complexity n². To appreciate the difference this makes, consider an array containing 1 million numeric values. For such an array, $log_2(1,000,000)$ is approximately 20. Therefore, the ratio of performance of Quick Sort compared to either Selection Sort or Bubble Sort would be:

$$10^{12} / (10^6 \times 20) = 50,000$$

Exercise 11.8

"Walk" through *Partition* for the following array:

3   1   6   4   7   2   9   0   3   5   6

A strange anomaly exists with Quick Sort. If the data set being sorted is already sorted (either in ascending or descending order), the efficiency of the algorithm breaks down and becomes equivalent to the much slower Selection Sort or Bubble Sort. This is because of the choice of always setting the partition value as the leftmost value. How ironic that the worst-case scenario involves an array that is already sorted!

To better understand this, consider the array given as follows:

1   2   3   4   5   6

After moving *index1* to the right until the first value larger than the leftmost partition value of 1 is found, *index1* becomes 1. After moving *index2* to the left until the first value that is equal or smaller than the partition value is found, *index2* becomes 0.

After performing the final interchange, the partitioned array is shown below with the partition value in large boldface.

1   2   3   4   5   6

Method *QuickSort* then proceeds to sort the right array containing 2, 3, 4, 5, 6. But this array has been reduced in size by only one. This pattern continues until the right array is reduced in size to one. So instead of producing an algorithm of complexity

$nlog_2(n)$, the complexity becomes n^2 because each of the n recursive calls requires the complexity n of the *Partition* method.

To verify this empirically, consider the following experiment. We load an array first with 1,000,000 random numbers and determine the execution time for Quick Sort. We then load an array with 10,000 numbers in ascending order and again determine the execution time for Quick Sort. The results on the author's computer are shown below.

Time for Quick Sort on 1,000,000 random numbers: **0.21875 seconds**.

Time for Quick Sort on 20,000 sorted numbers: **0.453125 seconds**.

Exercise 11.9

Implement the experiment that compares the execution time for Quick Sort on an array of 1,000,000 numbers and a sorted array of 10,000 numbers. What are the results for your computer?

The results dramatize the efficiency of Quick Sort when the numbers are not ordered. It takes more than twice as long to sort 20,000 numbers using Quick Sort when the numbers are ordered as it does to sort 1,000,000 unordered numbers.

What effect does ordering the numbers have on the performance of Quick Sort?

Exercise 11.10

How might you devise an experiment that would determine the effect of partially ordering the data on the performance of Quick Sort? You are not expected actually to perform the experiment; simply outline the steps that might be undertaken.

With Quick Sort having the Achilles' Heel demonstrated earlier, the natural question that needs to be asked and answered is, "What measures can be taken to avoid the pitfall in Quick Sort that causes its performance to degrade dramatically when the data is ordered?"

Listing 11.10 shows a revised Quick Sort method, *ProtectedQuickSort*, and a revised *Partition*, *ProtectedPartition*.

LISTING 11.10 Revised Quick Sort

```
// Fields
private static Random randomValue = new Random();

public static void ProtectedQuickSort(double[] data, int low,
                                      int high) {
    int partitionIndex;

    if (high - low > 0) {
        partitionIndex = ProtectedPartition(data, low, high);
        ProtectedQuickSort(data, low, partitionIndex - 1);
        ProtectedQuickSort(data, partitionIndex + 1, high);
    }
}
```

LISTING 11.10 Revised Quick Sort (continued)

```
private static int ProtectedPartition(double[] data,
                                      int low,
                                      int high) {
    int index1, index2;
    double temp, partitionValue;
    int initialPartitionIndex = randomValue.Next(low, high + 1);
    // Swap data[initialPartitionIndex] with data[low];
    temp = data[initialPartitionIndex];
    data[initialPartitionIndex] = data[low];
    data[low] = temp;

    partitionValue = data[low];

    // Rest of code identical to Listing 11.9.

}
```

Now using *ProtectedQuickSort*, the sorting time of 1,000,000 ordered numbers is compared to the sorting time of 1,000,000 random numbers. The results are:

Time for Quick Sort on 1,000,000 sorted numbers using *ProtectedQuickSort*:
0.140625 seconds.
Time for Quick Sort on 1,000,000 random numbers using *ProtectedQuickSort*:
0.28125 seconds.

It takes about half as long to execute *ProtectedQuickSort* on sorted numbers compared to random numbers. But it is noted that it takes about 29 percent longer to sort the random numbers compared to the ordinary *QuickSort*.

The performance penalty associated with *ProtectedQuickSort* (having to generate a random value between low and high and having to perform a swap for each invocation of *ProtectedPartition*) is expected, but perhaps not as high as anticipated.

But what about the performance gain in using *ProtectedQuickSort* to sort an ordered sequence of numbers? The gain results from choosing a random value between *low* and *high* as the partition value in each invocation of *ProtectedPartition*. Given that the numbers are already sorted, this random value tends, on the average, to be halfway between *low* and *high*. This has the effect of better ensuring that the partition index bisects the interval from *low* to *high*. This benefit does not occur if the numbers are already randomly distributed between *low* and *high*. This is a surprising result!

Exercise 11.11

Implement the experiment that compares the execution time for *ProtectedQuickSort* on an array of 1,000,000 random numbers and a sorted array of 1,000,000 numbers. What are the results for your computer?

11.4.2 Merge Sort

Merge Sort, like Quick Sort, is based on a recursive divide-and-conquer algorithm. The array to be sorted is split in half. Each half is sorted separately. Then the two sorted parts are merged together to form a sorted whole.

Listing 11.11 presents the recursive *MergeSort* method and two supporting methods.

The sentinel test on the parameters *high* and *low* in *MergeSort* allow the recursion to continue until *high* − *low* is no longer greater than the *threshold*. In that case, the portion of the array between *low* and *high* is sorted using the nonrecursive *InsertionSort* method.

Exercise 11.12

Carefully explain how the nonrecursive *InsertionSort* method works.

By sorting a portion of the array that is less than *threshold* in size using *InsertionSort*, the recursive overhead that would be required when *high* − *low* is small is avoided. The larger the threshold, the more recursive overhead is avoided. But the larger the threshold, the less efficient *InsertionSort* is in sorting a portion of the array. The optimum value of *threshold* must be determined experimentally. If it is too large, the penalty imposed by *InsertionSort* is too great. If it is too small, the penalty created by recursive overhead is too great.

Method *Merge*, invoked within *MergeSort*, compares the two sorted arrays and builds a resultant array that merges the values of the two sorted arrays. This resultant array is returned to *MergeSort* and copied into the input array, *data*.

LISTING 11.11 Method MergeSort

```
public static void MergeSort(
                double[] data, int low, int high) {
    const int threshold = 256;
    if (high - low > threshold) {
        // Split the array data in half and sort each half
        int middle = (low + high) / 2;
        MergeSort(data, low, middle);
        MergeSort(data, middle + 1, high);
        double[] result = Merge(data, low, middle, high);
        // Copy result into data
        for (int index = low; index <= high; index++) {
            data[index] = result[index];
        }
    } else {
        InsertionSort(data, low, high);
    }
}

// Sorts the values in the numbers array from low to high
private static void InsertionSort(double [ ]numbers,
                            int low, int high) {
    int firstIndex, secondIndex;
    double value;
```

LISTING 11.11 Method MergeSort (continued)

```
        for (firstIndex = low + 1; firstIndex <= high; firstIndex++) {
            value = numbers[firstIndex];
            secondIndex = firstIndex;
            while (secondIndex > low &&
                        numbers[secondIndex - 1] > value) {
                numbers[secondIndex] = numbers[secondIndex - 1];
                secondIndex--;
            }
            numbers[secondIndex] = value;
        }
    }

    // Returns a single sorted array from data where
    // data is sorted from low to middle and from middle + 1 to high
    private static double[] Merge(double[] data,
                                  int low, int middle, int high) {
        double[] toReturn = new double[high + 1];
        int i = low;
        int k = low;
        int j = middle + 1;
        while (i <= middle && j <= high) {
            // Put the smaller value from the two sorted arrays into
            // toReturn
            if (data[i] < data[j]) {
                toReturn[k] = data[i];
                i++;
            } else {
                toReturn[k] = data[j];
                j++;
            }
            k++;
        }
        if (i > middle) { // Copy the values from the right array into
                          // toReturn
            for (int index = j; index <= high; index++) {
                toReturn[k] = data[index];
                k++;
            }
        } else { // Copy the values from the left array into toReturn
            for (int index = i; index <= middle; index++) {
                toReturn[k] = data[index];
                k++;
            }
        }
        return toReturn;
    }
}
```

Exercise 11.13

Modify the code given in Listing 11.11 so that *InsertionSort* is not used at all. Determine the sorting time of *MergeSort* and compare it to the sorting time when the threshold is 256.

Exercise 11.14

Create an application that allows *threshold* to be varied, and find the value of *threshold* that minimizes the sorting time using *MergeSort*.

Exercise 11.15

Explain in detail method *Merge* given in Listing 11.11.

11.4.3 GUI Application for Sorting

An application is presented that allows one to visualize the process of sorting by displaying snapshots of the relative values of the numbers within the array at various instants during the sorting process.

Two such snapshots are shown in the screenshots of the completed application in Figures 11.1 and 11.2. You are encouraged to download the application from the book's Web site.

The divide-and-conquer nature of the Quick Sort algorithm is immediately evident when watching the sampled output as the numbers are sorted.

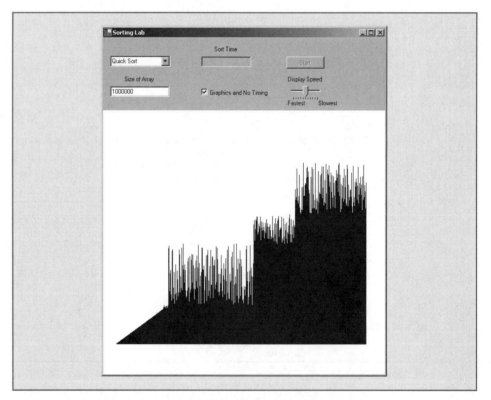

FIGURE 11.1 First screen shot of Quick Sort in action

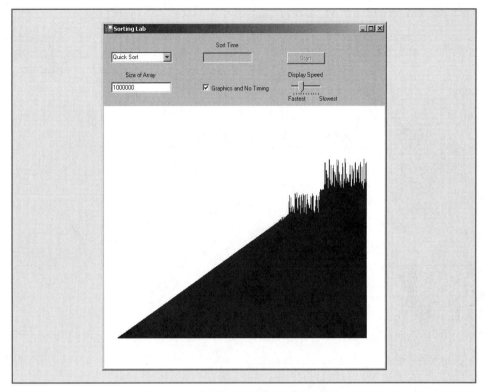

FIGURE 11.2 Second screen shot of Quick Sort in action

The GUI application is constructed using the Observer Pattern discussed in Chapters 9 and 10.

Within namespace *Sorting*, a *Notify* delegate, a *Timing* class, and a *SortingAlgorithms* class are defined. Listing 11.12 presents their details. These classes are the model classes in the Sort Lab application.

LISTING 11.12 Model classes in the Sort Lab

```
using System;
using System.Threading;

namespace Sorting {

    public delegate void Notify(double [] data, int size);

    public class Timing {
        // Fields
        private long startTicks, endTicks;

        public void StartTiming() {
            DateTime t = DateTime.Now;
            startTicks = t.Ticks;
```

LISTING 11.12 Model classes in the Sort Lab (continued)

```csharp
        }

        public void EndTiming() {
            DateTime t = DateTime.Now;
            endTicks = t.Ticks;
        }

        public double ElapsedTime() {
            return (endTicks - startTicks) / 10000000.0;
        }
    }

    public class SortingAlgorithms {

        // Fields
        private Random randomValue = new Random();
        private int size;
        private double[] data;
        private int count = 0;
        private bool noTiming = true;

        // Events
        public event Notify notify;

        // Properties
        public int Size {
            set { // Write-only
                size = value;
                data = new double[size];
                for (int i = 0; i < size; i++) {
                    data[i] = randomValue.NextDouble();
                }
                count = 0;
            }
        }

        public bool NoTiming { // Write-only
            set {
                noTiming = value;
            }
        }

        // Commands
        public void TriggerNotify() {
            notify(data, size);
        }

        public void Register(Notify handler) {
            notify += new Notify(handler);
        }
```

LISTING 11.12 Model classes in the Sort Lab (continued)

```
public void QuickSort(int low, int high) {
    count++;
    int partitionIndex;

    if (high - low > 0) {
        partitionIndex = Partition(low, high);

        if (noTiming) {
            int displayFactor = size / 20;
            if (count % displayFactor == 0) {
                notify(data, size);
            }
        }

        QuickSort(low, partitionIndex - 1);
        QuickSort(partitionIndex + 1, high);
    }
}

public void MergeSort(int low, int high) {
    const int threshold = 256;
    count++;
    if (noTiming) {
        int displayFactor = size / 20;
        if (count % displayFactor == 0) {
            notify(data, size);
        }
    }
    if (high - low > threshold) {
        // Split the array data in half and sort each half
        int middle = (low + high) / 2;
        MergeSort(low, middle);
        MergeSort(middle + 1, high);
        double[] result = Merge(low, middle, high);
        // Copy result into data
        for (int index = low; index <= high; index++) {
            data[index] = result[index];
        }
    } else {
        InsertionSort(data, low, high);
    }
}

// Internal support methods
private int Partition(int low, int high) {
    // See Listing 11.9
}

// Sorts the values in the numbers array from low to high
private void InsertionSort(double[] numbers,
                           int low, int high) {
    int firstIndex, secondIndex;
    double value;
```

LISTING 11.12 Model classes in the Sort Lab (continued)

```
                    for (firstIndex = low + 1;
                        firstIndex <= high; firstIndex++) {
                        value = numbers[firstIndex];
                        secondIndex = firstIndex;
                        while (secondIndex > low &&
                            numbers[secondIndex - 1] > value) {
                            numbers[secondIndex] = numbers[secondIndex - 1];
                            secondIndex--;
                        }
                        numbers[secondIndex] = value;
                    }
                }

        private double[] Merge(int low, int middle, int high) {
            // See Listing 11.11
        }
    }
}
```

The public *Size* property not only sets the size of the array *data* to be sorted but initializes this array and loads it with uniformly distributed random values from 0 to 1.

Class *SortingAlgorithms* contains a public *notify* event of delegate type *Notify*. This event provides the mechanism for each sorting method to communicate with the GUI class. The GUI class must register an event handler with class *SortingAlgorithms* so that it can respond appropriately.

Each time a recursive call to either *QuickSort* or *MergeSort* occurs, an internal *count* field is incremented by one. When the *count* reaches a predetermined threshold, the *notify* event is dispatched to the GUI. This allows the GUI to output a snapshot of the array as the sort progresses.

Class *SortLabUI* is presented in Listing 11.13. Portions of the class not generated by the IDE are shown.

LISTING 11.13 Class SortLabUI

```
using System;
using System.Collections.Generic;
using System.ComponentModel;
using System.Data;
using System.Drawing;
using System.Windows.Forms;
using Sorting;
using System.Threading;

namespace SortingLab {

    partial class SortLabUI : Form {
```

LISTING 11.13 Class SortLabUI (continued)

```
// Fields
private SortingAlgorithms sorting = new SortingAlgorithms();
private int tickBarValue = 0;

public SortLabUI() {
    InitializeComponent();
    this.SetBounds((Screen.GetBounds(this).Width / 2) -
                   (this.Width / 2),
                   (Screen.GetBounds(this).Height / 2) -
                   (this.Height / 2),
                   this.Width, this.Height,
                   BoundsSpecified.Location);
    comboBox.SelectedIndex = 0;
    sorting.Register(DisplayData);

    // To enable double buffering
    SetStyle(ControlStyles.UserPaint, true);
    SetStyle(ControlStyles.AllPaintingInWmPaint, true);
    SetStyle(ControlStyles.OptimizedDoubleBuffer, true);
    this.UpdateStyles();
}

// The event handler
private void DisplayData(double[] data, int size) {
    int sleepDuration = 50 + tickBarValue * 100;
    Thread.Sleep(sleepDuration);
    int xInterval = size / 500; // Divide interval into 500
                                // equal parts
    int x;

    /*
     * We wish to avoid flicker in the graphics.
     * We clear and write to the offScreen graphics context.
     */
    Bitmap offScreenBmp = new Bitmap(panel.Width,
                                     panel.Height);
    Graphics offScreen = Graphics.FromImage(offScreenBmp);
    offScreen.Clear(Color.White);
    for (int index = 0; index < size; index++) {
        if (xInterval > 0 && index % xInterval == 0) {
            x = index / xInterval; // Sample array every
                                   // xInterval
            offScreen.DrawLine(new Pen(
                            new SolidBrush(Color.Black)),
                         x + 25, 450, x + 25,
                         450 - (int)(data[index] * 350.0));
        }
    }

    Graphics onScreenGraphics = panel.CreateGraphics();
    // Dump offscreen graphics to the screen
    onScreenGraphics.DrawImage(offScreenBmp, 0, 0);
```

LISTING 11.13 Class SortLabUI (continued)

```
            onScreenGraphics.Dispose();
            offScreen.Dispose();
    }

    private void sortBtn_Click(object sender, EventArgs e) {
        sortTimeBox.Text = "";
        Timing timer = new Timing();
        sortBtn.Enabled = false;
        int arraySize = 0;
        try {
            arraySize = Convert.ToInt32(sizeBox.Text.Trim());
            if (arraySize < 5000) {
                MessageBox.Show("Size must be at least 5000.");
                sizeBox.Text = "5000";
                sortBtn.Enabled = true;
                return;
            }
            sorting.Size = arraySize; // Creates a new array of
                                      // data
            sorting.TriggerNotify();  // Displays the unsorted
                                      // data
                                      // for 1/2 second
            Thread.Sleep(500);
        } catch (Exception) {
            MessageBox.Show("Must enter a valid array size.");
        }
        if (comboBox.SelectedIndex == 0) {
            sorting.NoTiming = noTimingCheckBox.Checked;

            if (!noTimingCheckBox.Checked) {
                timer.StartTiming();
            }
            sorting.QuickSort(0, arraySize - 1);
            if (!noTimingCheckBox.Checked) {
                timer.EndTiming();
                sortTimeBox.Text = String.Format("{0:f4}",
                        timer.ElapsedTime()) + " seconds.";
            }
            sorting.TriggerNotify();
            sortBtn.Enabled = true;
        } else if (comboBox.SelectedIndex == 1) {
            sorting.NoTiming = noTimingCheckBox.Checked;

            if (!noTimingCheckBox.Checked) {
                timer.StartTiming();
            }
            sorting.MergeSort(0, arraySize - 1);
            if (!noTimingCheckBox.Checked) {
                timer.EndTiming();
                sortTimeBox.Text = String.Format("{0:f4}",
                        timer.ElapsedTime()) + " seconds.";
            }
```

LISTING 11.13 Class SortLabUI (continued)

```
                    sorting.TriggerNotify();
                    sortBtn.Enabled = true;
            }
        }

        private void trackBar_ValueChanged(object sender,
                                           EventArgs e) {
            tickBarValue = trackBar.Value;
        }

        public static void Main() {
            Application.Run(new SortLabUI());
        }
    }
}
```

Class *SortLabUI* contains a field *sorting* of type *SortingAlgorithm*. Through this field, the *DisplayData* method is registered as an event handler with the model class.

To enable double buffering, the following code is invoked in the constructor:

```
SetStyle(ControlStyles.UserPaint, true);
SetStyle(ControlStyles.AllPaintingInWmPaint, true);
SetStyle(ControlStyles.OptimizedDoubleBuffer, true);
this.UpdateStyles();
```

In addition, the event handler *DisplayData* updates the graphical display using an off-screen graphics context and then writes the entire graphics image to the screen at once. This provides for a flicker-free presentation of the graphics display. The code to accomplish this flicker-free presentation is the following:

```
Bitmap offScreenBmp = new Bitmap(panel.Width, panel.Height);
Graphics offScreen = Graphics.FromImage(offScreenBmp);
offScreen.Clear(Color.White);
for (int index = 0; index < size; index++) {
    if (xInterval > 0 && index % xInterval == 0) {
    x = index / xInterval; // Sample array every xInterval
        offScreen.DrawLine(new Pen(new SolidBrush(Color.Black)),
            x + 25, 450, x + 25, 450 - (int)(data[index] * 350.0));
    }
}
Graphics onScreenGraphics = panel.CreateGraphics();
onScreenGraphics.DrawImage(offScreenBmp, 0, 0);
```

The remaining code in method *sortBtn_Click* is straightforward and should be examined carefully.

11.5 SUMMARY

◆ The programming technique and design principle of recursion is examined in this chapter. Recursive methods generally satisfy the following conditions:

    ◆ The method invokes itself one or more times.

    ◆ The method contains a sentinel parameter that is used to stop further recursive calls from occurring, thus eventually stopping the recursion from continuing forever.

    ◆ The body of the recursive method must drive the value of the sentinel parameter in a manner that will eventually stop the recursion from continuing.

◆ To understand the mechanics of recursion, we need to understand that before a recursive call, all local variables and parameters are copied onto an internal stack and held until the recursive call is completed. This internal stack is managed by the runtime system and is not directly accessible to the programmer. Furthermore, when a recursive call is completed (the end brace of the recursive method has been reached), the local variables and parameters that were saved on the internal stack are removed from this stack and restored. The flow of control is returned to one line below the recursive call.

◆ A relatively simple, but important, application of recursion is performing a binary search of an array. A more complex application involves producing every permutation of an array of objects stored in an array.

◆ Two classic and important sorting algorithms are Quick Sort and Merge Sort. Quick Sort is considered the fastest sorting algorithm ever devised, and provides an example of a divide-and-conquer algorithm in which a large problem is partitioned into a series of smaller and smaller problems. Using recursion, the solutions to the smaller problems are woven together to form the solution to the larger problem. Merge Sort is also based on a recursive divide-and-conquer algorithm. The array to be sorted is split in half. Each half is sorted separately, and then the two sorted parts are merged together to form a sorted whole.

11.6 ADDITIONAL EXERCISES

Exercise 11.16

Write a recursive method that computes the nth Fibonacci number, F(n) where:
$F(n) = F(n-1) + F(n-2)$; for n >= 2 and $F(0) = F(1) = 1$.

Exercise 11.17

Using the recursive method created in Exercise 11.13, write an application that forms a table with n in the first column and F(n) in the second column as n goes from 0 to 30.

Exercise 11.18

For method *DoAgain*, if the input value were 50, diagram the inner workings of the recursion and show the output.

```
public void DoAgain (int value) {

    if (value < 100) {
      value *= 5;
      Console.WriteLine(value / 2);
      value -= 10;
      DoAgain(value / 3);
      Console.WriteLine(value);
    }

}
```

Exercise 11.19

Repeat Exercise 11.18 if the method *DoAgain* is as shown below and the value 40 were input.

```
public void DoAgain (int value) {
    if (value < 120) {
      value *= 3;
      Console.WriteLine(value / 2);
      value -= 20;
      DoAgain(value / 2);
      Console.WriteLine(value);
    }

}
```

Exercise 11.20

Show that if the value being searched for in an ordered array is not present, the recursive binary search method presented earlier in this chapter requires approximately $\log_2 n$ recursive calls.

Exercise 11.21

Write a recursive method for finding the greatest common divisor of two integers, a and b. The greatest common divisor (GCD) is defined as follows (where % means remainder):

GCD(a, b) = b if b <= a and a % b is 0

GCD(a, b) = GCD(b, a) if a < b

GCD(a, b) = GCD(b, a % b) otherwise

Exercise 11.22

List three problems from mathematics or elsewhere that should yield in a reasonable way to a recursive solution.

Exercise 11.23

Rewrite the binary search method (Listing 11.5) using iteration instead of recursion.

Exercise 11.24

Perform an experiment that allows you to compare the execution time of the recursive versus iterative binary search methods.

Exercise 11.25

Write and test a recursive method that computes the sum of the numbers in an array.

CHAPTER 12

Linear Data Structures and Their Applications

Container types in software development are used to hold and efficiently access information. Data structures represent the implementation of a container type. The study of data structures, including the algorithms for inserting information into a container, deleting information from a container, and accessing information within a container, has served as the foundation and basis for CS 2 courses for several decades.

Data structures such as stack, queue, deque (pronounced "deck"), tree, and hash table continue to be used in countless applications and have been studied extensively. In fact, they form the building blocks of many important applications.

To the novice, programming may appear to be an ad hoc process. Data structures provide the programmer an intellectual framework from which to construct many diverse applications. The mechanisms for efficiently structuring information often provide the skeletal structure of an application. It is for this reason that the study of data structures has been an important part of the education of computer science students.

To underscore the importance of data structures in programming, the title of Niklaus Wirth's classic reference, *Data Structures + Algorithms = Programs* (Prentice-Hall, 1975), says it all.

In older programming languages such as Pascal, Ada, and C, the construction of data structures was solely the responsibility of the programmer. With the advent of modern object-oriented languages such as Java and C#, standard data structure classes, referred to as collection classes, have emerged. We examine these standard C# collection classes in Chapter 14 and strongly encourage their use.

It is not the goal of this chapter or the next to provide an alternative to the standard collection classes provided in the .NET framework. Rather, these chapters present the thought processes and important algorithms that have become a key part of a computer scientist's intellectual base. The reasoning used in constructing these data structures is often needed in customizing an information structure for a particular application. Understanding the subtleties of how information can be efficiently stored and accessed is of fundamental importance in computer science.

Data structures are ubiquitous. A box of paper clips, a room full of desks, a tray holder that contains stacks of trays in a cafeteria, a bag of groceries, a collection of names and phone numbers in a phone directory, a dictionary of English words, and a database of patient records are all examples of containers of objects where each may be modeled using a data structure.

It is important to distinguish a container from the objects that it contains. In this and the next two chapters, containers are examined in detail. The focus is on how to represent and access the information that is held by the container. The type of information that is held, although ultimately important, will not be the primary concern. A well-constructed container class can usually hold a diversity of information types. The mechanism for inserting, deleting, and accessing this information is usually independent of the specific type of information that is contained within the data structure or may require that the information satisfy some constraint such as being comparable. Therefore, generic classes with unconstrained or constrained generic parameters play an important role in modeling containers and will be used throughout this and the next chapter.

Containers may be distinguished by considering the following properties:

◆ Objects within the container may be ordered or unordered.

◆ If the objects are ordered, their order may depend on the structure of the container or may depend on the contained objects.

◆ Duplicate objects may or may not be allowed.

◆ Objects may be restricted to a particular type or classification of types.

◆ Objects in the container may be accessible by index.

◆ Objects in the container may be accessible based on relative position.

◆ Objects in the container may be accessible based on their value.

◆ Containers may be distinguished by their connectivity (linear versus nonlinear).

This chapter focuses on the implementation of stacks, queues, deques, and lists and their applications. These are linear data structures because information is stored sequentially. Every element, except the first, has a predecessor and every element, except the last, has a successor. This is illustrated in Figure 12.1.

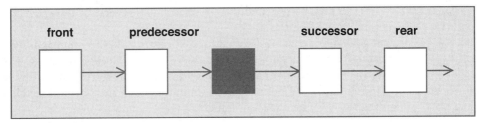

FIGURE 12.1 Linear data structure

What distinguishes a stack from a queue from a deque or from various list types are the ways that information can be inserted, removed, and accessed within the structure.

In constructing taxonomy of data structures, we begin with the most general container. Its properties are:

◆ It holds objects of arbitrary type.

◆ The order of the objects is arbitrary.

◆ It accepts duplicate objects.

◆ It has a command for emptying itself.

◆ It has queries for returning the number of objects in the container and whether the container is empty.

Interface *IContainer*, shown below, encapsulates the behavior of a generic container.

```
public interface IContainer<T> {

    // Commands

    // Remove all objects from the container
    void MakeEmpty();
```

```
// Queries

// Returns true if one or more objects are in the container
bool IsEmpty();

// Returns the number of objects in the container
int Size();
}
```

12.1 THE STACK DATA STRUCTURE

Perhaps the simplest classic data structure is the stack. A stack defines a last-in, first-out structure so that the first item to have been inserted is the last item to be removed, the second item to have been inserted is the next to the last item to be removed, ..., and the last item to have been inserted is the first item to be removed.

The name stack derives from the metaphor of a stack or pile of objects in which the only object that is accessible is the object on the top of the pile. The order in which objects may be removed from a stack is the reverse of the order in which the objects are inserted on the stack.

The operations that are defined for a stack include the commands *Push* and *Pop* and the query *Top*. The *Push* command inserts a new object on the stack. The *Pop* command removes the object that is on the top of the stack. The *Top* query returns the object that is on the top of the stack without removing this object. The following code shows the interface for a stack, *IStack*:

```
public interface IStack<T> : IContainer<T> {

    // Commands

    // Add element to the top of the stack
    void Push(T element);

    // Remove the top element of the stack
    void Pop();

    // Queries

    // Return the top object on the stack
    T Top();
}
```

The first implementation of *IStack* to be considered is a fixed-size implementation. The objects in the stack are stored in an internal array. Once the size of this stack is set, it cannot be changed. If an attempt is made to exceed the capacity of the stack, an exception is thrown. Also, if an attempt is made to pop an empty stack, an exception is thrown.

Listing 12.1 presents the details of *ArrayStack*.

LISTING 12.1 Class ArrayStack

```csharp
using System;

namespace Containers {

    public class ArrayStack<T> : IStack<T> {

        // Fields
        private int capacity;
        private T[] elements;
        private int topIndex;

        // Constructors
        public ArrayStack(int size) {
            capacity = size;
            elements = new T[size];
            topIndex = -1;
        }

        public ArrayStack() {
            capacity = 100; // default size
            elements = new T[100];
            topIndex = -1;
        }

        // Properties
        public int Capacity { // Read-only
            get {
                return capacity;
            }
        }

        // Commands
        public void Push(T element) {
            topIndex++;
            if (topIndex < capacity) {
                elements[topIndex] = element;
            } else {
                throw new IndexOutOfRangeException(
                    "Capacity of stack is full.");
            }
        }

        // Remove the top element of the stack
        public void Pop() {
            if (topIndex < 0) {
                throw new IndexOutOfRangeException(
                    "Cannot pop empty stack.");
            } else {
                topIndex--;
            }
        }
```

LISTING 12.1 Class ArrayStack (continued)

```
        public void MakeEmpty() {
            topIndex = -1;
        }

        // Queries
        public T Top() {
            if (topIndex < 0) {
                throw new IndexOutOfRangeException(
                    "Cannot access empty stack.");
            } else {
                return elements[topIndex];
            }
        }

        public bool IsEmpty() {
            return topIndex == -1;
        }

        public int Size() {
            return topIndex + 1;
        }
    }
}
```

In class *ArrayStack*, the array field, *elements*, is used to hold the objects. The field *topIndex* is used to select the object that is currently on the top of the stack.

Consider the operation of adding an object to the stack. This is done in method *Push*. The field *topIndex* is incremented by one. If the value goes beyond the predetermined size of the *elements* array, an *IndexOutOfRangeException* containing the message "Capacity of stack is full" is generated. Otherwise the new object is inserted in the *topIndex* location of the *elements* array.

The *Pop* command first checks the value of *topIndex* and ensures that it is not less than 0. If it is, an *IndexOutOfRangeException* containing the message "Cannot pop empty stack" is generated. Otherwise the value of *topIndex* is decremented by 1. Nothing is actually erased from the array because that is inefficient. By having decremented the *topIndex* value, the next time an object is pushed onto the stack, it will overwrite the previous object.

The remaining commands and queries are straightforward and require no explanation.

Listing 12.2 presents a short and simple application class, *StackApp*. This class exercises a few of the features of *ArrayStack*.

LISTING 12.2 Simple application class StackApp

```
using System;

namespace Containers {
```

LISTING 12.2 Simple application class StackApp (continued)

```
public class StackApp {

    public static void Main() {
        ArrayStack<int> myStack = new ArrayStack<int>();
        for (int i = 0; i < 100; i++) {
            myStack.Push(i);
        }
        Console.WriteLine("myStack.Top() = " + myStack.Top());
        for (int i = 0; i < 50; i++) {
            myStack.Pop();
        }
        Console.WriteLine("myStack.Top() = " + myStack.Top());

        Console.ReadLine();
    }
}
}
/* Output
myStack.Top() = 99
myStack.Top() = 49
myQueue.Front() = 3
reverseQueue.Front() = 9
*/
```

Exercise 12.1

In terms of defensive programming, what should one always do before pushing an object onto an *ArrayStack*? What should one always do before popping an object from an *ArrayStack*?

Exercise 12.2

Modify Listing 12.2 so that the *ArrayStack* holds objects that are each of type *ArrayStack<String>*. Create three such *ArrayStack<String>* objects containing one, two, and three *String* objects, respectively. Push these *ArrayStack<String>* objects onto the *ArrayStack*. Pop the stack once and access the top of the stack. Verify that it contains the object that it should contain.

We next consider a dynamic-sized stack implementation. Such a stack grows and shrinks as objects are pushed and popped from the stack.

In implementing class *LinkedStack*, the important notion of a linked structure is introduced.

Figure 12.2 shows the linked structure associated with *LinkedStack*.

Each of the three node objects shown in Figure 12.2 contains an object in the stack. The element that represents the top of the stack is in the left-most node.

The implementation of *LinkedStack* is presented in Listing 12.3. No constructor is needed because a capacity value does not need to be specified.

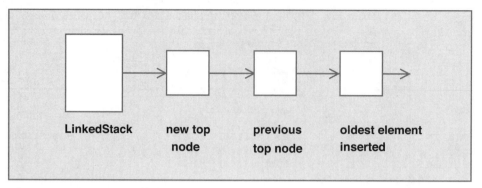

FIGURE 12.2 Linked structure

LISTING 12.3 Class LinkedStack

```
public class LinkedStack<T> : IStack<T> {

  // Fields
  private Node top;
  private int numberElements;

    // Commands
    public void Push(T element) {
        Node newNode = new Node(element, top);
        top = newNode;
        numberElements++;
    }

    public void Pop() {
        if (IsEmpty()) {
            throw new InvalidOperationException(
                "Cannot pop empty stack.");
        } else {
            Node oldNode = top;
            top = top.Next;
            numberElements--;
            oldNode = null;
        }
    }

    public void MakeEmpty() {
        top = null;
    }

    // Queries
    public T Top() {
        if (IsEmpty()) {
            throw new InvalidOperationException(
                "Cannot access top of stack.");
        } else {
            return top.Item;
        }
```

LISTING 12.3 Class LinkedStack (continued)

```
        }

        public bool IsEmpty() {
            return numberElements == 0;
        }

        public int Size() {
            return numberElements;
        }

        private class Node {
            // Fields
            private T item;
            private Node next;

            // Properties
            public T Item { // Read-only
                get {
                    return item;
                }
            }

            public Node Next { // Read-only
                get {
                    return next;
                }
            }

            // Constructor
            public Node(T element, Node link) {
                item = element;
                next = link;
            }
        }
    }
```

The private inner class *Node* contains two fields, *item* of type *T* and *next* of type *Node*. This is a recursive definition because *Node* is defined in terms of *Node*. We will see many such recursive definitions as we explore other linked data structures in this chapter. Class *Node* is an inner class in order to prevent client classes from accessing or attempting to manipulate *Node* objects directly.

It is recommended that whenever you analyze methods involving linked structures, you have a writing instrument in hand and sketch a diagram of the actions associated with each line of code. We shall do this for method *Push*.

Let us assume that we have three nodes already present, as shown in Figure 12.2. The first line of code,

```
Node newNode = new Node(element, top);
```

produces a freshly minted node, *newNode*, that links to the current *top* node. We visualize this in Figure 12.3. The last node links to the sentinel value of null.

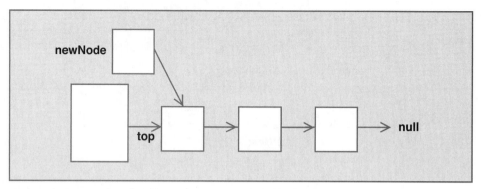

FIGURE 12.3 Visualization of line 1 of method *Push*

Line 2 of *Push*,

```
top = newNode;
```

causes the link from *ArrayList* to *newNode* to be forged, establishing *newNode* as the top of the stack. The resulting linked structure is shown in Figure 12.4.

When method *Push* is exited, the local variable *newNode* goes out of scope, but the field *top* persists and continues to "point" to the newly created node.

Exercise 12.3

Sketch a diagram that shows the effects of each line of code in method *Pop*.

Exercise 12.4

If a black box contained either the *ArrayStack* or the *LinkedStack*, devise an experiment that you could perform to determine whether the black box contained an *ArrayStack* or *LinkedStack* implementation.

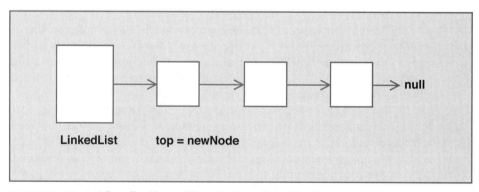

FIGURE 12.4 Visualization of line 2 of method *Push*

The method *MakeEmpty* sets *top* to *null*. Whenever an object no longer has any references to it, the automatic garbage collector will reclaim the storage of the object. So when *top* is assigned to null, the first node is reclaimed. This results in the reference to the second node being destroyed so the second node can be reclaimed. This chain of events continues so that all the nodes can be reclaimed.

LinkedStack is more flexible than *ArrayStack* because of its dynamic nature. It is also less efficient, because it is faster to access an object in a specified index within an array than to access the object through a link (*top* in this case). Pushing and popping are more efficient as well; it is more efficient to increment or decrement an array index than to allocate storage for a new node and readjust links, as done in methods *Push* and *Pop* in class *LinkedStack*.

A GUI that enables one to compare the time it takes to push a user-specified number of objects onto each type of stack and then pop all the objects from the stack has been developed. The user specifies the number of objects to be pushed and later popped.

A screenshot of the benchmark application is shown in Figure 12.5.

Exercise 12.5

Write a GUI application with an interface approximately the same as that shown in Figure 12.5. Using your application, compare the performance of *ArrayStack* and *LinkedStack* on your computer.

The results for 10 million pushes and pops show *ArrayStack* to be more than 10 times as efficient as *LinkedStack*. The flexibility of *LinkedStack* has its price!

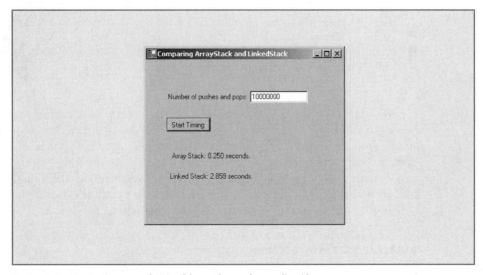

FIGURE 12.5 Screenshot of benchmark application

12.2 THE QUEUE DATA STRUCTURE

The classic data structure queue is perhaps the second simplest, being only slightly more complex than the stack.

A queue is a first-in, first-out structure. The first object to be added to a queue is the first that can be removed. The second object to be added is the second that may be removed, and so on. A queue is a model of a waiting line.

The operations that are defined for a queue include the commands *Add* and *Remove* and the query *Front*.

The interface for a queue, *IQueue*, is presented in Listing 12.4.

LISTING 12.4 Interface IQueue

```
using System;

namespace Containers {

    public interface IQueue<T> : IContainer<T> {

        // Commands

        // Adds element to the rear of the queue
        void Add(T element);

        // Removes the front element of the queue
        void Remove();

        // Queries

        // Returns the front element of the queue without changing it
        T Front();
    }
}
```

Henceforth, only dynamic implementations of linked structures shall be presented in this chapter because they are more interesting and challenging. The goal is not to produce commercial-quality data structure classes, because one should use the standard data structure classes provided in the .NET framework for any application programming. Once again, the goal of this chapter is to uncover the thought processes and algorithms that have served as the underpinning of classic data structures.

Listing 12.5 presents the details of class *LinkedQueue*.

LISTING 12.5 LinkedQueue

```
public class LinkedQueue<T> : IQueue<T> {

        // Fields
        private Node first;
        private Node last;
```

LISTING 12.5 LinkedQueue (continued)

```
        private int numberElements;

        // Commands
        public void Add(T element) {
            Node newNode = new Node(element, null);
            if (numberElements == 0) {
                first = newNode;
                last = first;
            } else {
                last.Next = newNode;
                last = newNode;
            }
            numberElements++;
        }

        // Removes the front element of the queue
        public void Remove() {
            if (IsEmpty()) {
                throw new InvalidOperationException(
                    "Cannot remove from empty queue.");
            } else {
                Node oldNode = first;
                first = first.Next;
                numberElements--;
                oldNode = null;
            }
        }

        public void MakeEmpty() {
            first = null;
        }

        // Queries
        public T Front() {
            if (numberElements == 0) {
                throw new InvalidOperationException(
                    "Cannot access front of empty queue.");
            } else {
                return first.Item;
            }
        }

        public bool IsEmpty() {
            return numberElements == 0;
        }

        public int Size() {
            return numberElements;
        }

        private class Node {
            // Fields
            private T item;
```

LISTING 12.5 LinkedQueue (continued)

```
        private Node next;

        // Properties
        public T Item {
            get {
                return item;
            }
        }

        public Node Next { // Read-write
            get {
                return next;
            }
            set {
                next = value;
            }
        }

        // Constructor
        public Node(T element, Node link) {
            item = element;
            next = link;
        }
    }
}
```

LinkedQueue contains two fields that point to the front and rear of the linked list, respectively. We explain the *Add* method through a series of diagrams.

Let us assume that the *LinkedQueue* contains two elements and we wish to add a third object to the queue. Figure 12.6 shows the queue before adding a third object.

The first line of code in method *Add* is:

```
Node newNode = new Node(element, null);
```

The diagram reflecting this line of code is given in Figure 12.7.

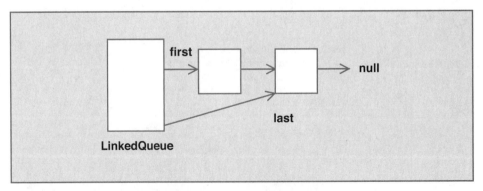

FIGURE 12.6 Initial configuration of linked queue

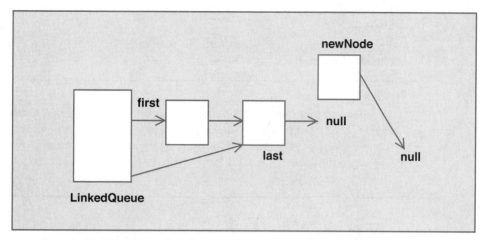

FIGURE 12.7 Diagram after first line of code in method *Add*

The line of code,

```
else {
    last.Next = newNode;
    last = newNode;
}
```

is diagrammed in Figure 12.8.

It is imperative that the user of a queue verify that the queue is not empty before attempting to invoke the *Remove* command or the query *Front*.

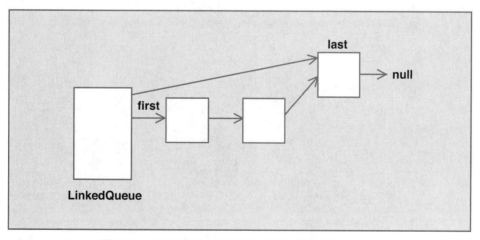

FIGURE 12.8 Diagram related to code in method *Add*

Exercise 12.6

Explain how method *Remove* works for *LinkedQueue* by sketching diagrams similar to those given previously.

Exercise 12.7

Write an application class that creates a *LinkedQueue* of type *LinkedStack<int>*. Create three separate *LinkedStack<int>* objects by pushing the values 1, 1 and 2, 1 and 2 and 3 onto the three stack objects, respectively. Add these three stack objects to the *LinkedQueue*. Perform a *Remove* operation, then examine and verify the front of the queue.

12.3 APPLICATIONS OF STACK AND QUEUE

12.3.1 Reversing the Objects in a Queue

The most obvious application of a stack is reversing the sequence of a collection of objects. Suppose we wish to write a method that reverses the sequence of objects stored in a queue. We can use one or more stacks to accomplish this as we shall show.

Consider the method *ReverseQueue* shown in Listing 12.6.

LISTING 12.6 Method ReverseQueue

```
public IQueue<T> ReverseQueue<T>(IQueue<T> input) {
    LinkedStack<T> stack = new LinkedStack<T>();
    LinkedQueue<T> resultQueue = new LinkedQueue<T>();
    LinkedQueue<T> copyQueue = new LinkedQueue<T>();
    // Empty the input queue, fill stack and copyQueue
    while (input.Size() > 0) {
        T first = input.Front();
        stack.Push(first);
        copyQueue.Add(first);
        input.Remove();
    }
    // Empty the stack and fill the resultQueue
    while (stack.Size() > 0) {
        T first = stack.Top();
        resultQueue.Add(first);
        stack.Pop();
    }
    // Empty the copyQueue and restore the input queue
    while (copyQueue.Size() > 0) {
        T first = copyQueue.Front();
        input.Add(first);
        copyQueue.Remove();
    }
    return resultQueue;
}
```

Exercise 12.8

Write a short application class that tests the method *ReverseQueue*.

Keep in mind that you must restore the *input* queue after removing its elements as the *stack* is being filled. This is the reason for defining *copyQueue*. Its purpose is to restore the *input* queue before returning *resultQueue*.

12.3.2 A Maze Application that Features a Stack

Note: This example is an adaptation of an example presented in Section 3.2 of *Data Structures Using Modula-2* by Richard Sincovec and Richard Wiener (John Wiley, 1986).

Consider the following example of an array of 0s and 1s that represents a maze. The 1s in the matrix represent barriers that block the movement of the mouse. The 0s in the matrix represent pathways that the mouse can take in navigating the maze. The S represents the starting position and the E, the ending position. To find a legal path from S to E, the mouse will be simulated by a computer algorithm.

```
1 1 1 1 1 1 1 1 1 1 1 1
1 S 0 0 0 0 0 0 0 0 0 1
1 0 1 0 1 1 0 1 0 1 0 1
1 1 0 0 0 1 1 0 0 1 0 1
1 0 1 0 1 0 1 1 0 1 0 1
1 1 0 1 0 1 0 1 0 1 1 1
1 0 1 1 1 1 1 0 0 0 0 1
1 0 1 1 0 0 1 0 1 0 0 1
1 1 0 1 1 1 0 1 0 0 1 1
1 0 0 0 0 0 1 1 1 1 1 1
1 0 1 0 1 0 0 0 0 0 E 1
1 1 1 1 1 1 1 1 1 1 1 1
```

The 1s in the first and last rows and first and last columns represent a wall that stops the mouse from escaping from the maze. The goal is to find an algorithm that allows the computer program to navigate from the specified starting and ending positions, if such a path exists. The maze itself is to be represented as a text file and read into the program as input.

The algorithm to be presented features a stack. At any coordinate in the maze, a move is made in one of eight directions (north, northeast, east, southeast, south, southwest, west, or northwest) providing there is a 0 in the given direction. The actual move direction is obtained randomly among the possible moves. This makes the search more interesting and allows for the possibility of different paths being found for the same maze if the program is run repeatedly.

After a legal and randomly chosen move is determined, the current position along with the direction of the move to be made is pushed onto a stack. If the path hits a dead end, the stack may be used to return to the last safe position.

The mouse must be prevented from traversing the same path twice or going in circles. This can be accomplished by changing the value from 0 to 1 each time we visit a coordinate. This prevents repeated visits to the position.

An algorithm for traversing the maze that uses a stack as its central mechanism is the following:

1. Get the maze data including the starting and ending positions.

2. Display the maze.

3. Show the starting and ending positions with special colors so they are easily discernable.

4. Initialize a stack that holds path objects.

5. A path object contains a coordinate within the maze, a current move direction, and an array of available move directions.

6. Choose an initial and legal move direction randomly from among the eight possible move directions.

7. As each move direction is attempted, delete it from the collection of eight possible move directions.

8. Construct a path object from the starting point, remaining move directions, and initial move direction.

9. Push the initial path object onto the stack.

10. While the stack is not empty, access the path object at the top of the stack to get a current path object (a position, a move direction, and a collection of available move directions).

11. Pop this top object from the stack.

12. Increment the total number of moves.

13. Start a loop as follows: while there are more available moves from this current path object and a move is possible (based on the barriers surrounding the current position that include positions already visited), choose one of the available move directions randomly until a valid move is possible. Each time an available move is randomly selected and attempted, it is removed from the array of available moves from the current path object.

    If a valid move is found:

    ◆ Make a move to the new position.

    ◆ Graphically display the move to the new position with a line.

    ◆ If the new position is equal to the ending position:
       Stop the simulation.

    ◆ Mark the new position as a barrier (to avoid going to it again).

    ◆ Push the current path object onto the stack.

    ◆ Construct a path object from the new position using the new position and a new collection of eight available move directions.

    ◆ Push the new path object onto the stack and set the current path object to the new path object.

    ◆ Indicate that no path can be found.

Our challenge is to create a GUI application that depicts the maze and allows the user to step ahead, one move at a time, graphically showing the result of the move.

As with earlier GUI applications, the Observer Pattern will be used. This requires the construction of two non-GUI classes. The first of these, *PathObject*, encapsulates the position, available move directions, and move direction associated with a particular maze coordinate. The second, *MazeModel*, encapsulates a computational model of the maze system including the barriers and the algorithm for moving ahead. This *MazeModel* class must provide four event sources that notify the UI class, *MazeUI*, when:

1. The maze is to be displayed.

2. A line connecting the current position to the new position needs to be drawn.

3. The total move count must be updated.

4. An announcement that the game is over must be generated.

Provisions for registering with these four event sources must be made in this model class. The *MazeUI* class must provide four event handlers to capture the appropriate model information and register these four handlers with the *MazeModel* class.

Listing 12.7 presents class *PathObject* and the *enum, Direction*.

LISTING 12.7 Class PathObject

```
using System;
using System.Collections.Generic;
using System.Text;
using System.Drawing;

namespace Maze {

    public enum Direction {
        North, Northeast, East,
        Southeast, South, Southwest,
        West, Northwest, NotAvailable
    };

    public class PathObject {
        // Fields
        private Point position; // Models the position of the mouse
        private Direction move; // Models the move direction
        private Direction [] movesAvailable;

        // Constructor
        public PathObject(Point point) {
            this.position = point;
            movesAvailable =
                new Direction[] {Direction.North,
                    Direction.Northeast, Direction.East,
                    Direction.Southeast, Direction.South,
                    Direction.Southwest, Direction.West,
                    Direction.Northwest};
```

LISTING 12.7 Class PathObject (continued)

```
        }

        // Properties
        public Direction Move {
            get {
                return move;
            }
        }

        public Point Position {
            get {
                return position;
            }
        }

        // Commands
        /*
         * Chooses a random direction from the array
         * movesAvailable. Remove this direction from the
         * movesAvailable.
         */
        public void MakeRandomMove() {
            // Sets the value of the field move, Direction.NotAvailable
            // if none is available
            int[] indicesAvailable = new int[8]; // Holds indices of
                                                 // moves that are available
            int count = 0;
            for (int index = 0; index < 8; index++) {
                if (movesAvailable[index] != Direction.NotAvailable) {
                    indicesAvailable[count] = index;
                    count++;
                }
            }
            if (count > 0) {
                int randomIndex = Global.randomValue.Next(count);
                move = movesAvailable[indicesAvailable[randomIndex]];
                movesAvailable[indicesAvailable[randomIndex]] =
                        Direction.NotAvailable;
            } else {
                move = Direction.NotAvailable;
            }
        }

        // Queries
        public override bool Equals(Object obj) {
            if (obj is PathObject) {
                PathObject other = (PathObject)obj;
                return other.position.Equals(position);
            } else {
                return false;
            }
        }
```

LISTING 12.7 Class PathObject (continued)

```
        public override int GetHashCode() {
            return position.GetHashCode();
        }
    }
}
```

The *enum Direction*, contained within namespace *Maze*, defines the eight possible move directions from any position as well as the sentinel value *NotAvailable*. Whenever a move has been attempted, the value of the move is changed to *NotAvailable* in order to prevent repeated attempts in the same direction. It is essential to provide this sentinel value because an *enum* has value semantics that prevent an assignment to the value *null*.

Class *PathObject* contains three fields: *position*, *move*, and *movesAvailable*. These fields correspond to the information that the algorithm requires be encapsulated.

The command *MakeRandomMove* assigns a value to the field *move*. This value may be accessed using the read-only property *Move*.

Exercise 12.9

Explain in detail how method *MakeRandomMove* works.

The constructor in class *PathObject* takes a *Point* as input and assigns this point to the *position* field. It also initializes an array of *Direction* objects.

An *Equals* method (and associated *GetHashCode* method) is needed because it is necessary to compare a path object with the ending position path object to determine whether the maze has been completed.

With class *PathObject* in place we turn our attention to class *MazeModel*. As indicated earlier, this class encapsulates the state of the maze and the move logic associated with solving the maze. Listing 12.8 presents the details of this class.

LISTING 12.8 Class MazeModel

```
using System;
using System.Collections.Generic;
using System.Text;
using System.Drawing;
using Containers;
using System.Windows.Forms;
using System.IO;

namespace Maze {

    public class MazeModel {
```

LISTING 12.8 Class MazeModel (continued)

```
public delegate void Display(bool [,]
        barriers, Point startPoint, Point endPoint);
public delegate void DrawLine(Point oldPoint,
                               Point newPoint, Color c);
public delegate void UpdateMoveCount(int count);
public delegate void AnnounceGameOver();

// Fields
private bool[,] barriers;
private LinkedStack<PathObject> pathStack;
private int dimension;
private Point startingPoint;
private Point endingPoint;
private int moveCount; // Records the number of move attempts
private PathObject current;
private bool gameOver = false;

// Events
public event Display display;
public event DrawLine drawLine;
public event UpdateMoveCount updateMoveCount;
public event AnnounceGameOver announceGameOver;

// Constructor
public MazeModel(int dimension,
        Point startingPoint, Point endingPoint) {
    pathStack = new LinkedStack<PathObject>();
    this.dimension = dimension;
    this.startingPoint = startingPoint;
    this.endingPoint = endingPoint;
    moveCount = 0;
    barriers = new bool[dimension + 1, dimension + 1];
    // Load maze from Maze.txt file
    StreamReader inputFile = new StreamReader("Maze.txt");

    for (int row = 1; row <= dimension; row++) {
        String line = inputFile.ReadLine();
        String delimiterString = " ";
        char[] delimiter = delimiterString.ToCharArray();
        String[] symbols = line.Split(delimiter); // Tokenizes
                                        // using space separator
        for (int col = 1; col <= dimension; col++) {
            barriers[row, col] =
                symbols[col - 1].Equals("1") ? true : false;
        }
    }
    // Construct a PathObject from the starting point
    current = new PathObject(startingPoint);
    pathStack.Push(current);
    barriers[startingPoint.X, startingPoint.Y] = true;
    inputFile.Close();
}
```

LISTING 12.8 Class MazeModel (continued)

```
// Commands
public void Register(Display handler) {
    display += new Display(handler);
}

public void Register(DrawLine handler) {
    drawLine += new DrawLine(handler);
}

public void Register(UpdateMoveCount handler) {
    updateMoveCount += new UpdateMoveCount(handler);
}

public void Register(AnnounceGameOver handler) {
    announceGameOver += new AnnounceGameOver(handler);
}

public void DisplayMaze() {
    display(barriers, startingPoint, endingPoint);
}

public void StepAhead() {
    bool validMove = false;
    while (!gameOver && !validMove && !pathStack.IsEmpty()) {
        validMove = false;
        current = pathStack.Top();
        pathStack.Pop();
        moveCount++;
        updateMoveCount(moveCount);
        current.MakeRandomMove();
        while (!validMove &&
          current.Move != Direction.NotAvailable) {
            Point newPosition =
              NewPosition(current.Position, current.Move);
            if (barriers[newPosition.Y, newPosition.X] ==
                                              false) {
                validMove = true;
                drawLine(current.Position,
                  newPosition, Color.Black);
                if (newPosition.Equals(endingPoint)) {
                    gameOver = true;
                    announceGameOver();
                }
                barriers[newPosition.Y, newPosition.X] = true;
                pathStack.Push(current);
                PathObject newPathObject =
                new PathObject(newPosition);
                pathStack.Push(newPathObject);
            } else {
                current.MakeRandomMove();
            }
```

LISTING 12.8 Class MazeModel (continued)

```
                    }
                    if (!validMove && pathStack.Size() > 0) {
                        drawLine(current.Position,
                            pathStack.Top().Position, Color.Red);
                    }
                }
                if (pathStack.IsEmpty()) {
                    MessageBox.Show("No solution is possible.");
                }
            }

            private Point NewPosition(Point oldPosition, Direction move) {
                switch (move) {
                    case Direction.North:
                        return new Point(oldPosition.X, oldPosition.Y - 1);
                    case Direction.Northeast:
                        return new Point(oldPosition.X + 1,
                                oldPosition.Y - 1);
                    case Direction.East:
                        return new Point(oldPosition.X + 1, oldPosition.Y);
                    case Direction.Southeast:
                        return new Point(oldPosition.X + 1,
                                oldPosition.Y + 1);
                    case Direction.South:
                        return new Point(oldPosition.X, oldPosition.Y + 1);
                    case Direction.Southwest:
                        return new Point(oldPosition.X - 1,
                                oldPosition.Y + 1);
                    case Direction.West:
                        return new Point(oldPosition.X - 1, oldPosition.Y);
                    case Direction.Northwest:
                        return new Point(oldPosition.X - 1,
                                oldPosition.Y - 1);
                }
                return new Point(-1, -1);
            }
        }
    }
```

The eight fields encapsulate the state of the maze.

Four delegate types, Display, DrawLine, UpdateMoveCount, and AnnounceGameOver, and associated public event types display, drawLine, updateMoveCount, and announceGameOver are defined.

The field *pathStack* with type *PathObject* plays the central role in defining the move logic. Specifically, the class *LinkedStack<PathObject>* is used to implement *pathStack*.

Four *Register* methods are defined that allow the soon-to-be-defined *MazeUI* class to register its event handlers with this *MazeModel* class.

The field *barriers* that defines the maze is declared as a two-dimensional array of *bool*. A value of true indicates the presence of a barrier at a particular coordinate, whereas a value of false indicates a pathway.

The constructor initializes barriers to contain one more row and one more column than needed in order to allow "natural" indexing to be used. This simplifies the logic of the *StepAhead* method considerably.

The *barriers* array is filled by reading the "Maze.txt" file. A row of data is read at once from the input file. Using a space delimiter and method *Split* from class *String*, each row of the two-dimensional array *barriers* is filled with values of true or false based on whether the *String* found in the input file is a "1" or a "0."

A path object is created from the specified starting point, and this object is pushed onto *pathStack*. The value of *barriers* for the starting point is set to true in order to prevent a return to this position.

The method *StepAhead* implements the maze move algorithm outlined previously. An outer while-loop executes as long as the value of the local Boolean *validMove* is false, *gameOver* is false, and as long as *pathStack* is not empty. After the *moveCount* field is incremented, the *updateMoveCount* event is fired with *moveCount* passed as a parameter. The *current* path object is commanded to make a random move. The support method *NewPosition* is used to obtain one of the available move directions. The *barriers* array is used to determine whether the randomly selected move is valid. If so, the *drawLine* event is fired and the move is tested to see whether the game is over (in which case the *announceGameOver* event is fired). The *barriers* array is used to create a barrier to block future visits to the position of the new move. The *current* path object is pushed onto *pathStack*. A new path object is created from the new position. This new path object is pushed onto *pathStack*.

If the new position generated randomly from the available positions has a barrier, another random move is generated.

If all available moves are exhausted and a valid move is not found, an event is fired that tells the *MazeUI* class to draw a red line from the current position to the next position to be taken from *pathStack*. This red line indicates backtracking along the existing path.

A screenshot that shows a completed maze is presented in Figure 12.9.

This particular run required 54 moves. The red lines indicate portions of a path that required backtracking. This backtracking is controlled by the path stack. Five dead-end paths are shown.

The application, as it stands, is incomplete because it provides no mechanism for refreshing the panel if the panel is resized or invalidated. It is a nontrivial task to provide this mechanism. An outline of the steps that one might consider follows:

1. Define handlers for panel repaint and resizing the user interface. Each of these handlers must invoke a method, say *RestorePanel*.

2. Restore the original maze with its barriers and pathways from the input file "Maze.txt".

3. As each line is created in the original maze, store the line and its associated color in an array that is added as a field, say *lines*, of class *MazeModel*. Another class, say *Line*, that encapsulates a line and its color should be added to the system. Then the array *lines* should store objects from this new class.

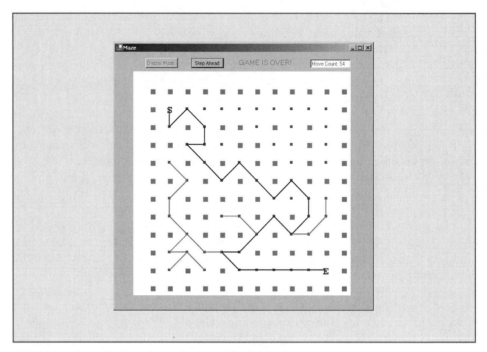

FIGURE 12.9 Screenshot of completed maze

4. After capturing the original maze from the input file, the *RestorePanel* method should access the array that contains all the lines drawn to date and their color. A new query method in class *MazeModel* should return this array to the UI class so that it can reconstruct all the lines along with their appropriate color. Once this is done, the application could continue where it left off because *pathStack* would still be intact as well as all the other important field values from *MazeModel*. All that is lost during a resize or repaint are the graphic details—the maze depiction and the lines drawn to date.

    Exercise 12.10 allows you to implement the panel repaint.

Exercise 12.10

Implement the mechanism for restoring the panel when it is resized or needs to be repainted.

12.4 PRIORITY QUEUE

In an ordinary queue with a first-in, first-out structure, objects are prioritized based on their time of entry in the queue—the oldest items have priority over the newer items. The content of the objects being inserted in the queue play no role in affecting their ordering.

Some applications require that objects be stored based on their priority rather than their time of entry in the queue. One such application might involve airplanes arriving in the controlled airspace near an airport and queuing to land. Ordinarily, landings would be prioritized based on the order in which planes enter this controlled airspace. But the ordering might be based on factors such as the aircraft's remaining fuel, its time in air, or whether it has VIP passengers. Such an application would require the services of a priority queue.

The supermarket queuing application presented in Chapter 3 could be modified so that customers with only a few items to check out might be granted priority over customers with a full basket of groceries. Again the services of a priority queue would be needed to construct such an application.

The interface that defines the contract of a priority queue is presented in Listing 12.9.

The generic type, *T*, is constrained. It must implement the *IComparable* interface. This allows the order of objects within the priority queue to be based on a comparison of the priority of the objects being inserted.

LISTING 12.9 Interface for priority queue

```
public interface IPriorityQueue<T> : IContainer<T>
                        where T : IComparable {

   // Commands

   // Inserts item based on its priority
   void Add(T item);

   // Removes first item in the queue
   void Remove();

   // Queries
   T Front();
}
```

Listing 12.10 presents the details of class *PriorityQueue*.

LISTING 12.10 Class PriorityQueue

```
public class PriorityQueue<T> : IPriorityQueue<T>
                    where T : IComparable {
      // Fields
      private Node first;
      private int numberElements;

      // Commands
      public void Add(T item) {
          if (numberElements == 0) {
              first = new Node(item, null);
          } else {
```

LISTING 12.10 Class PriorityQueue (continued)

```
                Node current = first;
                Node previous = null;
                // Search for the first node in the linked structure
                // that is smaller than item
                while (current != null &&
                            current.Item.CompareTo(item) >= 0) {
                    previous = current;
                    current = current.Next;
                }
                Node newNode = new Node(item, current);
                if (previous != null) {
                    previous.Next = newNode;
                } else {
                    first = newNode;
                }
            }
        numberElements++;
    }

    public void Remove() {
        if (IsEmpty()) {
            throw new InvalidOperationException(
                "Cannot remove from empty queue.");
        } else {
            Node oldNode = first;
            first = first.Next;
            numberElements--;
            oldNode = null;
        }
    }

    public void MakeEmpty() {
        first = null;
    }

    // Queries
    public T Front() {
        if (!IsEmpty()) {
            return first.Item;
        } else {
            throw new InvalidOperationException(
                "Cannot obtain front of empty queue.");
        }
    }

    public bool IsEmpty() {
        return numberElements == 0;
    }

    public int Size() {
        return numberElements;
    }

    private class Node {
```

LISTING 12.10 Class PriorityQueue (continued)

```
                // Fields
                private T item;
                private Node next;

                // Properties
                public T Item { // Read-only
                    get {
                        return item;
                    }
                }

                public Node Next { // Read-write
                    get {
                        return next;
                    }
                    set {
                        next = value;
                    }
                }

                public Node(T value, Node link) {
                    item = value;
                    next = link;
                }
            }
        }
```

The most interesting method is *Add*. Consider the following segment of code:

```
// Search for the first node in the linked structure
// that is smaller than item
while (current != null && current.Item.CompareTo(item) >= 0) {
    previous = current;
    current = current.Next;
}
Node newNode = new Node(item, current);
if (previous != null) {
    previous.Next = newNode;
} else {
    first = newNode;
}
```

It traverses the linked structure with node *current* starting at node *first*. The loop ends when *current* is null or a value within the linked structure is less than the item being inserted (remember that the items are being inserted from largest to smallest where elements are compared based on their priority). Assuming that such a value is found (less than the item being inserted), the new node is linked to this first smaller value. The node *previous* always trails the node *current* by one node so that *previous* can be linked to the new node which, in turn, is linked to the first smaller value.

Exercise 12.11

Sketch a diagram of the nodes, based on method *Add*, that clarifies the insertion of *item* into the priority queue.

A simple demonstration of class *PriorityQueue* in action is presented next. A support class, *MyClassWithPriorities*, is presented in Listing 12.11. This class contains two fields: *priorityValue* of type *int* and *name* of type *String*.

The *CompareTo* method that serves as the basis for comparing two objects of type *MyClassWithPriorities* uses the *priorityValue* field as the basis for the comparison.

LISTING 12.11 MyClassWithPriorities

```
public class MyClassWithPriorities : IComparable {
    // Fields
    private int priorityValue;
    private String name;

    // Properties
    public int PriorityValue {
        get {
            return priorityValue;
        }
    }

    // Constructor
    public MyClassWithPriorities(int priority, String name) {
        this.name = name;
        priorityValue = priority;
    }

    public int CompareTo(Object obj) {
        if (obj is MyClassWithPriorities) {
            MyClassWithPriorities other =
                (MyClassWithPriorities)obj;
            return priorityValue - other.priorityValue;
        } else {
            throw new InvalidDataException(
                "Cannot compare object with MyClassWithPriorities.");
        }
    }

    public override String ToString() {
        return name + " with priority " + priorityValue;
    }
}
```

Listing 12.12 shows an application class that builds a *PriorityQueue* and exercises some of its functionality.

LISTING 12.12 Application of PriorityQueue App

```
using System;

namespace Containers {

    public class PriorityQueueApp {

        public static void Main() {
            MyClassWithPriorities myObject1 =
            new MyClassWithPriorities(6, "Object 1");
            MyClassWithPriorities myObject2 =
            new MyClassWithPriorities(6, "Object 2");
            MyClassWithPriorities myObject3 =
            new MyClassWithPriorities(6, "Object 3");
            MyClassWithPriorities myObject4 =
            new MyClassWithPriorities(2, "Object 4");
            MyClassWithPriorities myObject5 =
            new MyClassWithPriorities(6, "Object 5");
            MyClassWithPriorities myObject6 =
            new MyClassWithPriorities(4, "Object 6");
            MyClassWithPriorities myObject7 =
            new MyClassWithPriorities(2, "Object 7");

            PriorityQueue<MyClassWithPriorities> queue =
                    new PriorityQueue<MyClassWithPriorities>();
            queue.Add(myObject1);
            queue.Add(myObject2);
            queue.Add(myObject3);
            queue.Add(myObject4);
            queue.Add(myObject5);
            queue.Add(myObject6);
            queue.Add(myObject7);

            // Output the values in the queue
            while (queue.Size() > 0) {
                Console.WriteLine(queue.Front().ToString());
                queue.Remove();
            }
            Console.ReadLine();
        }
    }
}

/* Program output
Object 1 with priority 6
Object 2 with priority 6
Object 3 with priority 6
Object 5 with priority 6
Object 6 with priority 4
Object 4 with priority 2
Object 7 with priority 2
*/
```

As shown in Listing 12.12, the generic parameter *T* is replaced by the actual type *MyClassWithPriorities*. The objects are indeed ordered by their priority. For objects of the same priority, those that get inserted first have de-facto priority over those that are inserted later.

12.5 DEQUE AND POSITIONABLE LIST

A deque has a linear structure. Elements are inserted from a well-defined front of a deque to its rear or from the rear to its front. As a minimum, we can access both ends of a deque. The objects in a deque have no inherent order except as a result of adding objects either to the front or to the rear of the deque.

A positionable list is a specialized kind of deque with the additional capability of being able to add or remove objects just before or just after an existing target object in the deque.

The implementation of linked lists has been an important part of data structure analysis for many decades. Through a careful analysis of such lists, the subtleties of linked structures are revealed. There are many implementations of lists that have been devised. These include singly linked, doubly linked, circular, and others.

An exhaustive presentation of these variations is not the mission of this chapter. Because the goal is to attain needed skills in manipulating linked structures, this can be achieved by closely examining one important variation—doubly linked lists. These are the most intricate and will serve to achieve this goal. Figure 12.10 depicts the structure of such a doubly linked list.

Each node has a forward link and a backward link. This allows the list to be traversed either from left to right or from right to left.

The contract for a deque is encapsulated in the interface *IDeque* in Listing 12.13.

A deque combines the functionality of a stack and queue. The command *AddFront* is identical to *Push* for a stack. The command *AddRear* is identical to *Add* for a queue. The command *RemoveFront* is identical to *Pop* for a stack or *Remove* for a queue. The command *RemoveRear* is not present in a stack or queue. The query *Rear* is also not present in a stack or queue.

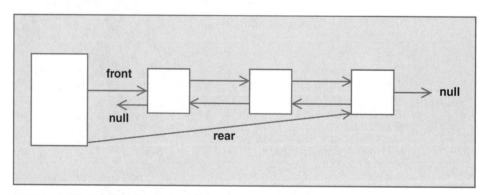

FIGURE 12.10 Doubly linked list

Finally, the query *Contains* is not present in a stack or queue. It allows a determination of whether a particular object is present in the deque container.

LISTING 12.13 Interface IDeque

```
public interface IDeque<T> : IContainer<T> {

    // Commands

    // Adds element to the front of the list
    void AddFront(T element);

    // Adds element to the rear of the list
    void AddRear(T element);

    // Removes the front element of the list
    void RemoveFront();

    // Removes the rear element in the list
    void RemoveRear();

    // Queries

    // Returns the front element in the list without changing it
    T Front();

    // Returns the rear element in the list without changing it
    T Rear();

    // Returns true if element is in the list.
    bool Contains(T element);
}
```

Listing 12.14 presents the interface *IPositionableList*.

LISTING 12.14 Interface IPositionableList

```
public interface IPositionableList<T> : IDeque<T>, IEnumerable<T>,
                                                    IEnumerator<T> {

        // Commands

        // Inserts element after target object
        void AddAfter(T element, T target);

        // Inserts element before target
        void AddBefore(T element, T target);

        // Removes object after target
        void RemoveAfter(T target);
```

LISTING 12.14 Interface IPositionableList (continued)

```
        // Removes object before target
        void RemoveBefore(T target);

        // Queries

        // Returns the object after target without changing it
        T ElementAfter(T target);

        // Returns the object before target without changing it
        T ElementBefore(T target);
    }
```

The four commands and two queries in *IPositionableList* allow objects to be added or accessed before or after some target object. Additional methods must be implemented to fulfill the contract of *IPositionableList*. These are mandated because *IPositionableList* is shown as inheriting from interfaces *IEnumerable<T>* and *IEnumerator<T>*. These additional methods, to be explored next, support iteration—our ability to visit the elements of a positionable list and iterate using the *foreach* construct.

With the interfaces *IContainer*, *IDeque*, and *IPositionableList* established, we turn our attention to the implementation of *DoublyLinkedDeque*.

Information inserted in *DoublyLinkedDeque* is inserted in nodes. The inner class *Node* that holds the information is given in Listing 12.15.

Each *Node* holds an item of generic type *T*. In addition a forward link, *next*, and backward link, *before*, are held as fields of *Node*.

The constructor for *Node* allows an item to be inserted and the *Node* object linked forward to the node directly in front of the given node and linked backwards to the node directly behind the given node. The fields *next* and *before* are designed to perform this linking. Each of these is recursively defined as type *Node*.

Node is declared as a *protected* class because it needs to be inherited in class *DoublyLinkedList* considered later.

LISTING 12.15 Private class Node for DoublyLinkedDeque

```
protected class Node {

    // Fields
    private T item;
    private Node next;
    private Node before;

    // Properties
    public T Item {
        get {
            return item;
        }
    }

    public Node Next { // Read-write
```

LISTING 12.15 Private class Node for DoublyLinkedDeque (continued)

```
        get {
          return next;
        }
        set {
          next = value;
        }
    }

    public Node Before { // Read-write
        get {
          return before;
        }
        set {
          before = value;
        }
    }

    // Constructor
    public Node(T element, Node link, Node backLink) {
        item = element;
            next = link;
        before = backLink;
    }
}
```

In exploring the details of class DoublyLinkedDeque, we focus first on the two add methods, *AddFront* and *AddRear*. As before, sketching diagrams that describe the actions is indispensable. Class *DoublyLinkedDeque* contains the following fields:

```
protected Node front, rear;
protected int numberElements;
```

Method *AddFront* is shown in Listing 12.16.

LISTING 12.16 Method AddFront

```
public void AddFront(T element) {
    Node newNode = new Node(element, front, null);
    if (numberElements == 0) {
        rear = newNode;
    } else {
        front.Before = newNode;
    }
    front = newNode;
    numberElements++;
}
```

The first line of code creates a new node with *element* inserted that links forward to the current *front* and backward to *null*. This is depicted in Figure 12.11.

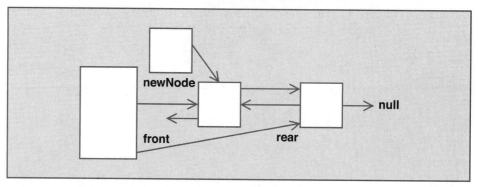

FIGURE 12.11 New node with *element* inserted that links forward to the current *front* and backwards to *null*

Exercise 12.12

Sketch the final linked structure when *AddFront* is completed.

Method *AddRear* is shown in Listing 12.17.

LISTING 12.17 Method AddRear

```
public void AddRear(T element) {
   Node newNode = new Node(element, null, rear);
   if (numberElements == 0) {
     front = newNode;
   } else {
     rear.Next = newNode;
   }
   rear = newNode;
   numberElements++;
}
```

The first line of code creates a new *Node*, inserts *element*, and has a forward link to *null* and a back link to *rear*.

This is shown in Figure 12.12.

Exercise 12.13

Sketch the final linked structure when *AddRear* is completed.

Next, method *RemoveFront* is considered. The details of this method are shown in Listing 12.18.

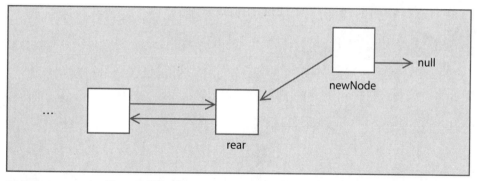

FIGURE 12.12 New *Node* with *element* and a forward link to *null* and a back link to *rear*

LISTING 12.18 Method RemoveFront

```
public void RemoveFront() {
   if (IsEmpty()) {
      throw new InvalidOperationException(
         "Cannot remove from empty deque.");
   } else {
      if (front.Next != null) {
         front.Next.Before = null;
         }
         front = front.Next;
         numberElements--;
         if (numberElements == 0) {
         rear = null;
         }
      }
   }
}
```

If the *Deque* is not empty and if *front.Next* is not *null* (ensuring that there are at least two nodes in the linked structure), the back link of the second node is assigned the value null because it is about to become *front*. It is essential that the test,

```
if (front.Next != null) {
```

be performed; otherwise a *NullPointerException* would be generated when *front.Next* were *null* (only one node in the linked structure).

Exercise 12.14

Sketch the steps involved in the linked structure for *RemoveFront*.

Next, method *RemoveRear* is examined. Its details are in Listing 12.19.

LISTING 12.19 Method RemoveRear

```
public void RemoveRear() {
   if (IsEmpty()) {
      throw new InvalidOperationException(
        "Cannot remove from empty deque.");
   } else if (numberElements == 1) {
      front = null;
      rear = null;
   } else { // 2 or more elements
      // Find node just in front of rear
         Node previous = rear.Before;
         previous.Next = null;
      rear = previous;
   }
}
```

Exercise 12.15

Explain the details of method *RemoveRear* and back up your explanation with diagrams showing the linked structure at each step in the method.

The remaining details of class *DoublyLinkedDeque* are shown in Listing 12.20.

LISTING 12.20 Remaining details of class DoublyLinkedDeque

```
public class DoublyLinkedDeque<T> : IDeque<T> {

    // Fields
    private Node front, rear;
    private int numberElements;

    // Commands
    public void AddFront(T element) {
        // See Listing 12.16
    }

    public void AddRear(T element) {
        // See Listing 12.17
    }

    public void RemoveFront() {
        // See Listing 12.18
    }

    public void RemoveRear() {
        // See Listing 12.19
    }
```

LISTING 12.20 Remaining details of class DoublyLinkedDeque (continued)

```
    public void MakeEmpty() {
        front = rear = null;
        numberElements = 0;
    }

    // Queries
    public T Front() {
        if (front == null) {
            throw new InvalidOperationException(
                "Cannot obtain front of an empty deque.");
        } else {
            return front.Item;
        }
    }

    public T Rear() {
        if (front == null) {
            throw new InvalidOperationException(
                "Cannot obtain rear of an empty deque.");
        } else {
            return rear.Item;
        }
    }

    public bool Contains(T element) {
        Node currentNode = front;
        while (currentNode != null) {
            if (currentNode.Item.Equals(element)) {
                return true;
            }
            currentNode = currentNode.Next;
        }
        return false;
    }

    public int Size() {
        return numberElements;
    }

    public bool IsEmpty() {
        return numberElements == 0;
    }

    private class Node {
        // See Listing 12.15
    }
}
```

Class *DoublyLinkedList*, which implements the interface *IPostionableList*, adds
four commands, *AddBefore*, *AddAfter*, *RemoveBefore*, and *RemoveAfter*, and two
queries, *ElementAfter* and *ElementBefore*, to those contained in *DoublyLinkedDeque*.
The implementation of the *DoublyLinkedDeque* commands *AddFront*, *AddRear*,
RemoveFront, and *RemoveRear* are identical in class *DoublyLinkedList*. The same holds

true for the queries *Front*, *Rear*, and *Contains*. This suggests the use of inheritance. Indeed much of the work in implementing *DoublyLinkedList* has already been done in the implementation of *DoublyLinkedDeque*.

The UML diagram in Figure 12.13 shows the relationships among the various interfaces and classes that provide the basis for class *DoublyLinkedDeque*.

Class *DoublyLinkedList* is presented in Listing 12.21.

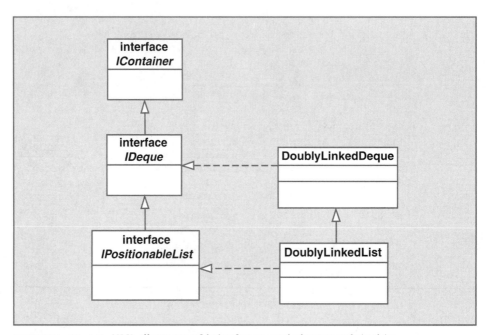

FIGURE 12.13 UML diagram of interfaces and classes related to
DoublyLinkedList

LISTING 12.21 Class DoublyLinkedList

```
public class DoublyLinkedList<T> : DoublyLinkedDeque<T>,
                                     IPositionableList<T> {

    // Fields
    private bool iterateLeftToRight = true; // Direction of
                                            // iteration
    private Node cursor;  // Points to the current node in an
                          // iteration

    // Properties
    public bool IterateLeftToRight {
        set {
            iterateLeftToRight = value;
            if (iterateLeftToRight) {
                cursor = front;
            } else {
                cursor = rear;
```

LISTING 12.21 Class DoublyLinkedList (continued)

```
            }
        }
    }

    public T Current { // Read-only
        get {
            return cursor.Item;
        }
    }

    // Commands
    public void Dispose() {
        // Required by the interface IEnumerator<T>
        front = rear = null;
        numberElements = 0;
    }

    public void AddAfter(T element, T target) {
        Node itemNode = GetNode(target);
        if (itemNode == null) {
            throw new InvalidOperationException(
                "Target does not exist in AddAfter.");
        } else {
            // Back link to itemNode and forward link to
            // itemNode.next
            Node newNode =
            new Node(element, itemNode.Next, itemNode);
            if (itemNode.Next != null) {
                itemNode.Next.Before = newNode;
            } else {
                rear = newNode;
            }
            itemNode.Next = newNode;
            numberElements++;
        }
    }

    public void AddBefore(T element, T target) {
        Node itemNode = GetNode(target);
        if (itemNode == null) {
            throw new InvalidOperationException(
                "Target does not exist in AddBefore.");
        } else {
            Node beforeNode = itemNode.Before;
            // Back link to beforeNode, forward link to itemNode
            Node newNode = new Node(element, itemNode, beforeNode);
            if (front == itemNode) {
                front = newNode;
            } else {
                beforeNode.Next = newNode;
            }
            itemNode.Before = newNode;
            numberElements++;
```

LISTING 12.21 Class DoublyLinkedList (continued)

```
        }
    }

    public void RemoveAfter(T target) {
        // Exercise
    }

    public void RemoveBefore(T target) {
        // Exercise
    }

    // Queries
    public T ElementAfter(T target) {
        if (!Contains(target) ||
            GetNode(target) == rear) {
            throw new InvalidOperationException(
                "target does not exist or is last node.");
        } else {
            return GetNode(target).Next.Item;
        }
    }

    public T ElementBefore(T target) {
        if (!Contains(target) || GetNode(target) == front) {
            throw new InvalidOperationException(
                "target does not exist or first in list.");
        } else {
            return GetNode(target).Before.Item;
        }
    }

// Iteration constructs

    public IEnumerator<T> GetEnumerator() {
        if (iterateLeftToRight) {
            cursor = front;
            Node currentNode = front;
            while (currentNode != null) {
                yield return currentNode.Item;
                currentNode = currentNode.Next;
            }
        } else {
            cursor = rear;
            Node currentNode = rear;
            while (currentNode != null) {
                yield return currentNode.Item;
                currentNode = currentNode.Before;
            }
        }
    }
    // Code needed since IEnumerable<T> inherits from IEnumerable
    IEnumerator IEnumerable.GetEnumerator() {
        return null;
```

LISTING 12.21 Class DoublyLinkedList (continued)

```
        }

        void IEnumerator.Reset() {
        }

        Object IEnumerator.Current {
            get {
                return null;
            }
        }

        public bool MoveNext() {
            if (iterateLeftToRight) {
                cursor = cursor.Next;
            } else {
                cursor = cursor.Before;
            }
            return cursor != null;
        }

        private Node GetNode(T value) {
            Node node = front;
            Node result = null;
            while (node != null) {
                if (node.Item.Equals(value)) {
                    result = node;
                    break;
                }
                node = node.Next;
            }
            return result;
        }
    }
}
```

Let us closely examine method *AddAfter* to get more practice in sketching and understanding linked structures. The node *itemNode* is obtained from *GetNode* using *target* as a parameter. It is initially linked, as shown in Figure 12.14, to node B.

The line of code, *Node newNode = new Node(element, itemNode.Next, itemNode)*, constructs a new node that is forward and back linked as shown in Figure 12.15.

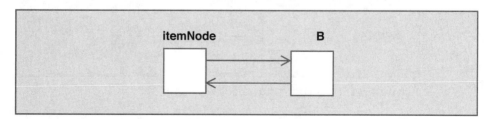

FIGURE 12.14 Node *itemNode* is linked to node B

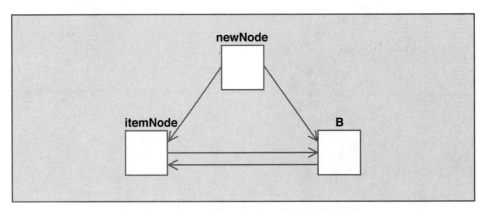

FIGURE 12.15 New node that is forward and back linked

The line of code *itemNode.Next.Before = newNode* produces the back link from B as shown in Figure 12.16.

The line of code *itemNode.Next = newNode* completes the two-way link as shown in Figure 12.17.

Exercise 12.16

Explain method *AddBefore* using a series of diagrams similar to those shown in Figures 12.14–12.17.

Exercise 12.17

Write the code for method *RemoveBefore* and use a series of diagrams to explain what you have done.

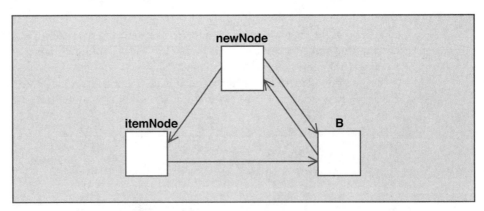

FIGURE 12.16 Producing a back link from B

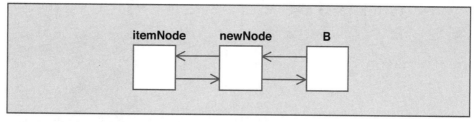

FIGURE 12.17 Completing the two-way link

Exercise 12.18

Write the code for method *RemoveAfter* and use a series of diagrams to explain what you have done.

The methods *GetEnumerator* and *MoveNext* and the property *Current* support iteration. A private field, *Cursor*, of type *Node* holds the node that is currently being pointed to as an iteration progresses. The command *MoveNext* advances the cursor either forward or backward depending on the value of another field *iterateLeftToRight*. A doubly linked structure enjoys the advantage of being able to traverse from left to right or from right to left, in contrast to a singly linked structure that permits navigation only from left to right. We will take advantage of this capability in Section 12.7 when we consider an application of lists. *MoveNext* returns true if the cursor has not gone beyond the boundaries of the linked structure (with value null) and false if it has. This enables a programmer to invoke *MoveNext* and test the outcome before accessing the new value through the property *Current*.

12.6 STACK AND QUEUE REVISITED

As indicated earlier, the operations of *Push* and *Pop* for a stack are identical to *AddFront* and *RemoveFront* for a deque. The operations of *Add* and *Remove* for a queue are identical to *AddRear* and *RemoveFront* for a *deque*.

Through a simple layering of abstractions, we can implement either a stack or queue using the services of an internal deque.

Listing 12.22 shows the details of a stack that is implemented using an internal *DoublyLinkedDeque*.

LISTING 12.22 DequeStack

```
public class DequeStack<T> : IStack<T> {

        // Fields
        private DoublyLinkedDeque<T> deque =
                new DoublyLinkedDeque<T>();

        // Commands
```

LISTING 12.22 DequeStack (continued)

```
        public void Push(T item) {
            deque.AddFront(item);
        }

        public void Pop() {
            if (deque.IsEmpty()) {
                throw new InvalidOperationException(
                    "Cannot pop an empty stack.");
            } else {
                deque.RemoveFront();
            }
        }

        public void MakeEmpty() {
            deque.MakeEmpty();
        }

        // Queries
        public T Top() {
            if (deque.IsEmpty()) {
                throw new InvalidOperationException(
                    "Cannot pop an empty stack.");
            } else {
                return deque.Front();
            }
        }

        public int Size() {
            return deque.Size();
        }

        public bool IsEmpty() {
            return deque.IsEmpty();
        }
    }
```

Although one could define a *DequeStack* class by having it inherit from *Deque*, this would violate the architectural principle that the methods of a subclass should add to and not subtract from those of its parent. The stack abstraction is narrower (contains fewer methods) than the deque abstraction, and therefore it would not be good design to have stack inherit from deque.

Exercise 12.19

Show the details of a class *DequeQueue* using the same type of layering of abstractions as used in *DequeStack*.

12.7 APPLICATION OF LISTS: LONG INTEGER MANIPULATIONS

Lists are used in many applications for holding information in which the order of information is based on where the insertion occurs (front, rear, before some target, after some target).

We shall consider an application where the use of a list may not be immediately obvious. We consider a long integer class that is capable of performing operations on integers that potentially contain thousands or hundreds of thousands of digits. Clearly integers that contain so many digits cannot be represented in terms of the basic data types defined within the .NET framework such as long and decimal. Such long integers have applications in cryptology as well as other areas of computer science.

A class *LongInteger* with limited functionality will be designed.

Its constructor creates a long integer instance from a string representation of the number. This string contains the potentially large number of numerals that represent the long integer.

The operations of addition and multiplication are supported. The *Equals* method and a *ToString* method are also defined so that long integers can be compared and output.

The long integers in this application are restricted to non-negative.

A *DoublyLinkedList* plays the central role in solving this problem and constructing this class.

As an example, consider the long integer 12345678901234567890123. This 23-digit integer can be divided from right to left into groups of integers, each of maximum length 10 as follows:

123   4567890123   4567890123

Each of the three potentially 10-digit integers can be represented as type *ulong*, an unsigned long integer. We can construct a *DoublyLinkedList<ulong>* with nodes as follows:

null <-Node 1: 123 <-> Node 2: 4567890123 <-> Node 3: 4567890123 -> null

Suppose we wish to add this long integer to the 23-digit long integer, 99999999999999999999999, whose doubly linked list representation is:

null <-Node 1: 999 <-> Node 2: 9999999999 <-> Node 3: 9999999999 -> null

A string *result* that holds the numerals that represent the resulting long integer is initialized to an empty string.

To perform the addition, we traverse each of the lists from right to left (thus the benefit of using a doubly linked structure). The unsigned long values of 4567890123 and 999999999 are extracted from each of the right-most nodes. They are added to produce the 11-digit sum, 14567890122.

If the sum is divided by the value 10000000000 (1 followed by 10 zeros, which is defined as the *groupSize*), a *carry* of 1 is obtained. Suppose we compute *sum* % *groupSize*, convert the value to a string and prepend sufficient 0s to make the resulting string contain 10 numerals. The string would be "**4567890122**".

Next, through a left-to-right iteration the nodes to the left of the right-most nodes are accessed and the unsigned long values extracted. We form the sum of these two unsigned long values and add *carry* from the previous step to the result. The *carry* is computed as before with a value of one. The same steps given previously are repeated producing a 10-numeral string, "**4567890123**". This string is prepended to the earlier string producing a resultant of "**45678901234567890122**".

Lastly the unsigned long values from the left-most node are accessed. The same steps result in the string "**0000001123**".

A new long integer is created from the resulting string "**000000112345678901234567890122**". In forming this long integer, the leading 0s are stripped out because they add clutter.

The doubly linked list that represents the sum is the following:

null <- Node 1: 1123 <-> Node 2: 4567890123 <-> Node 3: 4567890122 -> null

This represents the long integer: **112345678901234567890122**

If the long integer 9999999999 (10 nines) were added to the long integer 1, the carry would be one and the *sum % groupSize* would produce the string "**0000000000**" because the sum of 10000000000 % 10000000000 equals 0 and nine more 0s would be prepended.

Listing 12.23 shows the details of class *LongInteger*.

LISTING 12.23 Class LongInteger

```
public class LongInteger {
    private const ulong groupSize = 10000000000L;
    // Fields
    private DoublyLinkedList<ulong> numberList =
                new DoublyLinkedList<ulong>();
    private int size; // Number of digits in integer

    // Constructor
    public LongInteger(String numerals) {
        numerals = numerals.Trim();
        size = numerals.Length;
        // Assign groups of 10 digits to each node in the
        // DoublyLinkedList
        String nodeString = "";
        ulong nodeValue = 0L;
        for (int groupCount = 1;
                groupCount <= numerals.Length / 10;
                groupCount++) {
        // Grab groups of 10 numerals from numerals
        // from right to left
            nodeString = numerals.Substring(
                numerals.Length - 10 * groupCount, 10);
            nodeValue = Convert.ToUInt64(nodeString);
            numberList.AddFront(nodeValue);
            nodeString = "";
        }
        if (numerals.Length % 10 != 0) {
        nodeString = numerals.Substring(0, numerals.Length % 10);
```

LISTING 12.23 Class LongInteger (continued)

```
            nodeValue = Convert.ToUInt64(nodeString);
            numberList.AddFront(nodeValue);
        }
    }

    // Properties
    public int Size {
        get {
            return size;
        }
    }

    public static LongInteger operator +
                (LongInteger operand1, LongInteger operand2) {
        ulong operandValue1 = 0;
        ulong operandValue2 = 0;
        ulong sum = 0;
        ulong carry = 0;
        String result = "";
        operand1.numberList.IterateLeftToRight = false;
        operand2.numberList.IterateLeftToRight = false;
        IEnumerator<ulong> operandIterator1 =
                operand1.numberList.GetEnumerator();
        IEnumerator<ulong> operandIterator2 =
                operand2.numberList.GetEnumerator();
        bool moreOperand1 = operandIterator1.MoveNext();
        bool moreOperand2 = operandIterator2.MoveNext();
        while (moreOperand1 && moreOperand2) {
        operandValue1 = operandIterator1.Current;
            operandValue2 = operandIterator2.Current;
            sum = operandValue1 + operandValue2 + carry;
            carry = sum / groupSize;
            ulong resultValue = sum % groupSize;

            int length = ("" + resultValue).Length;
            String prepend = "";

            for (int index = 1; index <= 10 - length; index++) {
              prepend += "0";
            }

          result = prepend + resultValue + result;
          moreOperand1 = operandIterator1.MoveNext();
          moreOperand2 = operandIterator2.MoveNext();
        }
        if (moreOperand1) {
          while (moreOperand1) {
            operandValue1 = operandIterator1.Current;
                sum = operandValue1 + carry;
                carry = sum / groupSize;
                ulong resultValue = sum % groupSize;

                int length = ("" + resultValue).Length;
```

LISTING 12.23 Class LongInteger (continued)

```
                    String prepend = "";

                    for (int index = 1;
                    index <= 10 - length; index++) {
                    prepend += "0";
                    }

                    result = prepend + resultValue + result;
                    moreOperand1 = operandIterator1.MoveNext();
                }
            } else {
            while (moreOperand2) {
                operandValue2 = operandIterator2.Current;
                    sum = operandValue2 + carry;
                    carry = sum / groupSize;
                    ulong resultValue = sum % groupSize;

                    int length = ("" + resultValue).Length;
                    String prepend = "";

                    for (int index = 1;
                        index <= 10 - length; index++) {
                            prepend += "0";
                    }

                    result = prepend + resultValue + result;
                    moreOperand2 = operandIterator2.MoveNext();
                }
        }
        if (carry > 0) {
        result = carry + result;
        }
        return new LongInteger(result);
    }

    public static LongInteger operator *
                (LongInteger operand1, LongInteger operand2) {
        /* The operand with fewer digits is chosen.
         * The operand with more digits is added to itself in a loop
         * that terminates after the value of the smaller operand is
         * reached. In other words, multiplication is achieved through
         * successive addition.
         */
        int size1 = operand1.Size;
        int size2 = operand2.Size;
        LongInteger larger = size1 > size2 ? operand1 : operand2;
        LongInteger smaller = size1 > size2 ? operand2 : operand1;

        LongInteger one = new LongInteger("1");
        LongInteger index = new LongInteger("0");
        LongInteger result = new LongInteger("0");
          while (!index.Equals(smaller)) {
          result = result + larger;
```

LISTING 12.23 Class LongInteger (continued)

```
            index = index + one;
        }
        return result;


    public override bool Equals(Object obj) {
        if (!(obj is LongInteger)) {
        return false;
        }
         LongInteger other = (LongInteger)obj;
        return this.ToString().Trim().Equals(other.ToString().Trim());
    }

    public override String ToString() {
        String result = "";
        numberList.IterateLeftToRight = false;
        int listSize = numberList.Size();
        int iterations = 1;
        foreach (ulong nodeValue in numberList) {
        int length = ("" + nodeValue).Length;
            String prepend = "";
            if (iterations < listSize) { // Prevents 0s on last
                                         // iteration
                for (int index = 1; index <= 10 - length; index++) {
                    prepend += "0";
                }
            }
            String nodeString = prepend + nodeValue;
            result = nodeString + result;
            iterations++;
        }
        return result;
    }
}
```

Using the *Substring* query from class *String*, the constructor creates a *DoublyLinkedList* with generic parameter of *ulong* by parsing the input string of numerals into groups of 10 from right to left. The *AddFront* method is used to construct the list nodes.

The addition operator (+) is overloaded and is defined, as required, as a static method with two operand parameters, each of type *LongInteger*. Using the *IEnumerator* constructs *MoveNext* and *Current*, the lists representing each of the operands are traversed from right to left. Enumerators can be used only to access objects in the collection. They cannot be used to modify the underlying collection. The operations described earlier are implemented. Provision is made for the case when one of the operands' lists is longer than the other. Lastly, provision is made for the case when both lists are exhausted but there is a final *carry* value that needs to be inserted. After the final *result* string is computed, a new *LongInteger* object is created and returned.

The multiply method is implemented by creating a loop that performs addition the necessary number of times.

Exercise 12.20

Explain the details of method multiply (*).

The *Equals* method is implemented by comparing the two strings that represent the two long integers that are being compared.

The *ToString* method is carefully designed to ensure that as values of type *ulong* are extracted from each node, the appropriate number of 0s is prepended within each group. The string associated with the left-most value does not have any 0s prepended because that would add unnecessary clutter.

In class *LongInteger*, although the operations work as expected, their computational efficiency is poor. This is evident if one attempts to multiply two relatively long integers.

Listing 12.24 presents a *Main* method that exercises most of the functionality of the class. A table containing the value of 2^n as n goes from 1 to 150 is produced.

LISTING 12.24 Simple test of class LongInteger

```
public static void Main() {
   String operandString1 =
      "12345678901234567890123456789012345678901 23";
   String operandString2 =
      "99999999999999999999999999999999999999999";
   LongInteger myInt1 = new LongInteger(operandString1);
   LongInteger myInt2 = new LongInteger(operandString2);

   LongInteger longInt4 = new LongInteger("9");
   LongInteger longInt5 = myInt1 * longInt4;
   Console.WriteLine(myInt1.ToString() + " * 9 = \n" +
      longInt5.ToString());
   LongInteger longInt6 = longInt5 * new LongInteger("100000");
   Console.WriteLine("Result multiplied by 100000 = \n" +
      longInt6.ToString());

   LongInteger value1 = new LongInteger("10000000000");
   Console.WriteLine("value1: " + value1.ToString());
   LongInteger value2 = new LongInteger("1000000");
   Console.WriteLine("value2: " + value2.ToString());
   LongInteger value3 = value1 * value2;
   Console.WriteLine("value3 = value1 * value2 = \n" +
      value3.ToString());

   // Compute table of powers of 2
   LongInteger two = new LongInteger("2");
   LongInteger result = new LongInteger("1");
   Console.WriteLine("power\t2 ^ power");
   for (int i = 1; i <= 150; i++) {
      result = result * two;
```

LISTING 12.24 Simple test of class LongInteger (continued)

```
        Console.Write(i + "\t" + result.ToString());
        Console.WriteLine();
        }

    Console.ReadLine();
}

/* Portion of program output
 12345678901234567890123456789012345678901234567890123 * 9 =
111111110111111111101111111110111111111011107
Result multiplied by 100000 =
111111110111111111101111111110111111111011110700000
value1: 10000000000
value2: 1000000
value3 = value1 * value2 =
10000000000000000

power    2 ^ power
1        2
2        4
3        8
4        16
5        32
6        64
7        128
8        256
9        512
10       1024
...
140      1393796574908163946345982392040522594123776
141      2787593149816327892691964784081045188247552
142      5575186299632655785383929568162090376495104
143      11150372599265311570767859136324180752990208
144      22300745198530623141535718272648361505980416
145      44601490397061246283071436545296723011960832
146      89202980794122492566142873090593446023921664
147      178405961588244985132285746181186892047843328
148      356811923176489970264571492362373784095686656
149      713623846352979940529142984724747568191373312
150      1427247692705959881058285969449495136382746624
*/
```

12.8 SUMMARY

◆ Container types in software development are used to hold and efficiently access information. Data structures represent the implementation of a container type.

◆ Data structures provide the programmer an intellectual framework from which to construct many diverse applications. Data structures are ubiquitous. A box of paper clips, a room full of desks, a stack of trays in a cafeteria, a bag of groceries, a collection of names and phone numbers in a phone directory, a dictionary of English words, and a database of patient records are all examples of containers of objects where each may be modeled using a data structure.

◆ It is important to distinguish a container from the objects that it contains.

◆ A well-constructed container class can usually hold a diversity of information types. The mechanism for inserting, deleting, and accessing this information is usually independent of the specific type of information that is contained within the data structure or may require that the information satisfy some constraint such as being comparable.

◆ What distinguishes a stack from a queue from a deque or from various list types are the ways that information can be inserted, removed, and accessed within the structure.

◆ A stack defines a last-in, first-out structure so that the first item to have been inserted is the last item to be removed, the second item to have been inserted is the next to the last item to be removed, …, and the last item to have been inserted is the first item to be removed.

◆ A queue is a first-in, first-out structure. The first object to be added to a queue is the first that can be removed. The second object to be added is the second that may be removed, and so on. A queue is a model of a waiting line.

◆ Some applications require that objects be stored based on their priority rather than their time of entry in the queue. A priority queue is designed to meet this need.

◆ A deque has a linear structure. Elements are inserted from a well-defined front of a deque to its rear or from the rear to its front. As a minimum, we can access both ends of a deque. The objects in a deque have no inherent order except as a result of adding objects either to the front or to the rear of the deque.

◆ A deque combines the functionality of a stack and queue. The command *AddFront* is identical to *Push* for a stack. The command *AddRear* is identical to *Add* for a queue. The command *RemoveFront* is identical to *Pop* for a stack or *Remove* for a queue. The command *RemoveRear* is not present in a stack or queue. The query *Rear* is also not present in a stack or queue. Finally, the query *Contains* is not present in a stack or queue. It allows a determination of whether a particular object is present in the deque container.

◆ A positionable list is a specialized kind of deque with the additional capability of being able to add or remove objects just before or just after an existing target object in the deque.

◆ Through a simple layering of abstractions, we can implement either a stack or queue using the services of an internal *deque*.

12.9 ADDITIONAL EXERCISES

Exercise 12.21

How is a queue data structure different than a priority queue?

Exercise 12.22

Why does interface *Container* not contain any methods for adding or removing objects?

Exercise 12.23

List one potential application for each of the classic data structures presented in this chapter.

Exercise 12.24

Implement a linked stack that allows one to access the value just beneath the top of the stack, if such an element exists. All the other methods of the stack must continue to be implemented (such as *Push*, *Pop*, and *Top*).

Exercise 12.25

Implement an *ArrayQueue*. This data structure, like the *ArrayStack*, uses an internal array to hold the data being stored.

Exercise 12.26

Implement a class *InefficientQueue* in terms of two internal stacks. All the methods required in *IQueue* are to be fully implemented. **You are not** to directly use class *Node* at all. The goal of this problem is to get you to use the *IStack* abstraction while implementing an *IQueue* abstraction.

This method for implementing a *Queue* is quite inefficient (thus the name of the class). Why is this so?

```
public class InefficientQueue implements Queue {
    // Fields
     protected LinkedStack stack1, stack2;

    // No other fields should be used
}
```

Exercise 12.27

Implement method *AddBefore* for a class *SinglyLinkedList*. The internal class *Node* in this class has only a single link, *next*, that links to the node just behind the given node.

Exercise 12.28

Implement method *AddAfter* for a class *SinglyLinkedList*. The internal class *Node* in this class has only a single link, *next*, that links to the node just behind the given node.

Exercise 12.29

Implement method *RemoveBefore* for a class *SinglyLinkedList*. The internal class *Node* in this class has only a single link, *next*, that links to the node just behind the given node.

Exercise 12.30

Implement method *RemoveAfter* for a class *SinglyLinkedList*. The internal class *Node* in this class has only a single link, *next*, that links to the node just behind the given node.

CHAPTER 13

Nonlinear Data Structures and Their Applications

The previous chapter introduced linear data structures in which there is a well-defined path from a first node to a last node or the last node to the first node. For such linear data structures the computational effort required to access information is generally linear—that is, doubling the size of the structure (the number of nodes) results in doubling the access time. Linear data structures include stack, queue, deque, and list.

This chapter shifts the focus to nonlinear classic data structures. These include trees of various types, heaps, and hash tables.

The benefit of using nonlinear data structures is efficiency. Access time to information stored in a tree or hash table is generally significantly faster than in a linear data structure.

13.1 TREE STRUCTURES

Tree structures are used to trace family ancestry, keep track of the winners in sports events, and define the chain of command within a business organization.

A tree has a single entry point called the **root**. From the root one may generally go in many directions, as the tree shown in Figure 13.1 demonstrates.

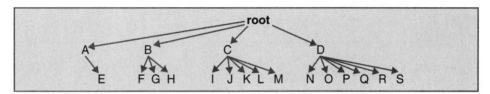

FIGURE 13.1 General tree structure

Here nodes E, F, G, H, I, J, K, L, M, N, O, P, Q, R, and S are leaf nodes because they do not "point" to any nodes below them. Each of these leaf nodes represents a possible termination point of a path that starts with the root node.

By long-standing convention, the root node of a tree is shown on top of the tree and the leaf nodes at the bottom (equivalent to looking at nature's trees from the vantage point of being upside down!).

Nodes A, B, C, and D are said to be the children of the root node. Nodes I, J, K, L, and M are the children of node C and the grandchildren of the root and so forth.

Only binary trees are discussed in this book.

13.2 BINARY TREE

A binary tree contains a root node as an entry point. If the tree is empty, the root is null. Each node in a binary tree is the root of a left sub-tree and a right sub-tree. These left and right sub-trees may be empty.

Figure 13.2 shows a typical binary tree.

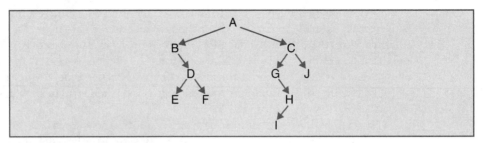

FIGURE 13.2 Binary tree

The left sub-tree from the root node A contains the nodes B, D, E, and F with B serving as its root. The right sub-tree from the root node A contains the nodes C, G, J, H, and I with node C serving as its root.

The root node is defined as being at level 0. Its children, if any, are at level 1. Its grandchildren, if any, are at level 2 and so on.

A binary tree is defined as perfectly balanced if each node has exactly two children except leaf nodes which have no children, and if every node has the same number of left and right descendents. Figure 13.3 shows a perfectly balanced tree that contains seven nodes.

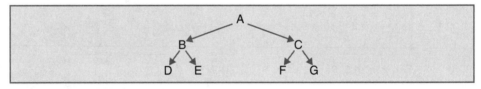

FIGURE 13.3 Perfectly balanced tree

Because a tree structure is nonlinear (there is no simple path that can take us from the entry point to the end of the tree), one challenge is determining how to traverse the tree. Such a traversal must visit each node exactly once.

13.3 BINARY TREE TRAVERSAL

There are three standard algorithms for traversing a binary tree. Each of these is recursive. The first of these to be discussed is pre-order traversal and is shown using the recursive method *Preorder* given in the following code:

```
public void Preorder(Node node) {
    if (node != null) { //
        Visit(node);
        Preorder(node.Left);
        Preorder(node.Right);
    }
}
```

The *Visit* command represents any operation that might be performed on a node when it is reached. The simplest operation might be outputting the value in the node.

For the balanced tree given in Figure 13.3, let us "walk" through the pre-order traversal. We always enter the tree through its root so the value of the root node A is passed to the recursive method *Preorder*. Because this node is not null, we visit the node. For our current purposes, we shall define *Visit* to mean output the node. So A is output.

The recursive call to the left takes us to node B. Because node B is not null we visit it and output B.

The recursive call to the left takes us to node D. Because node D is not null we visit it and output D.

The recursive call to the left next takes us to the left child of D, which is null. This causes the sentinel condition, *node != null*, to fail. The end brace of this recursive call is reached. The recursive runtime stack is popped, and the value of *node* equal to D is restored.

The recursive call to the right of D again takes us to null. This causes the stack to be popped once again and causes us to reach another ending brace of the recursive method. This causes the value of D's parent, B, to be restored from the stack, and the recursive call to its right takes us to node E. Because both of E's children are null, several pops from the recursive stack move us back to node A, which is restored from the stack.

The recursive call to the right of A takes us to node C. From there we go to F and then G. Further backtracking (restoring node values from the stack) empties the stack, and we exit the recursive method. The final sequence of nodes visited is: A, B, D, E, C, F, and G.

There is no need to make a table that records the runtime stack because the tree structure itself serves as a good roadmap. Each node has a clear parent so the sequence of recursive calls is always evident from the tree itself.

We next consider another recursive algorithm for traversing the tree, in-order traversal. The recursive method that accomplishes this is given in the following code:

```
public void Inorder(Node node) {
    if (node != null) { //
        Inorder(node.Left);
        Visit(node);
        Inorder(node.Right);
    }
}
```

Here the *Visit* method is sandwiched between ("In") the recursive call to the left and the recursive call to the right.

For the same tree as before (see Figure 13.3), the order of visitation is: D, B, E, A, F, C, and G.

Exercise 13.1

Explain the *Inorder* sequence of visitation and show the sequence of output when the tree shown in Figure 13.3 is used.

The third algorithm for binary tree traversal is post-order traversal. The recursive method that accomplishes this is given in the following code:

```
public void Postorder(Node node) {
    if (node != null) { //
        Postorder(node.Left);
        Postorder(node.Right);
        Visit(node); // Some arbitrary method that uses node
    }
}
```

Exercise 13.2

Show that the *Postorder* recursive method visits the nodes of Figure 13.3 in the order:

D, E, B, F, G, C, and A.

If the visit operation were defined as destroying the node, only the *Postorder* method would make any sense because it proceeds from the bottom of the tree to the top and does not cut any links in front of it.

13.4 BINARY SEARCH TREE

A special type of binary tree—binary search tree—provides the basis for efficient information storage and retrieval. We focus on such trees for the remainder of this chapter.

A binary search tree satisfies the following three conditions:

◆ Every node in a binary search tree has a value that is greater than any node in its left sub-tree.

◆ Every node in a binary search tree has a value that is smaller than any node in its right sub-tree.

◆ No duplicate values are allowed in a binary search tree.
Figure 13.4 shows a binary search tree with integer valued nodes.

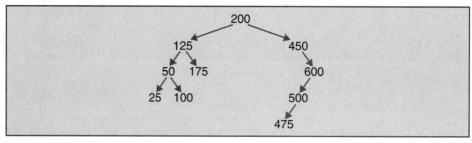

FIGURE 13.4 Binary search tree

Every node in the tree of Figure 13.4 satisfies the two conditions stated for binary search trees. For example, if the value of node 475 were changed to 400, the tree would no longer be a binary search tree because all the nodes in the right sub-tree of node 450 must be larger than 450 and this condition would be violated.

To see why a binary search tree offers the potential of efficiency, consider how one would search for the value 175, for example.

Starting at the root node the value being sought would be compared to the value of the root node. Because 175 is smaller than the root of 200, the binary search tree property guarantees that node 175, if present, must be in the left sub-tree of the root. Based on this, we descend to the left taking us to node 125. Because the node being sought (175) is larger than 125, we know that if 175 were present it would have to be in the right sub-tree of 125. Thus we descend to the right. A match-up occurs after three nodes are compared to 175. If the node we were searching for were 180 instead of 175, we would descend to the right of 175, hitting null. That would indicate that node 180 is not in the tree.

To insert a node into a binary search tree we employ a strategy similar to that of searching for a node. Consider the insertion of a node with value 75. We compare 75 against the root and descend to the left (because 75 is smaller than 200 and therefore must be placed in the left sub-tree). For the same reason, we descend to the left of 125, then to the right of node 50, and finally to the left of node 100. When we finally reach the value null (to the left of node 100) we place node 75 to the left of 100, as shown in Figure 13.5.

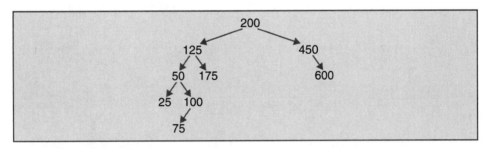

FIGURE 13.5 Insertion of value 75 into binary search tree

The computational effort required for searching for a node or inserting a node into a binary search tree is dependent on the depth of the tree. The more balanced the tree, the smaller the depth.

For a balanced or near-balanced binary search tree, the depth of the tree (number of levels below the root) is approximately equal to $log_2(n)$, where n is the number of nodes in the tree.

To appreciate the power of this relationship, consider a binary search tree that contains one million nodes and assume that it is reasonably balanced. The $log_2(1000000)$ is about 20. It would therefore take about 20 comparison operations to search for and locate a node in such a tree, compared with the possible one million comparison operations that might be needed in a linked list. This represents a gain of 50,000 to 1 in search performance. It is the search tree property of the tree that makes this efficiency possible, in addition to the assumption that the tree is reasonably balanced.

Is it reasonable to assume that a binary search tree is reasonably balanced? Consider the search tree formed by the following sequence of insertions: 10, 20, 30, 40, ...

Such a tree, shown in Figure 13.6, is essentially a linked list.

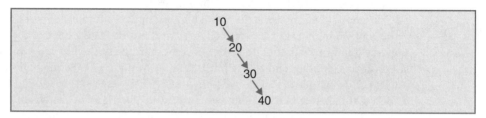

FIGURE 13.6 A linked-list type of binary search tree

How can we quantify the search efficiency of a binary search tree? As done in Chapter 14 of the book *Fundamentals of OOP and Data Structures in Java* by Richard Wiener and Lewis Pinson (Cambridge University Press, 2000), we define a metric called the Average Computational Effort (ACE).

The ACE metric represents the average number of comparison operations that would be required in searching for a randomly selected node assuming that all nodes have an equal likelihood of being chosen. The larger the ACE metric is for a given tree, the lower its search efficiency.

Let us consider the ACE values for the two trees shown in Figure 13.7.

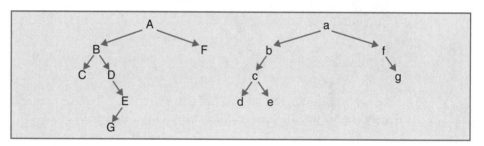

FIGURE 13.7 Comparing the ACE values of two binary search trees

To compute the ACE value of the tree on the left, if the A were sought, it would take one comparison operation. If either B or F were sought, each would take two comparison operations. If either C or D were sought, each would take three comparison operations. If E were sought, it would take four comparison operations. Finally, if G were sought, it would take five comparison operations. Therefore, the average number of comparison operations is:

$(1 + 2 + 2 + 3 + 3 + 4 + 5)/ 7 = 20 / 7$

The ACE value of the second tree is computed as:

$(1 + 2 + 2 + 3 + 3 + 4 + 4) / 7 = 19 / 7$

The second tree is therefore marginally more efficient than the first in its average search efficiency.

Exercise 13.3

What is the smallest possible ACE value for a tree with seven nodes? What is the largest possible ACE value for such a seven-node tree?

We next consider the more complex algorithm for deleting a node from a binary search tree. The tree that remains after a specified node is deleted must also be a binary search tree.

There are three special cases to consider. The easiest case is when the node being deleted is a leaf node. In this case we simply clip the node from the tree by cutting its stem. This is illustrated in Figure 13.8.

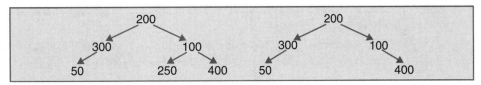

FIGURE 13.8 Deletion of node 250

The resulting tree must satisfy the search tree condition because the removal of the leaf node has no effect on nodes above it.

The second case to consider is the deletion of a node with only one child, such as node 100 in Figure 13.8. In this case we perform a linked-list type deletion by relinking the tree around the deleted node.

Figure 13.9 shows the result of removing node 100.

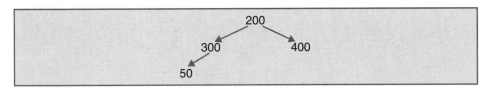

FIGURE 13.9 Deletion of node 100

The most challenging case is the deletion of a node that contains two children such as node 200 in Figure 13.8.

The algorithm for deletion when the node being deleted has two children is the following:

1. Find the in-order successor to the node being deleted. This is the next node to be visited after the node being deleted if an in-order traversal were applied.

2. Overwrite the item stored in the node being deleted with the item in the in-order successor node.

3. Delete the in-order successor node.

For the case of node 200 in Figure 13.9, the in-order successor node is node 400. If this value of 400 is used to overwrite the value of 200, and then the node containing 400 is deleted, the resulting tree is shown in Figure 13.10.

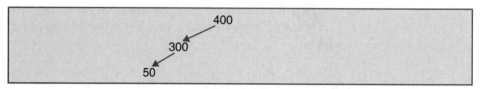

FIGURE 13.10 Tree after deletion of node 200

Exercise 13.4

Show that the value stored at the in-order successor node is always the value just larger than the value in the node being deleted.

Why is it useful to replace the problem of deleting a node with two children with the problem of deleting the in-order successor node, as is the case for the three-step algorithm given earlier?

It is easy to show that the in-order successor node never has more than a single child and is therefore easier to delete.

Consider the following example in Figure 13.11 in which we delete node 200.

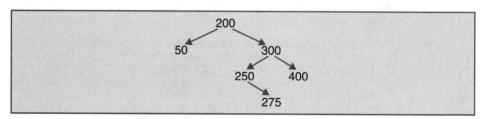

FIGURE 13.11 Another deletion example

The in-order successor of node 200 is node 250. It is evident that node 250 has only one child.

Exercise 13.5

Why is it impossible for the in-order successor node ever to have two children?

It is now time to go from concepts to C# implementation.

13.5 IMPLEMENTATION OF BINARY SEARCH TREES

A binary search tree is an implementation of the search table abstraction. The interface, *ISearchTable*, that defines the contract of a search table is given in Listing 13.1.

LISTING 13.1 Interface ISearchTable

```
public interface ISearchTable<T> : IContainer<T>, IEnumerable<T> {
    // Commands

    // Adds the unique object item since duplicates are not allowed
    // Generates an exception if a duplicate item is added.
    void Add(T item);

    // Removes the given item, if present. If the item is not
    // present, an exception is generated.
    void Remove(T item);

    // Queries

    // Return true if the item is present, otherwise false
    bool Contains(T item);
}
```

The *IEnumerable<T>* interface mandates that any class that implements *ISearchTable* implements *GetEnumerator*.

Listing 13.2 presents the *enum TypeOfTraversal* and the public methods of class *BinarySearchTree<T>*. The important private support methods are presented and discussed in separate listings.

LISTING 13.2 Public methods of class BinarySearchTree

```
public enum TypeOfTraversal { Preorder, Inorder, Postorder };

public class BinarySearchTree<T> : ISearchTable<T>
                            where T : IComparable {

    // Fields
    protected Node root;
    protected int numberElements;
    protected TypeOfTraversal traversalType;
    protected DoublyLinkedList<T> elements =
          new DoublyLinkedList<T>(); // Supports GetEnumerator
    protected int maxLevel; // Supports MaxLevel
    protected bool matchup = false;  Supports Contains

    // Properties
    public TypeOfTraversal TraversalType {
      set {
        traversalType = value;
      }
```

LISTING 13.2 Public methods of class BinarySearchTree (continued)

```
}
// Commands
public virtual void Add(T item) { // Redefined in AVLTree
    root = InsertNode(root, item);
    numberElements++;
}

public virtual void Remove(T item) { // Redefined in AVLTree
    root = DeleteNode(root, item);
      numberElements--;
      if (numberElements == 0) {
        root = null;
      }
}

public void MakeEmpty() {
    root = null;
    numberElements = 0;
}

// Queries
public bool Contains(T item) {
    matchup = false;
    Contains(root, item);
    return matchup;
}

public bool IsEmpty() {
    return numberElements == 0;
}

public int Size() {
    return numberElements;
}

public double ACEValue() {
    if (numberElements == 0) {
       return 0;
    } else {
        return (double) ComputeAceValue(root, 1) / numberElements;
    }
}

public int MaxLevel() {
    maxLevel = 0;
      ComputeMaxLevel(root, 0);
    return maxLevel;
}

public IEnumerator<T> GetEnumerator() {
    elements.MakeEmpty();
    if (traversalType == TypeOfTraversal.Preorder) {
      PreOrder(root);
    } else if (traversalType == TypeOfTraversal.Inorder) {
```

LISTING 13.2 Public methods of class BinarySearchTree (continued)

```
            InOrder(root);
        } else {
            PostOrder(root);
        }
        foreach (T value in elements) {
            yield return value;
        }
    }


    IEnumerator IEnumerable.GetEnumerator() {
        return null;
    }



    // Private methods presented in later source listings

    protected class Node {
        // Fields
        private T item;
        private Node left, right;
        private int balance; // Needed in class AVLTree later

        // Constructor
        public Node(T item) {
            this.item = item;
            left = right = null;
        }

        // Properties
        public Node Left {
            // Read-write get and set—details not shown
        }

        public Node Right {
            // Read-write get and set—details not shown
        }

        public T Item {
            // Read-write get and set—details not shown
        }

        public int Balance {
            // Read-write get and set—details not shown
        }

    }
}
```

Class *Node* includes the field *balance*. This field is not needed in class *BinarySearchTree* but is needed in class *AVLTree*, to be discussed later, so it is included.

For the same reason, the fields of *BinarySearchTree<T>* are protected. The methods *Add* and *Remove* are declared *virtual* because they will be redefined (using override) in the subclass *AVLTree*.

Many of the public methods do their work by invoking private support methods that are recursive. The root of the tree is passed to these private methods. Because nested class *Node* is hidden from the user of *BinarySearchTree*, the public methods take *item* of generic type *T* as input and cannot expect the user to pass the root node of the search tree because they have no access to this private information.

One of the fields of *BinarySearchTree* is of type *DoublyLinkedList<T>*, discussed in Chapter 12. This dynamic list is used to hold the items associated with one of the three traversal methods.

We consider method *Add* first. As shown in Listing 13.2, the private recursive support method *InsertNode* is used to accomplish most of the work. This method is presented in Listing 13.3.

LISTING 13.3 Method InsertNode

```
private Node InsertNode(Node node, T item) {
   if (node == null) {
     return new Node(item);
   } else if (item.CompareTo(node.Item) < 0) {
     node.Left = InsertNode(node.Left, item);
     return node;
   } else if (item.CompareTo(node.Item) > 0) {
     node.Right = InsertNode(node.Right, item);
     return node;
   }  else {
     throw new InvalidOperationException(
             "Cannot add duplicate object.");
   }
 }
```

The subtlety associated with the details of *InsertNode* needs to be discussed. Consider a binary search tree with integer values and a root node with value 200. *InsertNode* is invoked with an integer item of value 300. Let us walk through the details and uncover the subtlety.

Because *item*, 300, is larger than *node.Item* (200), the second else-if clause is executed. A recursive invocation of *InsertNode* with parameters *node.Right* and *item* occurs. The result is returned to *node.Right*. But *node.Right* is *null* because only the root node with value 200 exists in the tree.

The recursive call to *InsertNode* with *node* equal to *null* causes the *if* clause to be executed. Consider the following statement:

```
return new Node(item);
```

It causes a new node to be created and *item* placed within it. A reference to this new node is returned to the previous level of recursion, specifically to *node.Right*. This **implicit linkage** causes the root node to be linked to the right to the newly created node with value 300, producing the tree shown in Figure 13.12.

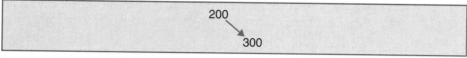

FIGURE 13.12 Implicitly linked tree

So the implicit linkage is a consequence of recursion—specifically the assignment at one level of recursion to a value returned by the one-deeper level of recursion.

For an arbitrary search tree, the recursive call causes the values of nodes in a search path to the leaf node just above the node to be inserted to be pushed onto the recursive stack. Then when the value of node becomes *null*, the newly created node is implicitly linked to the leaf node either to the right, as in the case shown in Figure 13.12, or the left, depending on whether the item being inserted is greater than or less than the value of the leaf node.

The private recursive *DeleteNode* method is more complex and requires the support of two additional recursive methods. These are presented in Listing 13.4.

LISTING 13.4 Method DeleteNode and methods that support it

```
private Node DeleteNode(Node node, T item) {
    if (node == null) {
        throw new InvalidOperationException(
                "item not in search tree.");
    }
    if (item.CompareTo(node.Item) < 0) {
        node.Left = DeleteNode(node.Left, item);
    } else if (item.CompareTo(node.Item) > 0) {
        node.Right = DeleteNode(node.Right, item);
    } else if (item.CompareTo(node.Item) == 0) { // Item found
        if (node.Left == null) { // No children or only a right child
            node = node.Right;
        } else if (node.Right == null) { // Only a left child
            node = node.Left;
        } else { // Two children
        // Deletes using the leftmost node of the right sub-tree
            T replaceWithValue = LeftMost(node.Right);
            node.Item = replaceWithValue;
            node.Right = DeleteLeftMost(node.Right);
        }
    }
    return node;
}

private T LeftMost(Node node) {
    if (node.Left == null) {
        return node.Item;
    } else {
        return LeftMost(node.Left);
    }
}
```

LISTING 13.4 Method DeleteNode and methods that support it (continued)

```
private Node DeleteLeftMost(Node node) {
   if (node.Left == null) {
     return node.Right;
   } else {
     node.Left = DeleteLeftMost(node.Left);
     return node;
   }
}
```

The recursive mechanism of implicit linkage is at work in method *DeleteNode* as it was in method *InsertNode* described previously.

We consider the case of deleting the root node in the tree shown in Figure 13.13.

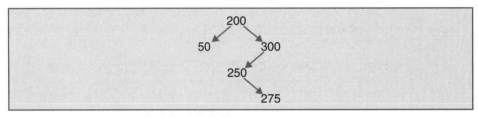

FIGURE 13.13 Root node to be deleted

When the node containing 200 is passed to *DeleteNode*, the *else* clause containing the comment "Two children" is executed.

The support method *LeftNode* with the node containing 300 as a parameter returns the node containing 250. The value 250 is assigned to the root node, and this overwrites the value of 200.

The method *DeleteLeftMost* is invoked with the node containing 300 as a parameter.

Exercise 13.6

Show how the *if* block in method *DeleteLeftMost*,

```
if (node.Left == null) {
   return node.Right;
}
```

causes the node containing 300 to be linked to the node containing 275 in the tree shown above. This is another example of implicit linkage resulting from recursion.

The *MakeEmpty* method, whose details are shown completely, assigns the root to *null*. With no further references to the root, it is eligible for automatic garbage collection. This in turn causes the two children of the root to have no further references to them, which make them eligible for garbage collection. This pattern propagates until every node of the tree is eligible for garbage collection.

Listing 13.5 presents the details of the private recursive support method *Contains*.

LISTING 13.5 Method Contains

```
private void Contains(Node node, T item) {
    if (node != null && !matchup) {
        if (node.Item.CompareTo(item) == 0) {
            matchup = true;
        }
        Contains(node.Left, item);
        Contains(node.Right, item);
    }
}
```

The private recursive *Contains* method is a pre-order traversal in disguise. The "visit" operation in this case compares the object in the visited node with the parameter *item*. If a matchup is found, the field *matchup* is set to true. As we shall see, many of the support methods in this and other tree-based classes use a traversal as the basis for accomplishing their work.

Listing 13.6 presents the support method *ComputeAceValue*.

LISTING 13.6 Method ComputeAceValue

```
private int ComputeAceValue(Node node, int level) {
    if (node != null) {
        return level + ComputeAceValue(node.Left, level + 1) +
                        ComputeAceValue(node.Right, level + 1);
    } else {
        return 0;
    }
}
```

This is a relatively simple recursion. At each succeding level, if the node is not *null*, the value returned equals the level plus the value at the next lower level. This corresponds to the number of comparison operations that are required to reach the node at the specified level. When the total value is divided by the number of nodes, the desired average computational effort (ACE) is computed.

Listing 13.7 presents the details of the support method *ComputeMaxLevel*.

LISTING 13.7 Method ComputeMaxLevel

```
private void ComputeMaxLevel(Node node, int level) {
    if (node != null) {
        ComputeMaxLevel(node.Left, level + 1);
        ComputeMaxLevel(node.Right, level + 1);
        if (node.Right == null &&
            node.Left == null && level > maxLevel) {
            maxLevel = level;
        }
    }
}
```

Exercise 13.7

Explain how the recursive support method presented in Listing 13.7 works.

Listing 13.8 presents the remaining support methods that perform the three types of traversal.

LISTING 13.8 Three traversal methods

```
private void PreOrder(Node node) {
   if (node != null) {
      elements.AddRear(node.Item);
      PreOrder(node.Left);
      PreOrder(node.Right);
   }
}

private void InOrder(Node node) {
   if (node != null) {
      InOrder(node.Left);
      elements.AddRear(node.Item);
      InOrder(node.Right);
   }
}

private void PostOrder(Node node) {
   if (node != null) {
      PostOrder(node.Left);
      PostOrder(node.Right);
      elements.AddRear(node.Item);
   }
}
```

As the traversals progress, the *DoublyLinkedList elements* are filled with the items contained within the search tree.

13.6 GRAPHICAL DISPLAY OF BINARY TREES

Suppose we want to display a binary tree such as a search tree as items are inserted and removed. Such a tree laboratory might be useful in allowing you to experiment with different sequences of insertions and deletions while being able to see immediately the effect of such operations on the appearance of the tree.

Only objects of type integer will be allowed in the tree. Although obviously not robust, this will suffice in meeting the goal of allowing the user to experiment with different input and deletion sequences. The number of displayable integer objects will also be limited by the available screen real-estate but sufficient to allow for useful experimentation.

The interface to the GUI application that will be constructed is shown in Figure 13.14.

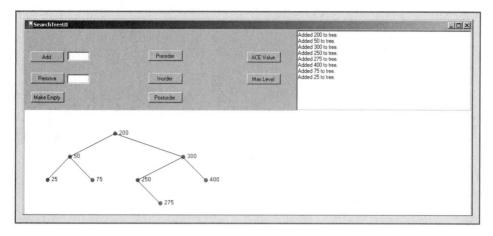

FIGURE 13.14 GUI application that displays tree

In addition to displaying the tree structure after each integer is added or removed, it displays a pre-order, in-order, post-order traversal of the tree, the ACE value, and the maximum level. A log of all events is written to a *RichEdit* panel in the upper-right portion of the interface.

A class *DrawTree* is added within class BinarySearchTree, as another nested class (in addition to class *Node*). Its details are presented in Listing 13.9.

LISTING 13.9 Class DrawTree

```
/*
 * This inner class renders a binary search tree to the Panel that is
 * passed in as a parameter in the constructor.
 */
public class DrawTree {

    // Fields
    private int size;
    private Node[] nodes;
    private int[] levels;
    private int nodesIndex = -1;
    private const int diameter = 4;
    private Panel panel;
    private Graphics g; // From panel
    private Color color;
    private Node root;

    // Constructor

    /*
     * root is the root node of the binary search tree.
     * size is the number of nodes in the tree.
     * panel is the Panel component upon which to
     * render the tree.
     * color is used for the nodes and links
     */
```

LISTING 13.9 Class DrawTree (continued)

```
public DrawTree(BinarySearchTree<T> tree,
                Panel panel,
                Color color) {
  root = tree.root;
    size = tree.Size();
    this.panel = panel;
  this.color = color;
    if (root != null) {
       ConstructTree();
    }
}

private void ConstructTree() {
  g = panel.CreateGraphics();
    g.Clear(Color.White);
    nodesIndex = -1;
    nodes = new Node[size];
  levels = new int[size];
    Build(root, 1);
    for (int index = 0; index < size; index++) {
      DrawNode(new Point(58 + index * 50,
                   levels[index] * 50-10),
         nodes[index].Item.ToString());
        if (nodes[index].Left != null) {
             Node left = nodes[index].Left;
             int indexLeft = Index(left);
             DrawLineSegment(new Point(50 + index * 50,
                             levels[index] * 50),
                          new Point(50 + indexLeft * 50,
                          levels[indexLeft] * 50));
       }
        if (nodes[index].Right != null) {
           Node right = nodes[index].Right;
           int indexRight = Index(right);
           DrawLineSegment(new Point(50 + index * 50,
                           levels[index] * 50),
                        new Point(50 + indexRight * 50,
                        levels[indexRight] * 50));
       }
    }
}

private void Build(Node node, int level) {
   if (node != null) {
      Build(node.Left, level + 1);
        nodesIndex++;
        nodes[nodesIndex] = node;
        levels[nodesIndex] = level;
      Build(node.Right, level + 1);
   }
}
```

LISTING 13.9 Class DrawTree (continued)

```
    private void DrawNode(Point pt, String str) {
        g.DrawArc(new Pen(new SolidBrush(color), 5),
            new Rectangle(pt.X-9, pt.Y + 8, diameter,
                    diameter), 0, 360);
            g.DrawString(str, new Font("Times Roman", 9,
                    FontStyle.Regular),
                        new SolidBrush(Color.Black), pt.X, pt.Y);
    }

    private void DrawLineSegment(Point pt1, Point pt2) {
        g.DrawLine(new Pen(new SolidBrush(Color.Black), 1), pt1, pt2);
    }

    private int Index(Node node) {
        for (int i = 0; i < size; i++) {
        if (nodes[i] == node) {
            return i;
            }
        }
        return -1;
    }
}
```

It will be largely left to you to determine the details of class *DrawTree*. Some guiding thoughts are the following:

◆ Method *Build* performs an in-order traversal of the search tree that is to be displayed.

◆ As it "visits" each node, it inserts the node into an array, *nodes*, and the level of the node into an array, *levels*.

◆ After invoking *Build*, the command *ConstructTree* invokes the commands *DrawNode* and *DrawLineSegment* in a for-loop that iterates through all the entries in the *nodes* and *levels* arrays.

Exercise 13.8

Walk through the details of method *ConstructTree* in class *DrawTree* and explain how this method renders the binary tree onto the *Panel* component that is input to the constructor.

The details of the class *SearchTreeUI* that contains the details of the GUI application that are not automatically generated by the IDE are presented in Listing 13.10.

LISTING 13.10 Class SearchTreeUI

```
using System;
using System.Collections.Generic;
using System.ComponentModel;
using System.Data;
using System.Drawing;
using System.Text;
using System.Windows.Forms;

namespace SearchTrees {

    partial class SearchTreeUI : Form {
        // Fields
        private BinarySearchTree<int> searchTree =
            new BinarySearchTree<int>();
        public SearchTreeUI() {
            InitializeComponent();
        }

        public static void Main() {
            SearchTreeUI app = new SearchTreeUI();
            Application.Run(app);
        }

        private void addBtn_Click(object sender, EventArgs e) {
            String addStr = addBox.Text.Trim();
            int addValue = 0;
            try {
                addValue = Convert.ToInt32(addStr);
                searchTree.Add(addValue);
                BinarySearchTree<int>.DrawTree drawTree =
                    new BinarySearchTree<int>.DrawTree(searchTree,
                                                panel, Color.Red);
                addBox.Text = "";
                addBox.Focus();
                actionBox.AppendText("Added " + addValue +
                            " to tree.\n");
            } catch (Exception) {
                MessageBox.Show("Cannot add specified value.");
            }
        }

        private void removeBtn_Click(object sender, EventArgs e) {
            String removeStr = removeBox.Text.Trim();
            int removeValue = 0;
            try {
                removeValue = Convert.ToInt32(removeStr);
                searchTree.Remove(removeValue);
```

LISTING 13.10 Class SearchTreeUI (continued)

```
                BinarySearchTree<int>.DrawTree drawTree =
                    new BinarySearchTree<int>.DrawTree(searchTree,
                            panel, Color.Red);
                removeBox.Text = "";
                removeBox.Focus();
                actionBox.AppendText("Removed " + removeValue +
                            " from tree.\n");
            } catch (Exception) {
                MessageBox.Show("Cannot remove specified value.");
            }


        }

        private void makeEmptyBtn_Click(object sender, EventArgs e) {
            searchTree.MakeEmpty();
            Graphics g = panel.CreateGraphics();
            g.Clear(Color.White);
        }

        private void SearchTreeUI_Resize(object sender, EventArgs e) {
            if (searchTree != null) {
                BinarySearchTree<int>.DrawTree drawTree =
                    new BinarySearchTree<int>.DrawTree(searchTree,
                            panel, Color.Red);
            }
        }

        private void preOrderBtn_Click(object sender, EventArgs e) {
            searchTree.TraversalType = TypeOfTraversal.Preorder;
            actionBox.AppendText("Preorder traversal: " );
            foreach (int value in searchTree) {
                actionBox.AppendText(value + " ");
            }
            actionBox.AppendText("\n");
        }

        private void inOrderBtn_Click(object sender, EventArgs e) {
            searchTree.TraversalType = TypeOfTraversal.Inorder;
            actionBox.AppendText("Inorder traversal: ");
            foreach (int value in searchTree) {
                actionBox.AppendText(value + " ");
            }
            actionBox.AppendText("\n");
        }

        private void postOrderBtn_Click(object sender, EventArgs e) {
            searchTree.TraversalType = TypeOfTraversal.Postorder;
            actionBox.AppendText("Postorder traversal: ");
            foreach (int value in searchTree) {
                actionBox.AppendText(value + " ");
            }
```

LISTING 13.10 Class SearchTreeUI (continued)

```
            actionBox.AppendText("\n");
        }

        // Restores graphics if the screen is "invalidated"
        private void SearchTreeUI_Validated(object sender,
                        EventArgs e) {
            if (searchTree != null) {
                BinarySearchTree<int>.DrawTree drawTree =
                    new BinarySearchTree<int>.DrawTree(searchTree,
                            panel, Color.Red);
            }
        }

        private void aceValueBtn_Click(object sender, EventArgs e) {
            actionBox.AppendText("ACE value: " +
                            searchTree.ACEValue());
            actionBox.AppendText("\n");
        }

        private void maxLevelBtn_Click(object sender, EventArgs e) {
            actionBox.AppendText("Max level: " +
                            searchTree.MaxLevel());
            actionBox.AppendText("\n");
        }
    }
}
```

It is interesting to note how an instance of the public nested class *DrawTree* is constructed. Such a nested class behaves as a static class.

```
BinarySearchTree<int>.DrawTree drawTree =
                new BinarySearchTree<int>.DrawTree(searchTree,
                            panel, Color.Red);
```

The remaining details, although tedious, are straightforward and left to the reader to study.

13.7 BALANCED SEARCH TREES

The ACE value of a search tree is minimum when the tree is perfectly balanced. This is possible only for trees that contain exactly $2^n - 1$ nodes, where n is an integer. Therefore it is impossible for most trees to be perfectly balanced. Nevertheless it is desirable to strive to obtain trees whose ACE value is as low as possible in order to provide the fastest average search time.

Before we delve more deeply into the theory and implementation of balanced search trees, it is useful to obtain a better grasp of what we are dealing with.

Consider a search tree constructed from a random sequence of double values. Such a search tree is called a random search tree. Consider in particular a random search tree that contains $2^{11}-1 = 2047$ nodes. Such a tree can in theory be perfectly balanced, although to achieve this would take a carefully chosen sequence of input values.

The smallest possible ACE value for a tree with 2047 perfectly balanced nodes is: $(1 + 2 * 2 + 4 * 3 + \ldots + 2^{10} * 11) / 2047 = 10.01$.

The largest possible ACE value would be for a tree with sequentially increasing or decreasing values (a linked list type of tree). Its ACE value is: $(1 + 2 + 3 + \ldots 2047) / 2047 = 1024$. There is therefore roughly a 100 to 1 ratio between the worst and best possible search tree containing 2047 nodes.

So where would a random search tree of 2047 fall within this range from roughly 10 to 1024?

It might be tempting to guess somewhere in the middle, because in the absence of any analysis or other information such guesses are generally safe—but in this case quite incorrect.

Exercise 13.9

Construct a console-based simulation experiment in which a set of 50 separate random search trees, each containing 2047 randomly generated double values, is constructed. Find the ACE value of each of these 50 trees and report the average of the 50 ACE values. Empty each search tree before creating the next search tree.

You will find after completing Exercise 13.9 that the ACE value for such a randomly generated tree containing 2047 nodes is approximately 13.6. This is only 36% worse than the best possible ACE value of approximately 10. It might therefore be tempting to conclude that most binary search trees have excellent search properties or are close to perfectly balanced.

As Exercise 13.10 demonstrates, this is simply not true.

Exercise 13.10

Construct another console-based simulation experiment in which an array of 2047 nodes is filled with randomly generated double values. Apply one iteration of bubble-sort to the values in this array. This has the effect of slightly ordering the data within the array. Construct a tree from this slightly ordered data and record its ACE value. Continue to perform additional iterations of bubble-sort, each time constructing a binary search tree from the increasingly ordered data and recording the ACE value of the tree so constructed. Present a table of ACE values as a function of the number of iterations of bubble-sort. Empty each search tree before creating the next search tree.

You will see upon completing Exercise 13.10 that the ACE value is sensitive to the ordering of data and increases rapidly as the ordering of data within the array increases. Expressed another way, as the data within the array deviates more and more from random, the ACE value grows quickly.

In "real-world" applications it can be assumed that it is rare to find circumstances in which the data sequence being used to construct a binary search tree satifies the stringent statistical requirements associated with pure randomness. This is because typically such input data has been processed and at least partially ordered upstream from where the binary tree gets this information. Therefore it is probable that the ACE value of a binary search tree constructed with such real-world data is closer to the middle of the range rather than at the lower end of the range as is the case with a random sequence of input data.

This then motivates the question, can one intervene during the process of constructing a binary search tree and take corrective measures to ensure that the resulting tree is well balanced? The answer is yes.

In 1962, two Russian mathematicians, Adelson-Velskii and E.M. Landis, defined a useful definition of balance and described algorithms for insertion and deletion that would guarantee that the tree resulting from the use of their insertion and deletion algorithms would continue to be balanced, in the sense that they defined such balance. In recognition of the significance of their work, their trees have become known as AVL trees.

We explore some of the theory of AVL trees first and then show an implementation.

13.8 DEFINITION OF AVL TREE

A binary search tree is an AVL tree if and only if for every node in the tree the difference between the maximum depth of the right sub-tree minus the maximum depth of the left sub-tree is less than 2 in magnitude. That is the difference can be -1, 0, or 1.

As an example, consider the balance of each node in the following tree shown in Figure 13.15. The balance for each node is shown next to the node. Balances of 0 are not shown.

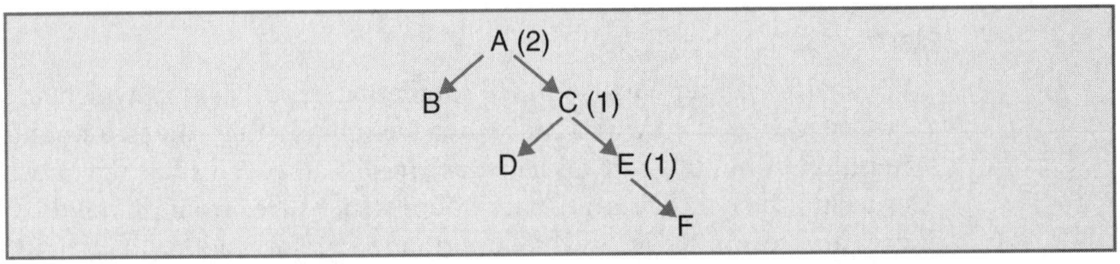

FIGURE 13.15 AVL balance for simple tree

The tree in Figure 13.15 is not an AVL tree because of the presence of a balance of 2 for node A.

The search tree in Figure 13.16 is AVL balanced.

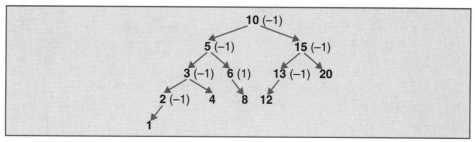

FIGURE 13.16 AVL balanced tree

13.9 NODE ROTATION

Before discussing the algorithms for insertion and deletion for AVL trees, it is necessary to understand the mechanics of node rotation within a search tree.

For example, a right rotation with respect to node 10 in Figure 13.16 is achieved by twisting the tree structure down to the right on node 10. In response to such a twist, node 5 rises to become the new root node as node 10 drops to its right. Most of the tree structure remains intact. The tree structure (without balances shown) resulting from such a right rotate on node 10 is shown in Figure 13.17.

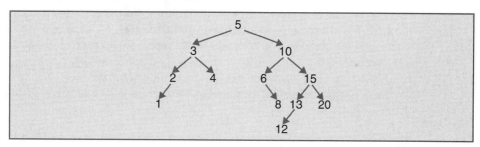

FIGURE 13.17 Result of right rotation on node 10 in Figure 13.16

When node 10 becomes the right child of node 5 because of the twist to the right, nodes 6 and 8 become orphans. They get placed back into the tree using the following reasoning: they are both greater than 5 and smaller than 10. This forces them to be placed as shown in Figure 13.17.

To illustrate node rotation further, consider a left rotate on node 10 in Figure 13.17. Node 15 rises upwards to replace node 10, which falls to the left and becomes the left child of 15. The resulting tree is shown in Figure 13.18.

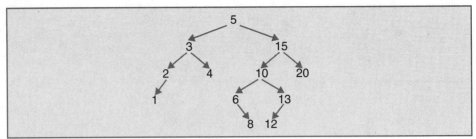

FIGURE 13.18 Result of left rotation on node 10 in Figure 13.17

The orphan nodes 13 and 12 are smaller than 15 and larger than 10 and are therefore placed where they are shown in Figure 13.18.

Exercise 13.11

Perform a right rotate on node 5 in Figure 13.18 and show the resulting tree.

Exercise 13.12

Perform a left rotate on node 5 in Figure 13.18 and show the resulting tree.

How much computational work is involved in achieving node rotation?

The answer is relatively little. Only two links in the entire tree are actually modified. This is true independent of the size of the tree. So it takes as much computational effort to perform a left or right rotation on a node in a tree of 10 nodes as a tree of 1,000,000 nodes.

Listing 13.11 presents the details of methods *LeftRotate* and *RightRotate*.

Each of these methods uses a ref parameter so that a different node is returned than is input.

Exercise 13.13

Using a diagram, walk through the details of *RightRotate* and demonstrate that it works properly for a binary search tree with the sequence of insertions 200, 50, 300 and the rotation performed on node 200.

LISTING 13.11 Method LeftRotate and RightRotate

```
private void RightRotate(ref Node node) {
    Node left = node.left;
    Node temp = left.right;
    left.right = node;      // Change a link
    node.left = temp;       // Change a link
    node = left;            // return a different node
}
```

LISTING 13.11 Method LeftRotate and RightRotate (continued)

```
private void LeftRotate(ref Node node) {
    Node right = node.Right;
    Node temp = right.Left;
    right.Left = node; // Change a link
    node.Right = temp; // Change a link
    node = right;      // return a different node
}
```

13.10 INSERTION INTO AN AVL TREE

The algorithm designed by Adelson-Velskii and Landis for insertion into an AVL tree is the following:

1. Perform an ordinary insertion into the search tree. Recompute the balances of all the nodes. If the tree is still an AVL tree, exit.

2. Starting at the node inserted, backtrack up the search path toward the root node. If a combination of nodes is found in which the parent has a balance of +/− 2 and the node a balance of +/− 1, if the signs of the node and parent balance are the same, a type 1 configuration exists, and if the signs of the node and parent balance are the opposite, a type 2 configuration exists.

3. If the configuration is type 1, perform a single rotation on the parent node whose balance is +/− 2 in a direction to restore balance.

4. If the configuration is type 2, perform a sequence of two rotations. The first rotation is on the node whose balance is +/− 1 in a direction to restore balance. The second rotation, always in a direction opposite the first rotation, is on the parent node whose balance is +/− 2.

    We illustrate this algorithm with the two examples that follow.

    Consider first the AVL tree shown in Figure 13.19.

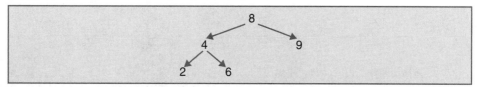

FIGURE 13.19 Initial AVL tree

The value 3 is to be inserted.

After an ordinary binary search tree insertion, the tree is as shown in Figure 13.20.

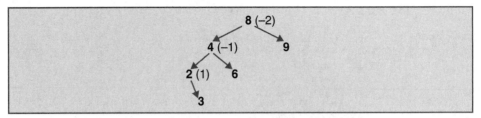

FIGURE 13.20 AVL tree just after ordinary insertion of node 3

Traversing up the search path from node 3 to the root, when the node is 4, the type 1 configuration is discovered because of the −1, −2 combination. Because the signs are the same, the configuration is type 1.

The AVL insertion algorithm specifies that a rotation needs to be performed on the node whose value is +/− 2 in "a direction to restore balance." Clearly this is a right rotation on the root node. After this rotation is performed, the resulting AVL tree is shown in Figure 13.21.

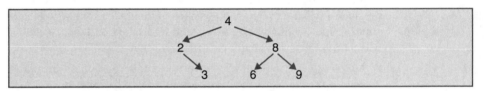

FIGURE 13.21 Final AVL tree after rotational correction

The fact that the algorithm works in this case does not of course demonstrate that it works in all cases. This proof was carried out by Adelson-Velskii and Landis as part of their landmark work in 1962 and is beyond the scope of this book.

Consider the insertion of node 5 into the initial AVL tree shown in Figure 13.19. After the ordinary insertion is completed, the tree is as shown in Figure 13.22.

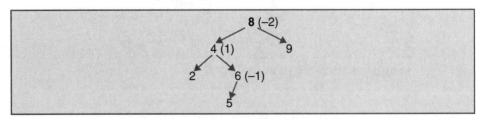

FIGURE 13.22 AVL tree after ordinary insertion of node 5

As we traverse upwards from the inserted node 5 toward the root, the 1, −2 combination suggests a type 2 configuration.

This requires that a left rotation on node 4 (the node with a 1 balance) and a right rotation on node 8 (the node with balance −2).

Figure 13.23 shows the two rotations and the resulting AVL tree.

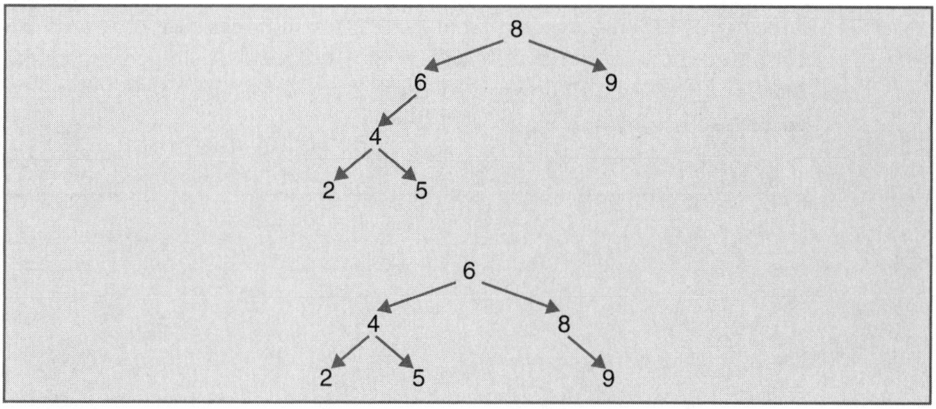

FIGURE 13.23 Type 2 pair of rotational corrections

13.11 DELETION FROM AN AVL TREE

The algorithm for deletion from an AVL tree follows closely the algorithm for insertion with only a few differences.

1. Perform an ordinary search tree deletion from the existing AVL tree.

2. Recompute the balances of each node.

3. If the tree continues to be an AVL tree, exit.

4. If the tree is not an AVL tree, traverse the search path from the node being deleted to the root node. Stop when one of the following combinations of balances is found concerning the node in the search path and its parent:

   (a) The node has a balance of $+/-1$ and its parent a balance of $+/-2$. Determine whether the configuration is type 1 or type 2, as before. Perform the necessary single or double rotations based on the type of configuration.

   (b) The node has a balance of 0 and its parent a balance of $+/-2$. This situation can never occur with AVL insertion. Consider this a type 1 configuration and perform the necessary single rotation on the parent node with balance of $+/-2$.

   (c) Re-evaluate the balances of all the nodes. There is a possibility that as a consequence of the rotation performed in steps (a) or (b), another configuration of either type 1 or type 2 exists because of a node that now has a balance of $+/-2$. After correcting the new imbalance, continue step (c) until the root node is reached or there are no further nodes going up the search path toward the root that have balances of $+/-2$.

The need for step (c) is demonstrated with the following example. Consider again the binary search tree given in Figure 13.16. Suppose node 20 is deleted.

This causes node 15 to acquire a balance of −2 and its left child, node 13, a balance of −1. Moving upward from node 20 being deleted to node 15, a −2, 0 type 1 configuration, as described in 4b previously, occurs. A single right rotate on node 15 brings 13 upwards, 15 downward, and 12 upwards. The tree following this rotational correction is shown in Figure 13.24.

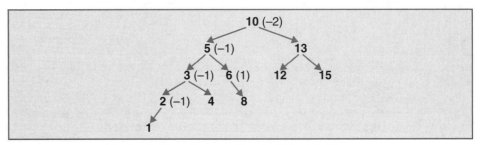

FIGURE 13.24 First rotational correction in AVL deletion

Figure 13.24 shows that the effect of bringing node 12 up from level 3 to level 2 as a result of the right rotate on node 15 causes node 10 to attain a balance of −2 instead of its earlier balance of −1.

Step 4c requires another rotation, a right rotate on node 10, to correct this latest imbalance.

Figure 13.25 shows the AVL tree resulting from this final rotational correction.

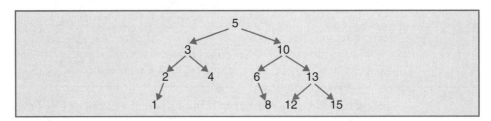

FIGURE 13.25 AVL resulting from final rotational correction during deletion

13.12 IMPLEMENTATION OF AVL INSERTION AND DELETION

Note: This section is for the more advanced reader and may be skipped.

The details of insertion and deletion are complex. Although the implementation for methods *Add* and *Remove* for an AVL tree are presented in class AVL in Listing 13.12, the details are not explained. Hopefully the variable names that provide self-documentation and the comments interspersed throughout the code will help the more advanced reader decipher the myriad details involved in the *Add* and *Remove* methods. The public versions of each of these methods invoke private overloaded support methods (methods with the same name but different signatures). The use of reference variables for several of the private support methods allows explicit linking. This linking is indicated with comments.

Class *AVLTree<T>* inherits from class *BinarySearchTree<T>* because the only two methods that are redefined are *Add* and *Remove*. The UML diagram that shows the relationship between the relevant classes is shown in Figure 13.26.

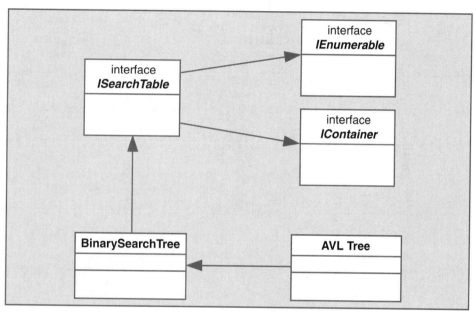

FIGURE 13.26 UML diagram of classes related to AVLTree

LISTING 13.12 Class AVLTree

```
using System;
using System.Collections.Generic;

namespace SearchTrees {

    public class AVLTree<T> : BinarySearchTree<T>
                    where T : IComparable {

        // Fields
        private bool sentinel; // Used in Add and Delete to control
                               // recursion
        private Node mark; // Support node for AVL deletion

        // Commands
        public override void Add(T item) {
            sentinel = false;
            Add(ref root, item);
            numberElements++;
```

LISTING 13.12 Class AVLTree (continued)

```
        }

    public override void Remove(T item) {
        if (numberElements == 0) {
            throw new InvalidOperationException(
                    "Cannot delete from empty tree.");
        }
        sentinel = false;
        Remove(ref root, item);
        numberElements--;
    }

    private void Add(ref Node node, T item) {
        Node child, grandChild;
        if (node == null) { // Bottom of tree is reached
            sentinel = true;
            node = new Node(item);
        } else if (item.CompareTo(node.Item) < 0) {
            Node left = node.Left;
            Add(ref left, item);
            node.Left = left; // Link to the node added
            if (sentinel) {
                switch (node.Balance) {
                    case 1:
                        node.Balance = 0;
                        sentinel = false;
                        break;
                    case 0:
                        node.Balance = -1;
                        break;
                    case -1:
                        child = node.Left;
                        if (child.Balance == -1) {
                            // Right rotate
                            node.Left = child.Right;
                            child.Right = node;
                            node.Balance = 0;
                            node = child;
                        } else {
                            // Left right rotate
                            grandChild = child.Right;
                            child.Right = grandChild.Left;
                            grandChild.Left = child;
                            node.Left = grandChild.Right;
                            grandChild.Right = node;
                            if (grandChild.Balance == -1) {
                                node.Balance = 1;
                            } else {
                                node.Balance = 0;
                            }
                            if (grandChild.Balance == 1) {
                                child.Balance = -1;
                            } else {
                                child.Balance = 0;
```

LISTING 13.12 Class AVLTree (continued)

```
                              }
                              node = grandChild;
                         }
                         node.Balance = 0;
                         sentinel = false;
                         break;
                    }
               }
          } else if (item.CompareTo(node.Item) > 0) {
               Node right = node.Right;
               Add(ref right, item);
               node.Right = right;  // Link to the node added
               if (sentinel) {
                    switch (node.Balance) {
                         case -1:
                              node.Balance = 0;
                              sentinel = false;
                              break;
                         case 0:
                              node.Balance = 1;
                              break;
                         case 1:
                              child = node.Right;
                              if (child.Balance == 1) {
                                   // Left rotate
                                   node.Right = child.Left;
                                   child.Left = node;
                                   node.Balance = 0;
                                   node = child;
                              } else {
                                   // Right left rotate
                                   grandChild = child.Left;
                                   child.Left = grandChild.Right;
                                   grandChild.Right = child;
                                   node.Right = grandChild.Left;
                                   grandChild.Left = node;
                                   if (grandChild.Balance == 1) {
                                        node.Balance = -1;
                                   } else {
                                        node.Balance = 0;
                                   }
                                   if (grandChild.Balance == -1) {
                                        child.Balance = 1;
                                   } else {
                                        child.Balance = 0;
                                   }
                                   node = grandChild;
                              }
                              node.Balance = 0;
                              sentinel = false;
                              break;
                    }
               }
          }
```

LISTING 13.12 Class AVLTree (continued)

```
        }

    private void Remove(ref Node node, T item) {
        if (node == null) {
            throw new InvalidOperationException(
                item.ToString() + " not present so cannot delete.");
        } else if (item.CompareTo(node.Item) < 0) {
            Node left = node.Left;
            Remove(ref left, item);
            node.Left = left; // Link node to value returned from
                              //    recursive call to Remove
            if (sentinel) {
                Rebalance1(ref node);
            }
        } else if (item.CompareTo(node.Item) > 0) {
            Node right = node.Right;
            Remove(ref right, item);
            node.Right = right; // Link node to value returned from
                                //    recursive call to Remove
            if (sentinel) {
                Rebalance2(ref node);
            }
        } else { // found a matchup
            if (node.Right == null) {
                Node temp = node;
                node = temp.Left;
                sentinel = true;
                temp = null;
            } else if (node.Left == null) {
                Node temp = node;
                node = temp.Right;
                sentinel = true;
                temp = null;
            } else {
                Node right = node.Right;
                Delete(ref right, node);
                node.Right = right; // Link node to return of
                                    //          Delete
                if (sentinel) {
                    Rebalance2(ref node);
                }
                mark = null;
            }
        }
    }

    private void Delete(ref Node r, Node node) {
        if (r.Left != null) {
            Node left = r.Left;
            Delete(ref left, node);
            r.Left = left;
```

LISTING 13.12 Class AVLTree (continued)

```
            if (sentinel) {
                Rebalance1(ref r);
            }
        } else {
            node.Item = r.Item;
            mark = r;
            r = r.Right;
            sentinel = true;
        }
    }

    private void Rebalance1(ref Node node) {
        Node child, grandChild;
        int balance1, balance2;
        switch (node.Balance) {
            case -1:
                node.Balance = 0;
                break;
            case 0:
                node.Balance = 1;
                sentinel = false;
                break;
            case 1:
                child = node.Right;
                balance1 = child.Balance;
                if (balance1 >= 0) {
                    // Single left rotate
                    node.Right = child.Left;
                    child.Left = node;
                    if (balance1 == 0) {
                        node.Balance = 1;
                        child.Balance = -1;
                        sentinel = false;
                    } else {
                        node.Balance = 0;
                        child.Balance = 0;
                    }
                    node = child;
                } else {
                    // Right left rotate
                    grandChild = child.Left;
                    balance2 = grandChild.Balance;
                    child.Left = grandChild.Right;
                    grandChild.Right = child;
                    node.Right = grandChild.Left;
                    grandChild.Left = node;
                    if (balance2 == 1) {
                        node.Balance = -1;
                    } else {
                        node.Balance = 0;
                    }
                    if (balance2 == -1) {
                        child.Balance = 1;
```

LISTING 13.12   Class AVLTree (continued)

```
                } else {
                    child.Balance = 0;
                }
                node = grandChild;
                grandChild.Balance = 0;
            }
            break;
    }
}

private void Rebalance2(ref Node node) {
    Node child, grandChild;
    int balance1, balance2;
    switch (node.Balance) {
        case 1:
            node.Balance = 0;
            break;
        case 0:
            node.Balance = -1;
            sentinel = false;
            break;
        case -1:
            child = node.Left;
            balance1 = child.Balance;
            if (balance1 <= 0) {
                // Single right rotate
                node.Left = child.Right;
                child.Right = node;
                if (balance1 == 0) {
                    node.Balance = -1;
                    child.Balance = 1;
                    sentinel = false;
                } else {
                    node.Balance = 0;
                    child.Balance = 0;
                }
                node = child;
            } else {
                // Left right rotate
                grandChild = child.Right;
                balance2 = grandChild.Balance;
                child.Right = grandChild.Left;
                grandChild.Left = child;
                node.Left = grandChild.Right;
                grandChild.Right = node;
                if (balance2 == -1) {
                    node.Balance = 1;
                } else {
                    node.Balance = 0;
                }
                if (balance2 == 1) {
                    child.Balance = -1;
                } else {
                    child.Balance = 0;
                }
```

LISTING 13.12 Class AVLTree (continued)

```
                                node = grandChild;
                                grandChild.Balance = 0;
                        }
                        break;
                }
            }
        }
    }
```

Some interesting facts related to AVL insertion and deletion follows.

◆ When inserting into an AVL tree, approximately 50 percent of such insertions require no rotational correction. Among the roughly 50 percent of insertions that require rotation, about half require one rotation (type 1 configuration) and half require two rotations (type 2 configuration).

◆ When deleting from an AVL tree, approximately 80 percent of such deletions require no rotational correction. Among the roughly 20 percent of insertions that require rotation, half are of type 1 and half of type 2. Only rarely are multiple rotations up the search path needed.

13.13 RED-BLACK TREES

A fascinating and important balanced binary search tree is the **red-black** tree. Rudolf Bayer invented this important tree structure in 1972, about 10 years after the introduction of AVL trees. He is also credited with the invention of the B-tree, a structure used extensively in database systems. Bayer referred to his red-black trees as "symmetric binary B-trees."

Red-black trees, as they are now known, like AVL trees, are "self-balancing." Whenever a new object is inserted or deleted, the resulting tree continues to satisfy the conditions required to be a red-black tree. The computational complexity for insertion or deletion can be shown to be $O(log_2 n)$, similar to an AVL tree.

Red-black trees are important in practice. They are used as the basis for Java's implementation of its standard *SortedSet* collection class. There is currently no comparable collection in the C# standard collections, so a C# implementation of red-black trees might be useful.

The rules that define a red-black tree are interesting because they are less constrained than the rather strict rules associated with an AVL tree. Each node is assigned a color of red or black. This can be accomplished using a field of type *bool* in class *Node* (true if the node is red and false if it is black).

The formal rules that define a red-black binary search tree are the following:

1. Every node is colored either red or black.

2. The root node is always black.

3. Every external node (null child of a leaf node) is black.

4. If a node is red, both of its children are black.

5. Every path from the root to an external node contains the same number of black nodes.

It is rule 5 that leads to a balanced tree structure. Because red nodes may not have any red children, if the black height from root to every leaf node is the same, this implies that any two paths from root to leaf can differ only by a factor of two. Using a relatively simple proof of mathematical induction, Kenneth Berman and Jerome Paul show on page 659 of their book, *Algorithms: Sequential, Parallel, and Distributed* (Thomson, Course Technology, 2005), that the relationship between the maximum depth of a red-black tree and the number of internal nodes is *depth = 2 log₂(n + 1)* where *n* is the number of internal nodes.

Let us consider some examples of red-black trees in Figure 13.27.

The first red-black tree has a black depth of 2 from the root to every leaf node. The second red-black tree has a black depth of 3 from the root to every leaf node. Each of these trees is generated by a search tree GUI application.

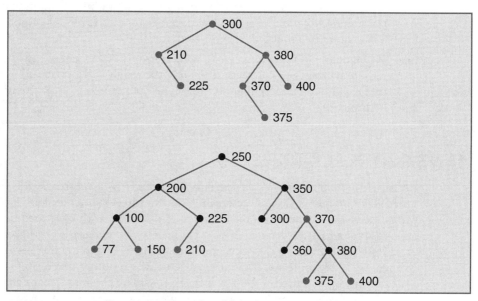

FIGURE 13.27 Two examples of red-black trees

The algorithms for insertion and deletion involve node rotations as well as node recoloring.

The algorithms with examples of insertion and deletion are presented first. Following this a complete implementation of class *RedBlackTree* is presented that includes all the implementation details for insertion and deletion.

13.14 MECHANISM FOR INSERTION INTO A RED-BLACK TREE

Following are steps for inserting into a red-black tree:

1. Perform an ordinary binary search tree insertion into the red-black tree.

2. If the path from root to the new leaf node that contains the information being inserted passes through a node that contains two red children, recolor these

nodes black and recolor the node with the two previously red children black, assuming that it is not the root node (if it is, leave the node black because the root node of a red-black tree must be black).

3.   Color the new leaf node just inserted red.

If these steps lead to a succession of two red nodes in moving from the root down the tree, a rotational correction is needed. Four rotations are possible. Two of these are illustrated in Figures 13.28 and 13.29. The other two are mirror images.

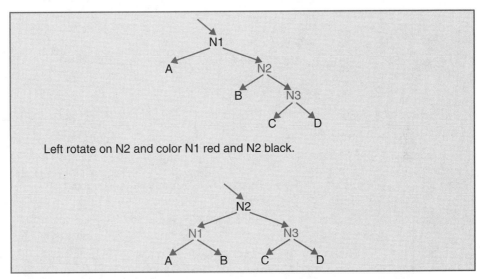

FIGURE 13.28 Rotational and recolor correction, part 1

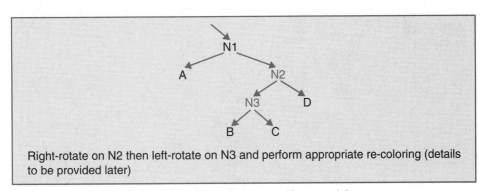

FIGURE 13.29 Rotational and recolor correction, part 2

Consider the sequence of insertions shown in Figure 13.30. After each insertion, the new red-black tree is displayed.

When node 50 is added, the search path passes through node 200 that contains two red nodes. This causes these nodes to be recolored black.

After node 250 is added, the insertion of 275 causes the rotation and recoloring shown in Figure 13.30 Part 4. After inserting 280, the final tree is shown in Part 5. No rotations are required.

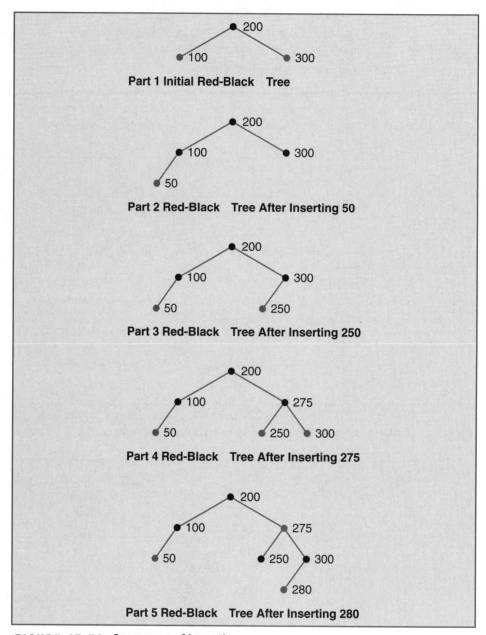

Part 1 Initial Red-Black Tree

Part 2 Red-Black Tree After Inserting 50

Part 3 Red-Black Tree After Inserting 250

Part 4 Red-Black Tree After Inserting 275

Part 5 Red-Black Tree After Inserting 280

FIGURE 13.30 Sequence of insertions

13.15 MECHANISM FOR DELETION FROM A RED-BLACK TREE

The algorithm for deletion is more complex than the algorithm for insertion. There are seven special cases to consider.

1. The first step is to perform an ordinary binary search tree deletion. In the case where the node being deleted has two children, we copy the value but not the color of the in-order successor. Then we delete the in-order successor, a node that can have at most one child.

2. If the node being deleted is colored red, no further corrections are needed. If the deleted node is black and it has a red right child, the red right child is recolored to black and this serves to restore the tree to red-black status.

3. When the node being deleted node is black and it has no right child or a black right child, the following table indicates which of the seven cases needs to be utilized.

Table 13.1 is an adaptation of Figure 21.8 in Berman and Paul's book cited earlier. The asterisk indicates any color. R indicates red and B indicates black.

TABLE 13.1 Cases to use when deleting from a red-black tree

Case	1	2a	2b	3	4	3'	4'
Parent	B	B	R	*	*	*	*
Sibling	R	B	B	B	B	B	B
Sibling (LC)	B	B	B	R	*	B	R
Sibling (RC)	B	B	B	B	R	R	*

From the starting state, any of the states can be reached. From state 1, a transition to either state 2b, state 3, or 4 occurs. When in state 2a, a transition back to state 2a, 2b, 3, or 4 occurs. When in state 3, a transition to state 4 occurs. When in state 3', a transition to state 4' occurs.

We consider states 1, 2a, 2b, 3, and 4 in the following sections. States 3' and 4' are mirror images of states 3 and 4. In each diagram, Current Node represents the right child of the actual node deleted (null in many cases). The R or B in parentheses indicates the node color.

13.15.1 State 1

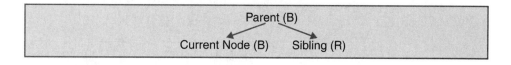

Change the color of Parent and Sibling and left rotate on Parent. Make a transition to case 2b, 3, or 4.

13.15.2 State 2a

(Same diagram as state 1)

Change the color of Sibling to red and then redefine Current Node as Parent. Compute the new Sibling and Parent. Make a transition back to state 2a or to case 2b, 3, or 4. Often Current Node gets moved up the tree in state 2a as transitions occur from 2b back to 2a.

13.15.3 State 2b

(Same diagram as state 1)

Change the color of Sibling to red and end.

13.15.4 State 3

(Same diagram as state 1)

Change the color of Sibling to red and its left child to black, and then right rotate on Sibling. Make transition to case 4.

13.15.5 State 4

(Same diagram as state 1)

Change the color of Sibling's right child to black, make Parent black, color Sibling the color of Parent and then left rotate on Parent and end.

Several examples are presented that demonstrate some of the cases defined above.

Consider the tree shown in Figure 13.31. We wish to delete node 250. The right child of 250 is null so the Current Node is null. Its parent is 225 (after the deletion when the left child of 350 becomes 225) and its sibling is null. Because its parent is colored red, the system goes from the start state to state 2b.

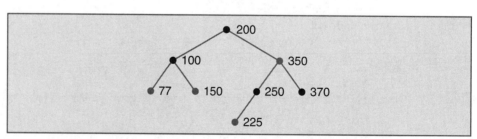

FIGURE 13.31 System changing from start state to state 2b

This leads to the result shown in Figure 13.32 in which the color of 225 is changed to black.

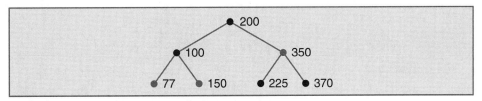

FIGURE 13.32 Color of 225 changed to black

Consider the deletion of 250 from the tree shown in Figure 13.33.

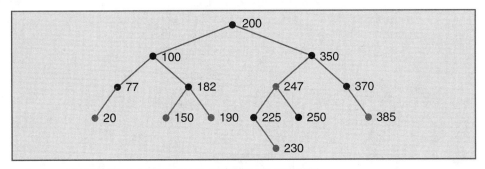

FIGURE 13.33 Tree from which 250 will be deleted

The table of states given above suggests that from the start state a transition to state 3' occurs. The Current Node is null, its parent is 247, its sibling is 225, and its sibling's right child is red. These are the conditions needed for state 3'. After the node recoloring indicated under state 3' above, a left rotate is done on the sibling node 225. A transition to state 4' occurs. After more recoloring, a right rotate on node 247 brings red node 230 to the left of 350. The tree resulting from states 3' and 4' is shown in Figure 13.34.

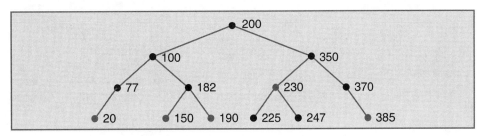

FIGURE 13.34 Tree resulting from states 3' and 4'

Consider the deletion of node 77 from the red-black tree shown in Figure 13.35.

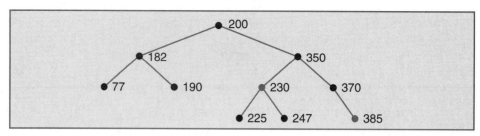

FIGURE 13.35 Red-black tree from which node 77 will be deleted

From the start state a transition is made to state 2a because the parent, node 182, is black, the sibling (190) is black, and the children of the sibling (null) are black.

From state 2a a transition is made to state 3 and then state 4. The final tree after these three states is shown in Figure 13.36.

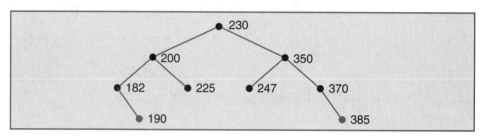

FIGURE 13.36 Final tree after three states

Unless one studies these transitions carefully, it simply looks like magic.

As the final example, consider the deletion of node 225 from the red-black tree shown in Figure 13.37.

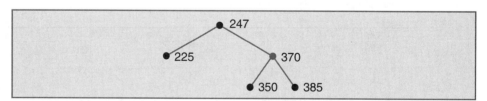

FIGURE 13.37 Red-black tree from which node 225 will be deleted

From the start state a transition to state 1 occurs. This is because the sibling, node 370, is red and the parent, node 247, is black.

13.16 TWO ALTERNATIVE DESIGNS OF RED-BLACK TREES

The algorithm for insertion requires that the ancestors (parent, grandparent, great-grandparent) of the inserted node be available. The implementation of deletion requires that the parent, sibling, and grandparent nodes be available from the node being deleted. This leads to an important implementation question: should each node of a red-black tree have a link "pointing" to its parent (the root would link to a parent of null)? The alternative is to stay with the same structure as used in the implementation of the binary search tree and AVL tree in which each node is linked to its two children and not to its parent. The tradeoff is replacing more complexity in the basic operations of insertion and deletion with easier implementations of the various rotational and recoloring "corrections" related to insertion and deletion.

The decision is to use the more complex node structure in which each node contains a link to its parent node because this leads to the most efficient implementation of the red-black tree, particularly for deletion. An implementation that does not use links from child to parent requires a field, *stack*, and a recursive *ConstructStack* method whose purpose is to determine the nodes in the path from root to any specified node. Because of the need to invoke this method frequently, the implementation for deletion is 100 times slower than an AVL tree with the same node values. This is unacceptable and leads to the focus on the version that contains links from child to parent nodes.

13.16.1 Comparing Performance of Binary Search Trees

The results of a simulation that compares the execution time required for inserting a sequence of values and later removing them from an unbalanced binary search tree, an AVL tree, and a red-black tree are presented first. The two types of red-black tree implementations, with and without links to parent nodes, are included in Table 13.2 even though only the implementation of the version with links to parent nodes will be presented. An ascending sequence of integers is used to construct each tree. Then all the values that were used to construct the tree are used in a sequence of deletions.

TABLE 13.2 Two types of red-black trees

Tree Type	Number of Nodes	Time for Insertion	Time for Deletion	ACE Value of Tree
Binary Search Tree	10,000	34.48 seconds		5000.5
Red-Black Tree (No links to parent nodes)	10,000	0.0312 seconds	2.844 seconds	12.88
Red-Black Tree (Links from child to parent nodes)	10,000	0.0156 seconds	0.0156 seconds	12.88
AVL Tree	10,000	0.0156 seconds	0.0156 seconds	12.36
Red-Black Tree (Links from child to parent nodes)	1,000,000	3.609 seconds	1.0625 seconds	19.33
AVL Tree	1,000,000	2.406 seconds	1.031 seconds	18.95

It is clear from Table 13.2 that the performance of the red-black tree with each node linking to its parent is superior to the red-black tree without such links to parent nodes and comparable to the performance of the AVL tree.

13.17 IMPLEMENTATION OF CLASS NODE WITH UPWARD LINKS

The details of class *Node* are presented in Listing 13.13. It is a nested class (similar to Java's static inner class) in a generic class with parameter *T* (as shown later), so it does not require its own generic parameter.

LISTING 13.13 Class Node

```
private class Node {
   // Fields
   private T item; // Generic object held by each node
   private Node left, right, parent;  // Links to children and parent
   private bool red = true; // Color of node

   // Constructor
   public Node(T item, Node parent) {
      this.item = item;
      this.parent = parent;
      left = right = null;
   }

   // Properties
   public Node Left {
     get {
        return left;
     }
     set {
        left = value;
     }
   }

   public Node Right {
      get {
         return right;
      }
      set {
         right = value;
      }
   }

   public Node Parent {
      get {
         return parent;
      }
      set {
```

LISTING 13.13 Class Node (continued)

```
            parent = value;
        }
    }

    // Similar get/set properties for Item and Red
}
```

13.18 TREE ROTATION WITH UPWARD LINKS TO PARENT NODES

The methods *LeftRotate* and *RightRotate* must take the *parent* link into account. Method *LeftRotate* is presented in Listing 13.14. Method *RightRotate* is the symmetrical opposite and not presented. The reference parameter capability of C# (*ref* parameter) is used in the two rotation methods. This allows explicit linking between the tree structure unaffected by the rotation and the new node that is passed back through the reference parameter.

LISTING 13.14 Revised methods LeftRotate

```
private void LeftRotate(ref Node node) {
    Node nodeParent = node.Parent;
    Node right = node.Right;
    Node temp = right.Left;
    right.Left = node;
        node.Parent = right;
    node.Right = temp;
        if (temp != null) {
        temp.Parent = node;

    }   if (right != null) {
        right.Parent = nodeParent;
    }
        node = right;
}
```

After setting the right child of ref variable *node* to *temp*, the parent of *temp* is set to *node* (if *temp* is not null). This reflects the new parent of *temp* after the rotation is completed. The parent of *right* is set to *nodeParent*, a local variable that is immediately assigned as the first line in the method. This reflects the upward connection between the node being passed back (*right*) and its parent (not affected by the rotation). These two assignments using *Parent* ensure that the two links that are modified by the rotation are linked in both directions.

13.19 IMPLEMENTATION OF INSERTION

The public method *Add* and its private support methods *InsertNode*, *GetNodesAbove*, and *FixTreeAfterInsertion* implement the red-black algorithm for insertion.

These methods are presented in Listing 13.15.

LISTING 13.15 Methods that support insertion in a red-black tree

```
public void Add(T item) {
    root = InsertNode(root, item, null);
    numberElements++;
    if (numberElements > 2) {
        Node parent, grandParent, greatGrandParent;
        GetNodesAbove(insertedNode, out parent,
                out grandParent, out greatGrandParent);
        FixTreeAfterInsertion(insertedNode, parent,
                grandParent, greatGrandParent);
    }
}

private Node InsertNode(Node node, T item, Node parent) {
    if (node == null) {
        Node newNode = new Node(item, parent);
        if (numberElements > 0) {
            newNode.Red = true;
        } else {
            newNode.Red = false;
        }
        insertedNode = newNode;
        return newNode;
    } else if (item.CompareTo(node.Item) < 0) {
        node.Left = InsertNode(node.Left, item, node);
        return node;
    } else if (item.CompareTo(node.Item) > 0) {
        node.Right = InsertNode(node.Right, item, node);
        return node;
    } else {
        throw new InvalidOperationException(
                "Cannot add duplicate object.");
    }
}

private void GetNodesAbove(Node curNode, out Node parent,
                           out Node grandParent,
                           out Node greatGrandParent) {
    parent = null;
    grandParent = null;
    greatGrandParent = null;
    if (curNode != null) {
        parent = curNode.Parent;
    }
```

LISTING 13.15 Methods that support insertion in a red-black tree (continued)

```
   if (parent != null) {
      grandParent = parent.Parent;
   }
   if (grandParent != null) {
      greatGrandParent = grandParent.Parent;
      }
}

private void FixTreeAfterInsertion(Node child, Node parent,
                                   Node grandParent,
                                   Node greatGrandParent) {
   if (grandParent != null) {
      Node uncle = (grandParent.Right == parent) ?
                      grandParent.Left : grandParent.Right;
      if (uncle != null && parent.Red && uncle.Red) {
         uncle.Red = false;
         parent.Red = false;
         grandParent.Red = true;
         Node higher = null;
         Node stillHigher = null;
         if (greatGrandParent != null) {
            higher = greatGrandParent.Parent;
         }
         if (higher != null) {
            stillHigher = higher.Parent;
         }
         FixTreeAfterInsertion(grandParent, greatGrandParent,
            higher, stillHigher);
      } else if (uncle == null || parent.Red && !uncle.Red) {
         if (grandParent.Right == parent &&
            parent.Right == child) { // right-right case
            parent.Red = false;
            grandParent.Red = true;
            if (greatGrandParent != null) {
               if (greatGrandParent.Right == grandParent) {
                  LeftRotate(ref grandParent);
                     greatGrandParent.Right = grandParent;
               } else {
                     LeftRotate(ref grandParent);
                     greatGrandParent.Left = grandParent;
                     }
            } else {
               LeftRotate(ref root);
            }
         }
      } else if (grandParent.Left == parent &&
         parent.Left == child) { // left-left case
         parent.Red = false;
         grandParent.Red = true;
         if (greatGrandParent != null) {
            if (greatGrandParent.Right == grandParent) {
               RightRotate(ref grandParent);
                  greatGrandParent.Right = grandParent;
            } else {
               RightRotate(ref grandParent);
```

LISTING 13.15 Methods that support insertion in a red-black tree (continued)

```
                    greatGrandParent.Left = grandParent;
                }
            } else {
                RightRotate(ref root);
            }
        } else if (grandParent.Right == parent &&
                parent.Left == child) {// right-left case
            child.Red = false;
            grandParent.Red = true;
            RightRotate(ref parent);
            grandParent.Right = parent;
            if (greatGrandParent != null) {
                if (greatGrandParent.Right == grandParent) {
                    LeftRotate(ref grandParent);
                    greatGrandParent.Right = grandParent;
                } else {
                    LeftRotate(ref grandParent);
                    greatGrandParent.Left = grandParent;
                }
            } else {
                LeftRotate(ref root);
            }
        } else if (grandParent.Left == parent &&
                parent.Right == child) {// left-right case
            child.Red = false;
            grandParent.Red = true;
            LeftRotate(ref parent);
            grandParent.Left = parent;
            if (greatGrandParent != null) {
                if (greatGrandParent.Right == grandParent) {
                    RightRotate(ref grandParent);
                    greatGrandParent.Right = grandParent;
                } else {
                    RightRotate(ref grandParent);
                    greatGrandParent.Left = grandParent;
                }
            } else {
                RightRotate(ref root);
            }
        }
    }
    if (root.Red) {
        root.Red = false;
    }
}
}
```

The recursive *InsertNode* contains a parameter, *parent*, which allows *node* at one level of recursion to be passed as *parent* to the next lower level of recursion.

The support method *GetNodesAbove* uses the *out* parameter facility of C# to return relevant nodes above the current node (*curNode*). This can be easily accomplished because of the upward links in the node structure.

The important support method *FixTreeAfterInsertion* with four nodes as input implements the details of the red-black insertion algorithm as outlined and illustrated previously. Care has been taken to use descriptive local variable and parameter names to make it easier for the code to be self-documenting.

13.20 IMPLEMENTATION OF DELETION

The implementation of deletion is more complex than the implementation of insertion. This reflects the additional complexity of the algorithm for deletion, which, as shown earlier, involves seven special cases and transitions from some of the cases to other cases. The remaining portion of class *RedBlack* that includes all the support for deletion is presented in Listing 13.16.

The generic class uses a constrained generic parameter *T* where *T* implements the *IComparable* interface.

LISTING 13.16 Remaining details of class RedBlackTree

```
using System;
using System.Collections.Generic;
using System.Text;
using System.Windows.Forms;

namespace SearchTrees {

    public class RedBlackTree<T> where T : IComparable {

        // Fields
        private Node root;
        private int numberElements;
        private Node insertedNode;
        private Node nodeBeingDeleted; // Set in DeleteNode
        private bool siblingToRight;   // Sibling of curNode
        private bool parentToRight;    // Of grand parent
        private bool nodeToDeleteRed;  // Color of deleted node

        // Commands
        public void Add(T item) {
        // Presented in previous listing
        }

        public void Remove(T item) {
            if (numberElements > 1) {
                root = DeleteNode(root, item, null);
                numberElements--;
                if (numberElements == 0) {
                    root = null;
                }
                Node curNode = null; // Right node being deleted
                if (nodeBeingDeleted.Right != null) {
                    curNode = nodeBeingDeleted.Right;
                }
```

LISTING 13.16 Remaining details of class RedBlackTree (continued)

```
                Node parent, sibling, grandParent;
                if (curNode == null) {
                    parent = nodeBeingDeleted.Parent;
                } else {
                    parent = curNode.Parent;
                }
                GetParentGrandParentSibling(curNode, parent,
                        out sibling, out grandParent);

                if (curNode != null && curNode.Red) {
                    curNode.Red = false;
                } else if (!nodeToDeleteRed && !nodeBeingDeleted.Red)
{
                    FixTreeAfterDeletion(curNode, parent,
                        sibling, grandParent);
                }
                root.Red = false;
            }
        }

        // Queries
        private Node InsertNode(Node node, T item, Node parent) {
            // Presented in previous listing
        }

        private void RightRotate(ref Node node) {
            // Presented earlier
        }

        private void LeftRotate(ref Node node) {
            // Presented earlier
        }

        private void GetNodesAbove(Node curNode, out Node parent,
                                   out Node grandParent,
                                   out Node greatGrandParent) {
            // Presented in previous listing
        }

        private void GetParentGrandParentSibling(Node curNode,
                            Node parent,
                            out Node sibling, out Node grandParent) {
            sibling = null;
            grandParent = null;

            if (parent != null) {
                if (parent.Right == curNode) {
                    siblingToRight = false;
                    sibling = parent.Left;
                }
                if (parent.Left == curNode) {
                    siblingToRight = true;
                    sibling = parent.Right;
                }
```

LISTING 13.16 Remaining details of class RedBlackTree (continued)

```
        }
        if (parent != null) {
            grandParent = parent.Parent;
        }
        if (grandParent != null) {
            if (grandParent.Right == parent) {
                parentToRight = true;
            }
            if (grandParent.Left == parent) {
                parentToRight = false;
            }
        }
    }

    private void FixTreeAfterInsertion(Node child, Node parent,
                    Node grandParent,
                        Node greatGrandParent) {
        // Presented in previous listing
    }

    private Node DeleteNode(Node node, T item, Node parent) {
        if (node == null) {
            throw new InvalidOperationException(
                "item not in search tree.");
        }
        if (item.CompareTo(node.Item) < 0) {
            node.Left = DeleteNode(node.Left, item, node);
        } else if (item.CompareTo(node.Item) > 0) {
            node.Right = DeleteNode(node.Right, item, node);
        } else if (item.CompareTo(node.Item) == 0) {
        // Item found
            nodeToDeleteRed = node.Red;
            nodeBeingDeleted = node;
            if (node.Left == null) {
            // No children or only a right child
                node = node.Right;
                if (node != null) {
                    node.Parent = parent;
                }
                } else if (node.Right == null) {
                // Only a left child
                  node = node.Left;
                  node.Parent = parent;
                } else { // Two children
                // Deletes using the leftmost node of the
                // right sub-tree
                T replaceWithValue = LeftMost(node.Right);
                node.Right =
                DeleteLeftMost(node.Right, node);
                node.Item = replaceWithValue;
            }
        }
        return node;
    }
```

LISTING 13.16 Remaining details of class RedBlackTree (continued)

```
    }

    private Node DeleteLeftMost(Node node, Node parent) {
      if (node.Left == null) {
          nodeBeingDeleted = node;
          if (node.Right != null) {
              node.Parent = parent;
          }
          return node.Right;
      } else {
          node.Left = DeleteLeftMost(node.Left, node);
          return node;
      }
    }

    private T LeftMost(Node node) {
      if (node.Left == null) {
          return node.Item;
      } else {
          return LeftMost(node.Left);
      }
    }

    private void FixTreeAfterDeletion(Node curNode, Node parent,
          Node sibling, Node grandParent) {
        Node siblingLeftChild = null;
        Node siblingRightChild = null;
        if (sibling != null && sibling.Left != null) {
            siblingLeftChild = sibling.Left;
        }
        if (sibling != null && sibling.Right != null) {
            siblingRightChild = sibling.Right;
        }
        bool siblingRed = (sibling != null && sibling.Red);
        bool siblingLeftRed = (siblingLeftChild != null
            && siblingLeftChild.Red);
        bool siblingRightRed = (siblingRightChild != null &&
            siblingRightChild.Red);

        if (parent != null && !parent.Red && siblingRed &&
            !siblingLeftRed && !siblingRightRed) {
            Case1(curNode, parent, sibling, grandParent);
        } else if (parent != null && !parent.Red &&
        !siblingRed && !siblingLeftRed && !siblingRightRed) {
            Case2A(curNode, parent, sibling, grandParent);
        } else if (parent != null && parent.Red &&
        !siblingRed && !siblingLeftRed && !siblingRightRed) {
            Case2B(curNode, parent, sibling, grandParent);
        } else if (siblingToRight && !siblingRed &&
            siblingLeftRed && !siblingRightRed) {
            Case3(curNode, parent, sibling, grandParent);
        } else if (!siblingToRight &&
        !siblingRed && !siblingLeftRed && siblingRightRed) {
```

LISTING 13.16 Remaining details of class RedBlackTree (continued)

```
                        Case3P(curNode, parent, sibling, grandParent);
            } else if (siblingToRight && !siblingRed &&
                        siblingRightRed) {
                Case4(curNode, parent, sibling, grandParent);
            } else if (!siblingToRight && !siblingRed &&
                        siblingLeftRed) {
                Case4P(curNode, parent, sibling, grandParent);
            }
        }

        private void Case1(Node curNode, Node parent,
                    Node sibling, Node grandParent) {
            if (siblingToRight) {
                parent.Red = !parent.Red;
                sibling.Red = !sibling.Red;
                if (grandParent != null) {
                    if (parentToRight) {
                        LeftRotate(ref parent);
                        grandParent.Right = parent;
                    } else if (!parentToRight) {
                        LeftRotate(ref parent);
                        grandParent.Left = parent;
                    }
                } else {
                    LeftRotate(ref parent);
                    root = parent;
                }
                grandParent = sibling;
                parent = parent.Left;
                parentToRight = false;
            } else if (!siblingToRight) {
                parent.Red = !parent.Red;
                sibling.Red = !sibling.Red;
                if (grandParent != null) {
                    if (parentToRight) {
                        RightRotate(ref parent);
                        grandParent.Right = parent;
                    } else if (!parentToRight) {
                        RightRotate(ref parent);
                        grandParent.Left = parent;
                    }
                } else {
                    RightRotate(ref parent);
                    root = parent;
                }
                grandParent = sibling;
                parent = parent.Right;
                parentToRight = true;
            }

            if (parent.Right == curNode) {
                sibling = parent.Left;
                siblingToRight = false;
```

LISTING 13.16 Remaining details of class RedBlackTree (continued)

```
        } else if (parent.Left == curNode) {
            sibling = parent.Right;
            siblingToRight = true;
        }

        Node siblingLeftChild = null;
        Node siblingRightChild = null;
        if (sibling != null && sibling.Left != null) {
            siblingLeftChild = sibling.Left;
        }
        if (sibling != null && sibling.Right != null) {
            siblingRightChild = sibling.Right;
        }
        bool siblingRed = (sibling != null && sibling.Red);
        bool siblingLeftRed = (siblingLeftChild != null &&
                siblingLeftChild.Red);
        bool siblingRightRed = (siblingRightChild != null &&
                siblingRightChild.Red);
        if (parent.Red && !siblingRed && !siblingLeftRed &&
                !siblingRightRed) {
            Case2B(curNode, parent, sibling, grandParent);
        } else if (siblingToRight && !siblingRed && siblingLeftRed
                && !siblingRightRed) {
            Case3(curNode, parent, sibling, grandParent);
        } else if (!siblingToRight && !siblingRed &&
                !siblingLeftRed && siblingRightRed) {
            Case3P(curNode, parent, sibling, grandParent);
        } else if (siblingToRight && !siblingRed &&
                siblingRightRed) {
            Case4(curNode, parent, sibling, grandParent);
        } else if (!siblingToRight && !siblingRed &&
                siblingLeftRed) {
            Case4P(curNode, parent, sibling, grandParent);
        }
    }

    private void Case2A(Node curNode, Node parent,
                Node sibling, Node grandParent) {
        if (sibling != null) {
            sibling.Red = !sibling.Red;
        }
        curNode = parent;
        if (curNode != root) {
            parent = curNode.Parent;
            GetParentGrandParentSibling(curNode, parent,
                    out sibling, out grandParent);
            Node siblingLeftChild = null;
            Node siblingRightChild = null;
            if (sibling != null && sibling.Left != null) {
                siblingLeftChild = sibling.Left;
            }
            if (sibling != null && sibling.Right != null) {
                siblingRightChild = sibling.Right;
            }
```

LISTING 13.16 Remaining details of class RedBlackTree (continued)

```
                bool siblingRed = (sibling != null && sibling.Red);
                bool siblingLeftRed = (siblingLeftChild != null &&
                        siblingLeftChild.Red);
                bool siblingRightRed = (siblingRightChild != null &&
                        siblingRightChild.Red);
                if (parent != null && !parent.Red && !siblingRed &&
                        !siblingLeftRed && !siblingRightRed) {
                    Case2A(curNode, parent, sibling, grandParent);
                } else if (parent != null && parent.Red && !siblingRed
                        && !siblingLeftRed && !siblingRightRed) {
                    Case2B(curNode, parent, sibling, grandParent);
                } else if (siblingToRight && !siblingRed &&
                        siblingLeftRed && !siblingRightRed) {
                    Case3(curNode, parent, sibling, grandParent);
                } else if (!siblingToRight && !siblingRed &&
                        !siblingLeftRed && siblingRightRed) {
                    Case3P(curNode, parent, sibling, grandParent);
                } else if (siblingToRight && !siblingRed &&
                        siblingRightRed) {
                    Case4(curNode, parent, sibling, grandParent);
                } else if (!siblingToRight && !siblingRed &&
                        siblingLeftRed) {
                    Case4P(curNode, parent, sibling, grandParent);
                }
            }
        }

        private void Case2B(Node curNode, Node parent,
                    Node sibling, Node grandParent) {
            if (sibling != null) {
                sibling.Red = !sibling.Red;
            }
            curNode = parent;
            curNode.Red = !curNode.Red;
        }

        private void Case3(Node curNode, Node parent,
                    Node sibling, Node grandParent) {
            if (parent.Left == curNode) {
                sibling.Red = true;
                sibling.Left.Red = false;
                RightRotate(ref sibling);
                parent.Right = sibling;
            }
            Case4(curNode, parent, sibling, grandParent);
        }

        private void Case3P(Node curNode, Node parent,
                    Node sibling, Node grandParent) {
            if (parent.Right == curNode) {
                sibling.Red = true;
                sibling.Right.Red = false;
```

LISTING 13.16 Remaining details of class RedBlackTree (continued)

```
                    LeftRotate(ref sibling);
                    parent.Left = sibling;
            }
            Case4P(curNode, parent, sibling, grandParent);
        }

        private void Case4(Node curNode, Node parent,
                        Node sibling, Node grandParent) {
            sibling.Red = parent.Red;
            sibling.Right.Red = false;
            parent.Red = false;
            if (grandParent != null) {
                if (parentToRight) {
                    LeftRotate(ref parent);
                    grandParent.Right = parent;
                } else {
                    LeftRotate(ref parent);
                    grandParent.Left = parent;
                }
            } else {
                LeftRotate(ref parent);
                root = parent;
            }
        }

        private void Case4P(Node curNode, Node parent,
                        Node sibling, Node grandParent) {
            sibling.Red = parent.Red;
            sibling.Left.Red = false;
            parent.Red = false;
            if (grandParent != null) {
                if (parentToRight) {
                    RightRotate(ref parent);
                    grandParent.Right = parent;
                } else {
                    RightRotate(ref parent);
                    grandParent.Left = parent;
                }
            } else {
                RightRotate(ref parent);
                root = parent;
            }
        }

        private class Node {
            // Details presented earlier
        }
    }
}
```

Care was again taken in choosing variable and parameter names so that the code would be self-documenting. The complexity of the code reflects the complexity of the algorithm for deletion.

C# has a requirement that *ref* or *out* parameters must be explicitly tagged when invoking a method, which is desirable. It makes the semantics of the method invocation clear without requiring the programmer to refer back to the method signature. There are many examples of such method invocations in Listing 13.16.

Exercise 13.14

Explain every occurrence of *ref* and *out* in Listing 13.16.

13.21 UPDATE OF SEARCH TREE GUI APPLICATION

The GUI application described in Section 13.6 is updated to allow left or right rotations about any node for binary search trees and insertion and deletion into AVL and red-black trees. A combo box allows the user to choose between an ordinary binary search tree, AVL tree, or red-black tree. If an AVL or red-black tree is chosen, the buttons that allow node rotations is disabled because the position of nodes within such trees must be strictly governed by the insertion and deletion algorithms. The user cannot be allowed to tamper with the results.

You are encouraged to download all the source code and experiment with this graphical tree laboratory.

13.22 HEAPS

The heap is a specialized type of binary tree and is useful in several important applications. We shall consider one such application—heap sort.

A **heap** is a **complete** binary tree in which the contents of any node must be greater than or equal to the contents of all its descendents.

A complete binary tree is one in which all possible nodes are present at each level, except the lowest level where leaf nodes are present from left to right. An example of a complete binary tree is shown in Figure 13.38.

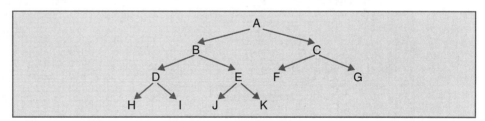

FIGURE 13.38 Complete tree structure

The nodes in Figure 13.38 may be mapped into an array containing the values:
A, B, C, D, E, F, G, H, I, J, K

Using natural indexing (indexing starting at 1), from any index location in the array representation of a complete tree, say index j, the two children are located in index locations 2 * j and 2 * j + 1. The parent is located in index location j / 2, assuming that j is equal or greater than 2.

So for example, the two children of node E (index 5 in the array) are found in index locations 10 and 11. The parent of node E is found in index 5 / 2 = 2.

The algorithm for heap sort is based on the following strategy. From the input array, build a heap by shuffling elements within the input array (details to be provided in the following sections). The consequence of building a heap from the input array is that the value in index 1 (we assume natural indexing), is the largest value in the array. This follows from the heap property that the value in every node is larger than all its descendents.

Interchange this largest value with the value in the largest index. Now the largest value is where it needs to be—on the right side of the input array. Rebuild the heap because the interchange performed above destroys the heap property of the input array. After rebuilding the heap, interchange the largest value (again in index 1) with the value in the next to the largest index. Continue this pattern until all the values are sorted.

This strategy resembles the strategy for the inefficient but simple selection sort algorithm. If you recall from Chapter 8, selection sort searches for the largest value in the array and swaps it with the value in the largest index location. It then finds the second largest value in the array (excluding the value in the largest index location) and swaps it with the value in the next largest index location. This pattern continues until selection sort has sorted all the values.

The only difference between heap sort and selection sort is the mechanism used to obtain the largest value at each stage. Using selection sort the computational complexity of accomplishing this is $O(n)$. It will be shown that when using heap sort the complexity is $O(log_2 n)$.

A class *Heap<T>* is constructed that implements the algorithms for building and later rebuilding a heap. We "walk" through an example to explain how each of these algorithms work. But first Listing 13.17 presents the details of class *Heap<T>*.

LISTING 13.17 Class Heap

```
using System;
using System.Collections.Generic;

namespace HeapStructure {

    public class Heap<T> where T : IComparable {

        // Fields
        private T[] data; // Natural indexing assumed
        private int size;

        // Constructor
        public Heap(T[] data, int size) {
            this.data = data;
            this.size = size;
```

LISTING 13.17 Class Heap

```
        }

        // Commands
        public void BuildHeap() {
            int parent, child;
            for (int nodeIndex = 2; nodeIndex <= size; nodeIndex++) {
                child = nodeIndex;
                parent = child / 2;
                while (parent >= 1 &&
                data[parent].CompareTo(data[child]) < 0) {
                    Interchange(child, parent);
                    child = parent;
                    parent = parent / 2;
                }
            }
        }

        public void RebuildHeap(int upTo) {
            int parent, child;
            parent = 1;
            child = 2 * parent;
            if (2 * parent + 1 <= upTo &&
                data[2 * parent + 1].CompareTo(data[2 * parent]) > 0) {
                child = 2 * parent + 1;
            }
            while (child <= upTo &&
                data[parent].CompareTo(data[child]) < 0) {
                Interchange(child, parent);
                parent = child;
                child = 2 * parent;
                if (2 * parent + 1 <= upTo &&
                    data[2 * parent + 1].CompareTo(data[2 * parent]) >
                                    0) {
                    child = 2 * parent + 1;
                }
            }
        }

        private void Interchange(int index1, int index2) {
            T temp = data[index2];
            data[index2] = data[index1];
            data[index1] = temp;
        }
    }
}
```

Consider the array with values in index locations 1 through 5 given by: 3.6, −2.7, 5.2, −1.3, 7.4.

The complete tree that represents this input array is shown in Figure 13.39.

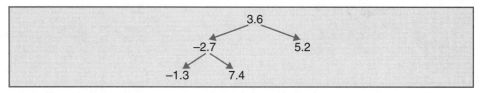

FIGURE 13.39 Complete tree representing input array

The method *BuildHeap* starts with parent equal to index 2 (value −2.7) and moves up the tree comparing parent to child. If they are out of order (child larger than parent), an interchange takes place.

When parent has the value 5.2, this causes an interchange leading to the tree shown in Figure 13.40.

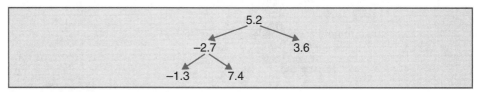

FIGURE 13.40 Tree when parent has value 5.2

When parent has the value −1.3, this causes the interchange leading to the next tree shown in Figure 13.41.

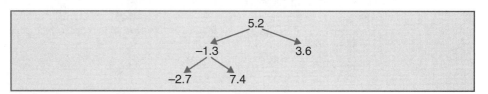

FIGURE 13.41 Tree when parent has value −1.3

Finally when parent has the value 7.4, multiple iterations of the inner while-loop produces the heap structure shown in Figure 13.42.

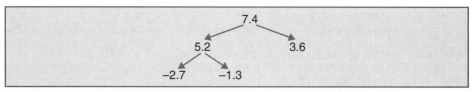

FIGURE 13.42 Tree when parent has value 7.4

After exchanging the values in index 1 with index 5, the tree, no longer a heap, looks as shown in Figure 13.43.

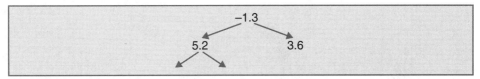

FIGURE 13.43 Tree after exchanging values in index 1 with index 5

The method *RebuildHeap* starts with the root node and finds the index of the larger child (index 2 in this case). It compares the child with the parent and performs an interchange if they are out of order. This leads to the tree shown in Figure 13.44. Node 7.4 is shown in boldface to indicate that it is excluded from further consideration (it is where it needs to be).

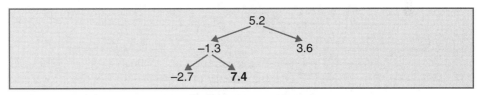

FIGURE 13.44 Tree after method RebuildHeap executes

The larger of the children of −1.3 (there is only one child remaining in contention) is −2.7. Because −1.3 is larger than −2.7 no further interchanges are required, otherwise another interchange would be performed. This would continue down to the bottom of the remaining tree.

It should be clear that the computational complexity of method *RebuildHeap* is $O(log_2 n)$; the number of interchanges is limited by the depth of the tree, which is logarithmically related to the number of nodes because the tree is almost balanced with its complete tree structure.

The generic and static *HeapSort* method is shown along with a simple test program in Listing 13.18.

LISTING 13.18 Generic heap sort method

```
using System;

namespace HeapStructure {

    public class Sort {

        public static void HeapSort<T>(T [] data, int size)
                            where T : IComparable {
            Heap<T> heap = new Heap<T>(data, size);
            heap.BuildHeap();
```

LISTING 13.18 Generic heap sort method (continued)

```
            for (int i = size; i >= 2; i--) {
                T temp = data[1];
                data[1] = data[i];
                data[i] = temp;
                heap.RebuildHeap(i-1);
            }
        }

        public static void Main() {
            double[] data = new double[6]; // Natural indexing
            data[1] = 3.6; data[2] = -2.7; data[3] = 5.2;
            data[4] = -1.3; data[5] = 7.4;
            Sort.HeapSort<double>(data, 5);
            for (int i = 1; i <= 5; i++) {
                Console.WriteLine(data[i]);
            }
            Console.ReadLine();
        }
    }
}
```

The overall computational complexity of heap sort is $O(nlog_2n)$ because the *BuildHeap* method has a complexity of $O(nlog2n)$ and within the for-loop, method *RebuildHeap* of complexity $O(log_2n)$ is executed n times.

Exercise 13.15

Discuss why method *BuildHeap* has a computational complexity of $O(nlog_2n)$.

Exercise 13.16

How long does the sort-time for heap sort compare to quick sort on your computer when sorting one million double values? (On the author's computer, it takes about nine times longer.)

13.23 HASH TABLES

Hash tables provide an efficient implementation of the set abstraction. The key operation of the set abstraction is the determination of whether an object is present or not present. In exchange for efficiency in determining set membership, a set does not support the ordering of information as a search tree does (see Exercise 13.2).

An important application that benefits from the use of a set is dictionary lookup of words in a spelling checker. If many words are being checked against a dictionary, it is desirable that the search time be as small as possible.

A hash table is frequently implemented as an array that contains the object type that needs to be stored in the table. The spelling checker application serves as a good frame of reference from which to discuss hash tables.

It is desired that over the collection of words (String objects) that are to be mapped to various index locations within the hash table, the index locations are randomly distributed across the collection of words. This would imply that two words that differ in only one character would map to index locations that are separated from each other.

The mapping from String objects (words) to their index location within the hash table is called the **hash function**. Hash functions have been studied extensively. An Internet search quickly produces dozens of good-quality algorithms for accomplishing the mapping from String to index location.

Happily, class *String* includes a good-quality hash function in the query method *GetHashCode* so no discussion about hashing algorithms is needed.

A perfect hash function would be one that produces a one-to-one mapping between any possible word and the hash index associated with the word. If we were to consider an alphabet of 27 characters (26 letters plus the apostrophe symbol), the following would provide a unique mapping between any word and its hash index:

$$\text{hashIndex} = \text{word}[0] + 27 * \text{word}[1] + 27^2 * \text{word}[2] + \ldots + 27^n * \text{word}[n] + \ldots$$

Exercise 13.17

How large would a perfect hash table have to be to accommodate words of up to 10 characters in length?

As Exercise 13.17 demonstrates, perfect hash functions, although theoretically desirable, are not practical because of their storage requirements.

A practical hash function such as *GetHashCode* in class String has equivalence classes of words that produce the same hash index. So there is not a one-to-one mapping between the string and the hash index. An immediate consequence of this is the need for collision resolution in constructing hash tables. If a word being placed in a hash table produces an index that is already spoken for by another word that is already in the table, it is necessary to resolve this collision by moving the second word with the same index to another empty location within the table. The algorithm for doing this is called a collision resolution algorithm.

The study of hashing is principally concerned with two problems:

♦ Designing an efficient hash function that appears to randomly associate the object being inserted with a hash index

♦ Designing an efficient collision resolution to move equivalence classes of words whose hash index values collide

We focus only on the second of these two basic issues because of the presence of the nicely designed *GetHashCode* method.

13.23.1 Linear Chaining Collision Resolution Algorithm

The simplest collision resolution algorithm is called **linear chaining**. With linear chaining, when a collision occurs, the word that has collided is placed in the first empty array location to the right of the existing word. That is, a search for an empty location begins at an index one larger than the location of the collision. If the highest index of the array is reached during this linear search, the next index to be searched is the smallest index location. This circular structure in which the right end of the array is attached back to the left end implies that a collision can be resolved providing that there is at least one empty cell in the array. For this reason the **load factor**, defined as the ratio of the number of words divided by the size of the table, must always be less than 1.

Consider a hash table that is half filled with words. Such a table has a load factor of 0.5. When the next word in such a table is inserted, it has a 50 percent chance of colliding with an existing word, if we assume that the hash index of the next word has a probability density function that is uniformly distributed across the index range of the hash table.

A collision chain of size two is thus born (the location of the original word in addition to the index location directly to its right). The likelihood of this collision chain being hit again is twice as high as any individual occupied cell being hit because the target is twice as large. If hit again, the collision chain grows to three in size and has three times the likelihood of being hit compared to any individual cell. So the tendency is for large chains to grow even larger because of their increased likelihood of being hit. These collision clusters tend to erode the performance of the hash table.

If the hash index of a word being sought is within a collision chain, the word must be compared against the remaining words in the collision chain before it can be determined whether the word is present or absent from the hash table. We define the number of such needed comparison operations as the **number of probes**. The smaller the average number of probes for a given hash table, the more efficient the hash table is.

Algorithm for Collision Resolution Using Linear Chaining During Word Insertion

1. Obtain the hash index for the word.
2. If the hash table is empty at the hash index, insert the word at this location.
3. If the table is occupied at this location, increment the index until the first free location is found. When the end of the table is reached, loop back to the beginning of the table.

Algorithm for Searching for a Word in Hash Table Using Linear Chaining

1. Obtain the hash index for the word.
2. If the table is empty at the given index, the word being sought is not present.
3. If the table contains a word at the given index, compare the word being sought against the word stored at the hash index. If they compare, the word is present. If not, increase the index by one. Continue to increase the index until a match-up occurs or until an empty location is found. During the search for the word, if the end of the table is reached, loop back to the beginning of the table.

13.23.2 Coalesced Chaining Collision Resolution Algorithm

Another collision resolution algorithm, coalesced chaining, has proven to be very effective. It is able to delay the buildup of collision chains, which results in superior performance even at high load factors.

Using coalesced chaining, instead of resolving a collision at the adjacent location, if it is empty, a collision resolution index (CRI) is used with initial value equal to the largest index in the hash table. If the location at the CRI is empty, the word is placed there. If the location at the CRI is filled, the CRI is decremented until the first empty location is found. There are some details that have been omitted and are described in a more formal statement of the algorithm in the following section.

A link array that contains integer values (index locations) and of size equal to the hash table is initialized to −1 in every cell. This array keeps track of collision chains. That is, the entry at a given index, if not −1, indicates the next index location in the hash table that must be searched.

Algorithm For Coalesced Chaining During Word Insertion

1. Initialize the link array so that every cell contains −1.

2. Initialize the collision resolution index (CRI) to the highest index in the hash table.

3. Obtain the hash index for the word being inserted.

4. If the hash table is empty at the value of hash index, insert the word and exit.

5. If the table is occupied with another word at the hash index, determine whether the link array contains an entry other than −1. If it does, trace through the link array until the first non-negative value is found. At each index in the link array, check to see whether the word being inserted is in the hash table. If it is, exit because no duplicates are allowed.

6. Determine the location at which to resolve the collision by starting at the present CRI location and seeing whether the hash table is empty at that value. If so, insert the word and update the link array. If not, decrement the CRI until the first empty location is found. Then insert the word and update the link array.

The algorithm is illustrated using a toy-sized problem in which seven words are inserted into a hash table of size 10, shown in Table 13.3.

TABLE 13.3 Hash table of size 10

Word	Hash Index
Ice	2
Tea	3
The	3
Gym	2
Ate	9
Dog	3
Cat	2

After each word is inserted, the hash table and link array are shown.

Insert Ice (hash index 2)

```
---   ---   Ice ---  ---  ---  ---  ---  ---  ---
-1    -1    -1   -1   -1   -1   -1   -1   -1   -1
```

Insert Tea (hash index 3)

```
---   ---   Ice Tea ---  ---  ---  ---  ---  ---
-1    -1    -1   -1   -1   -1   -1   -1   -1   -1
```

Insert The (hash index 3)

```
---   ---   Ice Tea ---  ---  ---  ---  ---  The
-1    -1    -1    9   -1   -1   -1   -1   -1   -1
```

Insert Gym (hash index 2)

```
---   ---   Ice Tea ---  ---  ---  ---  Gym The
-1    -1     8    9   -1   -1   -1   -1   -1   -1
```

Insert Ate (hash index 9)

```
---   ---   Ice Tea ---  ---  ---  Ate Gym The
-1    -1     8    9   -1   -1   -1   -1   -1    7
```

Insert Dog (hash index 3)

```
---   ---   Ice Tea ---  ---  Dog Ate Gym The
-1    -1     8    9   -1   -1   -1    6   -1    7
```

Insert Cat (hash index 2)

```
---   ---   Ice Tea ---  Cat Dog Ate Gym The
-1    -1     8    9   -1   -1   -1    6    5    7
```

The average number of probes required to find one of the words in the hash table given above is determined by computing the number of probes for each word and taking the sum and dividing by the number of words.

Probes to find **Ice**: 1
Probes to find **Tea**: 1
Probes to find **The**: 2
Probes to find **Gym**: 2
Probes to find **Ate**: 2
Probes to find **Dog**: 4
Probes to find **Cat**: 3
Total probes: 15
Average number probes = 15 / 7

Using linear chaining, the hash table is shown after each insertion and the average number of probes computed.

Insert Ice (hash index 2)

```
--- --- Ice --- --- --- --- --- --- ---
```

Insert Tea (hash index 3)

```
--- --- Ice Tea --- --- --- --- --- ---
```

Insert The (hash index 3)

```
--- --- Ice Tea The --- --- --- --- ---
```

Insert Gym (hash index 2)

```
--- --- Ice Tea The Gym --- --- --- ---
```

Insert Ate (hash index 9)

```
--- --- Ice Tea The Gym --- --- --- Ate
```

Insert Dog (hash index 3)

```
--- --- Ice Tea The Gym Dog --- --- Ate
```

Insert Cat (hash index 2)

```
--- --- Ice Tea The Gym Dog Cat --- Ate
```

Probes to find **Ice**: 1
Probes to find **Tea**: 1
Probes to find **The**: 2
Probes to find **Gym**: 4
Probes to find **Ate**: 1
Probes to find **Dog**: 4
Probes to find **Cat**: 6
Total probes using linear chaining: 19 / 7

The performance of the table using linear chaining is therefore slower because the average number of probes is 27 percent greater.

13.23.3 Simulation Experiment to Compare Linear Chaining and Coalesced Chaining

A simulation experiment is designed to compare the performance of a hash table that is constructed using linear chaining with one that is constructed using coalesced chaining. For each collision resolution algorithm, the average number of probes is estimated as a function of the load factor. A hash function of size 100,000 words is simulated using a random number generator. A random index across the range from the smallest to the largest available index is used to determine the hash index of the simulated word. Instead of actually storing the word in the hash table, a Boolean value of true is used to indicate the presence of the word and false to indicate an empty location. It is assumed that no duplicate words are inserted in the table. The table is initially set to empty by setting each value in the simulated table to false.

Listing 13.19 presents the details of this simulation experiment. The results are displayed after the source listing and are interesting.

LISTING 13.19 Simulation to evaluate the performance of linear chaining

```
using System;

namespace CollisionResolution {

    public class Chaining {

        // Fields
        private const int SIZE = 100000;
        private int probes;
        private bool[] words = new bool[SIZE];
        private Random randomValue = new Random();
        private int [] link = new int[SIZE];
        private int collisionResolutionIndex = SIZE-1;
        private int count;

        public void
            GenerateTableWithLinearChaining(double loadFactor) {
            // Empty the table
            for (int i = 0; i < SIZE; i++) {
                words[i] = false;
            }
            count = (int)(SIZE * loadFactor);
            probes = 0;
            for (int i = 0; i < count; i++) {
                int hashIndex = randomValue.Next(SIZE);
                while (words[hashIndex] == true) {
                    hashIndex++;
                    probes++;
                    if (hashIndex == SIZE) {
                        hashIndex = 0;
                    }
                }
                words[hashIndex] = true;
                probes++;
            }
        }

        public void
            GenerateTableWithCoalescedChaining(double loadFactor) {
            // Empty the table
            for (int i = 0; i < SIZE; i++) {
                words[i] = false;
            }
            count = (int)(SIZE * loadFactor);
            probes = 0;
            collisionResolutionIndex = SIZE-1;
            // Reset the link array
            for (int i = 0; i < SIZE; i++) {
                link[i] = -1;
            }

            for (int i = 0; i < count; i++) {
                int hashIndex = randomValue.Next(SIZE);
```

LISTING 13.19 Simulation to evaluate the performance of linear chaining (continued)

```
            if (words[hashIndex] == false) {
                words[hashIndex] = true;
                probes++;
            } else {
                // Scan to end of collision chain
                int index = hashIndex;
                while (link[index] != -1) {
                    probes++;
                    index = link[index];
                }
                while (words[collisionResolutionIndex]) {
                    collisionResolutionIndex--;
                }
                words[collisionResolutionIndex] = true;
                link[index] = collisionResolutionIndex;
                probes++;
            }
        }
    }

    static void Main() {
        Chaining app = new Chaining();
        Console.WriteLine("Load Factor\t\tAverage Probes");
        Console.WriteLine("\n\t\tUsing Linear Chaining");
        for (double loadFactor = 0.1; loadFactor <= 0.9;
            loadFactor += 0.1) {
            app.GenerateTableWithLinearChaining(loadFactor);
            Console.WriteLine(loadFactor + "\t\t\t" +
                    String.Format("{0:f3}",
                        (double) app.probes / app.count));
        }
        for (double loadFactor = 0.91;
            loadFactor <= 0.999; loadFactor += 0.01) {
            app.GenerateTableWithLinearChaining(loadFactor);
            Console.WriteLine(loadFactor + "\t\t\t" +
              String.Format("{0:f3}",
                    (double)app.probes / app.count));
        }

        Console.WriteLine("\n\t\tUsing Coalesced Chaining");
        app = new Chaining();
        for (double loadFactor = 0.1; loadFactor <= 0.9;
            loadFactor += 0.1) {
            app.GenerateTableWithCoalescedChaining(loadFactor);
            Console.WriteLine(loadFactor + "\t\t\t" +
                    String.Format("{0:f3}",
                        (double) app.probes / app.count));
        }
        for (double loadFactor = 0.91;
            loadFactor <= 0.999; loadFactor += 0.01) {
            app.GenerateTableWithCoalescedChaining(loadFactor);
```

LISTING 13.19 Simulation to evaluate the performance of linear chaining (continued)

```
                    Console.WriteLine(loadFactor + "\t\t\t" +
                        String.Format("{0:f3}",
                            (double)app.probes / app.count));
            }
            Console.ReadLine();
        }
    }
}


/* Program output
Load Factor               Average Probes

                 Using Linear Chaining
0.1                      1.056
0.2                      1.119
0.3                      1.204
0.4                      1.325
0.5                      1.499
0.6                      1.759
0.7                      2.165
0.8                      2.920
0.9                      5.431
0.91                     6.202
0.92                     6.666
0.93                     7.704
0.94                     8.723
0.95                    11.115
0.96                    12.347
0.97                    19.442
0.98                    26.759
0.99                    44.370


                 Using Coalesced Chaining
0.1                      1.002
0.2                      1.008
0.3                      1.017
0.4                      1.032
0.5                      1.054
0.6                      1.081
0.7                      1.120
0.8                      1.169
0.9                      1.228
0.91                     1.234
0.92                     1.237
0.93                     1.249
0.94                     1.261
0.95                     1.254
0.96                     1.266
0.97                     1.273
0.98                     1.285
0.99                     1.283
*/
```

As shown in the output, for linear chaining the average number of probes grows slowly until the load factor reaches about 0.5. As the load factor increases towards 1, the average number of probes shoots upwards asymptomatically approaching infinity. The reason for the rapid deterioration in performance with load factor for linear chaining is the buildup of collision chains.

For linear chaining, there is clearly a trade-off between memory usage and execution time. If less empty space is used (better memory usage—a larger dictionary of words can be fit into a table of given size), the higher the load factor and the higher the average probes and the lower the performance.

For coalesced chaining, the average number of probes is only slightly greater than 1 even for a load factor of 0.99. This is significant. High performance is attainable while getting good utilization of the available memory. There is no dramatic trade-off between memory usage and execution time. This is unusual and a counter example to the usual trade-off between memory usage and execution time.

13.24 SUMMARY

♦ The benefit of using nonlinear data structures is efficiency. Access time to information stored in a tree or hash table is generally significantly faster than in a linear data structure.

♦ A tree has a single entry point called the root.

♦ A binary tree contains a root node as an entry point. If the tree is empty, the root is null. Each node in a binary tree is the root of a left sub-tree and a right sub-tree. These left and right sub-trees may be empty.

♦ There are three standard algorithms for traversing a binary tree. Each of these is recursive: in-order, pre-order, and post-order traversal.

♦ A binary tree search satisfies the following three conditions:

   ♦ Every node in a binary search tree has a value that is greater than any node in its left sub-tree.

   ♦ Every node in a binary search tree has a value that is smaller than any node in its right sub-tree.

   ♦ No duplicate values are allowed in a binary search tree.

♦ The ACE metric represents the average number of comparison operations that is required in searching for a randomly selected node in a binary tree. The larger the ACE metric is for a given tree, the lower its search efficiency.

♦ The ACE value of a search tree is minimum when the tree is perfectly balanced. This is possible only for trees that contain exactly $2^n - 1$ nodes where n is an integer.

♦ A binary search tree is an AVL if and only if for every node in the tree the difference between the maximum depth of the right sub-tree minus the maximum depth of the left sub-tree is less than 2 in magnitude. That is, the difference can be −1, 0, or 1.

♦ The algorithm designed by Adelson-Velskii and Landis for insertion into an AVL tree has the following characteristics:

♦ Perform an ordinary insertion into the search tree. Recompute the balances of all the nodes. If the tree is still an AVL tree, exit.

♦ Starting at the node inserted, backtrack up the search path towards the root node. If a combination of nodes is found in which the parent has a balance of $+/-2$ and the node a balance of $+/-1$, if the signs of the node and parent balance are the same, a type 1 configuration exists, and if the signs of the node and parent balance are the opposite, a type 2 configuration exists.

♦ If the configuration is type 1, perform a single rotation on the parent node whose balance is $+/-2$ in a direction to restore balance.

♦ If the configuration is type 2, perform a sequence of two rotations. The first rotation is on the node whose balance is $+/-1$ in a direction to restore balance. The second rotation, always in a direction opposite the first rotation, is on the parent node whose balance is $+/-2$.

♦ The algorithm for deletion from an AVL tree follows closely the algorithm for insertion with only the following differences:

♦ Perform an ordinary search tree deletion from the existing AVL tree.

♦ Recompute the balances of each node.

♦ If the tree continues to be an AVL tree, exit.

♦ If the tree is not an AVL tree, traverse the search path from the node being deleted to the root node. Stop when one of the following combinations of balances are found concerning the node in the search path and its parent:

♦ The node has a balance of $+/-1$ and its parent a balance of $+/-2$. Determine whether the configuration is type 1 or type 2, as before. Perform the necessary single or double rotations based on the type of configuration.

♦ The node has a balance of 0 and its parent a balance of $+/-2$. This situation can never occur with AVL insertion. Consider this a type 1 configuration and perform the necessary single rotation on the parent node with balance of $+/-2$.

♦ Re-evaluate the balances of all the nodes. There is a possibility that as a consequence of the rotation performed in steps (a) or (b), another configuration of either type 1 or type 2 exists because of a node that now has a balance of $+/-2$. After correcting the new imbalance, continue the step until the root node is reached or there are no further nodes going up the search path toward the root that have balances of $+/-2$.

♦ When inserting into an AVL tree, approximately 50 percent of such insertions require no rotational correction. Among the roughly 50 percent of insertions that require rotation, about half require one rotation (type 1 configuration) and half require two rotations (type 2 configuration).

◆ When deleting from an AVL tree, approximately 80 percent of such deletions require no rotational correction. Among the roughly 20 percent of insertions that require rotation, half are of type 1 and half of type 2. Only rarely are multiple rotations up the search path needed.

◆ The formal rules that define a red-black binary search tree are the following:

  ◆ Every node is colored either red or black.

  ◆ The root node is always black.

  ◆ Every external node (null child of a leaf node) is black.

  ◆ If a node is red, both of its children are black.

  ◆ Every path from the root to an external node contains the same number of black nodes.

◆ The efficiency of the red-black implementation that does not employ upward links to parent nodes is poor compared to AVL trees. The deletion inefficiency of such red-black trees is caused by the need to frequently construct a stack from root to a given node in order to obtain parent and sibling information. The computational overhead associated with this is unreasonable.

◆ After implementing a red-black tree with nodes that link upward to their parent, the performance of a red-black tree compares very favorably to an AVL tree.

◆ A complete binary tree is one in which all possible nodes are present at each level except the lowest level where leaf nodes are present from left to right.

◆ A heap is a complete binary tree in which the contents of any node must be greater than or equal to the contents of all its descendents.

◆ Hash tables provide an efficient implementation of the set abstraction. The key operation of the set abstraction is the determination of whether an object is present or not present. In exchange for efficiency in determining set membership, a set does not support the ordering of information as a search tree does.

◆ A perfect hash function would be one that produces a one-to-one mapping between any possible word and the hash index associated with the word.

◆ The study of hashing is principally concerned with two problems:

  ◆ Designing an efficient hash function that appears to randomly associate the object being inserted with a hash index

  ◆ Designing an efficient collision resolution to move equivalence classes of words whose hash index values collide

◆ With linear chaining, when a collision occurs, the word that has collided is placed in the first empty array location to the right of the existing word.

◆ The load factor is defined as the ratio of the number of words (or objects in general) divided by the size of the table.

◆ Another collision resolution algorithm, coalesced chaining, has proven to be very effective. It is able to delay the buildup of collision chains, which results in superior performance even at high load factors.

◆ For linear chaining, there is clearly a trade-off between memory usage and execution time.

13.25 ADDITIONAL EXERCISES

Exercise 13.18

Sketch the binary search tree that results from the insertion of the following sequence of integers: 200, 50, 300, 250, 275, 400, 75, and 80.

Exercise 13.19

Sketch the AVL tree that results from the insertion of the same sequence of integers as given in Exercise 13.18.

Exercise 13.20

Compute the ACE value for the trees produced in Exercises 13.18 and 13.19 and compare them.

Exercise 13.21

Perform a sequential deletion of all the nodes in the AVL tree of Exercise 13.19. Delete the nodes in the same sequence as they were inserted.

Exercise 13.22

Add a method *IsAVL* to class *BinarySearchTree<T>*. This method returns true if the binary search tree is an AVL tree; otherwise it returns false.

Exercise 13.23

Implement a query *IsPerfectlyBalanced* in class *BinarySearchTree<T>* that returns true if the search tree is perfectly balanced; otherwise it returns false.

Exercise 13.24

Implement a query *MinimumDepth* in class *BinarySearchTree<T>* that returns the level of the leaf node whose level is closest to the root level.

Exercise 13.25

Implement a query *Level (T item)* in class *BinarySearchTree<T>* that returns the level of item.

Exercise 13.26

Implement a public query method *LeafNodes* that returns a *DoublyLinkedList<T>* of the items in the leaf nodes of a *BinarySearchTree<T>*.

Exercise 13.27

Implement a public query method *ItemsAtLevel(int level)* that returns a *DoublyLinkedList<T>* of the items at the specified level in a *BinarySearchTree<T>*.

Exercise 13.28

Show the red-black tree after each of the following integers are inserted into the tree:

100, 200, 300, 50, 75, 125, 225, 10, 15.

Exercise 13.29

Show the red-black tree after each deletion if the nodes are deleted in the same sequence as they were inserted in Exercise 13.28.

Exercise 13.30

Construct a deletion problem that requires case 1.

Exercise 13.31

Construct a deletion problem that requires case 2a.

Exercise 13.32

Construct a deletion problem that requires case 2b.

Exercise 13.33

Construct a deletion problem that requires case 3.

Exercise 13.34 (Major Project)

Implement class *RedBlackTree* using a nested class *Node* that contains only links to *left* and *right* child and no upward link to parent nodes.

CHAPTER 14

Standard Collections and Serialization

Chapters 12 and 13 discussed the construction of linear and nonlinear classic data structures from the inside out. The focus was on how to "roll your own" collection types. The skills associated with manipulating linked structures such as stack, queue, deque, list, and tree are fundamental in problem solving. There are numerous occasions when one needs to construct a customized collection class to meet the needs of a more advanced application.

Recognizing that collections of various types are important building blocks in many software development applications, the .NET framework provides a useful assortment of standard collection types. Given a choice between using one of your own collection types versus using an appropriate standard collection type, it is always better to choose the standard collection type. In all likelihood the standard collection is more efficiently implemented. But most importantly, the use of standard types promotes easier maintenance because standard types are universally available.

The namespaces *System.Collections* and *System.Collections.Generics* provide the basis for standard C# collection classes. This chapter introduces these collection classes and demonstrates their use. Several applications that require the use of standard collections are presented.

It is important to be able to store collections of objects. C# supports such "object persistence" through the mechanism of serialization. This subject is briefly examined and an example is presented that illustrates this important capability.

14.1 STANDARD COLLECTIONS FROM THE SYSTEM.COLLECTIONS NAMESPACE

Namespace *System.Collections* includes the following standard nongeneric concrete collection classes:

◆ ArrayList

◆ Stack

- Queue
- BitArray
- Hashtable
- SortedList

Standard generic collections are considered in Section 14.2.

14.1.1 ArrayList

ArrayList is an important and versatile collection class. It models an indexable list with index zero as the first index in the list. An *ArrayList* is a dynamic array—its size grows on demand as objects are inserted into it. Because a get/set indexer is defined, objects can be inserted and accessed in much the same way as in an ordinary array. The example, *myList[15] = 12.6*, assumes that index 15 is within the index range of the existing *myList*.

The initial default capacity of an *ArrayList* is 16. The capacity grows automatically if more than 16 objects are added to the collection. The *TrimToSize()* method causes the capacity to be reduced to the current number of objects in the collection. Table 14.1 lists many of the public properties and methods of class *ArrayList*.

TABLE 14.1 Methods and properties of *ArrayList*

Method	Description
Add	Adds an object to the end of the *ArrayList*
AddRange	Adds any *ICollection* to the end of the *ArrayList*
BinarySearch	Searches for object in sorted *ArrayList*
Clear	Removes all objects from *ArrayList*
Clone	Creates a shallow copy of the *ArrayList*
Contains	Determines whether an object is present in *ArrayList*
CopyTo	Copies all or part of an *ArrayList* to a one-dimensional array
GetEnumerator	Supports iteration through an *ArrayList*
GetRange	Returns an *ArrayList* that is a subset of the original *ArrayList*
IndexOf	Returns the index of the first occurrence of an object in *ArrayList*
Insert	Inserts an object at a specified index in *ArrayList*
InsertRange	Inserts any *ICollection* at specified index in *ArrayList*
LastIndexOf	Returns index of the last occurrence of object in *ArrayList*
Remove	Removes the first occurrence of object in *ArrayList*
RemoveAt	Removes object at specified index from *ArrayList*
RemoveRange	Removes a subset of *ArrayList* at specified index
Repeat	Replicates given value a specified number of times in *ArrayList*
Reverse	Reverses part of or an entire *ArrayList*
SetRange	Copies an *ICollection* over a specified portion of an *ArrayList*
Sort	Sorts the objects in the *ArrayList* using *CompareTo* or a specified implementation of *IComparer*

TABLE 14.1   Methods and properties of *ArrayList* (continued)

ToArray	Copies an *ArrayList* to an array
TrimToSize	Sets the capacity equal to the current size of the *ArrayList*
Property	**Description**
Capacity	The current size of the *ArrayList* (grows on demand)
Count	Returns the number of objects in the *ArrayList*
this	Get/set indexer that allows an array-like mechanism for access and assignment

Listing 14.1 presents a short application that exercises some of the important methods of class *ArrayList*.

LISTING 14.1   Short application that exercises *ArrayList*

```
using System;
using System.Collections;

namespace StandardCollections {

    public class StandardCollections {

        static void Main() {

            ArrayList myList = new ArrayList();
            for (int value = 5; value <= 20; value += 5) {
                myList.Add(value);
            }
            int[] values = {21, 22, 23, 24, 25};
            myList.AddRange(values);
            myList.Reverse(2, 5);
            myList[0] = 1;
            foreach (int value in myList) {
                Console.Write(value + "  ");
            }
            Console.WriteLine();

            int[] data = new int[10];
            myList.CopyTo(data);
            foreach (int value in data) {
                Console.Write(value + "  ");
            }
            Console.WriteLine();
            if (myList.Contains(22)) {
                Console.WriteLine("22 in myList");
            }
```

LISTING 14.1 Short application that exercises *ArrayList* (continued)

```
                    myList.RemoveRange(3, 3);
                    myList.Sort();
                    foreach (int value in myList) {
                        Console.Write(value + "  ");
                    }
                    Console.WriteLine();

                    Console.ReadLine();
                }
            }
        }
        /* Program output
        1   10   23   22   21   20   15   24   25
        1   10   23   22   21   20   15   24   25   0
        22 in myList
        1   10   15   23   24   25
        */
```

Exercise 14.1

Explain the output of Listing 14.1.

14.1.2 Stack

The stack abstraction is defined and explained in Chapter 12. Table 14.2 presents many methods and properties of this simple first-in, last-out standard collection.

TABLE 14.2 Methods and properties of *Stack*

Method	Description
Clear	Removes all objects from the *Stack*
Clone	Produces a shallow copy of *Stack*
Contains	Determines whether an object is present in *Stack*
CopyTo	Copies all or a portion of a *Stack* to an array
GetEnumerator	Supports iteration through a *Stack*
Peek	Accesses the top object in the *Stack* without removing it
Pop	Removes and returns the object on top of the *Stack*
Push	Inserts an object onto the top of the *Stack*
ToArray	Copies the *Stack* objects into an array
Property	**Description**
Count	Returns the number of objects in the *Stack*

The standard stack abstraction with methods and property given in Table 14.2 represents a richer abstraction than the one defined in Chapter 12. The stack abstraction defined in Chapter 12 does not support iteration, *Contains*, or the ability to transfer objects to an array directly. Furthermore, the *Pop* operation is defined as a command in Chapter 12, consistent with the command/query mechanism for constructing classes.

Suppose we add the following code to Listing 14.1:

```
Stack myStack = new Stack(myList);
myStack.Push(7);
myStack.Push(6);
myStack.Push(5);
foreach (int value in myStack) {
    Console.Write(value + " ");
}
Console.WriteLine();
```

Here *myStack* is constructed from *myList*. Note that the objects are effectively reversed by the stack because of the first-in, last-out nature of the stack. The new line of output confirms this:

```
5  6  7  25  24  23  15  10  1
```

14.1.3 Queue

The queue abstraction is presented in Chapter 12. Table 14.3 lists many methods and properties of this first-in, first-out standard collection.

TABLE 14.3 Methods and properties for *Queue*

Method	Description
Clear	Removes all objects from the *Queue*
Clone	Produces a shallow copy of *Queue*
Contains	Determines whether an object is present in *Queue*
CopyTo	Copies all or a portion of a *Queue* to an array
Dequeue	Removes and returns the object at the front of the *Queue*
Enqueue	Inserts an object at the end of the *Queue*
GetEnumerator	Supports iteration through a *Queue*
Peek	Accesses front of *Queue* without removing it
ToArray	Copies the *Queue* objects into an array
TrimToSize	Sets the capacity equal to the current size of the *Queue*
Property	**Description**
Count	Returns the number of objects in the *Queue*

As with the *Pop* method of the *Stack*, the *Dequeue* method both changes the internal state of the *Queue* and returns the front. This practice has been avoided in the classes developed throughout this book.

Consider the following code:

```
Queue myQueue = new Queue();
myQueue.Enqueue("CCC");
myQueue.Enqueue("BBB");
myQueue.Enqueue("AAA");
myQueue.Dequeue();
foreach (String value in myQueue) {
    Console.WriteLine(value);
}
Console.WriteLine();
```

If this code is added to method *Main* in Listing 14.1, the output is:

```
BBB
AAA
```

14.1.4 BitArray

The *BitArray* collection provides support for bit manipulation. Many of its methods and properties are given in Table 14.4. The *BitArray* collection is stored as an array of Boolean values where true indicates that the bit is on and false indicates that the bit is off.

TABLE 14.4 Methods and properties of *BitArray*

Method	Description
And	Performs the bitwise AND operation on the elements in the current *BitArray* against the corresponding elements in the specified *BitArray*
Clone	Creates a shallow copy of the *BitArray*
CopyTo	Copies all or a portion of a *BitArray* to an array
Get	Gets the value of the bit at a specific position in the *BitArray*
GetEnumerator	Supports iteration through a *BitArray*
Not	Inverts all the bit values in the current *BitArray*, so that elements set to true are changed to false, and elements set to false are changed to true
Or	Performs the bitwise OR operation on the elements in the current *BitArray* against the corresponding elements in the specified *BitArray*
Set	Sets the bit at a specific position in the *BitArray* to the specified value

TABLE 14.4 Methods and properties of *BitArray* (continued)

SetAll	Sets all bits in the *BitArray* to the specified value
Xor	Performs the bitwise exclusive OR operation on the elements in the current *BitArray* against the corresponding elements in the specified *BitArray*

Property	**Description**
Count	Returns the number of elements in the *BitArray*
this	Enables get/set for indexable access to *BitArray*
Length	Gets/sets number of elements in *BitArray*

A classic application that uses a *BitArray* collection is the Sieve of Eratosthenes algorithm for computing prime numbers.

The values in the *BitArray* are used to record the presence of a prime number. A value true at a given index indicates the presence of a prime number corresponding to that index, and a value false at a given index indicates that the index is not a prime number.

All the values in the *BitArray* are initialized to true. Starting with the first known prime number, 2, the bits at 4, 6, 8, ..., are set to false because any multiple of a prime number cannot be prime. For the next prime number, 3, the bits at 6, 9, 12, ... are set to false. Then for the next prime number, 5, the bits at 10, 15, 20, ... are set to false.

Class *Sieve* presented in Listing 14.2 encapsulates this Sieve of Eratosthenes algorithm in its *GeneratePrimes* command. An application class *PrimesApp* is shown in Listing 14.3.

LISTING 14.2 Class *Sieve*

```
using System;
using System.Collections;

namespace BitManipulation {

    /*
     * Generates prime numbers from 2 to upTo
     * using BitArray collection.
     */
    public class Sieve {

        // Fields
        private ArrayList primes = new ArrayList();
        private int numberPrimesFound;
        private int upTo;

        public Sieve(int upTo) {
            this.upTo = upTo;
        }
```

LISTING 14.2 Class *Sieve* (continued)

```
        // Properties
        public ArrayList Primes {
            get {
                return primes;
            }
        }

        public int NumberPrimesFound {
            get {
                return numberPrimesFound;
            }
        }

        // Commands
        public void GeneratePrimes() {
            BitArray bitset = new BitArray(upTo + 1);
            numberPrimesFound = 0;
            int i = 2;
            // Set all the bits
            bitset.SetAll(true);
            /*
             * If i is prime, add i to ArrayList of primes
             * and disable the following bits:
             * 2 * i, 3 * i, 4 * i, ...
             * since those values are multiples of i and cannot be
             * prime.
             */
            while (i * i <= upTo) {
                if (bitset[i]) {
                    primes.Add(i);
                    numberPrimesFound++;
                    // Disable multiples of the prime value i
                    int k = 2 * i;
                    while (k <= upTo) {
                        bitset.Set(k, false);
                        k += i;
                    }
                }
                i++;
            }
            //Fill out the bitset of primes from sqrt(upTo) to upTo
            while (i <= upTo) {
                if (bitset[i]) {
                    primes.Add(i);
                    numberPrimesFound++;
                }
                i++;
            }
        }
    }
}
```

LISTING 14.3 Class *PrimesApp*

```
using System;
using System.Collections;

namespace BitManipulation {

    public class PrimesApp {

        public static void Main(String [] args) {
            if (args.Length != 0) {
                Console.WriteLine("Usage:  BitManipulation #UpTo");
            } else {
                try {
                    int upTo = Convert.ToInt32(args[0]);

                    Sieve sieve = new Sieve(upTo);
                    sieve.GeneratePrimes();
                    ArrayList result = sieve.Primes;
                    int count = 0;
                    foreach (int prime in result) {
                        if (count % 10 == 0) {
                            Console.WriteLine();
                        }
                        Console.Write(prime + "\t");
                        count++;
                    }
                    Console.WriteLine();
                    Console.ReadLine();
                } catch (Exception) {
                    Console.WriteLine("Usage: BitManipulation #UpTo");
                }
            }
        }
    }
}
```

LISTING 14.3 Class *PrimesApp* (continued)

```
/* Program output when input is 1000
2     3     5     7     11    13    17    19    23    29
31    37    41    43    47    53    59    61    67    71
73    79    83    89    97    101   103   107   109   113
127   131   137   139   149   151   157   163   167   173
179   181   191   193   197   199   211   223   227   229
233   239   241   251   257   263   269   271   277   281
283   293   307   311   313   317   331   337   347   349
353   359   367   373   379   383   389   397   401   409
419   421   431   433   439   443   449   457   461   463
467   479   487   491   499   503   509   521   523   541
547   557   563   569   571   577   587   593   599   601
607   613   617   619   631   641   643   647   653   659
661   673   677   683   691   701   709   719   727   733
739   743   751   757   761   769   773   787   797   809
811   821   823   827   829   839   853   857   859   863
877   881   883   887   907   911   919   929   937   941
947   953   967   971   977   983   991   997
*/
```

14.1.5 Hashtable

The standard *Hashtable* collection is important because it provides an implementation of the *Set* abstraction. Key/value pairs are stored where a key cannot be null and duplicate key values are not allowed. Separate enumerations of keys and values are provided.

Many of the methods and properties of *Hashtable* are given in Table 14.5.

TABLE 14.5 Methods and properties of *Hashtable*

Method	Description
Add	Adds an element with the specified key and value into the *Hashtable*; an attempt to add a duplicate key results in an exception being generated
Clear	Removes all key-value pairs from *Hashtable*
Clone	Creates a shallow copy of the *Hashtable*
Contains	Determines whether the *Hashtable* contains a specific key
ContainsKey	Determines whether the *Hashtable* contains a specific key
ContainsValue	Determines whether the *Hashtable* contains a specific value
CopyTo	Copies all or a portion of a *Hashtable* to an array
Remove	Removes specified key (and its value) from *Hashtable*

TABLE 14.5 Methods and properties of *Hashtable* (continued)

Property	Description
Count	Returns the number of key/value pairs in *Hashtable*
this	Get/set allows insertion or access like an array. The index represents the key. If the key already exists, the key-value pair overwrites the current entry. This is in contrast to *Add*, which disallows a key that is already present. The array index approach should be used when there is no concern about overwriting an existing key-value pair. The *Add* approach should be used to protect against overwriting an existing key-value pair.
Keys	Returns an *ICollection* of the keys in the *Hashtable*
Values	Returns an *ICollection* of the values in the *Hashtable*

Suppose we want to remove duplicate words from some text. Listing 14.4 presents an application that takes text from the command line and outputs all duplicate and distinct words.

LISTING 14.4 Class *IdentifyDuplicates*

```
using System;
using System.Collections;

namespace Hashtables {

    public class IdentifyDuplicates {

        static void Main(string[] args) {
            Hashtable hashTable = new Hashtable();
            for (int index = 0; index < args.Length; index++) {
                try {
                    hashTable.Add(args[index], null);
                } catch (ArgumentException) {
                    System.Console.WriteLine("Duplicate detected:
                                        " + args[index]);
                }
            }
            System.Console.WriteLine("The following " +
                hashTable.Count + " distinct words detected: ");

            foreach (String str in hashTable.Keys) {
                System.Console.Write(str + " ");
            }
            Console.WriteLine();
            Console.ReadLine();
        }
    }
}
```

Here the *Add* method is used to insert a new key with the value null into the hash table. If the key is already present (a duplicate key), control is diverted to the catch block, which outputs the duplicate word. If the key is unique, it is added to the hash table.

More interesting applications of the *Hashtable* collection are presented later in the chapter.

14.1.6 SortedList

The standard *SortedList* collection contains key/value pairs that are sorted by the keys and are accessible by key and by index. The *SortedList* acts as a blend of an array and *Hashtable*. When a key is accessed by its key (using the indexer property), it acts like a *Hashtable*. When a key is accessed by *GetByIndex* or *SetByIndex*, it acts like an array. Many of its methods and properties are presented in Table 14.6.

TABLE 14.6 Methods and properties of *SortedList*

Method	Description
Add	Adds an element with the specified key and value to the *SortedList*
Clear	Removes all key-value pairs from *SortedList*
Clone	Creates a shallow copy of the *SortedList*
Contains	Determines the presence of a key
ContainsKey	Determines the presence of a key
ContainsValue	Determines the presence of a value
CopyTo	Copies all or a portion of a *SortedList* to an array
GetByIndex	Gets the value at the specified index of the *SortedList*
GetKey	Gets the key at the specified index of the *SortedList*
GetKeyList	Gets the keys in the *SortedList*
GetValueList	Gets the values in the *SortedList*
IndexOfKey	Returns the zero-based index of the specified key in the *SortedList*
IndexOfValue	Returns the zero-based index of the first occurrence of the specified value in the *SortedList*
Remove	Removes the element with the specified key from *SortedList*
RemoveAt	Removes the element at the specified index of *SortedList*
SetByIndex	Replaces the value at a specific index in the *SortedList*
TrimToSize	Sets the capacity to the actual number of elements in the *SortedList*

TABLE 14.6 Methods and properties of *SortedList* (continued)

Property	Description
Capacity	Gets or sets the capacity of the *SortedList*
Count	Gets the number of elements contained in the *SortedList*
this	Gets and sets the value associated with a specific key in the *SortedList*; same conditions as *Hashtable*
Keys	Returns the keys in the *SortedList*
Values	Returns the values in the *SortedList*

An application that compares the performance of the *SortedList* and *Hashtable* collections is presented in Listing 14.5.

LISTING 14.5 Comparing the performance of *SortedList* and *Hashtable*

```
using System;
using System.Collections;
using ElapsedTime;

namespace PerformanceHashtableAndSortedList {

    public class Performance {

        private static int SIZE = 50000;

        public void BuildAndDelete(IDictionary dictionary) {
            for (int i = 0; i < SIZE; i++) {
                dictionary[i] = i;
            }
            for (int i = 0; i < SIZE; i++) {
                dictionary.Remove(i);
            }
        }

        static void Main() {
            Performance p = new Performance();
            Timing time = new Timing();
            time.StartTiming();
            p.BuildAndDelete(new Hashtable());
            time.EndTiming();
            System.Console.WriteLine("Using Hashtable: time for " +
            Performance.SIZE +
                " insertions and deletions: " + time.ElapsedTime());
            time.StartTiming();
            p.BuildAndDelete(new SortedList());
            time.EndTiming();
            System.Console.WriteLine("Using SortedList: time for " +
                Performance.SIZE + " insertions and deletions: " +
```

LISTING 14.5 Comparing the performance of *SortedList* and *Hashtable* (continued)

```
                    time.ElapsedTime());
                System.Console.ReadLine();


            }
        }
    }
/* Program output
Using Hashtable: time for 50000 insertions and deletions: 0.015625
Using SortedList: time for 50000 insertions and deletions: 4.1875
*/
```

Because both *Hashtable* and *SortedList* implement *IDictionary*, this interface is used as the formal parameter type for the method *BuildAndDelete*. Polymorphic substitution allows *Hashtable* or *SortedList* to be the actual type passed into *BuildAndDelete*.

The results show *Hashtable* as more than 250 times faster than *SortedList* for the multiple operations of insert and remove. This is true because after each insertion, the *SortedList* must rearrange its values to maintain order within the collection.

This reordering can be seen if the following code is added to *Main*:

```
Hashtable wordTable = new Hashtable();
wordTable.Add("Star", null);
wordTable.Add("Lamp", null);
wordTable.Add("Car", null);
wordTable.Add("Barge", null);
wordTable.Add("Domestic", null);
wordTable.Add("Computer", null);
foreach (String value in wordTable.Keys) {
    Console.WriteLine(value);
}
Console.WriteLine();
SortedList list = new SortedList();
list.Add("Star", null);
list.Add("Lamp", null);
list.Add("Car", null);
list.Add("Barge", null);
list.Add("Domestic", null);
list.Add("Computer", null);
foreach (String value in list.Keys) {
    Console.WriteLine(value);
}
```

The output is:

```
Domestic
Computer
```

```
Barge
Star
Car
Lamp

Barge
Car
Computer
Domestic
Lamp
Star
```

Exercise 14.2

Compare the search time using method *Contains* between a *Hashtable* and *SortedList* if 500,000 integers are loaded into each table and a determination is made whether each integer is present in the *Hashtable* and in the *SortedList*.

14.2 STANDARD COLLECTIONS FROM THE SYSTEM.COLLECTIONS.GENERIC NAMESPACE

The recently added *System.Collections.Generic* namespace in .NET 2005 contains a much larger list of classes than the older *System.Collections* namespace. Each of these classes has one or two generic parameters. A generic version of *ArrayList* is not included but is replaced with *List<T>* in this new namespace. The classes and structs in the new namespace include:

- Stack<T>
- Queue<T>
- Dictionary<K, V>
- KeyValuePair<K, V>
- Dictionary.KeyCollection<K, V>
- Dictionary.ValueCollection<K, V>
- LinkedList<T>
- LinkedListNode<T>
- List<T>
- ReadOnlyCollection<T>
- SortedDictionary<K, V>
- struct Stack.Enumerator<T>
- struct Queue.Enumerator<T>
- struct Dictionary.Enumerator<K, V>
- struct KeyValuePair<K, V>
- struct Dictionary.KeyCollection.Enumerator<K, V>

- ◆ struct Dictionary.ValueCollection.Enumerator<K, V>
- ◆ struct LinkedList.Enumerator<T>
- ◆ struct List.Enumerator<T>

Two of these generic collection classes will be examined: *Dictionary<K, V>* and *LinkedList<T>*. The class *List<T>* will be skipped because it is identical to *ArrayList* except that it is generic.

14.2.1 Dictionary<K, V>

This class is a generalization of the older *Hashtable* class. Key-value pairs with generic types K and V may be added to the *Dictionary*.

Table 14.7 presents all the methods and properties of this new generic collection.

TABLE 14.7 Methods and properties of Dictionary<K, V>

Method	Signature	Comments
Add	```public sealed void Add(K key, V value);```	Adds key-value pair of types K and V, respectively
Clear	`public sealed void Clear();`	Removes all objects
ContainsKey	```public sealed bool ContainsKey(K key);```	Returns true if key is present
ContainsValue	```public bool ContainsValue(V value);```	Returns true if value is present
Enumerator	`public Dictionary.Enumerator<K, V> GetEnumerator();`	Allows enumeration
Remove	```public sealed bool Remove(K key);```	Removes the key
Properties		
Count	`public virtual int Count {get;}`	Returns the number of key-value pairs
this	```public virtual V this (K key) {get; set;}```	Set/get indexer
Dictionary.KeyCollection	```public Dictionary.KeyCollection<K, V> Keys {get;}```	Returns keys
Dictionary.ValueCollection	```public Dictionary.ValueCollection<K, V> Values {get;}```	Returns values

A dictionary is implemented as a hash table. A generic *struct*, *KeyValuePair<K, V>*, is used to hold key/value entries. In the enumeration, *foreach (KeyValuePair<K, V> dictionaryEntry in dictionary) { ... }*, where *dictionary* is an instance of *Dictionary<K, V>*, the *dictionaryEntry* instances are copies of the values in the dictionary so changes made to *dictionaryEntry* have no effect on *dictionary*.

Listing 14.6 shows the construction of a dictionary of 109,580 English words that is constructed from a text file that contains one distinct word per line. This file is available from the Course Technology Web site.

LISTING 14.6 Using *Dictionary* to build a collection of words

```
using System;
using System.Collections.Generic;
using System.Collections;
using System.IO;
using ElapsedTime;

namespace GenericCollections {

    public class BuildDictionaryFromWords{

        static void Main(string[] args) {
            String[] words = new String[110000];
            Dictionary<String, String> dictionary =
                new Dictionary<String, String>();
            StreamReader inputFile = new StreamReader
            ("distinct.txt");
            int numberWords = 0;
            String word = inputFile.ReadLine();
            while (word != null) {
                try {
                    dictionary.Add(word, word);
                    words[numberWords] = word;
                    numberWords++;
                } catch (Exception) { }
                word = inputFile.ReadLine();
            }
            Console.WriteLine("numberWords: " + numberWords);
            Timing timer = new Timing();
            // Lookup every work
            timer.StartTiming();
            bool result = false;
            for (int i = 0; i < numberWords; i++) {
                result = dictionary.ContainsKey(words[i]);
                // result = dictionary.ContainsValue(words[i]);
            }
            timer.EndTiming();
            Console.WriteLine("The time to look up " + numberWords +
                            " words in dictionary = " +
                                timer.ElapsedTime());
            int count = 0;
```

LISTING 14.6 Using Dictionary to build a collection of words (continued)

```
                foreach (String wrd in dictionary.Keys) {
                    Console.WriteLine(wrd);
                    count++;
                    if (count == 30) {
                        break;
                    }
                }
                Console.ReadLine();
            }
        }
    }
/* Program output
numberWords: 109580
The time to look up 109580 words in dictionary = 0.015625
*/
```

Exercise 14.3

If the commented line,

```
result = dictionary.ContainsValue(words[i]);
```

were used instead of the line above it, what effect would this have on the time it takes to look up the 109,580 words in the dictionary?

14.2.2 LinkedList<T>

The *LinkedList<T>* is implemented as a doubly linked list. Many of its methods and properties are given in Table 14.8.

TABLE 14.8 LinkedList<T>

Method	Signature	Comments

AddAfter	```public void AddAfter(```
	``` LinkedListNode<T> node,```
	``` LinkedListNode<T> newNode```
	```);```
		Adds *newNode* after node

AddBefore	```public void AddBefore(```
	``` LinkedListNode<T> node,```
	```); LinkedListNode<T> newNode```
		Adds *newNode* before node

AddFirst	```public void AddFirst(```
	``` LinkedListNode<T> node```
	```);```
		Adds node to the front of the list

AddLast	```public void AddLast(```
	``` LinkedListNode<T> node```
	```);```
		Adds node to the end of the list

TABLE 14.8 LinkedList<T> (continued)

Clear	`public sealed void Clear();`	Removes all nodes from the list

CopyTo	`public sealed void CopyTo(`
	`    T[] array,`
	`    int index`
	`);`
		Copies list to array

Find	`public LinkedListNode<T> Find(`
	`    T value`
	`);`
		Finds the first occurrence of *value*, if any

FindLast	`public LinkedListNode<T>`
	`FindLast(`
	`    T value`
	`);`
		Finds the last occurrence of *value*, if any

Remove	`public void Remove(`
	`    LinkedListNode<T> node`
	`);`
		Removes node from list

RemoveFirst	`public void RemoveFirst();`	Removes the first node from list
RemoveLast	`public void RemoveLast();`	Removes the last node from list
Property	**Signature**	**Description**
Count	`public virtual int Count` `{get;}`	Returns the number of elements in the list
First	`public LinkedListNode<T> First` `{get;}`	Returns the first node in the list
Last	`public LinkedListNode<T> Last` `{get;}`	Returns the last node in the list

A significant difference between the standard *LinkedList<T>* class and the *DoublyLinkedList<T>* class presented in Chapter 12 is the explicit exposure of nodes in the standard collection class. The *DoublyLinkedList<T>* class hides the existence of nodes and uses the generic parameter *T* in methods *InsertBefore*, *InsertAfter*, *RemoveBefore*, and *RemoveAfter*.

A short code segment is presented following that exercises class *LinkedListNode<T>*.

```
LinkedList<int> doublyLinkedList = new LinkedList<int>();
LinkedListNode<int> node10 = new LinkedListNode<int>(10);
doublyLinkedList.AddFirst(node10);
LinkedListNode<int> node15 = new LinkedListNode<int>(15);
```

```
doublyLinkedList.AddLast(node15);
doublyLinkedList.AddAfter(node10, 12);
doublyLinkedList.AddAfter(node15, 18);
LinkedListNode<int> node20 = new LinkedListNode<int>(20);
doublyLinkedList.AddLast(node20);
doublyLinkedList.Remove(18);
foreach (int value in doublyLinkedList) {
   Console.Write(value + "  ");
}
Console.WriteLine();
// Output
10  12  15  20
```

14.3 APPLICATIONS OF COLLECTIONS

Several applications of collections are presented in this section, including a spelling checker, permutation groups of English words, a palindrome tester, a concordance application, and infix to postfix conversion. Standard collections play a central role in each of these applications.

14.3.1 Spelling Checker

Listing 14.6 demonstrated how to construct a dictionary of English words from a text file containing 109,580 distinct words. This can serve as the core of a complete spelling checker application.

Screenshots of the running application are shown in Figure 14.1.

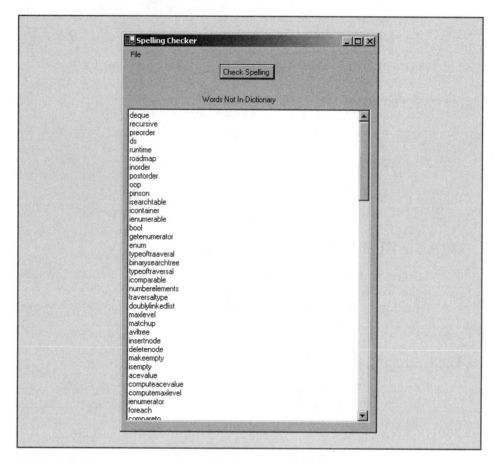

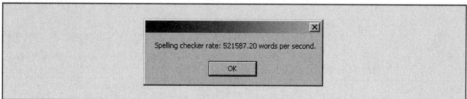

FIGURE 14.1 Screenshots of spelling checker application

Listing 14.7 presents the portion of the source code not automatically generated by the IDE. The throughput on the author's PC is more than one-half million words per second.

LISTING 14.7 Spelling checker application

```
using System;
using System.Collections.Generic;
using System.Collections;
using System.ComponentModel;
using System.Data;
```

LISTING 14.7 Spelling checker application (continued)

```
using System.Drawing;
using System.Windows.Forms;
using System.IO;
using ElapsedTime;


namespace SpellingChecker {

    partial class SpellCheckApp : Form {

        // Fields
        private String filename;
        private StreamReader dictionaryFile;
        private StreamReader inputFile;
        private Dictionary<String, String> dictionary =
            new Dictionary<String, String>();
        private Hashtable notInDictionary = new Hashtable();
        // Filter

        public SpellCheckApp() {
            InitializeComponent();
            dictionaryFile = new StreamReader("distinct.txt");
            String word = dictionaryFile.ReadLine();
            while (word != null) {
                try {
                    dictionary.Add(word, word);
                } catch (Exception) { }
                word = dictionaryFile.ReadLine();
            }
        }

        private void Open_Click(object sender, EventArgs e) {
            openFileDialog.Filter = "txt files (*.txt)|*.txt";
            openFileDialog.Title =
                "Opening file for spelling checking";
            openFileDialog.RestoreDirectory = true;
            if (openFileDialog.ShowDialog() == DialogResult.OK) {
                filename = openFileDialog.FileName;
                inputFile = new StreamReader(filename);
            } else {
                filename = "";
                return;
            }
        }

        private void Exit_Click(object sender, EventArgs e) {
            dictionaryFile.Close();
            inputFile.Close();
            Application.Exit();
        }
```

LISTING 14.7 Spelling checker application (continued)

```
private void checkSpellingBtn_Click(object sender,
                    EventArgs e) {
    notInDictionary.Clear();
    richTextBox.Text = "";
    String delimiterString =
    "\t<>_=;?#!:',[.](){}  \\\n\"-+/* ";
    char[] delimiter = delimiterString.ToCharArray();
    if (inputFile != null) {
        inputFile = new StreamReader(filename);
        String line = inputFile.ReadLine();
        int wordCount = 0;
        Timing timer = new Timing();
        timer.StartTiming();
        while (line != null) {
          String[] symbols = line.Split(delimiter);
          foreach (String str in symbols) {
             wordCount++;
             String word = str.Trim().ToLower();
             int last = word.Length - 1;
             if (word.Length > 1 &&
                 word[0] != '0' && word[0] != '1' &&
                 word[0] != '2' && word[0] != '3' &&
                 word[0] != '4' && word[0] != '5' &&
                 word[0] != '6' && word[0] != '7' &&
                 word[0] != '8' && word[0] != '9' &&
                 word[last] != '0' && word[last] != '1' &&
                 word[last] != '2' && word[last] != '3' &&
                 word[last] != '4' && word[last] != '5' &&
                 word[last] != '6' && word[last] != '7' &&
                 word[last] != '8' && word[last] != '9') {
                 if (!notInDictionary.ContainsKey(word) &&
                         !dictionary.ContainsKey(word)) {
                     richTextBox.AppendText(word);
                     notInDictionary.Add(word, word);
                     richTextBox.AppendText("\n");
                 }
             }
          }
          line = inputFile.ReadLine();
        }
    timer.EndTiming();
    double rate = (double) wordCount / timer.ElapsedTime();
    MessageBox.Show("Spelling checker rate: " +
             String.Format("{0:f2}", rate) +
                     " words per second.");
    }
  }
 }
}
```

The following parsing of the input file using the delimiter is the most interesting part of the application:

```
String delimiterString =
          "\t<>_=;?#!:',[.](){}  \\\n\"-+/* ";
```

The characters that are considered delimiters are included in *delimiterString*. Words are read one line at a time and parsed using the Split query that uses *delimiterString* as its input parameter.

Words are filtered as follows:

1. Words that are one character are not output.

2. Words that are present in *Hashtable notInDictionary* are not output. This prevents duplicate words that are not in the dictionary from being listed.

3. Characters that are present in the delimiter string are not output and are used to separate words.

4. Words that start or end with a numeral are not output.

5. Words that are in the dictionary are not output because they are correctly spelled.

Exercise 14.4

Show how the filtering specified above is performed in the spelling checker application presented in Listing 14.7.

14.3.2 Permutation Groups of English Words

The next application is inspired by the Java tutorial on collections (see Sun's Web site). Permutation groups of words are generated from the text file of words, *distinct.txt*. Every word in the permutation group is constructed from the same collection of characters. An example of a permutation group of size five is:

[**amblers**(walks slowly), **blamers**, **lambers** (meek and mild) **marbles**, **rambles** (talks or writes aimlessly)]

Each of these words is formed from the same basic set of characters 'a', 'b', 'e', 'l', 'm', 'r', 's'.

Two standard collections are featured in this relatively short application: *Dictionary<K, V>* and *SortedList*.

Listing 14.8 presents the details of the application.

LISTING 14.8 Permutation groups of words

```csharp
using System;
using System.Collections;
using System.Collections.Generic;
using System.IO;
using System.Text;


namespace PermutationGroupsOfWords {

    public class PermutationGroupsApp {
```

LISTING 14.8 Permutation groups of words (continued)

```
        // Rearranges the characters in str so that they are in
        // alphabetical order.
        private String Alphabetize(String str) {
            int[] count = new int[256];
            int len = str.Length;
            for (int i = 0; i < len; i++) {
                count[str[i]]++;
            }
            StringBuilder result = new StringBuilder();
            for (char c = 'a'; c <= 'z'; c++) {
                for (int i = 0; i < count[c]; i++) {
                    result.Append(c);
                }
            }
            return result.ToString();
        }

        static void Main(String[] args) {
            PermutationGroupsApp app = new PermutationGroupsApp();

            if (args.Length != 1) {
                System.Console.WriteLine(
                    "Usage:  PermutationGroupsOfWords(size)");
                return;
            }

            try {
                int groupSize = Convert.ToInt32(args[0]);
                Dictionary<String, SortedList> dictionary =
                    new Dictionary<String, SortedList>();
                StreamReader streamReader =
                    new StreamReader("distinct.txt");

                String word;
                while ((word = streamReader.ReadLine()) != null) {
                    String alphabetized = app.Alphabetize(word);
                    SortedList sortedList = null;
                    if (dictionary.ContainsKey(alphabetized)) {
                        sortedList = dictionary[alphabetized];
                    } else { // alphabetized not present in table
                        dictionary[alphabetized] = sortedList =
                            new SortedList();
                    }
                    sortedList.Add(word, word);
                }

                // Output all permutation groups
                ICollection keys = dictionary.Values;
                foreach (SortedList list in keys) {
```

LISTING 14.8 Permutation groups of words (continued)

```
                if (list.Count == groupSize) {
                    System.Console.Write(list.Count + " [");
                    foreach (String wrd in list.Keys) {
                        System.Console.Write(wrd + " ");
                    }
                    System.Console.WriteLine("]");
                }
            }
        } catch (IOException ex) {
            Console.WriteLine(ex.ToString());
        }
        System.Console.ReadLine();
    }
}
```

The private method *Alphabetize* is the computational core of this application. In this method, a *count* array is filled with the frequency count of each letter in the input String. A mutable *StringBuilder* object, *result*, is constructed from the *count* array from smallest letter to largest letter.

Each word that is found in the distinct.txt list of words is reduced to the alphabetized "normal form." These words form the keys in the dictionary. The values are a *SortedList* of all the words that can be reduced to the same normal form.

Following is an application in which the value objects are themselves collections of *String* objects held in a *SortedList*.

The output when the size that is input from the command line is 6 is given after the application.

```
6 [nastier retains retinas retsina stainer stearin ]
6 [dearths hardest hardset hatreds threads trashed ]
6 [arrest rarest raster raters starer terras ]
6 [arils lairs liars liras rails rials ]
6 [esprits persist priests spriest sprites stripes ]
6 [keats skate stake steak takes teaks ]
6 [notes onset seton steno stone tones ]
6 [lavers ravels salver serval slaver versal ]
6 [artiest artiste attires iratest striate tastier ]
6 [earls lares laser rales reals seral ]
6 [aretes easter eaters reseat seater teaser ]
6 [alerting altering integral relating tanglier triangle ]
6 [lusters lustres results rustles sutlers ulsters ]
6 [parties pastier piaster piastre pirates traipse ]
6 [stater strate taster taters tetras treats ]
6 [estrange grantees greatens negaters reagents sergeant ]
6 [leasts slates stales steals tassel teslas ]
6 [esprit priest ripest sprite stripe tripes ]
```

```
6 [paste pates peats septa spate tapes ]
6 [deltas desalt lasted salted slated staled ]
6 [enviers inverse veiners veneris venires versine ]
6 [luster lustre result rustle sutler ulster ]
6 [apter parte pater peart prate taper ]
6 [reigns renigs resign sering signer singer ]
6 [ester reset steer stere terse trees ]
6 [acred arced cadre cared cedar raced ]
6 [parts prats sprat strap tarps traps ]
6 [aspirer parries praiser rapiers raspier repairs ]
6 [laves salve slave vales valse veals ]
6 [reins resin rinse risen serin siren ]
6 [abets baste bates beast beats betas ]
6 [angriest astringe gantries granites ingrates rangiest ]
6 [earings erasing gainers regains reginas searing ]
6 [petrous posture pouters proteus spouter troupes ]
6 [opts post pots spot stop tops ]
```

14.3.3 Palindrome Tester

Palindromes are sequences of words that are spelled the same forward or backward.

The *LinkedList<T>* standard collection can be effectively used to detect the presence of a palindrome. A short application, Palindrome Tester, is shown in Figure 14.2.

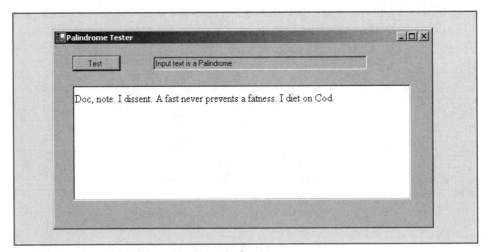

FIGURE 14.2 Palindrome Tester window

Listing 14.9 presents the details of the application.

LISTING 14.9 Palindrome tester

```
using System;
using System.Collections.Generic;
using System.ComponentModel;
using System.Data;
using System.Drawing;
using System.Windows.Forms;

namespace Palindromes {

    partial class PalindromeTesterApp : Form {

        // Fields
        private LinkedList<char> linkedList;

        public PalindromeTesterApp() {
            InitializeComponent();
        }

        private bool IsPalindrome() {
            bool result = true;
            while (linkedList.Count >= 2) {
                char front = linkedList.First.Value;
                while ((front < 'a' || front > 'z') &&
                        (front < 'A' || front > 'Z')) {
                    linkedList.RemoveFirst();
                    front = linkedList.First.Value;
                }
                char rear = linkedList.Last.Value;
                while ((rear < 'a' || rear > 'z') &&
                        (rear < 'A' || rear > 'Z')) {
                    linkedList.RemoveLast();
                    rear = linkedList.Last.Value;
                }
                if (linkedList.Count > 0) {
                    linkedList.RemoveFirst();
                }
                if (linkedList.Count > 0) {
                    linkedList.RemoveLast();
                }
                if (front != rear) {
                    result = false;
                    break;
                }
            }
            return result;
        }
```

LISTING 14.9 Palindrome tester (continued)

```
private void testBtn_Click(object sender, EventArgs e) {
    String textToTest = inputBox.Text.Trim().ToLower();

    linkedList = new LinkedList<char>();
    for (int i = 0; i < textToTest.Length; i++) {
        linkedList.AddLast(textToTest[i]);
    }
    outputBox.Text = IsPalindrome() ?
      "Input text is a Palindrome" :
        "Input text is not a Palindrome";
}
}
}
```

A *LinkedList<char>* is constructed by adding characters to the tail of the list. Characters are then sequentially stripped from the front and rear of the list, ensuring that they are letters. If the front letter does not match the rear letter, the result is changed to false.

14.3.4 Concordance

A concordance is a list of words and associated list of line numbers in which the words appear. Using the generic *Dictionary<K, V>* standard collection as well as a simple regular expression parser, a concordance generator is constructed.

The subject of regular expression searching in C# is discussed in Chapter 15. A small feature of the *Regex* class, designed for regular expression parsing, is used in this application. This class is found in the namespace *System.Text.RegularExpressions*.

An instance, delimiter, of class *Regex* is defined using the expression,

```
Regex delimiter = new Regex("[^a-zA-Z]+");
```

The search string, *"[^a-zA-Z]"*, allows an input string to be parsed into an array of individual strings that contain the alphabetic characters (lower- and uppercase letters).

The query, *Split*, from class *Regex*, is used to form an array of strings based on the regular expression passed to the delimiter given above.

```
String [] wordsOnLine = delimiter.Split(line); // line contains words
```

Class *ConcordanceGenerator* is shown in Listing 14.10.

LISTING 14.10 Class ConcordanceGenerator

```
using System;
using System.Collections.Generic;
using System.Text;
using System.Text.RegularExpressions;
using System.IO;
```

LISTING 14.10 Class ConcordanceGenerator (continued)

```
namespace Concordance {

    public class ConcordanceGenerator {

        // Fields
        private String filename;
        private Dictionary<String, List<int>> dictionary =
            new Dictionary<String, List<int>>();
        private StreamReader inputFile;

        // Constructor
        public ConcordanceGenerator(String filename) {
            this.filename = filename;
        }

        // Properties
        public Dictionary<String, List<int>> Concordance {
            get {
                return dictionary;
            }
        }

        // Commands
        public void GenerateConcordance() {
            inputFile = new StreamReader(filename);
            /* The pattern supplied to the Regex constructor
               indicates that an entire string containing alphabetic
               characters or numerals is to be
               filtered.
            */
            Regex delimiter = new Regex("[^a-zA-Z0]+");
            int lineNumber = 0;
            String line;
            while ((line = inputFile.ReadLine()) != null) {
                String [] wordsOnLine = delimiter.Split(line);
                lineNumber++;
                foreach (String word in wordsOnLine) {
                    if (word != "") {
                        if (!dictionary.ContainsKey(word)) {
                            dictionary[word] = new List<int>();
                        }
                        dictionary[word].Add(lineNumber);
                    }
                }
            }
            inputFile.Close();
        }
    }
}
```

The method *GenerateConcordance* uses the following block of code to construct a *Dictionary<String, list<int>>*:

```
foreach (String word in wordsOnLine) {
   if (word !=  "") {
     if (!dictionary.ContainsKey(word)) {
        dictionary[word] = new List<int>();
        }
        dictionary[word].Add(lineNumber);
   }
}
```

As evident in the preceding code segment, if a word not currently present in the dictionary is encountered, a new list is created and the line number is added to this new list. Otherwise, the line number is added to the existing list of integers.

Exercise 14.5

Write a short application class that exercises the methods of class *ConcordanceGenerator*.

14.3.5 Conversion from Infix to Postfix

A classic application of the *Stack* collection is presented in this section. In addition to being an interesting application of a standard C# collection, the subject of infix to postfix conversion is important in its own right and has been a standard subject in CS 2 courses.

Infix and Postfix Representations

Consider the following arithmetic expressions:

1. a + b
2. a + b * c
3. (a + b) * c
4. a + (b − c) / (d * e)

Each of these expressions is considered to be in infix format because each operator (+, −, *, /) is fixed between two operands. Parentheses are used to override the natural precedence of the operators.

An alternative and important format for representing these and all other arithmetic expressions is the postfix format. In this format, each operator is preceded by two operands. Because the operator occurs after the operands, the name "postfix" is used.

We consider each of the four arithmetic expressions and show the equivalent postfix representation.

For the infix expression, **a + b**, the equivalent postfix form is **ab+**. Reading from right to left, the "+" (addition) operation is performed on the two immediately preceding operands, a and b in this case.

For the infix expression, **a + b * c**, the equivalent postfix form is **abc*+**. Again reading from right to left, the "+" operation is performed on the immediate two operands, *a* and *bc**. In other words, we add the quantities a with b times c.

The infix expression **(a + b) * c** has a postfix representation given by **ab+c***. Reading from right to left, the multiply operation is performed on the two quantities *ab+* (a plus b) and *c*.

Finally, the infix expression **a + (b − c) / (d * e)** has an equivalent postfix representation given by **abc−de*/+**. Reading from right to left, the "+" operation is performed on the quantities *a* and *bc−de*/* (b minus c divided by d times e).

It certainly seems easier to interpret and understand the infix representations, particularly as the complexity of the expressions increase. So why is it useful to have a postfix representation?

The answer is that it is easier to evaluate the postfix representation than the infix representation. This can be accomplished using a relatively simple algorithm that uses a stack as its core information structure.

Algorithm for Evaluating Postfix Expression

1. Initialize an operand stack (holds objects of type double).

2. Read the sequence of symbols in the postfix expression from left to right.

3. If an operand symbol is read, push its real value (we assume that every operand symbol is associated with a real value) onto the operand stack.

4. If an operator symbol is read, pop the stack twice, obtaining two numeric values. Perform the operation indicated by the operator symbol. Push the resulting value onto the operand stack.

5. After all the symbols have been read, the value of the expression is found by popping the stack one final time and returning the value to the user.

As an example, consider the problem of evaluating the postfix expression, **abc−de*/+**. If you recall, this postfix expression corresponds to the infix expression, a + (b − c) / (d * e).

The values of each operand are listed in Table 14.9.

TABLE 14.9 Value of operands

Operand	Value
a	10
b	5
c	2
d	4
e	3

The values associated with the symbols abc are pushed onto the operand stack as follows:

Top of Stack

2

5

10

When the first operator symbol (–) is encountered, the stack is popped twice (stripping the values 2 and 5 from the stack), the operation of subtraction is performed on these values (the second value of 5 minus the first value of 2), and the result 3 is pushed onto the stack, producing:

Top of Stack

3

10

Next, the values associated with the symbols d and e are pushed onto the stack, producing:

Top of Stack

3

4

3

10

When the multiply symbol (*) is encountered, the stack is popped twice (stripping the values 3 and 4 from the stack), the operation of multiplication is performed on these values (the second value of 4 multiplied by the first value of 3), and the result 12 is pushed onto the stack, producing:

Top of Stack

12

3

10

When the division operator (/) is encountered, the stack is popped twice (stripping the values 12 and 3 from the stack), the operation of division is performed on these values (the second value of 3 divided by the first value of 12), and the result 0.25 is pushed onto the stack, producing:

Top of Stack

0.25

10

Finally, when the addition operator (+) is encountered, the stack is popped twice (stripping the values 0.25 and 10 from the stack), the operation of addition is performed on these values (the second value of 10 added to the first value of 0.25), and the result of 10.25 is pushed onto the stack, producing:

Top of Stack

10.25

Because there are no further symbols in the infix expression, the stack is popped one final time, producing the answer 10.25.

For several decades, Hewlett-Packard calculators have been designed around this algorithm. The user is responsible for entering the data in postfix format. An internal stack within the calculator implements the preceding algorithm in producing the answer.

It should be noted that postfix expressions never contain parentheses but only operands and operators. It may therefore be argued that the postfix format is more expressive than the infix expression.

The obvious question is, how can we convert an infix expression to its equivalent postfix form? Once this is answered, the machinery will be in place to perform infix expression evaluation.

Algorithm for Converting from Infix to Postfix Representation

The algorithm for converting an infix expression to its equivalent postfix representation is more complex than the algorithm for evaluating the postfix expression. It is given next and it, too, depends on a *Stack* of operator symbols (objects of type *char*).

1. Initialize an operator stack.

2. Ignoring white-space, and reading from left to right, read a symbol from the infix expression.

3. If the symbol read is a character (we assume here that all operands are represented by lowercase alphabetic characters), append the symbol to the infix expression.

4. If the symbol read is one of the six possible operator symbols—+, −, /, *, (,)—and if the operator stack is not empty, obtain the operator on top of the stack. If the precedence of the stack's top symbol is higher than the precedence of the symbol just read, then if the stack's top symbol is not (, append the stack's top symbol onto the postfix string. Pop the operator stack.

5. If the symbol read is not), push this symbol onto the operator stack.

6. If the symbol read is), pop the operator stack until the first (is found, sequentially appending each operator symbol onto the postfix string.

7. When there are no further symbols in the infix string, pop the leftover operator symbols from the operator stack, sequentially appending them to the postfix string.

Consider the conversion from the infix expression considered earlier, a + (b − c) / (d * e), to postfix using the algorithm given above.

The first symbol, "a", is appended to an empty postfix string producing, the string "a". The next symbol "+" is pushed onto the operator stack, producing:

Top of Stack

+

The stack's top symbol, +, has lower precedence than the next symbol read, (. Therefore push the symbol read, (, onto the operator stack, producing:

Top of Stack

(

+

The next non-white-space symbol, "b", is appended to the postfix string yielding, "ab". The stack's top symbol (has lower precedence than the next symbol read, −. This read symbol is pushed onto the operator stack, producing:

Top of Stack

-

(

+

The next symbol, "c", is appended directly to the postfix string, yielding "abc".

The next symbol,), causes the stack to be popped down to the first (, with the symbol − appended to the postfix string, yielding a postfix string abc- and the following operator stack:

Top of Stack

+

The top of the stack, +, has lower precedence than the new symbol read, /, so the / is pushed onto the operator stack, producing:

Top of Stack

/

+

The top of the stack, /, has lower precedence than the new symbol read, (, so this new symbol is pushed onto the operator stack, producing:

Top of Stack

(

/

+

The symbol "d" is appended directly to the postfix string, yielding "abc−d" for the postfix string.

The top of the operator stack, (, has lower precedence than the new symbol read, *. This new symbol is pushed onto the operator stack, producing:

Top of Stack

*

(

/

+

The next symbol read, "e", is appended directly to the postfix string, yielding "abc−de".

The final symbol,), causes the stack to be popped down to the first (, causing * to be appended to the postfix string, yielding abc−de* and the following operator stack:

Top of Stack

/

+

The remaining symbols are sequentially popped from the operator stack and appended to the postfix expression, producing the final result, abc−de*/+.

The operator stack holds the operators in non-increasing order of precedence viewing the stack from top to bottom. An operator can be added to this stack only if its precedence is not lower than the operator currently at the top of this stack.

Implementation of Algorithms

The algorithms for converting from infix to postfix and then evaluating the postfix expressions are included in a class *ExpressionEvaluation*, as presented in Listing 14.11. Central to the implementation of these algorithms are the two generic stacks, one with base type *double* and the other with base type *char*. In addition, a generic list, *List<char>*, and generic dictionary, *Dictionary<char, double>*, are used.

LISTING 14.11 Class ExpressionEvaluation

```
using System;
using System.Collections.Generic;
using System.Text;

namespace InfixPostfix {

    public class ExpressionEvaluation {

        // Fields
        private String infix, postfix;
        private char [] operators = {'a', 'b'};
        private List<char> operatorList = new List<char>(
            new char[] { '+', '-', '*', '/', '(', ')'});
        private Dictionary<char, double> values =
            new Dictionary<char, double>();

        // Constructor
        public ExpressionEvaluation(String infixExpression) {
            infix = infixExpression.ToLower();
            InfixToPostfix();
        }

        // Properties
        public String Postfix { // Read-only
            get {
                return postfix;
            }
        }

        // Commands
        public void InfixToPostfix() {
            Stack<char> operatorStack = new Stack<char>();
            char newSymbol, topSymbol;
            postfix = "";
            for (int infixIndex = 0; infixIndex < infix.Length;
                               infixIndex++) {
                newSymbol = infix[infixIndex];
```

LISTING 14.11 Class ExpressionEvaluation (continued)

```
                    if (newSymbol == ' ' || newSymbol == '\t' ||
                    newSymbol == '\n') { // white space
                        continue;
                    }
                    if (newSymbol >= 'a'&& newSymbol <= 'z') { //
                    operand
                        postfix += newSymbol;
                    }
                    if (operatorList.Contains(newSymbol)) {
                        if (operatorStack.Count > 0) {
                            topSymbol = operatorStack.Peek();
                            if (Precedence(topSymbol, newSymbol)) {
                                if (topSymbol != '(') {
                                    postfix += topSymbol;
                                }
                                operatorStack.Pop();
                            }
                        }
                        if (newSymbol != ')') {
                            operatorStack.Push(newSymbol);
                        } else {
                            char ch;
                            // Pop the operator stack down to the first
                            // left parenthesis
                            do {
                                ch = operatorStack.Pop();
                                if (ch != '(') {
                                    postfix += ch;
                                }
                            } while (ch != '(');
                        }
                    }
                }
                // Pop leftover operands
                while (operatorStack.Count > 0) {
                    if (operatorStack.Peek() != '(') {
                        postfix += operatorStack.Pop();
                    }
                }
            }
        }

        public void SetValue(char key, double value) {
            values[key] = value;
        }

        // Query
        public double Evaluate() {
            double operand1, operand2;
            Stack<double> operandStack = new Stack<double>();
```

LISTING 14.11 Class ExpressionEvaluation (continued)

```
        for (int postfixIndex = 0; postfixIndex < postfix.Length;
        postfixIndex++) {
            char ch = postfix[postfixIndex];
            if (ch >= 'a' && ch <= 'z') { // operand
                operandStack.Push(values[ch]);
            } else { // operator
                operand1 = operandStack.Pop();
                operand2 = operandStack.Pop();
                switch (ch) {
                    case '+':
                        operandStack.Push(operand2 + operand1);
                        break;
                    case '-':
                        operandStack.Push(operand2 - operand1);
                        break;
                    case '*':
                        operandStack.Push(operand2 * operand1);
                        break;
                    case '/':
                        operandStack.Push(operand2 / operand1);
                        break;
                }
            }
        }
        return operandStack.Pop();
    }

    private bool Precedence(char symbol1, char symbol2) {
        if ((symbol1 == '+' || symbol1 == '-') &&
            (symbol2 == '*' || symbol2 == '/')) {
            return false;
        } else if (symbol1 == '(' && symbol2 != ')' ||
                    symbol2 == '(') {
            return false;
        } else {
            return true;
        }
    }

    public static void Main() {
        ExpressionEvaluation eval =
            new ExpressionEvaluation("a + (b - c) / (d * e)");
        Console.WriteLine(
        "Postfix expression for a + (b - c) / (d * e) = " +
            eval.Postfix);
        eval.SetValue('a', 10);
        eval.SetValue('b', 5);
        eval.SetValue('c', 2);
        eval.SetValue('d', 4);
```

LISTING 14.11 Class ExpressionEvaluation (continued)

```
                eval.SetValue('e', 3);
                Console.WriteLine(
                    "The expression evaluates to: " +
                        eval.Evaluate());

            eval = new ExpressionEvaluation("a + b * c");
            eval.SetValue('a', 10);
            eval.SetValue('b', 5);
            eval.SetValue('c', 2);
            Console.WriteLine("Postfix expression for a + b * c
                            = "+ eval.Postfix);
            Console.WriteLine("The expression evaluates to: " +
                            eval.Evaluate());


            eval = new ExpressionEvaluation("(a + b) * c");
            eval.SetValue('a', 10);
            eval.SetValue('b', 5);
            eval.SetValue('c', 2);
            Console.WriteLine("Postfix expression for (a + b) * c
                            = " + eval.Postfix);
            Console.WriteLine("The expression evaluates to: " +
                            eval.Evaluate());
            Console.ReadLine();
        }
    }
}
/* Program output
Postfix expression for a + (b - c) / (d * e) = abc-de*/+
The expression evaluates to: 10.25
Postfix expression for a + b * c = abc*+
The expression evaluates to: 20
Postfix expression for (a + b) * c = ab+c*
The expression evaluates to: 30
*/
```

The following field is used to filter operators in the input in method *InfixToPostfix*.

```
private List<char> operatorList = new List<char>(
        new char[] { '+', '-', '*', '/', '(', ')'});
```

Note how the generic operator list is initialized at its point of declaration.

The important private support query *Precedence* compares two operator symbols, *symbol1* and *symbol2*.

Exercise 14.6

Explain in words how the *Precedence* query works.

The public command *SetValue* allows an operand symbol to be associated with a numeric value.

The command *InfixToPostfix*, invoked within the constructor, uses *Stack<char>* to implement the algorithm. There are no distracting downcasts used because of the specification of the base type within the generic stack.

The query *Evaluate* uses *Stack<double>* to implement the evaluation algorithm. It uses the values dictionary to convert each operand symbol in the postfix string to a numeric value.

Method *Main* creates three *ExpressionEvaluation* objects, loads the operands with values, and outputs the postfix expressions and the values of the expressions based on the assigned operand values.

14.4 OBJECT SERIALIZATION

The subject of object serialization is briefly introduced in this section. Many of the details of this important subject are beyond the scope of this book. This includes the use of serialization in remote computing, XML serialization, and the low-level details about the mechanics of serialization.

Object serialization is the process of converting an object into a stream of bits so that it can be stored and later reconstructed. The process is fundamental to object persistence—the ability to store and retrieve objects. Object serialization is also used when it is necessary to transmit an object across a network. The object is first serialized into a stream of bits, the bits are transmitted, and the object is reconstructed at the receiving end.

In the .NET framework, formatter objects are used to accomplish object serialization. A concrete formatter class that implements the *System.Runtime.Serialization.IFormatter* interface is *System.Runtime.Serialization.Formatters.Binary.BinaryFormatter*.

The *BinaryFormatter* class produces an efficient and reasonably compact binary representation of an object.

In order for the objects of a class to be serialized, it is necessary that the *Serializable* attribute be used as an annotation as shown in the following code sample. Attributes are declarations embedded in rectangular brackets that annotate programming elements such as types, fields, methods, and properties. Attributes are saved with the metadata in an assembly and are used to affect application behavior at run time.

```
[Serializable]
public class SomeClass {
    // Details not shown
}
```

Without this annotation, objects of *SomeClass* cannot be serialized.

The *[NonSerializable]* attribute can be used to prevent specific fields tagged from being serialized. When an object of such a class is saved, the fields tagged as *[NonSerializable]* are not saved.

Consider the simple example in Listing 14.12.

A formatter object of formal type *IFormatter* and actual type *BinaryFormatter* is created. The *Serialize* command takes a *FileStream* (*outstream* in this case) as the first parameter and the object being serialized as the second parameter.

To recover the object, an input stream of type *FileStream* is opened. The query *Deserialize* with parameter *instream* (of type *FileStream*) is used to produce the object that was previously saved. The downcast is needed because the formal type returned by *Deserialize* is *Object*, whereas the actual type in this case is *Persistent*.

The field *value2* is tagged with the attribute *[NonSerialized]*. This explains the value 0 for this field in the output.

LISTING 14.12 Simple example of object serialization

```
using System;
using System.IO;
using System.Runtime.Serialization;
using System.Runtime.Serialization.Formatters.Binary;


namespace Serialization {

    public class PersistentApp {
        static void Main() {
            Persistent obj = new Persistent(50, 100, "ABCDEFG");
            FileStream outstream =
            new FileStream("myData.binary",
                    FileMode.OpenOrCreate, FileAccess.Write);
            IFormatter formatter = new BinaryFormatter();
            formatter.Serialize(outstream, obj);
            outstream.Close();

            /* Now reopen the "myData.binary" file and restore the
             * persistent object.
             */
            FileStream instream = new FileStream("myData.binary",
                                    FileMode.Open, FileAccess.Read);
            Persistent newObject =
                (Persistent)formatter.Deserialize(instream);
            instream.Close();
            Console.WriteLine(
            "newObject.Value1 = " + newObject.Value1 +
                    " newObject.Value2 = " + newObject.Value2 +
                    " newObject.Value3 = " + newObject.Value3);
            Console.ReadLine();
        }
    }
}
/* Program output
newObject.Value1 = 50 newObject.Value2 = 0 newObject.Value3 =
ABCDEFG
*/
```

LISTING 14.12 Simple example of object serialization (continued)

```csharp
using System;

namespace Serialization {

    [Serializable]
    public class Persistent {

        // Fields
        private int value1;
        [NonSerialized]
        private int value2;
        private String value3;

        // Constructor
        public Persistent(int value1, int value2, String value3) {
            this.value1 = value1;
            this.value2 = value2;
            this.value3 = value3;
        }

        // Properties
        public int Value1 {
            get {
                return value1;
            }
        }

        public int Value2 {
            get {
                return value2;
            }
        }

        public String Value3 {
            get {
                return value3;
            }
        }
    }
}
```

If a class is tagged with the *[Serializable]* attribute, each of its fields must be of a type that is also serializable. If this is not the case, a runtime exception will be generated if an attempt is made to serialize an object of the class.

Classes that you construct are not serializable by default. We have already seen that using the *[Serializable]* attribute in front of your class is one way to ensure that its objects may be serialized as long as each of the fields of your class are serializable.

Another way to achieve this is to make your class implement the *ISerializable* interface. Implementing this interface allows more customization and control regarding how objects of your class are serialized.

The contract of *ISerializable* and the requirements of serialization mandate that your class that implements this interface implement the method *GetObjectData* and implement a serialization constructor with the parameter set *(Serialization info, StreamingContext context)* as shown following.

The *GetObjectData* method allows complete control over the data that is to be serialized. The serialization constructor allows complete control over the data that is to be deserialized.

We consider an example presented in Listing 14.13.

LISTING 14.13 Example of a class that implements ISerialization

```
using System;
using System.Collections.Generic;
using System.Collections;
using System.Runtime.Serialization;
using System.Text;
using System.IO;
using System.Runtime.Serialization.Formatters.Binary;

namespace Serialization {

    [Serializable]
    public class Grades : ISerializable {
        // Fields
        private String[,] scores; // Matrix of names and grades
        private int rows;         // Number of rows
        private int cols;         // Number of columns

        // Constructor
        public Grades(String[,] grades, int rows, int cols) {
            scores = grades;
            this.rows = rows;
            this.cols = cols;
        }

        public override string ToString() {
            String retString = "";
            for (int row = 0; row < rows; row++) {
                retString += "\n";
                for (int col = 0; col < cols; col++) {
                    retString += scores[row, col] + "  ";
                }
            }
            retString += "\n";
            return retString;
        }
```

LISTING 14.13 Example of a class that implements ISerialization (continued)

```
        // Deserialization constructor
        public Grades(SerializationInfo info, StreamingContext
            context) {
            scores = (String [,]) info.GetValue("scores",
                                    typeof(String[,]));
            rows = (int) info.GetValue("rows", typeof(int));
            cols = (int) info.GetValue("cols", typeof(int));
        }

        // Required by ISerializable contract
        public void GetObjectData(SerializationInfo info,
                            StreamingContext context) {
            info.AddValue("scores", scores);
            info.AddValue("rows", rows);
            info.AddValue("cols", cols);
        }
    }

    public class CustomSerializationApp {

        static void Main() {
            // Hardwire a 3 x 3 matrix of students and grades on
            // two exams
            String[,] scores = {{"Student 1", "90", "75"},
                            {"Student 2", "40", "60"},
                            {"Student 3", "95", "100"}};
            Grades grades = new Grades(scores, 3, 3);

            // Serialize the grades
            FileStream stream = new FileStream("Grades.data",
                                FileMode.Create);
            BinaryFormatter bf = new BinaryFormatter();
            bf.Serialize(stream, grades);
            stream.Close();

            // Deserialize the grades
            FileStream inputStream = new FileStream("Grades.data",
                        FileMode.Open);
            Grades inputGrades = (Grades) bf.Deserialize
            (inputStream);
            inputStream.Close();

            // Output the grades that are read
            Console.WriteLine(inputGrades.ToString());
        }
    }
}
```

LISTING 14.13 Example of a class that implements ISerialization (continued)

```
/* Program output
Student 1   90   75
Student 2   40   60
Student 3   95   100
*/
```

Class *Grades* is declared as implementing interface *ISerializable*. It contains three fields, each of which is serializable The two methods shown following are needed to enable *Grades* objects to be serializable.

```
// Deserialization constructor
public Grades(SerializationInfo info, StreamingContext context) {
    scores = (String [,]) info.GetValue("scores",
                                        typeof(String[,]));
    rows = (int) info.GetValue("rows", typeof(int));
    cols = (int) info.GetValue("cols", typeof(int));
}


// Required by ISerializable contract
public void GetObjectData(SerializationInfo info,
                          StreamingContext context) {
    info.AddValue("scores", scores);
    info.AddValue("rows", rows);
    info.AddValue("cols", cols);
}
```

These two methods precisely specify the fields that can be serialized and deserialized when objects of type *Grades* are saved and restored.

The code shown below, in method *Main*, creates and restores an object of type *Grades*.

```
// Serialize the grades
FileStream stream = new FileStream("Grades.data",
                             FileMode.Create);
BinaryFormatter bf = new BinaryFormatter();
bf.Serialize(stream, grades);
stream.Close();

// Deserialize the grades
FileStream inputStream = new FileStream("Grades.data",
                                  FileMode.Open);
Grades inputGrades = (Grades) bf.Deserialize(inputStream);
inputStream.Close();
```

The *ToString* method of *Grades* allows the output of the restored *inputGrades* object to be displayed.

14.5 SUMMARY

- Recognizing that collections of various types are important building blocks in many software development applications, the .NET framework provides a useful assortment of standard collection types.

- Given a choice between using one of your own collection types versus using an appropriate standard collection type, it is always better to choose the standard collection type.

- The namespaces *System.Collections* and *System.Collections.Generics* provide the basis for standard C# collection classes.

- Namespace *System.Collections* includes the following standard nongeneric concrete collection classes:
    - ArrayList
    - Stack
    - Queue
    - BitArray
    - Hashtable
    - SortedList

- Namespace *System.Collections.Generics* includes the following standard generic concrete collection classes:
    - Stack<T>
    - Queue<T>
    - Dictionary<K, V>
    - KeyValuePair<K, V>
    - Dictionary.KeyCollection<K, V>
    - Dictionary.ValueCollection<K, V>
    - LinkedList<T>
    - LinkedListNode<T>
    - List<T>
    - ReadOnlyCollection<T>
    - SortedDictionary<K, V>
    - struct Stack.Enumerator<T>
    - struct Queue.Enumerator<T>
    - struct Dictionary.Enumerator<K, V>
    - struct KeyValuePair<K, V>
    - struct Dictionary.KeyCollection.Enumerator<K, V>
    - struct Dictionary.ValueCollection.Enumerator<K, V>
    - struct LinkedList.Enumerator<T>
    - struct List.Enumerator<T>

◆ Converting an expression in ordinary infix format to postfix is useful because it is easier to evaluate the postfix expression than the corresponding infix expression.

◆ The class *ExpressionEvaluation* that includes facilities for converting an infix expression to postfix and then evaluating the postfix expression uses four standard collections: *Stack<double>*, *Stack<char>*, *List<char>*, and *Dictionary<String, double>*.

◆ Object serialization is the process of converting an object into a stream of bits so that it can be stored and later reconstructed. The process is fundamental to object persistence—the ability to store and retrieve objects.

◆ In the .NET framework, formatter objects are used to accomplish object serialization. A concrete formatter class that implements the *System.Runtime.Serialization.IFormatter* interface is *System.Runtime.Serialization.Formatters.Binary.BinaryFormatter*.

◆ The *[NonSerializable]* attribute can be used to prevent specific fields so tagged from being serialized. When an object of such a class is saved, the fields tagged as *[NonSerializable]* are not saved.

14.6 ADDITIONAL EXERCISES

Exercise 14.7

Explain how an *ArrayList* is different than a *List<T>*.

Exercise 14.8

How might you implement a Set in C#?

Exercise 14.9

Explain the difference between inserting a key, value pair in a *Hashtable* using:

```
hashTable.Add(key, value);
```

versus using:

```
hashTable[key]  = value;
```

Exercise 14.10

Set up a simulation experiment that investigates the difference in efficiency between an *ArrayList* and a *SortedList*. For what types of operations would each list be more efficient?

Exercise 14.11

Write a class *MyStack<T>* that is a subclass of *Stack<T>* and allows one to access the value just under the top of the stack using the query:

```
public T JustUnderTop( );
```

Exercise 14.12

Using a *Stack*, show how to reverse the objects within an *ArrayList* using the command *Reverse* with signature:

```
public void Reverse(ArrayList list) {

    // You write the details

}
```

Exercise 14.13

What data structure from Chapter 13 might you consider using if you were to implement a *SortedDictionary<K, V>* collection?

Exercise 14.14

Write an application that inputs a text file and outputs a table showing the number of words of size 1, 2, ..., 25 used in the text file. Indicate precisely how you define a word.

Exercise 14.15

Convert each of the infix expressions given to their postfix equivalent:

1. (a * b) / c + d
2. a / (b + c)
3. a / b + c
4. (a + b) * (c + d)
5. (a + b) * c + d

Exercise 14.16

Convert each of the postfix expressions to their infix equivalent:

1. ab*c*ef−/gh+*
2. ab/cd+*e−

CHAPTER 15

Regular Expressions

Sometimes it is useful to extract, edit, replace, or delete text substrings. Applications that deal with large text files such as those that read and display HTML documents or parse HTTP headers often use a pattern-matching notation to process text files. Data is often available in one format but needed in a different format for output purposes. Invalid characters sometimes must be stripped, and often strings of characters must be checked to verify their format prior to processing. These types of pattern matching applications form the basis for using regular expressions.

A regular expression is a string that precisely describes a search pattern. For example, as you will see shortly, the regular expression **a[^bcd]** means find the first occurrence of text that has an "a" followed by a character that is not a "b" or "c" or "d". All regular expressions used in this chapter will be presented in a larger bold-faced font to make them easier to read and dissect.

The formulation and use of regular expressions has been important in automata theory, compiler design, and text searching and parsing. Regular expression-processing forms the core of the Perl language.

C#/.NET provides strong support for regular expression processing in the name-space *System.Text.RegularExpressions*. The classes that support regular expressions provide support for searching text, replacing text within a string, and splitting text into separate sections based on delimiters. Applications involving each of these problem areas will be presented and discussed in this chapter.

The classes that comprise the *System.Text.RegularExpressions* namespace include: *Capture, CaptureCollection, Group, GroupCollection, Match, MatchCollection, Regex, RegexCompilationInfo, RegexRunner,* and *RegexRunnerFactory*.

15.1 INTRODUCTION TO REGULAR EXPRESSIONS

The simplest regular expression consists of a single character, such as the character "b". If the string "I love babies" were searched using the regular expression (regex) **b**, the first character "b" in "babies" would be found.

The following 12 meta-characters have special meaning:

^ (the caret)

[(open square bracket)

] (closed square bracket)

\ (backslash escape symbol)

$ (dollar sign)

. (dot)

| (vertical bar)

? (question mark)

* (star)

+ (plus sign)

((open round bracket)

) (closed round bracket)

Table 15.1 summarizes some important patterns and their explanations.

TABLE 15.1 Some important patterns

Pattern	Explanation	Simple Example
[^b]	Matches any character except "b"; the symbols [and] define a character class; the caret represents negation	**[^\{]*;** Matches zero or more occurrences of any character except "{" and terminated by ";"
\{	Escape character to suppress the special meaning of the meta-character	**[\{\}\;]** Matches "{" or "}" or ";"
\d \w \s	Special characters for any digit, any word character and a space	**\w+\s+\w+** Matches a word followed by one or more spaces followed by another word
.	Matches any characters except new-line	**\w+\s+.*;** Matches a word followed by one or more spaces followed by zero or more non new-line characters followed by ";"
^ $	Caret anchors to beginning of a line and dollar to end of a line	**^public class \w+ \{$** Matches the beginning of a line followed by literal "public class " a word followed by "{" and the end of a line

TABLE 15.1 Some important patterns (continued)

Pattern	Explanation	Simple Example
\b	Matches the boundary between a word and a non-word character	**\bclass\b** Matches every occurrence of "class" preceded and followed by non-word characters
+ +?	One or more occurrences (greedy) or one or more occurrences (non-greedy)	**\w+?;** Does a non-greedy search for a word followed by ";"
?	Makes the previous character optional	**A?BCD** Matches an optional A followed by BCD

If you want to include special characters in a regular expression, you must precede the character with the backslash escape symbol.

C#/.NET uses a regular expression-directed engine. The leftmost match will be used even if another and perhaps better match could be found later in the string.

Consider the following simple example: regex **dog** used to search the string: **"The doing is in the doggerel"**. The first character of the regular expression is matched against the first character of the string. No match occurs. The "d" in the regular expression continues to be matched against the string until a match occurs in the fifth character of the string. The "o" in the regular expression is matched against the sixth character of the string. Another match occurs. The "g" in the regular expression is compared with the seventh character of the string. No match occurs. The "d" in the regular expression is then matched against the eighth character of the string. No match occurs. This continues until the dog in "doggerel" is matched. The search ends.

The open and closed square brackets can be used to match any one of a collection of characters. For example, consider the regex **rec[ei][ie]ve**. It will match the string "receive". It will also match the string "recieve". It will not match the string "receieve". The order within the square brackets does not matter. Matches are based on any string with the sequence "rec" followed by either "i" or "e" followed by either "i" or "e" followed by "ve".

The regex **[0-9]** matches a single character between 0 and 9. A single hexadecimal digit can be found with the regex **[0-9a-fA-F]**. Here three sequences are used to match a single character. A caret character immediately following the open square bracket means "not". The regex **a[^bcd]** means "a" followed by a character that is not "b" or "c" or "d". If this regex were used on the string "a bc" it would match the "a" followed by the space because the space is a character that is not a "b" or a "c".

There are several important shorthand character classes. The **\d** matches any numeral and is short for **[0-9]**. The **\w** matches any word character **[A-Za-z]**. The shorthand **\s** matches any whitespace character **[\t\r\n]**. Each of these shorthand character classes has a negated version. **\D** matches any character that is not a numeral, **\W** matches any character that is not a word character, and **\S** matches any character that is not a space.

The dot matches any single character except the new-line character. It must be used with great care because misuse usually captures strings other than the ones you intend to be captured.

Suppose we want to match all the characters between quotes. We might be tempted to use the regex, **".*"**. If we use this regular expression on the string, **This is "the first" and "the second" string**, we get a match, **"the first" and "the second"**. The quote after the word "first" is matched by the dot. This is an example where the filter is not fine enough to capture the first word between a single set of quotes. The solution is to use **"[^"\r\n]*"**. The * matches zero or more occurrences of the preceding expression.

Anchors match a position before, after, or between characters. They can be used to "anchor" the regular expression match at a certain position. The caret (^) matches the position before the first character in the string. The dollar ($) matches the position just after the last character in the string. If multi-line mode is chosen, the caret matches the position before the first character in every line and the dollar matches the last character in every line. The meta-character, **\b**, is also an anchor. It matches a word boundary as follows:

- Before the first character in the string, if the first character is a word character.

- After the last character in the string, if the last character is a word character.

- Between a word character and a non-word character immediately following the word character.

- Between a non-word character and a word character immediately following the non-word character.

If we want to locate the word "public" in a C# source file, we could use the regex **\bpublic\b**. The regex \B is the logically negated version of \b.

The vertical bar meta-character allows us to employ alternatives. If we want to search for the first word that is either **public**, **private**, or **protected** in a C# source file, we could use the regex **\b(public | private | protected)\b**.

The question mark meta-character makes the token immediately in front of the question mark optional. The regular expression **\bSept(ember)?\b** matches both the words "Sept" and "September".

The meta-character star (*) matches the previous character zero or more times. The meta-character plus (+) matches the previous character one or more times. The regex **a+b*c+** will match "aaaccc", "abbbc", but not "abbb". The regular expression search is greedy—it will attempt to match each character as many times as possible. This can cause problems.

Suppose we want to search for tags in an XML expression. These are words bounded by < and >. A typical expression might be **<Important>first token</Important>**. It is tempting to use the regex **<.+>** to capture the first tag. Unfortunately because of the greedy application of **.+**, the entire string will be captured.

We can fix this problem using a question mark after the "+" in the regex. This mandates a non-greedy, lazy search based on the dot (any character). The repaired regex is **<.+?>**. The presence of the '?' indicates that the search is a non-greedy lazy search. Another solution would be to use **<[^>]+>**.

Curly braces allow us to specify a repetition count for the previous token. The regex **\b[1-2]\d{3}\b** means match either a 1 or 2 followed by exactly three digits. The regex **\b[1-2]\d{1,3}\b** means match either a 1 or 2 followed by a minimum of one digit and a maximum of three digits.

The round parentheses meta-characters are used to group part of a regular expression together. This is useful if you want to indicate repetition. However, round parentheses are also used to create a back reference that stores the part of the string matched by the part of the regular expression inside the parentheses. Suppose you want to determine the presence of "Get" and "GetEnumerator" in a string. You might create a regex **Get(Enumerator)?**.

A back reference to "Enumerator" will be created even though it is probably not needed. The back reference is saved, which consumes computational resources. We will see useful applications of back references later. But for now, suppose we want to use the round parentheses only to group the optional "Enumerator" part of the string and not save a back reference. We can turn the back reference off using the meta-characters **:?** as follows: **Get(?:Enumerator)?**.

Back references can be used in a regular expression. Consider the regex **([u-z])a\1b\1**. This regular expression will capture the match of the first character from "u" to "z" into back reference 1. It will then look for the character "a", followed by the back reference character, the character "b", and then the back reference character. So the string "wawbw" will match, but the string "wacbw" will not match. As another example, consider the regex **([u-z])([a-f])\1\2**. This regular expression will capture the first character from "u" to "z" and then capture the second character if it is within the range from "a" to "f", and then match the first character followed by the second character. The string "zbzb" will be matched, but the string "zbbz" will not be matched.

Suppose you want to design a regular expression that finds the triple repetitive occurrence of a word in a text. The regex **\b(\w+)\s+\1\b\s+\1\b** does the job. The string "The word word word is out" matches "word word word".

Round brackets cannot be used around a character class to hold back references. They are treated as character literals. For example, [(A)] looks for the single character "(" or "A" or ")".

Although back references always receive the default names "1", "2", "3", … in the order in which they are defined, it is sometimes useful to name back references explicitly. This can make a regular expression easier to read. C#/.NET uses one of the two following approaches to naming back references:

(?<firstName>pattern1)(?'secondName'pattern2)

where the name of the group is placed in angle brackets or in a single quote and *pattern1* and *pattern2* are the sub-regex expressions to be captured. The angle bracket or single quoted group name can be used interchangeably.

Let us revisit the example **([u-z])([a-f])\1\2** given earlier. This could be written: **(?'first'[u-z])(?<second>[a-f])\k<first>\k'second'**. The character "k" must be used in front of the group name when making reference to the group in the regular expression.

It is recommended that you either name all groups or use the default numbered group names.

Although C# supports Unicode matching, this subject is beyond the scope of this chapter and will not be discussed.

Look-ahead and look-back capability has been introduced into regular expression processing recently. Negative look-ahead is useful if you want to match some pattern not followed by another pattern. Suppose, as a quick example, we want to detect any words that have the character "e" not followed by "i". The string "receive" would not be captured but the string "believe" would be captured.

Let us compare the regex solution $\mathbf{\backslash b\backslash w^*e[\wedge i]\backslash w^*\backslash b}$ with the regex solution $\mathbf{\backslash b\backslash w^*e(?!i)\backslash w^*\backslash b}$. Let us use each on the string, "Be well my friend".

The first regex solution puts an anchor at the beginning of a word, allows for zero or more word characters followed by "e", followed by any character that is not "i", followed by zero or more word characters, followed by the end of word anchor. This causes **"Be well"** to be captured in the string. The "e" is followed by a space character, which is not an "i" character.

The second regex solution uses a look-back, $\mathbf{(?!i)}$. This causes "Be" to be matched because the "e" is not followed by the word character "i" and the space matches the anchor. Look-ahead and look-back bring extra power to string matching. Because of their complexity, they will be discussed further only if they are needed in later examples.

The equivalent of an *if-else* conditional can be embedded in a regular expression. An example follows:

$$([a\text{-}c])?d(?(1)e\,|\,f)$$

A back reference to "a", "b", or "c" is created. The back reference may be empty because the question mark character indicates that the presence of one of these three letters is optional. The next character "d" must be present. The expression that begins with $(?$ defines the conditional. The "if" part is given by (1). If the back reference is not empty, then the next character to be matched will be "e", otherwise it will be "f".

In the next section we apply some of the concepts presented in this section by considering several practical examples.

15.2 SOME EXAMPLES

Some of the examples that will be presented are fairly typical—they appear in tutorials and other books. Other examples will be unique. The first several examples are standard but nevertheless quite important.

15.2.1 Regular Expression that Captures the Syntax of a Floating-point Number

A quick but not necessarily totally thought-out formulation yields the following first attempt at capturing a floating-point number:

$$[-+]?[0\text{-}9]^*\backslash.?[0\text{-}9]^*$$

In words, this regular expression allows a match for an optional leading "+" or a "-" character. Following this, zero or more numerals are followed by an optional decimal point (notice that the dot is preceded by the escape slash meta-character) followed by zero or more numerals. This seems correct at face value.

The problem is not that it does not correctly match a properly constructed floating-point number, but that it matches strings that are not correctly constructed floating-point numbers. For example, the string "-" is matched by the regex. The string "." is also matched by this regular expression. We need to repair the expression so that it does not accept strings that are not properly constructed floating-point expressions. The following regex does the job: $[-+]?([0-9]*\.)?[0-9]+([eE][-+]?[0-9]+)?$

Exercise 15.1

Explain in detail how the regular expression given above works.

15.2.2 Regular Expression that Captures the Syntax of a Valid Date

To match a date in month/day/year (mm/dd/yyyy) format, use the following regex: $(0[1-9]|1[012])[- /.](0[1-9]|[12][0-9]|3[01])[- /.](19|20)\d\d$

A careful analysis of this expression reveals:

◆ Match either a leading "0" followed by a "1" to "9" or a leading "1" followed by a "0", "1", or "2". A back reference 1 is created.

◆ Match a single character among the characters "-", "/" or ".".

◆ Match either a "0" followed by "1" to "9", or a "1" or a "2" followed by "1" to "9", or a "3" followed by "0" or "1". A back reference 2 is created.

◆ Match a single character among the characters "-", "/" or ".".

◆ Match either a "19" or a "20" followed by any two integer values.

Even this regular expression fails if one is very strict. For example, the date "02/31/2099" is accepted. It is much easier to use the facilities of the programming language to filter out an illegal date than to repair the regular expression.

15.2.3 Regular Expression that Matches a Zip Code with an Optional Five-digit Extension

Consider the regular expression, $^\wedge\d{5}(-\d{4})?$$

Exercise 15.2

Explain the regular expression given above for matching a zip code.

15.2.4 Regular Expression for an E-mail Address

In many practical applications, it is necessary to parse e-mail addresses from a text. Consider the following regular expression:

$\b[A-Za-z0-9._%-]+@[A-Za-z0-9._%-]+\.[A-Za-z]{2,4}\b$

Exercise 15.3

Explain the regular expression given previously for matching an e-mail address.

15.2.5 Regular Expression for a North American Phone Number

A regex for matching North American phone numbers is:

$$\backslash b(\backslash(?\backslash d\{3\}\backslash)?\backslash\text{-})?\backslash d\{3\}\backslash\text{-}\backslash d\{4\}\backslash b$$

An optional "(" is followed by three digits, followed by an optional ")", a required "-", three digits, a required "-", and then four digits.

15.2.6 Regular Expressions for Parts of a C# Program

In building system tools for C# programming (program editors, formatters, and obfuscators), it is useful to be able to select different parts of a C# class. Regular expressions for several key parts of a C# program file are formulated in this section.

Single-line Comment

Suppose we want to capture single-line comments such as the one in the following code:

```
if (value1 > value2) { // This is a single-line comment
   SomeAction();
}
```

A regular expression that we could apply to the source code to capture such a comment would be: $//.*\$$

Multi-line Comment

Suppose we want to capture multi-line comments such as the one in the following code:

```
if (value1 > value2) {
   /* This is a multi-line
        comment. It spans
        three lines.
    */
   SomeAction();
}
```

A regular expression that captures any multi-line comment is: $/\backslash*.*?\backslash*/$

This expression matches a forward slash followed by an asterisk. Using a non-greedy search for any character (including new-line), the contents of the comment is matched. Then the asterisk and forward slash are matched at the end of the comment.

if-else Construct

Suppose we want to capture an if-else construct within a C# program file such as:

```
if (value1 > value2) {
    /* This is a multi-line
       comment. It spans
       three lines.
    */
  SomeAction();
} else if (value1 == value2) {
  OtherAction();
} else {
  ThirdPossibleAction();
}
SomeOtherCommand();
if (someOtherValue1 < someOtherValue2) {
  someOtherValue3 = 17;
}
AnotherCommand();
if (myValue == 19) {
  Console.WriteLine("Value is 19");
} else {
  Console.WriteLine("Value is not 19");
}
FinalStatement();
```

A regular expression that does the job is:

$$\texttt{(if\textbackslash s*\textbackslash(.*?\textbackslash)\textbackslash s*\textbackslash\{.*?\textbackslash\})(\textbackslash s*else\textbackslash s*if\textbackslash s*\textbackslash(.*?\textbackslash)\textbackslash s*\textbackslash\{.*?\textbackslash\})*(\textbackslash s*else\textbackslash s*\textbackslash\{.*?\textbackslash\})*}$$

Like many regular expressions, the one given above looks incomprehensible. Let us dissect it, at least part of it. The first back reference matches (and stores) an *if* block. The literal "if" is first matched. This is followed by zero or more spaces, followed by "(", zero or more characters (including new-line), the character ")", zero or more spaces, the character "{", zero or more characters (including new-line), and then "}".

Exercise 15.4

Dissect and explain the remaining portion of the regular expression given above for matching if-else blocks.

The regular expression given above will match an if-else block that appears within a comment or within a string. This is probably not desirable and would need to be corrected, probably outside of the regular expression.

Method Signature

Suppose we want to capture all method signatures in a C# application such as the signatures shown in the code segment following. As in all the examples given earlier, it is assumed that the C# file is syntactically correct. The fact that the regular expression would accept illegal constructs such as *FourthComputation() {* is of no concern because the goal is not to use the regular expression as a substitute for the C# parser but to select properly formed method signatures from the source listing.

```
public class SomeClass : ParentClass {
  // Fields
  private int value1, value2;

  // Constructor
  public SomeClass() {
    value1 = 5;
    value2 = 7;
  }

  public override void Method1(int value1, int value2) { // Comment
    SomeAction(value1, value2);
  }

  protected int FirstComputation() { // Another comment
    return SomeOtherAction() * SomeOtherAction();
  }

  private int SecondComputation() { /* Third comment */
    Return value1 * value2;
  }

  String ThirdComputation() {
    Return "hello";
  }
}
```

Consider the regular expression:

```
^\s*(\w+\s+)?(\w+\s+)?(\w+\s+)?(\w+\s+)?
(\w+\s+)?(\w+\s+)?(\w+\s*)\(.*\)\s*\{
```

The caret symbol anchors the string at the beginning of a line. This is important because the previous line may end with a word that is part of a single-line comment. After zero or more spaces, a series of six optional words followed by one or more spaces, a required word, and zero or more spaces, which must be followed by "(", then zero or more arbitrary characters, then ")", then zero or more spaces, and finally "{". The reason for the six optional words, each followed by one or more spaces is to allow for modifiers such as static, override, and other modifiers included in the method signature.

What would happen if the constructor in the code given earlier were changed as follows:

```
// Constructor
  public SomeClass() : base(value1, value2) {
    value1 = 5;
    value2 = 7;
}
```

The regular expression would continue to capture the method. That is because the greedy selection mechanism would match the first left parenthesis followed by many characters and closed by the final right parenthesis.

Unfortunately, the regular expression given previously, as often happens, matches other legal C# constructs that are not method signatures, as an example:

```
if (regex.Length == 0) {
```

This perfectly legal C# expression matches the pattern given previously for method signatures. We need to tighten the filter given by the regular expression.

The regular expression:

$$\verb|^\s*(private|protected|public|static)\s*|$$
$$\verb|(\w+\s+)?(\w+\s+)?(\w+\s+)?(\w+\s+)?|$$
$$\verb|(\w+\s+)?(\w+\s+)?(\w+\s*)\(.*\))\s*\{|$$

achieves the objective of tightening the filter and eliminating constructs such as *if (…) {* and *for (…) {* and *while (…) {*. But it will not match the legal method signature:

```
bool SomeQuery() {
```

Further work needs to be done if the goal is to capture all valid method signatures while maintaining this tight filter. This work would best be done outside of the regular expression in the application that needs to match all valid C# method signatures.

Many examples of regular expressions have been presented in this section. It is time to examine the mechanisms available in C#/.NET for performing regular expression processing. Some of the mechanisms that are provided by the classes in the *System.Text.RegularExpressions* namespace are examined in the next section along with practical applications that utilize regular expression processing.

15.3 REGULAR EXPRESSION PROCESSING IN C#

There are three categories of problems that we shall focus on:

1. Finding one or more occurrences of a pattern specified by a regular expression within some multi-line text.

2. Replacing one or more occurrences of a pattern specified by a regular expression within some multi-line text.

3. Splitting text into an array of *String* based on a delimiter that is specified by a regular expression.

15.3.1 Matching One or More Occurrences of a Pattern Given by a Regular Expression

A GUI application shown in Figure 15.1 is developed. A text box allows the user to enter any regular expression. If the regular expression entered is invalid, an error message is emitted in a modal dialog box.

A scrollable *RichTextBox* control is used to allow the user to paste or type the text that is to be searched. A scrollable read-only *RichTextBox* control is used to capture the matches that represent the output.

Two radio buttons allow the user to determine whether a single-line or multi-line search mode is used.

The source code for the GUI application itself is used in the screenshot. The regular expression:

```
^\s*(private|protected|public|static)\s*
(\w+\s+)?(\w+\s+)?(\w+\s+)?(\w+\s+)?(\w+\s
+)?(\w+\s+)?(\w+\s*)\(.*\)\s*\{
```

discussed earlier for matching valid method signatures is used, and the matches are shown in the bottom pane.

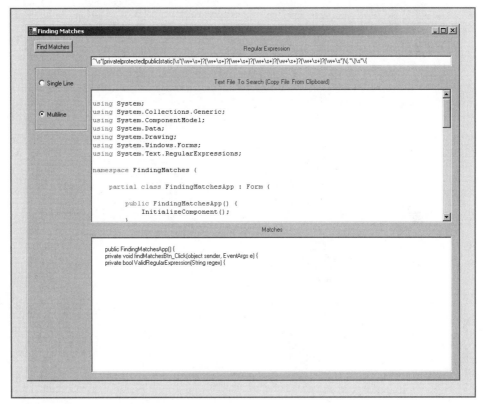

FIGURE 15.1 Screenshot of GUI application

Listing 15.1 presents the code that implements this GUI application. The code shown in boldface larger font shows the regular expression mechanisms from namespace *System.Text.RegularExpressions*. We examine this code carefully.

LISTING 15.1 Class FindingMatchesApp

```csharp
using System;
using System.Windows.Forms;
using System.Text.RegularExpressions;

namespace FindingMatches {

    partial class FindingMatchesApp : Form {

        public FindingMatchesApp() {
            InitializeComponent();
        }

        /* This method clears matchesBox.
         * It then constructs an instance of Regex using the
         * regular expression. It finally uses the static Matches
         * query to obtain all matches.
         */
        private void findMatchesBtn_Click(object sender, EventArgs e) {
            matchesBox.Clear();
            String regExpression = regexBox.Text.Trim();
            // Test the validity of regExpression before finding
            // matches
            if (ValidRegularExpression(regExpression)) {
                String searchString = textToSearchBox.Text.Trim();
                Regex regularExpression = new
                Regex(regExpression,
                        singleLineBtn.Checked ?
                        RegexOptions.Singleline :
                        RegexOptions.Multiline);
                    MatchCollection matches =
                        regExpression.Matches(searchString);
                    foreach (Match match in matches) {
                    matchesBox.AppendText(match.ToString() +
                        "\n");
                    }
            } else {
                MessageBox.Show("Invalid regular expression.");
            }
        }

        /* This method uses the exception generated
         * if an invald regular expression is used
         * to find a match to set the local
         * variable isValid to false in this case.
         */
        private bool ValidRegularExpression(String regex) {
            bool isValid = true;
            if (regex.Length == 0) {
                isValid = false;
            } else {
                try {
                    Regex.Match("", regex);
                } catch (Exception) {
                    isValid = false;
                }
            }
            return isValid;
        }
    }
}
```

An instance of class *Regex* is created as follows:

```
Regex regularExpression = new
    Regex(regExpression,
        singleLineBtn.Checked ?
        RegexOptions.Singleline : RegexOptions.Multiline);
```

The first parameter is the regular expression input as a *String*. The second parameter is the static *RegexOptions* value, either *RegexOptions.Singleline* or *RegexOptions.Multiline* in this case.

The query *Matches* is sent to the instance of *Regex*, and it returns a *MatchCollection* object as follows:

```
MatchCollection matches = regExpression.Matches(searchString);
```

Finally, each separate *Match* object is output to the *matchesBox* control using a *foreach* enumeration as follows:

```
foreach (Match match in matches) {
    matchesBox.AppendText(match.ToString() + "\n");
}
```

Exercise 15.5

Explain the operation of the query *ValidRegularExpression*.

You are encouraged to download the source code for this GUI and experiment with the different regular expressions and text to improve your skills at pattern matching.

15.3.2 Extracting Groups from a Matched Collection

The **Regex** Object model allows us to define *groups* within the specified regular expression. These groups are exposed using the "**Match.Groups**" property.

We can get each group by name, and get its value using the **Group.Value** property.

The application is modified so that it can capture the groups defined in the regular expression. Figure 15.2 shows the revised GUI.

The *foreach* loop in Listing 15.1 is changed as follows:

```
foreach (Match match in matches) {
  matchesBox.AppendText(match.ToString() + "\n");
    for (int groupNumber = 1; groupNumber < match.Groups.Count;
        groupNumber++) {
        if (match.Groups[groupNumber].Success) {
        groupsBox.AppendText(match.Groups[groupNumber].Value +
                                    "  ");
      }
    }
  groupsBox.AppendText("\n");
}
```

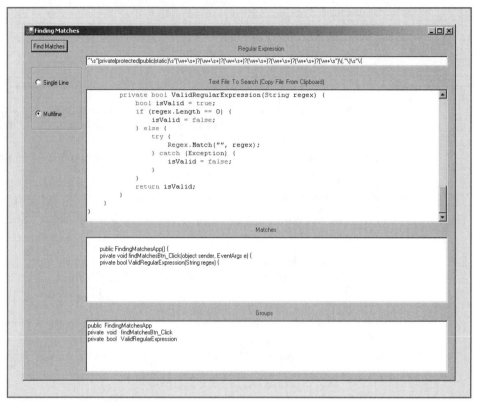

```
private bool ValidRegularExpression(String regex) {
    bool isValid = true;
    if (regex.Length == 0) {
        isValid = false;
    } else {
        try {
            Regex.Match("", regex);
        } catch (Exception) {
            isValid = false;
        }
    }
    return isValid;
}
```

FIGURE 15.2   Revised GUI

Another *RichEditBox* control is added to the GUI to hold the results of the group output.

The *get* indexer property *Groups* and the *Value* property are used to obtain each group. *Groups[0].Value*, not used, holds the match result.

15.3.3 Using Regular Expressions for Replacing Portions of Text

The *Regex.Replace* method replaces any matches in the input text with a specified replacement string. An overloaded version of *Replace* allows the specification of the maximum number of replacements and the starting position within the text. Finally, another overloaded version of *Replace* takes a *MatchEvaluator* delegate as a parameter. For each match that occurs, the delegate is invoked. The delegate is passed an instance of *Match*. The delegate returns the substitution string and has the following signature:

```
public delegate String MatchEvaluator(Match match);
```

Listing 15.2 shows a simple application that demonstrates the use of *Replace*.

LISTING 15.2 Using the Replace method

```
using System;
using System.Text.RegularExpressions;
namespace UsingReplace {

    public class ReplaceApp {

        // Match evaluator delegate instance
        public String Evaluator(Match match) {
            switch (match.Value) {
                case "dog" : return "cat";
                case "cat" : return "dog";
                case "horse" : return "cow";
                case "cow": return "horse";
                default: return match.Value;
            }
        }

        static void Main(string[] args) {
            ReplaceApp app = new ReplaceApp();
            String inputText = "The dog ran faster than the cat " +
                                "who was being chased by the horse " +
                                "who tried to avoid the cow.";
            Regex regExpression = new Regex(@"\w+[o,a]\w+");
            Console.WriteLine(regExpression.Replace(inputText,
                                app.Evaluator));

            Console.ReadLine();
        }
    }
}
/* Program output
The cat ran faster than the dog who was being chased by the cow  who
tried to avoid the horse.
*/
```

Exercise 15.6

Explain the operation of class *ReplaceApp*.

15.3.4 Splitting Text Based on Regular Expressions

Suppose that we want to parse a text file, *inputText*, into individual tokens. This can be accomplished using a regular expression as follows:

```
Regex regex = new Regex(regexStringForTokenizing);
String[] tokens = regex.Split(inputText);
```

As a trivial example, suppose *inputText* is given as:

"The man and the dog went walking into the forest to see the rain on the ground."

Suppose that the regular expression is **"the"**.
The *tokens* array would be:

```
"The man and"
"dog went walking into"
"forest to see"
"rain on"
"ground"
```

As a less trivial and more useful example, suppose we want to build a C# formatter—a program that takes poorly formatted source code and produces formatted output source code. Section 15.4 presents portions of this interesting and challenging application.

An important early step in formatting source code is to tokenize the code based on key operators. Specifically, consider the regular expression *regexStringForTokenizing*:

$$([\%|;|\(|\)|\{|\}|[|]]|\<|\=|\>|\+|*|\-|/|\-]|\s)$$

We could use the regular expression given earlier in the method *TokenizeInput*. This method is presented in Listing 15.3. Here, *inputTextBox* is a *RichEditBox* control to which the tokenized expression is written.

If the token is ";" or "{" or "(" or "]" or "}" or "[", it is appended directly to the text within the *inputTextBox*. Otherwise, it is appended directly and followed by a space.

LISTING 15.3 Method TokenizeInput

```
private void TokenizeInput() {
  inputText = inputTextBox.Text.Trim();
   Regex regex = new Regex(regexStringForTokenizing);
  String[] tokens = regex.Split(inputText);
  inputTextBox.Clear();
  foreach (String tok in tokens) {
    String token = tok.Trim();
    if (token.Length > 0) {
        Regex r = new Regex(@"([;|\{|\(|\}|\[)");
        if (r.IsMatch(token)) {
            inputTextBox.AppendText(token);
        } else {
            inputTextBox.AppendText(token + " ");
        }
    }
  }
    inputText = inputTextBox.Text;
}
```

Exercise 15.7

Using the regular expression *regexStringForTokenizing* given previously, convert the following segment of C# based on method *TokenizeInput* in Listing 15.3:

```
if (r.IsMatch(token)) {
  inputTextBox.AppendText(token);
} else {
  inputTextBox.AppendText(token + " ");
}
```

15.4 A C# FORMATTER APPLICATION USING REGULAR EXPRESSIONS

Portions of a C# formatter application are presented in this section. In addition to being practical, this application is challenging and interesting. It will allow us to carefully examine many nontrivial regular expressions in a meaningful context.

One of the more complex aspects of formatting C# source code is comment handling. Because it is not the purpose of this section to develop a commercial quality formatter, this most complex aspect of formatting is bypassed. Single-line double-slash comments preceded by code, single-line double-slash comments not preceded by code, and single- or multiline comments delimited by "/*" and */ are stripped out of the input source file before formatting.

To dramatize what the finished product will be able to accomplish, consider a compilable C# source file that is given in Listing 15.4.

LISTING 15.4 Poorly formatted C# source file

```
using System;

namespace Formatter {abstract public class TestCode3 {public
    TestCode3() {int value1 = 10,

value2 = 12, value3; if (value1 < value2) {
value1 = 14;} else if (value1 == value2) {value1 = 15;} else if
    (value1 % value2 == 6) {
value1 = 16;}}public void ControlConstructs() {int value1 = 4,
    value2 = 3;
if (value1<value2) value2=1;else value1 = 20;}
public void SomeMethod() {
Console.WriteLine("{a,b,c} def;ghij");
} abstract public void SomeAnotherMethod();}}
```

Listing 15.5 shows the output of the program.

LISTING 15.5 C# source file after formatting

```csharp
using System;

namespace Formatter {

    abstract public class TestCode3 {

        public TestCode3() {
            int value1 = 10, value2 = 12, value3;
            if (value1 < value2) {
                value1 = 14;
            } else if (value1 == value2) {
                value1 = 15;
            } else if (value1 % value2 == 6) {
                value1 = 16;
            }
        }

        public void ControlConstructs() {
            int value1 = 4, value2 = 3;
            if (value1 < value2) {
                value2 = 1;
            } else {
                value1 = 20;
            }
        }

        public void SomeMethod() {
            Console.WriteLine("{a,b,c} def;ghij");
        }

        abstract public void SomeAnotherMethod();
    }
}
```

The application is organized into four major steps:

1. Remove all comments.

2. Add open and closed curly braces to convert single-line statements to single-line blocks.

3. Split the input source file into tokens and format the source file into one large paragraph.

4. Format the paragraph.

Step 2 would convert the following code segment as shown:

```
if (someExpression)
    someStatement;
```

```
if (someExpression) {
    someStatement;
}
```

The same conversion could be used for a *while*-loop, *for*-loop, *foreach*-loop, *else if*, or *else*, each followed by a single statement.

15.4.1 Removal of Comments

We use two carefully constructed regular expressions to detect and remove comments. First we consider the following code:

```
private String
   regexStringForCapturingSingleLineCommentsPrecededByCode =
      @"(?<!^\s*)(//.*)$(?=(\s*).*)$";
```

This regular expression uses "negative look-back." The $(?<!L)$ that precedes the $(//.*)\$$ means that the expression L ($^\s^*$ in this case) cannot be matched. This is a useful construct whenever you need to assert NOT A followed by B.

The $(?=(\s^*).^*)\$$ is an example of "positive look-ahead." It might be useful if we wanted to capture the number of spaces of indentation on the line immediately following the comment. The back reference $(\s^*)$ is used to capture this indentation.

Next we consider the following code:

```
private String
   regexStringForCapturingSingleLineCommentsNotPrecededByCode =
      @"^(\s*//.*)$(?=(\s*).*)$";
```

Exercise 15.8

Explain the regular expression given above.

Exercise 15.9

Write a regular expression *String* that captures single or multi-line comments that are delimited by "/*" and "*/".

Listing 15.6 presents the details of method *RemoveComments*.

LISTING 15.6 Method RemoveComments

```
private void RemoveComments() {
   inputText = inputTextBox.Text.Trim();

   // Remove all multi-line comments
   Regex regex = new Regex(regexStringForCapturingMultiLineComments,
                    RegexOptions.Singleline);
   replacementText = regex.Replace(inputText, "");
   inputText = replacementText;

   // Remove all single-line comments that are not preceded by code
   regex = new
   Regex(regexStringForCapturingSingleLineCommentsNotPrecededByCode,
           RegexOptions.Multiline);
```

LISTING 15.6 Method RemoveComments (continued)

```
replacementText = regex.Replace(inputText, "");
inputText = replacementText;

// Remove all single-line comments that are preceded by code
regex = new
    Regex(regexStringForCapturingSingleLineCommentsPrecededByCode,
          RegexOptions.Multiline);
replacementText = regex.Replace(inputText, "");
inputText = replacementText;

// Mark the begin and end index of all strings
regex = new Regex(regexStringForCapturingStrings);
MatchCollection matches = regex.Matches(inputText);
foreach (Match match in matches) {
Point pt =
    new Point(match.Index, match.Index + match.Value.Length);
    strings.Add(pt);
}

/* Mark every {, } and ; inside either a string, single-line or
 * multi-line comment as follows: { => ~@, }=> ~#, ; => ~$
 */
regex = new Regex(@"([;\{\}])");
replacementText = regex.Replace(inputText, StringCommentEvaluator);
inputText = replacementText;

inputTextBox.Clear();
inputTextBox.Text = replacementText;
}
```

The following field is used to hold the starting and ending position of every *String* in the source file:

```
private List<Point> strings = new List<Point>();
```

The regular expression for capturing each *String* is:

```
private String regexStringForCapturingStrings =
  @"""".*?"""";
```

We want to temporarily replace every "{", "}", and ";" with the tokens "~@", "~#", and "~$", respectively. The reason for this is that later we will replace "{" with "{\n" and appropriate spaces to accomplish the correct level of indentation. Similar replacements will be made for "}" and ";". We do not want these replacements to occur within a string literal, so in order to avoid this, we initially replace these three symbols with the tokens given above.

The following code segment allows us to accomplish this:

```
regex = new Regex(@"([;\{\}])");
replacementText = regex.Replace(inputText, StringCommentEvaluator);
```

This allows us to showcase one of the important overloaded versions of the *Replace* method in class *Regex*.

Method *StringCommentEvaluator* is presented in Listing 15.7.

LISTING 15.7 Method StringCommentEvaluator

```
private String StringCommentEvaluator(Match match) {
    String retString = "";
    int matchIndex = match.Index;
    switch (match.Value) {
        case ";":
            // Determine whether { is inside of a String
            foreach (Point strPt in strings) {
                if (strPt.X <= matchIndex && matchIndex <= strPt.Y) {
                    return "~$";
                }
            }
            return ";";
        case "{":
            // Determine whether { is inside of a String
            foreach (Point strPt in strings) {
                if (strPt.X <= matchIndex && matchIndex <= strPt.Y) {
                    return "~@";
                }
            }
            return "{";
        case "}":
            // Determine whether } is inside of a String or comment
            foreach (Point strPt in strings) {
                if (strPt.X <= matchIndex && matchIndex <= strPt.Y) {
                    return "~#";
                }
            }
            return "}";
        default:
            return match.Value;
    }
}
```

List<Point> plays a key role in determining whether a particular symbol is inside of a *String*. All the values in *strings List<Point>* are enumerated using the *foreach* loop. If the symbol is inside a string, the replacement token (e.g. "~$") is used, otherwise the symbol is replaced with itself (nothing is changed).

15.4.2 Adding Open and Closed Curly Braces to Convert Single-line Statements to Single-line Blocks

The regular expression that enables us to detect the presence of one of several constructs that include a single-line statement that we wish to convert to a block delimited by "{" and "}" is:

```
private String regexStringForAddingOpenCloseBraces =
    @"(?:if|for|while|foreach|else)\s*\(.*?\)([^{]*?);";
```

The (?: within the parenthesized expression indicates that we do not want to capture a back-reference. The back-reference that we want to capture is given by ([^{]*?);. This represents a line-beginning anchor followed by zero or more characters other than "{" terminated by a semicolon.

Listing 15.8 presents method *AddOpenCloseBraces*.

LISTING 15.8 Method AddOpenCloseBraces

```
private void AddOpenCloseBraces() {
    Regex regex = new Regex(regexStringForAddingOpenCloseBraces);
    inputText = inputTextBox.Text.Trim();
    MatchCollection matches = regex.Matches(inputText);
    String backReference = "";
    replacementText = "";
    int matchIndex = 0;
    foreach (Match match in matches) {
        backReference = match.Groups[1].Value + ";";
        matchIndex = inputText.IndexOf(backReference, matchIndex);
        replacementText = inputText.Substring(0, matchIndex) + " {" +
        backReference + "}" +
            inputText.Substring(matchIndex + backReference.Length);
        inputText = replacementText;
    }
    if (replacementText.Length > 0) {
      inputTextBox.Clear();
        inputTextBox.Text = replacementText;
        inputText = replacementText;


    /* Code for replacing
     *  else
     *            someStatement;
     *  by
     *
     *          else {
     *              someStatement;
     *          }
     */
    }
}
```

In the *foreach* enumeration, the expression *match.Groups[1].Value* is used to capture the statement that needs to be replaced by " *{"* + *backReference* + *"}"*.

Exercise 15.10

Write the code for replacing the else followed by a single-statement shown in the comment in the previous code.

Listing 15.3 presented the details of tokenizing the input source file into one big paragraph. Now we are ready to tackle the most interesting and challenging part of the formatter—the actual formatting.

15.4.3 Formatting the Paragraph of Text

The preparations have been completed. Comments have been removed from the input source. Single-line statements have been bracketed by open and closed curly braces. The entire source file has been split into chunks delimited by a collection of operators. Now a formatted output file must be created. The code for accomplishing this is voluminous and involves the use of many more regular expressions. Listing 15.9 presents the details of method *basicFormattingBtn_Click*, an event-handler for a button click in the GUI application that supports formatting (you are invited to download and run the application).

Only selected parts of this method will be discussed in detail. Comments are used throughout to indicate the purpose of each segment of code.

LISTING 15.9 Method for Basic Formatting

```
private void basicFormattingBtn_Click(object sender, EventArgs e) {
    RemoveComments();
    AddOpenCloseBraces();
    TokenizeInput();

    // Remove spaces before each semicolon produced during tokenization
    Regex regex = new Regex(@"\s+;");
    replacementText = regex.Replace(inputText, ";");
    inputText = replacementText;

    // Create new-lines below ;, {, }
    regex = new Regex(@"([;\{\}]|else)");
    replacementText = regex.Replace(inputText,
                    MatchEvaluatorDelegateInstance);
    inputText = replacementText;

    // Remove spaces before each ) produced during tokenization
    regex = new Regex(@"\s+\)");
    replacementText = regex.Replace(inputText, ")");
    inputText = replacementText;

    // Remove spaces before each ( produced during tokenization
    regex = new Regex(@"\s+\(");
```

LISTING 15.9 Method for Basic Formatting (continued)

```
inputText = replacementText;
replacementText = regex.Replace(inputText, "(");
inputText = replacementText;

// Add space back in after while(, for(, foreach(, if(
// to offset previous task
regex = new Regex(@"while\(");
replacementText = regex.Replace(inputText, "while (");
inputText = replacementText;

regex = new Regex(@"for\(");
replacementText = regex.Replace(inputText, "for (");
inputText = replacementText;

regex = new Regex(@"foreach\(");
replacementText = regex.Replace(inputText, "foreach (");
inputText = replacementText;

regex = new Regex(@"if\(");
replacementText = regex.Replace(inputText, "if (");
inputText = replacementText;

// Replace + [+|=] and remove space produced during tokenization
regex = new Regex(@"([\+\-\*/\%]) \=");
Match match = regex.Match(inputText);
replacementText =
  regex.Replace(inputText, match.Groups[1].Value + "=");
inputText = replacementText;

// Replace + + with ++, replace - - with - (cause: tokenization)
regex = new Regex(@"\- \-");
replacementText = regex.Replace(inputText, "--");
inputText = replacementText;

regex = new Regex(@"\+ \+");
replacementText = regex.Replace(inputText, "++");
inputText = replacementText;

// Replace = = with == (produced during tokenization)
regex = new Regex(@"\= \=");
replacementText = regex.Replace(inputText, "==");
inputText = replacementText;

// Replace <   XXX  > with <XXX>
regex = new Regex(@"\<\s*(.*?)\s*\>");
Match m = regex.Match(inputText);
replacementText =
  regex.Replace(inputText, "<" + m.Groups[1].Value + ">");
inputText = replacementText;

// Convert ~+, ~-, ~* back to { } and ;
regex = new Regex(@"~\@");
replacementText = regex.Replace(inputText, "{");
inputText = replacementText;
```

LISTING 15.9 Method for Basic Formatting (continued)

```
    regex = new Regex(@"~\#");
    replacementText = regex.Replace(inputText, "}");
    inputText = replacementText;

    regex = new Regex(@"~\$");
    replacementText = regex.Replace(inputText, ";");
    inputText = replacementText;

    // Put a new-line in front of every
    (public|protected|private|partial|public abstract)? class
    regex = new // Cannot break the next line
Regex(@"\s*(public abstract|abstract public|public|protected|private|
partial)?\s*class");
    matches = regex.Matches(inputText);
    foreach (Match match in matches) {
      replacementText = regex.Replace(inputText,
                   "\n" + match.Value, 1, match.Index);
      inputText = replacementText;
    }

    // Put a new-line in front of every method signature
    // Exercise 15.11

    // Put a new-line in front of every namespace identifier
    // Exercise 15.12

     // Put a new-line in front of every class declaration
     // Exercise 15.12

    inputTextBox.Clear();
    inputTextBox.Text = inputText;
}
```

A sequence of tasks is performed in method *basicFormattingBtn_Click* and each is described with a detailed comment. Many of the tasks are designed to undo spaces introduced during the tokenization process. The most significant task is described following. We shall focus on the task given by the following code:

```
// Create new-lines below ;, {, }
regex = new Regex(@"([;\{\}]|else)");
replacementText = regex.Replace(inputText,
                  MatchEvaluatorDelegateInstance);
inputText = replacementText;
```

It is here that the unformatted tokenized paragraph is reformed into a formatted entity by introducing new lines and leading spaces to create consistent indentation. The support method *MatchEvaluatorDelegateInstance* is used to accomplish the replacement of "}", "{", and ";" with appropriate replacements.

Method *MatchEvaluatorDelegateInstance* is presented in Listing 15.10. References are made to the variable *indent*, a field whose scope covers the entire class.

LISTING 15.10 Method MatchEvaluatorDelegateInstance

```
private String MatchEvaluatorDelegateInstance(Match match) {
   String retString = "";
      String nextToken = match.NextMatch().Value;
      int matchIndex = match.Index;
   switch (match.Value) {
      case ";":
      // Determine whether next non-whitespace token is }
            retString = "";
            if (!nextToken.Equals("}")) {
               retString = ";\n";
                  for (int spaces = 0; spaces < indent; spaces++) {
                  retString += " ";
                  }
            else { // if next token is ;
               retString = ";";
            }
             return retString;
         case "{":
            indent += 4;
            retString = "{\n";
            for (int spaces = 0; spaces < indent; spaces++) {
                retString += " ";
            }
            return retString;
         case "}":
            indent -= 4;
             if (inputText[matchIndex - 1] != '\n') {
               retString = "\n";
            }
            for (int spaces = 0; spaces < indent; spaces++) {
                retString += " ";
             }
             if (nextToken.Equals("}")  ||
                (nextToken.Equals(";") &&
                inputText[matchIndex + 1] == ';')) {
                 retString += "}";
            } else if (nextToken.Equals("else")) {
               retString += "} ";
            } else {
               retString += "}\n";
                for (int spaces = 0; spaces < indent; spaces++) {
                 retString += " ";
                }
            }
            return retString;
       default :
            return match.Value;
    }
}
```

The query *NextMatch.Value* is used to obtain the token immediately following the given match. Each of the cases is relatively self-explanatory. We consider one case in detail, the symbol "}".

The level of indentation is decremented by four. A return string is initialized with leading spaces given by the current level of indentation. If the next token is a ";" or a "}", the return string is completed with the "}" character. If the next token is "else", a "}" followed by a space completes the return string. Otherwise the "}" is followed by another new-line character followed by spaces given by the indentation.

Another interesting task is adding a new-line character above each class declaration in the source file. The code for accomplishing this uses another overloaded version of *Replace* as follows:

```
matches = regex.Matches(inputText);
foreach (Match match in matches) {
    replacementText = regex.Replace(inputText,
                    "\n" + match.Value, 1, match.Index);
    inputText = replacementText;
}
```

The third and fourth arguments indicate the number of replacements and the starting position of the replacement. Because the regular expression finds all lines that represent a class declaration, it is essential to limit the number of replacements to one; otherwise all the class declarations will become the same as the last one that is replaced.

A similar strategy needs to be used in solving Exercises 15.11 and 15.12.

Exercises 15.11 and 15.12

Write the code for the tasks given directly above each exercise in Listing 15.9 (adding a new line above each method and namespace declaration).

Having completed our discussion of the highlights of this formatting application, it must be emphasized that the formatter is not complete. A commercial formatter is a complex software product. In addition to comment handling that is not done in this formatter, many other important formatting issues have not been addressed. These include logic for breaking long lines of source code at appropriate places while using appropriate indentation, logic for vertical white-space handling, and other practical options too numerous to mention.

It is quite a testimony to the power of regular expression handling that the basic formatting operations that have been described and implemented were accomplished using only regular expression text processing.

15.5 SUMMARY

◆ A regular expression is a string that precisely describes a search pattern.

◆ C#/.NET provides strong support for regular expression processing in the namespace *System.Text.RegularExpressions*. The classes that support regular expressions provide support for searching text, replacing text within a string, and splitting text into separate sections based on delimiters.

◆ The following table summarizes the construction of regular expressions.

Pattern	Explanation	Simple Example
[^b]	Matches any character except "b"; the symbols [and] define a character class; the caret represents negation	**[^\{]*;** Matches zero or more occurrences of any character except "{" and terminated by ";"
\{	Escape character to suppress the special meaning of the meta-character	**[\{\}\;]** Matches "{" or "}" or ";"
\d \w \s	Special characters for any digit, any word character and a space	**\w+\s+\w+** Matches a word followed by one or more spaces followed by another word
.	Matches any characters except new-line	**\w+\s+.*;** Matches a word followed by one or more spaces followed by zero or more non new-line characters followed by ";"
^ $	Caret anchors to beginning of a line and dollar to end of line	**^public class \w+ \{$** Matches the beginning of a line followed by literal "public class", a word followed by "{" and the end of a line
\b	Matches the boundary between a word and a non-word character	**\bclass\b** Matches every occurrence of "class" proceeded and followed by non-word characters
+ +?	One or more occurrences (greedy) or one or more occurrences (non-greedy)	**\w+?;** Does a non-greedy search for a word followed by ";"
?	Makes the previous character optional	**A?BCD** Matches an optional A followed by BCD

15.6 ADDITIONAL EXERCISES

For Exercises 15.13–15.17, explain in words the following regular expressions. The remaining exercises provide instructions particular to each exercise.

Exercise 15.13

```
(.*?) //\s*.*?;
```

Exercise 15.14

```
(the|dog|cat|person) buys
```

Exercise 15.15

```
(?!\w+)(.*)$
```

Exercise 15.16

```
\\\\(\w)\\\\
```

Exercise 15.17

```
(public|private|protected|internal)? class (?=.*$)
```

Exercise 15.18

Write a segment of C# code that replaces every occurrence of "the" with "a" in some text.

Exercise 15.19

Write a segment of C# code that replaces the first three occurrences of "private" with "protected" in a C# source file and leaves the rest alone.

Exercise 15.20

Write a segment of C# code that replaces every occurrence of "(" followed by a character with "(" followed by a space and the character.

Exercise 15.21

Write a segment of C# code that replaces every occurrence of a character followed by ")" with the character followed by a space followed by ")".

Exercise 15.22

In the current formatter, new-lines are generated after each semicolon in a *for*-loop. Show how this deficiency can be corrected.

PART 5

PUTTING IT ALL TOGETHER

This final section of the book contains only a single chapter. It presents an interesting application that puts together many of the important concepts and techniques presented in the book. These include analysis and design with UML diagrams, principles of class construction, threads, event-notification and handling and the Observer Pattern, use of standard collections, and graphical user interface development.

CHAPTER 16

Ecological Simulation

This chapter presents an application that uses some of the important concepts and techniques discussed earlier in the book. It is an interesting application in its own right with some history; it forms the basis of an emergent system—one whose behavior is complex, unpredictable, and engaging.

The application was first inspired by an article in *Scientific American*, "Wa-Tor" by A.K. Dewdney (*Scientific American*, December 1984). The problem continues to be interesting because it sets the foundation for modeling and understanding many complex predator-prey ecologies. Many variants of the problem have been used by the author in teaching object-oriented analysis and design over the years. Implementations have been done by the author in Modula-2, C, C++, Objective-C, Delphi Pascal, Eiffel, Java, and most recently C#/.NET. The problem does not require specialized expertise. The problem domain contains enough richness to provide the basis for interesting design and implementation decisions. Hopefully you will find this application a useful, fun, and fitting way to end this book. It will allow you to exercise many of the skills learned earlier.

Because of the unique nature of this chapter, there is not a separate end-of-chapter section with exercises. The exercises that are embedded within the body of the chapter are designed to enhance your understanding of the design and implementation of this software system.

16.1 EXAMINING THE SPECIFICATIONS FOR THE SIMULATION

In the artificial world of this simulation, marine animals live in a two-dimensional grid. Some of the animals behave as predators, some as prey, and most as both. The grid is defined so that it "wraps" along all four of its boundaries. See Figure 16.1. A marine animal moving up from the top row arrives at the bottom row. Moving to the left of the leftmost column brings the animal to the rightmost column. Moving right from the rightmost column brings the animal to the leftmost column. Finally, moving down from the bottom row brings the animal to the top row. To illustrate this using the grid in Figure 16.1, the animals in the cells marked A and B are adjacent (B is to the "left" of A or A to the "right" of B). D is adjacent to C (D is "above" C or C is "below" D). E and F are also adjacent because F is one cell "down" and one cell "left" of E.

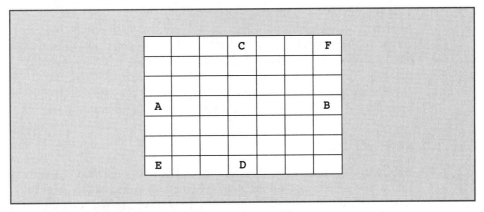

FIGURE 16.1 Marine animal positions in a grid

Every grid location has **neighboring** cells and **nearby** cells. These are shown in Figure 16.2 for a grid position marked with "X". The eight neighboring cells are marked with "N". The 24 nearby cells include the eight neighboring cells as well as those marked with "X".

X	X	X	X	X
X	N	N	N	X
X	N	X	N	X
X	N	N	N	X
X	X	X	X	X

FIGURE 16.2 Neighboring and nearby cells

At the top of the food chain is **shark**. Next in the chain is **dolphin**. Below dolphin is **tuna**. At the bottom of the chain is **minnow**. Sharks hunt for dolphin (their favorite food) and tuna. Dolphins prefer tuna but are capable of eating shark if they have the opportunity and conditions are right. Tuna feed on minnow. Minnow are at the bottom of the food chain in this simulation and do not feed on any other species. The life of a minnow, measured in number of move opportunities, is assigned at birth. In addition to shark, dolphin, tuna, and minnow, we have **scavenger**. These animals feed on dead shark, dead dolphin, dead tuna, and dead minnow, performing garbage collection.

Three of the five species (shark, dolphin, and tuna) must eat within a specified time period after last eating (measured in the number of move opportunities and called the STARVATION_INTERVAL); otherwise they starve to death and become dead shark, dead dolphin, or dead tuna. These remnants of live marine animals occupy space in the grid until they are eaten by a scavenger. All of the species except scavenger can reproduce within a specified time period measured since the last reproduction (measured in number of move opportunities and called the REPRODUCTION_INTERVAL).

The rules of engagement for the four predator-prey species (shark, dolphin, tuna, and minnow) and for the scavenger species are described in the following sections.

16.1.1 Rules for Minnow

A minnow moves to a nearby empty cell, if one is available. If two or more are available, one is chosen at random. A **nearby cell**, as stated earlier, is defined as one that is reachable by moving a distance of up to two cells in any direction from its current location in the grid. If no empty cell is found from its current grid position, it does not move even though the move counts as a move opportunity in considering its assigned lifetime or reproduction opportunity. The minnow can jump over an occupied adjacent cell if it chooses to move to an empty cell that is a distance of two cells away.

After a preset number of moves since its last reproduction (specified at the time of a minnow's birth and called the REPRODUCTION_INTERVAL), a minnow is allowed to reproduce. It can reproduce only after it has moved. If it cannot move and therefore reproduce on a given turn to move, it is eligible again to reproduce the next time it can actually move. Reproduction for a minnow involves creating a new minnow and placing it in the cell previously occupied by the minnow before it moved.

After a preset number of moves, a minnow perishes. This number of moves is specified by its MINNOW_PERISH_INTERVAL.

16.1.2 Rules for Tuna

A tuna hunts for minnow in a nearby cell, if one is available. As before, a nearby cell is a distance of up to two cells away from the current grid position of the tuna. If two or more minnow are available in nearby cells, it will choose one that is not adjacent to a shark or dolphin. If all the minnow are adjacent to a shark or dolphin, it will take its chances and pick a minnow at random and eat it. If a minnow cannot be found in a nearby cell, the tuna attempts to move to a nearby empty cell. If two or more empty cells are available among the nearby cells, it chooses a cell that is not adjacent to a dolphin or a shark. If all available empty cells would place the tuna adjacent to either a dolphin or shark, it does not move and therefore cannot reproduce on this move opportunity. In other words, a tuna will never move to an empty cell that is adjacent to a dolphin or shark. It will move adjacent to a shark or dolphin if it eats a minnow providing there is no minnow that is not adjacent to a dolphin or shark. If no empty cell is found among the nearby cells, it does not move or reproduce.

A tuna can reproduce only after it has moved and after REPRODUCTION_INTERVAL move opportunities have occurred since the last reproduction. Reproduction for a tuna involves creating a new tuna and placing it in the cell previously occupied by the tuna before it moved.

A tuna must feed on its prey, minnow, within another specified number of move opportunities since its last feeding. This interval, the STARVATION_INTERVAL, is set at its time of birth. Failure to accomplish this results in starvation and death and a conversion to a dead tuna.

16.1.3 Rules for Dolphin

A dolphin first hunts for a tuna, which is its primary prey, among its immediate neighbors (eight cells that are a distance of one cell away). If two or more tuna are found among the eight adjacent locations, one of these tuna is chosen at random and becomes the dolphin's next meal. If no tuna are found among neighboring grid locations, the next hunt is for shark in its neighboring eight cell locations. If two or more are found, one is chosen at random. 25 percent of the time, this shark is eaten. If the shark is not eaten (75 percent of the time), the dolphin dies of its wounds and becomes a dead dolphin. If neither primary prey (tuna) nor secondary prey (shark) is among the eight neighboring grid locations, the dolphin next looks for an empty location among the neighboring locations (one cell away). It then moves to an empty location, choosing one at random if two or more are available. The rules for reproduction or starvation are the same as for a tuna.

16.1.4 Rules for Shark

Before moving, a shark can consume a school of minnow residing in neighboring cells (a distance of one from the shark position). These minnow are removed from the ocean. In consuming all minnow that are in the neighborhood of the shark, the shark does not actually move to any of the minnow positions, but simply swallows all these minnow (they disappear from the ocean).

A shark's behavior is similar to a dolphin's. Its primary prey is dolphin and secondary prey is tuna. Dolphins are hunted for first in the shark's neighborhood (eight surrounding cells). If one is found (random choice as before in the event that two or more are found), the shark moves to that location and devours the dolphin (with 100 percent certainty). If a dolphin is not found, the shark next searches for a neighboring tuna. If one is found, the shark moves to the tuna's location and eats the tuna. (If two or more are found, one is chosen at random.) Two tuna must be eaten within the time frame, STARVATION_INTERVAL, set for the shark at birth in order to stave off starvation, but only one dolphin needs to be eaten in this time interval since the last feeding. Finally, if neither dolphin nor tuna are found, the shark moves to an empty neighboring location (one cell away) if one exists (with random choice if two or more exist).

16.1.5 Rules for Scavenger

A scavenger cannot die of starvation and cannot reproduce. When given a turn to move, it moves only if a dead dolphin, dead shark, dead tuna, or dead minnow are among the nearby grid locations (up to two cell positions away). It continues to move on the same turn until no dead dolphin, dead shark, dead tuna, or dead minnow are in its nearby cells.

The simulation should be controlled by a graphical user interface (GUI) that allows the user to specify the following parameters with default values provided to the user:

1. Reproduction interval for shark, dolphin, tuna, and minnow (the minimum number of move opportunities required since its last reproduction before reproduction can take place). The actual value assigned to a marine animal at birth is a uniformly distributed integer value between the specified value minus one to the specified value plus one.

2. The starvation interval for shark, dolphin, and tuna. If the species has not eaten since its last meal during the number of move opportunities specified by the starvation interval, it is converted to a dead species of the same type. A minnow does not have to eat, so its perish interval represents its lifetime. The actual starvation or perish interval for a minnow assigned at birth is uniformly distributed between the specified value minus one to the specified value plus one.

16.1.6 Examining the GUI

Each time the GUI is refreshed because of the movement or reproduction of an animal, the clock is incremented by one. The population dynamics for each species must be displayed as a graph that evolves as the simulation progresses (a new point after every 25 events). The movement of animals within the two-dimensional grid that models the ocean must be shown after each move or reproduction occurs. The average lifetime measured in the number of move opportunities before the death of minnow, tuna, dolphin, and shark must also be updated each time the GUI is refreshed. The actuarial data is obtained when each marine animal perishes. The number of times it was given the opportunity to move is recorded after its death. These evolving actuarial averages provide interesting insights into the ecological interactions between the species.

Figure 16.3 shows a screen shot of the GUI application.

The initial values that drive the simulation are shown in the "Initial Values" panel. The values used in this case are the default values. These may be changed by the user.

The current population values are shown and change rapidly over time. The population dynamics are shown with color-coded lines (green for minnow, goldenrod for tuna, blue for dolphin, and red for shark). The actual positions of each marine animal are shown in the middle panel. These change rapidly as the simulation evolves.

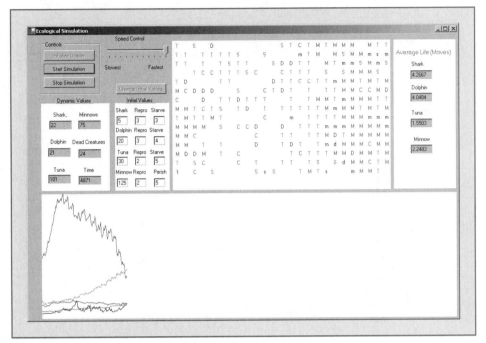

FIGURE 16.3   Screenshot of GUI

16.2 ANALYZING THE SIMULATION

Based on the rules given earlier, we examine in more detail how each marine species moves. This will help in the identification of classes and their relationships to each other.

We use sequence diagrams to codify the rules of movement for each species. Figure 16.4 contains a sequence diagram that defines the "move" rules for minnow.

The minnow has the least complicated move rules compared to the other marine animals. Six objects are shown in this diagram. They include the minnow that is moving, its location, the ocean in which it is moving, the GUI that displays its movement, a dead minnow, and a baby minnow.

The reproduction count and lifetime of the minnow are incremented. The position of the minnow is obtained from the location object. A collection of empty cells is also obtained from the location object within the ocean. This implies that each location object in the ocean is aware of its neighboring and nearby locations and contains the coordinate within the grid of the marine animal—minnow in this case.

If there are one or more nearby empty locations, the minnow's new position is chosen at random from this collection.

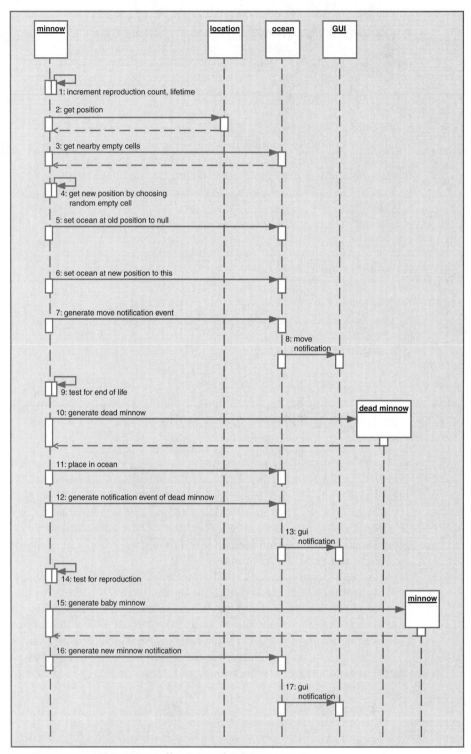

FIGURE 16.4   Sequence diagram of minnow move

The ocean is updated with the position of the minnow. In addition, the ocean receives a move notification event. It then generates a move notification event and transmits it to the GUI. This implies that the GUI must register an event listener with the ocean and the ocean must register an event listener with each minnow. The advantage of this separation is that the marine objects do not have to know anything about the GUI. They only need to know about the ocean. However, the ocean must know about the GUI. The ocean serves as a broker capturing event notifications from each marine object as it moves and transmits that information to the GUI. The marine objects live in their own space and operate independently of the GUI.

A test is then conducted to see whether the minnow perishes because it has moved the allowed number of times before it dies. If its lifetime equals the perish interval (a value randomly assigned to each minnow at its birth), a dead minnow object is generated and placed in the ocean in place of the previous minnow object. Further event notifications are sent to the ocean and to the GUI to update the view.

Finally, a test is conducted to see whether the minnow can reproduce. If it qualifies (its number of move opportunities equals or exceeds its assigned reproduction interval and it has moved), a baby minnow (new minnow) is generated. Again the ocean and GUI are notified. (In other words, the minnow notifies the ocean and the ocean notifies the GUI.)

The move logic for a tuna is more complex and is shown in Figure 16.5.

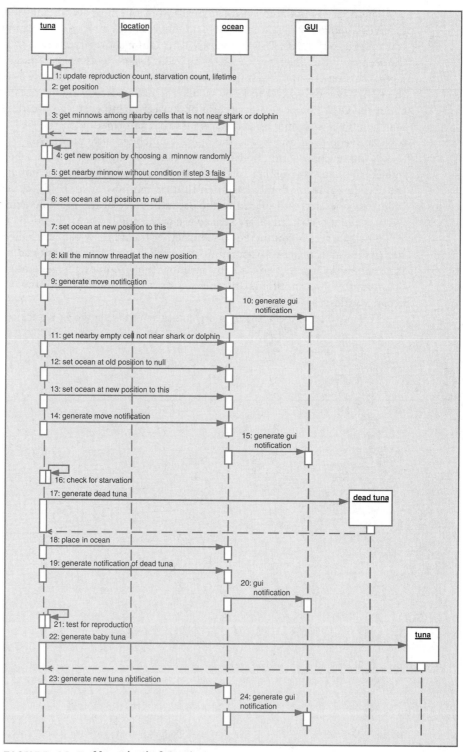

FIGURE 16.5 Move logic for a tuna

Exercise 16.1

Explain in words the move logic for a tuna based on the sequence diagram given in Figure 16.5.

Exercise 16.2

Draw a sequence diagram for the move logic of a dolphin based on the specifications given in Section 16.1.

Exercise 16.3

Draw a sequence diagram for the move logic of a shark based on the specifications given in Section 16.1.

The move logic for a scavenger is given in Figure 16.6.

The position of the scavenger is obtained. In a loop, while there is at least one dead animal among the nearby cells (obtained from the location object in the ocean), the scavenger is moved to the position previously occupied by the dead animal. A move notification is sent to the ocean which in turn sends a notification to the GUI.

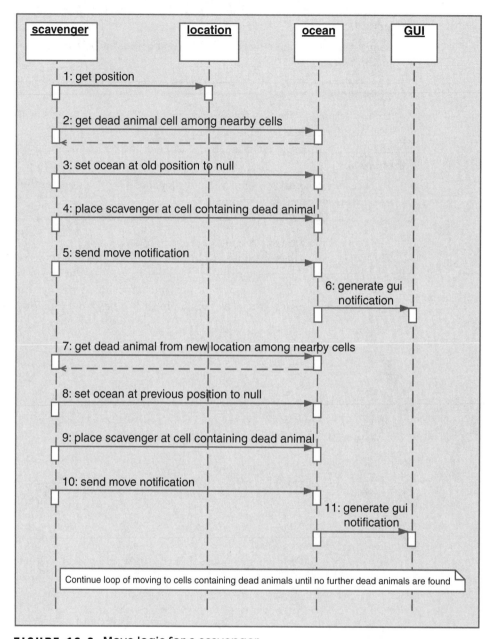

FIGURE 16.6 Move logic for a scavenger

16.3 DESIGNING THE SIMULATION

The problem domain classes include: *Minnow, Tuna, Dolphin, Shark, Scavenger, Location, DeadAnimal,* and *Ocean.* An abstract super class, *MarineAnimal,* is created that has *Minnow, Tuna, Dolphin, Shark, Scavenger,* and *DeadAnimal* as subclasses. This *MarineAnimal* class includes the utility methods that enable any marine animal to locate neighboring or nearby empty cells or prey.

Class *Ocean* is designed as a singleton. Only one instance of this class is allowed.

A UML class diagram that shows the relationships among the classes is shown in Figure 16.7.

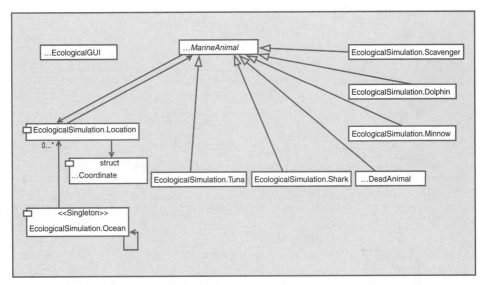

FIGURE 16.7 Design class diagram

Why is there only one class, *DeadAnimal,* which models dead minnow, dead tuna, dead dolphin, and dead shark?

Because each dead species is inert, its behavior is identical to the other species. They do not move from their location once placed there. They differ only in their name ("m" for dead minnow, "t" for dead tuna, "d" for dead dolphin, and "s" for dead shark). This difference is better accounted for with an attribute name (a field of class *MarineAnimal*) than separate classes for each species of dead animal.

16.4 IMPLEMENTING THE SIMULATION

A set of static constants that characterize the population of marine animals is defined in a class *Constants.* The default values for these constants are specified. These can be overridden in the GUI. Class *Constants* is presented in Listing 16.1.

LISTING 16.1 Class Constants

```
using System;

namespace EcologicalSimulation {

    public class Constants {

        // Static constants

        // Time delay between moves for each marine animal
        public static int TIME_DELAY = 200;
        public static int DELAY;

        public static Random RANDOM = new Random();

        // Ocean data
        public static int ROWS = 15;
        public static int COLS = 25;


        // Population data
        public static int NUMBER_TUNA = 30;
        public static int NUMBER_DOLPHIN = 20;
        public static int NUMBER_SHARK = 5;
        public static int NUMBER_MINNOW = 125;
        public static int NUMBER_SCAVENGER= 25;

        // Creature data
        public static int TUNA_REPRODUCTION_INTERVAL = 2;
        public static int TUNA_STARVATION_INTERVAL = 5;
        public static int DOLPHIN_REPRODUCTION_INTERVAL = 3;
        public static int DOLPHIN_STARVATION_INTERVAL = 4;
        public static int SHARK_REPRODUCTION_INTERVAL = 3;
        public static int SHARK_STARVATION_INTERVAL = 3;
        public static int MINNOW_REPRODUCTION_INTERVAL = 2;
        public static int MINNOW_PERISH_INTERVAL = 5;

        static Constants() {
            // Warm-up random number generator
            for (int i = 0; i < 100000; i++) {
                RANDOM.NextDouble();
            }
        }
    }
}
```

The static constructor in the *Constants* class generates 100,000 random number calls in order to "warm-up" the random number generator. This is supposed to result in better statistical properties.

Class *Coordinate* is presented next. This simple class models a row and column location within the ocean. It is implemented as a *struct* to promote efficiency. Listing 16.2 shows its details.

LISTING 16.2 Class Coordinate

```
using System;
using System.Collections.Generic;
using System.Text;

namespace EcologicalSimulation {

    // Models a row and column in the Grid
    public struct Coordinate {
        // Fields
        private int row, col;

        // Constructor
        public Coordinate(int row, int col) {
            this.row = row;
            this.col = col;
        }

        public Coordinate(Coordinate position) :
                this(position.Row, position.Col) {
        }

        public int Row {
            get {
                return row;
            }
            set {
                row = value;
            }
        }

        public int Col {
            get {
                return col;
            }
            set {
                col = value;
            }
        }

        public override bool Equals(Object obj) {
            Coordinate other = (Coordinate)obj;
            return row == other.Row && col == other.Col;
        }
        public override int GetHashCode() {
          return row ^ col;
        }
    }
}
```

Two constructors initialize an instance of *Coordinate*. The first takes a row and column and the second takes a *Coordinate*. The second constructor uses *this* (a reference to the first constructor) to do its work.

Abstract class *MarineAnimal* is presented in Listing 16.3. This important class establishes the foundation for all the concrete sea critter classes.

LISTING 16.3 Abstract class MarineAnimal

```
using System;
using System.Collections.Generic;
using System.Text;
using System.Threading;
using System.Drawing;
using System.Windows.Forms;

namespace EcologicalSimulation {

    public delegate void MoveNotify(Coordinate from, Coordinate to,
                                    String fromName, String toName);

    public abstract class MarineAnimal {

        // Fields
        protected Color color;
        protected String name;
        protected Location location;
        protected int reproductionInterval;
        protected int reproductionCount;
        protected int starvationInterval;
        protected int starvationCount;
        protected event MoveNotify moveNotify;
        protected Thread thread;
        protected bool stop;
        protected int lifetime; // Number of move opportunities

        // Constructor
        public MarineAnimal(Color color, String name, int row, int col,
                            int reproInterval, int starveInterval) {
            this.color = color;
            this.name = name;
            location = new Location(row, col);
            this.reproductionInterval = reproInterval;
            this.starvationInterval = starveInterval;
            reproductionCount = 0;
            starvationCount = 0;
        }
```

LISTING 16.3 Abstract class MarineAnimal (continued)

```
    // Properties
    public String Name {
        get {
            return name;
        }
    }

    public Color Color {
        get {
            return color;
        }
    }

    // Commands
    public void Register(MoveNotify handler) {
        moveNotify += new MoveNotify(handler);
    }

    public void StartMoveThread() {
        thread = new Thread(new ThreadStart(Move));
        thread.Start();
        stop = false;
    }

    public void FireMoveEvent(Coordinate from, Coordinate to,
                              String fromName, String toName) {
        if (moveNotify != null) {
            moveNotify(from, to, fromName, toName);
        }
    }

    public void StopMoveThread() {
        stop = true;
        this.UpdateMortality(lifetime);
        if (Ocean.OCEAN[location.Row, location.Col].MarineAnimal !=
            null && Ocean.OCEAN[location.Row,
                location.Col].MarineAnimal.thread != null &&
            Ocean.OCEAN[location.Row,
            location.Col].MarineAnimal.thread.IsAlive) {
            Ocean.OCEAN[location.Row,
            location.Col].MarineAnimal.thread.Abort();
        }
    }

    public List<Coordinate> NearbyEmptyCells(Coordinate position) {
        List<Coordinate> nearby = new List<Coordinate>();
```

LISTING 16.3 Abstract class MarineAnimal (continued)

```
            foreach (Coordinate pt in
                Ocean.OCEAN[location.Position].Nearby) {
                if (Ocean.OCEAN[pt].MarineAnimal == null) {
                    nearby.Add(pt);
                }
            }
        }
        return nearby;
    }

    public List<Coordinate> NearbyEmptyCellsWithName(
            Coordinate position, String name1, String name2,
            String name3, String name4) {
        List<Coordinate> nearby = new List<Coordinate>();
        foreach (Coordinate pt in Ocean.OCEAN[position].Nearby) {
            if (Ocean.OCEAN[pt].MarineAnimal != null &&
                (Ocean.OCEAN[pt].MarineAnimal.Name.Equals(name1) ||
                 Ocean.OCEAN[pt].MarineAnimal.Name.Equals(name2) ||
                 Ocean.OCEAN[pt].MarineAnimal.Name.Equals(name3) ||
                 Ocean.OCEAN[pt].MarineAnimal.Name.Equals(name4)) ) {
                nearby.Add(pt);
            }
        }
        return nearby;
    }

    public List<Coordinate> NeighboringEmptyCells(
                                    Coordinate position) {
        List<Coordinate> neighbors = new List<Coordinate>();
        foreach (Coordinate pt in
        Ocean.OCEAN[location.Row, location.Col].Neighbors) {
            if (Ocean.OCEAN[pt.Row, pt.Col].MarineAnimal == null) {
                neighbors.Add(pt);
            }
        }
        return neighbors;
    }

    public bool NeighborsWithName(Coordinate position,
                                    String name) {
        List<Coordinate> neighbors = new List<Coordinate>();
        foreach (Coordinate pt in
        Ocean.OCEAN[location.Row, location.Col].Neighbors) {
            if (Ocean.OCEAN[pt].MarineAnimal != null &&
                    Ocean.OCEAN[pt].MarineAnimal.Name == name) {
                return true;
            }
        }
        return false;
    }
```

LISTING 16.3 Abstract class MarineAnimal (continued)

```
    public List<Coordinate> NeighboringCellsWithName(
            Coordinate position, String name) {
      List<Coordinate> neighbors = new List<Coordinate>();
      foreach (Coordinate pt in
      Ocean.OCEAN[location.Row, location.Col].Neighbors) {
          if (Ocean.OCEAN[pt.Row, pt.Col].MarineAnimal != null &&
                  Ocean.OCEAN[pt].MarineAnimal.Name == name) {
              neighbors.Add(pt);
          }
      }
      return neighbors;
    }

    public List<Coordinate> NearbyCellsWithName(
            Coordinate position, String name) {
      List<Coordinate> nearby = new List<Coordinate>();
      foreach (Coordinate pt in
      Ocean.OCEAN[location.Row, location.Col].Nearby) {
          if (Ocean.OCEAN[pt.Row, pt.Col].MarineAnimal != null &&
                  Ocean.OCEAN[pt].MarineAnimal.Name == name) {
              nearby.Add(pt);
          }
      }
      return nearby;
    }

    public List<Coordinate> NeighboringCellsWithNameNotAdjacentTo(
    Coordinate position,
       String name, String notAdjacentTo1, String notAdjacentTo2) {
       List<Coordinate> neighbors = new List<Coordinate>();
       foreach (Coordinate pt in
              Ocean.OCEAN[location.Position].Neighbors) {
          if (Ocean.OCEAN[pt].MarineAnimal != null &&
                  Ocean.OCEAN[pt].MarineAnimal.Name == name) {
              if (!NeighborsWithName(pt, notAdjacentTo1) &&
                      !NeighborsWithName(pt, notAdjacentTo2)) {
                  neighbors.Add(pt);
              }
          }
       }
       return neighbors;
    }

    public List<Coordinate> NearbyCellsWithNameNotAdjacentTo(
       Coordinate position,
       String name, String notAdjacentTo1, String notAdjacentTo2) {
       List<Coordinate> nearby = new List<Coordinate>();
       foreach (Coordinate pt in
              Ocean.OCEAN[location.Position].Nearby) {
```

LISTING 16.3 Abstract class MarineAnimal (continued)

```
            if (Ocean.OCEAN[pt].MarineAnimal != null &&
                    Ocean.OCEAN[pt].MarineAnimal.Name == name) {
                if (!NeighborsWithName(pt, notAdjacentTo1) &&
                        !NeighborsWithName(pt, notAdjacentTo2)) {
                    nearby.Add(pt);
                }
            }
        }
        return nearby;
    }

    public abstract void Move();

    public abstract void UpdateMortality(int lifetime);
    }
}
```

Class *MarineAnimal* contains two abstract methods: *Move* and *UpdateMortality*.

A major implementation decision is implicit in class *MarineAnimal*. A field *thread* is included that assigns method *Move* to be in a separate thread. This has the effect of treating each marine creature as an autonomous entity that interacts with other autonomous entities (other marine creatures) much like real organisms. Each marine animal appears to run in parallel with the other marine animals. In principle, there could be as many threads running "in parallel" as there are cells in the grid. The public method *StartMoveThread* assigns the *Move* method to the thread object and starts the thread.

A delegate class *MoveNotify* with four parameters *from* (type *Coordinate*), *to* (type *Coordinate*), *fromName* (type *String*), and *toName* (type *String*) is defined. Associated with this delegate type a field *moveNotify* is declared to be a *MoveNotify* event. A public *Register* method allows a handler to be added to the invocation list of the *moveNotify* event.

The abstract method *UpdateMortality* is redefined in each concrete marine animal class and is used to inform the *Ocean* about the number of move opportunities for each marine animal after it dies.

The public method *StopMoveThread* uses the *Abort* command to terminate the thread associated with the marine animal. The Boolean *stop* field is changed to true. As we shall see when we examine the concrete subclasses of *MarineAnimal*, the effect of setting *stop* to true is to terminate the loop embedded in the *Move* method. The method *UpdateMortality* is invoked in order to notify the ocean and the GUI about the life of the thread that is being stopped.

A public *FireMoveEvent* tests to see whether *moveEvent* is null, and if it is not, fires *moveEvent*. A listener in class *Ocean* responds to *moveEvent* by firing its own event that is broadcast to the GUI class (as indicated in Section 16.2).

The field *lifetime* is used to capture the number of move opportunities that a marine creature is given before it dies. The public utility methods *NearbyEmptyCells*, *NearbyEmptyCellsWithName*, *NeighboringEmptyCells*, *NeighboringCellsWithName*, *NearbyCellsWithName*, *NeighboringCellsWithNameNotAdjacentTo*, and *NearbyCellsWithNameNotAdjacentTo* return an instance of *List<Coordinate>*. The query *NeighborsWithName* returns true if a neighbor with the specified name is in the neighborhood surrounding the specified position.

We examine one of the utility methods closely. The others are based on a similar principle.

Consider method *NeighboringCellsWithNameNotAdjacentTo*.

```
public List<Coordinate> NeighboringCellsWithNameNotAdjacentTo(
        Coordinate position,
            String name, String notAdjacentTo1, String notAdjacentTo2) {
            List<Coordinate> neighbors = new List<Coordinate>();
    foreach (Coordinate pt in
        Ocean.OCEAN[location.Position].Neighbors) {
        if (Ocean.OCEAN[pt].MarineAnimal != null &&
                Ocean.OCEAN[pt].MarineAnimal.Name == name) {
        if (!NeighborsWithName(pt, notAdjacentTo1) &&
                !NeighborsWithName(pt, notAdjacentTo2)) {
                neighbors.Add(pt);
            }
        }
    }
    return neighbors;
}
```

A *foreach* iteration through the collection *Neighbors*, a read-only property defined in class *Location* to be considered next, is used to find the eight neighboring cells with respect to *location.Position* (the current position of the marine animal). For each coordinate, *pt*, in a neighboring location, if the location contains a marine animal (is not null) and the name of the animal does not match either of the input values *notAdjacentTo1* and *notAdjacentTo2*, the coordinate is added to the field *neighbors*, of type *List<Coordinate>*.

Exercise 16.4

Explain the other utility methods that return *List<Coordinate>*.

With much of the behavior of each concrete marine creature established in the abstract class *MarineAnimal*, we examine class *Location* and then the many concrete subclasses of *MarineAnimal*.

Class *Location* is presented in Listing 16.4.

LISTING 16.4 Class Location

```
using System;
using System.Collections.Generic;
using System.Text;

namespace EcologicalSimulation {

    public class Location {

        // Fields
        private Coordinate position;
        private List<Coordinate> neighbors = new List<Coordinate>();
        private List<Coordinate> nearby = new List<Coordinate>();
        private MarineAnimal marineAnimal;

        // Constructor
        public Location(int row, int col) {
            position = new Coordinate(row, col);
        }

        public Location(Coordinate position) {
            this.position = new Coordinate(position.Row, position.Col)
;
        }

        public void SetNeighbors() {
            int row = position.Row;
            int col = position.Col;

            // North neighbor
            int rowPos = row - 1;
            if (rowPos < 0) {
                rowPos = Constants.ROWS - 1;
            }
            neighbors.Add(new Coordinate(rowPos, col));
            // North west neighbor
            rowPos = row - 1;
            if (rowPos < 0) {
                rowPos = Constants.ROWS - 1;
            }
            int colPos = col - 1;
            if (colPos < 0) {
                colPos = Constants.COLS - 1;
            }
            neighbors.Add(new Coordinate(rowPos, colPos));
            // West neighbor
            colPos = col - 1;
            if (colPos < 0) {
                colPos = Constants.COLS - 1;
```

LISTING 16.4 Class Location (continued)

```
        }
        neighbors.Add(new Coordinate(row, colPos));
        // South west neighbor
        colPos = col - 1;
        if (colPos < 0) {
            colPos = Constants.COLS - 1;
        }
        rowPos = row + 1;
        if (rowPos == Constants.ROWS) {
            rowPos = 0;
        }
        neighbors.Add(new Coordinate(rowPos, colPos));
        // South neighbor
        rowPos = row + 1;
        if (rowPos == Constants.ROWS) {
            rowPos = 0;
        }
        neighbors.Add(new Coordinate(rowPos, col));
        // South east neighbor
        rowPos = row + 1;
        if (rowPos == Constants.ROWS) {
            rowPos = 0;
        }
        colPos = col + 1;
        if (colPos == Constants.COLS) {
            colPos = 0;
        }
        neighbors.Add(new Coordinate(rowPos, colPos));
        // East neighbor
        colPos = col + 1;
        if (colPos == Constants.COLS) {
            colPos = 0;
        }
        neighbors.Add(new Coordinate(row, colPos));
        // North east neighbor
        rowPos = row - 1;
        if (rowPos < 0) {
            rowPos = Constants.ROWS - 1;
        }
        colPos = col + 1;
        if (colPos == Constants.COLS) {
            colPos = 0;
        }
        neighbors.Add(new Coordinate(rowPos, colPos));
    }

    public void SetNearbyValues() {
        /*
         * Fillup nearby by adding all the neighboring points of
```

LISTING 16.4 Class Location (continued)

```
                    * each neighboring point
                    * providing that the point is not already in the List of
                    * points.
                    */
                    foreach (Coordinate neighborPt in neighbors) {
                        if (!nearby.Contains(neighborPt)) {
                            nearby.Add(neighborPt);
                        }
                        foreach (Coordinate neighborOfNeighborPt in
                        Ocean.OCEAN[neighborPt.Row, neighborPt.Col].
                            Neighbors) {
                            if (!nearby.Contains(neighborOfNeighborPt)) {
                                nearby.Add(neighborOfNeighborPt);
                            }
                        }
                    }
                    // Remove the point from which NEARBY is computed
                    nearby.Remove(new Coordinate(position.Row, position.Col));
            }

            // Properties
            public int Row {
                get {
                    return position.Row;
                }
                set {
                    position.Row = value;
                }
            }

            public int Col {
                get {
                    return position.Col;
                }
                set {
                    position.Col = value;
                }
            }

            public Coordinate Position {
                get {
                    return position;
                }
            }

            public MarineAnimal MarineAnimal {
                get {
                    return marineAnimal;
                }
```

LISTING 16.4 Class Location (continued)

```
            set {
                marineAnimal = value;
            }
        }

        public List<Coordinate> Neighbors {
            get {
                return neighbors;
            }
        }

        public List<Coordinate> Nearby {
            get {
                return nearby;
            }
        }
    }
}
```

Every location object contains a *MarineAnimal* (using polymorphic substitution because it is a placeholder for one of the concrete subclasses of *MarineAnimal*), a position (type *Coordinate*), and two collections *neighbors* and *nearby*, each of type *List<Coordinate>*.

We examine the method *SetNearbyValues* because it uses nested *foreach* enumerators on the standard collection *List<Coordinate>*.

```
public void SetNearbyValues() {
    /*
     * Fillup nearby by adding all the neighboring points of
     * each neighboring point
     * providing that the point is not already in the List of
     * points.
     */
    foreach (Coordinate neighborPt in neighbors) {
      if (!nearby.Contains(neighborPt)) {
          nearby.Add(neighborPt);
          }
          foreach (Coordinate neighborOfNeighborPt in
             Ocean.OCEAN[neighborPt.Row, neighborPt.Col].
                     Neighbors) {
          if (!nearby.Contains(neighborOfNeighborPt)) {
              nearby.Add(neighborOfNeighborPt);
              }
          }
    }
    // Remove the point from which NEARBY is computed
    nearby.Remove(new Coordinate(position.Row, position.Col));
}
```

The outer *foreach* enumerator captures each *neighborPt* of type *Coordinate* and adds it to the collection *nearby*. The inner *foreach* enumerator finds the neighbor, *neighborOfNeighborPt*, of *neighborPt*. If *nearby* does not already contain *neighborOfNeighborPt*, it is added to the *nearby* collection. Finally, the coordinate *position* is removed because it should not be considered to be a nearby coordinate.

The collections *neighbors* and *nearby* must be computed only once for each *Location* object within the ocean.

The first concrete marine animal class that we consider is *Minnow*. Its details are presented in Listing 16.5.

LISTING 16.5 Class Minnow

```
using System;
using System.Collections.Generic;
using System.Text;
using System.Drawing;
using System.Threading;
using System.Windows.Forms;


namespace EcologicalSimulation {

    public class Minnow : MarineAnimal {

        // Constructor
        public Minnow(Color color, String name, int row, int col,
                    int reproInterval, int starveInterval) :
                        base(color, name, row, col, reproInterval,
                            starveInterval) {
        }

        // Commands
        public override void Move() {
            for (; !stop; ) {
                lock (Ocean.OCEAN) {
                    Thread.Sleep(Constants.TIME_DELAY *
                            Constants.DELAY);
                    starvationCount++;
                    reproductionCount++;
                    lifetime++;
                    Coordinate oldPos = location.Position;
                    List<Coordinate> nearby =
                    this.NearbyEmptyCells(location.Position);

                    bool ableToMove = false;
                    if (nearby.Count > 0) {
                        ableToMove = true;
                        // Move minnow
                        Coordinate moveTo =
                    nearby[Constants.RANDOM.Next(0, nearby.Count)];
                        Ocean.OCEAN[oldPos].MarineAnimal = null;
```

LISTING 16.5 Class Minnow (continued)

```
                        Ocean.OCEAN[moveTo].MarineAnimal = this;
                        location = Ocean.OCEAN[moveTo];
                        FireMoveEvent(oldPos, moveTo, "M", " ");
                    }

                    if (starvationCount == starvationInterval) {
                        // Must kill minnow thread
                        stop = true;

                        Ocean.OCEAN[location.Position].MarineAnimal =
                            new DeadAnimal(Color.Black, "m",
                            location.Position.Row,
                                location.Position.Col, 0, 0);
                        FireMoveEvent(location.Position,
                            location.Position, "M", "m");
                        this.StopMoveThread();
                    }

                    if (ableToMove && reproductionCount >=
                            reproductionInterval) {
                        reproductionCount = 0;
                        Minnow babyMinnow =
                            new Minnow(Color.Green, "M", oldPos.Row,
                                oldPos.Col,
                                    Constants.RANDOM.Next(
                                    Constants.
                                    MINNOW_REPRODUCTION_INTERVAL - 1,
                                    Constants.
                                    MINNOW_REPRODUCTION_INTERVAL + 2),
                                    Constants.MINNOW_PERISH_INTERVAL);
                        babyMinnow.Register(Ocean.OCEAN.MoveHandler);
                        Ocean.OCEAN[oldPos].MarineAnimal = babyMinnow;
                        // Notify the ocean which notifies the GUI
                        FireMoveEvent(oldPos, oldPos, "M", "M");
                        babyMinnow.StartMoveThread();
                    }
                }
            }
        }

    public override void UpdateMortality(int lifetime) {
        Ocean.OCEAN.UpdateMinnowMortality(lifetime);
    }
    }
}
```

Exercise 16.5

Compare the details of method *Move* in class *Minnow* with the details given in the sequence diagram given in Figure 16.4.

It is noted that when a baby minnow is created, a *MoveHandler* defined in class *Ocean* (to be examined later) is registered with the newly created *Minnow* object.

It is also noted that when a minnow dies of starvation, the last line of code in the relevant block of code terminates the minnow's thread. It is important not to terminate this thread until no further work has to be done because that will cause *Move* to be aborted prematurely.

Listing 16.6 presents the details of class *Tuna*.

LISTING 16.6 Class Tuna

```
using System;
using System.Collections.Generic;
using System.Text;
using System.Drawing;
using System.Threading;
using System.Windows.Forms;

namespace EcologicalSimulation {

    public class Tuna : MarineAnimal {

        // Constructor
        public Tuna(Color color, String name, int row, int col,
                    int reproInterval, int starveInterval) :
                    base(color, name, row, col, reproInterval,
                        starveInterval) {
        }

        // Commands
        public override void Move() {
            for (; !stop; ) {
                lock (Ocean.OCEAN) {
                    Thread.Sleep(Constants.TIME_DELAY *
                                    Constants.DELAY);
                    reproductionCount++;
                    starvationCount++;
                    lifetime++;

                    bool ableToMove = false;
                    Coordinate oldPos = location.Position;
                    Coordinate moveTo;
                    List<Coordinate> minnowsNotNearSharkOrDolphin =
                        this.NearbyCellsWithNameNotAdjacentTo(
                            location.Position, "M", "S", "D");
```

LISTING 16.6 Class Tuna (continued)

```
                  List<Coordinate> minnowsNearby =
                      this.NearbyCellsWithName(location.Position,
                                              "M");
              if (minnowsNotNearSharkOrDolphin.Count > 0) {
                  ableToMove = true;
                  moveTo =
                      minnowsNotNearSharkOrDolphin[
                      Constants.RANDOM.Next(0,
                          minnowsNotNearSharkOrDolphin.Count)];
                  // Must kill minnow thread
                  if (Ocean.OCEAN[moveTo].MarineAnimal != null) {
                  Ocean.OCEAN[moveTo].
                          MarineAnimal.StopMoveThread();
                  }
                  Ocean.OCEAN[oldPos].MarineAnimal = null;
                  Ocean.OCEAN[moveTo].MarineAnimal = this;
                  location = Ocean.OCEAN[moveTo];
                  FireMoveEvent(oldPos, moveTo, "T", "M");
                  starvationCount = 0;
              } else if (minnowsNearby.Count > 0) {
                  ableToMove = true;
                  moveTo =
                      minnowsNearby[Constants.RANDOM.
                              Next(0, minnowsNearby.Count)];
                  // Must kill minnow thread
                  if (Ocean.OCEAN[moveTo].MarineAnimal != null) {
                      Ocean.OCEAN[moveTo].
                  MarineAnimal.StopMoveThread();
                  }
                  Ocean.OCEAN[oldPos].MarineAnimal = null;
                  Ocean.OCEAN[moveTo].MarineAnimal = this;
                  location = Ocean.OCEAN[moveTo];
                  FireMoveEvent(oldPos, moveTo, "T", "M");
                  starvationCount = 0;
              } else {
                  // Find possible empty space not near shark or
                  // dolphin among nearby cells.
                  List<Coordinate> nearby =
                  NearbyEmptyCells(location.Position);
                  List<Coordinate>
                  emptyNearbyCellsNotNearSharkOrDolphin =
                      new List<Coordinate>();
                  foreach (Coordinate pt in nearby) {
                      if (!NeighborsWithName(pt, "S") &&
                              !NeighborsWithName(pt, "D")) {
                      emptyNearbyCellsNotNearSharkOrDolphin.
                              Add(pt);
                      }
                  }
```

LISTING 16.6 Class Tuna (continued)

```
                    if (emptyNearbyCellsNotNearSharkOrDolphin.Count
                        > 0) {
                      ableToMove = true;
                      moveTo =
                        emptyNearbyCellsNotNearSharkOrDolphin[
                          Constants.RANDOM.
                          Next(0,
                          emptyNearbyCellsNotNearSharkOrDolphin.
                          Count)];
                      Ocean.OCEAN[oldPos].MarineAnimal = null;
                      Ocean.OCEAN[moveTo].MarineAnimal = this;
                      location = Ocean.OCEAN[moveTo];
                      FireMoveEvent(oldPos, moveTo, "T", " ");
                    }
                  }

                  if (starvationCount == starvationInterval) {
                    // Must kill tuna thread
                    stop = true;
                    Ocean.OCEAN[location.Position].MarineAnimal =
                      new DeadAnimal(Color.Black, "t",
                          location.Position.Row,
                              location.Position.Col, 0, 0);
                    FireMoveEvent(location.Position,
                        location.Position, "T", "t");
                    this.StopMoveThread();
                  }

                  if (ableToMove && reproductionCount >=
                      reproductionInterval) {
                    reproductionCount = 0;
                    Tuna babyTuna =
                        new Tuna(Color.Goldenrod, "T", oldPos.Row,
                        oldPos.Col,
                    Constants.RANDOM.Next(Constants.
                    TUNA_REPRODUCTION_INTERVAL - 1,
                        Constants.TUNA_REPRODUCTION_INTERVAL +
                        2),
                        Constants.RANDOM.Next(
                        Constants.TUNA_STARVATION_INTERVAL - 1,
                        Constants.TUNA_STARVATION_INTERVAL +
                        2));
                    babyTuna.Register(Ocean.OCEAN.MoveHandler);
                    Ocean.OCEAN[oldPos].MarineAnimal = babyTuna;
                    // Notify the ocean which notifies the GUI
                    FireMoveEvent(oldPos, oldPos, "T", "T");
                    babyTuna.StartMoveThread();
                  }
                }
```

LISTING 16.6 Class Tuna (continued)

```
            }
        }

        public override void UpdateMortality(int lifetime) {
            Ocean.OCEAN.UpdateTunaMortality(lifetime);
        }
    }
}
```

Exercise 16.6

Compare the details of method *Move* in class *Tuna* with the details given in the sequence diagram given in Figure 16.5.

Other than the presence of more logical contingencies that reflect the more complex move logic of a tuna, the details in Listing 16.6 are straightforward.

When a minnow object is eaten, its thread must be stopped.

Listings 16.7 and 16.8 present classes *Dolphin* and *Shark*.

LISTING 16.7 Class Dolphin

```
using System;
using System.Collections.Generic;
using System.Text;
using System.Drawing;
using System.Threading;
using System.Windows.Forms;

namespace EcologicalSimulation {

    public class Dolphin : MarineAnimal {

        // Constructor
        public Dolphin(Color color, String name, int row, int col,
          int reproInterval, int starveInterval) :
            base(color, name, row, col, reproInterval starveInterval) {
        }

        // Commands
        public override void Move() {
            for (; !stop; ) {
                lock (Ocean.OCEAN) {
                    Thread.Sleep(Constants.TIME_DELAY *
                            Constants.DELAY);
                    reproductionCount++;
                    starvationCount++;
```

LISTING 16.7 Class Dolphin (continued)

```
                    lifetime++;

        bool ableToMove = false;
        Coordinate oldPos = location.Position;
        Coordinate moveTo;
        List<Coordinate> tunaInNeighborhood =
            this.NeighboringCellsWithName(
                location.Position, "T");
        List<Coordinate> sharkInNeighborhood =
            this.NeighboringCellsWithName(
            location.Position, "S");
        if (tunaInNeighborhood.Count > 0) {
            ableToMove = true;
            moveTo =
                tunaInNeighborhood[Constants.RANDOM.
                    Next(0, tunaInNeighborhood.Count)];
            // Must kill tuna thread
            if (Ocean.OCEAN[moveTo].MarineAnimal != null) {
                Ocean.OCEAN[moveTo].
            MarineAnimal.StopMoveThread();
            }
            Thread.Sleep(100);
            Ocean.OCEAN[oldPos].MarineAnimal = null;
            Ocean.OCEAN[moveTo].MarineAnimal = this;
            location = Ocean.OCEAN[moveTo];
            FireMoveEvent(oldPos, moveTo, "D", "T");
            starvationCount = 0;
        } else if (sharkInNeighborhood.Count > 0) {
            moveTo =
                sharkInNeighborhood[Constants.RANDOM.
                    Next(0, sharkInNeighborhood.Count)];
            // Decide who wins battle
            if (Constants.RANDOM.NextDouble() <= 0.25) {
            // Dolphin wins
                ableToMove = true;
                // Must kill shark thread
                if (Ocean.OCEAN[moveTo].MarineAnimal !=
                                        null) {
                    Ocean.OCEAN[moveTo].
                MarineAnimal.StopMoveThread();
                }
                Thread.Sleep(100);
                Ocean.OCEAN[oldPos].MarineAnimal = null;
                Ocean.OCEAN[moveTo].MarineAnimal = this;
                location = Ocean.OCEAN[moveTo];
```

LISTING 16.7 Class Dolphin (continued)

```
                         FireMoveEvent(oldPos, moveTo, "D", "S");
                         starvationCount = 0;
                     } else {
                         // Shark wins and dolphin turns to a dead
                         // animal.
                         stop = true;
                         Ocean.OCEAN[location.Position].
                                 MarineAnimal =
                             new DeadAnimal(Color.Black, "d",
                                 location.Position.Row,
                                 location.Position.Col, 0, 0);
                         FireMoveEvent(location.Position,
                                 location.Position, "D", "d");
                         this.StopMoveThread();
                     }
                 } else {
                     // Find possible empty space
                     List<Coordinate> emptyNeighbors =
                         NeighboringEmptyCells(location.Position);
                     if (emptyNeighbors.Count > 0) {
                         ableToMove = true;
                         moveTo =
                             emptyNeighbors[Constants.RANDOM.
                                 Next(0, emptyNeighbors.Count)];
                         Ocean.OCEAN[oldPos].MarineAnimal = null;
                         Ocean.OCEAN[moveTo].MarineAnimal = this;
                         location = Ocean.OCEAN[moveTo];
                         FireMoveEvent(oldPos, moveTo, "D", " ");
                     }
                 }

                 if (starvationCount == starvationInterval) {
                     // Must kill dolphin thread
                     stop = true;
                     Ocean.OCEAN[location.Position].MarineAnimal =
                         new DeadAnimal(Color.Black, "d",
                         location.Position.Row,
                             location.Position.Col, 0, 0);
                     FireMoveEvent(location.Position,
                         location.Position, "D", "d");
                     this.StopMoveThread();
                 }

                 if (ableToMove && reproductionCount >=
                     reproductionInterval) {
                     reproductionCount = 0;
                     Dolphin babyDolphin =
                         new Dolphin(Color.Blue, "D", oldPos.Row,
                             oldPos.Col,
```

LISTING 16.7 Class Dolphin (continued)

```
                                   Constants.RANDOM.Next(Constants.
                        DOLPHIN_REPRODUCTION_INTERVAL - 1,
                              Constants.DOLPHIN_REPRODUCTION_INTERVAL
                                 + 2),
                              Constants.RANDOM.Next(Constants.
                        DOLPHIN_STARVATION_INTERVAL - 1,
                              Constants.DOLPHIN_STARVATION_INTERVAL +
                                 2));
                        babyDolphin.Register(Ocean.OCEAN.MoveHandler);
                        Ocean.OCEAN[oldPos].MarineAnimal = babyDolphin;
                        // Notify the ocean which notifies the GUI
                        FireMoveEvent(oldPos, oldPos, "D", "D");
                        babyDolphin.StartMoveThread();
                    }
                }
            }
        }

        public override void UpdateMortality(int lifetime) {
            Ocean.OCEAN.UpdateDolphinMortality(lifetime);
        }
    }
}
```

Exercise 16.7

After studying Listing 16.7, outline the major logical steps that govern the move of a dolphin.

LISTING 16.8 Class Shark

```
using System;
using System.Collections.Generic;
using System.Text;
using System.Drawing;
using System.Threading;
using System.Windows.Forms;

namespace EcologicalSimulation {

    public class Shark : MarineAnimal {
```

LISTING 16.8 Class Shark (continued)

```
// Fields
private int tunaKilled = 0;

// Constructor
public Shark(Color color, String name, int row, int col,
            int reproInterval, int starveInterval) :
            base(color, name, row, col, reproInterval,
                starveInterval) {
}

// Commands
public override void Move() {
    for (; !stop; ) {
        lock (Ocean.OCEAN) {
            Thread.Sleep(Constants.TIME_DELAY *
                Constants.DELAY);
            reproductionCount++;
            starvationCount++;
            lifetime++;

            bool ableToMove = false;
            Coordinate oldPos = location.Position;
            Coordinate moveTo;

            // Swallow an entire school of minnow in
            // neighborhood
            List<Coordinate> neighboringMinnows =
              NeighboringCellsWithName(
                location.Position, "M");
            if (neighboringMinnows.Count > 0) {
                ableToMove = true;
                foreach (Coordinate pt in neighboringMinnows) {
                    if (Ocean.OCEAN[pt].MarineAnimal != null) {
                        Ocean.OCEAN[pt].MarineAnimal.
                            StopMoveThread();
                    }
                    Thread.Sleep(100);
                    Ocean.OCEAN[pt].MarineAnimal = null;
                    FireMoveEvent(oldPos, pt, "", "M");
                }
            }

            List<Coordinate> dolphinInNeighborhood =
                this.NeighboringCellsWithName(
                    location.Position, "D");
            List<Coordinate> tunaInNeighborhood =
                this.NeighboringCellsWithName(
                location.Position, "T");
            if (dolphinInNeighborhood.Count > 0) {
```

LISTING 16.8 Class Shark (continued)

```
                              ableToMove = true;
                              moveTo =
                                  dolphinInNeighborhood[Constants.RANDOM.
                                  Next(0, dolphinInNeighborhood.Count)];
                              // Must kill dolphin thread
                              if (Ocean.OCEAN[moveTo].MarineAnimal != null) {
                                  Ocean.OCEAN[moveTo].
                              MarineAnimal.StopMoveThread();
                              }
                              Thread.Sleep(100);
                              Ocean.OCEAN[oldPos].MarineAnimal = null;
                              Ocean.OCEAN[moveTo].MarineAnimal = this;
                              location = Ocean.OCEAN[moveTo];
                              FireMoveEvent(oldPos, moveTo, "S", "D");
                              starvationCount = 0;
                          } else if (tunaInNeighborhood.Count > 0) {
                              moveTo =
                                  tunaInNeighborhood[Constants.RANDOM.
                                          Next(0, tunaInNeighborhood.Count)];
                              ableToMove = true;
                              // Must kill tuna thread
                              if (Ocean.OCEAN[moveTo].MarineAnimal != null) {
                                  Ocean.OCEAN[moveTo].
                              MarineAnimal.StopMoveThread();
                              }
                              Thread.Sleep(100);
                              Ocean.OCEAN[oldPos].MarineAnimal = null;
                              Ocean.OCEAN[moveTo].MarineAnimal = this;
                              location = Ocean.OCEAN[moveTo];
                              FireMoveEvent(oldPos, moveTo, "S", "T");
                              tunaKilled++;
                              if (tunaKilled == 2) {
                                  starvationCount = 0;
                                  tunaKilled = 0;
                              }
                          } else {
                              // Find possible empty space
                              List<Coordinate> emptyNeighbors =
                                  NeighboringEmptyCells(location.Position);
                              if (emptyNeighbors.Count > 0) {
                                  ableToMove = true;
                                  moveTo =
                                      emptyNeighbors[Constants.RANDOM.
                                          Next(0, emptyNeighbors.Count)];
                                  Ocean.OCEAN[oldPos].MarineAnimal = null;
                                  Ocean.OCEAN[moveTo].MarineAnimal = this;
                                  location = Ocean.OCEAN[moveTo];
                                  FireMoveEvent(oldPos, moveTo, "S", " ");
                              }
```

LISTING 16.8 Class Shark (continued)

```
                }

                if (starvationCount == starvationInterval) {
                    // Must kill shark thread
                    stop = true;
                    Ocean.OCEAN[location.Position].MarineAnimal =
                        new DeadAnimal(Color.Black, "s",
                    location.Position.Row,
                            location.Position.Col, 0, 0);
                    FireMoveEvent(location.Position,
                    location.Position, "S", "s");
                    this.StopMoveThread();
                }

                if (ableToMove && reproductionCount >=
                        reproductionInterval) {
                    reproductionCount = 0;
                    Shark babyShark =
                        new Shark(Color.Red, "S", oldPos.Row,
                    oldPos.Col,
                            Constants.RANDOM.Next(Constants.
                    SHARK_REPRODUCTION_INTERVAL - 1,
                            Constants.SHARK_REPRODUCTION_INTERVAL +
                                2),
                            Constants.RANDOM.Next(Constants.
                    SHARK_STARVATION_INTERVAL - 1,
                            Constants.SHARK_STARVATION_INTERVAL +
                                2));
                    babyShark.Register(Ocean.OCEAN.MoveHandler);
                    Ocean.OCEAN[oldPos].MarineAnimal = babyShark;
                    // Notify the ocean which notifies the GUI
                    FireMoveEvent(oldPos, oldPos, "S", "S");
                    babyShark.StartMoveThread();
                }
            }
        }
    }

    public override void UpdateMortality(int lifetime) {
        Ocean.OCEAN.UpdateSharkMortality(lifetime);
    }
    }
}
```

Exercise 16.8

After studying Listing 16.8, outline the major logical steps that govern the move of a shark.

Listing 16.9 presents the details of class *Scavenger*.

LISTING 16.9 Class Scavenger

```
using System;
using System.Collections.Generic;
using System.Text;
using System.Drawing;
using System.Threading;
using System.Windows.Forms;

namespace EcologicalSimulation {

    public class Scavenger : MarineAnimal {

        // Constructor
        public Scavenger(Color color, String name, int row, int col,
                        int reproInterval, int starveInterval) :
                        base(color, name, row, col,
                            reproInterval, starveInterval) {
        }

        // Commands
        public override void Move() {
            for (; !stop; ) {
                lock (Ocean.OCEAN) {
                    List<Coordinate> deadAnimalNearby;
                    Coordinate oldPos = location.Position;
                    deadAnimalNearby =
                        this.NearbyEmptyCellsWithName(
                        location.Position, "s", "d", "t", "m");
                    do {
                        Coordinate moveTo = new Coordinate(-1, -1);
                        Thread.Sleep(Constants.TIME_DELAY *
                            Constants.DELAY);
                        if (deadAnimalNearby.Count > 0) {
                            moveTo =
                                deadAnimalNearby[Constants.RANDOM.Next(
                            0, deadAnimalNearby.Count)];
                            Ocean.OCEAN[oldPos].MarineAnimal = null;
                            Ocean.OCEAN[moveTo].MarineAnimal = this;
                            location = Ocean.OCEAN[moveTo];
                            FireMoveEvent(oldPos, moveTo, "C", "  ");
                            deadAnimalNearby =
```

LISTING 16.9 Class Scavenger (continued)

```
                              this.NearbyEmptyCellsWithName(
                      moveTo, "s", "d", "t", "m");
                    oldPos = moveTo;
                }
            } while (deadAnimalNearby.Count > 0);
        }
    }
}


    public override void UpdateMortality(int lifetime) {
    }
    }
}
```

The ability for a scavenger to move repeatedly is evident in the *do-while* loop of method *Move*.

Class *DeadAnimal* is presented in Listing 16.10.

LISTING 16.10 Class DeadAnimal

```
using System;
using System.Collections.Generic;
using System.Text;
using System.Drawing;

namespace EcologicalSimulation {

    public class DeadAnimal : MarineAnimal {

        // Constructor
        public DeadAnimal(Color color, String name, int row, int col,
                          int reproInterval, int starveInterval) :
                          base(color, name, row, col,
                                reproInterval, starveInterval) {

        }

        // Commands
        public override void Move() {
        }

        public override void UpdateMortality(int lifetime) {
        }
    }
}
```

The commands *Move* and *UpdateMortality* both have null implementations. This reflects the inert behavior of dead animals.

The singleton class *Ocean* has some subtleties and is presented in Listing 16.11.

LISTING 16.11 Singleton class Ocean

```
using System;
using System.Collections.Generic;
using System.Text;
using System.Drawing;
using System.Threading;
using System.Windows.Forms;

namespace EcologicalSimulation {

    public delegate void MoveNotifier(Coordinate from, Coordinate to,
                                      String fromName, String toName);

    // Implemented as a singleton class
    public sealed class Ocean {

        // Fields
        private Location [,] locations;

        private static readonly Ocean OCEAN_INSTANCE = new Ocean();

        private event MoveNotifier notifyGUI;

        private List<int> sharkMortality = new List<int>();
        private List<int> dolphinMortality = new List<int>();
        private List<int> tunaMortality = new List<int>();
        private List<int> minnowMortality = new List<int>();

         // Constructor
        private Ocean() { }

        // Static constructor
        static Ocean() {
            OCEAN_INSTANCE.locations =
            new Location[Constants.ROWS, Constants.COLS];
            for (int row = 0; row < Constants.ROWS; row++) {
                for (int col = 0; col < Constants.COLS; col++) {
                    OCEAN_INSTANCE.locations[row, col] =
                    new Location(new Coordinate(row, col));
                }
            }
            for (int row = 0; row < Constants.ROWS; row++) {
                for (int col = 0; col < Constants.COLS; col++) {
                    OCEAN_INSTANCE.locations[row, col].SetNeighbors();
```

LISTING 16.11 Singleton class Ocean (continued)

```
                }
            }
        for (int row = 0; row < Constants.ROWS; row++) {
            for (int col = 0; col < Constants.COLS; col++) {
                OCEAN_INSTANCE.locations[row,
                    col].SetNearbyValues();
            }
        }
    }


    // indexer
    public Location this[int row, int col] {
        get {
            return locations[row, col];
        }
        set {
            locations[row, col] = value;
        }
    }


    public Location this[Coordinate position] {
        get {
            return locations[position.Row, position.Col];
        }
        set {
            locations[position.Row, position.Col] = value;
        }
    }


    // Property
    public static Ocean OCEAN {
        get {
            return OCEAN_INSTANCE;
        }
    }


    public double SharkLife {
        get {
            if (sharkMortality.Count == 0) {
                return -1.0;
            }
            double sum = 0.0;
            foreach (int value in sharkMortality) {
                sum += value;
            }
            return sum / sharkMortality.Count;
        }
    }
```

LISTING 16.11 Singleton class Ocean (continued)

```
public double MinnowLife {
    get {
        if (minnowMortality.Count == 0) {
            return -1.0;
        }
        double sum = 0.0;
        foreach (int value in minnowMortality) {
            sum += value;
        }
        return (double )sum / minnowMortality.Count;
    }
}

public double TunaLife {
    get {
        if (tunaMortality.Count == 0) {
            return -1.0;
        }
        double sum = 0.0;
        foreach (int value in tunaMortality) {
            sum += value;
        }
        return sum / tunaMortality.Count;
    }
}

public double DolphinLife {
    get {
        if (dolphinMortality.Count == 0) {
            return -1.0;
        }
        double sum = 0.0;
        foreach (int value in dolphinMortality) {
            sum += value;
        }
        return sum / dolphinMortality.Count;
    }
}

// Commands
public void Register(MoveNotifier guiHandler) {
    OCEAN_INSTANCE.notifyGUI += new MoveNotifier(guiHandler);
}

public void MoveHandler(Coordinate from, Coordinate to,
                        String fromName, String toName) {
    OCEAN_INSTANCE.notifyGUI(from, to, fromName, toName);
}
```

LISTING 16.11 Singleton class Ocean (continued)

```
public void Initialize() {
    for (int minnowIndex = 0; minnowIndex <
        Constants.NUMBER_MINNOW; minnowIndex++) {
        int colPos = Constants.RANDOM.Next(0, Constants.COLS);
        int rowPos = Constants.RANDOM.Next(0, Constants.ROWS);
        while (OCEAN_INSTANCE[rowPos, colPos].MarineAnimal !=
                    null) {
            colPos = Constants.RANDOM.Next(0, Constants.COLS);
            rowPos = Constants.RANDOM.Next(0, Constants.ROWS);
        }
        Minnow minnow =
            new Minnow(Color.Green, "M", rowPos, colPos,
                    Constants.RANDOM.Next(Constants.
            MINNOW_REPRODUCTION_INTERVAL - 1,
                Constants.MINNOW_REPRODUCTION_INTERVAL + 2),
                Constants.MINNOW_PERISH_INTERVAL);
        minnow.Register(OCEAN_INSTANCE.MoveHandler);
        OCEAN_INSTANCE.locations[rowPos, colPos].MarineAnimal =
            minnow;
    }

    for (int tunaIndex = 0; tunaIndex < Constants.NUMBER_TUNA;
            tunaIndex++) {
        int colPos = Constants.RANDOM.Next(0, Constants.COLS);
        int rowPos = Constants.RANDOM.Next(0, Constants.ROWS);
        while (OCEAN_INSTANCE[rowPos, colPos].MarineAnimal !=
                null) {
            colPos = Constants.RANDOM.Next(0, Constants.COLS);
            rowPos = Constants.RANDOM.Next(0, Constants.ROWS);
        }
        Tuna tuna =
            new Tuna(Color.Goldenrod, "T", rowPos, colPos,
                    Constants.RANDOM.Next(Constants.
            TUNA_REPRODUCTION_INTERVAL - 1,
                Constants.TUNA_REPRODUCTION_INTERVAL + 2),
                Constants.RANDOM.Next(
                Constants.TUNA_STARVATION_INTERVAL - 1,
                Constants.TUNA_STARVATION_INTERVAL +
                    2));
        tuna.Register(OCEAN_INSTANCE.MoveHandler);
        OCEAN_INSTANCE.locations[rowPos, colPos].
            MarineAnimal = tuna;
    }

    for (int dolphinIndex = 0; dolphinIndex <
        Constants.NUMBER_DOLPHIN; dolphinIndex++) {
        int colPos = Constants.RANDOM.Next(0, Constants.COLS);
        int rowPos = Constants.RANDOM.Next(0, Constants.ROWS);
        while (OCEAN_INSTANCE[rowPos, colPos].MarineAnimal !=
```

LISTING 16.11 Singleton class Ocean (continued)

```
                    null) {
                colPos = Constants.RANDOM.Next(0, Constants.COLS);
                rowPos = Constants.RANDOM.Next(0, Constants.ROWS);
            }
            Dolphin dolphin =
                new Dolphin(Color.Blue, "D", rowPos, colPos,
                    Constants.RANDOM.Next(Constants.
                DOLPHIN_REPRODUCTION_INTERVAL - 1,
                        Constants.DOLPHIN_REPRODUCTION_INTERVAL +
                2), Constants.RANDOM.Next(Constants.
                DOLPHIN_STARVATION_INTERVAL - 1,
                        Constants.DOLPHIN_STARVATION_INTERVAL + 2));
            dolphin.Register(OCEAN_INSTANCE.MoveHandler);
            OCEAN_INSTANCE.locations[rowPos, colPos].MarineAnimal =
                dolphin;
        }
        for (int sharkIndex = 0; sharkIndex <
            Constants.NUMBER_SHARK; sharkIndex++) {
            int colPos = Constants.RANDOM.Next(0, Constants.COLS);
            int rowPos = Constants.RANDOM.Next(0, Constants.ROWS);
            while (OCEAN_INSTANCE[rowPos, colPos].MarineAnimal !=
                null) {
                colPos = Constants.RANDOM.Next(0, Constants.COLS);
                rowPos = Constants.RANDOM.Next(0, Constants.ROWS);
            }
            Shark shark =
                new Shark(Color.Red, "S", rowPos, colPos,
                    Constants.RANDOM.Next(Constants.
                DOLPHIN_REPRODUCTION_INTERVAL - 1,
                    Constants.DOLPHIN_REPRODUCTION_INTERVAL +
                2), Constants.RANDOM.Next(Constants.
                DOLPHIN_STARVATION_INTERVAL - 1,
                    Constants.DOLPHIN_STARVATION_INTERVAL + 2));
            shark.Register(OCEAN_INSTANCE.MoveHandler);
            OCEAN_INSTANCE.locations[rowPos, colPos].MarineAnimal =
                shark;
        }

        for (int scavengerIndex = 0; scavengerIndex <
            Constants.NUMBER_SCAVENGER; scavengerIndex++) {
            int colPos = Constants.RANDOM.Next(0, Constants.COLS);
            int rowPos = Constants.RANDOM.Next(0, Constants.ROWS);
            while (OCEAN_INSTANCE[rowPos, colPos].MarineAnimal !=
                    null) {
                colPos = Constants.RANDOM.Next(0, Constants.COLS);
                rowPos = Constants.RANDOM.Next(0, Constants.ROWS);
            }
            Scavenger scavenger =
                new Scavenger(Color.MediumPurple, "C", rowPos,
```

LISTING 16.11 Singleton class Ocean (continued)

```
                        colPos, 0, 0);
            scavenger.Register(OCEAN_INSTANCE.MoveHandler);
            OCEAN_INSTANCE.locations[rowPos, colPos].MarineAnimal =
                scavenger;
        }
    }

    public void UpdateSharkMortality(int lifetime) {
        sharkMortality.Add(lifetime);
    }

    public void UpdateDolphinMortality(int lifetime) {
        dolphinMortality.Add(lifetime);
    }

    public void UpdateTunaMortality(int lifetime) {
        tunaMortality.Add(lifetime);
    }

    public void UpdateMinnowMortality(int lifetime) {
        minnowMortality.Add(lifetime);
    }

    }
}
```

What makes class *Ocean* a singleton (only one instance can be created)?

The keyword *sealed* stops any subclasses from being created. The private constructor prevents a default constructor from being used. The following would not be legal:

```
Ocean myOcean = new Ocean();
```

The static property *OCEAN* returns the static read-only *Ocean* instance, *OCEAN_INSTANCE*. This is the only copy of the ocean that can be produced.

The static constructor *Ocean* sets the neighbors and nearby cells for each location in *OCEAN_INSTANCE*.

The fields *minnowMortality*, ..., *sharkMortality*, of type *List<int>* contain actuarial statistics relating to the life of each marine object. The read-only properties *MinnowLife*, *TunaLife*, *DolphinLife,* and *SharkLife* return the average number of move opportunities for each of these species respectively.

Two indexer properties allow ocean objects to access *Location* objects by specifying a row and column index. Class *Ocean* presents a compelling context in which indexers promote greater readability of the code. The notation *Ocean.OCEAN[row, col]* returns the *Location* object at the specified row and column indices in the one ocean that is present.

Another delegate class, *MoveNotifier*, is defined. A private event field, *notifyGUI*, is defined. A public *Register* method provides an opportunity for the GUI class to register an event handler with the ocean. The event *notifyGUI* provides the needed connection from marine animal objects that notify the ocean when they move, die, or reproduce and the ocean that notifies the GUI.

The public method *MoveHandler* fires the *notifyGUI* event passing the values *from*, *to*, *fromName*, and *toName* to the GUI handler.

The lengthy method *Initialize* populates the location objects within the OCEAN_INSTANCE with the requisite number of marine critters while registering the *MoveHandler* method with each critter.

Finally, the *UpdateSharkMortality*, …, *UpdateMinnowMortality* methods update the lifetime statistics for each species.

Listing 16.12 presents the aspects of the GUI class, *EcologicalGUI*, not automatically generated by the IDE.

LISTING 16.12 Class EcologicalGUI

```
using System;
using System.Collections.Generic;
using System.ComponentModel;
using System.Data;
using System.Drawing;
using System.Windows.Forms;
using System.Threading;


namespace EcologicalSimulation {

    partial class EcologicalGUI : Form {

        // Fields
        private int numShark, numDolphin, numTuna, numMinnow, numDead;
        private Graphics oceanGraphics;
        private Graphics graph;
        private int events = 0;
        private List<int> sharkPopulation = new List<int>();
        private List<int> tunaPopulation = new List<int>();
        private List<int> dolphinPopulation = new List<int>();
        private List<int> minnowPopulation = new List<int>();
        private List<int> deadAnimalPopulation = new List<int>();


        public EcologicalGUI() {
            InitializeComponent();
            Ocean.OCEAN.Register(MoveHandler);

            // Display initial values
            sharkPop.Text = Constants.NUMBER_SHARK.ToString();
            dolphinPop.Text = Constants.NUMBER_DOLPHIN.ToString();
            tunaPop.Text = Constants.NUMBER_TUNA.ToString();
            tunaPop.Text = Constants.NUMBER_TUNA.ToString();
            minnowPop.Text = Constants.NUMBER_MINNOW.ToString();
```

LISTING 16.12 Class EcologicalGUI (continued)

```
            sharkRepro.Text =
            Constants.SHARK_REPRODUCTION_INTERVAL.ToString();
            dolphinRepro.Text =
            Constants.DOLPHIN_REPRODUCTION_INTERVAL.ToString();
            tunaRepro.Text =
            Constants.TUNA_REPRODUCTION_INTERVAL.ToString();
            minnowRepro.Text =
            Constants.MINNOW_REPRODUCTION_INTERVAL.ToString();

            sharkStarve.Text =
            Constants.SHARK_STARVATION_INTERVAL.ToString();
            dolphinStarve.Text =
            Constants.DOLPHIN_STARVATION_INTERVAL.ToString();
            tunaStarve.Text =
            Constants.TUNA_STARVATION_INTERVAL.ToString();
            minnowStarve.Text =
            Constants.MINNOW_PERISH_INTERVAL.ToString();
        }

        public void DisplayOcean() {

            oceanGraphics = oceanPanel.CreateGraphics();
            oceanGraphics.Clear(Color.White);

            numTuna = numDolphin = numShark = numMinnow =
            numDead = 0;
            oceanGraphics.FillRectangle(new SolidBrush(Color.White),
                        new Rectangle(0, 0, 500, 300));
            // Count the sea creatures
            for (int row = 0; row < Constants.ROWS; row++) {
                for (int col = 0; col < Constants.COLS; col++) {
                    MarineAnimal animal = Ocean.OCEAN[row,
                        col].MarineAnimal;
                    if (animal != null) {
                        if (animal.GetType().ToString() ==
                                "EcologicalSimulation.Tuna") {
                            numTuna++;
                        } else if (animal.GetType().ToString() ==
                                "EcologicalSimulation.Dolphin") {
                            numDolphin++;
                        } else if (animal.GetType().ToString() ==
                                "EcologicalSimulation.Shark") {
                            numShark++;
                        } else if (animal.GetType().ToString() ==
                                "EcologicalSimulation.Minnow") {
                            numMinnow++;
                        } else if (animal.GetType().ToString() ==
                                "EcologicalSimulation.DeadAnimal") {
```

LISTING 16.12 Class EcologicalGUI (continued)

```
                        numDead++;
                    }
                }
                if (animal != null) {
                    oceanGraphics.DrawString(animal.Name, Font,
                                new SolidBrush(animal.Color),
                                5 + col * 20,
                                5 + row * 20);
                }
            }
        }
    }
    sharkBox.Text = numShark.ToString();
    dolphinBox.Text = numDolphin.ToString();
    tunaBox.Text = numTuna.ToString();
    minnowBox.Text = numMinnow.ToString();
    deadBox.Text = numDead.ToString();
}


public void MoveHandler(Coordinate from, Coordinate to,
                        String fromName, String toName) {
    lock (this) {
        if (oceanGraphics == null) {
            oceanGraphics = oceanPanel.CreateGraphics();
        }
        if (graph == null) {
            graph = graphPanel.CreateGraphics();
        }

        if (fromName.Length == 0) {
        // Shark swallowing school of minnow
            oceanGraphics.DrawString(toName, Font,
                            new SolidBrush(Color.White),
                            5 + to.Col * 20,
                            5 + to.Row * 20);

        } else {
            // Erase sea creature from old and new position
            Color color = Color.Black;
            if (Ocean.OCEAN[to].MarineAnimal != null) {
                color = Ocean.OCEAN[to].MarineAnimal.Color;
            }

            oceanGraphics.DrawString(fromName, Font,
                new SolidBrush(Color.White),
                    5 + from.Col * 20,
                    5 + from.Row * 20);
            if (Ocean.OCEAN[to].MarineAnimal != null) {
                oceanGraphics.DrawString(toName, Font,
                    new SolidBrush(Color.White),
                    5 + to.Col * 20,
                    5 + to.Row * 20);
```

LISTING 16.12 Class EcologicalGUI (continued)

```
                }
                if (fromName.Equals("C")) { // A scavanger
                    oceanGraphics.DrawString("s", Font,
                        new SolidBrush(Color.White),
                        5 + to.Col * 20,
                        5 + to.Row * 20);
                    oceanGraphics.DrawString("d", Font,
                        new SolidBrush(Color.White),
                        5 + to.Col * 20,
                        5 + to.Row * 20);
                    oceanGraphics.DrawString("t", Font,
                        new SolidBrush(Color.White),
                        5 + to.Col * 20,
                        5 + to.Row * 20);
                    oceanGraphics.DrawString("m", Font,
                        new SolidBrush(Color.White),
                        5 + to.Col * 20,
                        5 + to.Row * 20);
                }

                // Display sea creature in new position
                if (!from.Equals(to)) {
                    oceanGraphics.DrawString(fromName, Font,
                        new SolidBrush(color),
                        5 + to.Col * 20,
                        5 + to.Row * 20);
                } else {
                    oceanGraphics.DrawString(toName, Font,
                        new SolidBrush(color),
                        5 + to.Col * 20,
                        5 + to.Row * 20);
                }
            }
            Census();
        }
    }

    private void Census() {
        numShark = numTuna = numDolphin = numMinnow = numDead = 0;
        events++;
        for (int row = 0; row < Constants.ROWS; row++) {
            for (int col = 0; col < Constants.COLS; col++) {
                MarineAnimal animal = Ocean.OCEAN[row,
                    col].MarineAnimal;
                if (animal != null) {
                    if (animal.GetType().ToString() ==
                            "EcologicalSimulation.Tuna") {
                        numTuna++;
                    } else if (animal.GetType().ToString() ==
```

LISTING 16.12 Class EcologicalGUI (continued)

```
                                "EcologicalSimulation.Dolphin") {
                        numDolphin++;
                    } else if (animal.GetType().ToString() ==
                            "EcologicalSimulation.Shark") {
                        numShark++;
                    } else if (animal.GetType().ToString() ==
                            "EcologicalSimulation.Minnow") {
                        numMinnow++;
                    } else if (animal.GetType().ToString() ==
                            "EcologicalSimulation.DeadAnimal") {
                        numDead++;
                    }
                }
            }
        }

        sharkBox.Text = numShark.ToString();
        dolphinBox.Text = numDolphin.ToString();
        tunaBox.Text = numTuna.ToString();
        minnowBox.Text = numMinnow.ToString();
        deadBox.Text = numDead.ToString();
        eventsBox.Text = events.ToString();

        String sharkLifeStr = String.Format("{0:f4}",
                    Ocean.OCEAN.SharkLife);
        sharkLifeBox.Text =
        sharkLifeStr.Equals("-1.0000") ? "N/A" :
                    sharkLifeStr;
        String dolphinLifeStr = String.Format("{0:f4}",
                    Ocean.OCEAN.DolphinLife);
        dolphinLifeBox.Text =
        dolphinLifeStr.Equals("-1.0000") ? "N/A" :
                    dolphinLifeStr;
        String tunaLifeStr = String.Format("{0:f4}",
                    Ocean.OCEAN.TunaLife);
        tunaLifeBox.Text =
        tunaLifeStr.Equals("-1.0000") ? "N/A" : tunaLifeStr;
        String minnowLifeStr = String.Format("{0:f4}",
                    Ocean.OCEAN.MinnowLife);
        minnowLifeBox.Text =
        minnowLifeStr.Equals("-1.0000") ? "N/A" :
                    minnowLifeStr;

        // Update the population graph after every 25 events
        if (events % 25 == 0) {
            sharkPopulation.Add(numShark);
            tunaPopulation.Add(numTuna);
            dolphinPopulation.Add(numDolphin);
            minnowPopulation.Add(numMinnow);
```

LISTING 16.12 Class EcologicalGUI (continued)

```csharp
            deadAnimalPopulation.Add(numDead);

            // Plot population history

            for (int i = 0; i < sharkPopulation.Count - 1; i++) {
                graph.DrawLine(new Pen(Color.Red, 1), i,
                    265 - sharkPopulation[i], i + 1,
                    265 - sharkPopulation[i + 1]);
                graph.DrawLine(new Pen(Color.Blue, 1), i,
                    265 - dolphinPopulation[i], i + 1,
                    265 - dolphinPopulation[i + 1]);
                graph.DrawLine(new Pen(Color.Goldenrod, 1), i,
                    265 - tunaPopulation[i], i + 1,
                    265 - tunaPopulation[i + 1]);
                graph.DrawLine(new Pen(Color.Green, 1), i,
                    265 - minnowPopulation[i], i + 1,
                    265 - minnowPopulation[i + 1]);
                graph.DrawLine(new Pen(Color.Black, 1), i,
                    265 - deadAnimalPopulation[i], i + 1,
                    265 - deadAnimalPopulation[i + 1]);
            }
        }
    }

    private void initializeOceanBtn_Click(object sender,
                EventArgs e) {
        displayOceanBtn.Enabled = false;
        changeInitialValuesBtn.Enabled = false;
        Ocean.OCEAN.Initialize();
        DisplayOcean();
    }

    private void startSimulationBtn_Click(object sender,
                EventArgs e) {
        for (int row = 0; row < Constants.ROWS; row++) {
            for (int col = 0; col < Constants.COLS; col++) {
                MarineAnimal marineAnimal =
                    Ocean.OCEAN[row, col].MarineAnimal;
                if (marineAnimal != null) {
                    marineAnimal.StartMoveThread();
                }
            }
        }
    }

    private void stopSimulationBtn_Click(object sender,
                EventArgs e) {
        for (int row = 0; row < Constants.ROWS; row++) {
            for (int col = 0; col < Constants.COLS; col++) {
```

LISTING 16.12 Class EcologicalGUI (continued)

```
                    MarineAnimal marineAnimal =
                        Ocean.OCEAN[row, col].MarineAnimal;
                    if (marineAnimal != null) {
                        marineAnimal.StopMoveThread();
                    }
                }
            }
        for (int row = 0; row < Constants.ROWS; row++) {
            for (int col = 0; col < Constants.COLS; col++) {
                MarineAnimal marineAnimal =
                    Ocean.OCEAN[row, col].MarineAnimal;
                if (marineAnimal != null) {
                    marineAnimal.StopMoveThread();
                }
            }
        }
        for (int row = 0; row < Constants.ROWS; row++) {
            for (int col = 0; col < Constants.COLS; col++) {
                MarineAnimal marineAnimal =
                    Ocean.OCEAN[row, col].MarineAnimal;
                if (marineAnimal != null) {
                    marineAnimal.StopMoveThread();
                }
            }
        }
        for (int row = 0; row < Constants.ROWS; row++) {
            for (int col = 0; col < Constants.COLS; col++) {
                MarineAnimal marineAnimal =
                        Ocean.OCEAN[row, col].MarineAnimal;
                if (marineAnimal != null) {
                    marineAnimal.StopMoveThread();
                }
            }
        }
    }

    private void speedControl_ValueChanged(object sender,
                EventArgs e) {
        int value = speedControl.Value;
        if (value < 1) {
            Constants.DELAY = 40;
        } else {
            Constants.DELAY = 10 / value;
        }
    }

    private void changeInitialValuesBtn_Click(object sender,
                EventArgs e) {
        try {
```

LISTING 16.12 Class EcologicalGUI (continued)

```
            Constants.NUMBER_SHARK =
               Convert.ToInt32(sharkPop.Text.Trim());
            Constants.NUMBER_TUNA =
               Convert.ToInt32(tunaPop.Text.Trim());
            Constants.NUMBER_DOLPHIN =
               Convert.ToInt32(dolphinPop.Text.Trim());
            Constants.NUMBER_MINNOW =
               Convert.ToInt32(minnowPop.Text.Trim());

            Constants.SHARK_REPRODUCTION_INTERVAL =
               Convert.ToInt32(sharkRepro.Text.Trim());
            Constants.DOLPHIN_REPRODUCTION_INTERVAL =
               Convert.ToInt32(dolphinRepro.Text.Trim());
            Constants.TUNA_REPRODUCTION_INTERVAL =
               Convert.ToInt32(tunaRepro.Text.Trim());
            Constants.MINNOW_REPRODUCTION_INTERVAL =
               Convert.ToInt32(minnowRepro.Text.Trim());

            Constants.SHARK_STARVATION_INTERVAL =
               Convert.ToInt32(sharkStarve.Text.Trim());
            Constants.DOLPHIN_STARVATION_INTERVAL =
               Convert.ToInt32(dolphinStarve.Text.Trim());
            Constants.TUNA_STARVATION_INTERVAL =
               Convert.ToInt32(tunaStarve.Text.Trim());
            Constants.MINNOW_PERISH_INTERVAL =
               Convert.ToInt32(minnowStarve.Text.Trim());

         } catch (Exception) {
            MessageBox.Show("Illegal entry among initial values.");
         }
      }
   }
}
```

The *EcologicalGUI* class contains five fields that are generic *List<int>* collections. These hold the mortality data for each of the species. There are two *Graphics* objects that support the display of the marine animals and their population dynamics.

The constructor registers its *MoveHandler* method as a listener with the one instance of the ocean (*Ocean.OCEAN*). It then displays the default population, reproduction, and starvation values for each species.

The *changeInitialValuesBtn_Click* button handler assigns the user's population, reproduction, and starvation values back to the static variables in class *Constants*.

The *MoveHandler* is the most important method in the class. It updates both the display of marine animals and the graph that depicts the population of each species as a function of time.

Using the *lock* construct, the objects that comprise the fields of the class are synchronized as *MoveHandler* does its work.

Each of the logical blocks in the selection construct is commented, indicating its purpose. These include a shark swallowing a school of minnow, erasing a marine animal from the old and new position (this is accomplished by writing the name of the marine animal using the background color white), dealing with the move of a scavenger, and displaying a marine animal in its new position.

Exercise 16.9

Briefly explain each of the logical blocks in method *MoveHandler* that are cited earlier.

The *Census* method is invoked at the end of method *MoveHandler*. Runtime type identification is done using as an example:

```
animal.GetType().ToString() == "EcologicalSimulation.Tuna"
```

This is done for each of the rows * cols cells in the ocean for each location that is associated with a non-null marine animal.

Exercise 16.10

What would the consequence of not using synchronization with the *lock* construct be in class *EcologicalGUI*?

The *startSimulationBtn_Click* button handler invokes the *StartMoveThread* method on all marine animals found among the rows * cols cell locations.

The *stopSimulationBtn_Click* button handler iterates repeatedly (four times) through all the marine animals, sending each the *StopMoveThread* command. The reason for the repetition is that some marine animals may move to regions of the ocean already scanned by this iteration because of the multiply threaded nature of the application. Only by repeating the iteration several times is it reasonable to assume that all the threads will be halted. It typically takes several seconds for the action to grind to a halt.

It is interesting to observe the ebb and flow of population dynamics. They do in fact typify real ecological systems. Sometimes in one's zeal to "help" a species by allowing it to reproduce more readily (easily achieved in this simulation by lowering the reproduction interval), it has the effect of killing the species because it runs out of food. You are invited to perform the myriad experiments that are possible by tweaking the default values given by the initial population, reproduction, and starvation values and observing what happens.

16.5 SOME FINAL WORDS

The case study presented in this chapter demonstrated many of the important modern software development principles featured in this book. Deploying each marine animal as an independent thread comes as close to the reality of mimicking real marine organisms as they reproduce, eat, and die of starvation. You may want to examine a much simpler case study that involves marine creatures given at *www.collegeboard.com/ prod_downloads/student/testing/ap/compsci_a/2002_mbcs.pdf*.

The C# language supported by the powerful .NET framework was shown in action in this case study. The principles of encapsulation, polymorphic substitution, and late-binding were used extensively. The separation between the model classes (*MarineAnimal* and all its descendents) and the singleton *Ocean* class, and its separation from the *EcologicalGUI* class, reinforce a powerful Observer Pattern design pattern. When critical events are generated by marine animals as they reproduce, kill a prey, or die of starvation or by being eaten by a predator, these events are propagated to the singleton ocean object, which in turn notifies the GUI.

It is hoped that the principles put forth in this book and the examples used to illuminate them will help you forge a successful career in modern software development.

16.6 ADDITIONAL EXERCISES

In this chapter, all of the exercises (Exercises 16.1–16.10) are directly related to the examples and the listings. They therefore appear only in context, and are not repeated here.

INDEX